AGAINST THE TIDE

Pro-Feminist Men in the United States, 1776–1990

A Documentary History

EDITED BY

Michael S. Kimmel and Thomas E. Mosmiller

BEACON PRESS
BOSTON

Beacon Press
25 Beacon Street
Boston, Massachusetts 02108-2892

Beacon Press books
are published under the auspices of
the Unitarian Universalist Association of Congregations.

Printed in the United States of America

99 98 97 96 95 94 93 8 7 6 5 4 3 2

Text design by Karen Savary

Library of Congress Cataloging-in-Publication Data

Against the tide : pro-feminist men in the United States, 1776–1990
: a documentary history / edited by Michael S. Kimmel and Thomas E.
Mosmiller.
p. cm.—(Men and masculinity)
Includes bibliographical references.
ISBN 0-8070-6760-1 (cloth)
ISBN 0-8070-6767-9 (paper)
1. Women's rights—United States—History—Sources. 2. Feminism
—United States—History—Sources. I. Kimmel, Michael S.
II. Mosmiller, Thomas E. III. Series.
HQ1236.5.U6A34 1992
305.42'0973—dc20 91-17649
CIP

To the women of the Women's Movement
in their continuing struggle for equality

and to the men who support them
especially the National Organization for Men against Sexism
and *Changing Men: Issues in Gender, Sex, and Politics*

CONTENTS

PREFACE *xix*

ACKNOWLEDGMENTS *xxvii*

INTRODUCTION *1*

PART I: BEFORE SENECA FALLS, 1775–1848 *53*

Thomas Paine
"AN OCCASIONAL LETTER ON THE FEMALE SEX" (1775) *63*

Benjamin Rush
THOUGHTS UPON FEMALE EDUCATION (excerpt) (1787) *66*

Charles Brockden Brown
ALCUIN (excerpt) (1798) *70*

Mathew Carey
"RULES FOR HUSBANDS AND WIVES" (1830) *73*

Robert Dale Owen
"MARRIAGE CONTRACT WITH MARY JANE ROBINSON" (1832) *75*

Thomas Herttell
"THE RIGHT OF MARRIED WOMEN TO HOLD AND CONTROL PROPERTY" (1839) *76*

William E. Channing
"EMANCIPATION" (1840) *79*

Wendell Phillips and George Bradburn
SPEECHES AT THE WORLD ANTI-SLAVERY CONVENTION (1840) 80

Jonathan Neal
"RIGHTS OF WOMEN" (1843) 82

Martin Robinson Delaney
"YOUNG WOMEN" (1844) 93

Rev. Samuel J. May
"THE RIGHTS AND CONDITION OF WOMEN" (1846) 94

PART II: THE STRUGGLE FOR EQUAL EDUCATION, 1850–1960 99

WOMEN'S RIGHT TO HIGHER EDUCATION

Thomas Wentworth Higginson
"OUGHT WOMEN TO LEARN THE ALPHABET?" (1859) 111

Frederick A. P. Barnard
"SHOULD AMERICAN COLLEGES BE OPEN TO WOMEN AS WELL AS TO MEN" (1882) 115

George W. Curtis
"THE HIGHER EDUCATION OF WOMEN" (excerpt) (1890) 121

ESTABLISHING COLLEGES FOR WOMEN

Matthew Vassar
"TO THE BOARD OF TRUSTEES" (1864) 123

Rev. L. Clark Seelye
"THE NEED FOR A COLLEGIATE EDUCATION FOR WOMEN" (1874) 125

Henry Fowle Durant
"THE SPIRIT OF THE COLLEGE" (1877) 132

THE ARGUMENT FOR COEDUCATION

Horace Mann
"DEDICATION OF ANTIOCH COLLEGE AND INAUGURAL ADDRESS" (1854) 133

James B. Angell
"SHALL THE AMERICAN COLLEGES BE OPEN TO BOTH SEXES?" (1871) 135

Editorial, the *Amherst Student*
"THE OTHER SIDE—A REPLY" (1871) 136

John M. Van Vleck
"LETTER TO THE BOARD OF TRUSTEES OF WESLEYAN UNIVERSITY" (1900) 138

John Dewey
"IS CO-EDUCATION INJURIOUS TO GIRLS?" (1911) 139

PART III: WOMEN'S STRUGGLES FOR ECONOMIC EQUALITY, 1850–1960 145

WOMEN'S ECONOMIC INDEPENDENCE

Robert Dale Owen
"THE PROPERTY RIGHTS OF WIDOWS" (1851) 159

William I. Bowditch
"HOW LONG SHALL WE ROB AND ENSLAVE WOMEN?" (1885) 161

George Herbert Mead
"A LETTER TO HIS DAUGHTER-IN-LAW" (1920) 163

WOMEN IN THE TRADES

Horace Greeley
"WOMAN AND WORK" (1852) 165

Horace Greeley
"LETTER TO PAULINA W. DAVIS" (1852) 167

William H. Sylvis
"A UNION'S POSITION" (1872) 169

Carrol D. Wright
"THE INDUSTRIAL EMANCIPATION OF WOMEN" (1893) 170

James Oppenheim and Caroline Kohlsaat
"BREAD AND ROSES" (1912) 172

George Creel
"THE 'PROTECTED SEX' IN INDUSTRY" (1915) 173

Joe Hill
"THE REBEL GIRL" (1915) 177

Industrial Workers of the World
"WHAT ABOUT THE WOMAN WHO WORKS" (1925) 178

Byron McG. West
"YOU CAN'T DO THIS TO WOMEN" (1930) 181

Woody Guthrie
"UNION MAID" (1947) 183

WOMEN IN THE PROFESSIONS

Joseph S. Longshore, M.D.
"A VALEDICTORY ADDRESS AT THE FIRST COMMENCEMENT OF THE FEMALE MEDICAL COLLEGE OF PENNSYLVANIA" (1851) 184

Rev. Luther Lee
"WOMEN'S RIGHTS TO PREACH THE GOSPEL" (1853) 187

Melvil Dewey
"LIBRARIANSHIP AS A PROFESSION FOR COLLEGE-BRED WOMEN" (1886) 189

James Cardinal Gibbons
"ON THE OPENING OF THE JOHNS HOPKINS MEDICAL SCHOOL TO WOMEN" (1891) 191

William T. Harris
"WHY MANY WOMEN SHOULD STUDY LAW" (1901) 192

PART IV: THE MOVEMENT FOR POLITICAL EQUALITY, 1850–1960 195

FROM ABOLITION TO SUFFRAGE

Frederick Douglass
"THE RIGHTS OF WOMEN" (1848) 211

William Lloyd Garrison
"INTELLIGENT WICKEDNESS" (1853) 212

Theodore Parker
"A SERMON OF THE PUBLIC FUNCTION OF WOMEN" (1853) 214

Ralph Waldo Emerson
"WOMAN" (1855) 217

P. P. Fowler and John W. Hutchinson
"KANSAS SUFFRAGE SONG" (1867) 220

Parker Pillsbury
"THE MORTALITY OF NATIONS" (1867) 221

George W. Julian
"THE SLAVERY YET TO BE ABOLISHED" (1874) 224

WORKING FOR SUFFRAGE

Gov. John W. Hoyt
"WOMAN SUFFRAGE IN WYOMING" (1882) 226

Daniel P. Livermore
"WOMAN SUFFRAGE DEFENDED" (1885) 229

Rev. Charles Clark Harrah
"JESUS CHRIST—THE EMANCIPATOR OF WOMEN" (1888) 230

James Freeman Clarke
"WOMAN SUFFRAGE" (1889) 234

Finley Peter Dunne
"MR. DOOLEY ON WOMAN'S SUFFRAGE" (1909) 236

J. A. Wayland
"BULLY FOR THE WOMEN" (1911) 239

Edward J. Ward
"WOMEN SHOULD MIND THEIR OWN BUSINESS" (1912) 240

Gen. E. Estabrook
"THE TAXATION TYRANNY" (1912) 242

David Lloyd Garrison
"SUFFRAGE AND ?S" (1913) 243

Arthur Neil Rhodes
WOMEN'S SUFFRAGE AND INTEMPERANCE (excerpt) (1914) 244

Samuel Fraser
"WHAT ARE YOU GOING TO DO NOVEMBER SECOND?" (1914) 245

Samuel McChord Crothers
MEDITATIONS ON VOTES FOR WOMEN (excerpt) (1914) 248

William Benedict
LETTER TO THE *NEW YORK TIMES* (1915) 249

Eugene Debs
"WOMAN—COMRADE AND EQUAL" (N.D.) 250

Hon. Robert H. Terrel
"OUR DEBT TO SUFFRAGISTS" (CA. 1915) 252

W. E. B. DuBois
"VOTES FOR WOMEN" (1917) 253

A. Phillips Randolph
"WOMAN SUFFRAGE AND THE NEGRO" (1917) 254

A. Caswell Ellis
"WHY MEN NEED EQUAL SUFFRAGE FOR WOMEN" (1918) 255

William Pickens
"THE KIND OF DEMOCRACY THE NEGRO RACE EXPECTS" (1918) 258

Frank McCullough
"SOME QUESTIONS FOR WOMAN SUFFRAGISTS, FROM A MERE MAN" (1919) 259

ORGANIZING MEN FOR FEMINISM: THE MEN'S LEAGUE FOR WOMAN SUFFRAGE

Rabbi Stephen Samuel Wise
"STATEMENT ON SUFFRAGE" (1907) 260

Editorial, the *New York Times*
"THE HEROIC MEN" (1912) 261

James Lee Laidlaw
"STATEMENT AT NATIONAL AMERICAN WOMAN SUFFRAGE CONVENTION" (1912) 262

Charles A. Beard
"THE COMMON MAN AND THE FRANCHISE" (1912) 263

Max Eastman
"WHO'S AFRAID? CONFESSION OF A SUFFRAGE ORATOR" (1915) 265

Omar Elvin Garwood
"FIFTEEN REASONS WHY I AM IN FAVOR OF UNIVERSAL EQUAL SUFFRAGE" (CA. 1915) *269*

Wilmer Atkinson
"NUTS TO CRACK" (1916) *270*

Lincoln Steffens
"WOMAN SUFFRAGE WOULD INCREASE CORRUPTION" (1917) *272*

POSTSUFFRAGE STRUGGLES

Henry A. Wallace
"STATEMENT ON THE EQUAL RIGHTS AMENDMENT" (1944) *273*

William Z. Foster
"ON IMPROVING THE PARTY'S WORK AMONG WOMEN" (1948) *274*

PART V: THE STRUGGLE FOR SOCIAL EQUALITY, 1850–1960 *279*

SOCIAL EQUALITY FOR WOMEN

Theodore D. Weld
"MAN'S DISPARAGEMENT OF WOMAN IN ALL TIMES AND CLIMES" (1855) *297*

Walt Whitman
"A WOMAN WAITS FOR ME" (1856) *299*

Ezra Heywood
CUPID'S YOKES (excerpt) (1879) *300*

Lester F. Ward
"OUR BETTER HALVES" (1888) *306*

Judge Ben Lindsey
"ANIMAL RIGHTS FOR WOMEN" (CA. 1890) *313*

Praxedis Guerrero
"THE WOMAN" (1910) *316*

Eugene Hecker
A SHORT HISTORY OF WOMEN'S RIGHTS (excerpt) (1910) *318*

Ricardo Flores Magon
"TO WOMEN" (1910) 319

Arthur Meier Schlesinger
"THE ROLE OF WOMEN IN AMERICAN HISTORY" (1922) 321

MARRIAGE AND DIVORCE REFORMS

Stephen Pearl Andrews
"LOVE, MARRIAGE AND DIVORCE" (1853) 323

Henry Brown Blackwell
"LETTERS TO LUCY STONE" (1853–1854) 325

Henry Brown Blackwell and Lucy Stone
"PROTEST" (1855) 329

Ramon Sanchez
"LETTER TO HIS SISTER" (1862) 330

B. O. Flower
"PROSTITUTION WITHIN THE MARRIAGE BOND" (1880?) 332

"SEX RIGHTS," SEXUALITY, AND BIRTH CONTROL

Robert Dale Owen
MORAL PHYSIOLOGY (excerpt) (1831) 335

John Humphrey Noyes
"MALE CONTINENCE" (1877) 338

Lester F. Ward
"SOCIO-SEXUAL INEQUALITIES" (1883) 341

Thorstein Veblen
"THE ECONOMIC THEORY OF WOMAN'S DRESS" (1894) 347

William Sanger
"STATEMENT AT HIS TRIAL" (1915) 349

EXPERIMENTING WITH EQUALITY: GREENWICH VILLAGE, 1900–1920

Upton Sinclair
"THE DOUBLE STANDARD—A PARABLE OF THE AGES" (1913) 354

Walter Lippmann
"A NOTE ON THE WOMAN'S MOVEMENT" (1914) 355

George Middleton
"WHAT FEMINISM MEANS TO ME" (1914) 358

Hutchins Hapgood
"LEARNING AND MARRIAGE" (CA. 1915) 360

Floyd Dell
"FEMINISM FOR MEN" (1917) 361

PART VI: CONTEMPORARY PRO-FEMINIST MEN 365

STANDING UP FOR WOMEN

Gore Vidal
"WOMAN'S LIBERATION MEETS MILLER-MAILER-MANSON MAN" (1972) 375

John Lennon
"WOMAN IS THE NIGGER OF THE WORLD" (1972) 378

Herbert Marcuse
"MARXISM AND FEMINISM" (1974) 379

Ed Asner
"SPEECH ON MEN SUPPORTING WOMEN" (1987) 385

Rev. Jesse Jackson
"ENSURING THE DIGNITY AND EQUALITY OF WOMEN" (1988) 387

EDUCATIONAL EQUALITY

Louis Kampf and Dick Ohmann
"MEN IN WOMEN'S STUDIES" (1983) 389

Alex McDavid
"FEMINISM FOR MEN 101" (1986) 394

Harry Brod
"SCHOLARLY STUDIES OF MEN" (1990) 396

ECONOMIC EQUALITY

Walter P. Reuther
"POLICY REGARDING CHALLENGE TO STATE PROTECTIVE LAWS" (1970) 398

Leonard Swidler
"NO PENIS, NO PRIEST" (1973) 399

Bishop Paul Moore, Jr.
"STATEMENT AT THE ORDINATION OF REV. MARY MICHAEL SIMPSON" (1979) 401

Fred Small
"59 CENTS" (1981) 403

Robert Reich
"WAKE-UP CALL" (1989) 404

POLITICAL EQUALITY

Howard Cosell
"WHY I SUPPORT THE ERA" (1975) 406

Alan Alda
"ALAN ALDA ON THE ERA: WHY SHOULD MEN CARE?" (1976) 407

Joseph H. Pleck
"MEN'S POWER WITH WOMEN, OTHER MEN, AND SOCIETY: A MEN'S MOVEMENT ANALYSIS" (1977) 413

Men Allied Nationally for the Equal Rights Amendment
"ELEVEN WAYS MEN CAN BENEFIT FROM THE ERA" (1978) 422

Tim Wernette, Alan Acacia, and Craig Scherfenberg
"MALE PRIDE AND ANTI-SEXISM" (1980) 424

Robert Brannon
"STATEMENT ON THE FORMATION OF THE NATIONAL ORGANIZATION FOR CHANGING MEN" (1983) 429

Rep. Don Edwards
"SPEECH REINTRODUCING THE ERA" (1989) 432

SOCIAL EQUALITY

William Jennings Bryan Henrie, D.O.
"A NEW LOOK AT ABORTION" (1966) 433

Isaac Asimov
"UNCERTAIN, COY, AND HARD TO PLEASE" (1969) 434

Carl Wittman
"A GAY MANIFESTO" (1972) 442

Kalamu ya Salaam
"THE STRUGGLE TO SMASH SEXISM IS A STRUGGLE TO DEVELOP WOMEN" (1980) 443

Peter Blood, Alan Tuttle, and George Lakey
"UNDERSTANDING AND FIGHTING SEXISM: A CALL TO MEN" (1981) 455

Tim Beneke
MEN ON RAPE (excerpt) (1982) 457

Abelardo Delgado
"AN OPEN LETTER TO CAROLINA" (1982) 459

Gordon Mott
"FOLLOWING A WIFE'S MOVE" (1985) 463

Men Who Care about Women's Lives
"WHY WE MARCH" (1989) 465

PRO-FEMINIST MEN INTO THE 1990S

Pi Kappa Phi Fraternity
"STATEMENT OF POSITION ON SEXUAL ABUSE" (1985) 466

John Stoltenberg
"THE PRO-FEMINIST MEN'S MOVEMENT: NEW CONNECTIONS, NEW DIRECTIONS" (1988) 467

Justice Harry Blackmun
"DISSENT ON *WEBSTER V. REPRODUCTIVE SERVICES*" (excerpt) (1989) 471

Sen. Joseph R. Biden, Jr.
"STATEMENT BEFORE THE SENATE JUDICIARY COMMITTEE ON THE 'VIOLENCE AGAINST WOMEN ACT OF 1990'" (1990) 473

National Organization for Men against Sexism
"STATEMENT OF PRINCIPLES" (1990) *477*

ABBREVIATIONS

SELECT BIBLIOGRAPHY *481*

CREDITS *519*

PREFACE

WHEN WE TOLD our feminist women friends and colleagues that we were compiling a documentary history of men who had supported women's struggles in U.S. history, some appeared bemused. "Men who supported feminism?" said one. "That will surely be the shortest book in history!" We were not sure what we would find six years ago when we began our research on "pro-feminist" men in U.S. history. We had a few leads, and we had some idea that several prominent men had lent their names or their voices in support of women's causes.[1] But we had no idea that we would find over one thousand documents that indicated men's support for women's rights.

This book presents a sample of the documents we found, a fraction of what we now understand to be a substantial number of writings and speeches by men who have supported women's struggles. Some of these men supported feminism quietly and without fanfare, leaving little record of their support save an occasional letter or diary entry. Others made their entire careers as vigorous, visible supporters of women's rights, campaigning for suffrage or birth control, arguing for better wages or working conditions, ensuring women's rights to an education. Some men who had become prominent in other fields lent their names and

1. Such an agenda was initially suggested in Tom Mosmiller, Mike Bradley, and Michael Biernbaum, "Are We the First? A Call for a Feminist Men's History," in *M.*, no. 4 (Fall/Winter 1980): 3–4, 21.

voices on behalf of women in an effort to influence other men to do the same.

What this book documents, then, is a history of men who have supported women's struggles since the founding of the nation. We call these men "pro-feminist" because we believe that their support of feminism formed an important part of their public or private life. Care should be used in labeling all the men in this book "pro-feminist." The term "feminism" is a recent one, dating only from the turn of the century, and is thus one that few of the men in this book would have recognized as a label that described their activities.

The pro-feminist men in this book made their support of women's struggles visible either in a public arena or in the private realm of the home, in their relationships with women, children, and other men. As we were researching a documentary history, we have of course been concerned mainly with the written record of those activities. At times, the written record is the support—a speech, for example, or a book, or an essay published in a magazine or journal. At other times, the written record documents the activity, as in a diary entry or a letter, and we have included a few of these as well. Because we wanted to include the voices of the men themselves, we have, however, excluded from this book the written record *about* men's activities in support of women's rights. We have noted some of this literature in the select bibliography at the end of the book, and we hope to pursue the larger historical picture of men's support for feminism in future research.

In researching this book, we have wrestled with several intellectual dilemmas. What criteria should we use to determine whether a work is pro-feminist? What if the *work* appears to support women but the *writer* of the work appears not to have supported feminism in his everyday actions? What if a particular writer, or even a specific work, supported feminist thinking on one issue and was opposed to that same perspective on another issue? Our criteria for selection have allowed a good deal of latitude and also tried to remain true to the historical record. We have tried to eliminate men who may have been supportive in their public utterances but mistreated the women in their lives. Thus, we have not included Ben Reitman, who was vigorous in his support of his lover Emma Goldman's efforts on the part of birth control—he was once tarred and feathered for putting up posters announcing one of her speeches—but was tyrannical in their relationship and obsessive in his flagrant promiscuity. Nor have we included Dudley

Field Malone, husband of mid-twentieth-century feminist Doris Stevens, whose mistreatment included efforts to constrain her public activities. As far as we know, we have included no men who committed any acts of violence against women in their private lives.

The men in this book are not, however, angels. Many felt a split between the public advocacy of women's rights and the relatively traditional roles to which they adhered at home. Others sought to transform those private relations, only to find themselves without adequate models of equality. Many of the Greenwich Village radicals at the turn of the century, for example, tried to challenge monogamy and marriage as bourgeois conventions that enslaved women but found it difficult to articulate or enact alternatives that did not precipitate the problems of jealousy, possessiveness, and the double standard that they were trying to overcome. Many supported one part of women's struggles only to oppose or ignore other significant struggles. (Obviously, we do not agree with every author.)

We have tried to respect those inconsistencies. It is historically inaccurate to apply contemporary standards to past behavior, to interpret the past only in terms articulated in the present. In the mid-nineteenth century, for example, the notion of the personal being political, the effort to examine personal life in terms of its political dynamics, was absent from common discourse, except, of course, in the religious and secular communes designed to transform everyday private life. Similarly, though we might today see the link between struggles for equal education, labor force participation, the ballot, and birth control, many people—both women and men—saw no connection, feeling that their support for suffrage, for example, had little, if anything, to do with their opposition to birth control. And the consistency that we would today expect among the critique of sexism offered by feminists and their supporters and the critiques of racism, class oppression, and other forms of discrimination was not nearly as clear throughout American history. Several southern suffragists supported woman suffrage precisely because they saw it as a way to offset the gains of newly emancipated blacks. Some northern urban suffragists saw suffrage as a hedge against the waves of European immigrants flooding into eastern cities.

In our selections, we have tried to present a cross section of male support for feminist issues. But we have deliberately sought out the writings of black men, ethnic men, and gay men. This has not been an easy task, and, while we have probably oversampled to include more minority men's voices, we do not believe that we have overrepresented the presence of those voices within the chorus of pro-feminist men. For one thing, these are men, and, as such, they benefit from male privilege, but they are simultaneously oppressed by other men. Thus, black men, ethnic men, and gay men have been drawn into their own struggles for liberation from the oppressive power of white middle-class heterosexual men. As both the oppressed and the oppressor, these men have also had their own histories distorted, repressed, or obliterated. Their support of feminism may well be part of a long-repressed history, and we had a difficult time retrieving it. This hidden history was ameliorated in part by the struggles of these groups to reclaim their history, and in the contemporary era we found more evidence of these men taking part in women's struggles.

Nonprivileged pro-feminist men fight on two fronts: for their own liberation and in support of women's struggles. Rarely does one see the connection in these struggles. Occasionally, however, those links are made. For example, there is a line of thought from Frederick Douglass in the mid-nineteenth century to W. E. B. DuBois in the early twentieth to Kalamu ya Salaam today—all write as black men whose confrontation with racism has forced them to examine the ways in which sexism and racism are connected. Similarly, a few gay or bisexual men, from Walt Whitman to Carl Wittman, have articulated this link.

The most searching inquiries into the history of gender relations in the United States have been carried out by feminist scholars. While it used to be true that "the history of women has been mainly written by men," as pro-feminist writer Eugene Hecker wrote in *A Short History of Women's Rights* (1914), it is now the case that the women's movement, both inside and outside the academy, has transformed historical research. Women's history has rescued from historical obscurity those prominent women whose lives remained hidden from history because male historians rarely recognized their contributions. It has also reconstructed the daily experiences of ordinary women as they went about their quiet efforts to accommodate and resist a historically developing system that deprived them of full personhood. Women's history has transformed the biographies of the great and written the social history of the often faceless masses who eked out lives of dignity and meaning.

Our research is inspired by both these themes in women's history. We have tried to round out the pictures of some famous U.S. men whose earlier biographers often minimize or ignore altogether their commitments to advancing women's causes. It is not well known, for example, that support for women's rights held such a central place in the lives and work of such prominent American men as W. E. B. DuBois, Wendell Phillips, Thomas Wentworth Higginson, William Lloyd Garrison, John Dewey, Max Eastman, Judge Ben Lindsey, or Bishop Paul Moore. We have also endeavored to retrieve the efforts of the less prominent men who made the campaign for women's rights part of their everyday lives. While we have tended to emphasize the former, largely because access to documents by the prominent enables us to round out their portraits, we have developed the latter project as evidence permitted.

We see this work, though, not as establishing a new field of "men's history," or even situated in some vaguely defined generic field of "men's studies," new fields that emerged in the past decade. Sometimes, men's studies has been seen as a reaction against women's studies, an attempt to return men to the center of academic inquiry, to give, as one journalist put it, "the men's side of the story." This is clearly not our intention, nor is it the intention of most of what has been called men's studies. Men's studies begins from the initial premise of women's studies—that gender is a central organizing concept of both social life and individual identity. Where women's studies brings to light the impact of gender and women's inequality on the lives of women, men's studies, inspired by the insights of women's studies, attempts to apply those insights to the lives of men. Specifically, men's studies attempts to do what no other study of men in the curriculum—which includes virtually every course offered in the collegiate curriculum that does not have the word "woman" in the title of the course—attempts: to study men not as generic but in their gendered specificity, that is, to study men *as men*. Central to that analysis must be an understanding of the relation between power and the construction of masculinities in society, specifically, as the title of Joseph Pleck's essay puts it, "Men's Power over Women, Other, Men, and Society." In this sense, men's studies is a complement to women's studies, hoping to apply a feminist analysis to the lives of men.

This volume does not attempt such an analysis. We have not attempted to examine the lives of men as gendered actors, and we do not detail the organization of men's lives in a field of power. In that sense, this is not a text in men's studies. More properly understood, it is a chapter of women's history—a chapter that happens to be about the men who supported women's struggles. Most were content to contribute, as men, to the revision of traditional androcentric U.S. history that finally gives a central place to women's struggles for freedom and equality. This volume would not have been possible without the pioneering research of feminist scholars over the past quarter century. Feminist scholars have named the problem and begun the arduous yet exhilarating tasks of historical and canonical reconstruction. We are inspired by their work and hope that our book contributes to that project.

The organization of the book is both historical and thematic. We begin and end with historical periods—the era from the founding of the nation until the first Woman's Rights Convention in Seneca Falls, New York, in 1848 and the era from the rebirth of the modern feminist movement in the 1960s to the present. In between, we have grouped men's support around the specific issues that were the subject of women's campaigns—education, economic participation, political enfranchisement, and social equality. These thematic divisions are not chronologically distinct; indeed, they are intended to overlap. The divisions are somewhat arbitrary, as is the assignment of any particular pro-feminist man to one section when he may also have written about other areas of concern to women. Such divisions may also obscure the inconsistencies in these men's thinking, just as they might if we were to present the history of women's struggles in this format. After all, Elizabeth Cady Stanton believed that suffrage would make marriages stronger and lower what she believed was an alarming divorce rate, while Crystal Eastman and others sought suffrage as a legal mechanism by which to make the case against conventional marriage as a form of chattel slavery. Emma Goldman passionately supported birth control but opposed suffrage, which she saw as legitimating capitalism, and sought to free women politically by participating in anarchist struggles. These divisions serve a heuristic function in organizing the rough arenas of struggle, but they in no way indicate hard and fast divisions within the overall women's movement.

The history of pro-feminist men in America is incomplete—in part because women have not achieved the equality that they have struggled for more than two centuries to achieve, and in part because even the rights that women have won are still fragile. Some, like women's right to choose, are ominously threatened in a society that is still uncomfortable with both women's sexuality and men's responsibility. So, while we begin this volume with Thomas Paine's sanguine musings about women's "equal right to virtue," Senator Joseph Biden's statement of shock at the increasing rate of date rape and Justice Harry Blackmun's dire warnings about the implications of the Supreme Court's 1989 decision in *Webster v. Reproductive Services* are among the final selections. (As we go to press, Justice Blackmun has again attempted to defend a "woman's fundamental right to self-determination" in his dissent on *Rust v. Sullivan*.) In between are men who have stood for women's rights and against the tide of vilification, scorn, indifference, and derision that has historically been men's response to women's struggle for equality. These men have stood against the tide, but they have not turned it; what successes women have achieved have been due to women's tireless campaigns. As long as women must struggle for their rights, however, there will be men on the barricades with them. It is to that movement, and to the men who today support it, that we dedicate this book.

M.S.K. and T.E.M.
May 1991

ACKNOWLEDGMENTS

RESEARCHING THE DOCUMENTARY EVIDENCE of activities that few people even knew existed has proved difficult and exciting. Along the way, we have relied on many people—other scholars, colleagues, friends—for the insights, inspiration, and support that we have needed to see this project through.

All work on the history of the women's movement begins with the encyclopedic *History of Woman Suffrage* that Elizabeth Cady Stanton, Susan B. Anthony, and Matilda Joslyn Gage assembled over a twenty-year period. We have also relied on a large body of research in women's history, especially works by Lois Banner, Susan Brownmiller, Jill Ker Conway, Nancy Cott, Barbara Epstein, Sara Evans, Eleanor Flexner, Linda Gordon, Blanche Glassman Hersh, Aileen Kraditor, Gerda Lerner, Ruth Milkman, Elizabeth Pleck, Mary Ryan, Joan Scott, and Catharine Stimpson. The research of Sylvia Strauss and Sally Roesch Wagner on pro-feminist men has been particularly helpful. And the work of several men, including William Chafe, Carl Degler, John D'Emilio, Martin Duberman, Philip Foner, Jonathan Katz, William Leach, and Keith Melder, has been both useful and inspiring.

We found the research staff at every archive and library at which we worked to be enthusiastic about the project and genuinely helpful. We are grateful to the following college and university libraries and archives (and archivists and librarians): Alabama State Department of Archives and History (Nioni Jones); the University of Alaska (Dennis

Walle); Amherst College (Daria D'Arienzo); the Boston Public Library (Roberta Zonghi); Brandeis University (Caldwell Titcomb); the John Hay Library, Brown University (Rosemary Cullen); the State University of New York at Buffalo (Joseph Barnes); the Buffalo and Erie County Historical Society Library; the Bancroft Library and the libraries of the University of California, Berkeley (Patricia Kreitz); the California Historical Society Library; the Essex Institute (Prudence Backman, Eugenia Fountain); the Harvard University Archives; the Henry Huntington Library (Alan Jutzi); the Historical Society of Iowa (Soudi Janssens); the Jewish Community Library, San Francisco (Jonathan Schwartz); the Milton S. Eisenhower Library; The Johns Hopkins University (Cynthia Requardt, Margaret Burris); the Library of Congress (George Hobert, Anna Keller, Kathy Loughney, Sarah Pritchard, Janice Ruth, Peter Van Wingen); the Library Company of Philadelphia (Phil Lapsansky); the Massachusetts Historical Society; the Men's Studies Collection, Massachusetts Institute of Technology Library (Davied Ferriero, Kathy Marquis); the William Clements Library, University of Michigan (Galen Wilson); the Nevada Historical Society (Philip Earl); the University of Nevada, Reno (Kathryn Totton); the Newberry Library (Cynthia Wall); the New York Public Library; Oberlin College (Ronald Baumann); the Ohio State University Archives (Bertha Ihnat); the Archives and Special Collections on Women and Medicine, the Medical College of Pennsylvania (Sandra Chaff); the Phillips Memorial Library, Providence College (Jane Jackson); the Enoch Pratt Public Library; the Fondren Library, Rice University; the Arthur and Elizabeth Schlesinger Library on the History of Women, Radcliffe College (Eva Mosely, Susan Van Salis); the Women's Research Center, Rice University (Nancy Boothe); the University of Rochester (Mary Huth); the San Francisco Lesbian and Gay History Society (William Walker); the Sophia Smith Library, Smith College (Amy Hague); the Perry-Castaneda Library, the University of Texas; Vassar College (Nancy MacKechnie); the Wellesley College Archives (Wilma Slaight); the Women's History Research Center, Berkeley; the American Heritage Center, University of Wyoming (Emmet Chisum); and the Beinecke Library, Yale University (Susan Brady).

We are especially grateful to the staffs at the Library of Congress, the Sophia Smith Library, and the Schlesinger Library for facilitating our research visits. A residential fellowship from the Henry Murray Center at Radcliffe College made the research at the Schlesinger Library possible, while the staff there made it profitable and pleasurable. Additional financial support for this project from the Spencer Foundation Small Grants program and the State University of New York Faculty Research Grant program is also gratefully acknowledged.

Our research assistants—Laurie Goldstein, Miriam Mason, Phyllis Rothblatt, Barry Tymes, and especially Bill Mack and Deborah Strauss—were dependable, diligent, and delightful to work with. Additional logistic assistance was provided by Deborah Gonzalez, Mary Muldowney, and Trish Nicolaus.

We are grateful to those scholars, writers, and colleagues, and relatives of pro-feminist men who generously shared their work with us: Joyce Antler, Steven Buechler, Jacqueline Osborn Buell, Dennis Carey, Candace Falk, Fritz Fleischmann, Rev. Carter Heyward, Bob Huff, Kevin Huff, Lucy Knight, Kate Michelman, William O'Neill, Kathy Royce, Kalamu ya Salaam, Kevin White, and Laura X. We also want to thank people with whom we consulted at various stages of the project: Joe Beame, Jeff Beane, Alan Bérubé, Harry Brod, Rudy Busto, Nancy Cott, Ruth Schwartz Cowan, Martin Duberman, Jeff Escoffier, Linda Gordon, David Gutterman, James Harrison, Harry Hay, Katharine Hepburn, Lani Kaahumanu, Richard Lakes, Dave Matteson, Mike Messner, Regina Morantz-Sanchez, Joseph and Elizabeth Pleck, Mike Riegle, Will Roscoe, Andy Rose, Alan Sica, Barry Shapiro, Tom Stoddard, and Sally Roesch Wagner. Colleagues at the State University of New York at Stony Brook—Tilden Edelstein, John Gagnon, Norman Goodman, and Robert Zussman—also pitched in with timely advice or warnings. In addition, Harry Brod, Lauren Bryant, Tricia Donahue, Jo Anne Hall, Michael Kaufman, Iona Mara-Drita, Tony Rotundo, and Alix Kates Shulman provided exceptionally helpful and critical readings of the narrative portion of the book.

Our literary agent, Frances Goldin, and our editors at Beacon, first Joanne Wyckoff and now Lauren Bryant, believed in this project from the beginning and were enormously supportive throughout its history. Both the project and the collaborators were difficult to work with, and these people deserve special thanks for their enthusiasm and their patience. Thanks also to Joe Brown for meticulous copyediting.

The contemporary pro-feminist men's movement has been an important source of support and inspiration for this work. For the past ten years, Mike Biernbaum and Rick Cote have edited *Changing Men*, the publication of record for pro-feminist men's writings. Sally Wagner's regular column on male supporters of women's rights has been an important source for our work. And the National Organization for Men Against Sexism (NOMAS) provides an organizational network of men and women working to support feminist struggles.

Finally, this book would not have been possible without the constant support of that circle of family and friends who make research and writing far less of a solitary activity than it might otherwise be. Our list is long and our debt great. Kimmel especially acknowledges Iona Mara-Drita, for reminding him that commitment to principles begins at home. These people kept us afloat—at times even buoyant—as we worked on this project: Margo Adair, Angela Aidala, Paul Attewell and Katherine Newman, Jeff Beane, Bob and Joanne Brannon, Judith Brisman, the late Russ Broadhead, Barbara and Herb Diamond, Martin Duberman and Eli Zal, Kate Ellis, Jeff Escoffier, Phyllis Frank, Jo Freeman, John Gagnon, Cathy Greenblat, Richard Darius Hutchinson, Fred and Anne Jealous, Michael Kaufman, Ed and Dottie Kimmel, Sandi Kimmel, David, Deborah, and Drew Levin, Martin Levine, Iona Mara-Drita, Bill Mack, Mike Messner and Pierette Hondagneu-Sotelo, Diane Miller, Katie and Mary Morris and Larry O'Connor, Steven Neilson, Steve Pechter, Joseph and Elizabeth Pleck, Steve Rankin, George Robinson, Hank and Lillian Rubin, Blair Sandler, Jim Shattuck, Ron Smith, Mitchell Tunick and Pam Hatchfield, Mary Wilson, and Nancy Young.

This cause is not altogether and exclusively woman's cause. It is the cause of human brotherhood as well as human sisterhood, and both must rise and fall together. Woman cannot be elevated without elevating man, and man cannot be depressed without depressing woman also.

—FREDERICK DOUGLASS, 1848

The interests of the sexes are inseparably connected and in the elevation of the one lies the salvation of the other. Therefore, I claim a part of this last and grandest movement of the ages, for whatever concerns woman concerns the race.

—HENRY BROWN BLACKWELL, 1853

Feminism is going to make it possible for the first time for men to be free.

—FLOYD DELL, 1914

INTRODUCTION

Michael S. Kimmel

The Female equally with the Male I Sing
—WALT WHITMAN,
LEAVES OF GRASS

AMERICAN WOMEN have been struggling for equality for over two centuries, ever since American men achieved their independence from British rule.[1] In May 1776, two months before the signing of the Declaration of Independence, Abigail Adams asked her husband, John, to make sure that the new laws of this fledgling nation would curb the "unlimited power" that husbands held over wives. "I cannot say that I think you are very generous to the ladies," she wrote to the man who would be our second president, "for whilst you are proclaiming peace and good will to men, emancipating all nations, you insist upon retaining an absolute power over wives." She threatened that, "if particular care and attention is not paid to the ladies, we are determined to foment a rebellion and will not hold ourselves bound by any laws in which we have no voice, or representation" (cited in Bowditch 1879, 14).

John Adams's response was a joking, casual dismissal, and Abigail's plea became prophecy—the women's movement has become the most far-reaching social movement in the history of the nation, seeking to elevate over half the country's population to a position of equality.

Women have struggled on many different fronts during every era of American history—for equality of economic opportunity, suffrage, reproductive rights, and equal education, among other rights. The development of feminism, both as a set of political strategies for attaining equality and as the theoretical justification for that equality, was the inevitable outgrowth of silencing and excluding women. Feminism is the rational response of people systematically denied their rights on account of their sex.

And men have supported women every step of the way. Not all men, of course—not even most men. Most men have responded with bemused indifference or hostile rejection, when they have not jokingly dismissed women's claims, as John Adams did. Feminism has been the object of derisive humor and angry vilification. This antipathy to feminism has been based in part on a furious and irrational fear of equality, and of change in general, and in part on a perception that feminism implies changes for men and will necessitate a loss of men's power. Many men have recognized that women's claims for equality would require changes in more than the institutional arrangements of American society; feminism requires changes in personal relationships between women and men, rebuilding them on a new foundation of equality and interdependence, having destroyed the old foundation of hierarchy and enforced dependency. Feminism challenges the distribution of power in American society, in both the public and the private spheres. In short, feminism requires men to change.

Yet there have been men who supported women in these struggles since the founding of the country. These "pro-feminist" men have embraced the notion of equality between the sexes. They have argued vigorously for women's right to control their own bodies and to have equal access within the public arena. Some of them have even attempted to implement these changes within their personal lives as husbands, friends, parents, lovers, and relatives. This book presents the ideas and arguments of these pro-feminist men from the late eighteenth century until the present day. Within are samples of their writings, from both public sources, such as speeches, books, essays, poems, songs, plays, and political pamphlets, and private sources, such as letters and diary entries. Taken together, they allow us to begin to reconstruct the history of men's support for women's struggles in U.S. history.

Let me make clear why I use the term "pro-feminist" and not such others as "feminist man" or "male feminist."[2] Stripped to its essentials, feminism involves the empirical observation that women and men are not equal in either the public or the private sphere and also the moral stance that such inequality is wrong and ought to be changed. Men may agree with this empirical assessment of women's subordinate status and the moral imperative to work toward equality. In that sense, men *believe* in feminism. But to *be* a feminist, I believe, requires another ingredient: the felt experience of oppression. And this men cannot feel because men are not oppressed but privileged by sexism. We benefit from existing gender relations, earning higher salaries, receiving greater educational, professional, political, and economic opportunities, and having fewer fears (rape, sexual harassment) to obstruct our paths. To be sure, some men do feel oppression, but we are not oppressed *as men*. Oppression requires a structural relationship between groups and a set of institutions in which that oppression is embedded and by which it is reproduced. Men may be oppressed by dynamics of class, race, age, ethnicity, or sexual orientation. And to *be* a feminist, one needs to share the feminist analysis and vision as well as to experience that oppression. Men who support the struggle for gender equality may be called "anti-sexist" or "pro-feminist." I have used "pro-feminist" because it better states their positive support for women's struggles.

To document the participation of men in the struggle for women's equality is not to claim that men's support was internally consistent or of a single piece. Men supported feminism within their historical context, and their statements reveal the limitations of their era. We have made no effort to conceal those inconsistencies and contradictions; indeed, they are an essential part of the story. In particular, many men supported some parts of the feminist vision while rejecting others. It is not surprising to find a man like Horace Greeley supporting women's rights to equal education but opposing suffrage.

More common are men who supported a feminist cause in public but were unable or unwilling to implement that vision in their private lives. Some men did not understand—or willfully misunderstood—that these larger-scale institutional changes would have important ramifications in their own family lives and relationships with women. Some supported women's equality in public and maintained rather traditional—and traditionally unequal—marriages. Men's support for women's equality in the private sphere is understandably more difficult to document, but it is also, I believe, historically far less common. Only with the emergence of the modern feminist movement has the personal become so irretrievably political and have women demanded that men who "talk a good line" also follow through in their relationships with women, both public, as colleagues and coworkers, and private, as friends, partners, or spouses. Today's pro-feminist man must struggle against the legacy of sexism in his own life as well as against the institutional embeddedness of sexism in the public arena.

Why did some men support feminism while the vast majority of men were opposed to it? This is an important question, but one that the documentary evidence leaves us ill equipped to explain. The complex set of motivations that inspired some men to support women's equality emerges only vaguely through anecdote or biographical material. It would require more than occasional speculation about motive to develop an adequate collective psychology of the pro-feminist men we have identified in this work. For some, families may have played a role. A strong role model provided by a mother or a sister was, in some cases, critical; in others, compassionate and supportive fathers who nurtured and encouraged their daughters as well as sons were the decisive element. Marriage to a feminist woman transformed some men's thinking, although many feminists also encountered resistance and occasionally sabotage of their political work from less-than-supportive husbands. A few men seem to have supported feminist political reforms precisely because they did feel threatened and believed that ameliorative reforms early on would forestall the possibility of dramatic transformation of the relations between women and men later. Still other men were galvanized by their involvement in such political campaigns as the abolitionist, temperance, civil rights, or antiwar movements, which accustomed them to working alongside women as equals and also made them aware of women's plight.[3]

Another claim that this book does not make is that "men are essential, often the leading figures, in the history of feminism to date," as Donald Meyer recently put it (letter to the editor, *New York Times Book Review* [29 November 1987]: 38). Men neither made nor led the feminist movement, but we have been there. A more accurate assessment comes from nineteenth-century political reformer Thomas Wentworth Higginson, himself a campaigner for women's causes. In his treatise *Women and the Alphabet* (an extract is included in this volume), Higginson wrote,

> The woman suffrage movement in America, in all its stages and subdivisions, has been the work of women. No doubt men have helped in it: much of the talking has been done by them, and they have furnished many of the printed documents. But the energy, the methods, the unwearied purpose of the movement, have come from women: they have led in all councils; they have established the newspapers, got up the conventions, addressed the legislatures, and raised the money.[4]

Men may have supported feminist demands, mobilized other men around those demands, and attempted to integrate feminist principles into everyday life, but women's advances are the result of the tireless and dedicated work of feminist women.

Men were nevertheless there, and many found their support of women's equality costly. They were routinely jeered and occasionally assaulted when they participated in suffrage demonstrations. Playwright George Middleton recalled of one demonstration that, "while the women were gazed upon with respect and frequent applause, the men every step of the two-mile walk had to submit to jeers, whistles, 'me-a-ows,' and such cries as, 'Take that handkerchief out of your cuff,' 'Oh, you gay deceiver,' 'You forgot to shave this morning,' etc. etc." Not one of the men "deserted the ranks," reported Middleton proudly (1947, 243). Supporters of equal economic opportunities for women were occasionally targets of economic reprisal themselves, from firing to demotion. One West Virginia senator was threatened with dismissal as attorney for the United Fuel Gas Company if he did not change his vote on suffrage (SL, A-63, box 9, folder 146).

Occasionally, pro-feminist men were reviled as sexual predators, luring women from their homes and hearths to obtain sexual favors without the costs of marriage. As the Reverend John Todd warned,

> O woman! your worst enemy is he who scouts at marriage, who tries to flatter you with honeyed words about your rights, while he sneers in his own circle boasting that 'it is cheaper to buy milk than to keep a cow;' who would cruelly lift you out of your sphere, and try to reverse the very laws of God; who tries to make you believe that you will find independence, wealth, and renown in man's sphere, when your only safety and happiness is in patiently, lovingly, and faithfully performing the duties and enacting the relations of your own sphere. [1867, 26]

But the most common theme in public reaction to men's support of women's rights has been a questioning of their masculinity, as if supporting equality made pro-feminist men less manly. Male participants in suffrage demonstrations were seen as traitors to their sex. "Any success women may achieve in their 'anti-man' crusade is entirely due to the help given them by 'rats' from the camp of men themselves," wrote critic Belfort Bax, simultaneously vilifying men's support for feminism and overstating men's importance in the movement (cited in Dell 1921, 352). Male participants in suffrage demonstrations were labeled "Aunt Nancy men," or "miss-Nancys," or "man-milliners," turn-of-the-century versions of "Momma's boys." Samuel Eliot recalled that, during his years as a member of the Harvard Men's League for Woman Suffrage, when he marched in suffrage parades in cap and gown, onlookers would shout, "Look at the skirts!" (HUA, Pusey Library, Woman Suffrage Collection, HUD 3514.5000). The anonymous author of the 1915 pamphlet "How it Feels to be the Husband of a Suffragette" confessed that he did not wash the dishes in his home (neither did his wife) despite the fact that "something over 11,863 of you requested me to go home and wash them on the occasion of that first [suffrage] parade" (SL. A-63, box 2).

Opponents of suffrage consistently implied that the male supporters of women's struggles had lost their virility. Senator Heflin, from Alabama, made this charge explicitly in a 1913 anti-suffrage tirade. "I do not believe that there is a red-blooded man in the world who in his heart really believes in woman suffrage. I think every man who favors it ought to be made to wear a dress," he inveighed. "The suffragette and a little henpecked fellow crawling along beside her; that is her husband," he concluded (cited in Hecker 1914, 293). The *Syracuse Daily Star* opined in an editorial,

> The poor creatures who take part in the silly rant of "brawling women" and Aunt Nancy men, are most of the "ismizers" of the rankest stamp, Abolitionists of the most frantic and contemptible kind, and Christian (?) sympathizers with such heretics as Wm. Lloyd Garrison, Parker Pillsbury, C. C. Burleigh, and S. S. Foster. These men are all Woman's Righters, and preachers of such damnable doctrines and accursed heresies, as would make demons of the pit shudder to hear. [Cited in Schlesinger 1949, 139]

Contemporary pro-feminist men have been satirized as "wimps," and suspicions are frequently raised about their sexual orientation.[5]

This volume documents the continuing presence of pro-feminist men in the struggle for women's equality in U.S. history. In the remainder of this essay, I will provide a lens through which to read the documents and a theoretical and historical framework with which to place them in context. First, I will place men's support within the larger context of men's responses to feminism. Second, I will examine the types of arguments men offered to support a struggle that was generally perceived as being against their interests. What types of moral, legal, and political logic did they use to ground those arguments? Third, I explore the personal foundation of pro-feminist men's support for feminist women. I conclude with a brief exploration of the ways in which pro-feminist men are today supporting women's struggles and suggest some of the problems that face us today.

Men's Responses to Feminism, 1848–1990

Women's challenges to existing gender arrangements have prompted a variety of reactions among American men from the late eighteenth century to the present day (see Kimmel 1987). But those reactions were not just responses to women's demands for equal rights; they were also responses to both perceived and real threats to men's sense that their traditional notions of masculinity were being threatened. Feminism provided a concrete expression of the shifting terms on which gender relations were based, and, by demanding a change in men's and women's roles, feminists gave men a ready target. Instead of confronting the changing structural foundations of masculinity directly, men attempting to defend traditional arrangements or to redefine the meaning of masculinity have attacked the women's movement.

Historically, the normative definition of masculinity has been based on social and geographic mobility, economic autonomy, and political individualism. Control over one's labor, regardless of the color of one's collar, the struggle to conquer the wilderness as the American frontier expanded, property ownership, and an individual's political freedom have all been central themes in American men's identity. But these bases of men's notions of masculinity have been steadily eroding, even in the process of being articulated and elaborated. Capitalist industrialization and the growth of the state transformed the foundations of masculinity. Workplace autonomy steadily disappeared as factories replaced workshops, corporations replaced small offices, and shopping malls replaced local shops. Men's experience of public power has declined as the central government has assumed many public functions once held by localities.

In the first half of the nineteenth century, the relatively peaceful coexistence between the Christian gentleman and the autonomous artisan was shaken by the emergence of the urban, middle-class entrepreneur, who in his obsessive drive for marketplace success embodied a new definition of masculinity (Rotundo 1988; Leverenze 1989). Driven to dominate, the new capitalist entrepreneur was chronically insecure, aggressive, and sensitive only to the seduction of the market. Many rebelled against this mid-nineteenth-century "new man." Artisans shored up threatened solidarity with fraternal organizations, which sprang up in small towns and cities across the nation before the Civil War (Carnes 1989; Clawson 1989). Patricians retreated to their estates or plantations, where they reconsolidated masculinity on the cruel racial subordination of black men. In literature, the great writers of the American Renaissance—Melville, Hawthorne, Emerson, Whitman, and Thoreau—resisted marketplace masculinity (Thoreau called the market a "site of humiliation") and sought alternative grounds to reinvent themselves as men (Leverenz 1989).

The end of the Civil War signaled the triumph of the northern urban industrial entrepreneur over the genteel southern patrician. As much as the Civil War was a struggle for the dominance of industrial over agrarian capitalism or a fratricidal struggle over the morality of slavery, it was also a gendered war, in which one version of masculinity emerged as dominant. But, by the late nineteenth century, "the walls of the male establishment began to crack," as social and economic changes again changed the meaning of men's lives (Dubbert 1980, 307). The frontier was declared closed, and rapid industrialization radically transformed men's relation to their work. Before the Civil War, almost nine of every ten American men were farmers or self-employed businessmen; by 1870, that figure had dropped to two of three, and, by 1910, less than one-third were so employed (Trachtenberg 1982, 141–42). By century's end, American men faced a seemingly endless string of structural problems—"the failures and corruption of reconstruction, the longest depression in American history, insatiable trusts, swarms of what were held to be sexually potent and racially inferior immigrants, and a government discredited at all levels" (Barker-Benfield 1976, 84; see also Leach 1980). All these shifted the grounds of manhood.

Against this background of dramatic structural and ideological change, the family and the relations between women and men were undergoing upheaval and conflict. Women's public emergence—the increasing agitation for suffrage, temperance, marriage reforms, education, and equal economic opportunity—precipitated a "crisis" of masculinity, as men grappled with new terms of relationships with women and new meanings for manhood. Men "were jolted by changes in the economic and social order which made them perceive that their superior position in the gender order and their supposedly 'natural' male roles and prerogatives were not somehow rooted in the human condition, that they were instead the result of a complex set of relationships subject to change and decay" (Hartman 1984, 13; see also Douglas 1977).

It is in this context of dramatic structural changes that men's responses to the growing women's movement must be set. Just as the grounding of a masculinity defined in the public sphere was eroding, women entered that sphere in unprecedented numbers. Women rebelled against a definition of feminity that was "narrow or even suffocating" (Filene 1986, 11). The opening of women's colleges and coeducation afforded new and expanded educational possibilities. Entry into the paid labor force and the professions and activities in the political arena, especially in the temperance and suffrage movements, suggested a new public role for women. Within the family, women were delaying childbearing and demanding birth control and "sex rights," all of which augured broad changes in the micropolitics of domestic life (Cott 1987). Feminism gave articulate voice to women's concerns, and, as women pressed for institutional reforms to remove constraints on public participation and demanded shifts in family and private life, men were pressed to respond to feminism as one of the most vital forces in our nation's history.

Responses to Feminism

We can discern three types of response to feminist claims, reacting to demands for women's right to the ballot, the classroom, and the workplace and to discussions of proper domestic relations, childrearing, and sexuality. An *anti-feminist* response consisted of a frightened retreat to traditional gender arrangements, supported ideologically by recourse to religious or quasi-religious arguments about the "natural law" of male supremacy and also by an assumed necessity for male dominance encoded in genetics or manifest in evolutionary biology. Anti-feminists accepted a natural division between work and home and demanded that women leave the public sphere and return to the home, where, they argued, women belonged. Anti-feminist authors yearned nostalgically for a mythic past in which the genders were complementary but unequal. It was not that women were to be prevented from enjoying suffrage, education, or work as much as they had a "right" to "exempted from certain things which men must endure," as the Reverend John Todd (1867, 25) wrote. Their delicate constitutions made them biologically and temperamentally unfit. Harvard professor Edward Clarke argued that college education was causing women to lose the capacity to breed. "If these causes should continue for the next half-century," he concluded, "it requires no prophet to foretell that the wives who are to be mothers in our republic must be drawn from transatlantic homes" (Clarke 1873, 152). Anti-feminist writers opposed women's economic participation and social reforms on similar grounds, implying that feminism threatened the abandonment of traditional motherhood and femininity.

The centerpiece of anti-feminist sentiment was, of course, opposition to suffrage. Suffrage presaged a repudiation of womanhood, so women must be exempted from its burden. In a debate about the question of suffrage in Sacramento, California, in 1880, one man summarized this strain of anti-suffrage opinion:

> I am opposed to woman's sufferage [*sic*] on account of the burden it will place upon her. Her delicate nature has already enough to drag it down. Her slender frame, naturally weakened by the constant strain attendant upon her nature is too often racked by diseases that are caused by a too severe tax upon her mind. The presence of passion, love, ambition is all to [*sic*] potent for her enfeebled constitution[,] and wrecked health and early death are all too common. [CSHL, MS 2334]

Others argued that suffrage was a privilege, not a right. The Reverend O. B. Frothingham argued that "no one should take part in government who was not ready to defend, by force, it necessary, the institutions of the country. Women could not be counted on [to fight]; therefore women should not vote" (Frothingham 1894, 5).

Anti-suffragism was an organized movement. Organizations sprang up around the nation, often funded and staffed by men and women who represented those industries most vulnerable to reform should women vote, as expected, for social reform efforts (Flexner 1970, 311). Opposition included active campaigning against state propositions and the publishing of several national magazines and newspapers. The Massachusetts Association Opposed to the Extension of Suffrage to Women published a monthly journal, the *Remonstrance*; the first issue (1890) makes the anti-suffrage philosophy clear:

> The belief that women will impart their tenderness and purity to politics is surely somewhat simple. They are tender and pure because their sphere has hitherto been the home, which is the abode of tenderness and purity. Thrown into the arena of political strife, the "angels," if experience may be trusted, instead of imparting the angelic character to the male combatants, would be in danger of losing it themselves. [SL, microfilm collection]

Contemporary anti-feminists continue this tradition. Some argue that feminism has duped women into abandoning marriage and children. Women, they argue, ought to be exempted from public participation because they are the bearers of morality; only they can constrain men's antisocial, amoral impulses (Gilder 1986, 41). Others use a false anthropological universality of male domination to reassert it in advanced industrial societies (Goldberg 1973). Some rail against feminism's reform of social and sexual relationships, complaining that feminism has created the "impossible situation" of "trying *not* to feel aggressiveness or dominance toward a woman when making love to her. . . . It will be a sad day when men no longer see women as the objects of their lust" (Davidson 1988).

The National Organization for Men (NOM), founded by divorce lawyer and *Penthouse* columnist Sidney Siller, opposes a feminism that is designed "to denigrate men, exempt women from the draft and to encourage the disintegration of the family" (Siller 1984). Under the guise of promoting equal rights for all, *including* men, NOM opposes affirmative action, abortion rights, imprisonment of men for nonpayment of alimony, and giving preference to women in custody issues. In the anti-feminist scheme, it is time for men to stand up to the "libbers' stridency and the brain damaged man-hating" (Freedman 1985, 284).

A second group of men was less distressed about women's increased power than about the enervation of American culture and men's loss of virility. *Masculinists* opposed this perceived cultural feminization and sought to create islands of untainted masculinity, purified pockets of virility in separate institutions that could socialize young men to the hardiness appropriate to their gender. If anti-feminists sought complementary but unequal gender relations, masculinists hoped to restore a separate but equal relationship between the sexes so that boys would be certain to grow up to be "real men."

In part, masculinism responded to the consequences that the separation of spheres had for men. Some men felt exiled from the home, over which women now reigned, and sought ways to dislodge women from control. Masculinism included distinctly male agencies of socialization, such as the initiation rituals in fraternal orders, and developed distinctly male centers around the household, such as the den, a clever innovation in vernacular architecture that allowed men to return to their homes without becoming feminized. Masculinism also involved an increasing emphasis on fathering, campaigns against coeducation, and the development of institutions designed to remove boys from the feminizing clutches of women—teachers, Sunday school teachers, and, above all, mothers—and allow them to experience a purified masculine world with adult men and other boys. One writer in the *Educational Review* in 1914 claimed that female teachers had created a "feminized manhood, emotional, illogical, non-combative against public evils" ("The Woman Peril" 1914, 109–17). Others opposed collegiate coeducation, fearing that the entry of women would sap the virility of the male students. "Where coeducation exists, there is invariably a noticeable weakness in the calibre of the large majority of men attending such institutions and a corresponding loss of rank of such institutions among the colleges in the country," observed the editor of Wesleyan University's college newspaper, the *Argus*, in 1898.

Women's influence was also countered by religious leaders, who sought to reverse the feminization of American men by reinventing the public image of Jesus. The Muscular Christianity movement sought to transform religious iconography, which often portrayed Jesus as soft and gentle and was accompanied by a liturgy that emphasized self-effacing compassion. Jesus was "no dough-faced, lick-spittle proposition," proclaimed evangelist Billy Sunday, but "the greatest scrapper who ever lived." "Lord save us from off-handed, flabby cheeked, brittle boned, weak-kneed, thin-skinned, pliable, plastic, spineless, effeminate, ossified, three karat Christianity," Sunday pleaded (cited in McLaughlin 1955, 179, 175; see also Hughes 1880; Case 1906; Conant 1904; and Pierce 1912).

An early effort to revirilize Jesus' masculine image led Luther Gulick to commit the Young Men's Christian Association (YMCA), to the project of developing a disciplined altruistic manhood. The YMCA and also the Boy's Club were efforts to segregate boys and girls, thereby ensuring appropriate gender socialization. So, too, was the Boy Scouts of America, founded in 1910 by Ernest Thompson Seton. Women were turning "robust, manly, self-reliant boyhood into a lot of flat chested cigarette smokers with shaky nerves and doubtful vitality," Seton wrote (cited in Macleod 1983, 49; see also Hantover 1980; and Dubbert 1980). This "disciplined vitality" was also promoted through sports, increasingly prescribed as restorative of vigorous manhood. The late nineteenth century witnessed a bicycle craze, a sudden interest in physical fitness, and the spectacular rise of baseball as both participant and spectator sport. Novelist Zane Grey may have put the case most pithily. "All boys love baseball," he wrote. "If they don't, they're not real boys" (cited in McKeever 1913, 91).

Masculinism also included the flourishing of fraternal orders—slightly less than one-fourth of American men belonged to a fraternal order by the end of the century.[6] The lodge was a homosocial preserve, celebrating a purified, nurturant masculinity. Men "need banding together to stimulate their better affections," the Reverend A. B. Grosh wrote simply, if ideologically, in *The Odd Fellows Improved Manual* (1871, 170). Recharged militarism at the turn of the century also celebrated male bonding as a hedge against feminization. The soldier was a "moral exemplar"—none more so than Theodore Roosevelt, symbolic hero of militaristic masculinism, whose triumph over youthful frailty and subsequent robust aggression served as a template for a revitalized American social character. Roosevelt elevated compulsive masculinity and military adventurism to the level of national myth; promoting the strenuous life and imperialist adventurism fused masculinism and militarism into a compelling synthesis. Nowhere, though, is the masculinist response better expressed than in Henry James's novel *The Bostonians*. James's hero, the dashing Basil Ransom, is afraid that the natural masculinity of political leaders will be rendered impotent by aggressive women:

> The whole generation is womanized; the masculine tone is passing out of the world; it's a feminine, nervous, hysterical, chattering, canting age, an age of hollow phrases and false delicacy and exaggerated solicitudes and coddled sensibilities, which, if we don't soon look out, will usher in the reign of mediocrity, of the feeblest and flattest and most pretentious that has ever been The masculine character, the ability to dare and endure, to know and yet not fear reality, to look the world in the face and take it for what it is . . . that is what I want to preserve, or rather . . . recover; and I must tell you that I don't in the least care what becomes of you ladies while I make the attempt! [James (1885) 1984, 293]

Many of these themes inform contemporary masculinist thinking. Some seek to dislodge women's primacy in the private sphere; others offer male camaraderie and support for men "wounded" in the struggle in the public sphere. Men's challenge to women's parental monopoly comes from "men's rights" groups, such as the Coalition for Free Men, Mens Rights International, and Men Achieving Liberation and Equality (MALE), which deny that men have power in society. Male supremacy is an illusion, they claim, along the lines of the chauffeur: "He's dressed in the uniform and he looks like he's in the driver's seat," writes Warren Farrell, "but from his perspective someone else is giving the orders" (cited in Woldenberg 1986, 10). (Masculinists conveniently ignore the fact that it is another man who is giving the orders.) Others insist that men, too, are oppressed, "emotionally and sexually manipulated by women, forced into provider roles where they work themselves to death for their gold-digger wives, kept from equal participation and power in family life, and finally dumped by wives only to have courts and lawyers give all the property, money, and child custody to the women" (Messner 1986, 32).

Others seek to provide support and solace for men and an opportunity for them to connect spiritually with other men in homosocial settings. Poet Robert Bly and his associates run weekend retreats for men to rediscover their deeply masculine animal natures. By donning totemic animal symbols (reminiscent of late nineteenth-century fraternal rituals) and retrieving ancient myths of male bonding, Bly hopes that men will tap a stream of essential masculinity, long buried by the feminizing worlds of work and home. Still others echo the Muscular

Christianity movement by recasting Jesus as a religious Rambo. Televangelist Jerry Falwell, for example, insists that "Christ wasn't effeminate. . . . The man who lived on this earth was a man with muscles. . . . Christ was a he-man!" (cited in Fitzgerald 1986, 166). Baseball player Brett Butler echoed this theme in a newspaper interview. "If Christ played this game, he'd slide right into the second baseman, and then he'd help him up. Christ was no wimp" (*San Francisco Chronicle* 15 August 1989). Some observers insist that the separation of the sexes is the only way to preserve what is different (and interesting) about either women or men. When the Century Club, founded in the late nineteenth century as a protected male island, lost its struggle to exclude women, member Lewis Lapham defended men's clubs as an example of the way in which

> nature divides the whole of its creation into opposing forces (proton and electron, positive and negative, matter and antimatter, masculine and feminine) in order that their dynamic symmetries might decode and organize the unlocked chaos. The clarity of gender makes possible the human dialectic. Let the lines of balanced tension go slack and the structure dissolves into the ooze of androgyny and narcissism. [*New York Times* (4 March 1983)]

Clearly, for some masculinists, the entire fate of the human race hangs on the question of homosociality and the exclusion of women from private domains of untrammeled masculinity. True masculinists do not often care what women are doing with their lives. All they want is to be left alone, to become real men among other men.

It is the third group of men, the *pro-feminist* men, who are the subject of this book. From the late eighteenth century, pro-feminist men have supported women's claims for enlarged public participation and a wider sphere of personal autonomy. What was the basis for men's support of feminist struggles? What types of theories did they draw on to ground their ideas? How did they respond to the biological and religious theories that were employed by the anti-feminists or to the psychological theories used by the masculinists? These questions beg another more basic one. Why would men support women's struggles in the first place? If an increase in women's power in the public or the private sphere implies a challenge to men's position of privilege, why would men act against what were commonly thought to be their interests *as men* and support women? Why have there been so many pro-feminist men throughout U.S. history? Why, indeed, have there been *any*?

Since the founding of the country, there has been a gradual evolution of men's thinking, a slow transformation of the reasons that men have supported feminism. This evolution has been neither linear nor even since its context has always been that a majority of American men were indifferent or hostile to feminism. We can discern three patterns of support, three types of argument advanced to justify their adherence to and support of women's rights. Until the mid-nineteenth-century, pro-feminist men supported feminism because, quite simply, it was "right" and "just." Basing their support on abstract conceptions of justice grounded in a classic liberal theory of the sanctity of the individual and individual rights, these men supported suffrage, education, or employment because women were human beings and all human beings, regardless of race or gender, were entitled to the same basic rights as individuals. Women had an "equal right to virtue," as Thomas Paine put it. Later in the century, pro-feminist men supported feminism, not because of abstract conceptions of morality, but for more concrete moral reasons. Women, they argued, actually expressed a higher level of morality. Extending rights to women, therefore, would create a moralizing force to temper male excess and help men resist the temptation to vice. Men who worked with women in the temperance movement, the social purity movement and other social reform efforts sought to extend women's role as the guardians of the home to include the national home and hearth. If women tamed the wild beast in the household, she, together with her sisters, could clean up this sordid national household.

By the turn of the century, a new group of men began to articulate new grounds for support. These men saw support for feminism as part of a larger project to transform personal life in adherence to feminist and socialist principles. In this sense, they supported feminism *as men* because the gains that feminists sought would benefit men. Feminism, many claimed, offered an antidote to the crisis of masculinity, a blueprint to liberate men from restrictive gender roles, and opened the possibilities of sexual relations among equals.

These differences among pro-feminist men's arguments emerged from a historical process that roughly paralleled the history of the women's movement. (This process did not develop in a fully sequential pattern, one form superceding another; rather, forms overlapped considerably.) Just as feminist women's discourse shifted from political incorporation (suffrage), to social redemption, to the advocacy of "sex rights" for women, so did pro-feminist male discourse shift. This ought not surprise us since pro-feminist men attempted to be responsive to the positions articulated by women.

"Conscience and Common Sense": Pro-Feminist Men before 1870

For the first century of U.S. history, most male support of feminism revolved around three issues: the extension of the ballot, equal education, and, for a few, personal autonomy. Much of the discourse by pro-feminist men claims that women's equality was their natural right, a right based on a presumed equality with men at birth and grounded in "an abstract, ideological commitment to equality" and an overarching belief in the sanctity of the individual (Klein 1984, 7). Long before Seneca Falls, men promoted women's rights as the logical extension of the rights recently won from the British. Thus, Thomas Paine wrote "An Occasional Letter on the Female Sex" (1775), and writers like Benjamin Rush and Joseph Tuckerman supported women's rights to education and employment, respectively. (Paine's letter and Rush's and Tuckerman's essays appear in this volume.)

Transcendentalist thinkers, such as Ralph Waldo Emerson and Henry David Thoreau, supported suffrage because the boundaries of the individual could not be compromised by political dependency and exclusion. In a lecture at the Woman's Rights Convention in 1855, Emerson explained that human society "is made up of partialities. Each citizen has an interest and a view of his own, which, if followed out to the extreme, would leave no room for any other citizen." To bring all these biases together ensures that "something is done in favor of them all." Equality before the law, Emerson reasoned, will allow women to participate as individuals and, therefore, to determine "whether they wish a voice in making the laws that are to govern them" (Emerson 1883, 352, 354). Many abolitionists echoed these sentiments, extending moral arguments about ending slavery to the position of women as disenfranchised individuals. A number of abolitionists—including William Lloyd Garrison, Thomas Wentworth Higginson, Theodore Weld, Wendell Phillips, James Mott, Parker Pillsbury, Theodore Tilton, and Samuel Gridley Howe—actively campaigned for woman suffrage.

That campaign began in earnest at the World Anti-Slavery Convention of 1840 in London, where divisions between radical and moderate strategies of feminist action became evident among pro-feminist men. When the American delegation, led by Wendell Phillips, arrived, they were informed that the women would not be seated on the floor of the convention. Anglican ministers insisted that the Bible prohibited it, and other reformers argued that women's feeble constitutions could stand neither the physical strain nor the foul language likely to be used. Phillips eloquently defended the women's right to be seated:

> In America we listen to no such arguments. If we had done so we [would have] never been here as Abolitionists. It is the custom there not to admit colored men into respectable society, and we have been told again and again that we have been outraging the decencies of humanity when we permit colored men to sit by our side. When we have submitted to brick bats, and the tar tub and feathers in America, rather than yield to the custom prevalent there of not admitting colored brethren into our friendship, shall we yield to parallel custom or prejudice against women in Old England? We cannot yield this question if we would; for it is a matter of conscience. [*HWS*, 1:58]

In the end, Phillips did yield to an overwhelmingly negative vote—although Henry Stanton surprised his wife, Elizabeth, by voting to seat the women delegates—and the women were forced to sit behind a curtain, unseen and unable to speak during the proceedings that they had been elected to participate in.

When William Lloyd Garrison finally arrived with Charles Remond and Nathaniel P. Rogers, after having been delayed at sea, the story took a novel turn. Garrison was the founder of the American Anti-Slavery Society and perhaps the most prominent abolitionist of his era; his presence and fiery oratory were eagerly awaited by the entire convention. On hearing of the refusal to seat the women, Garrison and his companions were furious, but there was little they could do. Verbal remonstrance was impossible since the question had been decided and the proceedings were already under way. So Garrison, Remond, and Rogers refused to participate in the convention. "After battling many long years for the liberty of African slaves," Garrison said, "I can take no part in a convention that strikes down the most sacred rights of all women" (*HWS*, 1:60). For the ten days of the convention's proceedings, they sat with the women, and never uttered a word.

Eight years later, the first Woman's Rights Convention was held in

Seneca Falls, New York. Garrison and Douglass were there. Over thirty men participated in the convention, and James Mott was its co-chair. The resolution calling for woman suffrage, the only resolution not passed unanimously, was approved only after an impassioned speech by Douglass. "We hold woman to be equally entitled to all we claim for man. We go farther, and express our conviction that all political rights which it is expedient for man to exercise, it is equally so for women," he argued from the convention floor (cited in Strauss 1982, 176). Douglass was quickly labeled a "hermaphrodite," an "Aunt Nancy Man," and a "woman's rights man" by an unsympathetic press. He was shocked that "a discussion of the rights of animals would be regarded with far more complacency by many of what are called the 'wise' and the 'good' of our land, than would a discussion of the rights of women. . . . Many who have at last made the discovery that negroes have some rights . . . have yet to be convinced that women are entitled to any" (cited in DeLeon 1988, 142).

Douglass did not shrink from laying responsibility on men's shoulders, insisting that to do otherwise would have been to blame the victim for her diminished capacities. "By nature, she is fitted to occupy a position as elevated and dignified as her self-created master," he wrote in the *North Star* (26 May 1848). "And though she is often treated by him as his drudge, or a convenient piece of household furniture, 'tis but a striking evidence of his mental imbecility and moral depravity." Garrison also rejected arguments that suggested that women's inferior condition was either their own fault or at least the shared responsibility of women and men. At the Fourth National Woman's Rights Convention in Cleveland in 1853, Garrison made a strong claim for male responsibility for women's oppression (his speech appears in this volume). Believing in "sin, therefore in a sinner; in theft, therefore in a thief; in slavery, therefore in a slaveholder; in wrong, therefore in a wrong-doer," he argued that, "unless the men of this nation are made by women to see that they have been guilty of usurpation, and cruel usurpation, I believe very little progress will be made." Nor did Garrison believe that men's oppression of women was accidental or the result of ignorance; it was "intelligent wickedness." Women in America "are the victims in this land, as the women of all lands are, to the tyrannical power and godless ambition of man."

Other abolitionists claimed that women's natural equality with men required political equality. "Woman is a human being; and it is a self-evident truth that whatever right belongs to man by virtue of his membership in the human family, belongs to her by the same tenure," wrote Henry C. Wright in a letter of support to the Woman's Rights Convention in Akron in 1854 (*HWS*, 1:310). Wendell Phillips used a literary allusion to ground his argument at the Tenth Woman's Rights Convention in New York in 1861: "Man has been allowed to grow. We ask the same for woman," he wrote. "Goethe said if you plant an oak in a flowerpot, one of two things will happen: either the oak will be dwarfed, or the flowerpot will break. . . . So we have planted woman in a flowerpot, hemmed her in by restrictions; and when we move to enlarge her sphere, society cries out, 'oh, you'll break the flowerpot!' Well," Phillips concluded, "let it break!" (Phillips 1891, 127).

Such sentiments were also sounded from pulpits around the country since many abolitionists were ministers. Samuel J. May's 1846 sermon "The Rights and Condition of Women" (included in this volume) is an articulate pre–Seneca Falls statement of individualist Protestantism's spiritual grounding of feminism. May presumes moral equality; men and women are "equal in rank, alike rational and moral beings." Thus, the disenfranchisement of women "is as unjust as the disenfranchisement of the males would be; for there is nothing in their moral, mental or physical nature, that disqualifies them to understand correctly the true interests of the community, or to act wisely on reference to them." Since men and women are equals before God, May argues that men may "with no more propriety assume to govern women, than they might assume to govern us."

Many of this first wave of pro-feminist men campaigned for equality in education. The founders and early presidents of women's colleges found the idea of exclusion anachronistic or offensive to individualist sensibilities. A poem in *Littell's Living Age* (1869, cited in Woody 1929, 1:114) posed the question:

> Ye fusty old fogies, Professors by name,
> A deed you've been doing, of sorrow and shame:
> Though placed in your chairs to spread knowledge abroad,
> Against half of mankind you would shut up the road.
> The fair sex from science you seek to withdraw
> By enforcing against them a strict Salic law:
> Is it fear? is it envy? or what can it be?
> And why should a woman not get a degree?

Why, indeed? No reason at all, according to Matthew Vassar and Milo Jewett at Vassar, William Allan Neilson and Joseph Taylor at Smith, and Henry Durant at Wellesley, all of whom expressed articulate claims for women's education. Durant claimed that the real meaning of higher education for women was "revolt." "We revolt against the slavery in which women are held by the customs of society—the broken health, the aimless lives, the subordinate position, the helpless dependence, the dishonesties and shams of so-called education," Durant wrote. "The Higher Education of Women . . . is the cry of the oppressed slave. It is the assertion of absolute equality" (cited in Horowitz 1985, 17).

Perhaps no one better synthesized the positions of this first wave of pro-feminist men than Thomas Wentworth Higginson. Long a fierce abolitionist, Higginson was also a strong advocate of woman suffrage and women's education (see Edelstein 1970). His series of essays *Women and the Alphabet* (an extract is included in this volume), published in the *Atlantic Monthly*, argued for suffrage and education and pierced the veneer of women's presumed superior morality. He also indicated a striking empathy for women's anger:

> I do not see how any woman can avoid a thrill of indignation when she first opens her eyes to the fact that it is really contempt, not reverence, that has so long kept her sex from an equal share of legal, political, and educational rights. In spite of the duty paid to individual women as mothers, in spite of the reverence paid by the Greeks and the Germanic races to certain women as priestesses and sibyls, the fact remains that this sex has been generally recognized, in past ages of the human race, as stamped by hopeless inferiority, not by angelic superiority.

Higginson did not advocate feminist ideas because of women's supposed moral superiority. "It is a plausible and tempting argument, to claim suffrage for woman on the ground that she is an angel," he wrote, "but I think it will prove wiser, in the end, to claim it for her as being human." Higginson countered arguments about complementarity and against coeducation; women need equal rights

> not because she is man's better half, but because she is his other half. She needs them, not as an angel, but as a fraction of humanity. Her political education will not merely help man, but it will help herself. She will sometimes be right in her opinions, and

> sometimes be altogether wrong; but she will learn, as man learns, by her own blunders. The demand in her behalf is that she shall have the opportunity to make mistakes, since it is by that means she must become wise.

For these men, women's participation in the public sphere simply extended individual rights to women, as many had earlier urged for black men. Suffrage was, as Wendell Phillips (1866 cited in *HWS* I) put it, "not alone woman's right, but woman's duty," and men's support of women's right was, in the words of Frederick Douglass, a matter of "conscience and common sense" (*Frederick Douglass' Paper*, 25 November 1853).

Woman as Moral Force: Pro-Feminist Men and Moral Redemption

By the last few decades of the nineteenth century, a new discourse entered the debate about women's equality. Woman's participation in the public sphere was justified on the grounds that it would bring more purity and beauty into the world. Most often this notion of woman as moralizer assumed the separation of spheres. But, where anti-feminists accepted the separation of spheres as a way to esteem women rhetorically while containing and subordinating them in practice, pro-feminist men sought to extend woman's sphere into the public realm, making the city or even the nation her domain to clean up. Some of these arguments rested on the old analogy between nation and family. Earlier, the parallel had kept women out of the public sphere: since the father was head of the household, men should therefore rule the political nation. After the upheavals of political revolution, this argument took a feminist turn: if there was no longer a king to whom one owed unquestioned allegiance, then perhaps the family could be refounded on more egalitarian lines. By the late nineteenth century, the argument had swung back again to the family: if women were the virtual heads of the household, responsible for the nurturing of emotions, the maintenance of the household, and the socialization of children, could women not apply these particular skills to the nation as a whole? "The mission of woman on earth," Lizzie Harbert wrote in her novel *Out of Her Sphere* (1871), is to "uplift purify and confirm, by her own gracious gift, the world, in despite of the world's dull endeavor to degrade and drag down and oppose it forever. The mission of woman? Born to soothe and to solace, to help and to heal the sick world that leans upon her" (cited in Buechler 1986, 111).

Supporters of women's education and coeducation, for example, claimed that equal education was necessary to combat the degeneracy and vice that pervaded American culture. Joseph Sayers argued that "a liberal, literary, moral, and virtuous female education [was] the only detergent remedy for vice, crime and immorality" (Sayers 1956, iv). Women's public participation in charity work was the natural extension of work in the home. Charles Stelzle, a preacher of the Social Gospel, argued in *American Social and Religious Conditions* that women's charity work was important for women's health and national moral health:

> Confined to the four walls of their kitchens, and made to listen to the crying and the shouting of the children, is it any wonder that many of them become insane? Here's a chance for some big-hearted women—the chance to minister to just *one* immigrant woman, putting into her life something of the abundance which has filled her own . . . not in a spirit of patronage or paternalism, but coming as a sister in the spirit of her Master. [1912, 114]

Advocates of suffrage employed arguments that stressed women as a moralizing force instead of the simple morality of political incorporation. Clifford Howard argued that "woman should have the ballot, not only for her own benefit, but for the benefit of you and me and every other man who stands for good government and public cleanliness and purity." Howard co-opted the separation of spheres and contended that women's participation in the public sphere was imperative precisely because women's sphere "*is* the home. But today would she serve the home she must go beyond the house. No longer is the home compassed by four walls. Many of its most important duties lie now involved in the bigger family of the city and state" (Howard, n.d., 3, 7). Edward Ward facetiously asserted the separate-sphere argument, writing that "women should mind their own business. That is, they should vote in the modern government, for this is their proper sphere, except in its destructive, anti-social, military expression" (Ward, n.d., 7). During the Kansas campaign of 1887–88, one newspaper urged suffrage because

> it is a crime not to vote; because it is their natural right; because they can do good by voting; because their votes will help to purify politics; . . . because every tramp and foreigner, and anarchist and socialist, and dynamiter and ignoramus, and hoodlum, if he is twenty-one can vote. The votes of intelligent Christian women are needed to save the homes of the nation. . . . [A]nd every woman who fears for the purity of her daughters, the sobriety and honesty of her husband or sons, has in the ballot, one means of lessening her anxiety and healing her heartache. [cited in McNall 1988, 22]

Frederic C. Howe, commissioner of the Port of New York Authority and the celebrated humane warden of Ellis Island, argued that social reforms were made possible only by woman's extension of her proper sphere into the public realm. In "What The Ballot Will Do For Women and For Men," he cast suffrage as the redemption from the "muddle we have made of politics"; woman alone was capable of ending poverty, hunger, suffering, and disease. In a lyrical romanticization of women's participation, Howe wrote,

> I want to live in a world that thinks of its people rather than of business; of consumers rather than producers; of users rather than makers; of tenants rather than owners; in a world where life is more important than property, and human labor more valuable than privilege.
>
> As women are consumers, users, and tenants rather than producers, makers, and owners, I have hopes for a society in which women have and use the ballot.
>
> I want woman suffrage because I believe women will correct many of these law-made wrongs that man has made. For women will vote in terms of human life rather than in terms of special privilege. [Howe, nb.d., 7–8]

Mark Twain's ideas about suffrage were quoted in a program of the Equal Franchise Society's meeting in 1909. "If the women of New York City had the ballot they would drive corruption out," Twain wrote (SL, WSC). "Each party would be compelled to put up its best candidates to stand any chance of winning. I would like to see the ballot in the hands of every woman."

Much of this sentiment reversed the anti-feminist contention that participation in politics would drag women down into the mire of male vice. After all, anti-feminists had argued, one may vote in a saloon, in which a proper lady would not ever be caught. Quite so, said these men. But woman suffrage would not lower women; it would raise men to women's level. If women voted, there could be no saloons in which to vote; temperance would be the natural corollary to suffrage. Walt Whitman took these ideas away from extolling women's asexual virtue. Whitman believed that women were equally sensual as men, as entitled to sexual pleasure as men, and as fully capable of it as men. In "Song of the Broad Axe" (1856), Whitman combined support for public participation with a celebration of women's physical strength and sensuous beauty:

> Where women walk in public processions in the streets the same as the men,
> Where they enter the public assembly and take places the same as the men;
> Where the city of the faithfulest friends stands
> Where the city of the cleanliness of the sexes stands,
> Where the city of the healthiest fathers stands,
> Where the city of the best-bodied mothers stands,
> There the great city stands.

Women, according to Whitman, could be both more moral than men and still equal in desire.

"Feminism for Men": The Greenwich Village Radicals

By the turn of the century, the suffrage campaign split between statewide efforts to get women the ballot and national campaigns to enact a constitutional amendment granting woman equal rights. Some believed that suffrage was the goal of the movement and that all energies should be spent in ensuring its enactment; others promoted a wider-ranging agenda of social reforms and advocacy of "sex rights." The split between suffragists and feminists was echoed among profeminist men, as many men like Henry Brown Blackwell, Thomas Wentworth Higginson, William Lloyd Garrison, and Wendell Phillips continued on the suffrage trail until their deaths early in the twentieth century. But a group of men in New York City embraced a much larger vision of feminist social reconstruction. While never renouncing suffrage, they saw voting as only a reformist palliative; deeper structural change was necessary in the private relations of women and men and the public positions of the sexes. Both feminist and socialist, this group embraced feminist ideas as much for their potential to liberate men as for their importance to women's liberation. The bohemian "sex radicals" of Greenwich Village were actively linked to feminist causes because the liberation of women implied the demoliton, not the beautification, of industrial capitalism. "I see the social movement with all its manifestations—feminism, socialism, social religion, internationalism, etc.—slowly linking the chains of social consciousness, and thus transforming the individual persons, the individual groups, lifting them to a higher level, giving them a more abundant sense of sympathy and unanimity," wrote Randolph Bourne in 1914 (cited in Abrahams 1986, 367). Linking their critique of social and sexual relations between women and men to a socialist critique of the relations between workers and owners under capitalism, they were as concerned with questions of women's sexual autonomy as they were with political enfranchisement.

What is more, these men sought to organize other men around feminist issues and to lead lives that were consistent with their beliefs. In this way, they embraced a new feminism that was "a reaction against . . . the stress in nurturant service and moral uplift" (Cott 1987, 37). The socially reformist wing of the women's movement had promoted reform as woman's duty; these turn-of-the-century feminists proclaimed a full range of women's rights, including sexual autonomy. To Floyd Dell, feminism was more than "a revolt of women against conditions which hamper their activities; it is also a revolt of women and men against the type of woman created by those conditions" (Dell 1921, 349). The Greenwich Village radicals attempted to create new relationships while they promoted and supported feminist causes. In this "moral health resort," as Floyd Dell (cited in O'Neill 1978, 29) called it, they confronted issues of monogamy and sexual fidelity, women's sexual autonomy and right to birth control, while they supported women's entry into the economic sphere, increased educational opportunities, and, of course, suffrage. Feminism had created a new type of woman; such new women would soon meet some "new" men, men who could thrill to women's sexual autonomy, were outraged at economic and political discrimination, and worked in both public and private spheres to bring about a system of sexual equality and gender justice.[7]

Such men included Max Eastman, Dell, Hutchins Hapgood, William Sanger, and Randolph Bourne. Eastman, editor of the *Masses* and secretary and organizer of the Men's League for Woman Suffrage, was (in his early years) an exemplary figure, organizing other men around feminist issues and struggling toward equality in his personal life. Eastman and his wife, Ida Rauh, caused a scandal when, on their return from a trip to Europe in the fall of 1911, they began a Village custom when they posted Rauh's full name on their mail box. Eastman said that he wanted his wife to be "entirely independent of men in every way—to be as free as she was before we were married" (cited in O'Neill 1978, 24). Eastman linked support for feminism with his understanding of masculinity. "There was nothing harder for a man with my mamma's-boy complex to do than stand up and be counted as a 'male suffragette,'" he wrote in *Enjoyment of Living* (1936, 316). "It meant not only that I had asserted my manhood, but that I had passed beyond the need of asserting it." Dell tried to write a sexually explicit poem, "I Doubted Not" (1906), from the point of view of the woman, including what he believed to be her experience of orgasm.[8]

In the political sphere, the Greenwich Village radicals were very visible in their campaigns for women's equality. Several prominent New Yorkers joined Eastman in founding the Men's League for Woman Suffrage in 1910; the officers included Oswald Garrison Villard, publisher of the *New York Evening Post*, Columbia professor John Dewey, and Rabbi Stephen Wise. Their purpose, according to Secretary Eastman, was to "give status to the cause . . . showing that equal suffrage was advocated by others besides the silly women who were thought to be behind it" (cited in O'Neill 1978, 19). The Men's League was the first organized pro-feminist men's organization in the United States and consisted of over thirty statewide branches and several in other countries. Its chief purpose was, in the words of the constitution of the California branch, "to express approval of the movement of women to attain the full suffrage" and "to aid them in their efforts toward that end by public appearances in behalf of the cause, by the circulation of literature, the holding of meetings, and in such other ways as may from time to time seem desirable," which included organizing men's contingents for suffrage parades (CSHL).

One year after its founding, the league experienced some organizational success. An editorial in *La Follette's* in May 1911 praised the eighty-five "courageous and convinced men" who marched in one recent demonstration; one marcher counted being "booed and hissed down the Avenue a very thrilling experience" and indicated his determination that, "if I can help to that end, there shall be a thousand men in line next year." He was not very far off. An editorial in the *New York Times* (included in this volume) one year later predicted that eight hundred men would march the next day in a suffrage demonstration, although Eastman counted far more. "Even when the Men's League occupied five blocks, four abreast," he wrote, "the press could see only a grudging thousand of them" (Eastman 1936, 351).

Members of the league were active speakers on the suffrage circuit during the decade preceding suffrage. John Dewey, "an ardent woman suffragist," according to his philosophy student and disciple Eastman, was especially active, linking issues of education and suffrage for numerous audiences (Eastman 1941, 675). Other members were less visible. For example, when William Benedict, a New York lawyer, read that two organizations, the Retail Liquor Dealers' Association of Montana and the Union League Club of New York, had gone on record in 1915 as opposing woman suffrage, he resigned his membership in the Union League Club. In a well-publicized yet anonymous letter to Harriet Laidlaw, chair of the Manhattan Borough Chapter of the Woman Suffrage Party (and wife of James Lee Laidlaw, national president of the Men's League for Woman Suffrage), Benedict wrote that "about this time of year I should have been paying my annual dues to the Union League Club had I not resigned on account of its action on the equal suffrage question. I accordingly take pleasure in sending you a check for the amount of said dues to be used as you may think best in furthering the cause" (SL, Laidlaw Papers, A-65, box 14). Barely a month later, Benedict wrote an anonymous letter to the *New York Times* (included in this volume) in response to an anti-suffrage editorial.

Eastman was clearest that his participation sprang from different theoretical assumptions than did that of earlier pro-feminist men. Stoutly, he declared that for his generation of pro-feminist men it was neither "justice as a theoretic ideal, nor feminine virtue as a cure for politics," that prompted their support for feminism. They did "not look to women's votes for the purification and moral elevation of the body politic. . . . The great thing to my mind is not that women will improve politics but that politics would develop women," Eastman wrote, reversing earlier arguments about woman as moralizing force (Eastman 1912, 8, 2). Many saw the social revolution offered by feminist demands for personal autonomy as the personal complement to socialist revolution, women's freedom as the fulfillment of social change, and believed that women were the leaders in such a revolution. Thus, Dell argued in "Feminism for Men" (included in this volume) that capitalism is opposed to feminism because "it wants men with wives and children who are dependent on them for support." Feminism, however, will allow men to rediscover women as equals.

Such personal autonomy required sexual freedom, and pro-feminist men supported women's struggles for birth control. William Sanger was arrested by Anthony Comstock in 1915 for distributing *Family Limitation*, his wife Margaret's birth-control pamphlet. Women's sexual autonomy was vital, perhaps even more than the vote, as Floyd Dell explained in his extraordinary *Women as World Builders*:

> Her development, for freedom, for independence, must come from and through herself. First, by asserting herself as a personality, and not as a sex commodity. Second, by refusing the right to anyone over her body; by refusing to bear children unless she wants them; by refusing to be a servant to God, the State, society, the husband, the family, etc.; by making her life simpler, but deeper and richer. That is, by trying to learn the meaning and substance of life in all its complexities, by freeing herself from the fear of public opinion and public condemnation. Only that, and not the ballot, will set woman free, will make her a force hitherto unknown in the world, a force for real love, for peace, for harmony; a force of divine fire, of life giving; a creator of free men and woman. [1913, 61–62].

Eastman claimed a similar motive for supporting feminism—an "unqualified liking for women with brains, character, and independence" (Eastman 1936, 315)—and was equally certain that feminism held an important message for men as well. In one short item in the *Masses* (1914, 7), Eastman recounted a brief (and possibly apocryphal) exchange with a new stenographer:

> "Are you a feminist?" we asked the stenographer.
> She said she was.
> "What do you mean by Feminism?"
> "Being like men," she answered.
> "Now you are joking!"

"No, I'm not. I mean real independence. And emotional independence too—living in relation to the universe rather than in relation to some other person."

"All men are not like that," we said sadly.

"Then they should join the Feminist movement!"

Feminism was the culmination of the revolutionary impulse of the first decades of the century, worth supporting because it would extend the revolution that feminists advocated. As Dell wrote,

> They will not exchange one place for another, nor give up one right to pay for another, but they will achieve all rights to which their bodies and brains give them an implicit title. They will have a larger political life, a larger motherhood, a larger social service, a larger love, and they will reconstruct or destroy institutions to that end as it becomes necessary. They will not be content with any concession or any triumph until they have conquered all experience. [1913, 51]

For all their contradictory arguments (and eventual abandonment of feminism), Dell, Eastman, and other Greenwich Village radicals had discovered the fusion of the personal and the political. Men had come to see that the success of feminism contained within it the seeds of their liberation, to understand that feminism, as Dell wrote in "Feminism for Men" (included in this volume), "is going to make it possible for the first time for men to be free."

Friends, Lovers, Fathers, Sons, and Husbands: Personal Experience and Pro-Feminist Politics

Although this essay makes no attempt to construct a social psychology of pro-feminist men's motivations—such a project would be both beyond the scope of this work and somewhat of a political distraction from their commitments and ideas (as if by shifting the focus from the ideas to personal idiosyncratic motives one can explain away the ideas)—personal experience has played such a central role in their decisions that we might look briefly at the personal lives of some of these men. Without attempting to put a rosy gloss on these lives, I want to focus here on the men who were exemplary in their commitment to enacting feminist principles on an everyday basis with the women in their lives.

Many men, after all, publicly supported feminism but had mixed results applying it in their own lives. Public advocacy of feminism was inconsistent with their conventionally traditional relationships with women. Many abolitionists, such as Garrison, Pillsbury, and May, had conventional marriages, although several notable ones did not, and a couple, Tilton and Beecher, were central figures in a gripping sexual scandal. The champions of women's education, such as Vassar, Raymond, Durant, and Hutchins, held fairly conventional views about what women should do with the education that they were providing them. Many of the communards of the mid- to late nineteenth century seem to have advocated women's sexual autonomy and male responsibility for ambiguous reasons—partly because they really did believe in women's sexual equality and partly because they sought ideological justifications for their own sexual infidelities. Few before the twentieth century could believe that a woman would *want* to work, but some supported their right to do so for economic necessity. A few, like Samuel Gompers, vacillated in his public pronouncements while in his personal life he consistently demeaned the women around him.

Eugene Debs maintained a complete separation between his public and private lives. While believing in suffrage, Debs also believed in the separation of spheres, prohibiting women from membership in the co-operative colony he proposed in 1897. "If man the titan makes the world big, woman, the enchantress, makes it beautiful," he wrote in 1920. "Man may make the nation but woman does more—she makes the home. . . . Woman is the guardian of the sacred fire" (1983, 215). His marriage to Kate Metzel was fully conventional: he struggled for socialism and suffrage while she stayed at home and nursed him when he fell ill.

Few of the men who publicly proclaimed their adherence to feminism were as personally reprehensible in their behavior towards their wives as Dudley Field Malone, best known as a member of the defense team during the Scopes trial. Married to Doris Stevens, the head of the National Women's Party, Malone was given to drunkenly insulting Stevens in public, numerous affairs, and, on one occasion, physical violence against her. Stevens noted another instance of his personal abdication of his public beliefs. "I am on record as standing for a proper division between husband and wife of family income. He himself has publicly stated the same belief," she wrote. "It was a source of great disappointment and humiliation for me that he would never consent to put my (and his) publicly stated beliefs into practice in our menage" (cited in White 1987, 53). Stevens waited patiently until she and Jonathan Mitchell could escape together. Thus, Malone, New York's most flamboyant divorce lawyer, was himself involved in a scandalous divorce.

Other men simply could not accept a full feminist package, supporting some reforms and not others. Some supported suffrage but not women's participation in the labor force or the professions. Others supported women's education but not suffrage. (After all, Emma Goldman, one of the fiercest advocates for women's sexual freedom, did not support suffrage, which she saw as a moderate reform that would help legitimate capitalism in the eyes of working classes.) Among the Greenwich Village radicals, the case is not as clear. Some writers have charged that these men appeared to support feminism because it granted them greater license in their sexual activities without commitment (Trimberger 1984). But the central role played by feminist political organizing in the early life of Max Eastman and in the personal lives of Hutchins Hapgood and George Middleton, both of whom worked closely and as equals with their wives, makes it hard to justify such a claim. Although Dell steered clear of political activity with the Men's League for Woman Suffrage, his later writings indicate that his personal wrestling with issues of monogamy and women's equality came from deeply held convictions. Certainly, the Greenwich Village radicals were not completely successful in integrating the legacy of nineteenth-century patriarchal traditionalism with their progressive views about the feminist reconstruction of sex, love, and emotional intimacy. That none of them was able to live out that integration of the personal and the political fully does not mean that we should dismiss them as self-serving phonies or repudiate their ideas. Flawed and contradictory, they had also made an effort at integration on a far greater scale than any of the earlier suffragist marriages in the nineteenth century, thus offering suggestive new possibilities to those of us for whom that integration is still a goal.

What kinds of personal experiences can we observe among those men whose lives evinced a higher degree of consistency between the personal and the political? How did their personal experiences with women reflect their politics, and how did their politics become expressions of the personal struggles in which they engaged? Many of the men in this book were married to feminist women; some joined their wives or sisters (or mothers) on the suffrage campaign trail, and others stayed at home supporting their wives' work or caring for the children. As early as 1833, Emma Willard wrote about her husband's support of her educational reform work,

> He entered into the full spirit of my views with a disinterested zeal for that sex, whom, he believed, his own had injuriously neglected. With an affection more generous and disinterested than ever man before felt, he, in his later life, sought my elevation, indifferent to his own. Possessing on the whole an opinion of me more favorable than any other human being will ever have, and, thus encouraging me to dare much, he yet knew my weaknesses and fortified me against them. [Willard 1833, 46]

In one study, Blanche Glassman Hersh (1978) found that, of the thirty-seven nineteenth-century suffragists she studied, twenty-eight had husbands who supported their activity. Only four of the husbands were actively unsympathetic (the views of the others could not be determined). Hersh argues tht many men's support came from a shared religious vision that sprang from the mid-century reformist sects, especially the Quakers, Unitarians, and Universalists. James Mott, for example, a Quaker, learned early in life that women and men ought to be equal. Daniel Livermore was a Universalist minister. Even if not religious, many pro-feminist men came from reformist families, in which the mothers were active in reform work outside the home. This was true of Livermore, Mott, Stephen Foster, and Henry and Samuel Blackwell.

Many of these men had to wrestle with public disapproval as well as personal anguish. Habitually dismissed by the popular press as "henpecked husbands" who "ought to wear petticoats," most of them stood by their faith in equality and progress. When Stephen Foster married Abby Kelley, he was chastised for being led astray by a "vile and dangerous woman." Foster and others certainly suffered under the additional pressure of being married to a woman who was clearly more famous than her husband. In an article entitled "Women's Husbands" in the *Woman's Journal* in 1873, Thomas Wentworth Higginson explored this dilemma, discussing James Mott's marriage to Lucretia. "In the existing state of prejudice," he wrote, "it may sometimes require moral courage in a man to recognize frankly the greater ability or fame of his wife" (Higginson 1873, 1).

Mott supported his wife's work unequivocally; although frequently called on to assist her in her public appearances, he always did so in her shadow, never delivering a lecture or drawing attention to himself. They maintained a model home, in which each was responsible for housework. When their granddaughter began a biography of her illustrious grandmother, she found that she could not "write of one without the other," so she decided to write about both. It was impossible to contemplate her grandparents' lives, she wrote, "without realizing that *his* life made *hers* a possibility" (*HWS*, 4:409).

Carrie Chapman was also fortunate enough to have a loving and supportive husband. When she told George Catt that she was determined to devote herself to suffrage, he replied that that was precisely what he wanted her to do, especially since the demands of his business meant that he would be unable to take an active part in the suffrage struggle directly. He said that he would earn the living for the two of them so that she could continue her political work without worrying about making ends meet. Their marriage, he declared, would be "a partnership for public service" (Severn 1967, 118). So too was the married life of suffragist and activitist Harriet Laidlaw and her husband, James Lee Laidlaw, the president of the Men's League for Woman Suffrage from 1912 to 1917. After Harriet had "converted" James to feminism, he actively supported her political work and believed that his career could free his wife to pursue her important political work (ibid., 118).

George Francis Train also supported feminist causes financially. Train was an eccentric millionaire who was active in a large number of causes, including the Irish Rebellion, the perpetuation of racist segregation in the South, Populism, the campaign for the eight-hour day, and women's rights—without giving much thought to the inconsistencies. A fiery orator, Train swayed midwestern crowds to the suffrage cause when campaigning with Susan B. Anthony in the 1870s. Determined to help Anthony, he first suggested the idea and then financed the publication of Anthony and Stanton's newspaper, *Revolution*. It was also Train who supplied the paper's motto: "Men, their rights and nothing more; women, their rights and nothing less" (ibid., 86–87).

Both Theodore Weld and Angelina Grimké, as well as Stephen Foster and Abby Kelley, used the occasion of their wedding ceremonies to denounce laws that rendered women the property of their husbands. (Foster and Kelley's contract is included in this volume.) Daniel Livermore gave up his newspaper editorship and pastorate in order to follow his wife Mary to Boston, where she became the editor of the *Woman's Journal.* She later wrote an essay in the *Journal* asking, "The Ideal Husband: Does He Really Exist?" (*HWS*, vol. 5). She bestowed the title on Wendell Phillips (although she also commented on her gratitude to her own husband). For many women, personal life was a "partnership of equals" with their pro-feminist husbands.

Perhaps the most famous of these egalitarian marriages were those entered into by the Blackwell brothers. Samuel Blackwell married Antoinette Brown, the first woman ordained into the ministry in the United States; she counted on his "sustained sympathy" during their forty-year marriage. At their wedding, they contracted to be the "joint owners of all properties, real estate and moneys" (cited in Hersh 1978, 236). Henry Brown Blackwell and Lucy Stone's marriage contract (included in this volume), written by him with her approval, remains a powerful critique of traditional marriage. Blackwell renounced all legal privileges accorded to men and repudiated a system in which "the legal existence of the wife is suspended during marriage." The contract inspired feminist couples for over fifty years; at a memorial service for Stone in 1894, a speaker from the National Woman Suffrage Association called it the "grandest chart of the absolute equality of man and women that has ever been made" (*HWS*, 5:266).

Stone herself was deeply appreciative. "You are the *best husband* in the world," she wrote Henry in 1856. "In the midst of all the extra care, hurry, and perplexity of business, you stop and look after all my little affairs . . . doing everything you can to save me trouble. How shall I ever pay you, for all your thoughtful kindness? I will *love you*, as I do, with *all my heart.*" Elizabeth Blackwell, Henry's sister, called him "one of the best husbands possible, [who] certainly modified his whole course . . . to adapt his life to hers" (cited in Wheeler 1981, 151, 357). Stone inspired hundreds of women at the turn of the century to retain their names as a badge of autonomy from their husbands. The "Lucy Stoners" were objects of public scorn and occasional scandal since nonmarital cohabitation was illegal.

One young woman whom Stone inspired was Catherine Waugh, a law student in Chicago. As she and Frank McCullough planned their wedding, Waugh decided, after a lengthy correspondence with Stone, to retain her own name *and* add McCullough's. "I have always been grateful to my husband for the loyal way he stood by me when we took the new but true road," Stone wrote Waugh (SL, MC 378, box 1, folder 2). Catherine and Frank were the two top graduates from Northwestern Law School in 1886. (Catherine, valedictorian, was the second woman to graduate from Northwestern, the first law school to graduate a woman.) They set up a joint practice in Chicago and shared the raising of their three sons, two of whom eventually joined their firm.

Frank and Catherine Waugh McCullough had more than an egalitarian relationship, in which the two partners were equal at work and at home; they had a *feminist* relationship, in which feminist issues were debated and discussed and became a part of everyday life. One can observe this from the events surrounding their law school reunion in 1909. The banquet that year was held in the Chicago Athletic Association's building, a club that did not admit women. When club officials refused to allow Catherine to enter the banquet, Frank protested that she was, after all, one of the most prominent graduates of the law school and was entitled to enter. The club staff held firm. Frank entered the hall alone and, after talking with other alumni, returned within thirty minutes leading a march out of the building of well over half those attending. The staff relented, and Catherine was permitted to attend the banquet, to the cheers of the male graduates in attendance. The next day, Frank drafted a letter to the Law School Alumni Association advising that, in the future, no establishment should be selected for banquets that hesitated about admitting women. Catherine signed the letter as well, and, thereafter, the association selected banquets sites after ascertaining their policies regarding women (SL, MC 378, box 2).

William Sanger, Margaret's husband, who was arrested for distributing *Family Limitation*, was also supportive at home. "You go ahead and finish your writing," she quotes him saying, "and I'll get the dinner and wash the dishes." But Margaret used to draw the kitchen curtains in their first-floor Greenwich Village apartment, lest any passersby notice this gender reversal (Forster 1985; Reed 1977). Suffrage and birth-control campaigner Katharine Houghton Hepburn was married to a physician who supported birth control and woman suffrage "enthusiastically," according to his obituary in the *Hartford Courant* (21 November 1962). Their daughter, Katharine, recalled that her father wrote an article in 1900 "about how women had very superior minds, and how even though they were not as strong physically as men, they were certainly as bright mentally" (*New York Times* [9 March 1989]).

Max Eastman saw his relationships with his mother and his feminist sister Crystal as decisive influences on his life and on his later decision to attempt a turn-of-the-century version of an open marriage to Ida Rauh. The bearer of a "momma's-boy complex," Eastman believed that his support of suffrage was possible only after he had worked through a significant amount of difficulty with his masculine identity. But the marriage took most of Eastman's "irrational joy in life" away because he had "committed the folly of growing up." Eastman tried to be egalitarian in his efforts to demolish traditional monogamous marriage; as his biographer William O'Neill observed. Eastman believed in "a single standard of immorality" and expected his lovers and mates to enjoy the same (O'Neill 1978, 70). Thus, only from a narrow moralistic lens that embraces traditional marriage could one claim this as "a degree of irresponsibility towards the woman's feelings that can be described as sexist" (White 1987, 54).

It is evident that many of the men whose words are presented in this book struggled to practice in their personal relationships what they preached in the public arena. That many of their efforts were limited and contradictory is not surprising since we often hold people in other eras to standards that we are attempting to enact or that we expect of ourselves in our own. "I would have giants, and I find but men," feminist philosopher Simone de Beauvoir lamented in *The Second Sex* ([1956] 1973, 390). What is surprising is how many of them were so supportive of the feminist women in their lives and how they saw their lives, as Frank and Catherine Waugh McCullough put it, as a "copartnership of equals" (SL, MC 378, box 2).

Contemporary Pro-Feminist Men

Today's feminist woman also has male allies. As in the past, most ground their support by reference to abstract morality and justice, while a few extend it to examine the impact that feminism will have on men. But, as earlier, it is difficult to find a large number of men who both visibly support feminist struggles in the public sphere and attempt to transform their personal lives in accordance with those principles. That fusion of personal life with support for feminism in the public arena is one of the central challenges for today's pro-feminist men.

The campaign for the Equal Rights Amendment (ERA) brought forth the single largest outpouring of male support, much of it echoing earlier arguments about the extension of individual rights and about abstract conceptions of freedom, justice, and democracy. "How long can we stand by and watch qualified people excluded from jobs or denied fair payment for their labor?" asked actor Alan Alda. "How long can we do nothing while people are shut out from their fair share of economic and political power merely because they are women?" (Alda 1976, 93). These claims lay behind the speeches of the various senators and congressmen who introduced the ERA into both houses of Congress—Senators Charles Mathias and Edward Kennedy, Representatives Bill Green and Donald Edwards. Moral claims also convinced sports broadcaster Howard Cosell (included in this volume), who wrote that he supported the ERA "because, simply, it's right and necessary. It relates to the betterment of society, it relates to principles upon which the nation was supposed to be founded, principles which have not been lived up to. You do what is right and you stand for what is right. And the way you do that is with your mind, your heart, your vocalizations, and your general influence. It's very simple."

Some writers went further than abstract morality. Alda claimed that men would benefit from the passage of the ERA because wider role options available to women would relieve men of a lot of pressure: "As women fill traditionally male roles as police chiefs, gas station attendants, baseball players, and bankers, we may also begin to realize that wisdom, aggressiveness, and physical courage are not solely male attributes. The pressure to provide these qualities all by ourselves will be taken from men's shoulders. We can still be strong and brave but we won't have to feel we're the only ones who are" (Alda 1976, 93).[9] In a 1975 essay, reminiscent of Dell's "Feminism for Men" (included in this volume), Alda embraces a feminist critique of masculinity. Men, he argued, will benefit from feminism because current standards of masculinity are often pathological, locking men into behavior that is destructive to women, children, and other men. As a prisoner of masculinity, as a sufferer of what he calls "testosterone poisoning," a man is "not someone you'd want to have around in a crisis—such as raising children or growing old together" (Alda 1975, 16).

As in suffrage campaigns, men also supported the ERA organizationally. Men Allied Nationally for the Equal Rights Amendment (M.A.N. for the E.R.A.), founded by Barry Shapiro, with chapters in various states, sponsored rallies and campaigned actively for the amendment. The group often marched in ERA demonstrations behind their organizational banner, much the way the Men's League for Woman Suffrage marched in suffrage parades. One difference between contemporary pro-feminist men and earlier generations is the level of organization. Not only M.A.N. for the E.R.A. but currently several grass-roots organizations confront men's violence against women. Rape and Violence End Now (RAVEN) in St. Louis, Emerge in Boston, and Men Overcoming Violence (MOVE) in San Francisco are but three of the many centers where violent men receive counseling about domestic violence and convicted spouse abusers are referred by courts. Pro-feminist men's organizations in several major cities, such as the Chicago Men's Gathering, the Pittsburgh Men's Collective, and the New York Center for Men, sponsor programs on how men can share the feminist vision and work with other men around issues of sexism and homophobia. Some local pro-feminist men's groups are more activist oriented, like Madison (Wisconsin) or Santa Cruz (California) Men against Rape, and work closely with local women's groups.

A few state and regional organizations have also sprung up. The California Anti-Sexist Men's Political Caucus (CAMP Caucus) organized men around feminist issues such as violence against women, and the California Men's Gathering holds biannual retreats for men. These retreats are constantly torn between pro-feminist and masculinist factions, the latter wanting to create an oasis of purified masculinity in the woods. Workshops on working with batterers are scheduled opposite ritualistic drumming and elaborate mythic apparatuses to facilitate male bonding. The New England Men's Emerging Network (NEMEN) sponsors regional conferences for men attempting to build male solidarity and community through working on feminist-defined issues.

This strategy—building community among men through active engagement in feminist issues—is also the organizational principle of the National Organization for Men against Sexism (NOMAS), an umbrella organization for pro-feminist men in the United States. Composed of activists and scholars, the organization serves as a home base for men involved in everything from pro-feminist men's culture to political organizing about rape and violence. The organization's "Statement of Principles" (included in ths volume) applauds "the insights and positive changes that feminism has stimulated for both women and men" and opposes continued economic and legal discrimination, rape, domestic violence, and sexual harassment. Recent statements from the organization about child-custody issues and feminist debates about pornography indicate a deepening of these men's pro-feminist commitments and a willingness to take on difficult moral questions confronting the feminist movement.[10]

Contemporary pro-feminist men work with feminist women on issues concerning sexuality and reproductive freedom. Some, like Dr. Bill Baird and Dr. William Jennings Bryan Henrie, operated abortion clinics before 1973, when abortion was still illegal. Many served time in prison for their activities supporting women's right to choose. These pro-feminist men are not "pro-abortion" as much as they are "pro-choice," working to expand women's sphere of moral action. A new group in San Francisco, Men Who Care about Women's Lives, has organized men's demonstrations in favor of women's reproductive rights. Among the men at the 9 April 1989 March on Washington for women's rights were Representative Don Edwards, Leonard Nimoy, and Alan Rosenfield, dean of the Columbia University School of Public Health, each of whom addressed the large crowd. Nimoy sported a badge that read "Honorary Woman." Given the Supreme Court's recent rulings on abortion, it appears that we will continue to need more pro-feminist men who are willing to speak and act alongside feminist women to support women's right to choose.

Other men have taken on the feminist debates about pornography and sexuality, attempting to understand the role that pornography plays in the shaping of male sexuality and the maintenance of sexist culture. My book *Men Confront Pornography* (1990) presents a group of men committed to a feminist vision who, for the first time, explore the role of pornography in men's lives. Although pro-feminist men disagree—some oppose pornography as violence against women, others see feminism as a way for women to claim sexual autonomy and express concern about censorship—men are finally examining the issue and breaking their complicit silence about the pornography industry.

At home, many contemporary pro-feminist men are simply trying to implement egalitarian relationships with wives or partners who have careers—sharing housework, child care, and domestic responsibilities. Changing diapers, ironing, or cleaning the bathroom may not sound like revolutionary political activity, but these things represent a man's effort to take his partner's commitment to her career as seriously as he takes his own. Some men are engaging in what was formerly thought to be "women's work"—child-care services, primary education, nursing, and the like—not because they are interested in pushing women out of the way but because a commitment to feminism has broadened their emotional repertoire to include affective behavior and nurturing skills.

On college campuses around the country, there are men who are working together with feminist women. Some are themselves academics conducting research on the effects of pornography on male viewers, or of competitive sports on male development, or of the structure of the male sex role and the ways in which traditional masculinity can hurt women (see, e.g., Brod 1987; Brannon and David 1974; Pleck and Sawyer 1974; Kaufman 1987; Kimmel and Messner 1989). Psychologist Joseph Pleck's feminist-inspired empirical review of the psychological literature on the male sex role, *The Myth of Masculinity* (1981), found traditional masculinity to be contradictory and confusing. Historical projects such as this book are the outgrowth of a commitment to reclaiming the voices of men who shared a feminist vision of social change.

Not only in the classroom, but also in the dormitories and among students, men are organizing around feminist issues. Groups such as Men Acting for Change (Duke University), Man to Man (Syracuse University), and Men Discussing Gender (Brown University) have organized workshops and lectures about date and acquaintance rape, which are epidemic on college campuses. Others staff crisis lines and escort services to attempt to make the campus safer for women students. At the University of Michigan in April 1990, 350 men held a support rally for the two thousand women who participated in a Take Back the Night march. Some work with the campus counseling center to raise issues of violence with other male students. One national fraternity recently broke ranks with the traditional misogyny of the national Greek system by producing a poster against date rape (included in this volume).

Feminist women are also receiving support from male allies on the job. While many men have opposed affirmative action, other support it as a way to undo past injustices to racial minorities and women. A few men have supported women's entry into the professions, even when there was hostile opposition. The Reverend Paul Moore, the Episcopal bishop of the city of New York, for example ordained the first women priests in the Anglican church's history (Moore 1979). Derrick Bell, a black Harvard law professor for over twenty years, requested a leave of absence without pay until the university appointed a tenured black woman to its law faculty (*New York Times* [24 April 1990]).

Some men support women in subtle and quiet ways. Cartoonist Garry Trudeau's "Doonesbury" has long portrayed strong, feisty feminists like Joanie Caucus and poked fun at the sensitive new man's self-congratulatory nurturing efforts. Matt Groening, creator of television's popular show "The Simpsons" and the comic strip "Life in Hell," tries to draw cartoons that women will like. "The rage against women in a lot of comics, and a lot of pop culture in general, is something that I never felt," he commented in a recent interview. "I could never figure out why cartoonists and rock stars who couldn't get laid in high school felt compelled to get their revenge for the rest of their lives in creative self-expression" (cited in Elder 1989, 31).

One particularly striking example of this subtle support concerns baseball player Jesse Barfield, former right fielder for the Toronto Blue Jays. After a game in 1987, Suzyn Waldman, a sportscaster for a local radio station, was in the locker room for postgame interviews with the players. At the time, women reporters had been allowed in the locker room for about fifteen years since postgame interviews are integral to a sportswriter's job (although this issue has recently resurfaced as contested). As Waldman joined the huddle around George Bell, the team's star left fielder, he began to scream obscenities in Spanish and English and refused to continue the interview. *New York Times* sportswriter Ira Berkow reports on what happened next:

> "It seemed like the entire clubhouse went silent," recalled Waldman. "I knew I had to leave and didn't want to make any more of a scene. And I didn't want anyone to see me break down. I started to go for the door—the room was still dead quiet—when I heard someone call me. It was Jesse Barfield."
>
> "Hey, Suzyn," called the Toronto right fielder. "I went 3 for 4 today. Don't you want to talk to me?"
>
> Waldman, who didn't know Barfield personally, but later learned that he had turned to someone and asked her name, now smiled and took her tape recorder to his locker.
>
> "He gave me a terrific interview, even quoting some poetry," she said. [*New York Times* (24 March 1989)]

Barfield laughed when he was asked recently about the incident. "She was just trying to do her job just like I'm trying to do mine," he said. "And I only did what I'd want done to me. As long as they respect us, they should be respected as well" (ibid.).

Such simple truths do not altogether conceal the significance of unheralded actions like Barfield's. "Barfield's act in the locker room was more than mere chivalry," writes Berkow. "It was an act of courage—the kind of courage that goes beyond hitting a home run, say, in the bottom of the ninth. This is the kind of courage that comes with standing up for another human being" (ibid.). And a woman, no less.

Other pro-feminist men are less subtle and self-effacing in their support. One impassioned statement of support for the rights of poor and minority women came on 4 July 1989 from an eighty-year-old upper-class white man. In his dissent on *Webster v. Missouri* (included in this volume), Justice Harry Blackmun went beyond traditional legalistic language to chastise an offensively politicized Supreme Court. Blackmun's defense of women's right to choose retained a respect for women's integrity, regardless of race or class, and regardless of their decision to be sexually active. Blackmun's support for women has been consistent since *Webster*. In his opinion striking down Johnson Controls "fetal protection" policy, which barred women from certain positions, Blackmun noted historical bases for economic discrimination: "Concern for a woman's existing or potential offspring historically has been the excuse for denying women equal employment opportunities" (cited in the *Miami Herald*, 23 March 1991, p. A-23).

Conclusion

The feminist struggle continues today, as women fight on every front—political, educational, economic, personal, and social—to create a society in which women and men will be equal. The battle is far from won, although the issues that will be of concern in the United States in the 1990s are markedly different from those of earlier eras and represent a significant amount of progress. No longer do women need to struggle to retain their own names or property when they get married; women are legally entitled to job equity, voting, equal pay, and educational equality, although these rights are often compromised in practice.

At this writing, women still have the right, however fragile it has become, to decide whether to prevent or terminate a pregnancy.

At the same time, women still earn less than seventy cents for every dollar earned by men. Men are still overly represented in all professional and graduate schools in this country (except for those, like education, librarianship, nursing, and social work, that are gendered as "female") and still compose an overwhelming number of the legislators, judges, and school administrators at every level. More than half of all women have experienced some form of unwanted sexual contact while on a date, and 25 percent of college women in one survey had experienced date rape. One in three women will be sexually assaulted in her lifetime; one in six will be raped (Warshaw 1988). Few, if any, women can walk comfortably down a city street without fear of verbal harassment or even physical assault. An increasing number of women are reporting cases of sexual harassment on the job. Too many men would still agree with Indiana University's basketball coach Bobby Knight, who commented in a television interview, "If rape is inevitable, relax and enjoy it" (Telander 1988, 122).[11] The continuance of such attitudes underscores the importance of the Violence Against Women Act, sponsored by Senator Joseph Biden (see the statement by Biden included in this volume), currently under debate in Congress—a bill that would make rape a gender-based hate crime and thus punishable under federal civil rights statutes as well as state criminal codes.

At home, women still do the overwhelming amount of housework and child care, although the percentage of that work done by women has decreased in the past twenty years from 80 to 70 percent of the total. Even at home, women are not always safe in their "haven in a heartless world." Marital rape is not even considered a crime in some states; legally, the women "belongs" to the man sexually, her consent to sex implicit in the marriage contract. Thus, rape per se cannot exist within marriage. Each year, thousands of women are battered or murdered by their husbands or lovers.

The contemporary women's movement is intent on changing the structure of relations between women and men, to make the world a safer place for women and to extend women's choices. The women's movement exists because it *must* exist until women and men can both build lives of mutual respect and equality. And, as long as there is a women's movement, there will be pro-feminist men, allies of the women's movement, maybe even its "Gentleman's Auxilary." We will be there, not because we particularly *want* to be there, but because we feel we *must* be there, because we need to put ourselves and our words and actions on the line, to support the women we love as well as women we will never meet. Contemporary pro-feminist men are not necessarily famous men, whose actions command a certain public deference. We are everyday men who are trying, like other men, to make a life of meaning and coherence in a difficult and often painful world.

It is said that Susan B. Anthony carried with her a quotation from Elizabeth Barrett Browning's poem "Aurora Leigh," a constant inspiration about the possibility of women and men working together in the public arena and in their private lives:

> The world waits
> for help, Beloved, let us work so well,
> Our work shall be better for our love
> And still our love be sweeter for our work.

Later in the poem, Browning provides a phrase that, for me, captures the potential for today's pro-feminist man both to proclaim his solidarity with his feminist sisters publicly and to struggle to live a life consistent with that feminist vision. All men, Browning writes, are "possible heroes."

NOTES

Several friends have provided critical readings of this essay. I am grateful to Lauren Bryant, Michael Kaufman, Iona Mara-Drita, Tony Rotundo, and Alix Kates Shulman for their criticism and support. I should make clear that there are several points at which my collaborator, Tom Mosmiller, disagrees with my analysis or demurs from full agreement with my emphasis. While this introduction has surely benefited from his critical reading, I alone am responsible for its argument.

1. The phrase "American men" is a fiction, containing a false universalism in both a geographic and a gendered sense that I should like to disclaim. To use "American" to refer solely to the United States renders invisible such other "Americans" as Canadians, Mexicans, and Latin Americans. I use the term here

in its colloquial sense, and I also use it when I engage in dialogue with writers and critics who debate the "American personality" or the "American character." When I mean the United States in particular, I try to use the more accurate, although more cumbersome, "U.S." or "United States."

Similarly, to speak of "the American man" requires that one remain aware of the enormous variety in the experiences of American men over the past two centuries. It is inappropriate to write of masculinity as if it were a unitary phenomenon experienced by all American men at all times in American history. Masculinity varies dramatically by class, race, ethnicity, sexual orientation, age, and region, among other things; in fact, it makes more sense to speak of "masculinities" when describing men's experiences. In this essay, I am describing the historical transformation of one particular definition of masculinity, the masculinity embodied in the experience of largely white, middle-class, heterosexual men originally in the Northeast. This delineation is not arbitrary but central to a definition of masculinity that has also been the normative definition, held out to other men as the standard against which they will be measured as men. White middle-class heterosexual masculinity is the hegemonic construction of masculinity, rendering other masculinities "problematic" in their perceived deviations from the norm. Attempting to make the normative definition also appear to be the "normal" construction is a sleight of hand accomplished by the powerful as a mechanism to preserve their power. While I do not accept such an elision of the normative and the normal, it is important to acknowledge that the "crisis" of masculinity that I am describing was perceived as a national problem of gender relations, not a problem specific to a particular minority of U.S. men.

2. Throughout, the reader should treat the term "pro-feminist" as if it appeared everywhere in quotation marks because the term is a recent one, one that few men in the book would have recognized.

3. It is not simply lack of information that prevents us from constructing a collective psychological portrait of pro-feminist men in America. Such a discussion would make men's support an artifact of men's family socialization and, in a sense, explain such support away. Many men, regardless of their early childhood socialization or the constellation of family members and their respective political commitments, have embraced a feminist vision simply because they have become convinced that such a vision is right and just. A search for psychological origins to one's commitment to social justice makes that commitment the object of psychological inquiry. Such a search would make pro-feminist men's nonconformity the problem, instead of the social inequality that prompted their participation in a social movement. Our analytic energies would be better served examining the inequalities in society that make such commitments necessary in the first place.

4. Contemporary political scientist Ethel Klein addresses this same issue, although she carefully distinguishes the different sources of political mobilization. She writes that, while "most of the activists in the feminist movement were women, many of the bystanders whose support was critical to the success of the movement were men. These men acknowl-

edged that women faced many problems due to inequitable social arrangements rather than to individual shortcoming or unalterable biological determinants. They promoted the ERA, day care, and equal economic opportunity as ways to address these inequities. Yet their support could hardly have been based on either self-interest or group consciousness" (Klein 1984, 94–95).

5. This reveals how the attack on pro-feminist men's masculinity links the oppression of women and the construction of dominant forms of masculinity. To oppose women's subordination is simultaneously to oppose hegemonic masculinity. (See, e.g., Hearn 1988; Connell 1988; and Kaufman, in press.)

6. Of a total adult male population of nineteen million, fraternal organizations claimed about five and a half million members in more than seventy thousand lodges nationwide—slightly less than one in every four American men. Indeed, this was, as W. S. Harwood (1897) proclaimed, the "Golden Age of Fraternity." By "constituting the lodge as a male only preserve, fraternalism rejected the claims of domesticity and asserted the moral authority of masculine community," writes Clawson (1989, 256).

7. While the Greenwich Village radicals celebrated women's emergence from the home into the public sphere, and while many supported men's struggle with equality within the relationship, only one or two seem to have put into practice the suggestions of the male editor of the magazine *American Homes and Gardens* in 1905. "There is no reason at all why men should not sweep and dust, make beds, clean windows, fix the fire, clean the grate, arrange the furniture," he wrote in an editorial. The next month he continued his campaign: "The responsibility for the home is not [the woman's] alone, but is equally the husband's" (cited in Marsh 1988, 175).

8. That this new ideological foundation for men's support emerged in the first two decades of the century does not mean that earlier justifications disappeared. By far the most consistent theme in men's support for feminism has been, and continues to be, the recourse to abstract conceptions of justice and fairness.

9. That men will benefit from the ERA is a potentially dangerous argument, also adopted by contemporary anti-feminists, who hoped that all laws that "discriminate" against men—e.g., military service, child custody, and alimony—would be eliminated. Their support was not for women achieving equality with men but for men, in their eyes the unequal gender, finally achieving equality with women.

10. Until 1990, NOMAS was known as the National Organization for Changing Men (NOCM). The change in name was intended to differentiate the organization more clearly from masculinist and anti-feminist organizations and to bring forward the organization's explicit pro-feminist political perspective.

11. I am grateful to George Robinson for helping me track down the original quote.

REFERENCES

Abrahams, Edward. *The Lyrical Left: Randolph Bourne, Alfred Stieglitz and the Origins of Cultural Radicalism in America*. Charlottesville: University Press of Virginia, 1986.

Alda, Alan. "What Every Woman Should Know about Men." *Ms.* 4, no. 4 (October 1975).

———. "Why I Support the E.R.A." *Ms.* 5, no. 1 (July 1976).

Argus. Wesleyan University, 1898. (OL)

Barker-Benfield, B. A. *The Horrors of the Half-Known Life: Male Attitudes toward Women and Sexuality in Nineteenth Century America*. New York: Harper & Row, 1976.

Bowditch, William. "Woman Suffrage a Right, Not a Privilege." 1879. (SL, May-Goddard Papers).

Brannon, Robert, and Deborah David, eds., *The Forty-Nine Percent Majority*. Reading, Mass.: Addison-Wesley, 1974.

Brod, Harry, ed. *The Making of Masculinities: The New Men's Studies*. Boston: Unwin Hyman, 1987.

Buechler, Steven. *The Transformation of the Woman Suffrage Movement: The Case of Illinois*. New Brunswick, N.J.: Rutgers University Press, 1986.

Carnes, Mark. *Secret Ritual and Manhood in Victorian America*. New Haven, Conn.: Yale University Press, 1989.

Case, Carl. *The Masculine in Religion*. New York, 1906.

Clarke, Edward. *Sex in Education, or a Fair Chance for the Girls*. Boston: James Osgood, 1873.

Clawson, Mary Ann. *Constructing Brotherhood: Class, Gender, Fraternalism*. Princeton, N.J.: Princeton University Press, 1989.

Conant, R. W. *The Manly Christ, A New View*. Chicago, 1904.

Connell, R. W. *Gender and Power*. Stanford, Calif.: Stanford University Press, 1988.

Cott, Nancy. *The Grounding of Modern Feminism*. New Haven, Conn.: Yale University Press, 1987.

Davidson, Nicholas. *The Failure of Feminism*. Buffalo, N.Y.: Prometheus, 1988.

de Beauvoir, Simone. *The Second Sex*. 1956. New York: Vintage, 1973.

DeLeon, Daniel. *Everything Is Changing: Contemporary U.S. Movements in Historical Perspective*. New York: Praeger, 1988.

Dell, Floyd. *Women as World Builders*. Chicago: Forbes, 1913.

———. "Feminism and Socialism." *New Masses* (1921).

Douglas, Ann. *The Feminization of American Culture*. New York: Knopf, 1977.

Dubbert, Joe. *A Man's Place: Masculinity in Transition*. Englewood Cliffs, N.J.: Prentice-Hall, 1980.

Eastman, Max. "Is Woman Suffrage Important?" New York: Men's League for Woman's Suffrage, 1912.

———. "What Do You Know About This?" *Masses* (March 1914).

———.*The Enjoyment of Living*. New York: Harper & Row, 1936.

———. "John Dewey." *Atlantic Monthly* 168 (1941).

Edelstein, Tilden. *Strange Enthusiasm: A Life of Thomas Wentworth Higginson*. New York: Atheneum, 1970.

Elder, Sean. "Is TV the Coolest Invention Ever Invented?" *Mother Jones* (December 1989).

Emerson, Ralph Waldo. "Woman." In *Emerson's Complete Works*, vol. 10, *Miscellanies*. Boston: Houghton, Mifflin, 1883.

Filene, Peter. *His/Her Self: Sex Roles in Modern America*. 2d ed. Baltimore: Johns Hopkins University Press, 1986.

Fitzgerald, Frances. *Cities on a Hill*. New York: Simon & Schuster, 1986.

Flexner, Eleanor. *Century of Struggle*. New York: Atheneum, 1970.

Forster, Margaret. *Significant Sisters: The Grassroots of Modern Feminism*. New York: Knopf, 1985.

Freedman, C. H. *Manhood Redux: Standing Up to Feminism*. New York: Samson, 1985.

Frothingham, O. B. *Woman Suffrage: Unnatural and Inexpedient*. Boston, 1894.

Gilder, George. *Men and Marriage*. Gretna, La.: Pelican, 1986.

Goldberg, Steven. *The Inevitability of Patriarchy*. New York: William Morrow, 1973.

Grosh, Rev. A. B. *The Odd Fellows Improved Manual*. Philadelphia: T. Bliss, 1871.

Hantover, Jeffrey. "The Boy Scouts and the Validation of Masculinity." In *The American Man*, ed. Joseph Pleck and Elizabeth Pleck. Englewood Cliffs, N.J.: Prentice-Hall, 1980.

Hartman, Mary. "Sexual Crack-Up: The Role of Gender in Western History." Rutgers University, 1984. Typescript.

Harwood, W. S. "The Golden Age of Fraternity." *North American Review* 164 (May 1897).

Hearn, Jeff. *The Gender of Oppression*. London: Wheatsheaf, 1988.

Hecker, August. *A Short History of Women's Rights*. New York: Putnam, 1914.

Hersh, Blanche. *The Slavery of Sex: Feminist-Abolitionists in America*. Urbana: University of Illinois Press, 1978.

Higginson, Thomas Wentworth. "Women's Husbands." *Woman's Journal* (April 1873).

Horowitz, Helen Lefkowitz. ". . . 'The Most Beautiful Female Seminary the World Has Ever Seen.'" *Wellesley Alumnae Magazine* (Spring 1985).

Howard, Clifford. "Why Man Needs Woman's Ballot." New York: National American Woman Suffrage Association, n.d.

Howe, Frederic C. "What the Ballot Will do for Women and For Men." New York: National American Woman Suffrage Association, n.d.

Hughes, Thomas. *The Manliness of Christ*. Boston: Houghton, Mifflin, 1880.

James, Henry. *The Bostonians*. 1885. New York: Bantam, 1984.

Kaufman, Michael, ed. *Beyond Patriarchy*. Toronto: Oxford University Press, 1987.

———. *Cracking the Armor*. New York: Ballantine, in press.

Kimmel, Michael. "Men's Responses to Feminism at the Turn of the Century." *Gender and Society* 1, no. 3 (1987).

———, ed. *Men Confront Pornography*. New York: Crown, 1990.

Kimmel, Michael, and Michael Messner, eds., *Men's Lives*. New York: Macmillan, 1989.

Klein, Ethel. *Gender Politics*. Cambridge, Mass.: Harvard University Press, 1984.

Leach, William. *True Love and Perfect*

Union: The Feminist Reform of Sex and Society. New York: Basic, 1980.

Leverenz, David. *Manhood and the American Renaissance*. Ithaca, N.Y.: Cornell University Press, 1989.

McKeever, William. *Training the Boy*. New York: Macmillan, 1913.

McLaughlin, William. *Billy Sunday Was His Real Name*. Chicago: University of Chicago Press, 1955.

Macleod, David. *Building Character in the American Boy: The Boy Scouts, YMCA, and Their Forerunners, 1870–1920*. Madison: University of Wisconsin Press, 1983.

McNall, Scott. *The Road to Rebellion*. Chicago: University of Chicago Press, 1988.

Marsh, Margaret. "Suburban Men and Masculine Domesticity, 1870–1915." *American Quarterly* 40 (June 1988).

Messner, Michael. Review of *Men Freeing Men*. ed. Baumli. *Changing Men* 15 (1986).

Middleton, George. *These Things Are Mine*. New York: Harcourt, Brace, 1947.

Moore, Paul. *Take a Bishop Like Me*. New York: Harper & Row, 1979.

O'Neill, William. *The Last Romantic: A Life of Max Eastman*. New York: Oxford University Press, 1978.

Phillips, Wendell. "Suffrage for Women." In *Wendell Phillips: Speeches, Lectures and Letters*. Boston: Lee & Shepard, 1891.

Pierce, Jason Noble. *The Masculine Power of Christ; or, Christ Measured as a Man*. Boston: Pilgrim, 1912.

Pleck, Joseph. *The Myth of Masculinity*. Cambridge, Mass.: MIT Press, 1981.

Pleck, Joseph, and Jack Sawyer, eds. *Men and Masculinity*. Englewood Cliffs, N.J.: Prentice-Hall, 1974.

Reed, James. *From Private Vice to Public Virtue: Birth Control in America*. New York: Basic, 1977.

Rotundo, E. Anthony. "Learning about Manhood: Gender Ideals and the Middle Class Family in Nineteenth Century America." In *Manliness and Morality: Middle Class Masculinity in Britain and America*, ed. J. A. Mangan and James Walvin. New York: St. Martin's, 1988.

Salvatore, Nick. *Eugene Debs: Citizen and Socialist*. Urbana: University of Illinois Press, 1983.

Sayers, Joseph. *Women's Rights: or, A Treatise on the Inalienable Rights of Women, Carefully Investigated and Inscribed to the Female Community of the U.S. of America*. Cincinnati: Applegate, 1856.

Schlesinger, Arthur. *New Viewpoints in American History*. New York: Harper & Row, 1949.

Severn, Bill. *Free but Not Equal: How Women Won the Right to Vote*. New York: Julian Messner, 1967.

Siller, Sidney. "Statement of Purpose." National Organization for Men, privately printed, 1984.

Stetzle, Charles. *American Society and Religious Conditions*. New York, 1912.

Strauss, Sylvia. *"Traitors to the Masculine Cause": The Men's Campaign for Women's Rights*. Westport, Conn.: Greenwood, 1982.

Telander, Rick. "Not a Shining Knight." *Sports Illustrated* (9 May 1988).

Todd, John. *Women's Rights*. Boston: Lee & Shepard, 1867.

Trachtenberg, Alan. *The Incorporation of America: Culture and Society in the Gilded Age*. New York: Hill & Wang, 1982.

Trimberger, Ellen Kay. "Feminism, Men and Modern Love: Greenwich Village, 1900–1925." In *The Power of Desire: The Politics of Sexuality*, ed. Ann Snitow, Christine Stansell, and Sharon Thompson. New York: Monthly Review Press, 1984.

Ward, Edward. "Woman Should Mind Their Own Business." New York: National American Woman Suffrage Association, n.d.

Warshaw, Robin. *I Never Called It Rape.* New York: Harper and Row, 1988.

Wheeler, Leslie, ed. *Loving Warriors: Selected Letters to Lucy Stone and Henry B. Blackwell, 1853–1893*. New York: Dial, 1981.

White, Kevin. "Men Supporting Women: A Study of Men Associated with the Women's Suffrage Movement in Britain and America, 1909–1920." *Maryland Historian* 18 (Spring 1987).

Whitman, Walt. *The Essential Whitman*. Selected and edited by Galway Kinnell. New York: Ecco, 1987.

Willard, Emma. *Advancement of Female Education*. Troy, N.Y.: N. Tuttle, 1833.

Woldenberg, S. "Modern Man Is Revolting!" *Los Angeles Reader* (5 December 1986).

"The Woman Peril." *Educational Review* 47 (February 1914).

Woody, Thomas. *A History of Women's Education in the United States*. 2 vols. New York: Science Press, 1929.

I

BEFORE SENECA FALLS, 1775–1848

1917 handbill. Photo courtesy of the Sophia Smith Collection, Smith College.

IN 1830–31, nearly twenty years before the first Woman's Rights Convention was called at Seneca Falls, French observer Alexis de Tocqueville was struck by the remarkable difference between women's position in the United States and in Europe. In the United States, he noted in his prescient *Democracy in America*, young single women were seized by an independence of spirit, a sense of honor, an intelligence and a courage that were unmatched by their European sisters. In fact, Tocqueville concluded that, if asked "to what the singular prosperity and growing strength of that people ought mainly to be attributed, I should reply—to the superiority of their women."

Tocqueville believed that the general movement toward democracy would lead to increased gender equality. "I believe," he wrote, "that the social changes which bring nearer to the same level the father and son, the master and servant, and superiors and inferiors generally speaking, will raise woman and make her more and more the equal of man (Tocqueville [1836] 1961, 2-251). Yet Tocqueville also observed significant obstacles in the path of women's equality (he was not, however, especially critical of them). Nowhere in Europe were women so independent before marriage and so submissive and dependent once wed—"the independence of woman is irrecoverably lost in the bonds of matrimony: if an unmarried woman is less constrained there than elsewhere, a wife is subjected to stricter obligations" (ibid., 240). Nowhere

An asterisk (*) indicates that a document is included in this volume.

were women so in need of education, which was "indispensable to protect women from the dangers with which democratic institutions and manners surround them" (ibid., 239). Nowhere was a separation of spheres so rigorously enforced.

Tocqueville's essay points to a contradiction, present at the founding of the United States, between the esteem in which women were held and their relative independence of movement before marriage, on the one hand, and, on the other, their virtually total exclusion from public life (from politics, the work world, and education) and subjugation to their husbands once they married. (Only in the early nineteenth-century church did women exert power in the public sphere [see Cott 1977].) Women's lives expressed the paradox of life on the pedestal, of being, as Thomas Paine put it on the eve of the American Revolution, "adored and oppressed"—a simultaneous sentimental veneration and painful exclusion.

Nearly three hundred women (and forty men) gathered in the Wesleyan Chapel at Seneca Falls, New York, on 19 July 1848, determined to transform women's position by demanding inclusion in public life as well as social reforms that would provide women with some degree of personal autonomy in the private sphere. They convened, not in a historical vacuum, but in a context of seventy five years of slow, quiet agitation for changes in women's position. As the former colonies confronted the challenges of building an American nation, American women pressed for a reconsideration of their position.

Some men supported women's rights even before Seneca Falls. Not many, of course, for to champion the rights of women before the mid-nineteenth century was to champion a struggle that had no name, a movement that had no organization; it meant an attempt to articulate claims with few precedents. Yet men did promote women's cause and, in so doing, raised virtually every issue that the women's movement would have to face in the coming two centuries. These men ranged from the radical patriot Thomas Paine, musing about how women might feel about their position in American society, to committed abolitionists such as Wendell Phillips, William Lloyd Garrison, Martin Delaney, Frederick Douglass, and the Reverend Samuel J. May taking to the lectern and the pulpit to champion women's rights.

Paine's "Occasional Letter on the Female Sex"* indicates his compassion for women's position but falls short of fully advocating the extension of the vote to women (see Ayer 1989, 37, 81). Paine seems to have favored a property qualification for voting in the United States, although one specifying a significantly smaller landholding than was required in England. At the same time, however, he recognized the paralyzing consequences of women's condition and lent his voice in support of reform at a time when virtually no other radical intellectual raised an eyebrow over any other issue than independence from the British. (Although the document's authorship is disputed, it appears in Paine's collected works.)

Several pro-feminist men in the era before Seneca Falls felt that women's participation in public life was of paramount importance. Renowned educator Benjamin Rush's *Thoughts upon Female Education** makes an eloquent plea for women's right to education. Rush argued that educated women would be more easily governed and that their education was therefore in men's interests. "If men believe that ignorance is favorable to the government of the female sex," he wrote, "they are certainly deceived, for a weak and ignorant woman will always be governed with the greatest difficulty." The Reverend James Gray (1810), speaking at the Mechanics Institute, made a similarly eloquent plea.

Others, like Joseph Tuckerman (1830) and Philadelphia industrialist Mathew Carey (see his "Rules for Husbands and Wives"*), argued for women's right to equal economic opportunity—their right to earn higher wages, to enter the workplace, and to own property. Thomas Herttell, in "The Right of Married Women to Hold and Control Property,"* pointed out the inconsistency that allowed unmarried women to own property but that placed that property under the control of her husband when she married: "After thus stripping her of her property, he may covertly and openly abuse her with impunity; or may abandon her to her fate, to fare and suffer as may happen, with little means and less hope of redress." If women are born free, Herttell argued, then they are born with the right to own property all their lives, regardless of their marital status.

Some men even advocated suffrage before 1848. Abolitionists such as David Ruggle and William E. Channing (see his "Emancipation,"*), in addition to Garrison, Phillips, and Douglass, made early pleas for women's enfranchisement. Many early suffragists traced their political roots to their participation in the abolitionist struggle; many of the male abolitionists made the logical extension of their argument about the enfranchisement of black men to include women. Wendell Phillips's eloquent plea* for the seating of women at the World Anti-Slavery Convention in London in 1840 develops the links between the two struggles.

Some men saw women's equality in the private sphere as of at least equal importance as her incorporation into public life, seeking to transform women's position by ensuring equality in marriage. Several restricted reform to private life, while others saw women's domestic equality as a corollary to enlarged public participation. Social reformer and abolitionist Theodore Weld, for example, wanted his marriage to feminist and abolitionist Angelina Grimké to provide a common and equal basis for their public work. He wrote to her (Weld 1838) that he saw their marriage as an "unexpected opportunity to give a *little* testimony against a vandal law which prostrates a woman at the feet of her husband the moment after marriage." While Mathew Carey subscribed to the separation of spheres, he tried to ameliorate its more painful consequences. The first of his "Rules for Husbands and Wives"* begins, "A good husband will always regard his wife as his equal." Robert Dale Owen, son of social reformer Robert Owen and himself a founder of the communal experiment at New Harmony, Indiana, wanted it clear at his wedding that he and his wife were to be considered equals and that, as far as they were concerned, the laws that gave him control over her property were unjust (see his "Marriage Contract with Mary Jane Robinson"*). If not legally, he would "morally divest" himself of this usurpation, and he demanded that others consider him so divested.

Perhaps the most far-reaching visions of women's equality in the era before Seneca Falls were articulated by Charles Brockden Brown and John Neal. In *Alcuin* (1798), the first novel by one of the late eighteenth-century America's most prominent writers, we find a sustained argument for the rights of women. Brown's literary style lies between the epistolary novel popular earlier in the eighteenth century and the more formal narrative of the nineteenth century; the first two sections of the novel contain a dialogue between a young man (Alcuin) and Mrs. Carter, who lectures her young interlocutor about the position of women. Mrs. Carter claims that she disapproves of the system of marriage because "it renders the female a slave to the man. It enjoins and enforces submission on her part to the will of her husband. It includes a promise of implicit obedience and unalterable affection. Secondly, it leaves the woman destitute of property. Whatever she previously possesses, belongs absolutely to the man." The novel's final two sections contain a late eighteenth-century version of a guided fantasy, as Alcuin tries to image a world in which women are equal. In the end, forced by the strength of logic, Alcuin admits that his views on women are based on illogical prejudice, not reason.

Brown's advocacy of women's rights waned later in his career as "the first professional man of letters in the United States," according to *Alcuin*'s* editor. But even his later novels, like *Ormand, Edgar Huntly*, and *Arthur Mervyn*, return to themes of sexual politics and women's rights. In *Ormond*, young Constantia is reluctant to marry because, as her friend Sophia recounts it, "Now she was at least mistress of the product of her own labor. Her tasks were toilsome, but the profits, though slender, were sure, and she administered her little property in what manner she pleased. Marriage would annihilate this power. Henceforth she would be bereft even of personal freedom. So far from possessing property, she herself would become the property of another" (cited in Fleischmann 1983, 117). Unlike many of his contemporaries, Brown was also sensitive to the consequences that the separation of spheres had for men's lives. Arthur Mervyn's world is one of "failed fathers and ruined families," and Edgar Huntly emerges as a pathetic young man who is so consumed with anxiety about his place in the public world of the competitive marketplace that he becomes, as Brown puts it, "a formidable engine of destruction" (cited in ibid., 137). Surely, this is one of the first instances in American literature of a man's insecurity over his masculinity in the public sphere contributing to his propensity for violence.

Not only was John Neal an articulate champion of women's rights before Seneca Falls, but he remained a committed activist all his life, evincing a "stubborn and systematic inclusion of women in all the areas he considered important enough to write about" (ibid., 157). Neal was a founding vice president of the New England Woman Suffrage Association in 1868, and he was named first in a list of "distinguished men and women of the New England states" present at its founding convention. Thirty years earlier, Margaret Fuller invited Neal to address her students at the Greene Street School in Providence "on the destiny and vocation of Woman." Neal wrote regularly for the *Revolution*, the newspaper of the National Women Suffrage Association, and the *History of Woman Suffrage* praises him as "foremost in all good work in Maine." Feminist social reformer Mary Gove Nichols went even further, calling him "the man who gave the first impetus to the cause of women in this country" (see ibid., 212, 213, 215, 143).

Several themes stand out in Neal's writing. He championed reform of marriage and property law and was an early advocate of woman suffrage, which he believed essential to changing women's second-class status. In 1845, after reading her new book *Woman in the Nineteenth Century*, he wrote Margaret Fuller,

> I tell you there is no hope for woman, till she has a hand in making the law—no chance for her till her *vote* is worth as much as a mans [*sic*] vote. When it is—woman will not be fobbed off with a six-pence a day for the very work a man would get a dollar for. . . . But enough—we must have a talk together, if I am ever going to persuade you into a right view of the subject. All you and others are doing to elevate woman, is only fitted to make her feel more sensibly the long abuse of her own understanding, when she comes to her senses. You might as well educate slaves—and still keep them in bondage. [cited in ibid., 144]

Neal frequently used the analogy of slavery to make his point. In one speech in 1868, he asked why, since women are taxed without representation and barred from property ownership and public office, "are they not slaves, as much as the blacks, though not often sold openly in the market? Are they ever their own mistresses? Who makes the law for them?" (cited in ibid., 156).

Neal's insistence that women's helplessness, passivity, and dependency were the results, not the causes, of their oppression anticipates arguments advanced a half century later. He claimed that fashion was a vehicle of women's subjugation; petticoats, for example, "were the contrivance of man not of woman. They are part of *his* machinery for enhancing the attractions of woman, and for keeping her satisfied with herself, and out of harm's way, and for making her a prisoner of her own consent, regardless not only of expense, but of her health, comfort, and usefulness" (cited in ibid., 211). Perhaps Neal's most eloquent plea on behalf of women is "Rights of Women,"* an 1843 editorial that appeared in two New York newspapers. Here he summarizes many of his arguments for women's rights and develops a rhetorical strategy he was to use with great effect throughout his career—inviting his male readers to imagine that the gender situation is reversed and that women have the power that men now have: "What a clamor there would be then, about *equal rights*, about a *privileged class*, about being *taxed without their own consent*, about *virtual reprsentation*, and all that!"

What a clamor indeed. And in the era before Seneca Falls, before women themselves organized to raise that clamor, Neal and other men helped prepare the political ground so that that movement could take root. Their ideas emerged gradually, and the theoretical bases on which their support of woman's rights rested were often inconsistent. Some saw women as endowed with a special morality that needed freer expression, while others minimized the differences between the sexes and proclaimed women to be as possessed by reason as men.

Isolated from one another, the visions of these early pro-feminist men emerged mostly from their private convictions, often, but not always, from their reformist religious beliefs (Neal and Brown were Quakers, and May and Channing were both ministers). But, even in the years before 1848, before women had developed the organizational vehicles to carry their message, men were raising their own voices in support of that struggle.

"AN OCCASIONAL LETTER ON THE FEMALE SEX"

Thomas Paine (1775)

O Woman! lovely Woman!
Nature made thee to temper man,
We had been Brutes without you.
OTWAY

IF WE TAKE A SURVEY of ages and of countries, we shall find the women, almost—without exception at all times and in all places, adored and oppressed. Man, who has never neglected an opportunity of exerting his power, in paying homage to their beauty, has always availed himself of their weakness. He has been at once then tyrant and then slave.

Nature herself, in forming beings so susceptible and tender, appears to have been more attentive to their charms than to their happiness. Continually surrounded with griefs and fears, the women more than share all our miseries, and are besides subjected to ills which are peculiarly their own. They cannot be the means of life without exposing themselves to the loss of it; every revolution which they undergo, alters their health, and threatens their existence. Cruel distempers attack their beauty—and the hour which confirms their release from those is perhaps the most melancholy of their lives. It robs them of the most essential characteristic of their sex. They can then only hope for protection from the humiliating claims of pity, or the feeble voice of gratitude.

Society, instead of alleviating their condition, is to them the source of new miseries. More than one half of the globe is covered with savages; and among all these people women are completely wretched. Man, in a state of barbarity, equally cruel and indolent, active by necessity, but naturally inclined to repose, is acquainted with little more than the physical effects of love; and, having none of those moral ideas which only can soften the empire of force, he is led to consider it as his supreme law, subjecting to his despotism those whom reason had made his equal, but whose imbecility betrayed them to his strength. "Nothing" (says

From The Complete Writings of Thomas Paine, *ed. Philip S. Foner. 2 vols. New York: Citadel, 1945.*

Professor Miller, speaking of the women of barbarous nations) "can exceed the dependence and subjection in which they are kept, or the toil and drudgery which they are obliged to undergo. The husband, when he is not engaged in some warlike exercise, indulges himself in idleness, and devolves upon his wife the whole burden of his domestic affairs. He disdains to assist her in any of those servile employments. She sleeps in a different bed, and is seldom permitted to have any conversation or correspondence with him."

The women among the Indians of America are what the Helots were among the Spartans, a vanquished people, obliged to toil for their conquerors. Hence on the banks of the Oroonoko, we have seen mothers slaying their daughters out of compassion, and smothering them in the hour of their birth. They consider this barbarous pity as a virtue.

"The men (says Commodore Byron, in his account of the inhabitants of South America) exercise a most despotic authority over their wives, whom they consider in the same view they do any other part of their property, and dispose of them accordingly. Even their common treatment of them is cruel; for though the toil and hazard of procuring food lies entirely on the women, they they are not suffered to touch any part of it till the husband is satisfied; and then he assigns them their portion, which is generally very scanty, and such as he has not a stomach for himself."

Among, the nations of the East we find another kind of despotism and dominion prevail—the Seraglio, and the domestic servitude of woman, authorized by the manners and established by the laws. In Turkey, in Persia, in India, in Japan, and over the vast empire of China, one half of the human species is oppressed by the other.

The excess of oppression in those countries springs from the excess of love.

All Asia is covered with prisoners, where beauty in bondage awaits the caprices of a master. The multitude of women there assembled have no will, no inclinations but his. Their triumphs are only for a moment; and their rivalry, their hate, and their animosities continue till death. There the lovely sex are obliged to repay even their servitude with the most tender affections; or, what is still more mortifying, with the counterfeit of an affection, which they do not feel. There the most gloomy tyranny has subjected them to creatures, who, being of neither sex, are a dishonor to both. There, in short, their education tends only to debase them; their virtues are forced; their very pleasures are involuntary and joyless; and after an existence of a few years—till the bloom of youth is over—their period of neglect commences, which is long and dreadful. In the temperate latitude where the climates, giving less ardor to passion, leave more confidence in virtue, the women have not been deprived of their liberty, but a severe legislation has, at all times, kept them in a state of dependence. One while they are confined to their own apartments, and debarred at once from business and amusement; at other times, a tedious guardianship defrauded their hearts, and insulted their understandings. Affronted in one country by polygamy, which gives them their rivals for their inseparable companions; enslaved in another by indissoluble ties, which often join the gentle to the rude, and sensibility to brutality. Even in countries where they may be esteemed most happy, constrained in their desires in the disposal of their goods, robbed of freedom of will by the laws, the slaves of opinion, which rules them with absolute sway, and construes the slightest appearances into guilt; surrounded on all sides by judges, who are at once tyrants and their seducers, and who, after having prepared their faults, punish every lapse with dishonor—nay, usurp the right of degrading them on suspicion! Who does not feel for the tender sex? Yet such, I am sorry to say, is the lot of women over the whole earth. Man with regard to them in all climates, and in all ages, has been either an insensible husband or an oppressor; but they have sometimes experienced the cold and deliberate oppression of pride, and sometimes the violent and terrible tyranny of jealousy. When they are not beloved they are nothing; and, when they are, they are tormented. They have almost equal cause to be afraid of indifference and of love. Over three-quarters of the globe nature has placed them between contempt and misery.

"The melting desires, or the fiery passions," says Professor Ferguson, "which in one climate take place between the sexes, are, in another, changed into a sober consideration, or a patience of mutual disgust. This change is remarked in crossing the Mediterranean, in following the course of the Mississippi, in ascending the mountains of Caucasus, and in passing from the Alps and the Pyrenees to the shores of the Baltic.

"The burning ardors and torturing jealousies of the seraglio and harem, which have reigned so long in Asia and Africa, and which, in the southern parts of Europe, have scarcely given way to the differences of religion and civil establishments, are found, however, with an abatement of heat in the climate, to be more easily changed, in one latitude, into a temporary passion, which engrosses the mind without enfeebling it, and which excites to romantic achievements. By a farther progress to the north it is changed into a spirit of gallantry, which employs the wit and fancy more than the heart, which prefers intrigue to enjoyment, and substitutes affection and vanity where sentiment and desire have failed. As it departs from the sun, the same passion is further composed into a habit of domestic connection, or frozen into a state of insensibility, under which the sexes at freedom scarcely choose to unite their society."

Even among people where beauty received the highest homage we find men who would deprive the sex of every kind of reputation. "The most virtuous woman," says a celebrated Greek, "is she who is least talked of." That morose man, while he imposes duties upon women, would deprive them of the sweets of public esteem, and in exacting virtues from them, would make it a crime to aspire at honor.

If a woman were to defend the cause of her sex, she might address him in the following manner:

"How great is your injustice? If we have an equal right with you to virtue, why should we not have an equal right to praise? The public esteem ought to wait upon merit. Our duties are different from yours, but they are not therefore less difficult to fulfil, or of less consequence to society: They are the fountains of your felicity, and the sweetness of life. We are wives, and mothers. 'Tis we who form the union and the cordiality of families. 'Tis we who soften that savage rudeness which considers everything as due to force, and which would involve man with man in eternal war. We cultivate in you that humanity which makes you feel for the misfortunes of others, and our tears forewarn you of your own danger. Nay, you cannot be ignorant that we have need of courage not less than you. More feeble in ourselves, we have perhaps more trials to encounter. Nature assails us with sorrow, law and custom press us with constraint, and sensibility and virtue alarm us with their continual conflict. Sometimes also the name of citizen demands from us the tribute of fortitude. When you offer your blood to the State think that it is ours. In giving it our sons and our husbands we give more than ourselves. You can only die on the field of battle, but we have the misfortune to survive those whom we love most. Alas! while your ambitious vanity is unceasingly laboring to cover the earth with statues, with monuments, and with inscriptions to eternalize, if possible, your names, and give yourselves an existence, when this body is no more, why must we be condemned to live and to die unknown? Would that the grave and eternal forgetfulness should be our lot. Be not our tyrants in all. Permit our names to be sometimes pronounced beyond the narrow circle in which we live. Permit friendship, or at least love, to inscribe its emblem on the tomb where our ashes repose; and deny us not that public esteem which, after the esteem of one's self, is the sweetest reward of well doing."

All men, however, it must be owned, have not been equally unjust to their fair companions. In some countries public honors have been paid to women. Art has erected them monuments. Eloquence has celebrated their virtues, and history has collected whatever could adorn their character.

THOUGHTS UPON FEMALE EDUCATION (excerpt)

Benjamin Rush (1787)

GENTLEMEN,

I have yielded with diffidence to the solicitations of the Principal of the Academy, in undertaking to express my regard for the prosperity of this seminary of learning by submitting to your candor a few thoughts upon female education.

The first remark that I shall make upon this subject is that female education should be accommodated to the state of society, manners, and government of the country in which it is conducted.

This remark leads me at once to add that the education of young ladies in this country should be conducted upon principles very different from what it is in Great Britain and in some respects different from what it was when we were a part of a monarchical empire.

There are several circumstances in the sit-

From Thoughts Upon Female Education, Accommodated to the Present State of Society, Manners, and the Government of the United States. *Philadelphia: S. Hall, 1787.*

uation, employments, and duties of women in America which require a peculiar mode of education.

I. The early marriages of our women, by contracting the time allowed for education, renders it necessary to contract its plan and to confine it chiefly to the more useful branches of literature.

II. The state of property in America renders it necessary for the greatest part of our citizens to employ themselves in different occupations for the advancement of their fortunes. This cannot be done without the assistance of the female members of the community. They must be the stewards and guardians of their husbands' property. That education, therefore, will be most proper for our women which teaches them to discharge the duties of those offices with the most success and reputation.

III. From the numerous avocations to which a professional life exposes gentlemen in America from their families, a principal share of the instruction of children naturally devolves upon the women. It becomes us therefore to prepare them, by a suitable education, for the discharge of this most important duty of mothers. . . .

IV. The equal share that every citizen has in the liberty and the possible share he may have in the government of our country make it necessary that our ladies should be qualified to a certain degree, by a peculiar and suitable education, to concur in instructing their sons in the principles of liberty and government.

V. In Great Britain the business of servants is a regular occupation, but in America this humble station is the usual retreat of unexpected indigence; hence the servants in this country possess less knowledge and subordination than are required from them; and hence our ladies are obliged to attend more to the private affairs of their families than ladies generally do of the same rank in Great Britain. "They are good servants," said an American lady of distinguished merit in a letter to a favorite daughter, "who will do well with good looking after." This circumstance should have great influence upon the nature and extent of female education in America.

The branches of literature most essential for a young lady in this country appear to be:

I. A knowledge of the English language. She should not only read but speak and spell it correctly. And to enable her to do this, she should be taught the English grammar and be frequently examined in applying its rules in common conversation.

II. Pleasure and interest conspire to make the writing of a fair and legible hand a necessary branch of female education. For this purpose she should be taught not only to shape every letter properly but to pay the strictest regard to points and capitals. . . .

III. Some knowledge of figures and bookkeeping is absolutely necessary to qualify a young lady for the duties which await her in this country. There are certain occupations in which she may assist her husband with this knowledge, and should she survive him and agreeably to the custom of our country be the executrix of his will, she cannot fail of deriving immense advantages from it.

IV. An acquaintance with geography and some instruction in chronology will enable a young lady to read history, biography, and travels, with advantage, and thereby qualify her not only for a general intercourse with the world but to be an agreeable companion for a sensible man. To these branches of knowledge may be added, in some instances, a general acquaintance with the first principles of astronomy and natural philosophy, particularly with such parts of them as are calculated to prevent superstition, by explaining the causes or obviating the effects of nature evil.

V. Vocal music should never be neglected in the education of a young lady in this country. Besides preparing her to join in that part of the public worship which consists in psalmody, it will enable her to soothe the cares of domestic life. The distress and vexation of a husband, the noise of a nursery, and even the sorrows that will sometimes intrude into her own bosom may all be relieved by a song, where sound and sentiment unite to act upon the mind. . . .

VI. Dancing is by no means an improper branch of education for an American lady. It promotes health and renders the figure and motions of the body easy and agreeable. I anticipate the time when the resources of conversation shall be so far multiplied that the amusement of dancing shall be wholly confined to children. But in our present state of society and knowledge, I conceive it to be an agreeable substitute for the ignoble pleasures of drinking and gaming in our assemblies of grown people.

VII. The attention of our young ladies should be directed as soon as they are prepared for it to the reading of history, travels, poetry, and moral essays. These studies are accommodated, in a peculiar manner, to the present state of society in America, and when a relish is excited for them in early life, they subdue that passion for reading novels which so generally prevails among the fair sex. . . .

VIII. It will be necessary to connect all these branches of education with regular instruction in the Christian religion. . . . A clergyman of long experience in the instruction of youth informed me that he always found children acquired religious knowledge more easily than knowledge upon other subjects, and that young girls acquired this kind of knowledge more readily than boys. The female breast is the natural soil of Christianity, and while our women are taught to believe its doctrines and obey its precepts, the wit of Voltaire and the style of Bolingbroke will never be able to destroy its influence upon our citizens. . . .

IX. If the measures that have been recommended for inspiring our pupils with a sense of religious and moral obligation be adopted, the government of them will be easy and agreeable. I shall only remark under this head that *strictness* of discipline will always render *severity* unnecessary and that there will be the most instruction in that school where there is the most order. . . .

It is with reluctance that I object to drawing as a branch of education for an American lady. To be the mistress of a family is one of the great ends of a woman's being, and while the peculiar state of society in America imposes this station so early and renders the duties of it so numerous and difficult, I conceive that little time can be spared for the acquisition of this elegant accomplishment.

It is agreeable to observe how differently modern writers and the inspired author of the *Proverbs* describe a fine woman. The former confine their praises chiefly to personal charms and ornamental accomplishments, while the latter celebrates only the virtues of a valuable mistress of a family and a useful member of society. The one is perfectly acquainted with all the fashionable languages of Europe; the other "opens her mouth with wisdom" and is perfectly acquainted with all the uses of the needle, the distaff, and the loom. The business of the one is pleasure; the pleasure of the other is business. The one is admired abroad; the other is honored and beloved at home. "Her children arise up and call her blessed, her husband also, and he praiseth her." There is no fame in the world equal to this, nor is there a note in music half so delightful as the respectful language with which a grateful son or daughter perpetuates the memory of a sensible and affectionate mother.

It should not surprise us that British customs with respect to female education have been transplanted into our American schools and families. We see marks of the same incongruity of time and place in many other things. We behold our houses accommodated to the climate of Great Britain by eastern and western directions. We behold our ladies panting in a heat of ninety degrees, under a hat and cushion which were calculated for the temperature of a British summer. We behold our citizens condemned and punished by a criminal law which was copied from a country where maturity in corruption renders public executions a part of the amusements of the nation. It is high time to awake from this servility—to study our own character—to examine the age of our country—and to adopt manners in everything that shall be accommodated to our state of society and to the forms of our government. In particular it is incumbent upon us to make ornamental accomplishments yield to principles and knowledge in the education of our women.

A philosopher once said, "let me make all the ballads of a country and I care not who makes its law." He might with more propriety have said, let the ladies of a country be educated properly, and they will not only make and administer its laws, but form its manners and character. It would require a lively imagination to describe, or even to comprehend, the happiness of a country where knowledge and virtue were generally diffused among the female sex. Our young men would then be restrained from vice by the terror of being banished from their company. The loud laugh and the malignant smile, at the expense of innocence or of personal infirmities—the feats of successful mimicry and the low priced wit which is borrowed from a misapplication of scripture phrases—would no more be considered as recommendations to the society of the ladies. A *double-entendre* in their presence would then exclude a gentleman forever from the company of both sexes and probably oblige him to seek an asylum from contempt in a foreign country.

The influence of female education would be still more extensive and useful in domestic life. The obligations of gentlemen to qualify themselves by knowledge and industry to discharge the duties of benevolence would be increased by marriage; and the patriot—the hero—and the legislator would find the sweetest reward of their toils in the approbation and applause of their wives. Children would discover the marks of maternal prudence and wisdom in every station of life, for it has been remarked that there have been few great or good men who have not been blessed with wife and prudent mothers. . . .

I cannot dismiss the subject of female education without remarking that the city of Philadelphia first saw a number of gentlemen associated for the purpose of directing the education of young ladies. By means of this plan the power of teachers is regulated and restrained and the objects of education are extended. By the separation of the sexes in the unformed state of their manners, female delicacy is cherished and preserved. Here the young ladies may enjoy all the literary advantages of a boarding school and at the same time live under the protection of their parents. Here emulation may be excited without jealousy, ambition without envy, and competition without strife.

The attempt to establish this new mode of education for young ladies was an experiment, and the success of it hath answered our expectations. Too much praise cannot be given to our principal and his assistants, for the abilities and fidelity with which they have carried the plan into execution. The proficiency which the young ladies have discovered in reading, writing, spelling, arithmetic, grammar, geography, music, and their different catechisms since the last examination is a less equivocal mark of the merits of our teachers than anything I am able to express in their favor.

But the reputation of the academy must be suspended till the public are convinced by the future conduct and character of our pupils of the advantages of the institution. To you, therefore, YOUNG LADIES, an important problem is committed for solution; and that is, whether our present plan of education be a wise one and whether it be calculated to prepare you for the duties of social and domestic life. I know that the elevation of the female mind, by means of moral, physical, and religious truth, is considered by some men as unfriendly to the domestic character of a woman. But this is the prejudice of little minds and springs from the same spirit which opposes the general diffusion of knowledge among the citizens of our republics. If men believe that ignorance is favorable to the government of the female sex, they are certainly deceived, for a weak and ignorant woman will always be governed with the greatest difficulty.

I have sometimes been led to ascribe the invention of ridiculous and expensive fashions in female dress entirely to the gentlemen in order to divert the ladies from improving their minds and thereby to secure a more arbitrary and unlimited authority over them. It will be in your power, LADIES, to correct the mistakes and practice of our sex upon these subjects by demonstrating that the female temper can only be governed by reason and that the cultivation of reason in women is alike friendly to the order of nature and to private as well as public happiness.

ALCUIN (excerpt)

Charles Brockden Brown (1798)

. . . BY MARRIAGE she loses all right to separate property. The will of her husband is the criterion of all her duties. All merit is comprised in unlimited obedience. She must not expostulate or rebel. In all contests with him, she must hope to prevail by blandishments and tears; not by appeals to justice and addresses to reason. She will be most applauded when she smiles with most perseverance on her oppressor, and when, with

From Alcuin: A Dialogue. *Pts. 1–2 (1798). Pts. 3–4 (1815), ed. Lee R. Edwards. Reprint. New York: Grossman, 1971.*

the undistinguishing attachment of a dog, no caprice or cruelty shall be able to estrange her affection. . . .

And let me (replied she) repeat my answer—What have I, as a woman, to do with politics? Even the government of our country, which is said to be the freest in the world, passes over women as if they were not. We are excluded from all political rights without the least ceremony. Law-makers thought as little of comprehending us in their code of liberty, as if we were pigs, or sheep. That females are exceptions to their general maxims, perhaps never occurred to them. If it did, the idea was quietly discarded, without leaving behind the slightest consciousness of inconsistency or injustice. . . . While I am conscious of being an intelligent and moral being; while I see myself denied, in so many cases, the exercise of my own discretion; incapable of separate property; subject, in all periods of my life, to the will of another, on whose bounty I am made to depend for food, raiment, and shelter: when I see myself, in my relation to society, regarded merely as a beast, or an insect; passed over, in the distribution of public duties, as absolutely nothing, by those who disdain to assign the least apology for their injustice—what though politicians say I am nothing, it is impossible I should assent to their opinion, as long as I am conscious of willing and moving. If they generously admit me into the class of existence, but affirm that I exist for no purpose but the convenience of the more dignified sex; that I am not to be entrusted with the government of myself; that to foresee, to deliberate and decide, belongs to others, while all my duties resolve themselves into this precept, "listen and obey;" it is not for me to smile at their tyranny, or receive, as my gospel, a code built upon such atrocious maxims. . . .

What for example is the difference which takes place in the education of the two sexes?

There is no possible ground for difference. Nourishment is imparted and received in the same way. Their is one diet, one regimen, one mode and degree of exercise, best adapted to unfold the powers of the human body, and maintain them for the longest time in full vigour. One individual may be affected by some casualty or disease, so as to claim to be treated in a manner different from another individual, but this difference is not necessarily connected with sex. Neither sex is exempt from injury, contracted through their own ignorance, or that of others. Doubtless the sound woman and the sick man it would be madness to subject to the same tasks, or the same regimen. But this no less true if both be of the same sex. Diseases, on whichsoever they fall, are curable by the same means.

Human beings in their infancy, continued my friend, require the same tendance and instruction: but does one sex require more or less, or a different sort of tendance or instruction than the other? Certainly not. If by any fatal delusion, one sex should imagine its interest to consist in the ill treatment of the other, time would soon detect their mistake. For how is the species to be continued? How is a woman, for example, to obtain a sound body, and impart it to her offspring, but, among other sources, from the perfect constitution of both her parents? But it is needless to argue on a supposition so incredible as that mankind can be benefitted by injustice and oppression. . . .

We are born with faculties that enable us to impart and receive happiness. There is one species of discipline, better adapted than any other to open and improve those faculties. This mode is to be practised. All are to be furnished with the means of instruction, whether these consist in the direct commerce of the senses with the material universe, or in intercourse with other intelligent beings. It is requisite to know the reasonings, actions and opinions of others, if we seek the improvement of our own understanding. For this end, we must see them, and talk with them if present, or if distant or dead, we must consult these memorials which have been contrived by themselves or others. These are simple and intelligible maxims proper to regulate our treatment of rational beings. The only circumstance to which we are bound to attend is that the subjects of instruction be rational. If any one observe that the consideration of sex is of some moment, how must his remark be understood. Would he insinuate that because my sex is different from yours, one of us only can be treated as rational, or that though reason be a property of both, one of us possesses less of it than the other. I am not born among a people who can countenance so monstrous a doctrine. . . .

But different persons, said I, have different employments. Skill cannot be obtained in them without a regular course of instruction. Each sex has, I doubt not, paths of its own into which the others must not intrude. Hence must arise a difference in their education.

Who has taught you, replied she, that each sex must have peculiar employments? Your doubts and your conjectures are equally amazing. One would imagine that among you, one sex had more arms, or legs, or senses than the other. Among us there is no such inequality. The principles that direct us in the choice of occupations are common to all. . . .

What, cried I, are all obliged to partake of all the labours of tilling the ground, without distinction of rank and sex?

Certainly. There are none that fail to consume some portion of the product of the ground. To exempt any from a share in the cultivation, would be an inexpiable injustice, both to those who are exempted and those who are not exempted. The exercise is cheerful and wholesome. Its purpose is just and necessary. Who shall dare to deny me a part in it? But we know full well that the task, which, if divided among many, is easy and salubrious, is converted into painful and unwholesome drudgery, by being confined to a sex, what phrenzy must that be which should prompt us to introduce a change in this respect? I cannot even imagine so great a perversion of the understanding. Common madness is unequal to so monstrous a conception. We must first not only cease to be reasonable, but cease to be men. Even that supposition is insufficient, for into what class of animals must we sink, before this injustice could be realized? Among beasts there are none who do not owe their accommodations to their own exertions. . . .

Well, said I, that is yet to appear. Meanwhile, I pray you, what are *your* objections to the present system?

My objections are weighty ones. I disapprove of it, in the first place, because it renders the female a slave to the man. It enjoins and enforces submission on her part to the will of her husband. It includes a promise of implicit obedience and unalterable affection. Secondly, it leaves the woman destitute of property. Whatever she previously possesses, belongs absolutely to the man.

This representation seems not to be a faithful one, said I. Marriage leaves the wife without property, you say. How comes it then that she is able to subsist? You will answer, perhaps, that her sole dependence is placed upon the bounty of her husband. But this is surely an error. It is by virtue of express laws that all property subsists. But the same laws sanction the title of a wife to a subsistence proportioned to the estate of her husband. But if law were silent, custom would enforce this claim. The husband is in reality nothing but a steward. He is bound to make provision for his wife, proportionately to the extent of his own revenue. This is a practical truth, of which every woman is sensible. It is this that renders the riches of an husband a consideration of so much moment in the eye of a prudent woman. To select a wealthy partner is universally considered as the certain means of enriching ourselves, not less when the object of our choice is an husband than when it is a wife.

"RULES FOR HUSBANDS AND WIVES"

Mathew Carey (1830)

HAVING SEEN VARIOUS SETS of maxims for the conduct of married life, which have appeared to me to contain some very injudicious items, degrading to wives, sinking them below the rank they ought to occupy, and reducing them in some degree to the level of mere housekeepers, and believing them radically erroneous, I annex a set which appear more rational and just than most of those which I have seen:

1. A good husband will always regard his wife as his equal; treat her with kindness, respect and attention; and never address her with an air of authority, as if she were, as some husbands appear to regard their wives, a mere housekeeper.

2. He will never interfere in her domestic concerns, hiring servants, &c.

3. He will always keep her liberally supplied with money for furnishing his table in a style proportioned to his means, and for the purchase of dress suitable to her station in life.

4. He will cheerfully and promptly comply with all her reasonable requests, when it can be done, without loss, or great inconvenience.

5. He will never allow himself to lose his temper towards her, by indifferent cookery, or irregularity in the hours of meals, or any other mismanagement of her servants, knowing the difficulty of making them do their duty.

6. If she have prudence and good sense, he will consult her on all great operations, involving the risque of ruin, or serious injury in case of failure. Many a man has been rescued from destruction by the wise counsels of his wife. Many a foolish husband has most seriously injured himself and family by the rejection of the advice of his wife, fearing, lest, if he followed it, he would be

From Miscellaneous Essays. *Philadelphia: Carey & Hart, 1830.*

regarded as ruled by her! A husband can never procure a counsellor more deeply interested in his welfare than his wife.

7. If distressed, or embarrassed in his circumstances, he will communicate his situation to her with candour, that she may bear his difficulties in mind, in her expenditures. Women sometimes, believing their husband's circumstances to be far better than they really are, expend money which cannot well be afforded, and which, if they knew their real situation, they would shrink from expending.

1. A good wife will always receive her husband with smiles,—leave nothing undone to render home agreeable—and gratefully reciprocate his kindness and attention.

2. She will study to discover means to gratify his inclinations, in regard to food and cookery; in the management of her family; in her dress, manners and deportment.

3. She will never attempt to rule, or appear to rule her husband. Such conduct degrades husbands—and wives always partake largely of the degradation of their husbands.

4. She will in every thing reasonable, comply with his wishes—and, as far as possible, anticipate them.

5. She will avoid all altercations or arguments leading to ill-humour—and more especially before company.

6. She will never attempt to interfere in his business, unless he ask her advice of counsel, and will never attempt to control him in the management of it.

Should differences arise between husband and wife, the contest ought to be, not who will display the most spirit, but who will make the first advances. There is scarcely a more prolific source of unhappiness in the married state, than this "*spirit*," the legimate offspring of pride and want of feeling.

Perhaps the whole art of happiness in the married state, might be compressed into these two maxims—"Bear and forbear"—and "let the husband treat his wife, and the wife treat her husband with as much respect and attention, as he would a strange lady, and she a strange gentleman." And surely this is not an extravagant requisition.

"MARRIAGE CONTRACT WITH MARY JANE ROBINSON"

Robert Dale Owen (1832)

New York, Tuesday, April 2, 1832.

THIS AFTERNOON I enter into a matrimonial engagement with Mary Jane Robinson, a young person whose opinions on all important subjects, whose mode of thinking and feeling, coincide more intimately with my own than do those of any other individual with whom I am acquainted. . . . We have selected the simplest ceremony which the laws of this State recognize. . . . This ceremony involves not the necessity of making promises regarding that over which we have no control, the state of human affections in the distant future, nor of repeating forms which we deem offensive, inasmuch as they outrage the principles of human liberty and equality, by conferring rights and imposing duties unequally on the sexes. The ceremony consists of a simply written contract in which we agree to take each other as husband and wife according to the laws of the State of New York, our signatures being attested by those friends who are present.

Of the unjust rights which in virtue of this ceremony an iniquitous law tacitly gives me over the person and property of another, I can not legally, but I can morally divest myself. And I hereby distinctly and emphatically declare that I consider myself, and earnestly desire to be considered by others, as utterly divested, now and during the rest of my life, of any such rights, the barbarous relics of a feudal, despotic system, soon destined, in the onward course of improvement, to be wholly swept away; and the existence of which is a tacit insult to the good sense and good feeling of this comparatively civilized age.

Robert Dale Owen.

Reprinted in HWS, *vol. 1.*

"THE RIGHT OF MARRIED WOMEN TO HOLD AND CONTROL PROPERTY"

Thomas Herttell (1839)

HAVING BROUGHT IN the Bill now under consideration, it is doubtless expected that I will not only state my motive for so doing, but assign also some of the reasons why it ought to become a law of this state. This I shall endeavor to do; and with full confidence that the facts and arguments by which I shall advocate the bill, ought to recommend it to the favourable consideration of this House. . . .

It is doubtless obvious to those who have paid due attention to the provisions of this *bill* that its primary *principle* is to preserve to *married women* the title, possession, and control of their estate, both real and personal *after* as *before* marriage;—and that no part of it shall innure to their husbands, solely by virtue of their *marriage*. Thus to protect it from injury and waste by means of the unprovident, prodigal, intemperate, and dissolute habits and practices of their husbands;—to save it from loss through the husband's misfortunes and crimes, and in short to make each, and the property of each exclusively answerable for his or her own misconduct. . . .

It needs hardly to be mentioned that the *common law* in question, besides divesting married women of the right of private property and giving it to their husbands, also rests the latter with such absolute and irresponsible power over the person of the wife, as renders her the abject and servile slave and "servant" of her "*legal lord* and *master*!" . . .

By virtue of existing laws, *unmarried* females can acquire, manage, and dispose of their estate both real and personal, and can exercise all the rights and powers relative thereto, as are possessed and exercised by *men*.

This is as it ought to be. The doctrine, or just and moral principle of "equal rights" cannot consistently, and does not righteously justify laws, giving to one *sex* powers and privileges relative to property which are denied to the other. The "natural and inalienable right of life, liberty, and the pursuit of happiness," is common to both sexes; and the law relative to the acquisition, possession and the management of property by *un*married females is in perfect harmony therewith.

Not so with *married* women. Existing laws divest them of rights which are retained and exercised not only by the male,

"The Right of Married Women to Hold and Control Property Sustained by the Constitution of the State of New York: Remarks in the House of Assembly of the State of New York in the Session of 1837 to Restore to Married Women 'The Right Of Property' as Guaranteed by the Constitution of This State." New York: Henry Durell, 1839.

but by the *un*married portion of the female sex. By marriage, the wife's personal property, whether acquired by will, deed, inheritance, or her own industry, becomes vested in her husband, and she is as fully deprived of her title to it, and her right to use or dispose of it, or to control the use and management of it, as if she instead of being *married*, had been sold a *slave* to a *master*.

Nor is she divested of her personal property only; she is also deprived of the *use* of her *real estate*; the rents, issues and profits of which, go the husband during coverture; and while they both live, the wife's right to receive the income of her own real estate, or to control its expenditure, is wrested from her. Nor do the *legal wrongs* consequent on her marriage end here. If during coverture, issue be born alive, and inspire but a single breath, and the mother survive her infant but a moment; the income of the wife's real estate goes to the husband during *his* life, to be appropriated as may be, to the use and benefit of any subsequent wife or wives and children he may have, or be spent and wasted as it frequently is, in riot and dissipation.

Again—a married woman may *inherit* property; her parents or others to whom she may be heir at law, dying intestate. In this case also, being totally unprotected, she becomes a victim to *law* and *matrimony*; and her rights, liberty, and property, are all involved in the sacrifice. Immediately after marriage, the husband may sell all the personal property of his wife, absolutely; and his *life estate* in her *real property*, and thus divest her of the benefit of the whole. After thus stripping her of her property, he may both covertly and openly abuse her with impunity; or may abandon her to her fate, to fare and suffer as may happen, with little means and less hope of redress. In truth all she can *legally* claim from him, is bare subsistence; the means of obtaining which are such as most women with the usual delicate feelings of those above the lowest grade, would revolt from pursuing against a husband, as bad as he may happen to be; and if injury, poverty, and suffering, should dispose her to appeal to the *law* for redress, she is in most cases unable to do so. It is the *law* that has produced her injuries and occasioned her sufferings. It is the *law* that has divested her of her rights and deprived her of her property, and placed it in the hands of her antagonist; to whose commands it compels her to implicit obedience, and enjoins patient submission to the almost absolute power with which the law also vests the husband over the wife. *He* therefore, more than any other man, has it in his power to oppose, annoy, and oppress her with impunity. Thus deprived of her rights, her liberty, and her property, and left destitute of the means of seeking redress in a judiciary court, with any rational chance or hope of success; then to tell her, that she is *entitled* to a *subsistence*, and can obtain it, if she will alone, empty-handed, and powerless, engage in a legal conflict against an antagonist to whom the law has given all her property and nearly unlimited authority over her person, is to tantalize the helpless, to add insult to injury, and a cruel mockery of justice. . . .

I take it for granted, because the fact will doubtless be conceded, that the government of this state was instituted by the people; and that the people, therefore, are the *sovereign source* of *political power* in the state. It is equally clear, that the government being instituted by the people, it must necessarily have been intended for the common benefit of *all* its constituents; and hence all within the sphere of its power, are *alike* entitled to the protection and security contemplated to be derived from it. The preservation and enjoyment of the *rights* possessed by each and all its constitutents, is the primary principle and legitimate purpose of political government.

That "all men are born free and with equal rights," is an admitted maxim in the moral and political creed of all advocates and friends of free government. That this truth is meant to apply exclusively to the *male* sex, will not be urged by any who have a due regard for their reputation for common sense. "All" women "are" also "born free and with equal rights;" "among which are" not only the right of "life, liberty, and the pursuit of happiness," but also *the right of private property*. Those rights are possessed by all, each and every citizen; and of course by females equally with male citizens. The right of private property is not exclusive with the male sex. The existing law itself, admits the right of property of unmarried females to be the same as that of male citizens; and the right to be protected by the government in the exercise and enjoyment of all the rights abovementioned, is common both to male and female citizens. It follows as a necessary consequence, and the conclusion cannot be illuded, that the right of private property is not only possessed by females equally with males, but by married equally with unmarried women. If therefore a law violating the rights of private property possessed by *men* or *unmarried* women, would be *wrong*, a law violating the rights of private property possessed by married women cannot be *right*. If a law by which the private property of *men* or *unmarried* women be taken from them and given to another without their free and voluntary consent, would be a violation of their rights of private property; no law can be just or justifiable by which the property of married women is taken from them without their consent, and given to another. . .

But what have married women done that they should be made the victims of an unnaturalized, foreign law; and be deprived of the rights of property, which is held sacred and inviolate in the cases of *unmarried* women, and males, married and unmarried? Why, to be sure, they got married! *That* they had a right to do. By what rule of law and justice, can any citizen be deprived of a *right*, who has done no *wrong*? By what rule of law, or justice, can any "member of this state," be deprived of *one right*, for having exercised *another*? and shall married women be deprived of their rights, and dispossessed of their property, barely for having exercised a natural and inalienable right? merely for having entered into the honourable state of wedlock? an action meriting praise and favour, rather than privations of property, or of rights, which in the case of males and unmarried women are held sacred and inviolable, though secured by no provisions of the Constitution, which are not equally applicable to females as males, and to married as to unmarried "members" or citizens of this state?

To repel the foregoing argument, to avoid its point and shun its conclusions, it will doubtless be said, that the law in question does not authorize the taking of the property of a married woman from her, and giving it to the husband *without* her *free and voluntary consent*. That she *voluntarily consents to the marriage, knowing* the legal *consequences of the contract*, and hence as *freely* and *voluntarily consents to the transfer of her property*, as she does to the marriage, of which it is the *legal* consequence!!

"EMANCIPATION"

William E. Channing (1840)

I WOULD CLOSE this topic with observing, that there is one portion of the community to which I would especially commend the cause of the enslaved, and *the duty of open testimony against this* form of oppression; and that is, our women. To them, above all others, slavery should seem an intolerable evil, because its chief victims are women. In their own country, and not very far from them, there are great multitudes of their sex exposed to dishonor, held as property by *man*, unprotected by law, driven to the field of the overseer, and happy if not consigned to infinitely baser uses, denied the rights of wife and mother, and liable to be stripped of husband and child when another's pleasure or interest may so determine. Such is the lot of hundreds of thousands of their sisters; and is there nothing here to stir up woman's sympathy, nothing for her to remember, when she approaches God's throne or opens her heart to her fellow-creatures? Woman should talk of the enslaved to her husband, and do what she can to awaken, amongst his ever-thronging worldly cares, some manly indignation, some interest in human freedom. She should breathe into her son a deep sense of the wrongs which man inflicts on man, and send him forth from her arms a friend of the weak and injured. She should look on her daughter, and shudder at the doom of so many daughters on her own shores. When she meets with woman, she should talk with her of the ten thousand homes which have no defence against licentiousness, against violation of the most sacred domestic ties; and through her whole intercourse, the fit season should be chosen to give strength to that deep moral conviction which can alone overcome this tremendous evil.

I know it will be said that, in thus doing, woman will wander beyond her sphere, and forsake her proper work. What! Do I hear such language in a civilized age, and in a land of Christians? What, let me ask, is woman's work? It is, to be a minister of Christian love. It is, to sympathize with human misery. It is, to breathe sympathy into man's heart. It is, to keep alive in society some feeling of human brotherhood. This is her mission on earth. Woman's sphere, I am told, is home. And why is home instituted? Why are domestic relations ordained? These relations are for a day; they cease at the grave. And what is their great end? To nourish a love which will endure for ever, to awaken universal sympathy. Our ties to our parents are to bind us to the Universal Parent; our fraternal bonds, to help us to see in all men our brethren. Home is to be a nursery of Christians; and what is the end of Christianity, but to awaken in all souls the principles of universal justice and universal charity? At home we are to learn to love our neighbor, our enemy, the stranger, the poor, the oppressed. If home does not train us to this, then it is woefully perverted. If home

---

From The Works of William E. Channing, *vol. 1. Boston: American Unitarian Association, 1867.*

counteract and quench the spirit of Christianity, then we must remember the divine Teacher, who commands us to forsake father and mother, brother and sister, wife and child, for his sake, and for the sake of his truth. If the walls of home are the bulwarks of a narrow, clannish love, through which the cry of human miseries and wrongs cannot penetrate, then it is mockery to talk of their sacredness. Domestic life is at present too much in hostility to the spirit of Christ. A family should be a community of dear friends, strengthening one another for the service of their fellow-creatures. Can we give the name of Christian to most of our families? Can we give it to women who have no thoughts or sympathies for multitudes of their own sex, distant only two or three days' journey from their doors, and exposed to outrages from which they would pray to have their own daughters snatched, though it were by death?

"SPEECHES AT THE WORLD ANTI-SLAVERY CONVENTION"

Wendell Phillips and George Bradburn (1840)

MR. PHILLIPS:

When the call reached America we found that it was an invitation to the friends of the slave of every nation and of every clime. Massachusetts has for several years acted on the principle of admitting women to an equal seat with men, in the deliberative bodies of anti-slavery societies. When the Massachusetts Anti-Slavery Society received that paper, it interpreted it, as it was its duty, in its broadest and most liberal sense. If there be any other paper, emanating from the Committee, limiting to one sex the qualification of membership, there is no proof; and, as an individual, I have no knowledge that such a paper ever reached Massachusetts. We stand here in consequence of your invitation, and knowing our custom, as it must be presumed you did, we had a right to interpret "friends of the slave," to include women as well as men. In such circumstances, we do not think it just or equitable to that State, nor to America in general, that, after the trouble, the sacrifice, the self-devotion of a part of those who leave their families and kindred and occupations in their own land, to come three thousand miles to attend this World's Convention, they should be refused a place in its deliberations. . . .

George Bradburn, of Mass.: We are told that it would be outraging the customs of England to allow women to sit in this Con-

London, 1840. Reprinted in HWS, *vol. 1.*

vention. I have a great respect for the customs of old England. But I ask, gentlemen, if it be right to set up the customs and habits, not to say prejudices of Englishmen, as a standard for the government on this occasion of Americans, and of persons belonging to several other independent nations. I can see neither reason nor policy in so doing. Besides, I deprecate the principle of the objection. In America it would exclude from our conventions all persons of color, for there customs, habits, tastes, prejudices, would be outraged by *their* admission. And I do not wish to be deprived of the aid of those who have done so much for this cause, for the purpose of gratifying any mere custom or prejudice. Women have furnished most essential aid in accomplishing what has been done in the State of Massachusetts. If, in the Legislature of that State, I have been able to do anything in furtherance of that cause, by keeping on my legs eight or ten hours day after day, it was mainly owing to the valuable assistance I derived from the women. And shall such women be denied seats in this Convention? My friend George Thompson, yonder, can testify to the faithful services rendered to this cause by those same women. He can tell you that when "gentlemen of property and standing" in "broad day" and "broadcloth," undertook to drive him from Boston, putting his life in peril, it was our women who made their own persons a bulwark of protection around him. And shall such women be refused seats here in a Convention seeking the emancipation of slaves throughout the world? What a misnomer to call this a World's Convention of Abolitionists, when some of the oldest and most thorough-going Abolitionists in the world are denied the right to be represented in it by delegates of their own choice. . . .

. . . But when I look at the arguments against the title of these women to sit amongst us, I can not but consider them frivolous and groundless. The simple question before us is, whether these ladies, taking into account their credentials, the talent they have displayed, the sufferings they have endured, the journey they have undertaken, should be acknowledged by us, in virtue of these high titles, or should be shut out for the reasons stated.

Mr. Phillips, being urged on all sides to withdraw his motion, said: It has been hinted very respectfully by two or three speakers that the delegates from the State of Massachusetts should withdraw their credentials, or the motion before the meeting. The one appears to me to be equivalent to the other. If this motion be withdrawn we must have another. I would merely ask whether any man can suppose that the delegates from Massachusetts or Pennsylvania can take upon their shoulders the responsibility of withdrawing that list of delegates from your table, which their constituents told them to place there, and whom they sanctioned as their fit representatives, because this Convention tells us that it is not ready to meet the ridicule of the morning papers, and to stand up against the customs of England. In America we listen to no such arguments. If we had done so we had never been here as Abolitionists. It is the custom there not to admit colored men into respectable society, and we have been told again and again that we are outraging the decencies of humanity when we permit colored men to sit by our side. When we have submitted to brick-bats, and the tar tub and feathers in America, rather than yield to the custom prevalent there of not admitting colored brethren into our friendship, shall we yield to parallel custom or prejudice against women in Old England? We can not yield this question if we would; for it is a matter of conscience. But we would not yield it on the ground of expediency. In doing so we should feel that we were striking off the right arm of our enterprise. We could not go back to America to ask for any aid from the women of Massachusetts if we had deserted them, when they chose to send out their own sisters as their representatives here. We could not go back to Massachusetts and assert the unchangeableness of spirit on the question. We have argued it over and over again, and decided it time after time, in every society in the land, in favor of the women. We have not changed by crossing the water. We stand here the advocates of the same principle that we contend for in America. We think it right for women to sit by our side there, and we think it right for them to do the same here. We ask the Convention to admit them; if they do not choose to grant it, the responsibility rests on their shoulders. Massachusetts can not turn aside, or succumb to any prejudices or customs even in the land she looks upon with so much reverence as the land of Wilberforce, or Clarkson, and of O'Connell. It is a matter of conscience, and British virtue ought not to ask us to yield.

"RIGHTS OF WOMEN"

Jonathan Neal (1843)

WHETHER THE WOMEN of this country are *slaves*, or not, depends upon the definition of slavery.

That they are not *free—free*, in the sense that Men are *free*, according to any definition of liberty, acknowledged among themselves, is undeniably true.

What then is Freedom, or Liberty—that Freedom or Liberty, which all the Nations are struggling for? that is held to be, not the shadow only, nor the sunshine, but the very substance of Christianity? that which all human beings endowed with reason, are fitted to enjoy, and if our faith be sound, "*created*" to enjoy? that, of which "we, the People," claim to be the only true interpreters, the only faithful expounders on earth? Is it of two sexes? Are there two kinds of Liberty—one for Man, and another for Woman, throughout the world? . . .

Have women *no* political rights? Are their legal and social rights everywhere, only just what men may choose to concede to them? In other words, are their best privileges and highest prerogatives, matters of right or matters of favor, wholly dependent upon the opinions and prerogatives of Men—observe the question, we beseech you, and weigh it well—have Women, either in this country, or in England, or throughout Christendom, properly speaking, any *rights* at all?

Everywhere, among Barbarians as well as Christians, they are admitted to a sort of

---

Brother Jonathan 5 *(17 June 1843).*

qualified companionship—everywhere, they are allowed to enjoy just what Man may happen to think will best promote *his* comfort—and nothing more. In countries, where they are believed to have no soul, just as in countries where they are supposed to have no understanding, and are classed by the lawgivers and the law, with infants, lunatics, and people beyond sea, they are brought up to believe that they enjoy all the liberty they are capable to enjoying. And wo to the man, who shall attempt to undeceive them!

Among the Hindoos, it is the *privilege* of women to burn themselves alive—on the death of their husbands. Among the Chinese, the better sort are made cripples from their birth—it is their *privilege*, and one of which they are exceedingly jealous and watchful; the lower orders being satisfied with another and much humbler privilege—that of plowing while the husband sows. In one part of the world, it is the woman's *privilege* to dig and plant, and carry her children upon her back, till the boys are old enough to beat her, while her husband lolls about in the shadow, and amuses himself with hunting and fishing: In another, she is not permitted to sit down in the presence of her lord and master—nor even to eat with him, her husband, and the father of her children; it is her chief privilege, her highest prerogative, to stand before him barefoot, with her arms crossed upon her bosom, and her eyes fixed upon the earth, and *hear* him eat: while in another, where the men treat the women with the greatest possible tenderness—taking care that the very "winds of Heaven shall not visit their faces too roughly"; where "they toil not, neither do they spin, though Solomon in all his glory was not clad like one of these"; where the highest prices are paid for them, and they are literally worshipped for a season—they are not allowed to speak to a stranger; to go to the door under any pretence, nor to look out of a window, with uncovered eyes, under pain of death. But these are all barbarians. And while our men pity them, and labor to convince them of their short-sighted folly, sending Missionaries among them for the purpose; and while our women are amazed at the dreadful ignorance and blindness that prevail in such lands—looking upon the men as downright savages, and wondering at the patience of the women—there is another country, and another people much nearer home, with whose habits and customs they are much better acquainted—whom they never think of pitying, and with whom they never dream of intermeddling, though there is a greater difference between the privileges of the men and the privileges of the women—the rights of the Men, and the rights of the Women there—than in any other country, or among any other people upon the face of the earth: all the Men being free and all the Women slaves at birth, and utterly incapable of becoming free, by any change of circumstances. In that country, women are under a perpetual guardianship, they are never mentioned but in the language of poetry, with uplifted hands, or a gentler intonation of the voice; they are flattered and fondled, if we may believe what we hear, from the cradle to the grave. There, instead of being what she is in the lands of barbarian pomp, a slave, a plaything, or a toy, she is the companion of man—his friend, his equal, and his pleasant counsellor, sharing his proud sovereignty and qualified for everlasting companionship—if we may believe the Men themselves, or even the Women. There, it is their *privilege* to be spoken to in a subdued voice—never to be contradicted—never to be reasoned with—and to grow up with a belief, that men are their slaves, and that women always have their own way at last, whether married or unmarried. There, too, it is the privilege of woman to be excluded from all participation in business—in the professions—in government—in power; to be excluded from all offices, whether of trust, profit, or honor, however well fitted she may be, for the discharge of their duties, and however much she may need their help and comfort—huge, able bodied men, being preferred to her in every case, even for the sorting of letters, or the mending of pens—to labor all her life long, for a price varying from a fifth to a fiftieth part of what is paid for the same labor; to make shirts for sixpence a day—to cry her eyes out, under pretence of being courted—take in washing, or to marry—and be satisfied for the rest of her life "to suckle fools and chronicle small beer."

In that country it is their *privilege* to be taxed without their own consent; to be governed by laws, made not by themselves, nor by their representatives, but by people, whose interest instead of being identical with theirs, is directly opposed to theirs, in every important question of self-government, as they prove by their whole course of legislation, and by their unwillingness to share what they call *liberty* with the very persons whose interest they say is identical with theirs, and who amount to one half of the whole population of the country.

There too, up to the time of her marriage, and after the death of her husband, a woman is nobody. Her property is taxed without her own consent—and she is allowed to share in no one of the three great powers of self-government; neither in the making of the laws, the administration of the laws, nor in the execution of the laws. No vote can she give—no office can she hold. After marriage, it is the same, with these additional disqualifications; all her personal property goes to her husband, or to her husband's creditors; the use of all her real property during the marriage; and, if they have a child born alive, up to the time of her husband's death; all her rents and profits, all she may acquire during marriage, by gift, or devise (with a few exceptions, not worth mentioning). Add to this, that while no part of the husband's earnings belong to the wife, all her earnings belong to him; *that she is bound by personal service during marriage*, and may be treated by him, like a servant, a child, or an apprentice, and actually beaten, if beaten moderately and with a wholesome regard to her amendment, if she falters in her allegiance. Lo! the privileges of women in the country we have in our eye! And who taught them that these were indeed their privileges? The same being who taught the Egyptian woman that to bury herself alive with her husband was a privilege. The same being who persuaded the poor Indian, that to cast herself headlong into the fire, was a privilege. The same being, who persuaded the Chinese woman to cripple herself, and the North American savage to stand still and be beaten by her lord and master, in the shape of a man-child, carried in her arms till they dropped with fatigue; and the beautiful women of Turkey, and Circassia, that to be the plaything of a hoary lecher is a privilege. And who was that being? Was it God? No. It was Man: the tyrant Man. Having usurped all power—and being entitled to it, by the right of the strongest, according to the avowed opinions of ex-President Adams, and others equally distinguished—do what he may, and say what he may, it is high treason, ay, and blasphemy, for women to question his supremacy.

It is vain that she proposes to argue the question. She is only laughed at, for her pains. If she quotes his own language against him, and convicts him out of his own mouth of the most egregious folly, or falsehood, the answer is a rude laugh, a sneer, a sarcasm, or an appeal to the newspapers.

But we are not to be so easily silenced. And if argument is wanted, argument they shall have—these mighty logicians and mightier statesmen, who have undertaken to justify the everlasting disfranchisement of one-half of the whole human race, with a sneer.

To the point then. What is freedom? Ask our fathers of the Revolutionary War. People are free, said they—and they fought a battle of eight years with the most powerful nation of all the earth, pouring out their blood like water, to establish the proposition—people are free, only so far as they are allowed to govern themselves: in other words, to make their own laws, to expound their own laws, and to carry their own laws into execution. Were they right, or were they wrong? Let us see.

All government is made up of three elements, or powers, differently combined: the power of making, the power of interpreting, and the power of administering laws: in other words, all government, whether a Despotism, a Monarchy, an Oligarchy, an Aristocracy, a Republic, or a Democracy, may be resolved into the legislative, the judiciary, and the executive powers. Men are agreed upon this, without going to Aristotle, to Montesquieu, to John Locke, or to the authors of the *Federalist*.

Where these three powers are united in one person, as in the Czar of Russia, the government is a Despotism. Where they are enjoyed by and confined to a privileged class, independent of, and separated from the people, it is either an Aristocracy, or an Oligarchy. Where the People are allowed to share in the government, along with the privileged class, or hereditary lawgivers, and a king by right of birth, as in Great Britain, it is a limited Monarchy—though Sir Francis Burdett calls it a Republic, and others, pleasantly enough it must be acknowledged, a Constitutional Monarchy. Where the people govern themselves directly, as in Athens, it is a Democracy: where they govern indirectly, a representation, as in the United States, it is a Republic—so far at least as the *men* are concerned.

Now—under which of these different forms of government do the *women* of this country live?

Where people do *not* govern themselves, either directly or indirectly by representation, they are slaves. Qualify it as we may, disguise the unpalatable truth as we may, they have no *rights* and all their *privileges* are at the mercy of the governing power. Steadfast as Death—steady as the everlasting Ocean, in their encroachments, Men have obtained the mastery over Women, not by superior virtue, nor by superior understanding, but by the original accident of superior strength; and after monopolizing all power, have extinguished her ambition, dwarfed her faculties, and brought her up to believe—the simpleton—that she was created, only for the pleasure of man.

But what is meant by governing themselves? Ask our Revolutionary Fathers. Lo! their answer, as with the voice of congregated armies. Having argued the question for eight long years, by the mouth of cannon having agreed upon a confession of faith—having sent it abroad over all the earth—publishing it everywhere by the sound of trumpet—among all nations, and kindreds and tongues: we appeal to *them*, and to *that*.

To be free—such is their doctrine—*To be free, Men must be allowed to govern themselves*. But if Men, why not Women? We shall see before we get through. In other words, they must be allowed to make their own laws, either in person, *or by delegates chosen for the purpose*: they must be allowed to explain, or interpret these laws after they are made, either in person, or by delegates *chosen for the purpose*: and they must be allowed to carry out these laws into execution, either by themselves in person, or by delegates *chosen for the purpose*. But chosen by whom?—by themselves, or by another and a different class? Propound that question to our Fathers, if you dare.

In other words, to be free, people must be allowed to vote as they like—*to choose*—they must not only be electors, but eligible to office. We need not stop to qualify the doctrine by saying that we mean what our Fathers meant, where majorities govern, with proper qualifications, *fairly* assented to. Nobody will understand us to maintain that all have the right to govern themselves, according to their own good pleasure, without reference to others—but only that all have a right to *share* in the government, under which they live—to share and share alike, if our noble Fathers were right—if they were not rebels and traitors, alike unjust, unprincipled, and shameless.

Abridge a people of these rights; deny to them free exercise of any, the least of the whole, under any pretence (where they have not been forfeited by crime) and you abridge them of their liberty; you wrong them of their birthright; you spoil them of their *natural* heritage. So say our Fathers, and they were "honorable men."

And now to apply this. Are Women *people*—or a part of the people? When our Fathers say, that all *Men* are created *equal*—that they have "certain inalienable rights," etc., etc., etc., do they mean Women or not? If not, how much better are they, than the Turks, who deny that Women have souls? And what confidence can Women have in their pretended reverence and affection? And with what face, can they, the mothers in Israel, venture to become the teachers of our youth, or to justify the course of our Revolutionary Fathers?

Women constitute one half of our whole population. They amount now, in round numbers, excluding those held in bondage at the South, to eight millions, or thereabouts. Have these women souls or not? Have they understanding or not? Have they any *rights*—have they anything indeed but what they enjoy by the favor and courtesy of Men? are they capable of governing our households; capable of bearing men, and of educating them, capable of assisting in our churches, and managing our elections—and yet incapable of governing themselves, or even in sharing in the government of themselves? Let the spirit of eternal truth and justice answer. Men will not, and women cannot, in their present stifled condition, either feel, or see the truth. As well might we ask the Hindoo women to see *why* she has been taught to destroy herself at the tomb of her cruel, selfish, unrelenting husband; or hope to persuade the Chinese woman to understand *why* she is crippled for life; as the English woman to see her own hopeless, dependent, and pitiable condition, among rational beings, claiming to be free, or the American woman, hers.

But still we do not despair. We have faith in Woman—much more than we have in Man, if the truth must be told. And it shall be no fault of ours, if she does not hear the truth, and feel it too, before she goes into her grave, and we into ours.

To return therefore, we mean to be understood. For these eight millions of human beings—free white women—who make the laws? Men. Who expound the laws? Men. Who carry the laws into execution? Men. Who occupy all the professions? all the places of trust, profit and power? and who have charge of all the resources of the country? of all the scientific and literary institutions? of the army and navy, and the entire wealth of the nation? Men, always men. Just reverse the condition of the two sexes: give to Women all the power now enjoyed by the Men—and would they not be able to keep it, think you? What a clamor there would be then, about *equal rights*, about a *privileged class*, about being *taxed without their own consent*, about *virtual representation*, and all that! And yet—mark our words—that is the true way of putting the question. In any given case, we have only to ask ourselves how we should bear such laws from women as they are called upon to bear from us—and not only to bear, but to be thankful for? But we are Men—and they are Women; *only* Women. Behold the answer, urged by the husbands and fathers and sons of the land, against their wives and mothers and daughters, eight millions strong!

And now to the second, and last branch of our subject. Some people must have authority—even for believing that two and two make four. Be it so—they shall be satisfied.

In a certain paper called a *Declaration of Rights*, published to the world in 1774, by a body called the American Congress, we find the following passage:

"Resolved, That the *Inhabitants* of the English Colonies in North America, by the *immutable laws of nature*, the principles of the English constitution, etc., etc., have the following RIGHTS;" and then follows a brief enumeration of these rights: after which it is *Resolved*,

"That the foundation of English liberty, *and of all free government*, is a right in the people to *Participate in their legislative council*: and as the English colonists *are not represented*, and from their local and other circumstances, cannot properly be represented in the British parliament, they are entitled to a free and exclusive power of legislation, in their several provincial legislatures," etc., etc.

Among the grievances complained of, with profound seriousness, as involving the dearest rights of Freemen was that of taxation without representation or that of being taxed without their own consent. As early as 1765, when the first Provincial Congress met, this was regarded as the principal grievance; and from that hour, up to the Declaration of Independence, that was the abominable thing chiefly complained of. The Stamp Act, and the Repeal of the Stamp Act, the emptying of a cargo of tea into Boston harbor, the battle of Lexington, and the battle of Bunker Hill—in fact the whole war of Independence, if we may believe our Fathers, grew out of a *tax on tea*; in other words, out of the pretensions of the mother country to tax our people without their own consent.

And now two questions arise here. First. Were the *women* of these English colonies of North America, *inhabitants*? If they were, then did our Fathers decide the whole question; that they have all the rights we contend for, by the *immutable* laws of Nature. By the constitution of New Jersey, all the *inhabitants*, having resided a certain time within the State, and being worth fifty pounds proclamation money, are entitled to vote. Under this provision, the women of New Jersey, have occasionally voted, up to the time, when finding they could neither be shamed out of their privilege, nor laughed out of it, the Legislature undertook to settle the constitutional question, by declaring that the word "*inhabitants*," meant *free white males*! So much for contemporaneous interpretation. Secondly. Are women a part of the People? If they are, then by the solemn adjudication of our Fathers, they are entitled to *participate* in their *legislative council*: and not being represented, have a right to legislate for themselves.

On the other hand, if women are neither *inhabitants*, nor *people*—they are not *persons*. They have no right to assemble together for any purpose, even to petition for the redress of grievances, that privilege being confined to the people; they are incapable of riots—incapable of crime—they are not moral agents—and cannot be justly punished for anything. The conclusion is inevitable.

Now let us see where we are. The builders

up to our political Faith, went to war with their own Fathers and brothers, and quarrelled for eight long years, pouring out rivers of blood, and millions of treasure, and counted the cost nothing, because they would not consent to be *taxed without their own consent*; nor to be governed *by laws to which they had never agreed*; nor to be *virtually represented*.

Having triumphed; having established the great Truth for which they were so ready to lay down their lives, and with it their independence, what do they next? Why they turn round to one half of their whole population—their wives and sisters and daughters—and beloved ones, and say: "We hold these truths to be self-evident: that all men are created equal: that they are endowed with certain inalienable rights, among which are life, liberty, and the pursuit of happiness." Nonsense, at best, but nonsense well calculated to show their temper and meaning; and just of a piece with the behavior of the Puritans, who having fled from persecution at home, were no sooner established here, than they fell to persecuting others with unrelenting bitterness. They swear to England, as the Lord liveth, *we will not be taxed without our own consent*! and then turning to one-half of their whole number, they say, as the Lord liveth, *you shall*. They say to England, *we will not be governed by laws, to which we have not given assent*: and then turning to those among them, whom they profess to love and venerate, beyond anything on earth, they say—*You shall*! They declare to their fathers and brothers, that *they will not endure virtual representation*, and turning round to their brothers and sisters, declare that *they shall*!

But, perhaps, the framers of that constitution, when they declared, that all Men were created equal, meant Women? Let us see. We may allow them to speak for themselves; to be their own interpreters. They class women with infants, idiots and lunatics. They hold her to perpetual service,—allow her to share in governing herself—permit her to enjoy no office, though we have twenty thousand offices much better fitted for women, than for able-bodied men—and do not permit her to choose her own master, by a vote. Before marriage, a woman is taxed without her own consent. After marriage, it is the same. During marriage, all her personal property belongs to her husband, all her acquisitions, all her earnings, all her rents, and profits, and she is *bound to personal service*, until set free by death or divorce. There are a few exceptions to be sure, as where property is secured to her by the intervention of trustees, or by chancery, or by declaring that it shall not be subject to the control, nor liable for the debts of her husband—but these are only exceptions: the rule is just what we have stated. While under coverture as it is called, that is, during marriage, the wife can neither acquire, nor bestow anything, as or right. She can neither educate nor portion her children off. She can neither provide for old age, nor help her husband, however much he may need help—all her property belonging to his creditors; and at his death, she may be left entirely destitute at the pleasure of that husband, if he happens to have nothing but personal property, or has been cunning enough to obtain her relinquishment of dower; and this, although they may have begun the world together—both poor—or he poor, and she rich; and although she may have been his partner for life, laborious, diligent, faithful and frugal; and he, a drunken spend-thrift—so that by the common laws of partnership, she would be entitled to at least one half of all their joint-savings and acquisitions. Oh! but we could tell such things, if this were the time, or place! But it is not, and we leave them for another.

Again that we may understand our *rights*

and our *duties* when wrongfully dealt with, let us take another passage from the Declaration of Independence. In it, our Fathers declare that "to secure *these rights* governments are instituted among men, deriving their powers just from the *consent of the governed*: that when any form of government became destructive of *these ends*, it is the right of the People to alter or abolish it, *and to institute a new government*," etc., etc. But that "when a long train of abuses and usurpations, having invariably the same object, evinces a design to reduce them under *absolute despotism*, it is their *right*, it is their *duty* to throw off such government, and provide new guards, for their future security." If all this be true,—and who will venture to question its truth?—What is the *right* of Woman, what her *duty* towards her oppressor Man? What say the authorities? We leave them to answer the question.

And now—what say you? Try it by what standard you please: adopt what definition of liberty you will—are not the women of this country *slaves*? Do they not enjoy all they enjoy at all, by sufferance, rather than by *right*? Are they not wholly dependent upon men? Are they allowed any share whatever in the government of the country; any participation in what men call *liberty*? Are they not as much bondwomen as any you ever read of? Is not their situation as deplorable, all things considered, as that of the women of Egypt, or Hindostan, or China, so far as a just *equality*, a true *companionship* is concerned? Tell us not that Chritianity has done everything for woman—it has done little more for women than for the beasts that perish. It has not narrowed by one hair's breadth the *difference* between the sexes—the great gulf between the *powers* of men, and the *privileges* of woman: It has added no jot nor tittle to her acknowledged rights. Everywhere—throughout Christendom, as throughout all the rest of the world, woman is kept, only in the best possible working condition for the comfort of man. . . .

The question is not, whether you shall *force* women to do as they like—and much less whether you shall force them to do what you like, and they do not,—but whether you will allow them the same liberty you allow other accountable beings of a different sex—and that is, to govern themselves, *if they please*, and to think for themselves, *if they dare*. . . .

. . . It is no part of my plan that woman should be *denied* the privileges and comforts of womanhood,—much less that she should be *obliged* to take upon herself the obligations of manhood.

Ah! but how shall she escape? you ask. If you grant to her the privileges of men, you must load her with the correspondent obligations of men.

Granted. And what are they? Are they what they are represented to be by those who have written longest, and talked loudest—and least to the purpose—against the rights of women? Are men *obliged* to bear arms? Are they *obliged* to serve on a jury? Are they *obliged* to go to congress,—to hold office,—or even to vote? Because they are *eligible* to office, must they take office? Because they may, *if they will*, serve in the militia, or make speeches, or help to make laws—*must* they do so?

Nothing of the sort. The quakers, and all who are conscientiously scrupulous, are exempted from bearing arms. They are not even called upon to pay a fine, or provide a substitute. Others are exempted because of their age—being either too young or too old; others on account of their office, *or their health*, or their *bodily unfirmities*; and yet all these persons are eligible to office,—and all enjoy the high privilege we contend for—and that, too, discharged of their correspondent obligations. In principle, therefore, the great majority of our *males* are at this moment enjoying just what we ask for our *females*!

And so with service upon the jury. Old age, ill health—other duties—business that would greatly suffer—are always good and sufficient reasons,—and if they were not, a fine, or at the most, a short imprisonment, is the penalty.

And so with voting—and so with office and official duties. If a man does not *choose* to vote, nor to make a speech, nor to go to congress, nor to hold office, there's no law,—no power on earth to *make* him.

And now—give me your whole attention, I beseech you—suppose all such persons were immediately *disfranchised*. Suppose it were instantly established by law that they should not be eligible to office, nor serve on juries, nor bear arms,—in other words, suppose they were put into the condition of the blacks, whether bond or free,—or of the WOMEN, whether bond or free; suppose they were forbidden to hold property,—that they were *taxed without their own consent*,—that they were no longer allowed to make, or interpret, or administer the laws,—how think you they would bear it? and what would be *their* definition of liberty? . . .

But woman's declaration of rights, you say, is, "I am a wife and a mother! To be these is my *freedom*,—to be other is *slavery*."

But suppose she happened to be neither,—according to your own definition, she is *a slave*. We have some hundreds of thousands of women in this country who are neither wives nor mothers—nor ever will be—would you leave them nothing to console them? . . .

You maintain that woman is unfitted by nature to enjoy them,—and you prove that she does not understand them,—nor desire them. So much the worse for her! This is the very thing we complain of. There are countless millions of men upon the earth who do not understand what we call liberty,—who are wholly unacquainted with it,—who are unfitted by nature to enjoy it,—and what then? Shall we leave them in their blindness and helplessness, and go by on the other side? *Or*, when we see their hands groping about in the darkness,—and their eyes straining after the unknown God,—shall we not lift our voices for their encouragement, and shout to them to be of good cheer, and that help cometh!

Just so should it be with woman. If they are *fitted* for entire companionship with man, then they are entitled to it. If they are not, they never will desire it; and all the laws that we can make will not change their character. . . .

But you are startled at the extraordinary assertion made by me, that "Christianity has done little more for woman than for the beasts that perish;" and you proceed to urge a number of questions, with great eloquence and power, which might perhaps have been spared—well put, as I acknowledge them to be—had you given your attention to what immediately follows:—"It has not narrowed, by one hair's breadth, the *difference* between the sexes—the great gulf between the *powers* of men, and the *privileges* of women. It has added no jot nor tittle to her acknowledged *rights*."

Nor has it. Man has all power in Christendom,—woman *none*. She is wholly dependent upon him—by *law*,—I say nothing of nature,—I say nothing of God's law—the law of God I do not complain of; and this while man, by *law*, is wholly independent of her. Whatever she enjoys by *law*, she enjoys not as a matter of *right*, but as a matter of favor. And just so is it among all the barbarians of earth. Where the condition of man is improved, that of woman must follow, and does follow throughout the world. But the *difference*, I say, is never lessened—even under the benignest influences of Christianity.

. . . [Has] *Christianity* . . . not taught the doctrine of equal moral responsibility in the sexes?

My answer will depend upon what is understood by "Christianity." If the question be whether Jesus of Nazareth so taught—my answer would be YES: but if it were whether his followers have so taught, my answer would be NO. The Teacher of truth and righteousness and love,—the Man of sorrows and acquainted with grief,—permitted his feet to be washed with the tears of the unhappy, and wiped with her hair; and when the woman taken in adultery was brought to him, *by his followers*, he let her go in peace, saying "*Sin no more*!"

And how has it been with *his followers* from that day to this? Have they not always had one moral standard for woman, and another for man? Throughout Christendom, for eighteen hundred years, among the countless millions of Christian men and woman that have lived and died, or still live, has it not been death to a woman to do that which men have been permitted to do almost withour reproach? and why? Simply because Men make the law, and public opinion follows the law, as the shadow the substance? . . .

"Has not Christianity made woman *in a great degree*, the equal of man in the marriage contract?"

Yes—'in a great degree' it has; but in a still greater degree, it has not. Under the French law, marriage is a partneship—and the rights and privileges of the parties, are somewhat alike. In the North of Europe, there is a feeble show of equality. But in England, and here, it is altogether a one-sided and most inequitable arrangement; all the property going to the husband, while but a *chance* remains to the wife, which he can defeat, at will.

True—Christianity *has* said—in substance—"One wife shalt thou have and unto her shalt thou cleave all the days of thy life." But who cares for that? We are speaking of what Christianity has *done*—not what she has *said*. Divorces happen every day—thousands and tens of thousands of mistresses, who are wives in all but the name—are to be met with, if not among Christians, certainly in Christendom. . . .

. . . [Y]ou ask, . . . "*Ought* woman to have any rights or enjoyments, but such as harmonise with those of man? *Can* she have any such? *Could* they be necessary to complete her happiness?" And then you answer, "not unless the wisdom of nature failed here, and she blundered into one of those gross errors which sometimes expose the weakness of human intellect."

Now—instead of answering your question, suppose I put another. What if I propound the same enquiry, changing the word *woman* to man? Let us see if it would not answer itself.

Ought *Man* to have any rights or enjoyments, but such as harmonise with those of *Woman*? *Can* he have any such? *Could* they be necessary to complete his happiness? . . .

. . . [Y]ou assert that women "has been denied all participation in government," by ONE "wiser than man"—by God himself, therefore. And you find the evidence in the fact that, she is not "six feet high," that she "does not possess the wide shoulders, brawny arms, and iron muscles" of man—in other words, you find the evidence in her inferior bodily strength. And you object, and in large capitals too—and more than once, to what I have chosen to call the *original accident*, whereby Man has acquired the mastery of woman; the *original accident* of superior bodily strength.

Now, if I am wrong, and you are right, only the men of greatest bodily strength, ought to have dominion upon earth. All who are *under* six feet high—all who have narrow shoulders—feeble arms—and flabby muscles—were intended from the first, by *God himself*, and their physical organization proves it, to be forever subject to the legislation of those who are *over* "six feet high, with broad shoulders, brawny arms and iron muscles!" If you are right, and I wrong, then other men were wrong to overthrow the giants; and the Paragonians are the natural rulers of the earth; and it should be high treason for such little men as now govern Europe—and all the rest of the world—to think of governing themselves: nay—if you are right, then was it rebellion for Alexander the Great, Julius Caesar, and Napoleon Bonaparte, to bestir themselves against their natural sovereigns—the six footers—the gladiators—and the sappers and miners of their day. . . .

But "Woman is appointed to all the labor and responsibility of rearing the human family: and is it rational to suppose," you ask, "that the Creator has added to these, with her weaker person, the same tasks, which he calls upon the strong frame of man (to perform,) untasked by any of these?"

Certainly not. If by the question you mean to ask if the *same* woman, *at the same time*, is called upon to perform the tasks of man and woman both. I answer no—God never meant this. But if you mean to ask, whether, *because* one woman is sick abed, another may not be allowed to attend a public meeting; or *because* one woman is wanted at home to nurse her baby, her next door neighbor shall not be allowed to read a newspaper, or cast a vote, or act as a judge or lawgiver, I answer that I see no *incompatibility* here; and acknowledge none. . . . Suppose we stop the first hundred men that go by us through Broadway, most of them busy men, with anxious, careworn faces, and with families at home to provide for—and say to the busiest and frailest, and least healthy looking—God never meant to impose a *double task* upon *you*! *You* cannot attend to your family, and business, and help govern the country too—and therefore we propose to spare you the trouble to vindicate the wisdom of God—and to let you free forever! *Your interest and ours, you know, is identical*. What we gain, you gain—*of course*; and therefore, as the country grows richer and wiser, you, being a part of the country, grow richer and wiser with it. In a word—what say you? If you go to Congress, your wives will have to take your places behind the counter—and keep the books—and swear *at* the workmen—and shin it every day through wall-street—and look after the boys—and, in short, your families and business would be in a shocking condition. What would be the answer, think you? . . .

But you deny that women are *taxed*, as I say they are, without their own consent. And you ask, "in what nation on the face of the earth can that body of men be found so dastardly as to lay any burthen upon women of property, which they do not equally *submit* to for the public good?" To which I answer—such men are found everywhere, throughout all Christendom—wherever Woman is *taxed without her own consent*. Men who tax *themselves* have nothng to complain of: Men who tax *others*—along with themselves—not much. But people who are not allowed to tax themselves, nor others, are not to be satisfied, in the present state of the world, by a declaration that they are *taxed for the public good*; or that they who lay the tax, share the burthen with them, by taxing themselves. Our Fathers had a different notion; and so have we. And if the Men of our country were taxed by the Women; and if they remonstrated—and were answered in this way—how think you the Men would bear it?

That woman is exempted from a capitation or poll tax—that most dangerous and foolish of all taxes; that she is exempted from public service, in the militia, on juries, and in office, I admit: and so are the *niggers.* But does this prove that these exemptions are *privileges*? That for certain offences she cannot be punished, if committed in the presence of her husband, I also acknowledge. But for whose sake?—for hers—or for his, that she may take care of his children and house? You cannot imprison a woman for debt, after marriage, where you may the husband. But why?—for the sake of the woman,—or for the sake of the man, whose children must be cared for? The law itself answers the question—her husband shall not be deprived of the comfort he finds in her society! *Her* privileges, indeed!—Bound to obey her husband, or be beaten!—Obliged to do whatever he commands her to do, either by the law of the land, or by the law or brute force—another law claimed to be very merciful, because it doesn't punish her for obeying him—*her* whom it classes with *infants, idiots,* and *lunatics*! . . .

"YOUNG WOMEN"

Martin Robinson Delaney (1844)

SEVERAL PERSONS have spoken to us, and lastly, an esteemed friend who writes to us, says "that a good many of our people think that you should not fault our women for living out at service, that we are a poor people, and they must do something for an honest living." This induces us to make the explanation, especially for the satisfaction of our industrious young females. Certain, we say, it is no disgrace, to live out, or to do any honest work for a living when necessity so compels us.

As the generality of our people are unacquainted with the logical meaning of the word necessity, we will explain it here, for their express satisfaction. Necessity simply means something that cannot be done without, this is the sole meaning of the word. When we say that we admit that our people are doing this of necessity, we simply mean that we admit of them doing it, when they can't do without it. A man eats, and also dies of necessity, that is he eats to keep from dying, and dies because he can't help it; he would not go to the trouble of either eating or dying, provided, it was left to his own choice. This is necessity; a thing done without your choice, a thing done that you can't do without doing.

But to make this plain, suppose that you knew of a young lady and gentleman, the son and daughter of a family in which you

---

From The Mystery. *Reprinted in* Palladium of Liberty *(Columbus, Ohio) (21 February 1844).*

live, with all the comforts of life around them, leave their parents' house and their acquaintances, and throw themselves about in peoples houses among their domestics, though such hired girls were white, would you not at once revolt at the idea, though you were at service yourselves, and strongly reprove them for thus traducing themselves?

Certainly you would. There's not a colored girl, but would feel indignant at the idea, and wish that she had the opportunities of such a young lady, that she might appreciate them. This is all we ask of the people; when you can do better, it is your duty to do so, if you can not, it is no shame to do the best you can. Yours is necessity, the young white lady's is choice. She's to blame, you are not.

"THE RIGHTS AND CONDITION OF WOMEN"

Rev. Samuel J. May (1846)

In the day that God created man, in the likeness of God made he him, male and female created he them; and blessed them, and called their name Adam.
—GENESIS 5:1

There is neither male nor female, for ye are all one in Christ Jesus.
—GALATIANS 3:28

ALLOW ME AGAIN to speak plainly to you of the rights and condition of Women. My thoughts were urgently drawn to this subject last Spring, by the fact that, at that time, the people of this State were called, in their primary capacity, to decide whether the sale of intoxicating drinks should be licensed—a question of the highest personal, domestic and social consequence—and yet more than half of the people, the women, were not only not expected, but not allowed to influence directly a decision, in which they were so much interested.

About the same time, the *men* of our nation presumed to plunge us into the multiform calamities, crimes and expenditures of a war, without so much as consulting the women, who will have to share equally, if not to endure the larger part of the losses and sufferings, that are inevitable upon such a measure of folly and wickedness.

Again, during the past summer, a large

8 November 1846. Syracuse, N.Y.: Stoddard & Babcock, 1846.

Convention of delegates, elected by the people of this State, have been in Session at the Capitol, framing a new Constitution, which is to affect as vitally the lives, liberties, properties, happiness of women as of men: and yet not a female was there to represent the interests of her sex; nor would one hardly suspect, from the document they have spread before their fellow citizens, that there were any women in the body politic. Nor is this all; but last Tuesday, when the constituents of that Convention were called upon to signify whether they would ratify the new Constitution, the women of New York were not expected, nor would they have been permitted to say, by their votes, whether or not they were willing to live under such a frame of government.

Now this is all unequal, all unrighteous—this utter annihilation, politically considered, of more than one half of the whole community. It is a piece of assumption just as egregious as it would be for the females to call a Convention, frame a state government, and go on to administer it by officers of their own choosing, without any recognition of the rights, and hardly any of the existence even of our sex.

This entire disfranchisement of females is as unjust as the disfranchisement of the males would be; for there is nothing in their moral, mental or physical nature, that disqualifies them to understand correctly the true interests of the community, or to act wisely in reference to them. . . .

To prove, however, that woman was not intended to be the equal of man, the argument most frequently alleged is, that she is the weaker vessel—inferior in stature, and has much less physical strength. This physiological fact of course cannot be denied; although the disparity in these respects is very much increased by neglect or mismanagement. But allowing women generally to have less bodily power, why should this consign them to mental, moral or social dependence? Physical force is of special value only in a savage or barbarous community. It is the avowed intention and tendency of Christianity to give the ascendancy to man's *moral* nature; and the promises of God, with whom is all strength and wisdom, are to the upright, the pure, the good,—not to the strong, the valiant, or the crafty. . . .

. . . Civilization implies the subordination of the physical in man to the mental and moral; and the progress of the melioration of the condition of our race, has been every where marked by the elevation of the female sex. . . .

Undoubtedly some of you are ready to say to me, "pray would you have women public instructors, lecturing upon moral and political science, and haranguing the people upon their special duties as citizens?" Hear my reply. It is not for me, nor for us men, to prescribe the mode in which the women shall operate. Let us leave this to their own good sense, and taste. There is a great deal of lecturing and haranguing, that doth not profit. Would that neither men nor women should ever speak in public, unless they have somewhat to say worth hearing. But if a valuable thought is suggested to any one, I see not why that thought should be suppressed, because it was started in the mind of a female. And if she, to whom it has come, has power to utter it, and is moved so to do, I see not why she should be forbidden. To me, it is as grateful to hear words of wisdom and eloquence from a woman as a man; and quite as uninstructive and wearisome to listen to a vapid, inane discourse from the one as from the other. I know not why silly men should be encouraged to speak, more than silly women; nor why the wise of one sex should be forbidden, any more than the wise of the other, to communicate what they possess to those who may need it, and in the manner they prefer. To whomsoever God has given the power to instruct and control others, by their learning, their eloquence or their wit, to them he has given the authority to do so. I have heard some women speak in a manner far more convincing and impressive than most men, that I have known, were able to; and so as amply to vindicate their right to stand up in the pulpit or the forum, as teachers of men.

"Ah" say some, "would you then have women engage in the acrimonious contests of the political parties, attend the angry meetings, witness the passion, hear the ribaldry and abuse, that are poured upon each other by the excited opponents; and be tempted perhaps to commit the same offences themselves?" No. Surely not. Neither would I have *men* guilty of such indecorum, folly and wickedness. If political meetings must needs be disgraced by such scenes, they ought not to be held; and those men who would attend them, show that they are careless of their own moral health. It were no more unseemly, no worse any way, for women to be thus defiled than for us men. We are called to be upright, pure and holy beings as well as they. Propriety of conduct, courtesy of manners, purity of speech, delicacy, refinement, gentleness, are just as becoming in one sex as the other. For one, I do not allow it to be a matter of course, that we men should be rough, violent, passionate, abusive, profane, obscene. It is unworthy of any man to be so. He is as much bound as a woman can be, "to keep himself unspotted from the world," and to keep himself away from places where, and from persons by whom, he may be tempted to become thus vile. Is it not indeed a mortifying confession—one that we men ought to be ashamed to make, that political meetings are occasions, from which the delicate and pure would shrink, and yet that we attend them? Nay more, friends, if it be true that they are such,—if our primary political gatherings, at which the people are called to consider their true interests and duties, and to exercise their high prerogatives as a self-governing community,—if these primary meetings are indeed such scenes, that our mothers, wives, sisters and daughters would be disgusted if not corrupted at them, may we not seriously apprehend, that our civil institutions are unsound, rotten at the very core? and anxiously look about us, for healing and purifying influences, from any quarter, to save us from the impending ruin? . . .

Here the question comes—"would you have women leave their homes, neglecting their children and the duties of their households, that they may take part in the management of public affairs?" No; certainly not. No more would I encourage men to do this great wrong, as they too often do. The *family* is the most important institution upon earth. If the duties of father and mother were generally well discharged, there would be little of importance left for civil governments to take care of. The family therefore ought never to be neglected for the service of the state, by the father any more than the mother. Indeed there is one reason, why the father should be even more especially careful to make himself an object of reverence and deep affection to his children. . . .

Women are coaxed, flattered, courted, but they are not respected by many men as they ought to be; neither do they respect themselves as they should. They are not regarded and treated as equals; nor do they claim to be. So long has this been the case, so long have they and we all been used to that organization of society, in which they are assigned to an inferior place, that most of us, and most too of themselves acquiesce in the wrong, as if it were right. But this does not make it so; nor avert the evil consequences, which are flowing through society, from the entire exclusion of the wisdom and virtue of half of mankind, from the councils of State, and the administrations of justice and mercy. The intellectual and moral powers of the female sex generally are not half developed, because no adequate demands are made upon them. Excluded as they are from all direct influence, in the decision of many of the greatest questions of social and national interest—they seldom take the trouble even to consider them; and so we lose the benefit we might derive from their perceptions of right, which are often clearer than our own. When we see what has been done for the redemption of mankind, by the few women, who have broken through the enclosure, in which custom would keep them, and have thought and spoken and written freely in behalf of humanity, we cannot repress the apprehension, that states and nations are suffering immeasurably, from that waste of intellect and moral sense, which are expending themselves upon the inanities of fashion, and the follies of personal or household display. . . .

Women are too dependent upon men. We have too much power over them; and they are often cruelly oppressed. See how pitifully their labors are requited. The disclosures that have been made of the incessant, wasting toils to which they are subjected, especially in or near large cities, for a compensation utterly insufficient to provide them amply with the bare necessaries of life; the degradation of their persons to which they are often driven by the pressure of absolute want; the ease with which the base, heartless seducer escapes the condemnation which his villany deserves; and the unforgiving censure, with which his victim is pursued—these disclosures alone are enough to show how unequal, how unfair is the dealing of our race with that portion, which, if either, should be treated with the greater leniency—enough to show how false, hypocritical is much of the adulation that is bestowed on women. Can those men feel any proper respect for females, who make them their drudges from morning to night,—or who are willing to pay them the miserable pittances which they do, for labors that consume the live long day, and oft the sleepless night? Yes, about as much as the slaveholders feel for their slaves. . . .

Furthermore, the current literature of the day—the fashionable novels, the poetry, and the newspapers, are inimical to the independence, and true welfare of women. These are continually intimating, that *marriage* is indispensable to the respectability and usefulness of females. Not only the silliest jokes, but often also the most cruel taunts are flung at "single" women. So that, in addition to the urgencies of pecuniary necessity, they are impelled by the dread of ridicule, (of which strong and wise men often stand in awe) to rush into wedlock, on the first opportunity, consenting it may be to the most ill-assorted alliances, from which only sorrow and sin can flow.

These circumstances operate powerfully to depress, and oppress women—to make them too dependent—to leave them at the mercy of men; and I do not believe their condition will be essentially improved, until their rights are recognized as equal every way; nor until these are secured in the very framework of society.

II

THE STRUGGLE FOR EQUAL EDUCATION, 1850–1960

Portrait of John Dewey by Edwin Burrage Child, 1929. Courtesy of Columbia University in the City of New York.

IF YOU COMPLAIN of neglect of Education in sons, What shall I say with regard to daughters, who every day experience the want of it," wrote Abigail Adams to her husband, John, in August 1776. "With regard to the Education of my own children," she confessed, "I find myself soon out of my depth, and destitute and deficient in every part of Education" (cited in Butterfield, Barrett, and Sprague 1963, 2:94). In this letter, Adams captured the themes that would dominate women's demand for higher education throughout American history: education was important to women because without it they could not be men's equals and they could not become better and more responsible mothers.

Several wealthy women opened schools for women in the late eighteenth and early nineteenth century—for example, Sarah Pierce's "respectable academy" in Litchfield, Connecticut, in 1791 and the Young Ladies Academy in Philadelphia in 1787. Emma Willard founded her school in 1814, arguing that the future of the nation demanded better-educated mothers, and Catherine Beecher's Hartford Seminary (1832) was also a success.

The era's most significant experiment, however, was Mary Lyon's Mount Holyoke Female Seminary in South Hadley, Massachusetts, inaugurated in 1837, whose goal was to train young women (the age of today's junior high school students) to be teachers as well as proper, devoted wives. A devout Congregationalist, whose informal ministry

An asterisk (*) indicates that a document is included in this volume.

inspired her students, Lyon saw her seminary as a way to elevate women to do good Christian work. She ardently favored the separation of spheres. Once married, she argued, "males should go forward in all public duties, the female should go forward in private duties with courage, patience, and submission. Men are to earn a support, and the women to save" (cited in Solomon 1985, 26). The seminary received significant funding from prominent men, mostly ministers who saw her work as part of the Great Awakening, the revival movement then sweeping across New England.

Higher Education for Women

Men had also begun to take up the cause of women's education, in some cases inspired by Lyon's experiment (see Woody 1929; and Newcomer 1959). Matthew Vassar, Milo Jewett (an Alabama seminarian who became one of Vassar's first presidents), and William Durant (founder of Wellesley College) all began to explore the possibility of supporting women's right to education by founding women's colleges. In doing so, these pioneers confronted widely held public perceptions that higher education would "unsex" women—rendering them less physically, psychologically, and emotionally capable of competent motherhood or forcing them to strive for an intellectual development for which they were biologically unfit. Anti-feminists argued that women would become physically deformed, developing larger brains while their wombs atrophied, and that the excessive mental strain would destroy their figures or complexions. Higher education was said to be simply beyond women's physical, emotional, or intellectual capacity.

Some men would have none of these efforts to veil sexism with what they saw as spurious biological distinctions. Some argued that women were born with a capacity to reason equal to men's. In 1852, abolitionist Gerrit Smith argued against the "nonsense that there is a feminine element in the human mind and a masculine element in the human mind" (SL, A/S646a). "These faculties belong to the two sexes equally; it is equally important that they should be cultivated in both; and both sexes are therefore equally fit subjects for the culture which colleges are designed to give," wrote Frederick Barnard in 1882 (see his "Should American Colleges Be Open to Women as Well as to Men"*)—but, as president of Columbia College, his effort to admit women was unsuccessful. Any subsequent divergence or atrophy of intellectual capacity was the consequence of women's exclusion from higher education, not the cause of it.

Other men were less concerned with women's equal claim to reason than they were with the elevation of the race. Women needed higher education, they argued, because they were the bearers of morality and would thus be better able to restrain men and instruct children morally. Those who proposed woman as moral force offered her a temporary residence in the public sphere of higher education but only to facilitate her ennobling of the private sphere.

From the middle of the nineteenth century, many of the men who founded colleges for women accepted women's right to education and sought to provide an education equal to that afforded men at men's colleges. Milo Jewett had convinced Vassar to leave his brewery fortune to the establishment of "an *endowed* College for young women in the world" that would be, to women, "what Yale and Harvard are to young men" (Jewett 1879, 5, 6). "It occurred to me that woman, having received from her Creator the same intellectual constitution as man, has the same right as man to intellectual culture and development," Vassar argued (cited in Curtis 1908, 417). Vassar's mission, according to John Raymond in his *Vassar College,* was "to found and perpetuate an institution which should accomplish for young women what our colleges are accomplishing for young men" (Raymond 1873, 15). Henry Durant's "The Spirit of the College"* was as direct and unequivocal.

Both Vassar and Durant were also convinced that women should be taught by women teachers as well as by men. One Vassar professor, John Orton, argued that the college aimed, "not to make women like men, but to make the best women" (Orton 1871, 56). This would be best accomplished by having women teach women. Durant believed this from the founding of Wellesley College; Vassar became convinced after his college had been in existence for three years. In his final address to the Board of Trustees, Vassar had prepared to deliver a summation of his work and an inspiration to continue. As he turned to this page of his prepared text, however, he suffered a fatal heart attack and died at the lectern (see MacCracken 1919). In that text, Vassar argued that the best method of ensuring equal education would be to "appoint a committee of Ladys whose duty it should be to organise and define the course of Education for Women" and that these women administrators would be able to invite "experienced and well known Lady Educators *outside of the college,* to cooperate with the experience which your Faculty must have attained by this time, and thus establish a regular Curriculum course for the future" (ibid). The college's reputation would be as a college *for* women, whose curriculum revolved around women's lives and was taught and administered, in large part, *by* women.

Some of the most visible supporters of colleges for women opposed coeducation because they believed that higher education should develop the traits peculiar to each sex; mixing the two would invariably be detrimental to women's intellectual development. "I do not see how it is possible for the girls to have a fair chance to develop the highest feminine traits," was how the Reverend L. Clark Seelye, the first president of Smith College (founded 1875), put the case against coeducation in "The Need for a Collegiate Education for Women."* Seelye's purpose was to allow women to develop to their highest capacity *as women,* and he surely did not have full equality with men in mind. He wanted "nothing that is suggestive of the student life of a man's college to prevail at Smith" and hoped that Smith students would not join in the movement for woman suffrage, which he saw as "unwomanly and unworthy of a refined and cultured womanhood" (SL, WRC, folder, 679). (This in contrast to MacCracken, who was pressured to resign as Vassar's president in 1918 because of his support of suffrage [VCA, Special Collections, MacCracken Papers, box 120, folder 5].)

Perhaps the most sustained assault against women's education came from Edward H. Clarke, whose *Sex in Education; Or a Fair Chance for the Girls* was published in 1873. A member of Harvard's Board of Overseers and a former medical professor, Clarke argued that higher education would threaten women's reproductive capacity. Clarke's attack prompted numerous rebuttals by both men and women, including George and Anna Comfort's *Woman's Education and Woman's Heath* (1874), which argued against Clarke's thesis that higher education would lead to the physical debilitation of women students. Even Henry Adams, no supporter of feminism, argued that "to resist the demand that women are making for education is a hopeless task" (cited in Kaledin 1981, 137). Julia Ward Howe collected many of these responses in *Sex and Education: A Reply to Dr. E. H. Clarke's "Sex in Education"* (1874), including reports of the good health of the women students from Vassar, Antioch, Michigan, and Oberlin. The Reverend C. H. Brigham, for example, was pleased to report that, at Michigan, the sex that some call weaker "here, at any rate, is shown to be equal in endurance, in courage, in perseverance, in devotion to study, and in cheerful confidence, to the strong and stalwart men" (ibid., 199). Howe's volume also included Thomas Wentworth Higginson's systematic refutation of Clarke's text, a methodological critique of his use of anatomical evidence.

Higginson was among the most visible pro-feminist men in the nineteenth century. A prolific social reformer, Higginson took a leading part in the temperance, Free Soil, and abolitionist movements, also remaining a tireless campaigner for women's education and suffrage. He edited the *Woman's Journal* from 1870 to 1884 (with Lucy Stone and Henry Brown Blackwell) and wrote scores of pamphlets in defense of women's causes. Higginson combined a passionate commitment to equality with a strong belief that women's enfranchisement and education would infuse public life with a much-needed dose of morality (see Edelstein 1970, 373). In *Women and the Alphabet* (an extract is included in this volume), Higginson argued that women's equality hinged on women's education. Education, he argued, was the "fulcrum" of equality, and all else would move from it.

For Higginson, temperamental differences between women and men were no reason that they should not be equal. He considered separate colleges and universities but a temporary measure necessary to bring women up to the level of the men; once this goal was achieved, coeducational institutions would become the norm. As he argued in an editorial in the *Woman's Journal*, "Sooner or later, I am persuaded, the human race will look upon all these separate collegiate institutions as most American travelers now look at the vast monastic establishments of Southern Europe; with respect for the pious motives of their founders, but with wonder that such a mistake should ever have been made" (Higginson 1874, 1). Higginson disapproved most vigorously of all-female faculties teaching at women's colleges because this practice bred "the special evil of separate education," the adolescent crushes or full-blown erotic relationships between women (Horowitz 1984, 96).

The Coeducation Question

Once women's right to higher education had been realized, the wisdom of separating women and men in its pursuit was questioned. Some "masculinists" argued that educating women and men together would enervate the collegiate curriculum, forcing the inclusion of subjects and temperaments better omitted, or slowing down the pace to allow the women to keep up. Others suggested that coeducation would distract men from the discipline of their studies or that contact between the sexes in school would "dilute" the mysteries of heterosexual attraction, thus promoting homosexuality. In his influential psychological treatise on adolesence, G. Stanley Hall warned that coeducation would undermine the progress of social evolution: it "harms girls by assimilating them to boys' ways and work and robbing them of their sense of feminine character, [and it] harms boys by feminizing them when they need to be working off their brute animal element" (Hall 1904, 2:569). Profeminist men countered that coeducation would benefit both women and men: women would be exposed to the same educational opportunities as were offered to men, opportunities that were often difficult or prohibitively expensive to duplicate at all-women schools, and men would be exposed to the moral, taming influence of women, whose presence would temper their social excesses and bring out the gentleman too often hidden beneath the wild college man.

Harvard's inconsistent attempts to grapple with women's education indicate the anxieties that lay beneath institutional indecision. Harvard president Charles W. Eliot was "a vocal foe of coeducation" (Rosenberg 1982, 31); he believed that "girls and boys are better taught separately than together, especially after the age of puberty" (letter to Lindley C. Kent, 30 March 1880, SL, A/K37 Lindley Kent). Uneasy about associating Harvard's name with women's education, he informally invited selected members of Harvard's all-male faculty to tutor in the Society for the Collegiate Instruction of Women, colloquially known as the Annex. Philosopher Josiah Royce taught there and found that "the supposed difficulty that women are said to meet in forming abstract ideas, and so in grasping philosophical subtleties, does not exist" although he was concerned that women's temperament led to a certain intellectual timidity, a fear of "seeming unduly obstinate in thought" (letter to Mrs. Arthur Gilman, 5 January 1886, SL, May-Goddard Papers). Only after 1893, when the Annex was constituted as Radcliffe College, did women have a formal presence at Harvard.

Harvard's experience reassured Columbia's trustees that "educating women did not necessarily put heavy demands on the host university"

(Horowitz 1984, 134). Though the trustees thwarted President Barnard's plans to admit women to Columbia in 1882, seven years later they founded the college that bears his name.

Several colleges were founded as coeducational, for example, Oberlin (1833) and Antioch (1854). (Here, the geography of women's educational struggles shifted from New England to the Midwest, where faculty, administrators, and trustees debated the question of women's education at the founding of the institution.) The Reverend James Fairchild, president of Oberlin, argued in 1867 that the benefits of coeducation were economic convenience, better moral order, convenience to patrons of the college, stronger community relations, and improved "harmony with society at large" (Fairchild 1883). Horace Mann, speaking at Antioch's founding,* noted that coeducation promised "both moral restraint and intellectual excitement." At Knox College, President Blanchard (1870) described his conversion to the idea of coeducation when he saw that it did not threaten the "natural" separation of spheres between women and men. Knox, like other Christian colleges, was founded on the principle of the equality of souls. By contrast, Carroll Cutler (1884) of Western Reserve University in Cleveland eloquently enumerated the reasons for coeducation by minimizing women's differences and celebrating the risk-taking spirit of the frontier as a place to try out innovative collegiate experiments.

Cornell and the University of Michigan each faced the question early, opening their doors to women in 1870 after vigorous debates. Cornell president Andrew White noted that, if coeducation had affected the quality of scholarship, "it had improved it," as well as raising the level of manners and morals (cited in Stevens 1883, 7). Michigan president, James Angell, in "Shall the American Colleges Be Open to Both Sexes,"* made a clever sociological argument that presumed that differences between women and men were less significant than differences among men or among women: "But let us ask whether the difference in the mental habits and processes of the sexes is really a more formidable obstacle to working in the same class than is found in the difference in temperament, talent, and attainments of young men now working in classes together."

One of the more interesting debates took place at Wesleyan University, whose short-lived experiment with coeducation began in 1872. Professor William North Rice supported the plan since the "average scholarship of the women has been superior to that of the men" and their conduct "above reproach or suspicion" (Rice 1900). But from the beginning the plan was criticized as overly tentative by Professor John Van Vleck, who sought to push the trustees beyond their original scope of reform (see his letter* to the Wesleyan Board of Trustees). Anything less, he felt, would perpetuate women's second-class status and prevent Wesleyan from becoming a first-rank university. On the other hand, even this moderate plan proved too much for many wealthy alumni, whose financial backing of the college dried up quickly. Wesleyan abandoned coeducation in 1912 and remained all male until 1970 (see Knight 1972).

Some argued that coeducation would also benefit men. An editorial* responding to an article against coeducation in the *Amherst Student* claimed that "every step in the advancement of woman has benefited our own sex no less than it has elevated her." In "Is Co-Education Injurious to Girls?"* John Dewey, the noted philosopher and educator, argued not only that coeducation benefited girls in theory but also that, in practice over twenty-five years, at all educational levels, it had proved beneficial to men: "Boys learn gentleness, unselfishness, courtesy; their natural vigor finds helpful channels of expression instead of wasting itself in lawless boisterousness." Girls, on the other hand, become less manipulative; they "acquire greater self-reliance and a desire to win approval by deserving it instead of by 'working' others. Their narrowness of judgment, depending on the enforced narrowness of outlook, is overcome; their ultra-feminine weaknesses are toned up."

Dewey was a vigorous champion of women's rights throughout his career. At Columbia in the late 1910s, Dewey was a founder of the Men's League for Woman Suffrage (whose organizer was his young assistant in the philosophy department, Max Eastman). Earlier in the century, at the University of Chicago, where he acted as mentor to several well-known feminist women as well as to a group of male social scientists who became well known for their support of women's rights (including Thorstein Veblen, W. I. Thomas, and George Herbert Mead), Dewey (1902) persuaded President William Rainey Harper that both male and female students would be better served by coeducation, not by separate educational spheres. The latter, he argued, was "sure to accomplish what it is supposed to obviate—the fixing of attention upon sex matters. It at once draws the attention of the students coming to the university to the matter of sex as a fundamental consideration in determining the instruction they are to receive." If men were uneasy about educational equality or opposed to women's education, Dewey had a simple response, one that might serve as a summation of the best sentiments of the pro-feminist men who supported women's right to equal education: "The kind of man that will be kept from the University simply because he will have to associate upon equal terms with his equals is not the kind the University wants or needs."

WOMEN'S RIGHT TO HIGHER EDUCATION

"OUGHT WOMEN TO LEARN THE ALPHABET?"

Thomas Wentworth Higginson (1859)

. . . OUGHT WOMEN to learn the alphabet? There the whole question lies. Concede this little fulcrum, and Archimedea will move the world before she has done with it: it becomes merely a question of time. Resistance must be made here or nowhere. . . . Woman must be a subject or an equal: there is no middle ground. What if the Chinese proverb should turn out to be, after all, the summit of wisdom, "For men, to cultivate virtue is knowledge; for women, to renounce knowledge is virtue"? . . . What sort of philosophy is that which says, "John is a fool; Jane is a genius: nevertheless, John, being a man, shall learn, lead, make laws, make money; Jane, being a woman, shall be ignorant, dependent, disfranchised, underpaid"? Of course, the time is past when one would state this so frankly, though Comte comes quite near it, to say nothing of the Mormons; but this formula really lies at the bottom of the reasoning one hears every day. The answer is, Soul before sex. Give an equal chance, and let genius and industry do the rest. *La carrière ouverte aux talens!* Every man for himself, every woman for herself, and the alphabet for us all.

Thus far, my whole course of argument has been defensive and explanatory. I have shown that woman's inferiority in special achievements, so far as it exists, is a fact of small importance, because it is merely a corollary from her historic position of degradation. She has not excelled, because she has had no fair chance to excel. Man, placing his foot upon her shoulder, has taunted her with not rising. But the ulterior question remains behind. How came she into this attitude originally? Explain the explanation, the logician fairly demands. Granted that woman

---

From Women and the Alphabet: A Series of Essays. *Cambridge, Mass.: Riverside, 1859.*

is weak because she has been systematically degraded: but why was she degraded? This is a far deeper question—one to be met only by a profounder philosophy and a positive solution. We are coming on ground almost wholly untrod, and must do the best we can.

I venture to assert, then, that woman's social inferiority has been, to a great extent, in the past a legitimate thing. To all appearance, history would have been impossible without it, just as it would have been impossible without an epoch of war and slavery. It is simply a matter of social progress,—a part of the succession of civilizations. The past has been inevitably a period of ignorance, of engrossing physical necessities, and of brute force,—not of freedom, of philanthropy, and of culture. During that lower epoch, woman was necessarily an inferior, degraded by abject labor, even in time of peace,—degraded uniformly by war, chivalry to the contrary notwithstanding. Behind all the courtesies of Amadis and the Cid lay the stern fact,—woman a child or a toy. The flattering troubadours chanted her into a poet's paradise; but alas! that kingdom of heaven suffered violence, and the violent took it by force. The truth simply was, that her time had not come. Physical strength must rule for a time, and she was the weaker. . . .

The reason, then, for the long subjection of woman has been simply that humanity was passing through its first epoch, and her full career was to be reserved for the second. As the different races of man have appeared successively upon the stage of history, so there has been an order of succession of the sexes. Woman's appointed era, like that of the Teutonic races, was delayed, but not omitted. It is not merely true that the empire of the past has belonged to man, but that it has properly belonged to him; for it was an empire of the muscles, enlisting, at best, but the lower powers of the understanding. . . .

Everybody sees that the times are altering the whole material position of woman; but most people do not appear to see the inevitable social and moral changes which are also involved. . . .

. . . [E]ven into modern days this same tyrannical necessity has lingered. "Go spin, you jades! go spin!" was the only answer vouch-safed by the Earl of Pembroke to the twice-banished nuns of Wilton. Even now, travellers agree that throughout civilized Europe, with the partial exception of England and France, the profound absorption of the mass of women in household labors renders their general elevation impossible. But with us Americans, and in this age, when all these vast labors are being more and more transferred to arms of brass and iron; when Rochester grinds the flour and Lowell weaves the cloth, and the fire on the hearth has gone into black retirement and mourning; when the wiser a virgin is, the less she has to do with oil in her lamp; when the needle has made its last dying speech and confession in the "Song of the Shirt," and the sewing-machine has changed those doleful marches to delightful measures,—how is it possible for the blindest to help seeing that a new era is begun, and that the time has come for woman to learn the alphabet?

Nobody asks for any abolition of domestic labor for women, any more than of outdoor labor for men. Of course, most women will still continue to be mainly occupied with the indoor care of their families, and most men with their external support. All that is desirable for either sex is such an economy of labor, in this respect, as shall leave some spare time to be appropriated in other directions. The argument against each new emancipation of woman is precisely that always made against the liberation of serfs and the enfranchisement of plebeians,—that the new position will take them from their legitimate business. "How can he [or she] get wisdom that holdeth the plough [or the broom],—whose talk is of bullocks [or of babies]?" Yet the American farmer has already emancipated himself from these fancied incompatibilities; and so will the farmer's wife. In a nation where there is no leisure class and no peasantry, this whole theory of exclusion is an absurdity. We all have a little leisure, and we must all make the most of it. If we will confine large interests and duties to those who have nothing else to do, we must go back to monarchy at once. If otherwise, then the alphabet, and its consequences, must be open to woman as to man. . . .

There are duties devolving on every human being,—duties not small nor few, but vast and varied,—which spring from home and private life, and all their sweet relations. The support or care of the humblest household is a function worthy of men, women, and angels, so far as it goes. From these duties none must shrink, neither man nor woman; the loftiest genius cannot ignore them, the sublimest charity must begin with them. They are their own exceeding great reward; their self-sacrifice is infinite joy; and the selfishness which discards them is repaid by loneliness and a desolate old age. Yet these, though the most tender and intimate portion of human life, do not form its whole. It is given to noble souls to crave other interests also, added spheres, not necessarily alien from these; larger knowledge, larger action also; duties, responsibilities, anxieties, dangers, all the aliment that history has given to its heroes. Not home less, but humanity more. . . .

Les races se féminisent, said Buffon,—"The world is growing more feminine." It is a compliment, whether the naturalist intended it or not. Time has brought peace; peace, invention; and the poorest woman of to-day is born to an inheritance of which her ancestors never dreamed. Previous attempts to confer on woman social and political equality,—as when Leopold, Grand Duke of Tuscany, made them magistrates; or when the Hungarian revolutionists made them voters; or when our own New Jersey tried the same experiment in a guarded fashion in early times, and then revoked the privilege, because (as in the ancient fable) the women voted the wrong way;—these things were premature, and valuable only as recognitions of a principle. But in view of the rapid changes now going on, he is a rash man who asserts the "Woman Question" to be anything but a mere question of time. The fulcrum has been already given in the alphabet, and we must simply watch, and see whether the earth does not move.

There is the plain fact: woman must be either a subject or an equal; there is no middle ground. Every concession to a supposed principle only involves the necessity of the next concession for which that principle calls. Once yield the alphabet, and we abandon the whole long theory of subjection and coverture: tradition is set aside, and we have nothing but reason to fall back upon. Reasoning abstractly, it must be admitted that the argument has been, thus far, entirely on the women's side, inasmuch as no man has yet seriously tried to meet them with argument. It is an alarming feature of this discussion, that it has reversed, very generally, the traditional positions of the sexes: the women have had all the logic; and the most intelligent men, when they have attempted the other side, have limited themselves to satire and gossip. What rational woman can be really convinced by the nonsense which is talked in ordinary society around her,—as, that it is right to admit girls to common schools, and equally right to exclude them from colleges; that it is proper for a woman to sing in public, but indelicate for her to speak in public; that a post-office box is an unexceptionable place to drop a bit of paper into, but a ballot-box terribly dangerous? No cause in the world can keep above water, sustained by such contradictions as these, too feeble and slight to be dignified by the name of fallacies. Some persons profess to think it impossible to reason with a woman, and such critics certainly show no disposition to try the experiment.

But we must remember that all our American institutions are based on consistency, or on nothing: all claim to be founded on the principles of natural right; and when they quit those, they are lost. In all European monarchies it is the theory that the mass of the people are children to be governed, not mature beings to govern themselves; this is clearly stated and consistently applied. In the United States we have formally abandoned this theory for one half of the human race, while for the other half it flourishes with little change. The moment the claims of woman are broached, the democrat becomes a monarchist. . . . Most men admit that a strict adherence to our own principles would place both sexes in precisely equal positions before law and constitution, as well as in school and society. But each has his special quibble to apply, showing that in this case we must abandon all the general maxims to which we have pledged ourselves, and hold only by precedent. Nay, he construes even precedent with the most ingenious rigor; since the exclusion of women from all direct contact with affairs can be made far more perfect in a republic than is possible in a monarchy, where even sex is merged in rank, and the female patrician may have far more power than the male plebeian. But, as matters now stand among us, there is no aristocracy but of sex: all men are born patrician, all women are legally plebeian; all men are equal in having political power, and all women in having none. This is a paradox so evident, and such an anomaly in human progress, that it cannot last forever. . . .

Meanwhile, as the newspapers say, we anxiously await further developments. According to present appearances, the final adjustment lies mainly in the hands of women themselves. Men can hardly be expected to concede either rights or privileges more rapidly than they are claimed, or to be truer to women than women are to each other. In fact, the worst effect of a condition of inferiority is the weakness it leaves behind; even when we say, "Hands off!" the sufferer does not rise. In such a case, there is but one counsel worth giving. More depends on determination than even on ability. Will, not talent, governs the world. Who believed that a poetess could ever be more than an Annot Lyle of the harp, to soothe with sweet melodies the leisure of her lord, until in Elizabeth Barrett Browning's hands the thing became a trumpet? Where are gone the sneers with which army surgeons and parliamentary orators opposed Mr. Sidney Herbert's first proposition to send Florence Nightingale to the Crimea? In how many towns was the current of popular prejudice against female orators reversed by one winning speech from Lucy Stone! Where no logic can prevail, success silences. First give woman, if you dare, the alphabet, then summon her to her career: and though men, ignorant and prejudiced, may oppose its beginnings, they will at last fling around her conquering footsteps more lavish praises than ever greeted the opera's idol,—more perfumed flowers than ever wooed, with intoxicating fragrance, the fairest butterfly of the ball-room.

"SHOULD AMERICAN COLLEGES BE OPEN TO WOMEN AS WELL AS TO MEN"

Frederick A. P. Barnard (1882)

If I were not well aware of the power of prescriptive usage in controlling opinion, and of the almost unconquerable tendency in the human mind to cling to the conviction that the thing which long has been is the thing which ought to be, I should be inclined to express astonishment that the question here proposed could be presumed to admit of more than one reply. For what is a college? Is there any thing in the nature of the functions it is instituted to fulfill, which should limit the possibilities of its usefulness to any particular class, or to a single sex? As to social classes we are apt to pride ourselves that this with us is not the case. It is matter of boasting that our colleges and our universities are open equally to young men in any condition in life; and that their highest honors have been often carried off by those who have been compelled, while enjoying their advantages, to labor with their own hands for their daily bread. The youth who resort to our educational institutions are admitted indiscriminately to a perfect equality of privileges. No presumption of superior rank or of superior wealth is recognized as entitling any one to precedence above another. And this is as it should be. For the proper function of a college is to deal with those capacities of men which the accidental conditions of human society have no power to control or influence. Its business is to develop and cultivate those intellectual faculties of the race which give to it its distinctive position as a race in organic nature. These faculties belong to the two sexes equally; it is equally important that they should be cultivated in both; and both sexes are therefore equally fit subjects for the culture which colleges are designed to give. Why then should women be excluded from the advantages which these institutions so freely extend to men?

A great deal of ingenuity has been exercised in seeking answers to this question, and the reasons found have been various in character, and not always consistent among themselves; but most of them seem to have been devised for the purpose of concealing, or evading the confession of the real reason, which is that such exclusion has been practiced by our fathers before us, and that we have not the courage nor the independence to venture on a measure unsanctioned by their example or unapproved by their presumed wisdom.

Many of the grounds on which, in the earlier discussion of this question, the exclu-

Paper presented at the Twentieth Annual Convocation of the University of the State of New York at Albany. 12 July 1882. Reprinted in Proceedings of the Convocation. *Albany: Weed, Parsons, 1882.*

sion of women from colleges was commonly defended, appear to have been more recently abandoned; at least, at the present time, we hear them less frequently mentioned. One of these used to be, the natural inferiority of the female intellect, an assumption which there is nothing in antecedent probability, nothing in the comparative cerebral organization of the sexes, and nothing in the study of observed facts to justify. The argument that the number of women distinguished in the past for intellectual superiority is smaller than that of men, is wholly without significance in view of the concomitant fact that, down to the present century, women have been almost universally dwarfed in their intellectual growth, and pressed down beneath the normal mental stature for which nature intended them, by the denial to them of the educational opportunities which men have so abundantly enjoyed. And it is neither fair nor just, when we point to such illustrations of what woman is capable of accomplishing, as we find in a De Staël, a Somerville, a George Eliot or a Harriet Martineau, to reply that these are only the brilliant exceptions which prove the rule; they illustrate, on the contrary, only the fact that no system of repression can entirely smother the fire of intellect, and indicate that, under favoring circumstances, the occasional scintillations which we now observe would be replaced by a general blaze.

Supposing, however, for the sake of argument, that women are naturally the intellectual inferiors of men. It cannot, nevertheless, be denied that women have intellects, nor that such intellects as they have should be properly cultivated. If the experience of some centuries is worth any thing, our colleges present the instrumentalities best adapted for developing the capacities of growing minds. These instrumentalities must be presumed to be adapted to the needs of the masculine mind in very tender years; for I find that until quite recently, it was not unusual in American colleges to receive boys at ages as low as from nine to thirteen. Now whatever we may assume to be the mental inequality between the sexes, no one can maintain that a young woman of seventeen or eighteen is likely to be inferior in mental capacity to a boy of ten or eleven. If such a boy can be improved therefore by the instruction which the college affords, so probably can a girl a few years older, and there is no just reason for denying her the opportunity for such improvement. The argument therefore, for the exclusion of women from colleges, derived from their presumed intellectual inferiority, is without foundation; and if it were not so, it is simply a piece of sophistry designed to conceal the deeper lying reason in the mind of the objector, which perhaps he is ashamed or unwilling to avow.

Another ground for such exclusion has been found in the more delicate physical organization and inferior muscular strength of woman. It is said that the strain put upon her by the severity of the university course of study, would be ruinous to her constitution and destructive to her health. The visible fact upon which this objection is based is too obvious to be denied, and if the question were of success in a boat race, or of triumph in what young men call the "tug of war," the inference would not be illogical. But muscular strength has nothing whatever to do with brain energy. Some of the profoundest thinkers the world ever saw, have been men of the most delicate physical constitution. We often hear it said that a literary man has been exhausted by over work; but I have never known an authenticated case in which the over work which has broken a man down has been the work of his brain. It is a fact known to every man's experience that the mind does not tire as does the body.

On the other hand the mind is always active, always ready for work, even when the bodily strength fails. The mind will often drive the body to effort, even when the wearied physical frame demands repose. Strong emotion, it is true, may wear upon the nervous system, of which the brain is the principal organ; but the calm exercise of the faculties of the pure reason, never. When therefore a scholar or a scientific man breaks down in harness and is said to be over-worked, his prostration is owing to the same cause which breaks down an over-driven horse; and it is no more the effect of an excess of mental labor in the one case than in the other. If the scholar neglects the ordinary hygienic precautions necessary to the preservation of the vigor of the physical frame, if he continues himself from morning till night, and from month to month, to a close, ill-ventilated study and perhaps to a wearisome posture; if he systematically neglects healthful exercise and either starves or overfeeds himself habitually, he cannot expect to escape the consequences which nature sooner or later exacts from those who violate her laws. It is possible, indeed, that a student in college may do himself this violence; but it is not necessary that anyone should do so. I presume that everyone in this assembly may be able to call to mind instances in which young men during their college-life have been so inobservant of the means necessary for the preservation of a sound body as the habitation of a sound mind, as to have broken down in mid-career, and to have been compelled perhaps to relinquish their hopes of a completed education. On the other hand, many of you can doubtless recall others, who, though possessed of the most delicate physical organization, and constantly liable to be injuriously affected by surrounding unfavorable conditions, have nevertheless, by prudence and careful self-control, safely surmounted all the difficulties of the academic course, and come to its close with distinguished honors. Injudicious habits of life will be followed by evil consequences, whether the sufferer be a student or an idler. This law is universal and is irrespective of age or sex.

So far as the effect upon health is concerned, I believe it cannot be successfully denied that the course of superficial study which it has heretofore been common to force upon women, in institutions devoted to their special education, is just as likely to be injurious, and in many instances is as injurious actually, as the presumably more difficult, and certainly more educationally efficacious, course presented in the college curriculum. To learn to draw or to paint in water colors, at least if it be intended that the pupil shall learn in fact and not merely in pretense, requires close application for many days and weeks in attitudes unfavorable to the free play of the vital organs. An equal amount of time devoted to the study of a treatise on philosophy, though exacting undeniably a more energetic exercise of thought, would be physically far less exhausting. To learn to embroider, an accomplishment which however perfectly acquired, is usually, in later life, treated as the useless thing it is and totally neglected, exacts the devotion of many weary hours to a task purely mechanical, very trying to the physical system, and of no educational value whatever. The same may be said of music, considered only as the power of execution, the end exclusively aimed at in its use as a part of woman's education. Now and then may be found an individual in whom the musical faculty is a native gift, but in the case of ninety-nine out of a hundred, the amount of weary confinement and of physically exhausting labor necessary for the attainment of a sufficient facility of performance to save the young lady subjected to it from being a terror to her friends, is something truly appalling to think of. Music as a science is certainly a most improving and even fascinating study. It is a study, which, educationally considered, may be regarded rather as a recreation than as a task. But music as an art is an accomplishment in which skill is attainable only by the few, and by those few only at the sacrifice of a fearful amount of time and strength: while to the great majority it is not attainable at all. Yet this is a part of the severe regimen to which it has been hitherto customary to subject all our school-girls, without regard to differences, of native capacity, and in the face of the certainty, a thousand times over experimentally demonstrated, that not one in a hundred can ever be a musician. . . .

. . . It is nonsense therefore to attempt to justify the exclusion of women from our colleges on sanitary grounds. They are as little in danger of suffering from excess of mental labor as men.

Were we on the other hand to admit that, to use the words of a recent writer, "the more abstract and severe branches and advanced courses [of collegiate study] put too heavy a strain upon female health and vitality," we shall be driven to the inevitable conclusion that, in endowing women with minds capable of unlimited cultivation, the Creator has at the same time committed the mistake of making such cultivation impossible and has thus defeated his own manifest design. For if to the fullest development of mental power in women what are here called "the more abstract and severe branches" of study are not necessary, neither are they any more so in men, and our scheme of collegiate education is no better than a huge bundle of blunders. If, in order to meet this objection, it is replied that there is no need that the mental capacities of women *should* be fully developed, we may rejoin that this is begging the question, for our entire argument rests on the assumption, which our opponents do not deny, that women ought to be educated.

Oh, yes, women ought to be educated—every one admits so much as this—but then the objector asserts, women ought not to receive *the same* education as men. Well, perhaps not in every respect. Women ought to know something about cookery, the use of the needle, and the management of a household, accomplishments which in the case of men are not entirely indispensable; but exceptions of this kind seem to have very little relation to mental culture. So far as women and men are alike, so far as they are endowed with faculties entirely similar in kind and capable of similar development, and so far as the cultivation of these faculties may equally increase their happiness or enlarge their power of usefulness in life, so far their educational training should unquestionably be the same. The writer from whom I have already quoted, while admitting that "the opportunities of young ladies for education should be 'equal' to those of young men," yet holds that "in view of the peculiarities of the female mind and constitution, and the sphere to which woman is normally adapted and destined, the educational opportunities of the women cannot be thus 'equal' unless they are in some important respects different." What the writer means by "peculiarities of the female mind" I do not pretend to understand; but to assume that the kind of mental culture which he describes as "what is known as liberal or college education," is designed to fit anybody, either man or woman, to fill some "sphere," is to contradict its whole theory and to misrepresent its universally admitted design. If, in the controversy which has been going on for the last half century or more between the champions of liberal and of what is called practical education, any doctrine has been maintained more energetically than any other, it is that our colleges are not and ought not to be made schools of preparation for any special department of human activity, but that the object of the culture imparted by them is simply to make the most that is possible of man as an intellectual and moral being, and so to prepare him to fit himself to enter with the largest prospect of success upon any "sphere" of duty or usefulness to which he may subsequently devote himself. If woman's proper province is, as the writer just quoted tells us, and as we seem to have heard once or twice before, "to be the queen of the household and of society," it is not probable that she will find in any American college, even in any one of those recently established and richly endowed colleges designed for the education of women exclusively, a chair of instruction designed to prepare her for the duties of that responsible station. It is not the business of colleges to make "queens of the household," any more than it is to make lawyers or physicians or architects, or engineers; but it is their business, and one which they accomplish well, to make women fit to *become* queens of society, and men fit to be successful in the several departments of professional life. . . .

The question therefore needs no longer to be argued whether the advantages of a liberal education should not, in some form or other, be thrown open to women, nor whether it is wise or safe to expose women to the asserted dangers of so "severe" a course of mental training as such an education exacts. These questions, after long and vigorous discussion, have been submitted to the tribunal of public opinion, and the decision upon them has been as emphatic as it will be final. The liberal education which has so long been monopolized by men as their exclusive privilege, has at length, in all the variety of its comprehensiveness, been thrown open in these special institutions to women also. . . .

We ask then that the existing colleges shall be opened to women because they exist, because they possess the means of doing the work desired, and because the right to receive an education, liberal in the highest sense, belongs to women no less than to men. . . .

. . . It is folly to suppose that a movement like this can ever be arrested until it shall have run its complete course; and this course will not be complete until all the repositories of knowledge and all the aids to educational improvement which past centuries have created shall have been made everywhere throughout the world equally accessible to all mankind, without any regard to age or sex or race or social condition. A consummation so desirable as this it may not be given to our generation to witness; but the privilege is granted us to lend our aid in bringing it to pass; and even the feeble efforts of individuals may not be wholly without effect in furthering the end so greatly to be desired.

To the student of history, political or social, no more curious psychological phenomenon presents itself, than the propensity in man to resist the indications of manifest destiny, and to flatter himself with the idea that he can successfully oppose the inevitable. . . .

. . . That all our American colleges will sooner or later be opened to women appears to me to be a matter of as assured certainty as that the sun will rise tomorrow. The opposition which the proposition at present encounters can have no other possible effect than somewhat to retard the accomplishment of that inevitable result. This opposition, in so far as it is conscientious and not purely the result of prejudice, is founded on the apprehension that the proposed measure, aside from the educational benefits it is intended to confer, may involve consequences of a social nature esteemed to be undesirable. . . . Young women might with just as much propriety be prohibited from going to church because young men are there; and the same suggestion is still more applicable to attendance at the opera or the theatre. . . .

There can be no doubt that it is this apprehension of a contaminating contact—contaminating simply in a social sense I mean,—that stimulates most energetically the opposition to the extension to woman of the educational privileges of our colleges. Some of the opponents of the measure, . . . may profess to be contending for the preservation of "female refinement and delicacy." . . .

. . . So indeed would I, so would anyone who honors and respects woman, and who would desire to see her always most worthy of honor and respect. I would favor no measure which would leave the slightest trace upon the delicacy of this bloom; but I would have the peach valuable for something more than its bloom merely. And therefore as I would carefully guard against anything which might impair that delicacy in woman which is to make her the ornament and admiration of a refined society, so I would at the same time cultivate her intelligence to an extent which may enable her equally to adorn the world of intellect in which she may be destined to move, and of which she may thus become the animating and inspiring spirit. . . .

In the sentence which I have noted, there occurs a word which I am unwilling to pass over in silence. It is the word *co-education.* By whom this word was invented I do not know. It is an odious word, and I presume the design of the inventor may have been to prejudice the cause we advocate, by making it seem to be our chief object to secure a result which is purely incidental and unimportant, the presence of students of both sexes in the same institution. We might with the same propriety apply the term *co-education* to the teaching of Sunday-schools, because boys and girls are there taught together the words of the Bible; we might as well characterize churches as co-educational institutions because we ourselves with our families receive in them from our parish clergymen instruction in religious truth. When I demand for women admission into our colleges, I am demanding for them education, and not the privilege of being educated along with men. . . .

. . . Let those continue to use this word co-education who choose. I have never used it, and I never shall use it. It does not express the thing which, in this struggle, I have at heart; and the thing which it does express is to me a thing in which I have no interest whatever. . . .

. . . Revolutions of opinion always go forward. In regard to the subject which occupies us today, we have seen such a revolution for some years proceeding under our own eyes. It is a genuine revolution. Every day that passes, its manifestations are becoming more and more decided. Every day that passes is adding to the number of men and women whose judgement commands the respect of the people, and whose championship of any cause may usually be regarded as a sure presage of victory, who are openly avowing themselves its advocates and lending their active efforts to stimulate its progress. The end of all this is not probable only, it is certain. Sooner or later, the whole community, with a single voice, is going to demand that the governors of our highest institutions of learning shall no longer keep them closed against half the human race. Let not then the present champions of this just measure of generous and enlightened liberality be cast down, if their praiseworthy efforts fail to meet the immediate success which they deserve. Let them not be discouraged by any rebuffs they may receive from those who happen to hold in their hands for the time being the power to thwart their aims. Let no present disappointment be allowed to chill their enthusiasm or to dampen their zeal; but let them continue to possess their souls in patience, animated and cheered by the assured conviction that the time is not far distant when it shall be as much among the curiosities of history that one sex should ever have been debarred from the educational privileges accorded to the other, as it will be that the curse of slavery should have continued to darken the escutcheon of our Republic for a century after its foundation.

"THE HIGHER EDUCATION OF WOMEN"

George W. Curtis (1890)

. . . THE TEST of civilization is the estimate of woman. The measure of that estimate is the degree of practical acknowledgment of her equal liberty of choice and action with men, and nothing is historically plainer than that the progress of moral and political liberty since the Reformation has included a consequent and constant movement for the abolition of every arbitrary restraint upon the freedom of women. It has been, indeed, very gradual. Compliment and incredulity have persistently bowed out justice and reason. But as usual the exiles have steadily returned stronger and more resolute. Their first definite demand was that of education. For this they have pleaded against tradition, prejudice, scepticism, ridicule, and superstition. There has been bitter contention not only over the end, but the means. Profuse eloquence and wit and learning have been expended in the discussion of the comparative excellence of co-education or separate education, of the limitations and conditions which Nature herself has prescribed to the range and degree of education for women, of the divine intentions, and of the natural sphere of the sexes. . . .

This debate of the sphere of the sexes as determining the character and limits of education is very amusing. For if the sexes have spheres, there really seems to be no more reason to apprehend that women will desert their sphere than men. I have not observed any general anxiety lest men should steal away from their workshops and offices

---

From "The Higher Education of Women: An Address Delivered at the Celebration of the Twenty-Fifth Anniversary of Vassar College." 1890. Reprinted in Orations and Addresses of George William Curtis, *ed. Charles Eliot Norton, vol. 1. New York: Harper & Bros., 1894.*

that they may darn the family stockings or cook the dinner, and I see no reason to suppose that it will be necessary to chain women to the cradle to prevent their insisting upon running locomotives or shipping before the mast. We may be very sure that we shall never know the sphere of any responsible human being until he has perfect freedom of choice and liberty of growth. All we can clearly see is that the intellectual capacity of women is an inexplicable waste of reserved power, if its utmost education is justly to be deprecated as useless or undesirable.

Our dogmatism in sheer speculation is constantly satirized by history. Education was not more vehemently alleged to be absurd for women than political equality to be dangerous for men. Happily our own century has played havoc with both beliefs, however sincerely supposed to be ordinances of nature. The century began with saying contemptuously that women do not need to be educated to be dutiful wives and good mothers. A woman, it said, can dress prettily and dance gracefully even if she cannot conjugate the Greek verbs in *mi;* and the ability to calculate an eclipse would not help her to keep cream from feathering in hot weather. But grown older and wiser the century asks, as it ends, "Is it then true that ignorant women are the best wives and mothers? Does good wifehood consist exclusively in skilful baking and boiling and neat darning and patching? No," says the enlightened century; "if the more languages a man hath the more man is he, the more knowledge a woman hath the better wife and mother is she." And if any skeptic should ask, "But can delicate woman endure the hardship of a college course of study?" it is a woman who ingeniously turns the flank of the questioner with a covert sarcasm at her own sex—"I would like you to take thirteen hundred young men, and lace them up, and hang ten to twenty pounds of clothes upon their waists, perch them on three-inch heels, cover their heads with ripples, chignons, rats, and mice, and stick ten thousand hairpins into their scalps. If they can stand all this they will stand a little Latin and Greek." . . .

ESTABLISHING COLLEGES FOR WOMEN

"TO THE BOARD OF TRUSTEES"

Matthew Vassar (1864)

IT IS MY HOPE—it was my early hope and desire—indeed, it has been the main incentive to all I have already done, or may hereafter do, or hope to do, to inaugurate a new era in the history and life of women.

The attempt you are to aid me in making fails wholly of its point if it be not in advance, and a decided advance. I wish to give one sex all the advantages too long monopolized by the other. Ours is, and is to be, an institution for women—not men. In all its labors, positions, rewards and hopes, the idea is the development and exposition, and the martialing to the front, and the preferment of women, of their powers, on every side, demonstrative of their equality with men. If possible, demonstrative of such capacity as, in certain fixed directions, may surpass those of men. This, I conceive, may be fully accomplished within the rational limits of true womanliness, and without the slightest hazard to the natural attractiveness of her character.

We are, indeed, already defeated before we commence, if development be in the least dangerous to the dearest attributes of her class. We are not the less defeated, if it be hazardous for her to avail herself of the highest educated powers when that point is gained. We are defeated, if we start upon the assumption that she has no powers save those she may derive or imitate from the other sex. We are defeated, if we recognize the idea that she may not, with every propriety, contribute to the world the matured faculties which education evokes. We are specially defeated, if we fail to express our practical belief in her preëminent powers as an instructor, of her own sex especially.

Gentlemen, no superior power has given, or will give us, an exclusive patent for originating the ability or genius of women out of nothing. We must proceed upon the conviction that these are in the world before us. We shall fail to make all coming women what many already are. We can and shall fill up many valleys, elevate many plains, and build higher many natural summits. But we can scarcely hope that every future height shall wear our family crest alone. Go as high as we may, or can hope to do, and genius, which will not call our College mother, will stand all the time abreast of us. It is my wish to recognize not only the *possibility,* but the *fact,* of that genius and those high abilities at the very outset. Let us prove the certainty of woman's higher possible future

---

From Communications to the Board of Trustees of Vassar College by Its Founder. *New York: Standard Printing Company, 1886. (VCA)*

by the best examples from the present. Let us recognize and honor her existing talent ourselves first, before we demand that recognition from the world. In my judgment, it is clearly due to the idea which underlies our entire structure that we do not hesitate here. Let us not add another to the examples of man's want of generosity, or of half-hearted recognition of the powers of one half of the world. We should be ashamed to do it, as least under the mask of an institution which professed to be her peculiar champion, and which is to be dedicated to her benefit alone.

We can not hope to maintain our belief before the world, when we voluntarily oppose it to our practice. We are to act upon our profession—to illustrate our idea at the very start; and I need not mention that this idea, since the commencement of our enterprise, has unfolded itself immensely. I have therefore no fear of its failure. Only aid me judiciously in the selection of the best instruments to be found among the highly educated and accomplished women of this country, and let them take the hazard, if there be one. I, at least, have gone too far already to allow me to shrink one instant from sharing, or being intimidated, by that risk. Let woman at least share the most prominent and responsible positions in our gift, and let them be proffered her accordingly, as her unquestioned right, as far as she can fill them equally as well as man.

I spare your time by omitting here the great variety of reflections which have brought me unhesitatingly to this point. These will doubtless occur to you. I verily believe a generous partition between the sexes of all the professorships, is due no less to the idea underlying this enterprise than to woman herself, and the immediate and permanent success of our efforts. Inaugurate woman's elevation and power, genius and taste, at the same moment you open the door to her sex; for it is vain to educate woman's powers of thought, and then limit their operation. Give her a present confidence, and not push her back again upon a future hope. I have already staked my means upon my belief in her present practical powers. Let the foremost women of our land be among the most advanced and honored pilots and guardians of coming women, and I cheerfully leave my name to be associated with the result. I do not urge this point from any consideration of an economical nature. We must pay fairly, and even generously, whatsoever instruments we use.

Nine male professors, or even six, at any time, much more at the opening of our doors, will cause a perpetual drain upon our resources, which we may wish we had avoided when too late. Now, at least, it seems to me the dictate of the only enlightened prudence to reduce that number by at least one-half, and to concentrate their duties of supervision and lectures, so that all the rest may be left to the natural province of woman as distinctly hers. I have not the slightest fear that those may be found fully equal to one half of the positions. Indeed, we have the testimony of our President that he finds the most distinguished student and copyist in Rome to be an American woman; and we also have his early recognition of the superior attainments of Miss Maria Mitchell. Music, languages, literature, the natural sciences, and hygiene are woman's native elements, and she has not failed to reach the highest point in astronomy and mathematics.

Against the time when the subject of appointment shall arrive, and even now, while the distribution of duties in the various departments will receive your attention, I shall venture to refresh your memories in regard to the care to be taken in the exclusion of sectarian influences, and to that end, that the appointees, in every grade, shall fairly represent the principal Christian denominations among us. I would rather be remembered as one who earnestly sought to fuse the Christian element of the world into one grand Catholic body—at any rate, as one who has endeavored to remove all barriers, rather than recognize or cherish any exclusively.

As the legitimate and practical result of this *idea,* I would on this point invite to the College Desk, on the days of public worship, alternately the representatives of every Christian church. I am assured that no difficulty need be apprehended in effecting a permanent arrangement of this kind in this city. Let our pupils see and know that beyond every difference there is, after all, but one God, one gospel; and that the spires of whatsoever church forever point toward one heaven. And upon this point again, without disparagement to any other religious source, permit me to add that the strongest incentives to goodness, and the most valuable religious tendencies, will be found to flow most of all, like an emanation, from the presence of gifted, cultivated Christian women. . . .

"THE NEED FOR A COLLEGIATE EDUCATION FOR WOMEN"

Rev. L. Clark Seelye (1874)

THUS FAR, I presume, I have had the sympathy of nearly all believers in the higher education of woman. There remains, however, a question, so closely identified with our subject that we cannot ignore it, upon which we may not be as fully agreed. It is this: Do we need separate institutions to give woman this collegiate education?

Some of our best educators, whose ability and eloquence we cannot but respect and admire, maintain we do not. There are colleges enough, they tell us; open those which already exist to both sexes, and it is all that woman needs.

It might indeed be said, that while the guardians of our best colleges refuse to admit women, and the large majority of intelligent parents refuse to send their daughters to mixed institutions, the only feasible way to secure a thorough collegiate education for women is by establishing female colleges; but we do not care thus to evade the issue. Let us meet it fairly, and see whether co-education in colleges would be the better course, irrespective of present restrictions.

The main arguments in favor of co-edu-

Paper presented at the American Institute of Instruction, North Adams, Mass., 28 July 1874. Springfield, Mass.: Bryan, 1874. (SSL)

cation may be reduced to three. The first is: the greater advantages which may be secured through the reciprocal influence of the two sexes; the second: its greater economy; the third: the impossibility of founding female colleges which shall give a culture as thorough and complete as that attained in male institutions.

The force of these arguments may be seen if we examine them separately, and in the order in which they have been stated.

First, then, is a more complete education likely to be secured by the reciprocal influence of the two sexes as students in the same college? To determine this question, let us see what the natural effect of such influence will be upon the health, the intellect, the manners and morals of those thus associated.

Will co-education benefit the health? Without entering into that discussion upon "Sex in Education," which has occupied so prominent a place in the public mind during the past year, I would simply call attention to the fact, that the leading physicians and physiologists in this country and in Europe maintain that the health of women will be seriously endangered if the two sexes study "in daily competition with each other and with equal expenditure of force at all times."

The most that has been said in reply is: that the dangers are exaggerated, and can easily be prevented. No one of any note, so far as I am aware, has maintained that the health of either sex will be improved by co-education; the highest authorities in medical science tell us there is good reason to apprehend serious injury from it.

Will co-education benefit the intellect?

If the intellects of both sexes are alike, and the apparent variety and diversity due to the varied circumstances and nurture of life, as Mill and others claim, then the intellectual benefit which would come from the admission of women to our colleges is simply that of a greater number of minds—valuable if the college has not students enough to secure its ends, and injurious if it has already more than it can profitably care for.

The question then would be narrowed down to this:—Shall the colleges which have not sufficient students to realize our ideal of what a college ought to be, supply their deficiencies with girls? That question we cannot answer till we have seen whether anything more than intellect is to be considered in co-education.

If the intellects are unlike, and each sex has faculties of mind peculiar to itself, then the question at once arises whether the masculine type is so much better that it is well to make it universal? This question the highest civilization always answers in the negative. As the culture of a people advances, the diversity between the sexes invariably increases. It is barbarism that reveals most frequently masculine women. The tales of Amazons and female soldiers are the traditions of savage life. In Africa travelers tell us that the women are often as muscular as the men, and the sex almost indistinguishable from the features of the face. Our own Teutonic women once accompanied their husbands to battle, and shared with them the arts of husbandry. The lower down we go in the social scale the nearer in appearance and thought the sexes become. Whoever has noticed the peasant woman of Europe still engaging, according to ancient usage, in the occupations which a higher civilization assigns to men, cannot fail to have remarked the masculine character of the face and physique. It is the tendency of low life to make the woman masculine and the man effeminate, although the sexual type is weakened in the interchange. As civilization advances each sex assumes more and more its distinctive traits. The female portraits of the old masters are sometimes criticised as being too masculine, but they were doubtless true to life. Three centuries have done much to intensify sexual characteristics. Even the tones of the voice are changed. Musicians tell us that pure tenor, which is nearest the woman's voice in a man, and deep alto, which is nearest the male voice in a woman, are becoming more and more difficult to find in highly civilized countries, while the pure base and soprano are more and more common. Perhaps these distinctions are in many instances unnaturally intensified. Still the fact remains that high culture demands that they shall be greater rather than less. Our highest ideals of manhood and womanhood grow more and more distinct. Is it nothing but a perverted taste, which causes so general a feeling of aversion to masculine women and effeminate men; or is it rather a natural healthy instinct which demands that each shall be perfect after its kind?

Now it becomes a serious question, whether these distinctive traits which give the richest bloom to our civilization are not in great danger of being rubbed off by the constant attrition of the two sexes in a collegiate institution. Even if the course of study in most of our colleges be designed to give a general culture to the human intellect, and woman's intellect needs substantially the same exercise in the humanities and sciences, for its most perfect growth, still we must remember the educational influences of a college are only partially represented by its courses of study and its instructors. It has its traditions, its sports, its esprit de corps, its intellectual and moral atmosphere, which mould and stimulate all who are connected with it. Every class has its peculiar characteristics as truly as the individuals who compose it, while all the classes feel the common and stronger impress of the institution to which they belong.

What then is the character of these forces unrecognized by any academic catalogue, but no less potent in shaping the mind of its students? Why, it is what we should naturally expect it would be, exclusively masculine. The masculine type of mind is everywhere predominant, and in all probability will be as long as the institutions exist. This indeed is no disadvantage to the young men; it increases their manliness; it perfects their intellectual capacities.

But when it is proposed to introduce young women into institutions whose educational influences are so exclusively designed to develop masculine habits of thought and action, we submit whether it is merely a blind conservatism and unreasoning prejudice to maintain that the result will be the repression rather that the development of any peculiar intellectual gifts. The advantage must be all on the masculine side. I do not see how it is possible for the girls to have a fair chance to develop the highest feminine traits. Many specious analogies, I know, are given to the contrary. Put a rose bush and a pine tree in the same soil, they tell us, and each will grow according to its own law of life. But what if the same climate which strengthens the pine blasts the rose; what if the same soil which nourishes and perfects the tree starve the flower? What if the same forces which develop all that is most manly in one sex repress and dwarf all that is most womanly in the other.

That the mental influence of the two sexes upon each other is beneficial, no one will question. It is not necessary, however, to educate them together in the same institutions in order to feel that influence. College students are not debarred from female society more than other young men; while men and women are so closely associated during most of life that the opportunities are unlimited to gain by reading and society the discipline which each can give the other. May not that discipline be stronger and more marked if during the formative period of life special care be taken to preserve and perfect the peculiar intellect which belongs to each?

Moreover if marked intellectual benefits are to follow from co-education it is time that they should appear. The experiment has been faithfully tried in institutions East and West. Is the mental culture of young men in these institutions broader, their scholarship higher and more exact than in those from which women are excluded? Do Oberlin, and Ann Arbor, and Cornell, lead the scholarship of the country? We wish to make no invidious comparisons, but in looking carefully at the comparative culture of the different institutions we cannot find a single one in which the influence of female students has made the scholarship of the men one whit superior to that in male institutions.

It would be discourteous as well as distasteful to criticise the brave women who have sought education where they could get it, but we shall be pardoned, I trust, for saying we find no evidence to show that the influence of their male fellow students has made them any better students than their compeers in Holyoke and Vassar. We have not yet had any opportunity to compare girls educated in male colleges with those educated in female institutions, where the educational facilities are as ample, and the course of instruction as thorough and complete. Until we can, it is unfair to say, that actual experiment has shown co-education to be the better for the female intellect. Looking both at the reasons and the facts, we find nothing which leads us to the conclusion that co-education will benefit the sexes intellectually, but good grounds for apprehending serious intellectual injury.

Will co-education benefit their manners and morals?

Those who demand it affirm that it will, and it is certainly a strong point in their favor, if they can establish it.

If co-education will put an end to all the puerile customs and disorders which disturb college life; if it will make our young men more gentlemanly and our young women more lady-like; if young men and women by merely pursuing their studies together become so philosophic, that the passions, which are very inflammable, and often regnant in others, lie dormant in them, and they are made purer in heart and life, then many indeed will be willing to make great sacrifices to secure results so desirable. Let us see however whether these have been the results where co-education has been tried, or whether there is any reasonable expectation that they will come in the future? What are the facts?

Are the young men more gentlemanly, more moral in their conduct, and the young ladies more modest, lady-like and virtuous in colleges where both sexes are admitted than in other institutions? To answer this question satisfactorily we must compare institutions which represent as nearly as possible the same classes in society. It is certainly an argument of very little worth in favor of co-education to cite a college where the proportion of wild students who enter is less than any other in the land, and say there are fewer expulsions and immoralities than in ordinary colleges. So there would be were the girls excluded. Bring a company of mature young men and women, most of them church members, into an institution where every influence tends to strengthen their religious sentiments, and we grant there will be less disorder and fewer lapses from virtue than among an equal number of young men, who represent the wild and vicious as fully as the virtuous and Christian elements of society. We will not dispute the statement so frequently made that there is greater order and less immorality in Oberlin than in any college exclusively male, but, if the fact be true, it can be more justly attributed to the smaller proportion of immoral students who enter it, than to the union of the sexes. There is no less decorum and virtue at Mt. Holyoke seminary than at Oberlin, and there has been no such fearful tragedy in its history as that which once shocked the American public at Oberlin as the direct result of co-education. Give the freshman class of other colleges as few wild students, and as strong Christian influences, as Oberlin possesses, and there is no reason why they may not present as immaculate a record. In colleges where all classes of society are fairly represented, co-education has produced no superiority of manners or morals. This summer in Michigan University over seventy students were suspended for hazing notwithstanding the influence of seventy young ladies. In eastern colleges our young men, without female aid, have nearly banished the absurdity. The young men, we are triumphantly told, do not treat their young lady fellow-students rudely; are young men in other institutions rude to ladies? The head of one of our Western colleges in defending his institution from the charge of match-making, naively remarks that the ladies in the town are more attractive to the students than those in college. We will not draw the natural inference, we will simply say there is not a particle of evidence to show that the young ladies in mixed institutions grow any more attractive than they do without collegiate relations to young men.

Do we find any more evidence that co-education changes the ordinary relation of the sexes to each other? The president of that college, where co-education has been tried the longest, frankly admits, that most of the students are engaged to each other before leaving college, and thinks it a good thing; another defends the courtships, which he admits are going on most of the time in mixed colleges, as a needed intellectual stimulus. Horace Mann, when asked if he had been successful in preventing all trouble from the association of the sexes, replied: "Yes, but the success has been more by a care and vigilance brought as near to omniscient supervision as it is possible to bring them." There is no evidence that co-education has eradicated or materially changed the most deeply-rooted passions of human nature. Is there any probability that it will? Is there not good reason to suppose that young people in college as elsewhere will continue to be in many respects what their fathers and mothers were; and can not most of us remember a youthful period when we were not entirely absorbed by philosophy?

I have confidence enough in the youth of this generation, in the moral and Christian influences of the homes they represent, to anticipate no greater evils in bringing four or five hundred young people together in a collegiate institution than frequently occur in other circumstances. But there is always danger from animal passion, and we are being taught in many a fearful tragedy that it is folly to ignore it. Any one who has any true conceptions of the early struggles, and temptations of life, must feel great solicitude for young people, when the restraints of expediency are weak, and the appetites most inflammable. It is a time of great anxiety to discerning parents, when their sons are first sent away from home to meet the temptations of college life. Would not many feel still more solicitude for sons and daughters, if to the ordinary dangers, were added those which might arise from the familiar intercourse away from home, of three or four hundred of both sexes? The great trouble with our most successful male colleges is, that the students are already becoming too numerous to receive the personal supervision they need. Is there no danger that we shall lack still more the care which Horace Mann says must be next to omniscient, when an equally large number of girls are added? . . .

The advocates of co-education point, I know, to the corruptions prevalent in medieval nunneries and monasteries as one of their strongest arguments; and when they wish any epithet peculiarly opprobrious to apply to male colleges, they call them monastic institutions. But it would be well to notice the state of morals outside monastic walls, before we judge too harshly that within. Notwithstanding all their vices, and these we should remember are learned mainly from Protestant sources, history clearly shows that the average morality of the nuns and monks was much higher than that of the great mass of the people to whom they ministered.

I have not the slightest disposition to defend monasticism. It arose to meet an exigency in society which it is to be hoped may never occur again. It outlived its usefulness, and, in the decrepitude and folly of its dotage, caused men to forget the inestimable services which it rendered public morals in its youth. But whatever be our opinion of its merits or defects, no argument can fairly be drawn from it, or from the facts of college life, to show that the separation of the sexes in our educational institutions promotes vice. Are the young men ordinarily in our communities so much purer and more exemplary, that they can afford to throw stones at their comrades in college? Is it not true that there is a higher type of manhood, and less dissipation among college students, than among young men in ordinary life? There are more traditions for good than evil in our colleges. Great as are their temptations, they are less than a young man ordinarily encounters in any of our larger communities and cities. Nor have I yet heard the complaint made that our female seminaries are in such a bad way, that they need the introduction of a few young men to improve their morals. The thought is preposterous! Yet why, if co-education be necessary for moral improvement. This argument must work both ways if it is good for anything. If the morality of the girls is in any way endangered by the admission of young men into female institutions, it is certainly more endangered by the admission of young ladies into male. There is now a purity of thought and sentiment among our young women which we do not find among the other sex. Who would see it otherwise? Who would see woman less sensitive to the very appearance of evil? Is there no danger that she would be, if placed at an early age away from home in institutions where the masculine influence is predominant?

They tell us that co-education is in the line of nature; brothers and sisters are brought up together in the same family, and young people associate freely in the same communities. But the young men and women in college are not generally brothers and sisters; nor do young people in our communities usually associate with the freedoms and familiarity which characterize college life. Would prudent parents, who have large families of sons or daughters, introduce into their homes large numbers of the opposite sex; or if they should, would they deem it advisable to go away for four years, and leave young people thus associated to keep house by themselves under the general supervision of their pastor and school-teacher? The college is family life on a large scale. There is danger, either of destroying one of its chief charms and benefits, or of making it productive of unspeakable evils, by admitting both sexes to the same institution.

Grant, if you please, to our Western colleges all the success they claim in the solution of this difficult problem. We have no disposition to disparage them, or to indulge in a single captious criticism. But whatever be their success, we do not think it can be safely taken as a universal criterion. Young ladies have thus far been admitted to college in comparatively limited numbers, and have generally been of the steady kind. We know little by actual experiment of the evils which would arise were both sexes as widely and numerously represented in our colleges.

Grant also, that the introduction of a few well-mannered girls in a company of young men, has had the effect to soften them, and that the girls have not been materially injured by it. We need more than this to justify us in adopting a course attended with so many disadvantages. It is not sufficient that woman does not grow masculine; we wish her to become much more womanly; we wish to contrive those educational influences which shall bring out in greatest perfection all her faculties; which shall intensify and strengthen all the qualities which are most desirable and distinctive in either sex. Thus far, co-education has produced no higher types of manhood or womanhood than have been secured through institutions in which the sexes are educated separately.

Looking then at the health, intellect, manners and morals of our youth, we think there is good reason to anticipate better results from female colleges which shall give young women equal educational advantages, than from any system of co-education which has thus far been proposed. . . .

Co-education, indeed, is better than no education. We can conceive that in our Western States it may have been the wiser course, in the poverty of their educational appliances and the condition of their society, to open their colleges to all. We cannot always do what is abstractedly the best; and it is not for us to criticise those, who, in altered circumstances, and with greater obstacles, have nobly done the best they could for the higher education of their youth. . . .

I will not, however, tax your patience with a farther discussion of this prolific theme. Whatever be our opinions concerning co-education, or separate education, shall we not at least agree that woman needs to be educated for her womanhood; that she needs the college not merely that she may better fulfill the varied duties of maternity and wifehood, or successfully compete with men in the learned professions; but that she may be perfect as her Father in Heaven is perfect; assured that the woman is more than her trade, and womanhood more to be prized than any thing she can gain by her toil.

"THE SPIRIT OF THE COLLEGE"

Henry Fowle Durant (1877)

In whom are hid all the treasures of wisdom and knowledge. —COLOSSIANS 2:3

THE WELLESLEY COLLEGE plan of education may properly be made a lesson for the Sabbath day, because it is religious throughout.

It asks the co-operation of teachers and students in that revolt which is the real meaning of the Higher Education of Women. We revolt against the slavery in which women are held by the customs of society—the broken health, the aimless lives, the subordinate position, the helpless dependence, the dishonesties and shams of so-called education. The Higher Education of Women is one of the great world battle-cries for freedom; for right against might. It is the cry of the oppressed slave. It is the assertion of absolute equality. The war is sacred, because it is the war of Christ against the principalities and powers of sin, against spiritual wickedness in high places.

Wellesley College desires to take the foremost place in the mighty struggle. All our plans are in outspoken opposition to the customs and the prejudices of the public. Therefore, we expect every one of you to be, in the noblest sense, reformers.

It is difficult in the midst of great revolutions, whether political or social, to read rightly the signs of the times. You mistake altogether the significance of the movement of which you are a part, if you think this is simply the question of a college education for girls. I believe that God's hand is in it; that it is one of the great ocean currents of Christian civilization: that He is calling to womanhood to come up higher, to prepare itself for great conflicts, for vast reforms in social life, for noblest usefulness. The higher education is but the putting on God's armor for the contest.

From "Notes of Mr. Durant's Sermon on 'The Spirit of the College.' " September 1877. Boston: Frank Wood, 1890.

THE ARGUMENT FOR COEDUCATION

"DEDICATION OF ANTIOCH COLLEGE AND INAUGURAL ADDRESS"

Horace Mann (1854)

I AM AWARE that, in proposing to educate males and females together, and to confer equal opportunities for culture upon both, we encounter some objections. . . .

That female education should be rescued from its present reproach of inferiority, and advanced to an equality with that of males, is a conviction which has already taken fast hold of the best minds in society, and is soon to mark the grand distinction between cultivated and uncultivated communities. But those who feel the necessity of this reform may still object to congregating both sexes in the same institutions of learning. To this objection, I consider it to be a complete answer, at least for many years to come, that, as separate institutions for the different sexes would nearly double all primary outlays and current expenditures, the plan would impoverish all; and the attempt to give an equal education to both sexes, by such means, would result in bringing male education down to the present level of female education, instead of carrying the latter up to the height of the former. For the present then, if not always, the only practicable way of securing the great end of high female education, is to educate both sexes at the same seats of learning. . . .

. . . [A] well-filled school assembles together a great variety of character; and a class-room, where the sexes recite in presence of each other, daily and for years, affords opportunities for a kind of acquaintance, infinitely superior to any that can ever be enjoyed, at Washington, at watering-places, or other matrimonial bazaars. For the exercise and manifestation of mental capacities and attainments, there is no reception-room like the recitation-room. Here too, there will be a daily observation of manners and appearance which either are a habit, or must become habitual, through practice. Dispositions will here be subjected to the severest trials; and unworthy passions, though hidden beneath the last folds of the heart, will be roused to a shameful exposure by excitement, or stifled into extinction by the divine discipline of conscience. If to all

---

Yellow Springs, Ohio: A. S. Dean; Boston: Grosby & Nichols, 1854.

this be added social interviews, at appropriate seasons, under guardian watchfulness and through a period of years, whatever errors of opinion may have been formed in the class-room can hardly fail to be rectified by views of other phases of character taken from these different points of observation. And when, in addition to all this, it is known that no precocious attachment that may spring up, can be consummated, until after the college life is completed, without forfeiting all connection with the college itself; and all these salutary arrangements are reinforced and corroborated by the parental counsels of the College Government, I ask whether there be any situation in life where the proprieties and the restraints, which belong to the social intercourse of the sexes, will be or can be better balanced or adjusted than here? I confidently ask, whether there be any situation in life, where the truly sacred, (though often horribly profaned,) principles and instincts which give birth and sanctity to the conjugal relation, will be likely to be better understood and guarded from harm; or will promise, in after-life, a richer amount of that bliss which God reserves as the special reward of a wise and virtuous wedlock?

Besides and beyond all this: I believe that the daily and thrice daily meetings of the sexes, with occasional interviews in social circles, will be mutually advantageous to them. It will work both moral restraint and intellectual excitement. That innate regard which each sex has for the other sex, over and above what it has for the same good qualities in its own,—the difference between friendship and love,—is too precious and too powerful an agency to be thrown away in the education of either. I believe it to be an agency which God meant we should make use of to promote the refinement, the progress and the elevation of them both. I believe it may be made to supersede many of our present coarse and crude instruments of discipline,—the goads and bludgeons of punishment which are now employed to rouse young men from the stupefaction of idleness, or beat them back from the gateways of sin.

And what a state of society does it invincibly argue, among parents, and in the community at large, if young men and young women cannot be brought together to pursue those ennobling studies and to receive those apt instructions which pre-eminently fit them for the highest duties of their common life, without mutual peril! And where in reason or in the divine commands, is there either warrant or pretext for the doctrine, that those whom God mingles together in the family, by birth; and whom, through the sacred ordinance of marriage, He designs for a still closer relation in after-life; where, I ask, is there any authority human or divine, for seizing and violently separating these same parties, for four or six or ten of the middle years of their existence?—those very years when they can best prepare themselves, by the elevation of whatever is in them of good and the suppression of whatever is in them of evil, for a future companionship so intimate as to be lost in identity. Such separation is obviously unnatural, and if it be necessary for the preservation of sexual purity, it is time that the whole community should take the alarm and hasten to devise a less monstrous remedy.

"SHALL THE AMERICAN COLLEGES BE OPEN TO BOTH SEXES?"

James B. Angell (1871)

I PROPOSE to consider briefly some of the reasons why an affirmative answer should be given to this question, and some of the objections, which are commonly raised to such an answer.

In the first place, it is desirable that our daughters as well as our sons should have the most generous intellectual culture which we can furnish them. . . . [It] would be a great gain if we could secure to every young woman who desires it, an education as thorough and generous and stimulating as our colleges afford to young men.

In the second place, it is plain that no considerable number of young women can at present obtain such an education unless our colleges are opened to them. Concede, if you please, that one or two colleges, specially devoted to the education of young women, furnish as valuable instruction as our better New England colleges,—though probably few would be ready to make that concession,—still they can meet the wants of but a small number. What then shall be done? The alternative is to multiply colleges for women or to open the doors of the colleges which are now accessible to young men alone. When can we complete the endowments of Yales and Harvards and Browns for young women alone? How can we duplicate the libraries, the scientific collections, and all the apparatus for illustrating instruction? Must our sisters and daughters wait for such achievements before they can enjoy equal intellectual privileges with our brothers and sons?

The argument then is very simple. The higher education is desired and needed by young women.

Unless it is furnished to them by our colleges, it cannot be provided at all in this generation, and not even in the future, except at an enormous expenditure. Do we not find in these facts a sufficient reason for opening the American colleges to young women, unless there are very serious practical obstacles to such action?

Let us notice the most prominent arguments which are adduced in opposition to the admission of women to our colleges. . . .

. . . [I]t is argued that the mental habits and processes of women are so different from those of men, that the two sexes cannot work profitably in the same classes or in the same institutions. But let us ask whether the difference in the mental habits and processes of the sexes is really a more formidable obstacle to working in the same class than is found in the difference in temperament, talent and attainments of young men now working in classes together. It is not found to be so up to the day when the brother and the sister leave the preparatory school. Is not the greater difference which

Rhode Island Schoolmaster *17, no. 8 (August 1871). (WCL, Pamphlet collection)*

subsequently appears, due in part to the difference in training and opportunities? After all that has been said on the difference of the minds of the sexes—and certainly there is a marked difference—are not the mental resemblances much greater than the mental differences? Do not these resemblances form the proper basis for the successful work of the instructor under an elastic system, which leaves opportunity for rational choices in departments of work? May not the difference in the mental constitution of the sexes be such that each sex may furnish suggestion, inspiration, and help to the other? It is believed by many that such is the fact. . . .

But if it be conceded that the doors of our colleges should be opened to young women, the trustees of any particular college must have regard to the state of public opinion among its constituency, in determining when and how to make the innovation on old usage. Until public sentiment is ripe for the change, young men may be turned from the college by the admission of young women. They may with a certain contempt look upon the institution as merely "a girls' school or academy," and so inferior to other colleges. . . .

. . . In more than one college corporation, and in many a college faculty, the subject is receiving increasing attention. It is improbable that the experience of the colleges which in other parts of the country are admitting both sexes into their classes, and the thorough discussion which the question before us must undergo, will soon bring some of our New England colleges to receive the young women who are desirous of a more generous and thorough culture than is now within their reach?

"THE OTHER SIDE—A REPLY"

Editorial, the *Amherst Student* (1871)

First, you say: "We should inevitably be placed under stricter surveillance, our actions would be more sharply scrutinized, and our privileges materially abridged." One unacquainted with the peculiarities of a college community would be at a loss to understand what "surveillance" or "scrutiny," unknown to all mixed society, would be made necessary, or what "privileges," which true gentlemen desire, would be "abridged" by the presence of women. Is it our religious privileges? Certainly women are as good as men. Is it our intellectual privileges? Surely women are mentally capable of studying

November 1871. Reprinted in The Liberal Education of Women: The Demand and the Method. Current Thoughts in America and England, *ed. James Orton. New York and Chicago: A. S. Barnes, 1873.*

side by side with men in any ordinary college course. What, then, are the privileges that the presence of women in our college would take from us? This question has been answered. What you intimate, a speaker upon the college stage has recently stated with great plainness of speech. The privileges which would be taken from us are the very same which our parents, our friends, the Faculty, and the trustees have been for years trying to induce us to forego. The privilege of abusing innocent Freshmen, the privilege of destroying college property, the privilege of making night dreadful with hideous noises, the privilege of transforming a literary society into an organized mob, the privilege of screaming our insults at the women who visit our cabinets or even ride through our grounds, and the privilege of being sent home in disgrace—these, forsooth, are the *"privileges"* which would be "materially abridged" by the admission of women to our monastic community. . . .

Now it is this restraining influence of woman's presence for which we are contending; this is the very point at issue. Many a student will resist all the checks which family affection can throw around him while he is absent from home, whom the presence of impersonated refinement and purity will improve and elevate. There are few who possess a love which absence will not weaken, and this few need help least of all. For the sake of the thoughtless many who constantly need restraint, we ask for the presence of women in our midst. We believe it is not only possible, but certain, that her presence would effect a complete reformation in many of those immoralities which now disgrace our college.

From the earliest times every step in the advancement of woman has benefited our own sex no less than it has elevated her. Slowly she has wrought her way from an abject position to one which commands the admiration of all right thinking people. She has demonstrated her power to adorn and to elevate every sphere into which she has been admitted. Society, literature, and art could not dispense with her own peculiar talent. We believe that in education also she has a yet more important place to occupy than has yet been assigned her. Twenty students firmly believe that her coming will "materially abridge" our dangerous privileges. She will prevail where College Law is a failure. "For what the law could not do in that it was weak," she, coming to us in all strength of purity, will speedily accomplish.

"LETTER TO THE BOARD OF TRUSTEES OF WESLEYAN UNIVERSITY"

John M. Van Vleck (1900)

GENTLEMEN:—As a member of the Joint Committee appointed by your authority on the Relation of Wesleyan University to the Higher Education of Women, I beg leave to submit, in dissent from the reports presented by other members of that committee, the following statement of my opinions on the subject:—

First. The establishment of a Woman's College at Wesleyan seems to me forbidden by sound educational and economical principles. It is, furthermore, in my opinion, at least for the immediate future, absolutely prohibited by the present and prospective financial condition of the University.

Second. I desire to protest against the establishment of a "Woman's Department of Wesleyan University," unless the male students be likewise designated as constituting the Men's Department of Wesleyan University,—in short, against any name or ruling which states or implies that women are students of Wesleyan University in any other relation than such as shall apply equally to men.

Third. I plead most strenuously against any actual or provisional separation of the sexes in class instructions, except in the few instances in which the peculiar nature of the study involved may render such separation appropriate and profitable. To authorize such a separation of instruction as has been proposed in the required studies of the Freshman and Sophomore years, by the use either of funds now in the possession of the University or of funds to be specially contributed therefor, would in my opinion be incapable of any logical significance or defence, except as the beginning of a policy looking toward the ultimate establishment of an institution for women largely separate from that for men,—a policy which, as I have said, seems to me, for the present at least, impossible. Granting as possible that the adoption of such a policy may be found wise in the future, it would nevertheless be in the highest degree unwise, either directly or by implication, to commit the college to that policy *now* while there is grave difference of opinion as to whether it ought to be adopted, and no assurance whatever that it can be successfully carried out.

I venture to suggest as desirable action at present the following:—

First, That the Board of Trustees declare it to be the fixed policy of Wesleyan University to continue to offer to women opportunities and facilities for education equal in all respects to those offered to men.

Second, That they authorize separation of

---

25 June 1900. (OL)

the women from the men in administration and organization, the details of this separation to be referred to the decision of a suitable committee, composed, perhaps, of members of the Board and of the Faculty.

Third, As essential to such separate administration and organization, that the Board appoint a woman as Dean of Women, who shall have authority in all matters pertaining to the women, the exact limits of her authority, as well as her precise relation to the Faculty, to be determined by the committee just suggested.

Fourth, That the Board, if they deem it necessary, should fix for a term of, say, five years, a definite percentage limit which the number of women be not allowed to exceed, that limit, however, to be large enough to permit the development of a healthy and attractive community life among the women. For this purpose, twenty per cent., as has been proposed by some, is in my opinion decidedly too small.

Fifth, That an appeal be made to the friends of women's education for funds for the speedy erection of a women's building or buildings, such as shall offer to women an attractive home, with facilities for social and physical culture now greatly needed.

Respectfully submitted,
J. M. Van Vleck
Middletown, Conn., June 25, 1900

"IS CO-EDUCATION INJURIOUS TO GIRLS?"

John Dewey (1911)

"Who excuses himself accuses himself," says the French proverb. A defense of co-education may suggest that its cause needs bolstering. As a matter of fact, however, the case for co-education does not depend upon balancing arguments. A plea for it is simply a record of what American experience has demonstrated; and few persons on the Atlantic seaboard are aware of the extent of this experience. Of the boys and girls in our public schools—high schools included—nineteen out of every twenty are educated together. Even in the colleges and universities there are five women in co-educational institutions of the first rank to one in women's colleges. And if we omit the women's colleges of only two states, Massachusetts and New York, the ratio in the colleges is almost that in the high schools—nineteen to one on the side of co-education. An ounce of practice is worth a pound of theory; it is absurd to treat the question of

Ladies Home Journal 28 *(June 1911).*

co-education as one to be debated on theoretical or abstract grounds.

Several years ago President Jordan declared: "Co-education is never a question where it has been fairly tried." These words are as true today as when spoken. The few cases recently exploited in newspaper headlines may be disposed of without quibbling about the word "fairly." Their nature is well brought out in a little incident President Jordan relates just before making the statement quoted: "An Eastern professor lately visiting a Western State university asked one of the seniors what he thought of co-education. 'I beg your pardon,' said the student, 'what question do you mean?' 'Why, co-education,' said the professor, 'the education of women *in colleges for men.*' " The italicized words tell the whole story. Permitting a few women to enter "colleges for men" is one thing; co-education, conjoint education of women and men, is quite another. If some colleges for men, that opened their doors to women for the sake of additional numbers—and fees—without having considered whether they could deal justly with them afterward, have been compelled to take back tracks toward segregation, it proves nothing about co-education—whatever it may prove about the judgment of the administrative authorities. That men in an institution which they regard as their exclusive monopoly should resent the presence of women is, doubtless, only too natural.

There was a time when males resented the presence of women, on equal terms, in any social relation, even putting to death all girl babies beyond the minimum needed to continue the tribal existence. Whether the tendency to perpetuate survivals of barbarism in exclusively male institutions is an argument against co-education or against the conditions that favor such survivals is not here to the point.

The Moral One Is the Most Definitely Established Advantage

The most definitely established of the advantages of co-education is the most important one: the moral one. Not one of the few remaining authorities opposed to mixed education will commit himself definitely to a statement that it has had a bad effect on sexual morality. The evils so profusely prophesied in advance are conspicuous by their absence. An English critic, opposed both to co-education and to our secular education, says that American experience is conclusive that in this country at least sexual tension and sexual perversion are reduced by co-education. The late Dr. W. T. Harris pointed out as one of its chief benefits its tendency to "desexualize" the school atmosphere. There is a natural irradiation of sexually aroused emotions into normal channels such as is quite impossible when the sexes are arbitrarily isolated. An English authority, referring to what an English schoolman had said of the prevalence of sex precocity in some of the boys' schools, adds: "I have no hesitation in saying that the evil he speaks of, which does so much to impair both the minds and the bodies of the young people of our day and to impair the powers of reproduction, might be largely mitigated by co-education. It is the stolen fruit which is the sweetest, and the don't look-on-the-other-side system has always the undesired, and, in this case, disastrous effect."

The moral case, however, is much wider than the sexual aspect, infinitely important as that is. It would be easy to fill my allotted space with quotations from experienced high-school teachers testifying to the wholesome and refining influence, in all directions, of companionship of boys and girls on the intellectual plane afforded by co-instruction. If the adolescents of the two sexes can meet anywhere to advantage it must be where conditions of contact are the most steadying and elevating. To think otherwise is not to question co-education, but to exhibit contempt for the moral possibilities of all education. The influences of association radiate throughout the whole of character. Boys learn gentleness, unselfishness, courtesy; their natural vigor finds helpful channels of expression, instead of wasting itself in lawless boisterousness. The natural attraction of the other sex unconsciously puts them on their honor with themselves to live up to the best in themselves rather than to descend to the lowest in their natures. Girls acquire greater self-reliance and a desire to win approval by deserving it instead of by "working" others. Their narrowness of judgment, depending upon enforced narrowness of outlook, is overcome; their ultra-feminine weaknesses are toned up.

Beneficial Influence of Co-Education upon Manners

Manners and morals run into each other and fuse. Even those who oppose co-education admit its beneficial influence upon manners. The utmost they urge is that its effect is a little too good—so to speak—or that boys are made unnaturally gentlemanly. The so-called feminization of our schools must be spoken of with all the solemnity befitting a secret mystery. Nobody has seen it; nobody has yet pointed out regiments of effete mollycoddles coming forth from our schools; on the contrary, they persist in sending forth wholesome, natural, boyish boys. It is simply a vague, impalpable fear that somehow hangs over the heads of Americans whom we have so foolishly regarded as a strenuous people. Such intangibly indefinite things cannot, of course, be argued against. A bit of history may, however, be better than argument. A British visitor, member of the Mosely Commission, is the first on record as experiencing this dread fear. Here are his official words: "The boy in America is not being brought up to punch another boy's head, nor to stand having his own punched, in a healthy and proper manner. There is a strange and indefinable feminine air coming over the men." Possibly some light is thrown on the value of this opinion when we find the same writer denying that Americans generally are a practical people, and saying "their tendency is to be guided by sentiment and emotion. I do not think the Americans can long claim to rank as a practical people."

As a matter of fact there is no serious difference between the opponents and the upholders of co-education as to its actual effects upon the morale of boys and girls. The difference is not in the facts, but in the medium of sentiment through which the facts are viewed. Says the chief American opponent: "There is a little charm and bloom rubbed off the ideal of girlhood by close contact, and boyhood seems less ideal to girls at close range. In place of the mystic attraction of the other sex that has inspired so much that is best in the world, familiar camaraderie brings a little disenchantment. The impulse to be at one's best in the presence of the other sex grows lax, and each comes to feel itself seen through, so that there is less motive to indulge in the ideal conduct which such contact inspires, *because the call for it is incessant.*"

No upholder of co-education has ever made any stronger claim for it than that it renders the call for courteous, decent and kindly conduct incessant, as this writer concedes. If anyone holds that a sporadic sentimental "jacking up" of conduct to some ideal plane—stimulated by contact whose sexual features are accentuated by its rarity—is better than an even, sexually unconscious raising of the general level of behavior, one can only say that there is no arguing about tastes, but that the tastes of most American parents do not run in that direction. They prefer a just and wholesome appreciation by men and women of the enduring good points of each other to the illusions of temporarily excited fancy. They are quite willing to have a "bloom" which is purely romantic and sentimental rubbed off, in order to lessen those illusions that lead to disaster in married life when their unreality becomes apparent.

As I have said, there is no serious difference as to the facts. The difference is one of social, ideal, and moral and intellectual standards of value. Those who retain the ideal of weak and dependent femininity bequeathed to us from the sentimentalism of the eighteenth century—it is no older—those who agree with the author whom I have quoted, that womanhood reaches "its ideal of beauty and perfection between the years of eighteen and twenty," will probably regret the substitution of a little common sense for an excess of romantic silliness. Others will not.

Intellectual Effects of Co-Education

What are the intellectual effects of co-education? Well it has at least forever laid at rest one old bugaboo—the notion of the inherent mental inferiority of the female sex. Hardly more than a generation ago the chief objection urged—next to the riot of sexual immorality that would follow—to co-education in colleges was that the standard of scholarship would have to be irretrievably lowered to bring studies down to the level of women. Today the objection is more likely to read that women do so much better than young men as to discourage the latter. But, in the main, the objection heard today on the intellectual side rests not on the difference in quantity, but quality. "Female botany," "female algebra"—and, for all I know, a female multiplication table—have been conceived, adapted to the "female mind." Most of this talk is, of course, sheer mythology; upon no subject has there been so much dogmatic assertion, based upon so little scientific evidence, as upon male and female types of mind. We know that traits are transmitted from grandfather to grandson through the mother, even the traits most specifically masculine in nature. This, with other accessible facts, demonstrates that such differences of mental characteristics as exist are those of arrangement, proportion and emphasis, rather than of kind or quality. Moreover, it is scientifically demonstrable that the average difference between men and women is much less than the range of *individual* differences among either men or women by themselves. Hence the argument is even stronger for abolition of all class instruction and the substitution of individual tutoring than it is for separation of men and women.

Moreover, such differences of outlook, interest and method of approach as do exist are, upon any sound theory of education, an argument in favor of joint instruction. The only available comparative statistics of any scientific standing are from Finland. They show what might have been expected: Scholarship averages somewhat better in mixed than in separate schools. A fair statement of the differences most likely to be found—overstated, if anything, and, of course, with many individual exceptions in both sexes—would be that boys are the more variable; girls depart less, for either better or worse, from the mean. Boys are slower or more deliberate; girls are more "intuitive" or discriminating, and hence quicker. Boys are more inert, and hence independent and refractory; girls are more responsive, and hence more docile and suggestible. Boys take more to the impersonal, the abstract and mechanical phases of things; girls more to their concrete—that is, their human and social—phases. Can any unprejudiced person deny that a balance of these features is desirable rather than an exaggeration in either direction? And will any unprejudiced person deny that the desired balance is most likely to be secured where each sex is confronted with and has to take account of the characteristic interests, methods, and mental reactions of the other sex?

Some Advantages to Both Sexes

One argument for separation reads that woman "better than man represents the feeling instincts that are higher, deeper and broader than mere mental culture; she is generic, being nearer the race; every individual of her sex is a better representative of the race." Discount the note of exaggeration in this; accept its measure of truth, and the moral points to co-education.

Is it desirable that young men shall pass through their most plastic years without coming into effective contact with those fundamental factors of humanity which woman is said to represent? And if the contact is not to be merely physical or merely sentimental it must take place under the intellectual and moral conditions of regulation afforded by co-instruction. Surely it is not desirable that young men should secure "mere mental culture" and nothing more. And it would seem equally clear that the "feeling instincts" of girls need to be steadied, clarified and purged—made fit for greater functional usefulness—by genuine and continued contact with serious intellectual culture. Oftentimes those who make the most extreme statements regarding the distinctive, innate traits of women seem to think that it is absolutely necessary for men to lay down the law regarding what traits really are—and what are not—natural to women; they have been totally unwilling to allow and encourage these traits to work themselves out by furnishing them a free and congenial environment in which to operate.

There is no important adjustment in society into which the proper relation of the sexes does not enter. The place of women in the family and the importance of right family life for all social ends do not need emphasis. But as a wife the woman is in relation to a man; whatever in prior training makes this relation opaque and strained is sure to make the family itself less successful and less efficient both in itself and for society at large. As a mother the woman is likely to have to train boys as well as girls, and as a father the man is likely to become responsible for the intellectual and moral nurture of girls as well as boys. To make these important and difficult tasks still more difficult by a forced prior isolation, thereby preventing natural acquaintance with the needs, capacities and reactions of the other sex—and to do it merely to relieve pedagogues of some of their schoolroom problems—would be a penny-wise, pound-foolish policy. . . .

III

WOMEN'S STRUGGLES FOR ECONOMIC EQUALITY, 1850–1960

Sheet music cover, 1915. Courtesy of the Labor Archives and Research Center, San Francisco State University.

IN HER INFLUENTIAL *Woman in the Nineteenth Century* (1845), Margaret Fuller called for an economic revolution that would allow women to choose whatever occupation they wished—even to "be sea captains if they will" (Fuller 1978, 43). But economic equality has been a difficult struggle. Social customs and deliberate policies have prevented women from entering the labor force, thrown barriers up against their entering the professions, made it difficult or impossible for them to keep what little they did earn, and ignored the large numbers of them who had been in the labor force all along. This last group has been the subject of much excellent research by feminist historians, who have shown that, in every occupation from which they were not formally excluded (and even in some of those), there have been large numbers of women working since the founding of the country (see Kessler-Harris 1982; Tentler 1979; Weiner 1985; and Milkman 1985, 1987).

Women have struggled on several fronts for equality in the economic sphere. Early struggles included that of married women to retain the economic rights they possessed (property and control over wages) before marriage and that for women's right to enter the labor force in the first place. Later issues included equal wages, bringing women into the growing union movement, and entry into the professions. Married women struggled against the ideology of domesticity, which removed them from the workplace after marriage.

An asterisk (*) indicates that a document is included in this volume.

Most pro-feminist men supported struggles for economic equality because they assumed a natural equality of women and men as individuals and citizens; women should be allowed to work, hold property, and receive equal wages because the physiological differences between women and men should make no difference in the public sphere. A second group of men supported *some* campaigns for economic equality, such as protective legislation, reforms of working conditions and hours, and higher wages, because they saw women as fragile creatures in need of the state's paternal protection against greedy entrepreneurs and industrialists. These men emphasized gender difference, not similarity, in their efforts to shield working women from the brutalities of economic competition. They also thought that working outside the home would make women better wives and mothers, much the same way as Emma Willard had argued for better-educated women. Finally, some men have supported women's economic struggles because women's equality is essential to improving the quality of men's lives. Many early twenty-century socialists saw women's economic inequality as a pillar on which capitalist society rested. Women's campaigns for economic justice were part of the larger struggle to liberate economic life from the evils of private property and exploitation.

To be taken seriously as economic actors, women had to confront traditional assumptions about "natural" delicacy. Anti-feminists argued that woman's proper job was maintaining the home as a sanctuary and that, so occupied, she need not bother herself with the realities of economic life. The ideology of domesticity set up a "cultural halo ringing the significance of home and family" to the rest of society (Cott 1977, 199). Women lost the right to own and control property when they married; after her wedding, a woman became herself the property of her husband. Perhaps the earliest effort to bring women onto the economic stage was to allow married women to retain their own property. "Husbands and wives cannot legally contract with each other, and they cannot legally testify as to private conversations with each other," wrote William Bowditch in "How Long Shall We Rob and Enslave Women?" (1885).* "Even criminals, may testify in their own behalf, but under laws framed by men alone, and to which no woman has ever consented, a wife cannot testify as to what sort of agreement her husband has made with her in private conversation, and the agreement itself is worthless." How, he asked, could one justify the *loss* of status that accompanied marriage?

Social reformer and Indiana senator Robert Dale Owen offered legislation permitting women to retain their property rights (see "The Property Rights of Widows"*). This was not an exceptionally popular idea; it was "met by some of the sticklers for old custom, as a terrible innovation, calculated to uproot the foundations of society, destroy the harmony of the domestic circle, invade the sanctity of the marriage relation, and a great deal more of the same nonsense," wrote Owen to his father, the celebrated reformer, in 1851 (see pt. 2 of Owen's "Rights of Women in the Old Immoral World" [1851]). By the end of the century, many states had eliminated restrictions on married women's property rights. The Connecticut state legislature, for example, passed a law in 1877 permitting women to retain property held before marriage and to control their earnings after marriage (*HWS*, 4:538).

Women as Workers

Women also demanded to be recognized as workers. Many women were already in the labor force and wanted to be acknowledged, while others sought to remove the barriers that prevented their full economic participation. Work was a priority for women and their male supporters. In 1852, in "Woman and Work,"* Horace Greeley wrote, "Before all questions of intellectual training or political franchises for women . . . do I place the question of enlarged opportunities for work; of a more extended and diversified field of employment."

By the last decades of the nineteenth century, women's labor force participation grew significantly. In 1870, 1.8 million women were working; ten years later, more than 2.6 million women, or 14.7 percent of all women over age ten, were working. That number more than doubled again by 1900, reaching 5.3 million women, one-fifth of all women over age fifteen, and by 1910 it had grown to 25 percent (Billington 1967, 78). To enter the work world, however, meant confronting the antifeminist charge that women would no longer be fit for life on the pedestal. "If [a woman] was to fight for her interests," one working woman complained in 1874, "they would say how 'rough' and 'coarse' she is. Society would put her finger of scorn on her. Why is it can a woman not be virtuous if she does mingle with the toilers?" (cited in Kessler-Harris 1982, 164).

Many men considered working women equally virtuous and thus entitled to the same treatment and the same wages as male workers.

In "The Industrial Emancipation of Women,"* for example, Carroll Wright, of the Massachusetts Bureau of Statistics of Labor, praised the working girls of Boston in 1889 for "making an heroic, an honest, and a virtuous struggle to earn an honorable livelihood." Here, again, pro-feminist men encountered those who argued that spheres must be separate so that women could perform their natural function as mothers. In 1845, for example, one Boston minister told the *Voice of Industry* that women's real purpose in life was "the nobler task of moulding the infant mind" and that they were also meant "to control the stormy passions of man, to inspire him with those sentiments which subdue his ferocity and make his heart gentle and soft . . . to open to him the truest and purest source of happiness, and prompt him to the love of virtue and religion" (cited in Kessler-Harris 1982, 52).

Pro-feminist men argued that women's equality at birth entitled them to equal wages. In 1874, Henry Brown Blackwell wrote in the *Woman's Journal* that "it is mainly in the want of respect and sympathy for Woman in her work and in social restraints upon the freedom of her movements as a laborer, that we find the explanation of her lower wages" (Blackwell 1874, 1). William Bowditch argued that, even when performing the same tasks, "the woman invariably receives less wages than the man" (Bowditch 1889, 1). Even Buffalo Bill Cody supported women's economic equality. "I'm not one of a kind that think God made woman to do nothing but sit at home in the ashes and tend to babies," Cody said. "If a woman can do the same work as a man can and do it just as well, she should have the same pay" (cited in *New York Times* [26 July 1987]). Other writers linked women's wages to suffrage, arguing that, as long as women were deprived of the ballot, they could not carry out their own campaign for higher wages.

Others saw suffrage as the vehicle by which women could enact protective legislation. For example, in "The 'Protected Sex' in Industry"* (1915), George Creel, secretary of the Men's League for Woman Suffrage, observed that "only in the states where the women have the vote to protect themselves [is] there adequate comprehension of the necessity for guarding the mother sex against the poison of fatigue." Some supported higher wages because women were more in need of protection by the state. Social reformers campaigning against prostitution argued that women who received adequate wages would have no need to turn to sin.

Women in the Labor Movement

Working women also sought to press their demands to a growing labor movement, with whom they have had a troubled relationship. Some trade unionists saw women workers as men's competitors for jobs and sought to exclude women from membership. As early as 1836, the National Trades Union urged women's exclusion from factories since women workers provided "ruinous competition" to male workers. "If every man engaged in useful labor was properly remunerated," declared the *National Laborer* a year later, "the female portion of their families would not need to leave their homes and domestic duties to earn their own subsistence" (cited in Andrews and Bliss 1911, 48, 35.) In 1854, the National Typographical Union prohibited some locals from allowing male members to work beside women. Some male workers were distressed that their wives and daughters were forced to work because they themselves were not earning sufficient wages to keep their women out of the labor force.

Many early unionists supported women's participation in the labor struggle. William Sylvis, leader of the National Labor Union (NLU), opposed women's entry into the labor force but argued that, since women were already there, the labor movement needed to incorporate them in order to present a united front to the employers (see his "A Union's Position"*). This meant including women (and also blacks) in the union, and in 1866 the National Labor Convention admitted them to membership, pledging "individual and undivided support to the sewing women, factory cooperatives, and daughters of toil" (in Balser 1987, 58). The next year, the NLU recommended that working men endorse the principle of equal pay for equal work and invite women to join labor organizations. (In 1868, *Revolution,* the feminist newspaper, published a biography of Sylvis and proclaimed, "The Principles of the National Labor Union are *our* principles" [cited in ibid., 59].) Later, the Knights of Labor stood for equal pay for equal work, ending child labor, and no discrimination against women or blacks. In 1886, Elizabeth Rogers was named head of the Knights' Chicago district office, the first woman to achieve such a high office.

At the same time, many unions did not include women, many did not acknowledge working women as equal workers, and many sought to push women out of the labor force altogether. Some supporters of labor employed the separate-spheres argument to maintain women's exclusion. At a mass meeting in Chicago in 1890, the Reverend V. P. Gifford argued that the "man should make the money and the woman remain at home to care for it. Work should not be added to her burden of childbearing" (cited in Tax 1980, 83). Many trade unionists argued that the inequality of wages between women and men was necessary because male workers were paid a "family wage" while women were working only for "pin money" or to feed their frivolous consumerist appetites.

Some unions did admit women, and pro-feminist men hailed their entry. An editorial in the *New Republic* in 1919, for example, noted that, "whatever may be the attitude of the masculine and capitalist state, surely in the eyes of labor there should be neither man nor woman but only workers, all helping each other in their fight" (14 June 1919: 209). Women workers proved to be fierce and dedicated unionists, leading strikes in Lawrence and Paterson. (So passionate was the women's participation that one Philadelphia newspaper warned that "the governor may have to call out the militia to prevent a gynecocracy" ([Andrews and Bliss 1911, 48].) Activists and songwriters like James Oppenheim, Joe Hill (see his "The Rebel Girl"*), and Woody Guthrie celebrated women's participation in the workers' struggle. Oppenheim's song* for the Lawrence, Massachusetts, mill strike of 1912 coined the phrase "bread and roses" to describe the beneficial transformation of the labor movement. "The rising of the women means the rising of the race," the strikers sang. Guthrie's "Union Maid"* celebrated the union woman's vigilance—"she always stood her ground"—however, he also suggested that the union maid ought to marry a union man and "join the Ladies' Auxiliary." (Several years after Guthrie's death, feminists complained about the last verse of the song, and Pete Seeger popularized a revised version.)

Joe Hill's union, the militant socialist Industrial Workers of the World (IWW, or Wobblies), consistently supported women's rights. In "What About the Woman Who Works,"* the IWW made it clear that women did not work because they *wanted* to any more than a man was a wage laborer because he wanted to work for the capitalists. Women worked because they had to work, because "no woman can consistently live on a man's wages any more." The "wage slavery" of capitalism necessitated women working, and male workers now must welcome women into their struggle against the capitalist system. The

IWW applauded women who cheered and inspired male rebels and whose "directness" was always "refreshing to men worn out in the fray" and welcomed them into the union. "The advent of women side by side with men in strikes, will soon develop a fighting force that will end capitalism and its horrors in short order" was how one editorial writer in *Solidarity* put it in 1910 (cited in Tax 1980, 127). The IWW was also the only labor organization to raise the nonworkplace issue of birth control (ibid., 128).

One of the more difficult struggles for women's economic rights was fought out within the American Federation of Labor (AFL). "The great principle for which we fight," commented the union's treasurer in 1905, "is opposed to taking . . . women from their homes to put them in the factory and the sweatshop." Another AFL leader argued that "it is wrong to permit any of the female sex of our country to be forced to work, as we believe that the man should be provided with a fair wage in order to keep his female relatives from going to work. The man is the provider and should receive enough for his labor to give his family a respectable living" (cited in Kessler-Harris 1982, 153). That women's participation in the labor force contributed to men's unemployment, underemployment, or depressed wages was a problem. "Every women employed," wrote one editor of the *American Federationist,* "displaces a man and adds one more to the idle contingent that are fixing wages at the lowest limit" (cited in ibid., 155). AFL president Samuel Gompers agreed. "It is the so-called competition of the unorganized defenseless woman worker, the girl and the wife, that often tends to reduce the wages of the father and husband," he wrote (Gompers 1906, 13).

In a few years, however, Gompers was persuaded that women workers were in the workplace to stay, not in competition with male workers, but as potential comrades. Under Gompers, the AFL organized women workers and supported equal pay for equal work, arguing that the organization offer "full and free opportunity for women to work whenever and wherever necessity requires" (cited in Kessler-Harris 1982, 155). In an editorial in the *American Federationist,* Gompers (1913, p. 3) wrote that the women's movement "is a movement for liberty, freedom of action and thought, tending toward a condition when women shall be accorded equal independence and responsibility with men, equal freedom of work and self-expression, equal protection and rights." His 1915 speech "Coming Into Her Own" went even further: "Industrial freedom must be fought out on the industrial field. It will be achieved when wage-earning women hold in their own hands the right and the power to participate in determining the conditions under which they shall work and the wages they shall receive. They can delegate this power and responsibility to no outside authority if they wish industrial freedom." For this reason, Gompers boasted that the AFL had been organizing women "on an equality with men and have equal rights and privileges in the organization." Yet women workers were not convinced of their equality within the AFL and moved to start the National Women's Trade Union League (NWTUL). This organization was designed to promote women's position and protect women workers since they could not count on the AFL.

The struggle to be included in the union movement was slow and difficult. By 1924, less than 5 percent of all working women were union members, according to a Women's Bureau study (Raybeck 1966, 259). Women's recognition as economic equals by both employers and fellow employees was constantly hampered by the transmutation of the ideology of separate spheres into the twentieth century. Once married, a woman was still expected to retreat to the home and devote herself to housekeeping and child-rearing tasks. But the shifting composition of the female labor force meant that this struggle would finally become a dominant theme in debates about women's work. Demographic factors—declining fertility, the growth of education, increasing urbanization, and the aging of the population—combined with such economic changes as the increased utilization of technological advances and the rise of white-collar and service occupations to bring increasing numbers of married women into the labor force. Married women made up about 15 percent of the total female labor force at the turn of the century, but by 1910 almost one-fourth of all working women were married. In 1940, over one-third were married and by 1950 more than half (ibid., 259 and passim).

Married women's increasing labor force participation aroused significant alarm. Writers warned of "race suicide," as educated native-born white women chose work over motherhood (while the "lower" races and immigrants bred rapidly). Arthur Calhoun argued that to the working woman "children are an embarrassment and interfere with a career, hence the tendency to avoid maternity"; Theodore Roosevelt branded her a "criminal against the race" (Calhoun 1917–19, 252). Not only was the working mother unsexing herself by contact with the coarse world of the public sphere, but she was committing political treason by abandoning her role as mother of the future defenders of the nation.

Against such illogic, unions slowly began to accept and organize women. Women's massive participation in the labor force during World War II boosted their efforts to be recognized as workers. Both the United Electrical Workers (UEW) and the United Auto Workers (UAW) encouraged the unionization of women workers in defense plants as well as in non-defense-related industries. For some, the effort was strictly pragmatic. "There are thousands and thousands of women being introduced into our industries," UEW president Albert Fitzgerald said in 1942. "If we do not encourage women to come into the organization, think what this will mean. After the war, you will have a group of unorganized women working in the factories taking your jobs and your living away from you" (cited in Milkman 1987, 87–89). But others were sincere. "Sisters, I know we have made some mistakes, dealing with you as you entered our industry and our union," confessed UAW president R. J. Thomas in 1944. "But we want, we need more women leaders" (cited in ibid., 89). At the war's end, however, women were again pushed out of these occupations as men returned home and were reintegrated into the work world. The ideology of domesticity was restated; raising children and housekeeping in the growing suburbs would provide women's fulfillment. It was in response to this re-creation of "the feminine mystique" that the modern feminist movement first took shape in the early 1960s.

Women Enter the Professions

Women attempting to enter the professions confronted arguments that they could not be adequately trained, that they would not be competent and reliable professionals after training, and that it was immoral for women to enter professional life and abandon their domestic role anyway. Against this, the Reverend C. C. Foote, for example, supported women's right to preach the gospel. That right "no human power can bequeath nor abridge," he wrote in "Woman's Rights and Duties" (1849, 68), since women had been priestesses in biblical times. Ordination would simply *restore* to women a right that formerly had been theirs. Four years later, the Reverend Luther Lee ordained Antoinette L. Brown (later married to Samuel Blackwell, brother of Henry Brown Blackwell), the first woman minister in the United States. "We are not here to make a minister," he argued in his sermon* to the Congregational Church of South Butler, New York. "It is not to confer on this our sister, a right to preach the gospel. If she has not that right already, we have no power to communicate it to her." Lee only acknowledged Brown's calling. Several prominent suffragists, including Lucretia Mott and Angelina and Sarah Grimké, were also ministers.

Women's entry into the health professions proved difficult. Before the Civil War, few medical schools would admit women. One exception was the Female Medical College of Pennsylvania, which graduated its first class in 1851, only two years after Elizabeth Blackwell graduated from the Geneva Medical College and became the nation's first female M.D. In the Female Medical College's first valedictory address,* Professor Joseph Longshore warned the students of the obstacles they would encounter: "Where men and women are engaged in the same vocations, and the labors are equal, and the products of their toil the same, the compensation of the latter seldom exceeds one half that of the former. Thus the profits of the employer are doubly enhanced by woman's incessant exertions for an honest and virtuous livelihood." Longshore knew something about these dual-career families. His brother Thomas, a physician who also taught at the college, had married Hannah E. Myers, a student in that first class, and they practiced medicine together for their entire careers.

Despite the removal of formal barriers, women still found it difficult to enter medicine. One problem was the "unreasonable" preference of the great majority of people of both sexes for a "mediocre man doctor to a first rate woman doctor," as Richard Cabot (1915) put it. To gain acceptance, women and their male supporters used a variety of rhetorical strategies. When anti-feminists argued that women were more fragile and could not handle the physical or intellectual rigor of medical training, pro-feminists pointed out that women's natural predisposition toward morality would enhance their work as healers. Women's "sympathy with suffering, their quickness of perception, and the aptitude for the duties of the sick room, render them peculiarly adapted for the ministrations of the healing art," argued Boston physician Samuel Gregory (1862, 243).

Other men argued that, if, indeed, women were not men's equals, those who wished to study medicine and had received appropriate training must truly be extraordinarily gifted and dedicated. "A woman who feels an irresistible impulse to study medicine, so strong as to overcome her natural timidity, or to be willing to take the obloquy and covert, if not overt, insults from the world in general, and very often her own family and friends in particular—she will make a better doctor than a stupid lout, of whom, being found good for nothing, his father makes either a minister or a doctor," wrote Dr. A. K. Gardner (1870). Still others asserted women's natural equality as evidence of their equal right to practice the science of medicine. "I am quite sure that there is no risk of lowering the intellectual standard of medical education if women and men study together," argued Dr. Charles Folsom (1872), as the medical school at the Johns Hopkins University became the first to open its doors to women and men together (SL MC-378). The celebrated Baltimore theologian, James Cardinal Gibbons, also spoke* at the opening of the school.

As in medical school, so too in the other professions. The law was closed to women until 1869, when Arabella Mansfield, self-taught and apprenticed, was admitted to practice in Iowa, and Phoebe Couzins and Lemma Barkaloo entered the first coeducational class at Washington University's law school. One year later, Ada Kepley graduated from the Law Department at the University of Chicago, after studying in her husband's law office. (She and her husband led the campaign to allow women to practice law in Illinois.)

Henry Noble MacCracken, chancellor of the City University of New York (prior to accepting Vassar's presidency in 1915), argued that the City University should open its law schools to women. In a column in the *New York Times* (11 March 1894), MacCracken supported legal education as a responsibility of the college. Since women can already practice law, he argued, he "did not think it fair . . . to keep them from a legal education." In "Why Many Women Should Study Law,"* William T. Harris argued that women lawyers would develop sharper and more inquisitive minds without sacrificing any of their femininity. Turning anti-feminist arguments on their heads, Harris claimed that women *were* temperamentally less fit for law. "Sentiment and impulse predominate those [women] rather than cold investigation of the forms of justice which protect society as a whole. An interest in legal studies is less likely to be a feminine than a masculine trait." But that was the reason, he argued, "one would say that the study of law is desirable on the part of many women."

Though the struggles for professional recognition continued through the century, feminist women and their male allies had found a justification for women's equality in the economic sphere. Women's natural equality predisposed them toward whatever they desired, and the changes in modern society had made women's sphere almost as unattractive to women as it was to men. This is well expressed in a letter that social psychologist George Herbert Mead wrote to his daughter-in-law* in 1920 as she faced the difficult decision about her career. "Being a wife and a mother [is] no longer a calling in itself, because the exercise of intelligence in those activities has passed out of the home and involves scientific method at every point. You must be a part of this intellectual world to which this method belongs," he wrote.

To many pro-feminist men, equality depended on the opening of the economic arena to allow woman to develop her equal capacities. It was not for women alone but for the benefit of humanity. We might extend the argument of Dr. S. Adolphus Knopf, who concluded an article about women doctors by saying, "This is not the age of either man or woman alone; let us work side by side with our sisters in medicine, open the doors of all the medical schools to women and give them equal opportunity, and they will do their share in advancing medical science, alleviating distress and suffering, sharing in social service as they are sharing nobly in other fields of human activity" (Knopf 1915, 160).

WOMEN'S ECONOMIC INDEPENDENCE

"THE PROPERTY RIGHTS OF WIDOWS"

Robert Dale Owen (1851)

No subject of greater importance has come up since we met here, as next in estimation to the right of enjoying life and liberty, our Constitution enumerates the right of acquiring, possessing, protecting property. And these sections refer to the latter right, heretofore declared to be natural, inherent, inalienable, yet virtually withheld from one-half the citizens of our State. Women are not represented in our legislative halls; they have no voice in selecting those who make laws and constitutions for them; and one reason given for excluding women from the right of suffrage, is an expression of confident belief that their husbands and fathers will surely guard their interests. I should like, for the honor of my sex, to believe that the legal rights of women are, at all times, as zealously guarded as they would be if women had votes to give to those who watch over their interests.

Suffer me, sir, in defense of my skepticism on this point, to lay before you and this Convention, an item from my legislative recollection.

It will be thirteen years next winter, since I reported from a seat just over the way, a change in the then existing law of descent. At that time the widow of an intestate dying without children, was entitled, under ordinary circumstances, to dower in her husband's real estate, and one-third of his personal property. The change proposed was to give her one-third of the real estate of her husband absolutely, and two-thirds of his personal property—far too little, indeed; but yet as great an innovation as we thought we could carry. This law remained in force until 1841. How stands it now? The widow of an intestate, in case there be no children, and in case there be father, or mother, or brother,

---

Reprinted in HWS, *vol. 1.*

or sister of the husband, is heir to no part whatever of her deceased husband's real estate; she is entitled to dower only, of one-third of his estate. I ask you whether your hearts do not revolt at the idea, that when the husband is carried to his long home, his widow shall see snatched from her, by an inhuman law, the very property her watchful care had mainly contributed to increase and keep together?

Yet this idea, revolting as it is, is carried out in all its unmitigated rigor, by the statute to which I have just referred. Out of a yearly rental of a hundred and fifty dollars, the widow of an intestate rarely becomes entitled to more than fifty. The other hundred dollars goes—whither? To the husband's father or mother? Yes, if they survive! But if they are dead, what then? A brother-in-law or a sister-in-law takes it, or the husband's uncle, or his aunt, or his cousin! Do husbands toil through a life-time to support their aunts, and uncles, and cousins? If but a single cousin's child, a babe of six months, survive, to that infant goes a hundred dollars of the rental, and to the widow fifty. Can injustice go beyond this? What think you of a law like that, on the statute book of a civilized and a Christian land? When the husband's sustaining arm is laid in the grave, and the widow left without a husband to cherish, then comes the law more cruel than death, and decrees that poverty shall be added to desolation!

Say, delegates of the people of Indiana, answer and say whether you, whether those who sent you here are guiltless in this thing? Have you done justice? Have you loved mercy?

But let us turn to the question more immediately before us. Let us pass from the case of the widow and look to that of the wife: First, the husband becomes entitled, from the instant of marriage, to all the goods and chattels of his wife. His right is absolute, unconditional. Secondly, the husband acquires, in virtue of the marriage, the rents and profits (in all cases during her life) of his wife's real estate. The flagrant injustice of this has been somewhat modified by a statute barring the marital right to the rent of lands, but this protection does not extend to personal property. Is this as it should be? Are we meting out fair and equal justice? . . . There is a species of very silly sentimentalism which it is the fashion to put forth in after-dinner toasts and other equally veracious forms, about woman being the only tyrant in a free republic; about the chains she imposes on her willing slaves, etc.; it would be much more to our credit, if we would administer a little less flattery and a little more justice. . . .

"HOW LONG SHALL WE ROB AND ENSLAVE WOMEN?"

William I. Bowditch (1885)

Every now and then we are shocked to hear of some great and successful robbery, some enormous defalcation, or some flagrant breach of trust.

But so long as our laws systematically rob women, and our courts aid in the theft, is there any cause for wonder? If men can rightly steal millions in one way, why may they not rightly enough steal millions in other ways? . . .

The governor's salary is paid partly out of money stolen from women! When our legislators appropriate money to pay their salaries, part of the money so appropriated will have been stolen from women! Even our judges are not free from this contamination. If one of them were found guilty of receiving stolen goods knowing them to be stolen, we should forthwith remove him from office, either by impeachment or address; and that man would remain black-marked for the rest of his life, and would be deemed forever incapable of holding any office of trust, honor, or emolument.

And yet every quarter day when our judges go up to the State House to receive payment of their salaries, part of the money which they receive was really stolen from women! That is, our judges are really receivers of stolen goods! But, nevertheless, nothing is or can be done, as matters now stand, about this great scandal, for it would be impossible to find within the limits of the Commonwealth a single man, whether in office or out of office, from the governor downwards who's not guilty of substantially the same offence.

It seems to me, if I were a judge that I could never forget the words of Lord Camden. It would be impossible for me ever to sentence a petty thief to the House of Correction without agitation of mind, for peradventure, the culprit might be bold enough to retort to me from the dock: "Does not your honor receive stolen goods?" The officers of the court would no doubt be able to suppress his voice, but how could I hope to silence the voice of my own conscience? We are told that Falstaff's companions could "steal anything and call it purchase" We Massachusetts men can steal millions, but we call it just taxation! . . .

In anti-slavery days, it was not an uncommon thing for a slave-hunter, after spotting his victim, to begin operations by complaining of him as a thief, and getting a warrant for his arrest, because he had stolen his own clothing, and having once got the victim safely in jail as a thief, and without public disturbance, the complaint on which the arrest was made was dropped, and the jailer was deputed to act as agent for the owner to hold a runaway slave. Of course, legally speaking, the clothing of a slave belonged to the master as much as his body. Do you ask

---

From The Woman's Journal, *1885. (Copy in EI, Bowditch Family Papers)*

what has this story to do with women in Massachusetts?

I answer: A few years since, a married woman in Massachusetts who earned wages agreed with her husband, who also earned wages, to form a common fund for the use of both, and the fund was accordingly so formed and placed in the husband's hands for safety and for mutual use. Afterwards, with the consent of her husband, she took part of this common fund to buy some clothing for herself, and our court, after solemn argument, decided that this clothing, which could only be used by a woman, belonged to the husband! (119, Mass. 596, 1876.)

If I had been this woman, I should have felt as if I really were a slave, even though on Massachusetts soil! She did not legally own the very shoes and stockings on her feet, any more than the slave in Leverett Street Jail owned the jacket on his back! This was the law in Massachusetts down to 1879, and would have been the law today, had it not been for the persistent efforts of woman suffragists. It is still the law in Ohio! (State vs. Clara Hepin) and no doubt in other States also. It took us three years' struggle before we could change the law in Massachusetts. (Stat. 1879, chap. 133.) . . .

. . . For husbands and wives cannot legally contract with each other, and they cannot legally testify as to private conversations with each other. All other men and women may contract with each other just as they please, all other men and women may testify as to private conversations with each other, but husbands and wives cannot do either of these things. Even criminals may testify in their own behalf, but under laws framed by men alone, and to which no woman has ever consented, a wife cannot testify as to what sort of an agreement her husband has made with her in private conversation, and the agreement itself is worthless.

So that all a husband in Massachusetts has got to do when he wishes to cheat his wife out of her property, is to make a contract with her in private, without other witnesses present, and then he may keep her money for his own use, although she has given it to him to invest for her benefit and he has promised her so to do! You will find reported in our law-books several cases where the wife has thus been stripped of her money, solely in consequence of these laws, which are really a legacy from the times when women were simply slaves, and which continue a sort of slavery even to this day.

In former days, at the South, it was no crime to seduce a slave woman, for she was a chattel personal, for all purposes whatsoever, and to the everlasting shame and disgrace of the men of Massachusetts, it is no crime here to seduce a woman!

Who can say with truth that women in Massachusetts are free as men are free?

And if a majority of the people of the State are not free, have we really a republican form of government in Massachusetts? And yet the son of the man who voted for the fugitive slave bill, and the successor of the clergyman who thought the mission of the Unitarians in reference to slavery should be silence, and other men like them, are opposed to enfranchising women! . . .

"A LETTER TO HIS DAUGHTER-IN-LAW"

George Herbert Mead (1920)

. . . A WOMAN AS WELL AS A MAN should have the training for a social calling apart from the family life, this for the sake of the best family life but principally for the independence of mind and self which every one legitimately craves. The training cannot naturally be put off in the case of a woman any more than in that of a man beyond the years within which such professional training is normally given. On the other hand these are the years within which you will naturally bear children, so that the training will have to be taken more slowly, but there is nothing in the family life nor in the training which detracts from either. The intellectual interest you will have in study will make you a finer woman and therefore a better mother and wife, and while the care of children will reduce the amount of time you can give to training, it will also give you a feeling for all the social values which give their meaning to professional activities. Society is not organized for this now, but the fortunate situation in which you and Henry find yourselves makes this more normal expression for a woman possible for you. If you have the will and the courage you can have both the social independence which comes with competence in some real social function, together with the breadth of view and the capacity to criticize life and the living of it—what Thomas calls the man's intellectual world into which woman as yet so seldom enters—and as well, the family life which should be yours in these years.

Hoffman's views on medicine are absurd—they arise as you indicate from the fact that he would rather do research work than practice medicine. What he says about medicine as the mere application of various pure sciences to practice, is true of all forms of engineering, of teaching, of every practical calling for which any man or woman wishes to fit himself or herself. If you have the impulse for research work only practical necessity would take you into practical medicine, but if either the practice of medicine or the various activities which are open to women who have had a medical training or even the capacity to understand the meaning of hygiene in its widest sense, i.e. in its bearing on the relations of men and women, on the birth and bringing up of children, on the very varied social problems of vice and crime, and on normal social life in its dependence on health and disease, are your interests, training for medicine is the natural training—for you need the method and clinical experience to raise you above the amateur, and to give you both the capacity and the standpoint that your interest demands. What Hoffman recommends is for

---

28 August 1920. Reprinted in "George Herbert Mead's Ideas on Women and Careers: A Letter to His Daughter-in-Law, 1920," by Steven J. Diner. Signs: Journal of Women in Culture and Society *4, no. 2 (1978): 407–9.*

you a sort of scientific culture, which would leave you in the class of those who appreciate but have no competent reaction nor independence of judgment. For the fullest normal development, an individual must be able to act competently—to have the method which intelligence demands, in some social field. If he does, his conduct in this field brings him into real relations with the rest of life.

It is a difficult thing you are undertaking but worthwhile things are all difficult. Being a wife and a mother is no longer a calling in itself, because the exercise of intelligence in those activities has passed out of the home and involves scientific method at every point. You must be a part of this intellectual world to which this method belongs, or you must accept the judgments of others without feeling competent to criticize them. Do not let the dependence on others which we all have for those whom we love carry with it intellectual dependence and you cannot have real intellectual independence, that which gives one the fundamental self respect on which one builds, without competence in some field of the society which is responsible for the very existence of ourselves. Cultural training never gives this—only training for a practical end. In this large sense, research is one of the most practical callings there is. Of course medicine is only one of the callings, and a difficult one, but it is the one that touches most intelligently the questions and interests in which you are most concerned. But if it isn't medicine it should be some other definite technique toward which your training should be directed. . . .

WOMEN IN THE TRADES

"WOMAN AND WORK"

Horace Greeley (1852)

WHETHER WOMEN should or should not be permitted to vote, to hold office, to serve on juries, and to officiate as lawyers, doctors, or divines, are questions about which a diversity of opinions is likely long to exist. But that the current rates of remuneration for woman's work are entirely, unjustly inadequate, is a proposition which needs only to be considered to insure its hearty acceptance by every intelligent, justice-loving human being. Consider a few facts:

Every able-bodied man inured to labor, though of the rudest sort, who steps on shore in America from Europe, is worth a dollar per day, and can readily command it. Though he only knows how to wield such rude, clumsy implements as the pick and spade, there are dozens of places where his services are in request at a dollar per day the year through, and he can even be transported hence to the place where his services are wanted, on the strength of his contract to work and the credit of his future earnings. We do not say this is the case every day in the year, for it may not be at this most inclement and forbidding season; but it is the general fact, as every one knows. And any careful, intelligent, resolute male laborer is morally certain to rise out of the condition of a mere shoveler, into a position where the work is lighter and the pay better after a year or two of faithful service.

But the sister of this same faithful worker, equally careful, intelligent, and willing to do anything honest and reputable for a living, finds no such changes proffered her. No agent meets her on the dock to persuade her to accept a passage to Illinois or Upper Canada, there to be employed on fair work at a dollar per day and expectations. On the contrary, she may think herself fortunate if a week's search opens to her a place where by the devotion of all her waking hours she can earn five to six dollars per month, with a chance of its increase, after several years' faithful service, to seven or eight dollars at most.

The brother is in many respects the equal of his employer; may sit down beside him at the hotel where they both stop for dinner; their votes may balance each other at any election; the laborer lives with those whose company suits him, and needs no character from his last place to secure him employment or a new job when he gets tired of the old one. But the sister never passes out of

---

New York Tribune. [*1852.*] *Reprinted in* HWS, *vol. 1.*

the atmosphere of caste—of conscious and galling inferiority to those with whom her days must be spent. There is no election day in *her* year, and but the ghost of a Fourth of July. She must live not with those she likes, but with those who want her; she is not always safe from libertine insult in what serves her for a home; she knows no ten-hour rule, and would not dare to claim its protection if one were enacted. Though not a slave by law, she is too often as near it in practice as one legally free can be.

Now this disparity between the rewards of man's and woman's labor at the base of the social edifice, is carried up to its very pinnacle. Of a brother and sister equally qualified and effective as teachers, the brother will receive twice as much compensation as the sister. The mistress who conducts the rural district school in summer, usually receives less than half the monthly stipend that her brother does for teaching that same school in winter, when time and work are far less valuable; and here there can be no pretence of a disparity in capacity justifying that in wages. Between male and female workers in the factories and mills, the same difference is enforced.

Who does not feel that this is intrinsically wrong? that the sister ought to have equal (not necessarily identical) opportunities with the brother—should be as well taught, industrially as well as intellectually, and her compensation made to correspond with her capacity, upon a clear understanding of the fact that, though her muscular power is less than his, yet her dexterity and celerity of manipulation are greater?

Where does the wrong originate? Suppose that, by some inexorable law in the spirit of Hindoo caste, it were settled that negroes, regardless of personal capacity, could do nothing for a living but black boots, and that red-haired men were allowed to engage in no avocation except horse-currying; who does not perceive that though boot-blacking and horse-currying might be well and cheaply done, black-skinned and also red-haired men would have but a sorry chance for making a living? Who does not see that their wages, social standing, and means of securing independence, would be far inferior to those they now enjoy?

The one great cause, therefore, of the inadequate compensation and inferior position of woman, is the unjust apportionment of avocation. Man has taken the lion's share to himself, and allotted the residue to woman, telling her to take that and be content with it, if she don't want to be regarded as a forward, indelicate, presuming, unwomanly creature, who is evidently no better than she should be. And woman has come for the most part to accept the lot thus assigned her, with thankfulness, or, rather, without thought, just as the Mussulman's wife rejoices in her sense of propriety which will not permit her to show her face in the street, and the Brahmin widow immolates herself on the funeral pyre of her husband.

What is the appropriate remedy?

Primarily and mainly, a more rational and healthful public sentiment with regard to woman's work; a sentiment which shall welcome her to every employment wherein she may be useful and efficient without necessarily compromising her purity or overtasking her strength. Let her be encouraged to open a store, to work a garden, plant and tend an orchard, to learn any of the lighter mechanical trades, to study for a profession, whenever her circumstances and her tastes shall render any of these desirable. Let woman, and the advocates of justice to women, encourage and patronize her in whatever laudable pursuits she may thus undertake; let them give a preference to dry-goods stores wherein the clerks are mainly women; and so as to hotels where they wait at table, mechanics' shops in which they are extensively employed and fairly paid. Let the ablest of the sex be called to the lecture-room, to the temperance rostrum, etc.; and whenever a post-office falls vacant and a deserving woman is competent to fill and willing to take it, let her be appointed, as a very few have already been. There will always be some widow of a poor clergyman, doctor, lawyer, or other citizens prematurely cut off, who will be found qualified for and glad to accept such a post if others will suggest her name and procure her appointment. Thus abstracting more and more of the competent and energetic from the restricted sphere wherein they now struggle with their sister for a meager and precarious subsistence, the greater mass of self-subsisting women will find the demand for their labor gradually increasing and its recompense proportionally enhancing. With a larger field and more decided usefulness will come a truer and deeper respect; and woman, no longer constrained to marry for a position, may always wait to marry worthily and in obedience to the dictates of sincere affection. Hence constancy, purity, mutual respect, a just independence and a little of happiness, may be reasonably anticipated.

"LETTER TO PAULINA W. DAVIS"

Horace Greeley (1852)

New York, Sept. 1, 1852.

MY FRIEND:—I have once or twice been urged to attend a Convention of the advocates of woman's rights; and though compliance has never been within my power, I have a right to infer that some friends of the cause desire suggestions from me with regard to the best means of advancing it. I therefore venture to submit some thoughts on that subject. To my mind the BREAD problem lies at the base of all the desirable and practical reforms which our age meditates. Not that bread is intrinsically more important to man than Temperance, Intelligence, Morality, and Religion, but that it is essential to the just appreciation of all these. Vainly do we preach the blessings of temperance to human beings cradled in hunger, and suffering at intervals the agonies of famine; idly do we commend intellectual culture to those whose minds are daily racked with the dark problem, "How shall we procure food for the morrow?" Morality, religion, are but words to him who fishes in the gutters for the means of sustaining life, and crouches behind barrels in the street for shelter from the cutting blasts of a winter's night.

Before all questions of intellectual training or political franchises for women, not to

---

Reprinted in HWS, *vol. 1.*

speak of such a trifle as costume, do I place the question of enlarged opportunities for work; of a more extended and diversified field of employment. The silk culture and manufacture firmly established and thriftily prosecuted to the extent of our home demand for silk, would be worth everything to American women. Our now feeble and infantile schools of design should be encouraged with the same view. A wider and more prosperous development of our Manufacturing Industry will increase the demand for female labor, thus enhancing its average reward and elevating the social position of woman. I trust the future has, therefore, much good in store for the less muscular half of the human race.

But the reform here anticipated should be inaugurated in our own households. I know how idle is the expectation of any general and permanent enhancement of the wages of any class or condition above the level of equation of Supply and Demand; yet it seems to me that the friends of woman's rights may wisely and worthily set the example of paying juster prices for female assistance in their households than those now current. If they would but resolve never to pay a capable, efficient woman less than two-thirds the wages paid to a vigorous, effective man employed in some corresponding vocation, they would very essentially aid the movement now in progress for the general recognition and conception of Equal Rights to Woman.

Society is clearly unjust to woman in according her but four to eight dollars per month for labor equally repugnant with, and more protracted than that of men of equal intelligence and relative efficiency, whose services command from ten to twenty dollars per month. If, then, the friends of Woman's Rights could set the world an example of paying for female service, not the lowest pittance which stern Necessity may compel the defenceless to accept, but as approximately fair and liberal compensation for the work actually done, as determined by a careful comparison with the recompense of other labor. I believe they would give their cause an impulse which could not be permanently resisted.

"A UNION'S POSITION"

William H. Sylvis (1872)

. . . THE SUBJECT of female labor is one that demands our attention and most earnest consideration. There are many reasons why females should not labor outside of the domestic circle. Being forced into the field, the factory, and the workshop, (and they do not go there from choice, but because necessity compels them), they come in direct competition with men in the great field of labor; and being compelled of necessity, from their defenceless condition, to work for low wages, they exercise a vast influence over the price of labor in almost every department. If they received the same wages that men do for similar work, this objection would in a great measure disappear. But there is another reason, founded upon moral principle and common humanity, far above and beyond this, why they should not be thus employed. Woman was created and intended to be man's companion, not his slave. Endowed as she is with all her loveliness and powers to please, she exercises an almost unlimited influence over the more stern and unbending disposition of man's nature. If there are reasons why man should be educated, there are many more and stronger reasons why woman should receive the soundest and most practical mental and moral training. She was created to be the presiding deity of the home circle, the instructor of our children, to guide the tottering footsteps of tender infancy in the paths of rectitude and virtue, to smooth down the wrinkles of our perverse nature, to weep over our shortcomings, and make us glad in the days of adversity, to counsel, comfort, and console us in our declining years.

"Woman's warm heart and gentle hand,
in God's eternal plan,
Were formed to soften, soothe, refine,
exalt, and comfort man."

Who is there among us that does not know and has not felt the powerful influences of a good and noble woman? one in whom, after the busy toil and care of the day are past, we can confide our little secrets and consult upon the great issues of life. These sir, are my views upon this question. This I believe to be the true and divine mission of woman, this her proper sphere; and those men who would and do turn her from it are the worst enemies of our race, the Shylocks of the age, the robbers of woman's virtue; they make commerce of the blood and tears of helpless women, and merchandise of souls. In the poverty, wretchedness, and utter ruin of their helpless victims, they see nothing but an accumulating pile of gold. In the weeping and wailing of the distressed, they hear nothing but a "metallic ring." To the abolition of this wrong imposed upon the tender sex should be devoted every attribute of our nature, every impulse of our heart, and every energy and ability with which we are endowed. . . .

From Life, Speeches, Labors and Essays of William H. Sylvis, *ed. James C. Sylvis. Philadelphia: Claxton, Remsen & Haffelfinger, 1872.*

"THE INDUSTRIAL EMANCIPATION OF WOMEN"

Carrol D. Wright (1893)

UNTIL WITHIN a comparatively recent period, woman's subjection to man has been well-nigh complete in all respects, whether such subjection is considered from a social, political, intellectual or even a physical point of view. At first the property of man, she emerged under civilization from the sphere of a drudge to that of a social factor and, consequently, into the liberty of cultivating her mental faculties. . . .

Industrial emancipation, using the term broadly, means the highest type of woman as the result, the word "industrial" comprehending in this sense all remunerative employment. The entrance of woman into the industrial field was assured when the factory system of labor displaced the domestic or hand labor system. The age of invention, with the wonderful ramifications which invention always has produced, must be held accountable for bringing woman into a field entirely unknown to her prior to that age. As an economic factor, either in art, literature or industry, she was before that time hardly recognizable. With the establishment of the factory system, the desire of woman to have something more than she could earn as a domestic or in agricultural labor, or to earn something where before she had earned nothing, resulted in her becoming an economic factor, and she was obliged to submit to all the conditions of this new position. It hardly can be said that in the lower forms of industrial pursuits she superseded man, but it is true that she supplemented his labors. . . .

Each step in industrial progress has raised her in the scale of civilization rather than degraded her. As a result she has constantly gone up higher and gained intellectual advantages, such as the opening to her of the higher institutions of learning, which have in turn equipped her for the best professional employment. The moral plane of the so-called workingwoman certainly is higher than that of the woman engaged in domestic service, and is equal to that of any class of women in the community. . . .

As women have occupied the positions of bookkeepers, telegraphers and many of what might be called semi-professional callings, men have entered engineering, electrical, mechanical and other spheres of work which were not known when women first stepped into the industrial field. As the latter have progressed from entire want of employment to that which pays a few dollars per week, men, too, have progressed in their employments, and occupied larger fields not existing before. . . .

Woman is now stepping out of industrial subjection and coming into the industrial system of the present as an entirely new

---

Speech presented to the National American Woman Suffrage Association Convention, Washington, D.C., 16–19 January 1893. Reprinted in HWS, *vol. 4.*

economic factor. If there were no other reasons, this alone would be sufficient to make her wages low and prevent their very rapid increase. . . . The growing importance of woman's labor, her general equipment through technical education, her more positive dedication to the life-work she chooses, the growing sentiment that an educated and skilful woman is a better and truer companion in marriage than an ignorant and unskilful one, her appreciation of the value of organization, the general uplifting of the principle of integrity in business circles, woman's gradual approach to man's powers in mental achievement also, her possible and probable political influence—all these combined, working along general avenues of progress and evolution, will bring her industrial emancipation, by which she will stand on an equality with man in those callings in life for which she may be fitted. As she approaches this equality her remuneration will be increased and her economic importance acknowledged. . . .

If woman's industrial emancipation leads to what many are pleased to call "political rights," we must not quarrel with it. It is not just that all other advantages which may come through this emancipation shall be withheld simply because one great privilege on which there is a division of sentiment may also come.

One of the greatest boons which will result from the industrial emancipation of woman will be the frank admission on the part of the true and chivalric man that she is the sole and rightful owner of her own being in every respect, and that whatever companionship may exist between her and man shall be as thoroughly honorable to her as to him.

"BREAD AND ROSES"

James Oppenheim and Caroline Kohlsaat (1912)

As we come marching, marching, in the beauty of the day,
A million darkened kitchens, a thousand mill lofts gray,
Are touched with all the radiance that a sudden sun discloses,
For the people hear us singing, "Bread and Roses, Bread and Roses."

As we come marching, marching, we battle too, for men,
For they are women's children and we mother them again.
Our lives shall not be sweated from birth until life closes.
Hearts starve as well as bodies:
Give us bread, but give us roses.

As we come marching, marching, unnumbered women dead
Go crying through our singing their ancient song of bread.
Small art and love and beauty their drudging spirits knew.
Yes, it is bread that we fight for,
But we fight for roses, too.

As we come marching, marching, we bring the Greater Days,
The rising of the women means the rising of the race.
No more the drudge and idler, ten that toil where one reposes,
But a sharing of life's glories,
Bread and Roses, Bread and Roses.

Reprinted in Rise Up Singing. *Edited by Peter Blood-Patterson. Bethlehem, Pa.: Sing Out, 1988.*

"THE 'PROTECTED SEX' IN INDUSTRY"

George Creel (1915)

In the United States today, nine million women are engaged in gainful occupations. They breathe the humid, lint-filled air of the cotton mills, watch needles that set 3,000 stitches a minute, scrub floors of office buildings from midnight to daybreak, creep on bruised knees across cranberry bogs, faint from nausea in the canneries, sew incredible hours in the squalor of tenements, toil in the heat of steam laundries, tear their fingers in the oyster shucking beds, strain their eyes in the silk mills, race through long days in department stores and roll cigars in filthy basements.

Yet the cry of these drudges of the world for a voice in the fixing of the laws that govern their industrial status is met by the incredible hypocrisy that *"woman's place is the home."*

These women receive less pay than men, they labor longer hours than men, they are subjected to fire hazards and health hazards that are not tolerated by men, and as if these were not disadvantages enough, they are called upon to endure a host of economic, political and legal disabilities inherited from a time when man supported his women folk.

Yet in the face of these grim facts there is a persistence in the amazing assumption that the American woman is an uncrowned queen who walks in ways of ease and beauty, guarded from the rougher airs by some uncrowned king whose one object in life is to minister to her slightest desire.

These cruelties and indifferences are due to omission, not commission. It is not that men have passed discriminatory laws deliberately, but that they have failed to pass laws made necessary by social upheaval that has thrown women out of the home into industry. The reason for it is a vanity that would be monstrous were it not so unconscious.

The average man laments the passing of the feudal state. He resents the fact that women *are* at work, and the more generous his instincts the greater his resentment. Out of the centuries during which his woman waited at home for him to return with the fruits of his forage, there grew a very definite protective sense, and it is this large and pleasurable feeling that the working woman *undermines.* Therefore he has tried to ignore her as much as possible, by way of conserving his vanity, and has redoubled his protective tenderness to those who have least need of it.

It is indeed true that the American man spoils his women by too much coddling, yet the slightest investigation soon develops that this manufacture of Noras is confined to houses of ease and comfort. Up to date the *working* woman has not been called upon to protest against being treated as a doll.

Plain enough for those who run to read, it

Harper's Weekly *40 (8 May 1915).*

stands proved that laws for the protection of the female worker now wait upon disaster and exposure, and that even when a shocked public opinion forces reforms, it is only a question of time when secret greed will attempt to nullify them.

The Triangle factory disaster, in which 147 girls lost their lives, was followed promptly enough by remedial legislation. The 1912 investigation into cannery conditions in New York, which proved that women had been working 117 hours a week, was also answered by laws designed to prevent a recurrence of this savagery. Yet the owner of the Triangle factory was never punished, and within the year he was arrested for locking the doors on 150 girls, and permitted to escape this second time with a nominal fine of $20. Nor is it less significant that these spring months have witnessed a concerted attempt to have the New York Legislature repeal the essential features of those laws which were passed in consequence of the Triangle disaster and the cannery horrors.

It is only in the states where the women have the vote to protect themselves that there is adequate comprehension of the necessity for guarding the mother sex against the poison of fatigue. Colorado, California, Washington and Arizona have decreed an eight hour day for the working woman, and Utah and Idaho have the nine hour day. The nearest approach to this humanity is a nine hour day for women, in four non-suffrage states, and the case of Massachusetts is admirably illustrative of the cautious manner in which the male voter approaches the problem.

There are 50,000 manufacturing establishments in Massachusetts, yet the total inspecting force is twenty-four. Although there are over 200,000 women and children at work in these factories, only four of the inspectors are women. Unlike the equal suffrage states, where all working women are included in the law, the Massachusetts statute excludes practically all women except those in factories and mills.

In the South, where chivalry still retains its ancient place and lustre, the working day for women is eleven and twelve hours in the mills and factories; in New Jersey the cranberry bogs feel the creeping knees of women and children from dawn to dark; in New York the machines of the tenements drive night and day, and in Pennsylvania the industrial conditions have changed but slightly since the not long distant time when half-naked women toiled tremendously in the hot glare of the blast furnaces.

Can anyone have forgotten the recent investigations into the conditions of department store employees, or the long discussions in the daily press as to whether $5 or $8 a week was a "living wage?" Surely the heart of chivalry must have throbbed with high pride to read the stories of underpaid drudgery, disregarded health and superhuman effort to safeguard character and chastity against the demoralizing effects of involuntary poverty.

As an instance of the manner in which the chivalric instinct finds expression where the working woman is concerned, the case of a Paterson manufacturer by the name of Straus may be mentioned. Mr. Straus felt that the happiness of his workers proceeded from their own weak submission to the grosser appetites. In various talks to the women he told them that they would "be all right" if they would only practice greater economy in their homes, for with his own eyes he had noticed that many things were thrown into the garbage can that could have been used to keep down the high cost of living. Among other things he noted that many of the girls did not eat all of the five cents worth of soup at the luncheon hour, and his suggestion was to the effect that two girls should contribute to the purchase of the pail, thereby saving two and a half cents.

Colorado, Washington, Oregon, Utah and California, of the equal suffrage states, have already enacted splendid minimum wage legislation with reference to women, while only four of the non-suffrage states have displayed a similar interest. In California, Washington, and Oregon, the voting woman has created welfare commissions empowered to explore all the dark corners of industry in order that old cruelties may be cleaned out, and room made for new justices.

Child labor is a rotting evil that even its paid apologists are compelled to gloss over with lies. Every equal suffrage state has a law forbidding the employment of children under fourteen, while in Georgia, South Carolina, Alabama, Mississippi (boys only) and New Mexico, little ones of twelve are permitted to drudge ten and even eleven hours a day. Let it be remembered that the child labor evil is a *woman* evil as well, for the girls, unless sent to the grave by exhaustion, must be regarded as the mothers of the future. . . .

There are few, even among men, who will deny that women teachers are as efficient as men, yet the fact remains that it is only in the equal suffrage states that equal pay for the same work is the rule. In Massachusetts, for instance, the average pay of the male teacher is three times that of the woman. In New York it took six years of fighting for the teachers to get an equal pay law, and it was the bitter experience of those years that made an ardent equal suffragist of Miss Grace Strachan, leader of the teachers. . . .

In the federal employment, four [wo]men pass the civil service examinations to three men, yet appointments are made in the ratio of two men to one woman. It is also the case that men are paid more than women for the same work.

In New York, a wife is not entitled to her own earnings when she works with her husband, or even if she works in his store or factory. According to a man's law, the joint earnings of a husband and wife belong to the husband, the wife acquiring no legal interest whatever in the product of their joint efforts.

In some non-suffrage states it is still the law that the husband may check out his wife's savings, and in many others the working mother has no rights in the earnings of a minor child, the commonwealth viewing them as the perquisites of the father.

It is a record of injustice that could be continued indefinitely, for only in the states where women have the vote do the statute books contain full measure of protection for the woman who is compelled to match her strength with man in the economic struggle. Intelligence points out the inevitableness of this fact, for even did a very perfection of the social sense urge men to legislate in behalf of the woman worker, he could still be without proper comprehension of her needs and desires.

It is when one compares these neglects with the tender solicitude shown to the working *man* that the true power of the ballot is fully realized. There is a federal law limiting the hours of labor in public employment to eight per day, an enactment that safeguards the thousands of letter-carriers, mail clerks, department employees and construction laborers. Twenty states have similar laws with respect to public employment, practically all of them specificially designed to protect the adult male worker.

Private employment of *men* in industry is also limited to eight hours a day as follows: in mines, twelve states; in smelters, eight states; in railroad labor, twenty-four states; telegraph or telephone operators engaged in handling trains, eighteen states; street car service, ten states; bakeries, brickyards, cement and plaster mills and drug clerks, one state each. Counted up there are sixty-five separate and distinct laws in the United States for the protection of the voting male against overwork.

Are there any fatuous enough to imagine that these laws would have been secured by the working man had he not been possessed of the ballot? The whole record of industrial reform is a story of bitter and continuous struggle, and success after many defeats. Mark the present progress of such an admittedly wise and humane measure as Workmen's Compensation! In eight states, the old common law defenses of "fellow servant" and "assumed risk" are still on the statute books, and in seventeen states their abrogation applies only to railroads. Even with the ballot in their hands, even with all the power of state and national organizations behind them, the fight of the male worker for justice is not yet won. How may women, unorganized for the most part, and burdened by prejudices carried down from a feudal society, be expected to make her fight for better conditions unless given the vote?

In view of the millions who are drudging for existence, equal suffrage cannot be put aside as a mere political question. It is a demand upon justice and humanity. In no sense can it be viewed as a capricious desire of Noras for a greater freedom, a larger field, a more expansive environment. It is a hunger cry, a child cry, a cry of distress and despair.

It is true that these millions work and suffer and die in seeming helplessness, but in money and tears they take heavy toll of the society that refuses them succor. Their slum homes foster disease, their rickety children fill the jails, asylums and hospitals, and out of it all comes a vast discontent that saps the foundations of our free institutions.

If the humanities mean nothing to us, if chivalry is a meaningless word and justice a joke, surely every instinct of social *self-preservation* should lead us to give the working woman a chance to secure the protection that man has withheld.

"THE REBEL GIRL"

Joe Hill (1915)

THERE ARE WOMEN of many descriptions
In this queer world, as everyone knows.
Some are living in beautiful mansions
And are wearing the finest of clothes.
There are blue-blooded queens and princesses
Who have charms made of diamonds and pearls:
But the only and thoroughbred Lady
Is the Rebel Girl.

Chorus
That's the Rebel Girl, That's The Rebel Girl,
To the working class she's a precious pearl.
She brings Courage, Pride and Joy
To the fighting Rebel Boy.
We've had girls before, But we need some more
In the Industrial Workers of the World
For it's great to fight for freedom with a Rebel Girl.

Yes, her hands may be hardened from labor,
And her dress may not be very fine:
But a heart in her bosom is beating,
Warm and true to her class and her kind.
And the grafters in terror are trembling
When her spite and defiance she'll hurl:
For the only and thoroughbred Lady
Is the Rebel Girl. *Chorus*

Reprinted in Songs of Struggle. *Chicago: Industrial Workers of the World, 1916.*

"WHAT ABOUT THE WOMAN WHO WORKS"

Industrial Workers of the World (1925)

WHAT ABOUT the woman who works? What message has Industrial Unionism for her?

The I.W.W. is the first and practically the only union which recognizes that a worker is a worker, without regard to sex. The members of the I.W.W. declare that a woman has exactly the same rights in the organization, pays the same dues, has the same duties, and is in every way an equal to the men members of the organization.

The I.W.W. stands ready to improve the lot of women as well as men, to abolish exploitation based on classes, to free workers from the rule of business men, and is necessarily making its appeal to the most exploited group of workers first, and expects to change their position most.

There is no group of workers more robbed and cheated than the women workers.

The Problem Is Urgent

The ills from which women suffer at the hands of property owners have lately so stirred the populace, that the governments of the world had to take notice of them. A Congress was held in Washington, D.C., January 11, 1923, to allow some of the indignant ones to express themselves, and to devise some ways and means of soothing them. At this congress a working woman scandalized the polite professionals and women property owners by declaring that women's affiliations are economic, that economic injustice injures all workers but hurts women workers the most. She said:

"We are more deeply concerned than the men with feeding, clothing and housing the world. We are not theorists. We know that we can not feed and clothe and house the children, we can not take them out of the factories into the schools, we can not warm our homes, on theories. We are realists. We are weary of the haggling, the debate, the theories of the masters of the world in the face of suffering and cold and hunger. The earth is rich in the means of life. We want bread and coal and the right to an education; we want our children in the schools and out of the factories; we want peace, not war. . . ."

There speaks the voice of six million women in the United States who work in the factories, the voice too of over six million more who teach school; act as nurses, stenographers, clerks, etc.

Women Must Work or Die

The time when women were the pets and slaves of individual men is long gone past. The time when girls needed no education, because all they had to do was to pick one

---

Chicago: Industrial Workers of the World, 1925.

of a troop of suitors, marry him, keep house for him and live on his wages, is gone forever, for the very simple reason that no woman can consistently live on a man's wages any more.

When the world began to produce goods on a large scale by machinery, about 150 years ago, the end to the dependence, and the support, of the wives of wage workers was in sight. The machines made work easy enough for women to do, and the owners of the machines promptly put down the wages until women had to do it. The more women were forced to work, the more workers there were, and the lower the wages could go, because the workers, both men and women, all wanted the jobs.

Look at it now: Dr. Clara P. Seippel, of Chicago, writing in the Monthly Labor Review, published by the U.S. Department of Labor, November 1921, states:

Always More Women Workers

"As manufacturing becomes more and more simplified through the invention of almost human machinery, and as each process becomes more and more highly specialized and divided, the opportunities for women increase rather than diminish.

"Woman is a permanent factor in industry and a factor of the greatest economic importance." The doctor might have added, "As the opportunities to use women increase, the boss will see to it that she is starved into the jobs," and history would support the statement.

Women Run Machines

Here is another example of the way women are being crowded into the factories and shops. The Monthly Labor Review reports that in a group of typical industries, in a typical manufacturing center, Rhode Island, the part of the working force that consisted of women was rather more than half.

In the rubber factories 42.6 per cent of the workers were women; in electrical manufacturing, 60.1 per cent women; jewelry, 48 per cent; paper boxes, 65 per cent; metal shops, 15.8 per cent; other manufacturers, 44.9 per cent; general merchandise, 60.8 per cent; in 5 & 10 cent stores, 88 per cent, and in laundries, 67.7 per cent.

In the textile industry most of the workers who tend the spinning machinery are girls, and so are many of the weavers.

That is the way it is all over the country. When the above survey was made by the government, these women workers on the average, did not earn as much as $15.50 per week the year around, a sum considered at that time necessary to support one person, give them food and clothing.

If you are interested, you can find in government figures many such reports, covering nearly the whole country. Just for another example, consider that in Kansas, in the fall of 1921, women wage earners (according to the government's own figures) got, two-fifths of them, no more than $9 per week, and one half of them less than $12 per week, at a time when a living wage was considered to be $16 per week.

Children Orphaned by Capitalism

What did these women do with such magnificent wages? Why, a good many of them supported children on the money! Is it any wonder then that the United States Children's Bureau in its Publication 102 (a government document) says: (reporting an investigation in the city of Chicago, 1922).

"The young children of wage-earning mothers are often inadequately cared for, or receive no care whatever during the day—many of the others were in very poor health, resulting apparently in some cases from undernourishment and overwork. . . . When the father was a member of the family group and was regularly employed, his wages in the greater number of cases were insufficient for the families' support. . . . One-third of the children of wage-earning mothers were below standard grade at school." (No wonder!)

Now there is the situation. Women are in the factories, the stores and the schools to stay. All workers need short hours and more pay, but women need them especially, because they are women, with different bodies from those of men, and because they have children to care for, and these children die like flies, grow up to be morally, mentally and physically crooked, grow up to be stunted wrecks, unfit and suffering, or, if by some cleverness on the mother's part they are saved this misery, they grow up to be cannon fodder, to be conscripted in the next war, and riddled with shrapnel, or with venereal diseases, sent home shell-shocked and gassed and mutilated.

The woman in industry fights for herself, and for the whole human race—she cannot help so doing—because she is a woman and because she is a worker.

How shall she fight? There is where the I.W.W. comes in. The Industrial Workers of the World wants to help, and it can help. We propose a complete overthrow of the conditions which make it possible to exploit anybody, man or woman, though the women have the most to gain, being most exploited. We propose to take the two-thirds of this world's wealth, which we produce day after day, and day by day turn over to masters, business men; we intend to take that and add it to the wages of the workers. Then if a man wants to work five or six hours a day, he can support a family in comfort, and the mother need not work. If a woman wishes to be independent, she can work the three hours a day which Dr. Clara Seippel thinks wouldn't hurt her, and she is independent, with all the privileges and rights of a man. She gets the same wages for the same work.

War we abolish altogether, for wars are fought because capitalists cannot agree on the division of the things they steal from us—they are fought for mines, oil fields and markets, in which to exploit labor.

Poverty, ignorance, crime and especially prostitution with all its menace of disease, and suffering and blindness of the innocent babes,—all this shall go, for no woman will need to sell herself, either to the general public, or in marriage to a man she cannot love—every woman can have congenial work, with which to support herself, if she wishes.

We can do all these things, if we overthrow capitalism, and let the workers own the industries. We can make things a whole lot better, if we stick together, at the right time, and force the boss to raise wages and cut down the hours.

We have to do it—if the world is to be a better place to live in—we workers must make it so. . . .

"YOU CAN'T DO THIS TO WOMEN"

Byron McG. West (1930)

AN ORGANIZATION, with headquarters in Chicago, has launched a campaign destined to be nationwide in scope to deny all married women the right to work for a living. It would not only drive married women out of jobs they now occupy, but would deny them the right to get jobs should those unfortunates find it necessary to work—lest they starve.

If this movement is not un-American and contrary to the Constitution, which guarantees certain rights and privileges to all American citizens—then we do not know our Constitution and all our thinking is haywire. Certainly here is a field for exploration by the Department of Justice and the Dies Congressional Committee on un-American activities. . . .

The ban on married women is called the Wage-Security Plan and its initial circular says, "The first guns to be fired in our campaign for jobs for men and single women only will be in Illinois, Missouri, Michigan, Ohio, Indiana and Minnesota."

So it is safe to assume that later—when it gets richer and bolder—the campaign will be extended.

Its unblushing slogan is "Put the Married Women Back in the Home."

Its folder, printed in red, white and blue, outlines its plan as follows:

1—Jobs for men and single women only (extenuating circumstances excepted).

2—To seek municipal, state and federal legislation creating laws to this effect. (Lawmakers throughout the nation are now being canvassed.)

3—To maintain a lobby in Washington and the different state capitols to further our cause.

4—To seek the cooperation of industrialists, storekeepers and employers in general.

5—To endorse candidates for public office who pledge themselves to actively support legislation to accomplish the aims of the plan.

6—To seek support through speakers' bureaus and through advertising via radio, newspapers and periodicals. . . .

Married women get just as hungry as any other human beings—male or female—married or single. That they must work for economic reasons is as pressing to them as it is to other groups. Few people work just for the sheer love of working. They labor because they must do so to survive. Countless married women have dependents to support as well as themselves and many of these dependents are husbands, who are either physically incapacitated, too lazy, or too incompetent to be bread winners. There are many hundreds of thousands of women in the United States supporting themselves and their children after worthless husbands have abandoned them.

Women represent a little more than fifty

Equal Rights: Magazine of the National Woman's Party *(Washington, D.C.)* [1930].

percent of the population of the United States. Probably ninety-nine out of every hundred single women have an idea that some day they may marry. And probably a large percentage of these women do not want a ban placed upon their right to work, should they so desire or should it become an economic necessity.

Movements such as this Wage-Security misnomer will eventually drive all women into a voting bloc and the way they will slaughter legislative candidates pledging themselves to vote for laws driving women out of jobs and putting them back in the home will be an interesting episode in American political history. . . .

Similarly, there is not a word of truth in any of its statements concerning the so-called "disasters" which will overtake the country unless married women are driven out of jobs. And the same goes for the "beneficial" results which it says will accrue to the nation if all married women are put back in the home. . . .

Such pernicious activity already has broken up many homes through divorce because married women, who had to work, could not afford marriage. It was not that they wanted divorce—it occurred in those cases where the combined salaries of men and wife made it possible for them to meet their joint obligations. When the wife was driven from her job and there was but one salary—divorce, through mutual agreement, followed. Likewise many pending marriages never materialized because the parties realized that if only one could be employed the situation was futile.

That the Congress of the United States once tried this dangerous experiment through the ill-starred Section 213 of the "Economy Act," ought to be a lesson to those who would attempt to perpetuate such an absurd and discriminatory policy against one-half of the population of free America.

But Section 213 was repealed, because women marshalled their forces and taught the country a lesson in political science.

That this sort of mental aberration could gain support from any one—except Morons—seems incredible. That it could even be proposed in the American democracy is still more incredible.

There is one thing the male ought to get through his thick skull and that is that the female is his equal in intelligence, his superior in many other attributes, and can no longer be brushed aside as a minor, held in bondage or legislated out of her inheritance as a human being that his vanity and economic security, without competition, might be protected.

Selfishness, born of fear of competition from women in business and industry, is one of a number of sinister motives behind this movement. Its sponsors are not so chivalrous that they want to put the woman back in the home that she might be sheltered from the rudeness and cruelties of a cold and sordid world. This is not the idea at all. The plan offers a lucrative return on the one hand and on the other it would protect all the jobs for men—married or single. Men want all the jobs at their disposal without competition.

Well, there is one natural law, which cannot be abrogated by man-made legislation or discrimination, and that law is the survival of the fittest. If man cannot meet the competition of women—then it is time to put the *men* back in the home and let the women work. . . .

"UNION MAID"

Woody Guthrie (1947)

There once was a union maid,
Who never was afraid
Of the goons and ginks and the company finks,
And the deputy sheriffs who made the raids.
She went to the union hall
When a meeting it was called,
And when the company boys came 'round,
She always stood her ground.

Chorus
Oh, you can't scare me, I'm sticking to the union,
I'm sticking to the union,
I'm sticking to the union.
Oh, You can't scare me, I'm sticking to the union,
I'm sticking to the union,
Till the day I die.

This union maid was wise
To the tricks of company spies,
She couldn't be fooled by Company stools,
She'd always organize the guys.
She'd always get her way
When she asked for higher pay,
She's show her card to the National Guard,
And this is what she'd say. *Chorus*

Now, you gals who want to be free,
Just take a little tip from me,
Get you a man who's a union man
And fight together for liberty.
Married life ain't hard
When you've got a union card.
A union man leads a happy life
When he's got a union wife. *Chorus*

[New last verse, added in 1970s:]

You women who want to be free
Take a little tip from me
Break outa that mold we've all been sold
You've got a fighting history
The fight for women's rights
With workers must unite
Like Mother Jones, move them bones
To the front of every fight! *Chorus*

From Woody Guthrie Folk Songs. *New York: Ludlow, 1963,*

WOMEN IN THE PROFESSIONS

"A VALEDICTORY ADDRESS AT THE FIRST COMMENCEMENT OF THE FEMALE MEDICAL COLLEGE OF PENNSYLVANIA"

Joseph S. Longshore, M.D. (1851)

LADIES OF THE GRADUATING CLASS:
The word farewell implies the parting of friends, the dissolution of agreeable associations, the severing of silken cords. The duty of uttering that often dreaded word, has today been assigned to me, by my colleagues. It is one both painful and pleasant. The relations that have existed between you as pupils, and us as your teachers, for months, have been the most harmonious and delightful; you have sympathised with us in our trials, and participated with us in our enjoyments. We have all been engaged in a new, but momentous enterprize. We have met alike the frowns and prejudices of the community, and labored hand in hand to sustain our institution against powerful opposing influences. These relations have bound us together in ties of friendship, only to be broken by death. These circumstances render the utterance of the parting word painful.—But the thought that you are about to return to the kindly greetings of the loved ones, from whom you have been so long separated, and the revival of early affections and associations in the society of parents, relations and friends, imparts pleasure to the otherwise painful duty assigned me. In returning to your homes, and to all the tender endearments that cluster around the domestic hearth, you bear with you the highest honors of the institution in which you have been educated, as the trophies of your toils and privations. And may these honors ever be as links, connecting you in friendship with your Alma Mater, and those who have labored with you, for the high distinction they confer.

Ladies, the circumstances under which we meet to-day differ essentially from those hitherto characterizing our coming together.—We have been accustomed, hereto-

---

"A Valedictory Address Delivered Before the Graduating Class at the First Annual Commencement of the Female Medical College of Pennsylvania, December 30, 1851," Philadelphia: Published by the graduates, 1852. (MCP, Archives and Special Collections on Women in Medicine)

fore, to assemble in the capacity of instructors and learners. But this relation, delightful to your teachers, and they flatter themselves, not unpleasant to you, has been dissolved. By a perseverance and industry characteristic of your sex, and worthy of the great enterprise in which you have enlisted, you have, with signal ability, completed your collegiate studies, and to-day, by virtue of your acquirements and the diploma of the Female Medical college of Pennsylvania, a reward of merit, and a passport to the honors and emoluments of the profession of your choice, we place you on the platform of *equal* professional and literary relations, with those who are your *seniors* in the healing art, as well as those who are *contemporary* with you, in assuming its duties and responsibilties. By an act of incorporation, by the legislature of the commonwealth of Pennsylvania, your Alma Mater has been placed on an *equality*, in chartered immunities, with the colossal Institution of our city, around which the names of Kuhne, Wistar, Rush, Godman, Physic, James and Dewees cast a halo of unfading glory; or her proud and successful rival, with the history of which are identified the imperishable names of Eberle, McClellan and Revere. . . .

. . . But from the honorable portion of those engaged in the practice of medicine, you will invariably receive the sympathy and assistance to which your abilities, zeal and perseverance, in acquiring your medical education, so justly entitle you. The true physician labors not for himself alone; benevolence constitutes the most prominent trait in his character. It is this that prompts him to toil on, and ever, in the cause of suffering humanity; it is this that leads him with cheerfulness, complaisance and smiles into the low hovels of the poor, with as much alacrity as the hope of rewards entices him into the statelier mansions of the wealthy. Forgetful of self, he "bides the peltings of the pitiless storm," he shrinks not from the wintry blasts; the poisoned malaria, the scorching rays, the chilling dews, the haunts of contagion, he disregards, and flies to the abode of misery, to relieve the suffering and to soothe the pangs of death. He labors for his fellow man, and angels applaud the act. Ladies, from such men you have nothing to fear—at their hands you may hope for much. Instead of rebuffs, contempt and derision, which you may expect from some, these will welcome you to the profession, and hail you as co-laborers in the great cause of benevolence and humanity. Your progress you will find to be impeded by obstacles, interposed by those from whom, rightfully, might be expected the greatest amount of encouragement and patronage. Woman having so long been regarded, and having so long regarded herself, alike *intellectually* and physically inferior to man, it will require *time* before she can justly realize the great fact, that her own sex can be rendered equally qualified to assume all the responsibilities of a profession hitherto wholly monopolized by him. Some of your own sex you will find your most earnest and determined opposers. Many there are who will make it a matter of conscience, believing that woman is sadly wandering from her legitimate sphere, when she attempts, scientifically, to administer to the necessities of the sick and suffering—though to do it ignorantly and emp[i]rically, would seem to be within her appropriate province, and title her to the beautiful appellation of "ministering Angel." Next, perhaps, to her spiritual adviser, does her medical attendant exert the greatest influence over the mind of woman; and among your professional brethren, (with deep humility I acknowledge the fact,) may not be wanting those, who, actuated by motives of selfishness, and feelings of jealousy, will not hesitate to make use of this means to prejudice against you those who should be your truest, firmest, fastest friends and supporters; for it is for their health, their comfort, their happiness, that you have, mainly, eschewed the pleasures of life, the charms of the social circle, and the delights of domestic enjoyment, and encloistered yourselves, for months and years, in the study and the lecture room, engaged in intense mental labor, and enduring severe physical privations. Ay! while hundreds, who would, I am pained to say, at this moment crush within you the faintest ray of rising hope, were reposing on their beds of down, or gaily whirling in the merry dance; for them—for the relief of their sufferings—for the amelioration of their woes—were you plodding by the midnight lamp, the rugged paths of science. Such is the ingratitude of the human heart!

But I would bid you take cheer; be not dismayed! Thousands of sympathizing hearts now palpitate in unison with your every struggle—thousands of willing hands are now extended to receive you; be then encouraged;—as the gloom of night recedes before the rising splendor of the morning sun, so will the dark clouds of ignorance and prejudice, that now envelope the mind of woman, vanish before the superior brightness of your many virtues and high professional attainments. . . .

Most of the occupations assigned to woman, are those of a subservient character, where the scale of remuneration is graded by the interests of parsimony of others. Where men and women are engaged in the same vocations, and the labors are equal, and the products of their toil the same, the compensation of the latter seldom exceeds one half that of the former. Thus the profits of the employer are doubly enhanced by woman's incessant exertions for an honest and virtuous livelihood. There are, at this moment, in this city, hundreds, nay thousands who are toiling from earliest dawn to midnight's hour, enriching their employers, while they are scarcely gleaning for themselves a comfortable subsistence. Many a true, noble heart, that would sooner cease its pulsations than consent to vice; many a brilliant intellect, that might adorn a palace, lie crushed and mangled beneath this oppressive system of outrage and wrong. See the taper glimmering at the window of yonder low attic at midnight, visit the apartment, and you will behold the pale, emaciated, careworn seamstress—there you will find intelligence—there an undying devotion to virtue. Thousands in the pursuit of pleasure, luxuriating in ease and competence, pass her abode, unmindful of her toils, her privations and her sorrows. Hundreds, from their close confinement in illy ventilated apartments, ruin their health irreparably. Time that should be devoted to exercise and recreation, would be so much loss, out of the means of a meagre subsistence. And in early life, while health should yet be glowing upon the cheek, and sprightliness beaming from the eye, they will be found presenting to you, ladies, shattered constitutions and diminished vital energies, craving your counsels and your sympathies. Let them be freely given—for those who ask are your suffering sisters. Treat them kindly, and whisper gently in their ears, words of encouragement and sympathy. Prescribe for their sufferings, and let it be a gratuitous act. Refuse to accept any pecuniary consideration for such services. Soil not your hands with the pittance wrung from their toil and suffering, but be content with the clear perception of the emotions of grateful hearts. Be attentive and charitable to the poor everywhere, and at all times. Refuse them not your services, because of their inability to compensate you. Remember their indignance adds additional pangs to their woes, and they stand the more in need of your consoling attentions. But when the competent and wealthy require your services, let a full and fair compensation be demanded. You are independent of and beyond the control of oppressing influences. You are as justly entitled to full fees as are your brethren of the profession. You will render equal services, and justice will award you an equal compensation.—Do not condescend to fall into the common error of your sex, and consent to receive less for the same duties than is demanded by the profession generally. In this particular forget that you are *women*, but remember that you are *physicians*—and as such, you expect to be rewarded for your labors—and the profession and the community will respect you the more. You must not expect the public to place a higher estimate upon you than you place upon yourselves. Respect yourselves and you will be the more respected. . . .

"WOMEN'S RIGHTS TO PREACH THE GOSPEL"

Rev. Luther Lee (1853)

THE THINKING PORTION of the assembly have, by this time, reasoned within themselves, "that is a singular text from which to preach an Ordination sermon." This may render it proper for me to remind my hearers, just at this point, that the text is no more unusual, as the basis of an Ordination sermon, than the occasion is unusual, upon which I am called to preach it.

The ordination of a female, or the setting apart of a female to the work of the Christian ministry, is, to say the least, a novel transaction, in this land and age. It cannot fail to call forth many remarks, and will, no doubt, provoke many censures.

For myself, I regard it in the light of a great innovation upon the opinions, prejudices and practices of nearly the whole Christian world. There have been some Christian communities who have allowed females to preach the gospel, but so far as I know, they have not ordained their ministers, male or female, or by any solemn form or service, set them apart to the work of the ministry, as I suppose is intended to be done at the conclusion of this discourse. . . .

It is with these views, and under these impressions that I have selected the text which I have read as the basis of my discourse. "There is neither male nor female; for ye are all one in Christ Jesus."

What does this text mean? and what was the Apostle's design in uttering these words? Whatever the text means, or does not mean, its application is to be limited to what is clearly and specifically Christian. It is in

"Women's Rights to Preach the Gospel: A Sermon at the Ordination of Rev. Miss Antoinette Brown." Syracuse, N.Y., 1853.

Christ Jesus that there is no difference, and that the sex become one. There may be differences of rights and positions growing out of incidental relations, and conventional rules and usages, in matters which do not affect the fundamental rights of humanity, which I need not discuss; but when we come to consider those rights and privileges, which we claim as Christians, and which belong to us as believers in Christ, there is no difference, we are all one in Christ Jesus. Without even presuming to discuss, on this occasion, the questions of civil and political rights, the text amply sustains me in affirming that in a Christian community, united upon Christian principles, for Christian purposes; or, in other words, in the Church, of which Christ is the only head, males and females possess equal rights and privileges; here there is no difference, "there is neither male nor female; for ye are all one in Christ Jesus." I cannot see how the text can be explained so as to exclude females from any right, office, work, privilege, or immunity which males enjoy, hold or perform. If the text means anything, it means that males and females are equal in rights, privileges and responsibilities upon the Christian platform. I am very frank to confess that I had never very thoroughly investigated the question, until called upon to preach on this occasion, though I have held an opinion loosely on the subject for many years. This call, in my own estimation laid me under obligation to do one of two things, either step forward and assist this church, or decline so to do, for good and satisfactory reasons. I might have evaded the question, by declining for want of time, or some other fictitious reason, but that would not only have been in bad keeping with my general character, but would have been false to Christianity and my brethren. If those inviting me here are right in proposing to ordain a female to the Gospel ministry, they needed my help, and were entitled to it; if they were wrong, they needed my reproof and reasons for it, and it was due to my own fidelity, and to truth, that I should administer it. But to do either, required thought beyond what I had ever bestowed upon the subject. You may then suppose me to have asked myself, "If I decline, what reason can I give for so doing? So far as I know there is no want of moral, or mental or educational qualification on the part of the candidate; if it be right to ordain any female, it is right to ordain this female." At this point, the text which I have selected for the occasion, presented itself to my mind, and I reasoned thus:—"I acknowledge the candidate to be in Christ, to be with me a sister in Christ; if I deny her the right to exercise her gifts as a Christian minister, I virtually affirm that there is male and female, and that we are not all one in Christ Jesus, by which I shall contradict St. Paul, and though he is not among us to reply to me, to know myself at variance with him, would give me more uneasiness than to differ from modern doctors of divinity, and divinity schools. I am then brought to this conclusion, which I will state in the form of a proposition as the sequence of the text.

FEMALES HAVE A GOD-GIVEN RIGHT TO PREACH THE GOSPEL.

I take it upon myself, as my portion of the effort on this occasion, to defend and substantiate the above proposition. To make any distinction in the church of Jesus Christ, between males and females, purely on the ground of sex, is virtually to strike this text from the sacred volume, for it affirms that in Christ there is no difference between males and females, that they are all one in regard to the gospel of the grace of God. If males may belong to a Christian church, so may females; if male members may vote in the church, so may females; if males may preach the gospel, so may females; and if males may receive ordination by the imposition of hands, or otherwise, so may females, the reason of which is found in my text; "there is neither male nor female, for ye are all one in Christ Jesus." . . .

We are here assembled on a very interesting and solemn occasion, and it is proper to advert to the real object for which we have come together. There are in the world, and there may be among us, false views of the nature and object of ordination. I do not believe that any special or specific form of ordination is necessary to constitute a gospel minister. We are not here to make a minister. It is not to confer on this our sister, a right to preach the gospel. If she has not that right already, we have no power to communicate it to her. Nor have we met to qualify her for the work of the ministry. If God and mental and moral culture have not already qualified her, we cannot, by anything we may do by way of ordaining or setting her apart. Nor can we, by imposition of our hands, confer on her any special grace for the work of the ministry, nor will our hands if imposed upon her head, serve as a special medium for the communication of the Holy Ghost, as conductors serve to convey electricity; such ideas belong not to our theory, but are related to other systems and darker ages. All we are here to do, and all we expect to do, is, in due form, and by a solemn and impressive service, to subscribe our testimony to the fact, that in our belief, our sister in Christ, Antoinette L. Brown, is one of the ministers of the New Covenant, authorized, qualified, and called of God to preach the gospel of his Son Jesus Christ.

"LIBRARIANSHIP AS A PROFESSION FOR COLLEGE-BRED WOMEN"

Melvil Dewey (1886)

THERE IS a large field of work for college-bred women in promoting the founding of new libraries, infusing new life into old ones, or serving on committees or boards of trustees where their education and training will tell powerfully for the common good. Active interest of this kind may fairly be expected of every college graduate.

In the more direct work for which salaries are paid there is an unusually promising field for college girls and in few lines of work have women so nearly an equal chance with

Address delivered before the Association of College Teachers, 13 March 1886. Boston: Library Bureau, 1886. (CU, Dewey Collection, P-16)

men. There is almost nothing in the higher branches which she cannot do quite as well as a man of equal training and experience; and in much of library work woman's quick mind and deft fingers do many things with a neatness and despatch seldom equaled by her brothers.

My experience is that an increasing number of libraries are willing to pay for given work the same price, whether done by men or women. Yet why are the salaries of women lower? In all my business and professional life I have tried to give woman more than a fair chance at all work which I had to offer. Experience has taught me why the fairest employers, in simple justice usually pay men more for what seems at first sight the same work. Perhaps these reasons may help you to avoid some of the difficulties.

1. Women have usually poorer health and as a result lose more time from illness and are more crippled by physical weakness when on duty. The difficulty is most common to women, as are bright ribbons and thin shoes and long hair, but it is a question of health, not of sex. A strong, healthy woman is worth more than a feeble man for the same reason that a strong man gets more than a weak woman.

2. Usually women lack business and executive training. Her brothers have been about the shops and stores and in the streets or on the farm hearing business matters discussed and seeing business transacted from earliest childhood. The boys have been trading jack knives and developing the business bumps while the girls are absorbed with their dolls. It would be a miracle at present if girls were not greatly inferior in this respect and it is this fact which accounts for so few prominent chief librarianships being held by women. But this is the fault of circumstances, not necessarily of sex, and women who have somehow got the business ideas and training and have executive force are getting the salaries that such work commands. When girls have as good a chance to learn these things, I doubt not that they will quite equal their brothers and will keep cash and bank accounts and double entry books for their private affairs. A man brought up girl-fashion, as not a few are, proves just as helpless on trial and as a result gets only a "woman's salary."

3. Lack of permanence in her plans is one of the gravest difficulties with women. A young man who enters library work and later thinks of a home of his own, is stimulated to fresh endeavors to make his services more valuable. Many a young man's success in life dates from the new earnestness which took possession of him on his engagement. But with women the probability or even the possibility that her position is only temporary and that she will soon leave it for home life does more than anything else to keep here value down. Neither man or woman can do the best work except when it is felt to be the life work. This lack of permanence in the plans of women is more serious than you are apt to realize. If woman wishes to be as valuable as a man she must contrive to feel that she has chosen a profession for life and work accordingly. Then she will do the best that is in her to do as long as she is in the service and if at any time it seems best to change her state, the work already done has not been crippled by this "temporary" evil.

4. With equal health, business training and permanence of plans, women will still usually have to accept something less than men because of the consideration which she exacts and deserves on account of her sex. If a man can do all the other work just as well as the woman and in addition can in an emergency lift a heavy case, or climb a ladder to the roof or in case of accident or disorder can act as fireman or do police duty, he adds something to his direct value just as

a saddle horse that is safe in harness and not afraid of the cars will bring more in nine markets out of ten than the equally good horse that can be used only in the saddle. So in justice to those who wish to be fair to women, remember that she almost always receives, whether she exacts it or not, much more waiting on and minor assistance than a man in the same place and therefore, with sentiment aside, hard business judgment cannot award her quite as much salary. There are many uses for which a stout corduroy is really worth more than the finest silk.

"ON THE OPENING OF THE JOHNS HOPKINS MEDICAL SCHOOL TO WOMEN"

James Cardinal Gibbons (1891)

It is perhaps not sufficiently understood that there is no obstacle in ecclesiastical or canon law to the education of women for the medical profession. Among the persons inhibited by the Church from pursuing the profession of medicine are included priests, monks, and clergymen generally, but not women. . . .

I do not hesitate to say . . . that in my opinion it is important to the well-being of society that the study of medicine by Christian women should be continued and extended. The difficulties that are said to attend their pursuing the necessary studies in the same schools with men may be obviated by judicious precautions, and these difficulties should not debar women from the profession of medicine. We permit women to exercise the art of painting, though its successful pursuit is not always free from danger to female modesty. In my judgment, in anatomical demonstrations men and women should be separated; but I learn that in the anatomical departments of Paris and Geneva, Zurich, Berne, and Basle, and in the universities of Belgium, Spain, and Italy, women work side by side with men, and that this, in the opinion of the professors, has been attended by good rather than bad results. I believe that in other departments, and wherever the proper restrictions are observed, the coeducation of the male and the female sex will exert a beneficial influence on the male.

The prejudice that allows women to enter the profession of nursing and excludes them from the profession of medicine cannot be

Century Magazine, *1891. (Copy in SL, Mary Putnam Jacobi Papers, A-26, Box 32)*

too strongly censured, and its existence can be explained only by the force of habit. It has been urged that women do not as a rule possess the intellectual powers of men, but their ability to pursue the usual medical studies has been sufficiently demonstrated; and it is admitted, even by those who concede to men a higher order of intellect and greater powers of ratiocination, that what women may lack in that direction seems to be supplied by that logical instinct with which they have been endowed by God. It is evident also that if female nurses may with propriety attend men as well as women, that privilege cannot reasonably be withheld from the female physician; indeed, the position of the nurse might be regarded as open to much graver objections, inasmuch as the physician makes but a transient visit to the patient, while the nurse occupies the sickroom day and night. The attendance of female physicians upon women is often of incalculable benefit. Much serious and continued suffering is undergone by women, and many beginnings of grave illness are neglected, because of the sense of delicacy which prevents them from submitting to the professional services of men. There is also an infinite number of cases, known to all who have been concerned in charitable or reformatory work, in which no influence or assistance can be so effectual as that of a physician who is also a woman and a Christian.

The alleviation of suffering, for women of all classes, which would result from the presence among us of an adequate number of well-trained female physicians cannot but be evident to all; but I wish to emphasize as strongly as possible the moral influence of such a body, than which there could be no more potent factor in the moral regeneration of society.

"WHY MANY WOMEN SHOULD STUDY LAW"

William T. Harris (1901)

According to the statistics of 1899 there were in the United States 96 law schools, enrolling in the aggregate, 11,874 students, 167 of this number being women. . . .

Here I base my argument in behalf of the necessity not only for an increase of law students in general, but especially of women students of law. I have heard it asked whether the profession is not overstocked? Are there not more lawyers than can make a living at their profession? I answer by calling attention to the increase of great business combinations and to the utter necessity of professionally skilled legal advice in every new issue. We need greater specialization

(SSL)

and more expert skill on the part of the legal counsel. Here is woman's opportunity. She will not be so much required as lawyers in criminal cases as lawyer in civil cases; she will not be required so much in actual control of civil cases in the courts, as in the office giving professional advice in advance, giving advice which will prevent law suits, rather than skillfully extricating the client who has been so unfortunate as to be brought into court. This, in my thinking, is a much more noble view of the profession of law. I hold that the lawyer of the future is to find his or her chief function in preventing law suits. . . .

. . . The natural characteristic of the feminine temperament is not favorable to the legal consideration of a subject. Sentiment and impulse predominate those rather than a cold investigation, of the forms of justice which protect society as a whole. An interest in legal studies is less likely to be a feminine than a masculine trait. By all means therefore one would say that the study of law is desirable on the part of many women. It has been often remarked by wise philosophers in politics that the United States succeeds in the experiment of self-government especially through the services of its lawyers. For the lawyers abound not only in the courts of justice but in the legislative chambers. The lawyer serves his country not only in helping interpret the law in the court but also in the legislature in making a law that does not contradict itself or subvert the fundamental law of the state.

It will add an element of strength to the mind of woman to acquire the judicial way of looking at human deeds and actions,—to acquire what is called a "legal mind." And it will not be at the expense of the high traits of character which are recognized as feminine.

I therefore predict great success and great influence ultimately from this movement which brings woman into the professions and especially into the profession of law.

IV

THE MOVEMENT FOR POLITICAL EQUALITY, 1850–1960

—Photo The Pictorial News Co.

EIGHTY-FIVE COURAGEOUS AND CONVINCED MEN

This picture shows the "men's division" of the suffrage parade in New York. They found the chaffing of the crowd that lined tne streets "inspiring."

From *LaFollette's Weekly Magazine*, May 27, 1911. Photo courtesy of Bancroft Library, University of California at Berkeley.

WHETHER WE WISH IT or not, the economic independence of women is taking place before our eyes," argued M. Carey Thomas, president of Bryn Mawr College, in 1908. These changes amounted to a "stupendous social revolution," she believed. "Women are one-half of the world, but until a century ago . . . women lived a twilight life, a half life apart, and looked out and saw men as shadows walking. It was a man's world." Now that "women have won the right to higher education and economic independence, the right to become citizens of the state is the next and inevitable consequence of education and work outside the home. We have gone so far; we must go farther. We cannot go back" (Thomas 1908, 59).

Women's struggle to become citizens of the state was formally launched in 1848 at the First Women's Rights Convention in Seneca Falls, New York. From its earliest days, that struggle was split: two different sources of activism led to two different visions of the egalitarian future (see Flexner 1970; Berg 1975; Kraditor 1981; and DuBois 1978). One group sought to minimize the differences between the sexes and supported women's rights because they believed that women were similar to men. The other group sought to maximize the differences between women and men; women's separate identities and separate spheres revealed a natural difference between the sexes. Women should be enfranchised *because* they were different; their presence would in-

An asterisk (*) indicates that a document is included in this volume.

fuse the dirty business of politics with the virtue, morality, and cleanliness that were women's natural gifts. Only occasionally could these positions be fused, as they were by Harriet Burton Laidlaw. Insofar as women were like men, she argued, they ought to have the same rights. Insofar as they were different, they must have the right to represent themselves (Laidlaw 1912, 10–11).

Most reformers, men and women, saw the separation of spheres as a social, not a natural, creation and believed that women were equally entitled, as individuals, to participate in political life. "Women have natural rights, no less than men; and because *natural* they are also inalienable, and can never be set at naught or disregarded with impunity," wrote the Reverend Samuel May in a letter to the Woman's Rights Convention in 1850 (*HWS,* 1:266). "Woman is a human being; and it is a self-evident truth that whatever rights belong to man by virtue of his membership in the human family, belongs to her by the same tenure," wrote Henry C. Wright (1851) the next year. "Woman has the same individual right to determine her aim in life, and to follow it" added Theodore Parker in "A Sermon of the Public Function of Woman"* (1853).

Abolitionism and Suffrage

"The history of the battle for woman's rights is . . . inseparable from the movement for the Negro's liberty." So wrote journalist Samuel Sillen (1955) introducing *Women against Slavery,* his collective biography of women who participated in the abolitionist struggle. The link was equally strong for some male abolitionists, whose support of woman suffrage sprang from their participation in the anti-slavery movement. These included white abolitionists like William Lloyd Garrison, James Mott, the Reverend Samuel May, Gerrit Smith, Henry Brown Blackwell, Theodore Tilton, Parker Pillsbury, and Wendell Phillips as well as many black abolitionists, including Frederick Douglass, Charles Remond, and Robert Purvis.

For Frederick Douglass, the fugitive slave who became the most famous black leader of the nineteenth century, there was, as he wrote in his autobiographical reminiscences, "no foundation in reason or justice for woman's exclusion from the right of choice in the selection of the persons who should frame the laws, and thus shape the destiny of all the people, irrespective of sex" (Douglass 1885, 473); See also

Douglass's "The Rights of Women,"*). This was also true for William Lloyd Garrison, one of the movement's most controversial leaders. A founder of the New England Anti-Slavery Society in 1831 and the American Anti-Slavery Society in 1833, and publisher of the *Liberator* until 1865, Garrison criticized politicians, theologians, and businessmen equally as the chief props of the slave system. Converted to perfectionism by John Humphrey Noyes, Garrison was an unrelenting critic of clerical hypocrisy about both slavery and the rights of women. He defended abolition and suffrage because all people were inherently equal. As early as 1840, Garrison demonstrated his radical support of suffrage when he refused to be seated at the World Anti-Slavery Society convention in London, where he was scheduled to be the key speaker. "After battling so many long years for the liberty of African slaves," he said, "I can take no part in a convention that strikes down the most sacred rights of all women." (cited in *HWS*, 1:164).

Garrison was a tireless speaker for suffrage. "I doubt whether a more important movement has ever been launched, touching the destiny of the race, than this in regard to the equality of the sexes," he wrote the Woman's Rights Convention in 1850 (*HWS*, 1:216). Perhaps his most compelling speech came in 1853, at the Fourth Women's Rights Convention in Cleveland ("Intelligent Wickedness"*). Garrison lays blame for women's oppression neither on immoral individuals nor on society as a whole but on men's "intelligent wickedness"; men as a group were the oppressor, not the equally oppressed victims.

Many prominent abolitionists and pro-feminist campaigners came from wealthy families, the sons of established northeastern families. Gerrit Smith, for example, son of a New York landowner, was involved in an unsuccessful effort to establish a black agricultural settlement and manual arts training school in New York State. Disillusioned by the federal government's pro-slavery position, he supported John Brown's effort to incite the insurrection at Harper's Ferry. In one speech, he argued that women "complain that they have been robbed of great and essential rights. They do not ask favors; they demand rights, the right to do whatever they have the capacity to accomplish, the right to dictate their own sphere of action, and to have a voice in the laws and rulers under which they live" (*HWS*, 1:526).

Wendell Phillips came from a patrician Massachusetts family. Next to Garrison, his good friend and political mentor, Phillips was perhaps the best-known abolitionist and suffrage supporter. A constant speaker at local, national, and international suffrage meetings, Phillips was less flamboyant and also less radical than Garrison or even Parker Pillsbury. He opposed inclusion of a clause about sex in the Fourteenth or Fifteenth Amendment because "this hour belongs to the negro. As Abraham Lincoln has said 'One War at a time,' so I say One question at a time" (cited in DuBois 1978; 59) (At the 1840 World Anti-Slavery Society's convention, after his plea* to seat the women delegates was denied, Phillips took his seat, leaving it to Garrison to make the more dramatic protest.) A passionate orator, Phillips's literary allusions won him respect from such notable intellectuals as Emerson and Thoreau:

> I take it America never gave any better principle to the world than the safety of letting every human being have the power of protection in its own hands. I claim it for woman. It is the beginning and end of my Woman's Rights speeches. The moment she has the ballot, I shall think the cause is won. Education, employment, equality, genius, the fine arts, places in college and everywhere else, follow in the train. They are written, they are endorsed upon the back of the ballot. They will come by necessity, the moment that you give her that. The moment you give women the ballot, the wealth of Wall Street will give bends that she shall have every other right, in order that she may constitute a safe trustee of its own prosperity. [cited in Higginson 1858, 32]

Phillips seems also to have led an exemplary private life; he was "the ideal husband," according to Mary Livermore. "Intellect, culture, eloquence, personal magnetism, remorseless moral logic, influence, money—all that he had and was were given to the service of the abolition movement," she writes. "But he always wrought with his heart leaning towards his wife, and her slightest needs of him was answered by his presence at her bedside" (Livermore 1895, 212–13).

One man who did not fit this mold was Parker Pillsbury, one of the most radical campaigners for suffrage. Son of a Massachusetts blacksmith, Pillsbury was self-educated (Higginson, May, Phillips, and Smith all went to Harvard) and eventually became a minister, only to lose his first pulpit because of his anti-slavery position. A devoted Garrisonian, Pillsbury edited the *Herald of Freedom* through the 1840s and 1850s, broke with the American Anti-Slavery Society because they assumed that black suffrage was more pressing than woman suffrage, and opposed the Fifteenth Amendment because it excluded women. After the Civil

War, Pillsbury devoted himself to woman suffrage and was coeditor of the *Revolution* in 1868–69. Not surprisingly, Pillsbury was sensitive to class issues. Women, "worth thousands and hundreds of thousands in gold, and whose money is the meanest part of their real value in society, are humbly petitioning their coachmen, their footmen and gardeners, the discharged State-Prison convicts, the idiots and lunatics, all of whom may and often do exercise the right of the ballot, to permit them also to share with them in making and executing the laws," he wrote in "The Mortality of Nations"* in 1867. At the 1867 meeting of the New England affiliate of the American Anti-Slavery Society, Pillsbury joined with Stephen Foster in supporting a suffrage plank. If the franchise would protect black man from slavery, Foster asked, who "is going to save the black woman from slavery?" From the floor came an answer: "Her husband." "Her husband!" exclaimed Pillsbury. "I say, God pity her then! . . . The right of suffrage, if it came from God, came for woman as well as man" (cited in DuBois 1978, 72).

Many pro-feminist men were clergymen in reformist churches. "We feel it is a duty to declare in regard to the sacred cause which has brought us together, that the most determined opposition it encounters is from the clergy generally, whose teaching of the Bible are intensely inimical to the equality of women with man," stated a resolution at the 1854 national convention (*HWS*, 1:383, cited in Dubois 1978, 35). Mott was a Quaker elder, Samuel May a Unitarian minister. Other clergymen who spoke out on both abolition and suffrage included Henry Ward Beecher, William Channing, and Theodore Parker as well as Higginson and Pillsbury.

Frederick Douglass was not the only black abolitionist to see the link between abolition and women's emancipation. Charles Remond, a northerner whose family had emigrated from Curaçao in 1798, was brought up in the heady abolitionist atmosphere of the New England Anti-Slavery Society. Remond attended the World Anti-Slavery Convention in 1840 with Garrison and was a prominent anti-slavery speaker (see Ward 1977). William Purvis, son of an anti-slavery cotton broker and his mulatto wife, was active in campaigns against fugitive slave laws. Married to Harriet Forten, daughter of black abolitionist James Forten, Purvis was a founder of the Pennsylvania Equal Rights Association, dedicated to suffrage for both women and blacks. Martin R. Delany, one of the earliest anti-slavery advocates, who urged emigration to Africa following emancipation, also supported woman rights. Half a century later, Judge Robert Terrell "believed ardently in woman suffrage when few men took that stand," according to his wife, Mary Church Terrell, first president of the National Association of Colored Women and herself a renowned suffragist (Terrell 1940, 144).

Later in the century, pro-feminist men extended the individual rights argument to include the fulfillment of democracy. In "Woman Suffrage Defended,* Daniel Livermore, husband of National Woman Suffrage Association president Mary Livermore, argued, "Women are people, and are as such entitled to the ballot as men, but they are defrauded by men of their right and privilege, and are unjustly excluded from all participation in the administration of government." In 1912, Representative Victor Berger of Wisconsin argued, "We can never have democratic rule until we let the women vote. We can never have real freedom until the women are free"—because, he continued, "they have much the same interests that we men have" (*HWS,* 5:361). Wisconsin's Amos Wilder extended this line of argument further, calling the denial of woman suffrage the "last form of caste lingering in the American system." "It is no answer to say that men vote for the women. Why are not workingmen shut out from the franchise because employers vote for them? Why not debar left-handed men because right-handed men kindly offer to relieve them of the duty and responsibility of voting," he wrote in 1895. "No class can get its fair representation by another class."

The other major ideological position took the separation of spheres as given. Encouraged by ideologies of domesticity and the cult of semtimentality and inspired by the evangelical revivalism and its organizational offshoots like the Female Moral Reform Society, some argued that women's capacities as mothers required public participation because qualities like compassion and nurturance were the missing ingredients in public life. Women, they argued, were a species apart from men, characterized by compassion, warmth, and a capacity to nurture. Theodore Parker argued that women's voice on all subjects would be incomparably superior to that of men. "In government as in housekeeping; or government as morality, I think Man makes a very poor appearance when he says Woman could not do as well as he has done and is doing. I doubt that Woman will ever, as a general thing, take the same interest as men in political affairs, or find therein an abiding satisfaction. But that is for women themselves to determine, not for men," he wrote in "A Sermon of the Public Function of Woman."*

Reformers active in the Women's Christian Temperance Union, the social purity movement, and various anti-vice crusades made similar arguments. Since women were the world's moralizers, by expanding their domain to the public arena the world would be cleansed of vice and depravity. "Woman's presence purifies the atmosphere," populist orator George Francis Train argued in a speech in 1867. "Give that woman a vote and she will keep the money she earns to clothe and feed her children, instead of it being spent in drunkenness and debauchery by her lord and master" (*HWS,* 2:164). This position was best summed up by George William Curtis, who argued that women's votes would purify politics. "I am asked," he wrote, "would you drag women down into the mire of politics? No sir. I would have them lift us out of it" (cited in Eastman's "Is Woman Suffrage Important" [1912, 3]).

Against the common anti-suffrage notion that voting would "unsex" women, making them more masculine, pro-feminist men argued that equality with men would "enhance their charms and not lessen their beauty," as one congressman put it in 1884 (cited in *HWS,* 4:34). One popular suffrage poem addressed this question directly:

> It doesn't unsex her to toil in a factory
> Minding the looms from the dawn till the night;
> To deal with a schoolful of children refractory
> Doesn't unsex her in anyone's sight;
> Work in a store—where her back aches inhumanely—
> Doesn't unsex her at all, you will note
> But think how exceedingly rough and unwomanly
> Woman would be if she happened to vote!

Others promised remarkable results should women receive the ballot. The Reverend Edward Eggleston argued, "If women can not make war, they can at least do something to stop war" (*HWS,* 3:810). An editorial in the *North Carolinian* urged men to "tear down the barriers, give woman an opportunity to show her wisdom and virtue; place the ballot in her hands so that she may protect herself and reform men, and ere a quarter of a century has elapsed many of the foulest blots upon the civilization of this age will have passed away" (cited in *HWS,* 3:827). In states where women already voted, men testified that such reforms had already occurred. Ben Lindsey, the celebrated Denver judge responsible for numerous landmark decisions on juvenile delinquency and child protection, reported that there were only three "dry towns" in

Colorado before woman suffrage but that there were now over fifty. The liquor interests, he suggested—in fact, all "corrupt and malign influences"—were united in opposition to suffrage. "The gambler, saloon-keeper, *macquereau* and barrel-house boss—the respectable criminals who fatten on franchises and the exploitation of the people—these are the people at the bottom of the anti-suffrage agitation!" (Lindsey 1904, 3).

Many adherents of this view were also clergymen, themselves involved in social reform movements. In "Woman Suffrage,"* the Reverend James Freeman Clarke suggested that the public arena be an extension of women's dominion in the home. "Women are the most religious, the most moral and the most sober portion of the American people, and it is not easy to understand why their influence in public life is dreaded," commented Bishop Spalding in 1889 (cited in Winston 1889, 1). In the arrestingly titled "Jesus Christ—the Emancipator of Women"* (1887) the Reverend Charles Clark Harrah argued that to "disenfranchise the women is to disenfranchise the family, and largely the virtue of the nation."

Others favored bringing women into the public arena to perform "public housecleaning." Edward J. Ward's clever pamphlet "Women Should Mind Their Own Business"* suggested that "government has become more and more the organization of women's sphere" since that sphere was the domain of arts and industry, the "caring for, keeping well-ordered, clean and comfortable the camp or village." In a brilliant rhetorical reversal, he argued that, although man may contribute little to the ordering and control of society, he should not be disenfranchised. Populist leader and presidential candidate William Jennings Bryan seemed to fuse these two positions. On one hand, he championed women as moralizers. "The liquor interests," he wrote in 1915, "are against woman suffrage. Every man who traffics in sin is opposed to woman suffrage." The reason was that all who made "a profession of wickedness understand that woman's conscience is *against* them" (Bryan, "Three Great Reforms," 1915). The next year, he posed the problem in terms of women's tendency to promote peace. "Is it just that men only shall determine when the mother must yield up her son to the battle-field, or when the ties that bind the husband to the wife shall be severed by the sword?" (Bryan 1916; see also Levine 1965, 128–29).

By the turn of the century, a new position linked women's emancipation to the struggle for social justice and democracy. These profeminist men and feminist women were often socialists, who saw the structural sources of women's disenfranchisement, not in society's failure to extend individual political rights to women as individual citizens, but in the mechanisms by which certain groups maintain collective power. Eugene Debs, unionist and Socialist party candidate for president, hailed the feminist movement in "Woman—Comrade and Equal."* Many Greenwich Village radicals at the turn of the century supported suffrage as part of a larger vision of social and political liberation—a program that often included a peculiar amalgam of socialism, free love, anarchism, birth control, and psychoanalysis.

The Campaign for Suffrage

The struggle for suffrage drew from differing philosophical or moral positions but was ultimately a political struggle fought out in the political arena. This meant mass demonstrations and rallies on the one hand and the slow business of political lobbying on the other. "The relation of suffragists to the existing parties could not become a major issue . . . until enough men had become converted to the cause to force the suffragists to consider practical ways and means of achieving their goal." Even then, however, the National American Woman Suffrage Association (NAWSA) "largely ignored parties and preferred to convert individuals who might respond to principle" (Kraditor 1981, 226, 247). At the national, state, and local levels, advocates of woman suffrage mounted an impressive campaign to convince male legislators—as individuals, as men, and as husbands—to vote for suffrage.

No president had been a sincere advocate of suffrage before the turn of the century. As close as anyone had come was the young Abraham Lincoln, who, in 1833, twenty-seven years before he became president (and 15 years before Seneca Falls), wrote, "I go for all sharing in the privileges of government who assist in bearing its burden, by no means excluding females." (cited in *HWS,* 1:11). Both William Howard Taft and Theodore Roosevelt were resolutely opposed to suffrage (see Taft 1915). When Roosevelt became a Progressive and ran for president again in 1912, he changed his position slightly, declaring himself a supporter, though not a very enthusiastic one. "I am," he wrote to Lyman Abbott in 1908, "what you would regard as lukewarm or tepid in my support of [suffrage] because, while I believe in it, I do not regard it as of very much importance" (*Remonstrance* [January 1909]: 3). Woodrow Wilson also offered tepid support, late and reluctant, as a war measure (Flexner 1970, 308).

Much of the divisiveness in statewide campaigns resulted from bitter political battles over Reconstruction programs. In 1867, in Kansas, for example, Wendell Phillips expressed anxiety over being allied with a pro-slavery Democrat like George Francis Train (in *HWS*,2:285). As the Republican party steadfastly refused to support suffrage, suffragists and pro-feminist men split over continued adherence to the Reconstruction program. Stanton, Anthony, and Pillsbury were critical; Higginson, Stone, and Blackwell remained loyal. This split led to the formation of two separate organizations, the National Woman Suffrage Association and the American Woman Suffrage Association, and the emergence of suffragism as an independent movement, no longer linked to a party (DuBois 1978, 163–64).

As separate statewide campaigns got under way (1870–1920), women often found enthusiastic support from the western states seeking admission to statehood. Women were enfranchised first in western territories and states. Wyoming granted them the vote as a territory in 1869 and retained woman suffrage when it became a state twenty years later. Three other western states, Colorado (1893), Utah (1896), and Idaho (1896), followed and these four were the only states in which women could vote before 1900. By 1914, Washington (1910), California (1911), Oregon (1912), Kansas (1912), Arizona (1912), Illinois (1913), Alaska (1913), Montana (1914), and Nevada (1914) joined them.

Suffrage passed most readily in the West partly because there was no organized opposition to it and partly because women's efforts in westward expansion gave the lie to notions about women's natural delicacy and debility. Many agreed with the Reverend W. C. Harvey, who said that he had come to Laramie, Wyoming, "prejudiced against woman suffrage, but I have been thoroughly converted" (*WSL*, no. 21 [1889]). (There is also a less sanguine reason for woman suffrage's success in the western territories: the Homestead Law allowed single women and widows to own 160 acres of land for a small fee and an agreement to farm the land for five years. Husbands and wives staked out adjoining plots and built their house exactly on the dividing line. By 1880, more than one-third of the land in the Dakota territory was owned by women [Wagner 1990, 39].) Campaigns in the North and East used testimonials from governors and state officials in western states to propel their campaigns in more hostile political environments (see Waite and Crounse 1894).

The difficulties faced by the southern campaign were compounded by persistent racism and the punitive Republican reconstruction policy. Many suffragists believed that any argument was acceptable as long as it advanced suffrage and played on southern racism. For example, in the pamphlet "What the South Can Do" (1867), circulated in Kansas, Henry Brown Blackwell provided statistics about white and black populations and then suggested that the votes of white females would exactly counterbalance those of black males and females. Under such circumstances, he asked, "can any Southerner fear to trust the women of the South with the ballot?"

Appeals to racism were motivated by political expediency, but most suffragists and pro-feminist men repudiated such strategies. Many black leaders, such as A. Phillips Randolph, supported woman suffrage at the turn of the century (see his "Woman Suffrage and the Negro"*), but few were as consistent as W. E. B. Du Bois. Du Bois published editorials for suffrage in the *Crisis* (see, e.g., "Votes for Women"*) and ran symposia in which prominent black leaders—men and women—would write in its favor (see Cott 1987). "The uplift of women is, next to the problem of the color line and the peace movement, our greatest modern cause," Du Bois wrote in the powerful essay "The Damnation of Women," which was published in his *Darkwater* (1920, 179). Du Bois's abiding respect and admiration for women, especially black women, "had its roots in his deep regard for his mother" (Rampersad 1976, 4). Women must have "a life work and economic independence" and the right to choose or reject motherhood (and the knowledge about how to do both). His critique of "the bestiality of free manhood" led to a conclusion that, "despite the noisier and more spectacular advance of my brothers, I instinctively feel and know that it is the five million women of my race who really count" (Du Bois 1920, 179).

The Men's League for Woman Suffrage

In 1910, Max Eastman, editor of the *Masses* and a young philosophy professor at Columbia, helped to organize the Men's League for Woman Suffrage in New York City, the first pro-feminist men's organization (see his "Who's Afraid? Confessions of a Suffrage Orator"*). Oswald Garrison Villard, editor of the *Nation* and the *New York Eve-*

ning Post, and Rabbi Steven Wise had already "agreed to share the ignominy" of founding the league and needed someone to take on the task of organizing it (see Wise's "Statement on Suffrage"*). Eastman populated the board with the era's most prominent reformers and social activists, such as George Foster Peabody, an eminent banker; Ward Melville; Hamilton Holt; Frederic Howe, husband of Marie Jenny Howe, the founder of the Heterodoxy Club in Greenwich Village; Vassar president Henry Noble MacCracken; and John Dewey. Columbia economist Charles Beard joined, arguing, in *The Common Man and the Franchise,** that suffrage would result from the "increasing economic independence of women." But it was Peabody, the blueblood financier, who really gave the league its impetus. "The league owed its pecuniary life" to Peabody, wrote Eastman, "and a great part of its early standing before the public" (*HWS,* 5:484–85).

League activities included organizing men's contingents to march in suffrage parades, mass meetings for suffrage speakers, and rallies and suffrage dinners for up to six hundred guests. The league sponsored benefit theatrical performances and balls and persuaded the New York Giants to sponsor an Annual Woman Suffrage Day on the Diamond, in which the New York Woman Suffrage Party received a percentage of the ticket price. In 1913, as a publicity stunt, the league organized a "Blue Button" campaign, in which members wore blue buttons on street cars and gave up their seats to women. "Women entering crowded street cars from now on should look for the man wearing a blue button," noted the *New York Times* (21 July 1913: 7). The wearer is a member of the Men's League for Woman Suffrage, and one of his principles is to give his seat to the first woman who needs it." He would then say, "That's all right, Madam: I am a woman suffragist and a member of the Men's League, and courtesy and consideration for women is the special feature of our creed."

Much of the league's attention was focused on lobbying male legislators. George Creel and Gilbert Roe organized a twentieth-century version of the Committees of Correspondence, inviting prominent men in other states to detail women's political participation and organizing a letter-writing campaign to newspapers that had published hostile articles or editorials (see Creel to Hamlin Garland, 11 September 1915, SL, H. B. Laidlaw Papers, box 8, folders 125–28). The great suffrage meetings at the Cooper Union featured Men's League members, including Peabody, Dewey, Eastman, George Middleton, as well as non-members Samuel Gompers and W. E. B. Dubois (see letter from DuBois, 7 May 1915, ibid., folder 124). Branches sprang up in cities across the country and also at colleges, where male students worked to bring suffrage speakers to campus. A national league, chaired by James Lee Laidlaw, served as an umbrella, and even some public schools organized branches (see letter to R. C. Beadle, 24 April 1915, SL, Laidlaw Papers, A-63, folder 123). The league commissioned prominent writers to answer one each of the major objections to suffrage (see Lincoln Steffens, "Woman Suffrage Would Increase Corruption"*).

Political Struggles after Suffrage

On the eve of ratification of the Nineteenth Amendment, one feminist newspaper, the *Suffragist,* ([5 July 1919]: 1), paid tribute to men's support:

> It has been said that the suffragists have only themselves to thank for the victory that marks the end of a long struggle, but while the fight has essentially been woman's own, there have been hundreds of men throughout the country, in politics and out of politics, from the beginning of the fight to its end, who have so truly understood the aspirations that lay at the bottom of woman's endeavor, that they have stood shoulder to shoulder with her, helping in an earnest, dependable, generous, brotherly fashion, to bring about the things she sought. . . . There have been an ever increasing number of true hearted men . . . who have been the kind of suffragists to actually seek ways to help, and if occasion demanded, to make sacrifices for the cause.

But women's struggle for political equality did not end with suffrage. Several prominent men supported the National Woman's Party, founded by Alice Paul, and especially the party's effort to enact an equal rights amendment to the Constitution, in order to accomplish for women what the Fifteenth Amendment had for blacks (see Henry Wallace's "Statement on the Equal Rights Amendment"*). Other political parties also addressed the issue. Robert LaFollette's Progressive Party platform included a plank on women's rights in 1924, advocating "removal of legal discriminations against women by measures not prejudicial to legislation necessary for the protection of women and for the advancement of social welfare" (cited in Cott 1987, 253). Socialist and Communist party leaders Daniel DeLeon's and William Z. Foster's support of women was notable in a political party in which women were so often ignored (see Foster's "On Improving the Party's Work Among Women"*). Foster launched a crusade against "male chauvinism" in the party, which marked the first time that that phrase was used with its current meaning.

After suffrage was granted, the battle lines again shifted, as some feminists thought new issues could assume center stage. As suffragists celebrated victory, some took up other causes—for workplace equality in the union struggles of the 1920s, for continued entry into the professions, for "sex rights" and birth control, and for sexual liberation. All these themes converged in the late 1960s with the rebirth of the women's liberation movement and the rebirth of modern feminism in the current era.

FROM ABOLITION TO SUFFRAGE

"THE RIGHTS OF WOMEN"

Frederick Douglass (1848)

ONE OF THE MOST INTERESTING events of the past week, was the holding of what is technically styled a Woman's Rights Convention at Seneca Falls. The speaking, addresses, and resolutions of this extraordinary meeting was almost wholly conducted by women; and although they evidently felt themselves in a novel position, it is but simple justice to say that their whole proceedings were characterized by marked ability and dignity. No one present, we think, however much he might be disposed to differ from the views advanced by the leading speakers on that occasion, will fail to give them credit for brilliant talents and excellent dispositions. In this meeting, as in other deliberative assemblies, there were frequent differences of opinion and animated discussion; but in no case was there the slightest absence of good feeling and decorum. Several interesting documents setting forth the rights as well as the grievances of women were read. Among these was a Declaration of Sentiments, to be regarded as the basis of a grand movement for attaining the civil, social, political, and religious rights of women. We should not do justice to our own convictions, or to the excellent persons connected with this infant movement, if we did not in this connection offer a few remarks on the general subject which the Convention met to consider and the objects they seek to attain. In doing so, we are not insensible that the bare mention of this truly important subject in any other than terms of contemptuous ridicule and scornful disfavor, is likely to excite against us the fury of bigotry and the folly of prejudice. A discussion of the rights of animals would be regarded with far more complacency by many of what are called the *wise* and the *good* of our land, than would a discussion of the rights of women. It is, in their estimation, to be guilty of evil thoughts, to think that woman is entitled to equal rights with man. Many who have at last made the discovery that the Negroes have some rights as well as other members of the human family, have yet to be convinced that women are entitled

---

North Star *(28 July 1848). Reprinted in* HWS, *vol. 1.*

to any. Eight years ago a number of persons of this description actually abandoned the anti-slavery cause, lest by giving their influence in that direction they might possibly be giving countenance to the dangerous heresy that woman, in respect to rights, stands on an equal footing with man. In the judgment of such persons the American slave system, with all its concomitant horrors, is less to be deplored than this *wicked* idea. It is perhaps needless to say, that we cherish little sympathy for such sentiments or respect for such prejudices. Standing as we do upon the watch-tower of human freedom, we cannot be deterred from an expression of our approbation of any movement, however humble, to improve and elevate the character of any members of the human family. While it is impossible for us to go into this subject at length, and dispose of the various objections which are often urged against such a doctrine as that of female equality, we are free to say that in respect to political rights, we hold woman to be justly entitled to all we claim for man. We go farther, and express our conviction that all political rights which it is expedient for man to exercise, it is equally so for woman. All that distinguishes man as an intelligent and accountable being, is equally true of woman, and if that government only is just which governs by the free consent of the governed, there can be no reason in the world for denying to woman the exercise of the elective franchise, or a hand in making and administering the laws of the land. Our doctrine is that "right is of no sex." We therefore bid the women engaged in this movement our humble Godspeed.

"INTELLIGENT WICKEDNESS"

William Lloyd Garrison (1853)

IT WAS this morning objected to the Declaration of Sentiments, that it implied that man was the only transgressor . . . and our eloquent friend, Mrs. Rose, who stood on this platform . . . told us her creed. She told us she did not blame anybody, really, and did not hold any man to be criminal. . . .

For my own part, I am not prepared to respect that philosophy. I believe in sin, therefore in a sinner; in theft, therefore in a thief; in slavery, therefore in a slaveholder; in wrong, therefore in a wrong-doer; and unless the men of this nation are made by woman to see that they have been guilty of usurpation, and cruel usurpation, I believe very little progress will be made. To say all

Speech at the Fourth National Women's Rights Convention, Cleveland, 1853. Reprinted in New York Daily Tribune *(7 September 1853), and* HWS, *vol. 1.*

this has been done without thinking, without calculation, without design, by mere accident, by a want of light; can anybody believe this who is familiar with all the facts in this case? Certainly, for one, I hope ever to lean to the charitable side, and will try to do so. I, too, believe things are done through misconception and misapprehension, which are injurious, yes, which are immoral and unchristian; but only to a limited extent. There is such a thing as intelligent wickedness, a design on the part of those who have the light to quench it, and to do the wrong to gratify their own propensities, and to further their own interests. So, then, I believe, that as man has monopolized for generations all the rights which belong to woman, it has not been accidental, not through ignorance on his part; but I believe that man has done this through calculation, actuated by a spirit of pride, a desire for domination which has made him degrade woman in her own eyes, and thereby tend to make her a mere vassal.

It seems to me, therefore, that we are to deal with the consciences of men. It is idle to say that the guilt is common, that the women are as deeply involved in this matter as the men. Never can it be said that the victims are as much to be blamed as the victimizer; that the slaves are to be as much blamed as the slaveholders and slave-drivers; that the women who have no rights, are to be as much blamed as the men who have played the part of robbers and tyrants. We must deal with conscience. The men of this nation, and the men of all nations, have no just respect for woman. They have tyrannized over her deliberately, they have not sinned through ignorance, but theirs is not the knowledge that saves. Who can say truly, that in all things he acts up to the light he enjoys, that he does not do something which he knows is not the very thing, or the best thing he ought to do? How few there are among mankind who are able to say this with regard to themselves. Is not the light all around us? Does not this nation know how great its guilt is in enslaving one-sixth of its people? Do not the men of this nation know ever since the landing of the pilgrims, that they are wrong in making subject one-half of the people? Rely upon it, it has not been a mistake on their part. It has been sin. It has been guilt; and they manifest their guilt to a demonstration, in the manner in which they receive this movement. Those who do wrong ignorantly, do not willingly continue in it, when they find they are in the wrong. Ignorance is not an evidence of guilt certainly. It is only an evidence of a want of light. They who are only ignorant, will never rage, and rave, and threaten, and foam, when the light comes; but being interested and walking in the light, will always present a manly front, and be willing to be taught and be willing to be told they are in the wrong.

Take the case of slavery: How has the anti-slavery cause been received? Not argumentatively, not by reason, not by entering the free arena of fair discussion and comparing notes; the arguments have been rotten eggs, and brickbats and calumny, and in the southern portion of the country, a spirit of murder, and threats to cut out the tongues of those who spoke against them. What has this indicated on the part of the nation? What but conscious guilt? Not ignorance, not that they had not the light. They had the light and rejected it.

How has this Woman's Rights movement been treated in this country, on the right hand and on the left? This nation ridicules and derides this movement, and spits upon it, as fit only to be cast out and trampled underfoot. This is not ignorance. They know all about the truth. It is the natural outbreak of tyranny. It is because the tyrants and usurpers are alarmed. They have been and are called to judgment, and they dread the examination and exposure of their position and character.

Women of America! you have something to blame yourselves for in this matter, something to account for to God and the world. Granted. But then you are the victims in this land, as the women of all lands are, to the tyrannical power and godless ambition of man; and we must show who are [*sic*] responsible in this matter.

"A SERMON OF THE PUBLIC FUNCTION OF WOMAN"

Theodore Parker (1853)

If woman is a human being, first, she has the Nature of a human being; next, she has the Right of a human being; third, she has the Duty of a human being. The Nature is the capacity to possess, to use, to develop, and to enjoy every human faculty; the Right is the right to enjoy, develop, and use every human faculty; and the Duty is to make use of the Right, and make her human nature, human history. She is here to develop her human nature, enjoy her human rights, perform her human duty. Womankind is to do this for herself, as much as mankind for himself. A woman has the same human nature that a man has; the same human rights, to life, liberty, and the pursuit of happiness; the same human duties; and they are as inalienable in a woman as in a man.

Each man has the natural right to the normal development of his nature, so far as it is general-human, neither man nor woman, but human. Each woman has the natural right to the normal development of her nature, so far as it is general-human, neither woman nor man. But each man has also a natural and inalienable right to the normal development of his peculiar nature as man, where he differs from woman. Each woman has just the same natural and inalienable right to the normal development of her peculiar nature as woman, and not man. All that is undeniable.

Now see what follows. Woman has the same individual right to determine her aim in life, and to follow it; has the same individual rights of body and of spirit—of mind and conscience, and heart and soul; the same physical rights, the same intellectual, moral, affectional, and religious rights, that man has. That is true of womankind as a whole; it is true of Jane, Ellen, and Sally, and each special woman that can be named.

Every person, man or woman, is an integer, an individual, a whole person; and also

---

"A Sermon of the Public Function of Woman—Preached at the Music Hall, March 27, 1853." Reprinted in Additional Speeches, Addresses, and Occasional Sermons, *vol. 2. Boston: Little, Brown, 1855.*

a portion of the race, and so a fraction of humankind. Well, the rights of individualism are not to be possessed, developed, used, and enjoyed, by a life in solitude, but by joint action. Accordingly, to complete and perfect the individual man or woman, and give each an opportunity to possess, use, develop, and enjoy these rights, there must be concerted and joint action; else individuality is only a possibility, not a reality. So the individual rights of woman carry with them the same domestic, social, ecclesiastical, and political rights, as those of man.

The Family, Community, Church and State, are four modes of action which have grown out of human nature in its historical development; they are all necessary for the development of mankind; machines which the human race has devised, in order to possess, use, develop, and enjoy their rights as human beings, their rights also as men.

These are just as necessary for the development of woman as of man; and, as she has the same nature, right, and duty, as man, it follows that she has the same right to use, shape, and control these four institutions, for her general human purpose and for her special feminine purpose, that man has to control them for his general human purpose and his special masculine purpose. All that is as undeniable as anything in metaphysics or mathematics.

If woman had been consulted, it seems to me theology would have been in a vastly better state than it is now. I do not think that any woman would ever have preached the damnation of babies new-born; and"hell, paved with the skulls of infants not a span long," would be a region yet to be discovered in theology. . . .

The popular theology leaves us nothing feminine in the character of God. How could it be otherwise, when so much of the popular theology is the work of men who thought woman was a "pollution," and barred her out of all the high places of the church? If women had had their place in ecclesiastical teaching, I doubt that the "Athanasian Creed" would ever have been thought a "symbol" of Christianity. The pictures and hymns which describe the last judgment are a protest against the exclusion of woman from teaching in the church. "I suffer not a woman to teach, but to be in silence," said a writer in the New Testament. The sentence has brought manifold evil in its train. So much for the employments of women.

By nature, woman has the same political rights that man has—to vote, to hold office, to make and administer laws. These she has a matter of right. The strong hand and the great head of man keep her down; nothing more. In America, in Christendom, woman has no political rights, is not a citizen in full; she has no voice in making or administering the laws, none in electing the rulers or administrators thereof. She can hold no office—can not be committee of a primary school, overseer of the poor, or guardian to a public lamp-post. But any man, with conscience enough to keep out of jail, mind enough to escape the poor-house, and body enough to drop his ballot into the box, he is a voter. He may have no character—even no money; that is no matter–he is male. The noblest woman has no voice in the State. Men make laws, disposing of her property, her person, her children; still she must bear it, "with a patient shrug."

Looking at it as a matter of pure right and pure science, I know no reason why woman should not be a voter, or hold office, or make and administer laws. I do not see how I can shut myself into political privileges and shut woman out, and do both in the name of inalienable right. Certainly, every woman has a natural right to have her property represented in the general representation of property, and her person represented in the general representation of persons. . . .

If the affairs of the nation had been under woman's joint control, I doubt that we should have butchered the Indians with such exterminating savagery, that, in fifty years, we should have spent seven hundred millions of dollars for war, and now, in time of peace, send twenty annual millions more to the same waste. I doubt that we should have spread slavery into nine new States, and made it national. I think the Fugitive Slave bill would never have been an act. Woman has some respect for the natural law of God.

I know men say woman can not manage the great affairs of a nation. Very well. Government is political economy—national housekeeping. Does any respectable woman keep house so badly as the Unites States? with so much bribery, so much corruption, so much quarrelling in the domestic councils?

But government is also political morality, it is national ethics. Is there any worthy woman who rules her household as wickedly as the nations are ruled? who hires bullies to fight for her? Is there any woman who treats one-sixth part of her household as if they were cattle and not creatures of God, as if they were things and not persons? I know of none such. In government as housekeeping, or government as morality, I think man makes a very poor appearance, when he says woman could not do as well as he has done and is doing.

I doubt that woman will ever, as a general thing, take the same interest as men in political affairs, or find therein an abiding satisfaction. But that is for women themselves to determine, not for men.

In order to attain the end—the development of man in body and spirit—human institutions must represent all parts of human nature, both the masculine and the feminine element. For the well-being of the human race, we need the joint action of man and woman, in the family, the community, the Church, and the State. A family without the presence of woman—with no mother, no wife, no sister, no womankind—is a sad thing. I think a community without woman's equal social action, a church without her equal ecclesiastical action, and a State without her equal political action, is almost as bad—is very much what a house would be without a mother, wife, sister, or friend. . . .

Oh, brother-men, who make these things, is this a pleasant sight? Does your literature complain of it—of the waste of human life, the slaughter of human souls, the butchery of woman? British literature begins to wail, in "Nicholas Nickleby" and "Jane Eyre" and "Mary Barton" and "Alton Locke," in many a "Song of the Shirt"; but the respectable literature of America is deaf as a cent to the outcry of humanity expiring in agonies. It is busy with California, or the Presidency, or extolling iniquity in high places, or flattering the vulgar vanity which buys its dross for gold. . . .

Well, we want the excellence of man and woman both united; intellectual power, knowledge, great ideas—in literature, philosophy, theology, ethics—and practical skill; but we want something better—the moral, affectional, religious intuition, to put justice into ethics, love into theology, piety into science and letters. Everywhere in the family, the community, the Church, and the State, we want the masculine and feminine element co-operating and conjoined. Woman is to correct man's taste, mend his morals, excite his affections, inspire his religious faculties. Man is to quicken her intellect, to help her will, translate her sentiments to ideas, and enact them into righteous laws. Man's moral action, at best, is only a sort of general human providence, aiming at the welfare of a part, and satisfied with achieving the "greatest good of the greatest number." Woman's moral action is more like a special human providence, acting without general rules, but caring for each particular case. We need both of these, the general and the special, to make a total human providence.

If man and woman are counted equivalent—equal in rights, though with diverse powers,—shall we not mend the literature of the world, its theology, its science, its laws, and its actions too? I can not believe that wealth and want are to stand ever side by side as desperate foes; that culture must ride only on the back of ignorance; and feminine virtue be guarded by the degradation of whole classes of ill-starred men, as in the East, or the degradation of whole classes of ill-starred women, as in the West; but while we neglect the means of help God puts in our power, why, the present must be like the past—"property" must be left, "law" the strength of selfish will, and "Christianity"—what we see it is, the apology for every powerful wrong.

To every woman let me say—Respect your nature as a human being, your nature as a woman; then respect your rights, then remember your duty to possess, to use, to develop, and to enjoy every faculty which God has given you, each in its normal way.

And to men let me say—Respect, with the profoundest reverence, respect the mother that bore you, the sisters who bless you, the woman that you love, the woman that you marry. As you seek to possess your own manly rights, seek also, by that great arm, by that powerful brain, seek to vindicate her rights as woman, as your own as man. Then we may see better things in the Church, better things in the State, in the Community, in the House. Then the green shall show what buds it hid, the buds shall blossom, the flowers bear fruit, and the blessing of God be on us all.

"WOMAN"

Ralph Waldo Emerson (1855)

PLATO SAID, Woman are the same as men in faculty, only less in degree. But the general voice of mankind has agreed that they have their own strength; that women are strong by sentiment; that the same mental height which their husbands attain by toil, they attain by sympathy with their husbands. Man is the will, and Woman the sentiment. In this ship of humanity, Will is the

"Woman: A Lecture Read Before the Woman's Rights Convention." Boston, 20 September 1855. Reprinted in Emerson's Complete Works. *Riverside ed. Boston: Houghton Mifflin, 1883–93.*

rudder, and Sentiment the sail: when Woman affects to steer, the rudder is only a masked sail. When women engage in any art or trade, it is usually as a resource, not as a primary object. The life of the affections is primary to them, so that there is usually no employment or career which they will not with their own applause and that of society quit for a suitable marriage. And they give entirely to their affections, set their whole fortune on the die, lose themselves eagerly in the glory of their husbands and children. Man stands astonished at a magnanimity he cannot pretend to. . . .

Women, are, by this and their social influence, the civilizers of mankind. What is civilization? I answer, the power of good women. . . .

One truth leads in another by hand; one right is an accession of strength to take more. And the times are marked by the new attitude of Woman; urging, by argument and by association, her rights of all kinds,—in short, to one-half of the world;—as the right to education, to avenues of employment, to equal rights of property, to equal rights in marriage, to the exercise of the professions and of suffrage. . . .

They have an unquestionable right to their own property. And if a woman demand votes, offices and political equality with men, . . . it must not be refused. It is very cheap wit that finds it so droll that a woman should vote. Educate and refine society to the highest point,—bring together a cultivated society of both sexes, in a drawing-room, and consult and decide by voices on a question of taste or on a question of right, and is there any absurdity or any practical difficulty in obtaining their authentic opinions? . . .

. . . [A]ll my points would sooner be carried in the state if women voted. On the questions that are important;—whether the government shall be in one person, or whether representative, or whether democratic; whether men shall be holden in bondage, or shall be roasted alive and eaten, as in Typee, or shall be hunted with bloodhounds, as in this country; whether men shall be hanged for stealing, or hanged at all; whether the unlimited sale of cheap liquors shall be allowed;—they would give, I suppose, as intelligent a vote as the voters of Boston or New York.

We may ask, to be sure,—Why need you vote? If new power is here, of a character which solves old tough questions, which puts me and all the rest in the wrong, tries and condemns our religion, customs, laws, and opens new careers to our young receptive men and women, you can well leave voting to the old dead people. Those whom you teach, and those whom you half teach, will fast enough make themselves considered and strong with their new insight, and votes will follow from all the dull.

The objection to their voting is the same as is urged, in the lobbies of legislatures, against clergymen who take an active part in politics;—that if they are good clergymen they are unacquainted with the expediencies of politics, and if they become good politicians they are worse clergymen. So of women, that they cannot enter this arena without being contaminated and unsexed.

Here are two or three objections; first, a want of practical wisdom; second, a too purely ideal view; and, third, danger of contamination. For their want of intimate knowledge of affairs, I do not think this ought to disqualify them from voting at any town-meeting which I ever attended. I could heartily wish the objection were sound. But if any man will take the trouble to see how our people vote,—how many gentlemen are willing to take on themselves the trouble of thinking and determining for you, and, standing at the door of the polls, give every innocent citizen his ticket as he comes in, informing him that this is the vote of his party; and how the innocent citizen, without further demur, goes and drops it in the ballot-box,—I cannot but think he will agree that most women might vote as wisely.

For the other point, of their not knowing the world, and aiming at abstract right without allowance for circumstances,—that is not a disqualification, but a qualification. Human society is made up of partialities. Each citizen has an interest and a view of his own, which, if followed out to the extreme, would leave no room for any other citizen. One man is timid and another rash; one would change nothing, and the other is pleased with nothing; one wishes schools, another armies, one gunboats, another public gardens. Bring all these biases together and something is done in favor of them all.

Every one is a half vote, but the next elector behind him brings the other or corresponding half in his hand: a reasonable result is had. Now there is no lack, I am sure, of the expediency, or of the interests of trade or of imperative class-interests being neglected. There is no lack of votes representing the physical wants; and if in your city the uneducated emigrant vote numbers thousands, representing a brutal ignorance and mere animal wants, it is to be corrected by an educated and religious vote, representing the wants and desires of honest and refined persons. If the wants, the passions, the vices, are allowed a full vote through the hands of a half-brutal intemperate population, I think it but fair that the virtues, the aspirations should be allowed a full vote, as an offset, through the purest part of the people.

As for the unsexing and contamination,—that only accuses our existing politics, shows how barbarous we are,—that our policies are so crooked, made up of things not to be spoken, to be understood only by wink and nudge; this man to be coaxed, that man to be bought, and that other to be duped. It is easy to see that there is contamination enough, but it rots the men now, and fills the air with stench. Come out of that: it is like a dance-cellar. The fairest names in this country in literature, in law, have gone into Congress and come out dishonored. And when I read the list of men of intellect, of refined pursuits, giants in law, or eminent scholars, or of social distinction, leading men of wealth and enterprise in the commercial community, and see what they have voted for and suffered to be voted for, I think no community was ever so politely and elegantly betrayed. . . .

. . . Let the laws be purged of every barbarous remainder, every barbarous impediment to women. Let the public donations for education be equally shared by them, let them enter a school as freely as a church, let them have and hold and give their property as men do theirs;—and in a few years it will easily appear whether they wish a voice in making the laws that are to govern them. If you do refuse them a vote, you will also refuse to tax them,—according to our Teutonic principle, No representation, no tax.

All events of history are to be regarded as growths and offshoots of the expanding mind of the race, and this appearance of new opinions, their currency and force in many minds, is itself the wonderful fact. For whatever is popular is important, shows the spontaneous sense of the hour. The aspiration of this century will be the code of the next. It holds of high and distant causes, of the same influences that make the sun and moon. When new opinions appear, they will be entertained and respected, by every fair mind, according to their reasonableness, and not according to their convenience, or their fitness to shock our customs. But let us deal with them greatly; let them make their way by the upper road, and not by the way of manufacturing public opinion, which lapses continually into expediency, and makes charlatans. All that is spontaneous is irresistible, and forever it is individual force that interests. . . .

. . . Slavery it is that makes slavery; freedom, freedom. The slavery of women happened when the men were slaves of kings. The melioration of manners brought their melioration of course. It could not be otherwise, and hence the new desire of better laws. For there are always a certain number of passionately loving fathers, brothers, husbands and sons who put their might into the endeavor to make a daughter, a wife, or a mother happy in the way that suits best. Woman should find in man her guardian. Silently she looks for that, and when she finds that he is not, as she instantly does, she betakes her to her own defences, and does the best she can. But when he is her guardian, fulfilled with all nobleness, knows and accepts his duties as her brother, all goes well for both.

The new movement is only a tide shared by the spirits of man and woman; and you may proceed in the faith that whatever the woman's heart is prompted to desire, the man's mind is simultaneously prompted to accomplish.

"KANSAS SUFFRAGE SONG"

P. P. Fowler and John W. Hutchinson (1867)

O, SAY what thrilling songs of fairies,
Wafted o'er the Kansas prairies,
Charm the ear while zephyrs speed 'em!
Woman's pleading for her freedom.

Clear the way, the songs are floating;
Clear the way, the world is noting;
Prepare the way, the right promoting,
And ballots, too, for woman's voting.

Reprinted in HWS, *vol.* 2.

We frankly say to fathers, brothers,
Husbands, too, and several others,
We're bound to win our right of voting,
Don't you hear the music floating?

We come to take with you our station,
Brave defenders of the nation,
And aim by noble, just endeavor
To elevate our sex forever.

By this vote we'll rid our nation
Of its vile intoxication.
Can't get rum? Oh, what a pity!
Dram-shops closed in every city.

Fear not, we'll darn each worthy stocking,
Duly keep the cradle rocking,
And beg you heed the words we utter,
The ballot wins our bread and butter.

All hail, brave Kansas! first in duty.
Yours, the meed of praise and beauty,
You'll nobly crown your deeds of daring,
Freedom to our sex declaring.

"THE MORTALITY OF NATIONS"

Parker Pillsbury (1867)

MY MAIN POINT is this—we have had enough of the past in government. It is time to change. Literally almost, more than metaphorically, the "times are rotten ripe." We come to-day to demand—first an extension of the right of suffrage to every American citizen, of whatever race, complexion or sex.

Manhood or *male*-hood suffrage is not a remedy for evils such as we wish removed. The Anti-Slavery Society demands that; and so, too, do large numbers of both the political parties. Even Andrew Johnson at first recommended it, in the reconstruction of the rebel States, for three classes of colored men. The New York *Herald*, in the exuberance of its religious zeal, demanded that "members of Christian Churches" as added as a fourth estate to the three designated by the President.

The Woman's Rights Society contemplated suffrage only for woman. But we, as an Equal Rights Association, recognize no distinctions based on sex, complexion or race. The Ten Commandments know nothing of any such distinctions. No more do we.

The right of suffrage is as old, as sacred and as universal as the right to life, liberty and the pursuit of happiness. It is indeed the complement and safeguard of these and all civil and political rights to every citizen. The right to life would be nothing without the right to acquire and possess the means of its support. So it were mockery to talk of liberty and the pursuit of happiness, until the ballot in the hand of every citizen seals and secures it.

The right of the black man to a voice in the government was not earned at Olustee or Port Hudson. It was his when life began, not when life was paid for it under the battle-axe of war. It was his with Washington and Jefferson, James Buchanan and Abraham Lincoln. Not one of them could ever produce a higher, holier claim. Nor can any of us.

We are prating about *giving* right of suffrage to black *male* citizens, as complacently as we once gave our compassion and corn to famishing Ireland. But this famine

---

An address to the first meeting of the American Equal Rights Association, 9 May 1867. Reprinted in HWS, *vol. 2.*

of freedom and justice exists because we have produced it. Had our fleets and armies robbed Ireland of its last loaf, and left its myriads of inhabitants lean, ghastly skeletons, our charity would not have been more a mockery when we sent them bread to preserve them alive, than it is now when we talk of *giving* the ballot to those whom God created free and equal with ourselves.

And in the plenitude of our generosity, we even propose to extend the *gift* to woman also. It is proposed to make educated, cultivated, refined, loyal, tax-paying, government-obeying woman equal to the servants who groom her horses, and scour the pots and pans of her kitchen. Unfortunate beings, without property, and scarcely knowing the English tongue, or any other, are entreated to grant to women, the superior of all the queens of the old world, the right to cooperate with them in the affairs of State. Women here in New York worth thousands and hundreds of thousands in gold, and whose money is the meanest part of their real value in society, are humbly petitioning their coachmen, their footmen and gardeners, the discharged State-prison convicts, the idiots and lunatics, all of whom may and often do exercise the right of the ballot, to permit them also to share with them in making and executing the laws.

Our Maria Mitchells, our Harriet Hosmers, Harriet Beecher Stowes, Lydia Maria Childs, and Lucretia Motts, with millions of the mothers and matrons of quiet homes, where they preside with queenly dignity and grace, are begging of besotted, debauched white male citizens, legal voters, soaked in whiskey, simmered in tobacco, and parboiled in every shameless vice and sin, to recognize them also as human, and graciously accord to them the rights of intelligent beings!

And singularly enough, in some of the States, it is proposed to grant the prayer. But the wisest and best men have no idea that they are only restoring what they have so long held by force, based on fraud and falsehood. They only propose to *give* woman the boon which they claim was theirs by heavenly inheritance. But they are too late with their sublime generosity. For God gave them when he gave life and breath, passions, emotions, conscience and will. Give gold, give lands, give honors, give office, give title of nobility, if you must; but talk not of giving natural inalienable and heaven-derived endowments. God alone bestows these. He alone has them to give.

Our trade in right of suffrage is contraband. It is bold buccaneering on the commerce of the moral universe. If we have our *neighbor's* right of suffrage and citizenship in our keeping, no matter of what color, or race, or sex, then we have stolen goods in our possession; and God's search-warrant will pursue us forever, if those goods be not restored.

And then we impudently assert that "all just governments derive their powers from the consent of the governed." But when was the consent of woman ever asked to one single act on all the statute books?

We talk of "trial by jury of our peers!" In this country of ours, women have been fined, imprisoned, scourged, branded with red hot irons and hung; but when, or where, or for what crime or offence, was ever woman tried by a jury of her peers?

Suffrage was never in the hands of tyrants or of governments, but by usurpation. It was never given by them to any of us. We *brought* it; not *bought* it; nor conquered it; nor begged it; nor earned it; nor inherited it. It was man's inalienable, irrepealable, inextinguishable right from the beginning. It is so still; the same yesterday, to-day and while earthly governments last.

It came with the right to see and hear; to breathe and speak; to think and feel; to love and hate; to choose and refuse; or it did not come at all.

The right to see came with the eye and the light; did it not? and the right to breathe, with the lungs and the air; and all these from the same infinite source.

And has not also the moral and spiritual nature its inalienable rights? Have the mere bodily organs, which are but the larder of worms, born of the dust, and dust their destiny—have they power and prerogative that are denied to the reason, the understanding, the conscience, the will, those attributes which constitute responsibility, accountability and immortality? . . .

Must we be told that woman herself does not ask the ballot! Then I submit to such, if such there be, the question is not one of privilege, but of duty—of solemn responsibility. If woman does not desire the ballot, demand it, take it, she sins against her own nature and all the holiest instincts of humanity, and cannot too soon repent.

After all, the question of suffrage is one of justice and right. Unless human government be in itself an unnatural and impious usurpation, whoever renders it support and submission, has a natural and inalienable, imperishable and inextinguishable right, to an equal voice in enacting and executing the laws. Nor can one man, or millions on millions of men acquire or possess the power to withhold that right from the humblest human being of sane mind, but by usurpation, and by rebellion against the constitution of the moral universe. It would be robbery, though the giving of the right should induce all the predicted and dreaded evils of tyrants, cowards, and white male citizens.

"THE SLAVERY YET TO BE ABOLISHED"

George W. Julian (1874)

. . . DEVOTION to humanity was the basis of the anti-slavery enterprise, and that devotion should find expression against every form of oppression. It should heed the logic of its work, and when one task is done proceed to another. The abolition of the chattel slavery of the southern negro only brought anti-slavery men to the threshold of their undertaking. It was the mere prelude to a far grander movement, looking to the emancipation of all races from all forms of slavery. It not only opens the way for systematic opposition to the several forms of slavery I have mentioned, but it makes inevitable the demand for the enfranchisement of woman; and thus I am naturally conducted to the principal subject of my present discourse. . . .

In the first place, I take it for granted that we are all agreed in the purpose to stand by our popular form of government. I assume that none of you desire to reopen the controversy between monarchy and aristocracy on the one hand, and democracy on the other, which was settled by our fathers a century ago in the forum of argument and by the ordeal of battle. You would not call in a king and reinstate an order of nobility if you could; or if such persons exist in our midst they are so few in numbers and so prudently non-committal that I need not notice them in dealing with the problem I am considering. You all believe in a "government of the people, by the people, and for the people," and you all concede that it must be carried on by a majority, through the instrumentality of the ballot. . . .

. . . We all agree that the right of suffrage does not depend upon property, or nativity, or race, or color, or religion, or any specific literary qualification. We have settled it that none of these mere accidents of humanity can be the basis of the right, and consequently that it must rest upon humanity itself. The right to the ballot, therefore, by which I mean the right to be represented in the organism which deals with your liberty, your property, and your life, is as natural and as inborn as the right to the breath of your nostrils. A responsible human being, innocent of crime, yielding his allegiance to the government, answerable to it in his person and property for disobedience, and yet denied any political right, is a slave. So thought Samuel Adams, James Otis, and the Fathers, and if it is not true, then nothing is true. "Taxation without representation is tyranny;" that is to say, a man who is taxed and governed, with no voice in the taxing and governing power, is not and can not be free. Dr. Franklin says that "they who have

---

"The Slavery Yet To Be Abolished: Delivered at Various Points in Michigan and Iowa in the Year 1874." Reprinted in Later Speeches on Political Questions with Select Controversial Papers, *ed. Grace Julian Clarke. Indianapolis: Carlon & Hollenbeck, 1889.*

no voice nor vote in the choosing of representatives do not enjoy liberty, but are absolutely enslaved to those who have votes." Will any American deny this? The essence of slavery is enforced obedience to irresponsible power, and therefore it can make no difference in principle whether that power is exercised by a single master or by society. . . .

. . . [F]ully one-half the human race is feminine. Woman stands related to us as wife, mother, sister and daughter. She is a citizen by the unmistakable words of the constitution. She is a tax-payer, and as to certain positions, in some of the states, she is already allowed to vote and hold office. We are enlarging her sphere of employment, and increasing her compensation for her work. We are recognizing her equality with man by securing to her the same educational opportunities. We imprison her for crime and hang her for murder. We baptize her as a Christian, and send her abroad as a missionary. I suppose Christ died for her in the same sense in which he died for man. She is endowed with the same faculties and affections, is animated by the same hopes, shares with man his joys and sorrows, and strives with him for the same blessings. Indeed, the case seems to me so plain that until those who deny woman's humanity are more particularly heard from, it can hardly be worth while to argue the question further. . . .

. . . Women, we are told, are unfit to vote. If enfranchised, they would vote on the wrong side. Undoubtedly, they would sometimes do so. They would make mistakes; but could they not profit by them? And if a careful search were made, is it not barely possible that cases could be found in which *men* have voted on the wrong side? I think I have known such cases myself, and probably you can recall others. How stands the account? Have we, in fact, such a record as makes it decent for us to sit in judgment upon the fitness of woman for politics? Look at our Sanborn contracts, our Moiety system, and our custom-house thieving. Look at our eminent Christian statesmen auctioning their consciences to a great railway corporation. Look at the great salary theft of the last Congress. Look at our civil service to-day, as foul and feculent a system of huckstering and plunder as our thoroughly debauched party politics could make it. Look at our drunken libertines elevated to high places by male voting. Look at the open and wholesale pollution of the ballot, and the spectacle of bribery and perjury we have witnessed in so many states. Look at the frightful decay of political morality in every section of the land, and listen to the prayers of good men for a speedy resurrection of conscience as the only possible salvation of the country!

Or look at the *wisdom* which male suffrage has made manifest in our parties and politicians. Take the tariff question. It is unsettled as it was a half century ago. Each of the great parties is divided upon it, and neither can define its position. So of the question of railway transportation. Neither is competent to deal with it, and neither, as a party, has any defined position respecting it. The same is true of the finance question. As national parties they are internally divided, while no man can name any vital point on which they stand opposed. Some of the leaders of both are for hard money and a return to specie payments, while others scout this idea, demand more printed money, and refer to Adam Smith and John Stuart Mill as theorists and dreamers whose doctrines of political economy are not applicable to the United States. Take the slavery question. Male suffrage could not settle it, and we were obliged to try it by battle. The labor question succeeds it, and no party has yet appeared that seems at all able to grapple with it. On the temperance question our parties have tried their hand at legislation for more than a generation, but thus far the result is a muddle. The picture thus imperfectly sketched is the picture of our country under the full blaze of masculine wisdom and virtue; and I respectfully submit that it does not warrant the arraignment of woman as unfit to share in our politics. On the contrary, I think it shows the need of her helping hand and saving grace, unless we decide to jump out of our democratic frying pan into the fire of kingly rule, which we have resolved not to do. . . .

WORKING FOR SUFFRAGE

"WOMAN SUFFRAGE IN WYOMING"

Gov. John W. Hoyt (1882)

WHAT, NOW, are the reasons that the work does not advance yet more rapidly? Why is there hesitation, a holding back on the part of the great majority? Let me see if I can point out the reasons.

In the first place, I am satisfied that it is feared by many that if women throughout the country had the ballot, certain evils would follow as the result. It is felt that there would be a disturbance of the social element, that the home would be deranged and desecrated by politics, that it would no longer have its charm as home. I am able to answer this from the experience of Wyoming, running through a period of thirteen years. I have been there four years myself, have made the most careful inquiry as to this matter, and find that nothing of the sort is to be heard of in any quarter. They have settled upon it there, as a principle, that the man may think one way and the woman another. They were not cast in the same mould, and why should they be bound together in matters of opinion like a bundle of faggots? Each should be free, as free in politics as in social questions. You never knew a husband and wife who agreed precisely on

An address delivered at Association Hall, Philadelphia, 3 April 1882. Reprinted in HWS, *vol.* 2.

every social question. I have never found a family of the kind, and I should be very sorry if my wife agreed with me upon everything; there would be no music in the house. We rather enjoy a quiet discussion of principles, or questions social, private, public, literary, scientific. Is it not a blessing, rather, to have a woman to compare notes with? No trouble of this sort comes of practical woman suffrage. I know of many families in which the husband is on one side of politics and the wife on the other, each fighting his own battles good naturedly, and joking each other when beaten just as two gentlemen do, who are friends.

Then, again, it is thought that women, if they had the ballot, would all the time be seeking office, that this would make things uncomfortable in the home; that the man would have to rock the babies, sew on the shirt buttons, and do a variety of disagreeable things, which *he* calls petty, you know, from his supreme height, and which he finds himself, when he comes to the trial, very ill fitted for. That is another great bugbear. There is nothing whatever in it. Two or three women in the Territory of Wyoming have held office; one was a school superintendent, and some have sat on juries a few times; but since I have been there I have never once heard the slightest intimation that any woman of Wyoming wanted office. The truth is, women do not care for the public life. I speak of women as a class. There are brilliant women, with remarkable powers, who could exercise the judicial function, or sit in the halls of Congress. I know women who, in the Senate, would be peers of any man there. If there are women of such remarkable powers and attainments, or of less ability, and they should be called to serve their State or country in official position, let them serve her, if willing so to do. But woman, *as a class,* do not desire public life. As before the magi of the old, woman stands to-day before the lawmakers of this new time, questioned as to what most pleases her, answering, as then, and as she ever will answer, "This is what woman most desires—to be loved, to be studied by her husband, and to be mistress of the house." The difference between the woman of the former time and of the present is in the manner of the response. The Persian representative of her sex stood in the twilight of a far-off time, asking for a veil behind which to conceal even from the gods, who held in their keeping those most precious gifts, her great joy in anticipation of their bestowal; the woman of to-day stands on platform and in press sternly demanding the things which have been denied her for all these centuries, and expressing her purpose to have something more than the promise of them. That is the only difference. "To be loved, to be studied by her husband, and to be mistress of the house," is the desire and hope of every woman, speaking in the broadest and most general terms. Now, my friends, please lay aside that ground of anxiety. It does not exist in a sound philosophy; it does not exist, in fact, where the experiment has been made.

Then, again, it has been thought by some that woman herself would suffer from contact with politics. The noisy, boisterous politicians at the polls, the rude men in office, in association with her on boards of one sort or another—with all these, it is said, women should not be brought in contact. Let them rather be saved from those trials. Well, I half thought so once myself, I must confess. I, too, was one of the women protectors. In my ignorance of what would practically work out, I saw through a glass darkly; I saw women subjected to all these disagreeable things, and I stepped right in between them and her and said, "I will protect you." But that was a *long* time ago. I have been ashamed of it for a good many years. I made up my mind long before going to Wyoming that it was entirely safe to leave to woman herself this question of what would affect her welfare. I said, "If woman is indeed the sensitive being, the refined and pure, angelic creature, which is supposed in the argument of her opponents, I can leave this question to her; she can better judge than I." Are women, or are men better judges of what a woman should undertake, or to what she should voluntarily subject herself? Touching the results of actual trial, I do not find that the women of Wyoming have suffered in the least degree from contact with politics. For delicacy and refinement they will bear favorable comparison with women of like social position anywhere.

Almost on the first day of my arrival in Wyoming there was an election. It was a general election for all the officers of the city, town, county, and territory, and I went early in the morning, you may be sure. I had assumed the role of student, and observed with great interest. I wanted to see what there was in this contact of delicate and refined women with the ruder elements of the population at the polls. The polls were opened in the office of the hotel, a very pleasant place. The window was on the side near the private entrance. There were steps there for the convenience of persons alighting from carriages, and they could pass easily to the window. Inside this pleasant office were the judges of the election—two women and one man. The secretary was a lady. There was considerable discussion of different questions outside, not boisterous, but lively and animated, and I was listening to it and observing. By-and-by I heard, running through the entire company, "Sh-h-h-h-h!" What does that mean? I turned, and saw ladies were coming to cast their ballots. Everything was quiet. Instantly the gentlemen pressed back, making a passage, and one of them, hat in hand, opened the carriage door. The lady stepped down and deposited her ballot, the gentlemen lifting their hats as she passed; she was politely helped back into the carriage, and drove away. I said, *"Surely that woman is not hurt."* As soon as the ladies came in sight there was a transformation among the men, in every case. There could not have been a more quiet place in the world while those women were present. It was the same whether they came in carriages or on foot. There was always a ripple when they approached, succeeded by a "Sh-h-h-h-h," then all was as still as the unruffled sea. The women seemed to be pleased with so courteous a reception; they felt that they had acquired a new dignity, a new power. To me, a stranger, it was very unexpected that there should be found so real a gentility in this new country, where men are supposed to be of ruder manners than in the older communities, but where they are in fact a noble, intelligent people from the East, with the best blood in their veins, and with much cultivation of the intellectual powers, as well as of the social amenities. How much of this was due to the influence of women I do not know, for this condition of things had existed a number of years before I arrived there. But I have no doubt that it should be in large measure ascribed to that influence. . . .

Fellow citizens: This movement for the emancipation of woman is in a right line toward that universal freedom which is the ideal condition of the human race. To doubt of its ultimate success is to question the wisdom and justice of God. It cannot fail, for the good of mankind demands that it triumph. It is a work which, in this enlightened Christian land, should, and I believe will, have early accomplishment. It but remains for us who are men to decide, with the least of further delay, whether this grandest of all the struggles for freedom since the beginning of history shall be carried through by woman alone, or whether, turning our backs on the false prejudices and groundless fears of the past, we, too, will join heroic hands for its furtherance.

"WOMAN SUFFRAGE DEFENDED"

Daniel P. Livermore (1885)

Our Government Not Democratic.

Notwithstanding our democratic theories and our Fourth of July "orations," which are largely "glittering generalities," our government is not a pure democracy. In no proper sense do "the people" govern, and hence we practically deny the fundamental principles upon which our government is based—the government of the people, when in fact, the few govern the many. . . .

This startling fact not only arrests our attention, but shows the fallacy of our democratic pretensions, that this is a government *of the people and by the people!* Women are "people," and are as much entitled to the ballot as men, but they are defrauded by men of their right or privilege, and are unjustly excluded from all participation in the administration of government.

When men *assume* the right to make laws for women to obey under penalty of fine, imprisonment and death, it is not merely a "stinging insult" to woman, it is the cruelest kind of depostism and subjugation, which *men* would not submit to for a moment! . . .

Boston: Lee & Shepard, 1885. (GERR)

"JESUS CHRIST—THE EMANCIPATOR OF WOMEN"

Rev. Charles Clark Harrah (1888)

NOTHING in Jesus' reform work has a pre-eminence over the recognition of women and their rights. In no instance does He appear in controversy with them. He defended their rights in marriage, and condemned the practice of husbands divorcing their wives for any cause but one. (Matt. xix:9.) Man and woman were to meet on equal terms in life-long union; each honoring the other, and both training their children amidst the sanctities of a pure family life. Through all time, men had taken for themselves the license of lust, and applied the law of purity to women. Jesus made chastity equally binding on both. He addressed men especially, and required of them even purity in *thought*. (Matt. v:28.) In cases of sin, the better circumstances and the superior power of man were recognized, and he was held to be the greater sinner. This is the lesson taught where that band of men, with the arrogance which belongs to those who have the power of law in their own hands, brought a woman, legally and physically helpless, to Jesus. Her sin was known, but the hollow-hearted men were able to conceal theirs. They quickly and sneakingly fled, when Jesus applied the principle of justice to the case, by saying: "He that is without sin among you, let him first cast a stone at her." All this was new to the world. Never before had men been addressed in such burning words, and with such authority. Bad men quickly learned to hate the Reformer, because He hated their lusts and evil deeds. The women rejoiced that they had found one who gave them justice, apologized for them in their hard circumstances, and respected their worth. One after another came to him with her sufferings, and no one went away heavy-hearted or unblest. Mothers' hearts were touched by such an unheard-of example of goodness and righteousness, and they brought their little children and begged His blessing upon them. The poor woman who had gone on in sin until she was known to the inhabitants of the city as "the sinner," heard of the man who had dared to demand justice for women, and who could see all the way from a crime back to its cause. A sad fact of the history of the sexes is, that, when the humanity of woman was counted as nothing, and she was robbed of her rights, women of ambition, and sometimes those belonging to illustrious families, resorted to the one way of getting influence with men—the representatives of power. Jesus' regard for woman as a responsible human being touched the heart of this "sinner," and led her to repentance. She wanted to see the just man, and found Him at a Pharisee's table. Unwelcomed by the host, she drew near, and fell upon her knees at Jesus' feet. With her hair she wiped away the tears from his feet,

---

Woman Suffrage Leaflet, 1, no. 8 (15 November 1888).

and anointed them from her alabaster box of ointment—probably all that she had in the world.

Before this time, Mary of Magdala had found a friend in the great Teacher. As Jesus went through the cities and villages preaching, this woman, and Joanna, the wife of Chuza, Herod's steward, and Susanna, and "*many others,*" ministered unto Him of their substance. *History has no record of any philosopher or rabbi who had such a following of women as Jesus had.* It is a fitting tribute to the devotion of the women, that the names of some of those who followed the Saviour are handed down to us; while the names of the men are lost, with the exception of the twelve.

In passing through Samaria at one time, Jesus gave a mighty impulse to the advancement of woman to a place of equality with man. At Jacob's well he met a humble woman, of poor antecedents, but in whom He recognized her better self. It was forbidden to a rabbi to speak to a woman in public, or to take any notice of her, and His disciples marvelled that He talked with this one. One rabbi says that the words of the Law should be burned rather than committed to women. But, as at other times, Jesus treated with contempt all the practices which had for their end the exaltation of one sex by humbling the other. Never did apostle or prophet receive a richer message to bear to the world than that which was given to this woman. Through her, Christ gave to mankind their charter of spiritual liberty. He abolished the exclusiveness of former creeds. He placed the life of worship in the espousal of our nature to truth, and made the temple of it in the spirit and heart. Our astonishment is still greater when we consider that to this woman Jesus made the first disclosure of Himself as the Messiah: "I that speak unto thee am He." Such an incident makes plain, as no mere words can, the respect that Jesus had for woman.

Even the wife of Pilate, who by her wealth and position knew not the hardships which come to the poor, appreciated Christ's work for her sex. It was left for this heathen woman to be the only human being who had the courage to plead the cause of our Lord at that dreadful time when the disciples forsook Him, and the fanatical multitude cried out for His crucifixion. She was distressed that such a righteous friend of humanity should be so cruelly treated. Her convictions were strengthened by a dream, and she sent word to her husband: "Have thou nothing to do with that just man."

It was the grandest tribute ever paid to a public teacher, and a testimony that His life work had been for them, that, when the rulers of the Jews, attended by the Roman soldiers and the cruel mob, were hurrying Jesus to the place of crucifixion, "a great company of women" followed, and with tears bewailed and lamented Him. Poor women! They had no more power in law to rescue Jesus than drunkards' wives now have to rescue their husbands and sons from the cruel clutches of liquor traffic. Like the millions of their sisters whose hearts have been broken by the existence of wrongs, all that they could do was to weep. How can any one who has Christ's spirit of reform keep silent, and let this crying of broken-hearted women unceasingly go on, because ours is not a government of the homes, and by the homes, and for the homes? As if thinking of all the injustice and sorrow yet to come upon women, and forgetting Himself, Jesus said: "Daughters of Jerusalem, weep not for Me, but weep for yourselves and for your children." . . .

Christ gave the Golden Rule—"All things whatsoever ye would that men should do to you, do ye even so to them." This will vitalize every humane movement while the world stands. It is eternally opposed to a civilization or a government where man is the integer and woman the cipher, having value only as appended to him. Its principle of fair dealing put the ballot into the hands of men, as the equals of each other. In the beginning of the nation, some of the wisest men doubted the capacity of the masses for self-government. It was declared that fraud and vice would become privileged, if all men could vote. But how groundless are fears, when the change is in the line of justice! Ben Hill, Georgia's great senator, feared that America would be ruined if the negroes were set free. He lived long enough to say that, while once he would have given one life rather than have slavery abolished, he then would give ten lives rather than have it re-established. Those who fear to give woman the ballot ought to learn from the past, and see their folly. It must come, for Christ began a reform that leads to it, and there is no sex in His Golden Rule. In his "History of Humane Progress" Mr. Brace says: "The progress of the religious sentiment and of right reason will be continually in this direction towards asserting the absolute legal independence of women. It will be asked: Does not this lead to the share of women in government? Undoubtedly it does ultimately. Christianity by itself no more teaches woman suffrage than it does man suffrage, or republicanism; but it throws into human society that sentiment of equality before God, that principle of equal rights and equal responsibility, and of universal brotherhood, which all lead logically to these results." The country needs a Golden Rule in religion and patriotism, when one class of the community heaps miseries upon the other class, because of unwillingness and stupid incapacity of the one to put itself in the other's place. Most of the miseries of the world have their cause here. The condition of the 3,000,000 women in the United States who earn their own living should be considered in the light of the Golden Rule. Those who are in bonds should be remembered, as if we were bound with them. I beg satisfied ladies of fortune, and gentlemen who boast of the perfection of "woman's sphere" and our Christian civilization, to imitate Christ by going among the people of want, and there learn the lessons of needed change. Go to the stores and shops where the products of women's labor are sold, and prove the truth of what the Bureau of Labor Statistics of Illinois has said: that there should be a "change in the policy of merchants who are passing the lives of women over their counters in every package of this ill-paid work they sell." Go to their homes, and see that these women with needles and thread are making, not their living only, but their shrouds. Go and learn how helpless women are driven to lives of shame, and then despised by the class of persons who have lived off their labor and their tears. Pity and be just, when you know that no woman tramp comes to your kitchen door begging for a breakfast. How many have you known of the great army of working-women who drink and gamble away the bread and butter of those dependent upon them, or return from their daily toil to a hungry household with empty hands and indifference to their needs? Among the 200,000 women in New York City who earn their own living was a widow who did sewing on boys' caps at thirty-six cents per dozen. I found her at a time when she was in great distress because of unpaid rent. She had nothing but the sewing-machine and stove that could be called furniture; and at times worked most of the night and went without necessary food for herself and children. I know it to be a fact that at this time of distress, favors were offered her by a man connected with the house for which she worked, if she would turn to an immoral life. Put yourself in that woman's place, and then consider, that, if we do not directly lead others into evil, we may aid in making the hard circumstances that result in evil. Hypocrites pretend to abhor wickedness, while by injustice and hard dealings they drive others into it. *Where the Golden Rule is true, the subordination of woman is a lie.* But if women have equal political rights with men, will that improve their condition? It looks like it, when the laboring men of the country regard their own ballots as the most effective means of defense against injustice. Women need this same means of protecting themselves in the maintenance of life, liberty, and happiness.

It looks like it, when one result of the equal rights agitation has been that women are now employed in 222 of the 265 different occupations enumerated in our census for 1880; while, when this agitation began, the number of occupations was less than a score.

It looks like it, when every father knows that his daughter would have a better chance for a living and for justice with the ballot than without it, if at some future time she should be left a mother and a widow, poor and alone—left to struggle through the hardships endured by hundreds of thousands of working women, and required to protect herself against the injustice and cruelty of the wicked and strong.

The method by which Jesus sought to liberate woman was not alone by giving her rights, but by making her personally responsible, equally with man, for the use of the talents God had intrusted to her. All noble characters are the product of the conviction of personal responsibility. Instead of its being a detriment to woman to occupy the offices of greatest responsibility in the Church, it will contribute to the beauty of her character and her womanhood. . . .

It will be a blessing to women and a happy day for the nation when responsibility for its laws and life rests equally upon its citizens. The virtue of the people never can be expressed in the laws until the unit of the nation is the family. One sex has equal significance with the other. Christianity is a family religion; and when the cottages govern, we shall have a Christian civilization. To disfranchise the women is to disfranchise the family, and largely the virtue of the nation. While we have in this country the best men on the face of the earth, still it is true that the overwhelming majority in the prisons, and almost all those in the dram-shops, are of their sex; while women are in the majority in the churches and all good work. God never would let the war between freedom and slavery end until the slaves were put into the army; and He will never let the conflict between good and evil now going on in the nation end until all the virtue of the Republic is expressed at the polls.

Applied Christianity means liberty to all. The want of liberty has cursed the world, and filled it with groans, and kept the hedged-in victims weak. The principles of Christ guarantee to men and women democratic liberty. It is not consistent for men to oppose woman's ballot by an apostolic command for wives to be "subject to their own husbands," when the same authority enjoins them, when a Nero is on the throne, to be "subject unto the higher powers," and to "honor the king." With as much reason, Tories once tried to barricade with Bibles and muskets our fathers' way to independence. The Gospel principles of personal responsibility and accountability forced our fathers into independence; and by them all the "bruised" ones of earth shall yet be set at liberty, and the reform that Jesus began at Nazareth shall be accomplished. Many understand our national constitution to contain already all that is necessary for the equal political rights of both sexes. But clear to all there is written in it: "There is neither Jew nor Greek, there is neither bond nor free." The same principles that have driven the darkness out of the world enough to make the changes already effected possible, will continue to work—shooting down through human convictions like rays of burning light from the throne of God—until, in the Constitution, is also clearly written: "There is neither male nor female." . . .

"WOMAN SUFFRAGE"

James Freeman Clarke (1889)

ONE OF the most important of the reforms proposed at the present time is that which shall give the suffrage to women. It is not merely a political question, but a social question, a moral question, and a religious question. Politically, it may make the greatest change in the character of our government, our laws, and our political institutions. Socially, it may alter the aspect of society and the manners and civilization of the people. Morally, it may either purify, elevate, and ennoble the character of the nation, or it may degrade it. This reform also connects itself with religion. Some religious writers think it opposed to the principles and the commands of the New Testament; others regard it as contradicting the providence of God, who has formed woman for a retired and subordinate position. Others, again, believe that it will tend to elevate religion by elevating women, on whom religious institutions so much depend.

What are the reasons why woman should vote? The principal one is that there is no reason why she should not vote. In this country we assume the ground of popular government; we say that the government is for the people, not the people for it; we say that the public opinion of the whole people is the safest guide; we make universal suffrage the corner-stone, deep, solid, broad, on which the whole building stands in stable equilibrium. Here every man votes, except where a good reason can be given why he should not. Foreigners just landed do not vote, because they do not understand our institutions, and do not yet belong to the nation. Idiots and insane people do not vote, because they have not the use of their faculties. Children do not vote, not having the necessary knowledge. Criminals do not vote, for they are public enemies. Now, if any similarly good reason can be given why women should not vote, they can properly be deprived of the suffrage; but not otherwise, on American principles. No such reason can be given. Women can understand our institutions as well as men; they have, like men, a faculty for judging what persons and measures are desirable; they are not public enemies, but friends to the common

Woman Suffrage Leaflet 2, no. 14 (15 February 1889).

weal. If no reason can be given to show that women, as women, cannot vote wisely and well, than, on American principles, they ought to vote. . . .

The philosophers who define the sphere of woman say that her sphere is home. But a woman who keeps house governs all the time. She governs her domestics, she governs her children, from rosy morn till dewy eve. This is all right, this is her sphere, this will do her no harm. But she must not drop a ballot into the box once a year because she is supposed to be inadequate to government.

With the common view of politics, no wonder it is thought that women should have nothing to do with it. Politics is assumed to be only a base, low struggle for office, power, and wealth. It is said that "the great objection to suffrage is that the primary assemblies are filled by the most rude and violent elements, and that good men are wholly out of place in them." But whose fault is this? It is the fault of "the good men" who will not go to the primary meeting, and then complain that it falls into the hands of the mob. When women have the ballot, they may attend to their duties better than we do, and so reform even primary meetings.

There is nothing greater, nobler, more important, than politics or the art of government, especially with democratic institutions. It is not a struggle for power. It is the combined action of all honest and intelligent people to organize and carry on a State so as to bring the greatest good to the greatest number. The happiness and virtue of every man, woman, and child in the land are influenced by the laws and institutions of the country.

Those whose highest idea of a woman is of an appendage to a man have not risen to the level of the Jewish Scriptures, much less to that of the Christian. Man's world they think, is to fight and quarrel with other men during the day; then he is to come home at night into a sweet atmosphere of peace prepared for him by his wife, sisters, and daughters. They are "to govern by graces the men who govern by forces." They are to live in "an atmosphere of silence," and "a field of peace." They are to "make a realm in which the poor bruised fighters, with their passions galled and their minds scarred with wrong, their hates, disappointments, grudges, and hard-won ambitions, must come in to be quieted and civilized, and get some touch of the angelic." "Government is not given them, but protectors are given them." Man is to protect woman, woman is to soothe man. He is necessarily, to be strong and coarse; she is necessarily, to be gentle and weak. Being gentle, she can soothe him and comfort him after the fierce and evil conflict which it is his business to carry on, and so restore his strength that he may go out to be as bitter and violent and coarse again to-morrow as he was to-day.

But is there not a higher work still for woman, namely, to be such a companion and true work fellow for man as to save him from this bitter warfare? Let the woman-nature take part with the man-nature in work, and his work will be saved from this coarseness. God has made man and woman to be together, and the Creator may be presumed to know what the result will be.

"MR. DOOLEY ON WOMAN'S SUFFRAGE"

Finley Peter Dunne (1909)

WELL SIR," said Mr. Dooley, "fr'm th' way this here female sufferage movement is sweepin' acrost th' counthry it won't be long befure I'll be seein' ye an' ye'er wife sthrollin' down th' sthreet to vote together."

"Niver," said Mr. Hennessy with great indignation. "It will niver come. A woman's place is in th' home darning her husband's childher. I mean—"

"I know what ye mean," said Mr. Dooley. "Tis a favrite argymint iv mine whin I can't think iv annything to say. But ye can't help it, Hinnessy. Th' time is near at hand whin iliction day will mean no more to ye thin anny other day with th' fam'ly. Up to th' prisint moment it has been a festival marked: 'For gintlemen on'y.' It's been a day whin sthrong men cud go foorth, unhampered be th' prisince iv ladies, an' f'r th' honor iv their counthry bite each other. It was a day whin it was proper an' right f'r ye to slug ye'er best frind.

"But th' fair sect are goin' to break into this fine, manly spoort an' they'll change it. No more will ye leap fr'm ye'er bed on iliction mornin', put a brick in ye'er pocket an' go out to bounce ye'er impeeryal vote against th' walls iv inthrenched privilege. No more will ye spind th' happy mornin' hours meetin' ye'er frinds an' th' akeely happy avenin' hours receivin' none but inimies.

"No sir, in a few years, as soon as ye've had ye'er breakfast, ye'er fellow citizen who, as th' pote says, doubles ye'er expinses an' divides ye'er salary, will say to ye: 'Well, it's about time we wint down to th' polls an' cast my votes. An' I do wish ye'd tie ye'er necktie sthraight. Honorya, bring me me new bonnet an' me Cashmere shawl an' get papa his stove pipe hat.' Thin ye'll be walked down th' sthreet, with a procission iv other married men in their best clothes an' their wanst a week shoes that hurt their feet. Th' sthreets will look like Easter Sundah. Ye'll meet ye'er frinds an' their wives comin' fr'm th' pollin' place an' talk with thim on th' corner.

" 'Good morning, Michael.'

" 'Ah, good morning, Cornelius.'

" 'A delightful morning is it not f'r th' exercise iv th' franchise.'

" 'Perfect! Howiver, I fear that such a morning may bring out a large republican vote.'

" 'I hope our frind Baumgarten will succeed in his candydacy.'

" 'I heartily agree with ye—he will make an excellent coroner, he's such good company.'

" 'Yes, indeed, a charming fellow f'r a Dutchman. Cud I prevail on ye an' ye'er lady to come an' have a tub iv ice cream sody with us?'

American Magazine 63 (*June 1909*).

" 'Thank ye, Cornelius, we wud be delighted, but three is all I can hold. Shall I see ye at th' magic lanthern to-night?'

"Th' pollin' place won't be in th' office iv a livry stable or a barber shop, but in a pleasant boodwar. As ye enter th' dure ye won't say to th' polisman on jooty: 'Good mornin', Pete; anny murdhers so far?'

"But wan iv th' judges will come forward an' bow an' say: 'Madam, can I show ye annything in ballots? This blue is wan iv our recent importations, but here is a tasty thought in ecru. F'r th' gintleman I'd ricommind something in dark brown to match th' socks. Will that be all? Th' last booth on th' right is unoccypied. Perhaps ye'er husband wud like to look at a copy iv th' *Ladies Home Journal* while ye'er preparin' th' ballots.'

"Ye neednt get mad about it, Hinnessy. Ye might as well face it. It's sure to come now that I see be th' pa-apers that female suffrage has been took up be ladies in our best s'ciety. It used to be diff'rent. Th' time was whin th' on'y female sufferigists that ye iver see were ladies, Gawd bless thim, that bought their millinery th' same place I buy mine, cut their hair short, an' discarded all iv their husband's names excipt what was useful f'r alimony.

"A fine lot iv rugged pathrites they were.

"I used to know wan iv thim—Docthor Arabella Miggs—as fine an old gintleman as ye iver see in a plug hat, a long coat an' bloomers. She had ivry argymint in favor iv female suffrage that ye iver heerd, an' years ago she made me as certain that women were entitled to a vote as that ye are entitled to my money.

"Ye are entitled to it if ye can get it. They ain't anny argymint against female sufferage that wudden't make me lible to arrest ivry time I'm seen near a pollin' place. But it isn't argymints or statistics that alters things in th' wurruld. Th' thick end iv a baseball bat will change a man's mind quicker an' more permanently thin anny discoorse.

"So th' first iv thim lady sufferigists had a hard time iv it, an' little boys used to go to their meetings to hoot at thim, an' they were took up in th' sthreet be polismen f'r pretindin' to look like gintlemen, an' th' pa-apers wud no more think iv printin' their speeches thin iv printin' a sermon in a church.

"Now be hivens, 'tis diff'rent. 'Tis far diff'rent. I pick up th' pa-apers an' read:

" 'Gr-reat sufferage revival. Society queens take up th' cause. In th' magnificent L. Quince dhrawin' rooms iv Mrs. Percy Lumley's mansion in Mitchigan avnoo yesterdah afthernoon wan iv th' most successful sufferage teas iv th' season was held. Mrs. Lumley, who presided, was perfectly ravishing in a blue taffeta which set off her blonde beauty to perfection. She wore pearls an' carried a bunch iv American beauty roses. On th' platform with her were Mrs. Archibald Fluff, in green bombyzine with a pink coal scuttle hat. Mrs. Alfonso Vanboozen in a light yellow creation cut demi thrain an' manny other leaders iv th' smart set.

" 'A spirited debate was held over th' pint whether something shudden't be done to induce th' department stores to put in polling places. Wan dhream iv beauty asked whether if it rained iliction day wud th' iliction be held or postponed f'r better weather. Th' chairman ruled that th' iliction wud have to go on rain or shine. "Iv coorse," says she, "in very bad weather we cud sind th' footman down with our votes. But we must not expict to gain this great reform without some sacrifice. (Applause.) In anny case th' tillyphone is always handy."

" 'A lady in th' aujeence wanted to know how old a lady wud have to be befure she cud vote. Says th' chairman: "To be effective th' reform must be thorough. I am in favor iv makin' it legal f'r ivry woman to vote no matter how old she is an' I, therefore, wud put th' maximum age at a lib'ral figure, say thirty years. This gives all iv us a chance." (Cheers.) Afther th' meetin', a few voters dhropped in f'r an informal dance. Among those presint was.'

"An' there ye are. Ain't I again female sufferage? Iv coorse I am. Th' place f'r these spiled darlings is not in th' hurly burly iv life but in th' home, be th' fireside or above th' kitchen range. What do they know about th' vast machinery iv governmint? Ye an' I, Hinnessy, are gifted with a supeeryor intilligence in these matthers. Our opposition to a tariff is based on large pathriotic grounds. We have thought th' subjick out carefully, applyin' to it minds so sthrong that they cud crush a mountain an' so delicate that they cud pick up a sheet iv gold foil. We are in favor iv abolishin' th' tariff because it has thrown around this counthry a Chinese wall; because we are bribed be British goold fr'm th' Parsee merchant who riprisints th' Cobden Republican Marchin' Club iv London, England; because th' foreigner does or does not pay th' tax; because Sam'l J. Tilden was again th' tariff; because th' ultimate consumer must be proticted.

"Larkin on th' other hand, blessed with a republican intelleck since eighteen eighty four whin he become a protectionist because James G. Blaine was a fine man, annyway ye took him, is in favor iv a tariff on borax, curled hair, copra, steel ingots, an' art because cheap clothes makes a cheap man; because th' star spangled banner an long may it wag; because th' party that put down th' rebellyon an' stormed th' heights iv Lookout Mountain an' sthrewed th' bloody field iv Anteetam is th' same party (applause) that to-day is upholdin' th' tax on hides undher th' leadership iv th' incomp'rable hero Seerinio D. Payne. Often had I set here listenin' to ye an' Larkin discussin' this here question, wan moment thinkin' that I was as fine a pathrite as th' goose that saved Rome, be payin' more f'r me pants thin they were worth an' another moment fearin' I was a thraitor to th' flag f'r buyin' pants at all undher this accursed tariff. Both iv ye want to do what's best f'r th' counthry.

"But if ye put th' question up to th' ladies, if women undherstood th' tariff, which th' poor crathers don't, ye'd find they were against it f'r no higher reason thin that it made thim pay too much f'r th' childher's shoes an' stockin's. Can ye imagine annything baser thin that, to rejooce a great question like th' tariff down to a personal level, take all th' music an' pothry out iv it an' say: 'I'm again it, not because it has lowered th' morality iv ivrywan that it has binifitted, but because it's a shame that I have to pay eighty-six cints a pair f'r stockin's.'

"Women take a selfish view iv life. But what can ye expict fr'm a petted toy iv man's whim that has spent most iv her life thryin' to get four dollars worth iv merchandise f'r two dollars an' a half? Th' foolish, impractical little fluffy things! It wud be a shame to let thim hurl thimselves into th' coorse battles iv pollyticks. How cud ye explain to wan iv these ideelists wy we have th' Philippeens an' th' Sandwich Islands, an' why we keep up a navy to protict Denver, Colorado.

"We don't hear much about sufferage up our way in Ar-rchy road an' th' ladies that have got out their noblest hats in behalf iv th' cause complain that they can't stir up anny excitement among th' more numerous ladies that prefer to wear a shawl on their heads. Maybe th' reason is that these fair dhreamers haven't been able to figure out that a vote is goin' to do thim anny good. P'raps if ye asked ye'er wife about it she'd say:

" 'Well, ye've had ye'er vote f'r forty years. F'r forty years ye've governed this counthry be a freeman's ballot an' ye'er salary an' perquisites at th' mill still amounts to a dollar an' eighty-five cints a day. If a vote hasn't done ye anny more good thin that I don't think I can spare time fr'm me domestic jooties to use wan. I will continue to look afther th' fam'ly, which is th' on'y capital a poor man can accumylate to protict him fr'm poverty in his old age. I'll stay at home an' see that th' boys an' girls are saved up ontil they are old enough to wurruk f'r us. An' if ye want to amuse ye'erself be votin' go on an' do it. Ye need recreation wanst in a while, an' ye'er vote don't do anny wan no harm.'"

"I wudden't talk to me wife about votin' anny more thin she'd talk to me about thrimmin' a hat," said Mr. Hennessy.

"Well," said Mr. Dooley, "if she gets a vote maybe she'll thrim it to please ye. Annyhow it won't be a bad thing. What this counthry needs is voters that knows something about housekeeping."

"BULLY FOR THE WOMEN"

J. A. Wayland (1911)

Do Socialists condemn suffrage because women helped to defeat Socialism at Los Angeles? Bless you, no. There is not a true Socialist in America who is not just as ardently in favor of woman suffrage today as he was before that election. If men have been going through election after election without turning to Socialism, what right have we to be angry at the women because they did not stampede to Socialism the first time they got to vote? The women will get their eyes open yet and shame many of the men by their understanding of public good. Yet even if they did not, even if they always voted against Socialism, Socialists would favor woman suffrage. They couldn't help it, from the fact that woman suffrage is on the line of further democracy and hence an essential feature of Socialist agitation. Get this idea: Socialists seek only to give both men and women the power over their own lives, the power over their own jobs. We know that when they get this power they may make mistakes; but that makes no difference. They should have the power anyhow.

Los Angeles Appeal (23 December 1911).

"WOMEN SHOULD MIND THEIR OWN BUSINESS"

Edward J. Ward (1912)

WOMEN SHOULD devote all their energies to the duties of their own sphere. Surely Mrs. Pankhurst and Colonel Roosevelt could agree on this proposition.

Women should not invade the realm of men's activities. That seems axiomatic.

Men should be willing to give up their own work to help bear the burdens which belong to women's realm. What gentleman will dissent from this?

In order to see clearly what the proper respective spheres of men and women are, we must turn back to the simple conditions of primitive living among the American aborigines, for instance. There we see two sorts of work fairly well divided. There we can see woman engaged in her proper sphere, and man busy with his characteristic activities. And we can answer the question: what is woman's sphere? The woman is engaged in grinding corn or other grains, preparing food, plaiting baskets, molding pottery, preparing wool and weaving blankets, drawing and fetching water, caring for and educating the children, ordering the care of the camp or village, transporting the burdens when the camp is moved—in short, in all the useful industries and arts of the primitive Indian.

And what was man's characteristic sphere? War and killing other animals with some minor avocations such as gambling between times—but mostly war.

Here we have the respective spheres of men and women, easily seen in the simple primitive division.

With the process of invention and discovery there have come great changes in the methods used to carry on the activities of women's sphere. For instance, instead of the little stone hand mortar and pestle with which the primitive woman ground corn, we have the gigantic roller mills; instead of the earthen jar in which she carried water, we have the municipal water system; instead of the primitive method by which she, with or without the aid of a horse, transported the burdens, we have this work of hers done by means of freight and express trains and vans and automobiles, and so on thru practically all of the lines of women's sphere. There has been an equally great enlargement of the work which was hers in caring for, keeping well-ordered, clean and comfortable the camp or village. With the increasing aggregation of people into the modern city and State, this phase of woman's work has grown tremendously.

And great changes have come also in the proper historic sphere of men's activities. Instead of the simple bow and arrow or tomahawk with which the primitive man could hurt people, there have been developed artificial volcanoes and various forms of hard-

New York: National American Woman Suffrage Association, [1912]. (URL)

ware and fireworks which are very much more harmful, expensive and noisy. Slaughter houses have been substituted for the hunt, except in the case of really dangerous wild beasts like the fly. Not much real improvement has, however, been made in his method of gambling.

Women should remain in their own sphere. They should devote themselves to useful civic, social, educational and industrial activities. For women to participate in carrying on the activities which belong to man's particular province would mean for them to go to war, and when there isn't a war on, to strut around with a band. This, it seems to me, they should not do.

On the other hand, men should continue to devote more and more of their thought and energy to the activities of woman's proper sphere, the useful work of the world, the industries and the arts, the work of preparing food and clothing and shelter, the work of transportation, the cleaning up and making comfortable of the living places. Men must be allowed to do this more and more, for tho we still set apart from this useful service some of our number and support them to carry on the work of destruction and hurting strangers, yet this proper sphere of man's activities for the majority of us isn't what it used to be. The average male individual has given up wearing feathers and stovelids and tinware, and the average man no longer regards it as a sign of sanity to carry butcher-knives and other violent junk around with him in the hope of chopping his neighbor's head open. That is, men have been turning away from their own particular vocation, and, if they didn't enter women's sphere of constructive service, there wouldn't be much for them to do.

In the old days, when man's sphere amounted to something, when practically all of them spent most of their time in war, government consisted chiefly in devising means and methods of doing harm, in "councils of war." Then government was man's business and for women to participate in it would have been to take up the work of men. But as we have come away from barbarism, as this sphere of man's activity has shrunken and fallen into disrepute, government has become more and more the organization and control of the means of human service, the promotion of human welfare. In other words, government has become more and more the organization of woman's sphere.

Man should have a voice in this, for in spite of the age-old habit of selfishness and hostility, developed through thousands of years of practice in hurting people, which tends to make him carry on even the useful activities which belong to woman's sphere with something of the war motive and manner, and with a good deal of the old gambling practice mixt in, and which makes it hard for him to think in terms of the common welfare, he is the child of his mother and he has in him a finer element, a latent capacity for constructive united service. Yes, men should have some voice in regulating and controlling the industries, the education of children, and all the matters relating to the welfare of the camp, that is, of society.

But of course, the fact that man participates does not limit the primary responsibility of woman in this sphere. She started this business of human service. She can no more shirk her share in the ordering and control of society, in the mutual interservice which we call government, without shirking her duty as a woman than in the old days she could shirk the duty of preparing the food and making the camp a pleasant, well-ordered, clean place in which to live.

Women then should mind their own business. That is, women should vote in the modern government, for this is their proper sphere, except in its destructive, anti-social, military expression, which has gone from local and city and State affairs and will be gone from national affairs as soon as we get sense enough to put through a few world bargains such as the neutralization of the Panama Canal, provided an international parliament with an international police force is established at The Hague.

And men ought also to vote in the modern government, in spite of the fact that this is women's sphere, because—well, because any number of reasons:—they pay taxes the same as women do and they should have a voice in saying how their money shall be spent; they have to submit to the laws just as women do, and they should have something to say in framing those laws; and anyway, it would not be honest for us to have a government by a sex when we pretend to have a democracy.

"THE TAXATION TYRANNY"

Gen. E. Estabrook (1912)

To tax one who's not represented
Is tyranny—tell, if you can,
Why woman should not have the ballot,
She's taxed just the same as a man.
King George, you remember, denied us
The Ballot, but sent us the tea,
And we, without asking a question
Just tumbled it into the sea.

Chorus

Then to justice let's ever be true
To each citizen render his due;
Equal rights and protection forever
To all 'neath the Red, White, and Blue!

That one man shall not rule another,
Unless by the other's consent,
Is the principle deep underlying
The framework of this government.
So, as woman is punished for breaking
The laws which she cannot gainsay,
Let us give her a voice in the making
Or ask her no more to obey.

Chorus

Reprinted in Songs America Voted By, *ed. Irwin Silber. Harrisburg, Pa.: Stackpole, 1971. Lyrics by Estabrook, sung to the tune of "The Red, White, and Blue."*

"SUFFRAGE AND ?S"

David Lloyd Garrison (1913)

WHAT ? s have antys got?
None ! ! !

We can ancer well any quejuns the antys poot to us.

Sometimes antys dear (dare) to think they have reasons, but the funny part is we all ways tern what they call quesjuns into reasons for suffrage.

Other funny things are, antys as you know, have no rell (real) reasons, and one person pootes a quejon, and then an other persons pootes a quejon, whitch is the obersit (opposite) of the other, and expectes it to go as a reson.

WJ (24 April 1913). It was noted that Garrison, grandson of William Lloyd Garrison, was eight years old.

Why the Woman Should Have the Vote

God made us all the same, and to all have the same rites.

It was not the woman's falt that they were born that way, nor it was not the blacks falt they were born that way.

It is not the falt of the poor that they are that way. Some times it means that they have binn robed, some times that they have bin cheated in traed (trade), and other such things.

What difference would there be iff woman dressed as men did, did as men did, and called them sellves men?

None.

Therefor the woman should shear equal rite to vote.

WOMEN'S SUFFRAGE AND INTEMPERANCE (excerpt)

Arthur Neil Rhodes (1914)

. . . I CAN PLAINLY SEE the reason why man is opposed to Equal Suffrage. Man does not want to be disturbed in his career of selfishness. He desires to have no one to dictate in the great field of drink. The liquor sellers are opposed. They see the handwriting on the wall: "Thus far shalt thou go and no farther." They know the vote of woman is a protection to home, family and friends. The hand of woman will dash aside the cup of the inebriate, and prevent the downfall of her boy. They know that when woman votes she will scourge the saloon keepers, as did Christ the money-changers from the church of God. They know that the wives and mothers will no longer remain idle and see their loved ones go down in shame and ruin.

This is why woman is not granted equality with man. It is Satan who uses man's propensities to fight his battles. . . .

We will admit there are a great many men that would enjoy having their wives and daughters help in making laws and helping to enforce them. They enjoy anything that has a tendency to elevate civilization in moral ways. Some probably might be ministers; they dare not speak their thoughts along this line, because, of course, they have to preach to suit the people and not take anything of this nature under consideration. Even using of intoxicating drinks is not hit as hard as it might be. Another class of men think their wives have no right to know their personal affairs, as long as they provide them livlihood. And they don't know any of his business career. Almost in every case this kind of a man would be opposed to his wife taking any part in woman's rights, or the elevating of anything that is good and just. But she must look on and let others go ahead to battle for the upliftment of their sex. There is still another class of men. I call them the selfish class. They dictate what their wives shall wear and they do the buying and paying for everything in the house and out of the house. She has no excess to the money matters whatever. He dictates to the whole married life. She knows no thing of his personal wealth, it seems she has no interest in view. She would not be allowed to tolerate the woman's rights movement; she must not recognize any charity society; she must live each week and year with the same old routine of work as simply a servant of man to meet his demands. Church going is not tolerated by him. This life may be all right if the woman believes that it is happiness, but you know it would almost try the patience of a saint.

There is another class of men who think they are doing right with their family. After working hours, supper over, they go to the saloon and fill up on alcoholic beverages and after closing time they stagger home, not fit to be in company with their family. They do

---

Minneapolis: McIntire & Dahlen, 1914. (GERR)

this stunt six days out of every week and Sunday they are chasing around perhaps to some beer party, their wife and family not knowing where they are. His wife becomes dissatisfied with his life of ignorance and dissipatious, and she leaves him and tries to better her conditions. Sometimes she does, but most always follows a blighted future. Of course she has been almost a saint to live as she did with a man of that stamp. And to make up caring nothing for her, leaving her at home continually alone. We have still another class of men caused by vice. We have the kind that cares nothing for their homes and family. They are doles and don't care to make a livelihood for their wife and family and the consequence is the woman has to get out and work. But still if his wife wanted to vote or encourage the woman's right movement he would holler his head off opposing it. We have still another class. We call it the ideal class. It is the man that encourages every movement of his wife along the line of woman's rights. He appreciates her as a real guiding angel. He is broad-minded enough to see it will uplift humanity, uplift civilization, bring harmony in their homes and adjust many wrongs we have to contend with at present. He also admires the true principles of equal rights to all. He admires her indignations along the line of special privileges. He believes in opening up new lives into light that have been kept in darkness, and new ideas to better man and woman in swift traveling pace of humanity. He admires her disposition of giving words of encouragement to everything that has the foundation of justice. And they travel along in life in harmony, in agreeableness and love for each other. And their love makes their hearts beat true, enjoying each others joys and suffering each others sorrows. And as they draw nearer to life's destination they look back and think what a beautiful dream is life. . . .

"WHAT ARE YOU GOING TO DO NOVEMBER SECOND?"

Samuel Fraser (1914)

. . . WOMAN SUFFRAGE is a man's question. It is not a woman's question. It concerns women but it is of the greatest moment to men, and what are you going to do about it? What will influence you to vote for it or against it? I will offer to buy your vote. I offer an American child's life for a vote. Your vote cast for woman suffrage will save

An address before the Livingston County Granges, Geneseo, N.Y., 1914. (Buffalo and Erie County Historical Society Library)

life: it will avert much misery and suffering. Your vote cast against woman suffrage will continue the present destruction of life, unnecessary and willful loss of life.

It is yours to say Yea or Nay. It is folly to put yourself in Pilate's position and continue to listen to the cry of "His blood be upon us and our children." The blood is upon you and me now. We live at a momentous time. Never before could we men say Yes or No to this question.

Read the story—Three hundred thousand babies under one year old die annually in this country, i.e., the annihilation of a city the size of Chicago or a State the size of New Jersey every ten years. One-half of these die needlessly.

In New York City in 1912 the mortality was 125 per 1,000.

In Washington, D.C., in 1912 the mortality was 152 per 1,000.

In Lowell, Mass., in 1912 the mortality was 231 per 1,000.

In Seattle, Wash., in 1912 the mortality was 82 per 1,000.

Take a place where women are political factors. New Zealand, in 1912, had 51 deaths per 1,000 less than half that of the United States. Taking cities of

Dunedin, New Zealand, in 1913, 38 per 1,000.

Los Angeles, Cal., in 1913, 97 per 1,000.

Pittsburg, Pa., in 1913, 150 per 1,000.

Lowell, Mass., in 1913, 230 per 1,000.

In Connecticut and Massachusetts the infant death rate is double that of New Zealand. In Rhode Island it is treble that of New Zealand.

Public health is purchasable. A community determines its own death rate to a large degree. The responsibility rests with the men here. They hold the purse. Do you want the women to look after the children? Why, yes; that is woman's work. Then let them. They wash the baby; they comb the boy's hair; they make the clothes. Do you see whether Johnny gets his home work done? No, Mother does. Why not let her have something to say about the school then, and about the healthfulness of the community in which the child lives. To do this she needs the tool to work with and that is the same one man uses—the Ballot.

The U.S. Census, 1911 report, estimates the death rate at 124 per 1,000.

In Russia it is 261 per 1,000.

In England it is 105 per 1,000.

In Australia it is 75 per 1,000.

In New Zealand it is 51 per 1,000.

Where women have full suffrage as in New Zealand and Australia, the death rate is lowest; the partial suffrage of England has helped to place the death rate lower than that of this country. Are you satisfied to leave it so? Let me get nearer to home. In Johnstown, Pa., 1,551 babies were born one year and 196 died that same year, namely, 134 per 1,000. This was the city average. In the poor parts of the city the death rate was 271 per 1,000, in the best part of the city about 50 per 1,000. Poverty, drunkenness and venereal diseases were primary causes. Public health is purchasable. It concerns you and me, your family and mine. Your vote has financial value to you and me, to your community and mine.

Nations holding women in subjection, India, Turkey, etc., decline; nations in which women fail to develop with men, die. In New England, famous for its strong men, the women have been a negligible factor politically and have as a consequence ceased to look upon themselves as economic factors. Out of 12,722 wives of well-known New England families, Prof. Crum found that the number of children per woman has declined. Look at this table carefully:

	No. of children per wife	Percentage of women with one child
1750–1799	6.43	1.88
1800–1849	4.94	4.07
1850–1869	3.47	5.91
1870–1879	2.77	8.10
1915	1.92	20.

In New Zealand with similar Anglo-Saxon stock the women have been shown that they are important political factors and as a consequence realize their economic importance and the birthrate is one of the highest in the world.

The past one hundred and fifty years is the transition in the United States. Men have worked out their political liberty. They have been allowed to exercise their judgment as to whether they would be mothers or not, but the responsibility of the maintenance of the State and Nation was left with the men. Woman has had an increasing life of ease and irresponsibility, especially among those families who were financially comfortable as these New England people are. Not having responsibility, these women shirked none; but the race is going to die that tries to live this way. It is doomed. Do the women want it? Do the men want it? If we continue as we are the American of whom we are so proud is a passing cloud. His sun has set, for he has no son. His glory is departed; his inheritance goes to the stranger within his gate. He has defied the laws of God. Nature abhors a vacuum. She sweeps those who defy her off the face of the earth. The remedy lies now with the men here. Give the women the chance to realize that this is their America; this is their nation. No nation can survive half slave and half free. No house can live half responsible and the other half irresponsible. It is not a case of whether all women want to be responsible. It is whether it is not in the best interest of all that all women be responsible for their own lives and action and take their place as thinking individuals among a people who have advanced so far since 1750. We do not plead for the introduction of woman suffrage; we merely ask that we move with the times. We stand on the tracks of time. Better get aboard the train of evolution rather than be run down by it. . . .

MEDITATIONS ON VOTES FOR WOMEN (excerpt)

Samuel McChord Crothers (1914)

AT A MEETING in opposition to the further extension of the suffrage I heard a charming woman object to such extension on the ground that a woman already has more influence than can be measured by a mere vote. And she proved her point, at least so far as women like herself are concerned. Almost every woman has some man whom she can influence. She has a husband or a son or a brother or a lover, or perhaps two or three nephews. In voting she would only count one for her cause, but in directing the votes of those nearest her she may easily count half a dozen. In standing apart from politics she may stand above it, now and then intervening like the Homeric goddesses while all the time being invisible. Like the King, she can do no wrong, having no direct responsibility, but as the fountain of honor she can hold out rewards to those who are responsible. In order to win her favor they are likely to adopt the righteous opinions she recommends. Why should she give up these prerogatives of royalty in order to assume the unromantic burdens of citizenship?

As I listened I was almost converted, and was prepared to believe that government by charm was to be preferred to any of the coarse methods of democracy. It was only when I seated myself in the street-car that my reflections took another turn. The car was filled with business men returning from their work. I could not but notice how deficient in charm these citizens were. There was no subtle witchery about them that could make the worse seem the better reason, or the good reason seem better than it is. Not one of these men was capable of changing my opinion by a subtle appeal to my emotions. Any cause they advocated must have some merit independent of them in order to succeed. They were unable to invest it with any irresistible personal attraction.

I considered how helpless these men would be when they returned to their homes and were beset by the propagandists who refused a vote of their own in order that they might vote by proxy. I could not but feel that an unfair advantage was being taken of these proxies, for they might have opinions of their own, which they would like to express.

For the voter who is a son I make no plea. It is doubtless better for him to vote as his mother tells him. The voter who is a brother is amply able to take his own part, and the lover-voter yields voluntarily. But the husband of the woman with a conscience elicits my sympathy. He is so helpless. He loves his wife dearly and is ready to share her joys and sorrows, but he does not share all her opinions in regard to local government. Of course she does not choose to exercise her

---

Boston: Houghton Mifflin, 1914.

influence except in a great moral issue. But she will find a great moral issue or make one. From this harvest field she expects to return bearing her sheaves with her. And her husband's vote is her most precious sheaf. To be deprived of that were treason to the cause of Anti-Suffrage.

When the husband and wife have set their minds on the same vote, the result is not doubtful. The husband, in voting according to the dictates of his wife's conscience, feels a bitterness that he is unable to express. It was not quite fair. If his wife could have used her conscience in a more impersonal way, it would have been a good diffused over the whole community. But she concentrated it all on him and bore down all opposition.

If instead of having only one vote for the family they could have their individual votes, what a convenience it would be! It would give the husband a sense of independence like having a check book of his own. . . .

LETTER TO *THE NEW YORK TIMES*

William Benedict (1915)

New York, February 8, 1915.

To the Editor of the "Times."

It is quite inconceivable that a writer of sufficient ability to be retained on the staff of so great and able a paper as the New York Times should have put forth an editorial such as appeared Sunday, against woman suffrage, with any real conviction that his arguments were sound or that they would appeal to any but the readers of mediocre intelligence, who presumedly had brought to the subject no knowledge, and but little thought.

To refer to a few points only: It was stated, "All the arguments of the suffragists are old and were long ago refuted and sent to limbo," yet in spite of that, those "old and refuted" arguments seem already to have appealed sufficiently to the *male* voters of twelve States of this great Union for them to grant the suffrage to women, and we have yet to hear that in these States the skies have fallen, or that a great upheaval has taken place in any of them, or even that the "affliction," (whatever that may mean), referred to in the editorial as the result of woman suffrage, has materialized.

Again, it states: "Without the counsel and guidance of men, no woman ever ruled a state wisely and well," but it might have been added that no state has ever been ruled wisely and well under universal male suffrage, and the New York Times has been most assiduous and useful in pointing out

(SL, Harriet B. Laidlaw Papers) The New York Times *did not publish this letter.*

almost daily in its admirable editorials, the lamentable mistakes of our male rulers.

To quote another statement: "Either women must work as men work, or they will never be qualified to vote as men vote. Men's work is different from woman's work," but it is a fact that the United States Census for 1910 shows only five occupations in which women are not represented, and we all know they are often driven to work at one thing or another because men cannot or will not exercise their "privilege of caring for them" referred to in the Times.

To refer to a dastardly slur, (for it cannot be called an argument), the editorial says, "The hackneyed cry that 'what is right for the man is right for the woman' is heard continually." Surely this is a "specious, shameless and unrighteous statement," to quote its own words, for the Times to make. The writer does not know where such a cry is "heard continually," but the cry which he has been in the habit of hearing from the women associated with woman suffrage is, "what is *wrong* for the woman is *wrong* for the man," which expresses a radically different idea.

Again, "If women suffer wrongs, it is the duty of men to right them; if bad laws hamper and afflict them, men should bestir themselves to have those laws repealed." A delightful truism, but hardly an argument against woman suffrage.

One more statement from the editorial, a pure assumption: " 'Heelers' and the manipulators of votes will all support woman suffrage." Now, if there is one element with which "heelers" are associated, "hand and glove," it is the liquor element which has stood solidly against woman suffrage from the beginning.

But enough has been quoted to show what a vulnerable editorial is that of Sunday, and to what desperate straits the Times must be driven in its efforts to influence public opinion, to have allowed it to appear.

A Saddened Admirer of the
New York Times.

"WOMAN—COMRADE AND EQUAL"

Eugene Debs (n.d.)

THE *London Saturday Review* in a recent issue brutally said: "Man's superiority is shown by his ability to keep woman in subjection." Such a sentiment is enough to kindle the wrath of every man who loves his wife or reveres his mother. It is the voice of the wilderness, the snarl of the primitive. Measured by that standard, every tyrant has been a hero, and brutality is at once the acme of perfection and the glory of man.

From Writings and Speeches of Eugene V. Debs. *New York: Hermitage, 1948.*

Real men do not utter such sentiments. He who does so prostitutes his powers and links himself once more to the chattering ape that wrenches the neck of the cowering female, glorying as he does so in the brute force that is his.

Yet the sentiment is not confined to a moral degenerate, who writes lies for pay, or to sycophants who sell their souls for the crumbs that arrogant wealth doles out to its vassals. It is embodied and embedded in the cruel system under which we live, the criminal system which grinds children to profits in the mills, which in the sweatshops saps women of their power to mother a race of decent men, which traps the innocent and true-hearted, making them worse than slaves in worse than all that has been said of hell. It finds expression in premiers hiding from petticoated agitators, in presidents ignoring the pleading of the mothers of men, in the clubbing and jailing of suffragettes; in Wall Street gamblers and brigands cackling from their piles of loot at the demands of justice. It is expressed in laws which rank mothers and daughters as idiots and criminals. It writes, beside the declaration that men should rebel against taxation without representation, that women must submit to taxation without representation. It makes property the god that men worship, and says that woman shall have no property rights. Instead of that, she herself is counted as property, living by sufferance of the man who doles out the pittance that she uses.

Woman is made the slave of a slave, and is reckoned fit only for companionship in lust. The hands and breasts that nursed all men to life are scorned as the forgetful brute proclaims his superior strength and plumes himself that he can subjugate the one who made him what he is, and would have made him better had customs and institutions permitted.

How differently is woman regarded by the truly wise and the really great! Paolo Lombroso, one of the deepest students of mind that time has ripened, says of her:

"The most simple, most frivolous and thoughtless woman hides at the bottom of her soul a spark of heroism, which neither she herself nor anybody else suspects, which she never shows if her life runs its normal course, but which springs into evidence and manifests itself by actions of devotion and self-sacrifice, if fate strikes her or those whom she loves. Then she does not wince, she does not complain nor give way to useless despair, but rushes into the breach. The woman who hesitates to put her feet into cold, placid water throws herself into the perils of the roaring, surging maelstrom."

Sardou, the analytical novelist, declares:

"I consider women superior to men in almost everything. They possess intuitive faculty to an extraordinary degree, and may almost always be trusted to do the right thing in the right place. They are full of noble instincts, and, though heavily handicapped by fate, come well out of every ordeal. You have only to turn to history to learn the truth of what I say."

Lester F. Ward, the economist, the subtle student of affairs, gives this testimony:

"We have no conception of the real amount of talent or of genius possessed by woman. It is probably not greatly inferior to that of man even now, and a few generations of enlightened opinion on the subject, if shared by both sexes, would perhaps show that the difference is qualitative only."

I am glad to align myself with a party that declares for absolute equality between the sexes. Anything less than this is too narrow for twentieth-century civilization, and too small for a man who has a right conception of manhood.

Let us grant that woman has not reached the full height which she might attain—

when I think of her devotion to duty, her tender ministries, her gentle spirit that in the clash and struggle of passion has made her the savior of the world, the thought, so far from making me decry womanhood, gives me the vision of a race so superior as to cause me to wonder at its glory and beauty ineffable.

Man has not reached his best. He never will reach his best until he walks the upward way side by side with woman. Plato was right in his fancy that man and woman are merely halves of humanity, each requiring the qualities of the other in order to attain the highest character. Shakespeare understood it when he made his noblest women strong as men and his best men tender as women.

Under our brutal forms of existence, beating womanhood to dust, we have raged in passion for the individual woman, for use only. Some day we shall develop the social passion for womanhood, and then the gross will disappear in service and justice and companionship. Then we shall lift woman from the mire where our fists have struck her, and set her by our side as our comrade and equal and that will be love indeed.

Man's superiority will be shown, not in the fact that he has enslaved his wife, but in that he has made her free.

"OUR DEBT TO SUFFRAGISTS"

Hon. Robert H. Terrell (ca. 1915)

Of all the elements in our great cosmopolitan population the Negro should be most ardently in favor of woman suffrage, for above all others, he knows what a denial of the ballot means to a people. He has seen his rights trampled on, he has been humiliated and insulted in public, and he has brooded over his weakness and helplessness in private, all because he did not possess the power given by the vote to protect himself in the same manner as other classes of citizens defend themselves against wrong and injustice. To those who oppose the right of women to vote it may be well to quote the stirring words of Benjamin Wade, of Ohio, uttered on the floor of the United States Senate, when he was advocating Negro Suffrage. He said: "I have a contempt I cannot name for the man who would demand rights for himself that he is not willing to grant to every one else."

Finally, as a matter of sentiment, every man with Negro blood in his veins should favor woman suffrage. Garrison, Phillips, Frederick Douglass and Robert Purvis and

---

(LOC, Mary C. Terrell Collection)

the whole host of abolitionists were advocates of the right. I often heard it said when I was a boy in Boston that immediately after the Civil War Susan B. Anthony, Julia Ward Howe, Elizabeth Cady Stanton and other leaders of the women's rights movement at the request of these men devoted all of their efforts towards obtaining the ballot for the Negro, even to the neglect of their own dearly cherished cause, hoping, indeed, that the black man, who would be in some measure the beneficiary of their work and sacrifice, would in turn give them the aid they so sorely needed at that time. Now what our fathers failed to do for these pioneers who did so much for our cause before and after the great war, let us do for those who are now leading the fight for woman suffrage. I believe that in supporting them we will render our country a great and much needed service.

"VOTES FOR WOMEN"

W. E. B. DuBois (1917)

LET US ANSWER frankly, there is not the slightest reason for supposing that white American women under ordinary circumstances are going to be any more intelligent, liberal or humane toward the black, the poor and unfortunate than white men are. On the contrary, considering what the subjection of a race, a class or a sex must mean, there will undoubtedly manifest itself among women voters at first more prejudice and petty meanness toward Negroes than we have now. It is the awful penalty of injustice and oppression to breed in the oppressed the desire to oppress others. The southern white women who form one of the most repressed and enslaved groups of modern civilized women will undoubtedly, at first, help willingly and zealously to disfranchize Negroes, cripple their schools and publicly insult them.

Nevertheless, votes for women must and ought to come and the Negroes should help bring this to pass for these reasons:

1. Any extension of democracy involves a discussion of the fundamentals of democracy.

2. If it is acknowledged to be unjust to disfranchise a sex it cannot be denied that it is absurd to disfranchise a color.

3. If the North enfranchises women, the proportion of unselfish intelligent voters among Negroes will be increased, and the proportion of Negro voters whom white politicians have trained to venality will be decreased.

4. If when the North enfranchises women the South refuses, or enfranchises only the

Crisis 15, no. 1 (November 1917).

whites, then the discrepancy between North and South in the votes cast will be even greater than now; at present the southern white voter has from five to seven times the power of the northern voter. How long would the nation endure an increase or even a doubling of this power? It would not take long before southern representatives in Congress would be cut down or colored women enfranchised.

5. Granting that first tendencies would make the woman voter as unfair in race rights as the man, there would be in the long run a better chance to appeal to a group that knows the disadvantage and injustice of disfranchisement by experience, than to one arrogant and careless with power. And in all cases the broader the basis of democracy the surer is the universal appeal for justice to win ultimate hearing and sympathy.

Therefore: Votes for Women.

"WOMAN SUFFRAGE AND THE NEGRO"

A. Phillips Randolph (1917)

WOMAN SUFFRAGE is coming.

Some women want it, and some women don't want it.

Women are taxpayers, producers and consumers just the same as men are, and they are justly entitled to vote.

The sentimental and puritanical objections advanced by the squeamish moralists won't stand. Sex is no bar to woman's participating in the industrial world and it should be none to her participating in the political world.

Negro men should realize their responsibility and duty in the coming election on the question of woman suffrage. Remember that if the right to vote benefits the Negro man, the right to vote will also benefit the Negro woman.

If white women ought to have the right to vote, then colored women ought to have the right to vote. If it will be beneficial to one, it will be beneficial to the other. Colored women are taxpayers, producers and consumers and they have a right to express their sentiment as regards the school systems, sanitation, the high cost of living, war, and everything which affects the general public. Of course, there are some colored women who will speak against woman suffrage, just as there are some white women who will speak for it. There were some Negro slaves who were opposed to freedom. Such kinks in the mind of the common people are not unusual.

Messenger 1, no. 2 (November 1917).

Of course, when they are seen among the aristocracy, the reason is not difficult to see. Throughout history the few have attempted to keep the many in economic and political slavery.

But the great sweep of democracy moves on. The artificial standards of sex or race should not stand against it.

All peoples, regardless of race, creed or sex will be drawn into the vortex of world democracy.

Just as there could not be any union while some men were slaves and some men were free, so there can be no democracy while white men vote and white women, colored women and colored men in the South don't vote.

Mr. Negro Voter, do your "bit."

"WHY MEN NEED EQUAL SUFFRAGE FOR WOMEN"

A. Caswell Ellis (1918)

THE MEN of America need equal suffrage for women immediately, because of four facts, one of which has reference only to American conditions, the other three are universal.

First, the men of this nation must grant equal suffrage to women fully, freely and cheerfully at *once,* in order to square their nation's acts with its declarations. We male citizens of the United States after three years of debate and deliberation solemnly and practically unanimously declared that a government without the consent of the governed was unjust and that the existence of such a government was a menace to all free governments. We both publicly pledged our nation to the principle of self government, and voted to consecrate every dollar of our wealth and every drop of our blood to the cause of human freedom and human justice, to the end that this world might be "made safe for democracy." England, France and Russia accepted our principle and our leadership in good faith. Russia had freed even her illiterate peasants. England has offered self government to the Irish, and Russia, France, England and Canada have all either already granted equal suffrage to their women, or have pledged to do so promptly. We alone lag behind. The United States can not lead in a war for democracy and be the last great nation to establish democracy. To pledge ourselves to democracy and then refuse to grant representation in our government to half of our adult educated popula-

From War Messages to the American People, *no. 3. New York: National Woman Suffrage Publishing, [1918]. (Barker Texas History Center, University of Texas at Austin)*

tion is to give support to the Kaiser's contention that our democratic pretentions are pure hypocrisy. The minute that this nation officially declared war upon autocratic Germany for the cause of democracy, the enfranchisement of our entire intelligent adult population, including the women, ceased to be a matter of personal judgment or state privilege, and became a sacred national pledge which Congress is in honor bound to redeem at once or brand us as a nation of knaves or fools before the bar of intelligent public opinion of the world. In short, we must grant women equal suffrage by federal amendment at once to demonstrate the sincerity of our nation's pretentions.

Second, we need woman's suffrage to protect us and our government from our own one-sided masculine view of life. This is not to say that our man's views are wrong or that the woman's views are right. We mean only that each view is partial and inadequate, and needs the other to balance and complete it. With few exceptions, men are more interested in problems of production, distribution and sale, in questions relating to economics and property interests, or in abstract speculation. Women are usually more concerned with problems of conservation; of personal relations, of human happiness and human welfare. The future welfare of men as well as of women is dependent upon proper governmental attention to questions of health and hygiene, of food and housing, of human protection in industry, of child welfare; in short, of municipal, state and national housekeeping. Women are by nature more concerned that men with these vital questions of personal relation and human welfare, and when women have adequate voice in our government we can hope for wiser and more speedy solution of these grave problems.

Third, men need to grant to women the privileges and duties of citizenship in order to strengthen the weakening family bond and enrich and elevate the home life for themselves and their children. It is obvious that the great problems of municipal, state and national government offer one a broader mental horizon than do those of a single family. The daily work of the mother, while demanding the highest intelligence, can very easily drop into a ceaseless round of petty routine. It is not always true that the family conversation becomes a mere recounting of commonplace details about foods and servants, clothing and neighborhood gossip, but this, alas, is the usual result. It is contrary to human nature that women who are not allowed to participate in public life should take enough interest in public welfare or governmental problems to inform themselves upon them or to enjoy discussing them in the home. If the husband is to find expression for his interests in the broader problems of life, he must leave the home and go to his club, the street, or the hotel lobby. The addition of women to the electorate would give a wholesome corrective for the narrowing effect of routine home duties of women, and by furnishing broad matters of common interest for father, mother, and children, would elevate and strengthen home life and contribute largely toward bringing up the next generation with higher and better ideals of citizenship and of home.

Fourth, and most far reaching of all, man must grant equal suffrage to woman in order to refine his own sense of justice which is inevitably dulled by the continued toleration of any act of injustice. Everyone knows that his ideas influence and modify his acts, but few recognize how much their ideas are colored and modified by their habits of acting. If we live under a social or civic system that leads us to act in a certain way, we soon begin to justify that act. If we habitually act towards any class of people as if they were of a certain character, we soon find ourselves either consciously or unconsciously accepting a view that is in accord with our conduct. This fact was deeply impressed upon me one day in Berlin. The social democrats were demanding equal suffrage for the men in Prussia with such vigor that the Kaiser brought about forty thousand troops into the city and filled the open square with machine guns in order to awe the population. At that time an honest, intelligent carpenter or stone-mason had about one two hundred and fiftieth of a vote in Prussia. I remarked to the wife of a distinguished German professor, at whose home I was staying at the time, "Why not let these honest, intelligent men have a vote?" She threw up her hands in genuine horror at the idea, and exclaimed: "Merciful Heavens! Let that herd vote! Why, they would steal everything we have away from us and tear everything to pieces." She regarded my proposal of universal male suffrage about as I had suggested that every wild cat, tiger, lion and hyena on the globe be given the ballot. She was personally a gentle, kind-hearted woman, she had a keen, active conscience in general, and was kind and considerate to her own servants, but she had lived under a system of government that through its suffrage law acted as if the laboring population were wild animals unfit to trust with the vote until she had acquired the idea that they were exactly the kind that the law in effect declared them to be.

Not only do our ideals tend to come into conformity with our conduct, but an ideal fostered by conduct in one field of life tends to modify our views even in other fields and bring us to commit acts that would otherwise have been abhorred. The institution of human slavery in many cases resulted in better care for the slaves than they gave themselves when freed, and yet slavery had to be abolished as much to protect the minds of those who owned the slaves from the corroding influence of the many indirect effects of the institutions as to protect the slaves from injustice.

For these reasons we men cannot quietly continue to keep women in a state of political slavery, denying them the fundamental right to participate in their own government, without blunting our own sense of justice, nor can we continue to act toward woman in her civic relations as if she were an infant or a civic imbecile without to some extent coming to accept this view. These false views and this dulled sense of justice acquired by the continued performance of this act of injustice unfortunately will spread their influence far beyond the incident which gave rise to them and injuriously affect much of our thinking and living. The only way to continually refine our sense of right is to live up to the highest that we now have, and the sure way to dull our sense of justice and lower our ideals is to allow prejudice, personal interest or cowardice to hold us back from following immediately the highest light that is in us.

If the men of this nation refuse to heed the light that our quickened consciences have brought to us in this hour of supreme peril, that light will vanish as we slip backward and downward. We must as brave, free men break the shackles of tradition and every unworthy tie that binds, face without blinking the dawn of this new day of freedom and justice and live up to the highest that is given us in order that we may become pure enough and strong enough to see yet more light.

"THE KIND OF DEMOCRACY THE NEGRO RACE EXPECTS"

William Pickens (1918)

DEMOCRACY is the most used term in the world today. But some of its uses are abuses. Everybody says "Democracy"! But everybody has his own definition. By the extraordinary weight of the Presidency of the United States many undemocratic people have had this word forced upon their lips but have not yet had the right ideal forced upon their hearts. I have heard of one woman who wondered with alarm whether "democracy" would mean that colored women would have the right to take any vacant seat or space on a streetcar, even if they had paid for it. That such a question should be asked, shows how many different meanings men may attach to the one word *democracy.* This woman doubtless believes in a democracy of me-and-my-kind, which is no democracy. The most autocratic and the worst caste systems could call themselves democratic by that definition. . . .

It is in order, therefore, for the Negro to state clearly what he means by *democracy* and what he is fighting for. . . .

Fourth. Democracy without Sex Preferment. The Negro cannot consistently oppose color discrimination and support sex discrimination in democratic government. This happened to be the opinion also of the First Man of the Negro race in America—Frederick Douglass. The handicap is nothing more nor less than a presumption in the mind of the physically dominant element of the universal inferiority of the weaker or subject element. It is so easy to prove that the man who is down and under, deserves to be down and under. In the first place, he is down there, isn't he? And that is three fourths of the argument to the ordinary mind; for the ordinary mind does not seek ultimate causes. The argument against the participation of colored men and of women in self-government is practically one argument. Somebody spoke to the Creator about both of these classes and learned that they were "created" for inferior roles. Enfranchisement would spoil a good field hand or a good cook. Black men were once ignorant, women were once ignorant. Negroes had no political experience, women had no such experience. The argument forgets that people do not get experience on the outside. But the American Negro expects a democracy that will accord the right to vote to a sensible industrious woman rather than to a male tramp.

Reprinted in The Voice of Black America, *ed. Philip S. Foner. New York: Simon & Schuster, 1972.*

"SOME QUESTIONS FOR WOMAN SUFFRAGISTS, FROM A MERE MAN"

Frank McCullough (1919)

DO YOU WANT the ballot? Do you want it as quickly as possible? The right of women to vote in Illinois for any officer mentioned in the Constitution of the State can be obtained only by the consent of the male voters. The Legislature has now given the male electors the opportunity to vote upon the question whether or not a convention shall be called to propose a new Constitution. If the vote for a convention be in the affirmative and a convention be called its members will decide what suffrage provisions to put into the proposed Constitution which must later be submitted to a vote of the men of the State. If the men voters elect to have a constitutional convention then the members of that convention may draft something favorable or something unfavorable to women. Would not favorable action be more likely if women were given the right to vote for members of the constitutional convention, and the right to be members?

No provision can be made for the election of members of such convention until the legislative session of 1919. They will not be elected until after that time. In the meantime our Constitution may be amended so as to permit women to vote for and be members of the constitutional convention and to vote upon the question of the adoption or rejection of the draft of Constitution which the convention may present. Ought not the women of the State to have a voice in the making of any new Constitution under which they are to be governed? The only way to give them any such power is to amend the Constitution in advance and give them the ballot. This can be done if the present Legislature will pass the pending resolution for a Suffrage Amendment which will then be voted on in November 1918.

Are you afraid to submit the question of woman suffrage to vote in 1918? If so what can happen to make its chances better three or four or more years later? The suffrage movement has never had such a favorable impetus as it has just now. During the last two months North Dakota and Ohio have given women the Presidential ballot; Indiana has given the right to vote for Presidential electors and all officers not mentioned in the Constitution and for members of the constitutional convention; New York, Maine, North Dakota and Oklahoma have submitted suffrage amendments; Minnesota, Wisconsin and Missouri have taken action which indicates that they will give women the right to vote for Presidential electors. Arkansas has given women the right to vote at primaries which in that one-

---

(SL, Catherine Waugh McCullough Papers)

party State amounts to practically the same thing as a vote at the election. Favorable votes have been given in one house of several other states. Victory is upon you. Why hesitate to take it?

But suppose that you are fearful. Can you ever win by inaction? Is there any better way to make suffrage propoganda than to have a suffrage campaign? How else can the indifferent or the unconvinced be so well found out and persuaded as by putting all to the test of an election? If education and appeal must be given what furnishes so good an opportunity as an election upon the very question to be decided?

Is it not wise to push for the ballot in Illinois just as fast as possible? More than 876,000 women voted in our State at the November election. While their interest is fresh and favorable action is being taken in all neighboring states is it not an opportune time to work for the suffrage amendment to our Constitution? Are you urging your State Senator and Representatives to vote for this Amendment?

ORGANIZING MEN FOR FEMINISM: THE MEN'S LEAGUE FOR WOMAN SUFFRAGE

"STATEMENT ON SUFFRAGE"

Rabbi Stephen Samuel Wise (1907)

WE ARE TOLD [the ballot] would be unwomanly. Whenever women begin to do something new, it is always called unwomanly. I can remember when it was thought unwomanly for a woman to know how to swim or to have good health or a good appetite.

Then we are told that woman ought not to vote because they already have so much influence for good. What an absurd argument! Woman now has a magnificent influence; if she gets the ballot will she at once become dangerous and permicious?

The most serious obstacle is the spirit of those who believe that manhood suffrage is a failure and ought to be wiped out. If you believe that, you will vote against equal suffrage, of course. But if you believe that democracy is the hope of the ages, vote for the amendment.

An eloquent minister of the gospel says that women ought not to vote because suffrage is not a natural but a derived right. So

From "The Field of Their Activity; the Position Taken on Suffrage by Rabbi Wise." 2 February 1907. (SSL)

is the right of your children to a common school education. So is our right to sanitary and police protection. It is not natural; heaven did not make policemen. But who will say that girls should be shut out from school or women from police protection, because it is not a natural right?

Another great force opposed is Mr. Sleek Contented Conservatism. He has three names like some ministers of the gospel. He has stood in the way of every reform in history because his father did not believe in it and his grandfather never heard of it.

"THE HEROIC MEN"

Editorial, the *New York Times* (1912)

THE FACTS are all in print now about the masculine adherents of the woman suffragists who will march in the parade tomorrow. There will be 800 of them surely. They will represent every trade and profession except the clergy. This is clearly an oversight which should be rectified. There is no lack of clergymen ready to support the cause of votes for women. For the rest the list includes bankers, manufacturers, students, librarians, dentists, musicians, booksellers, journalists, as well as dancing teachers, egg inspectors, capitalists, watchmen, ladies' waistmakers—and authors. A lawyer will carry the banner, and a drum and fife corps will head the division.

This is important news and not to be trifled with. The men who have professed to believe in woman suffrage have always been numerous. But these men are going to do more than profess, they are going to march before the eyes of the more or less unsympathetic multitude. It is one thing to sit on the platform and smile at a woman's meeting, quite another to march behind a gaudy banner to the inspiration of the squeaking fife, in order to indicate one's belief in the right of women to the ballot. The men will be closely scanned, but they will not mind that. They will be called endearing names by small boys on the sidewalk. But doubtless they will study to preserve their gravity. They will not march as well as the women. Only trained soldiers can compete with the amazons in keeping step. There must be strong inducement to make men march in a woman's parade. Some may be looking for customers. We suspect both the waistmakers and the dentists, for instance. But the majority must firmly believe in the righteousness of the cause, and also in the value to it of their public appearance in line. They are courageous fellows. The march of the 800 may be renowned. We hope they will all hold out from Thirteenth Street to Carnegie Hall, and we extend to all the 800 our sympathy and admiration.

---

3 May 1912.

"STATEMENT AT NATIONAL AMERICAN WOMAN SUFFRAGE CONVENTION"

James Lee Laidlaw (1912)

Mr. Chairman, as Dr. Shaw says, the men in this country, who are now beginning to realize that the question of woman suffrage is a vital one, have formed an organization which has spread all over the country. We have organizations in nearly all the leading cities, and they are now uniting in one great national association, which we expect will have hundreds of thousands of members.

About 100 years ago, when the question of the expediency of manhood suffrage was under consideration, women had few rights under the law; they had few property rights, not even the right to the body of their own children, and boys only were admitted to education in the public schools. At that time perhaps it was not such an obvious injustice to exclude the women from the right of franchise as it is now. Since that time the laws concerning women have been somewhat liberalized in certain of the States after a hard fight made step by step by the leaders of the women's rights movement; so that now, in the State of New York, for instance, women, either married or single, may hold property and their investments in securities and real estate, are a considerable proportion of the total.

Reprinted in HWS, *vol. 5.*

Most important of all is the change of women's position in industrial, commercial, and educational fields. We are all familiar with the exodus of millions of women from the home to the industries which have taken them out into the world—into the mill and into the factory. To-day they may enter into business either as principal or as employee. The public schools and many of the institutions of learning are open to them. I was astonished to hear reported at a recent meeting of the Chamber of Commerce of New York, that in the commerical high schools of New York City, where a business education is given, 85 percent of the pupils are girls. We have to-day a great body of intelligent citizens with many interests in the Government besides their primary interests as mothers and home keepers.

If men are not going to take the next logical step, they have made a great mistake in going thus far. Why give women property rights if we give them no rights in making the laws governing the control and disposition of their property and no vote as to who shall have the spending of the tax money? Why give women the right to go into business or trades, either as employees or employers, without the right to control the conditions surrounding their business or trades? Why train women to be better mothers and better housekeepers and refuse them the right to say what laws shall be passed to protect their children and homes? Why teach women to be teachers, lawyers, doctors, and scientists, and say to them, "Now you have assumed new responsibilities, go out into the world and compete with men," and then handicap them by depriving them of the right of political expression? Women now have the opportunity for equal mental development with men. Is it right, or is it politically expedient, that we should not avail ourselves of their special knowledge concerning those matters which vitally affect the human race? . . .

"THE COMMON MAN AND THE FRANCHISE"

Charles A. Beard (1912)

It is a favorite practice of privileged persons in all times to base their prerogatives upon natural law, divine will, right reason, or some other respectable foundation. King James I. of England, whose unhappy son lost his head during the Puritan revolution, ordered Parliament and the judges not to interfere with his affairs, saying: "That which concerns the mystery of the king's power is not lawful to be disputed; for that is to wade into the weakness of princes, and to take away the mystical reverence that belongs to them that sit in the throne of God. . . . It is atheism and blasphemy to dispute what God can do. . . . So it is presumption and high contempt in a subject to dispute what a king can do, or say that a king cannot do this or that; but rest in that which is the king's revealed will in his law." Bossuet, the famous theologian and orator of Louis XIV.'s reign, celebrated the divine origin of absolute monarchy in his treatise on "Politics Drawn from the Very Words of the Holy Scripture," and boasted of the special advantage enjoyed by the French constitution in the exclusion of women from the throne. To him, France had "the best constitution possible, and the one most conformable to that which God Himself has established; all of which shows the wisdom of our ancestors and the special protection which God extends to this kingdom." . . .

. . . [T]he average male opponent of woman suffrage to-day, is constantly assuming that his right to vote rests on natural, if not divine, sanctions. He knows nothing about the origin of it. He is ignorant of the fact that not many generations ago kings, priests and nobles regarded the common man of his

New York: Men's League for Woman Suffrage, 1912. (SL)

class and intelligence just exactly as he regards woman to-day. James I.'s motto was, "Let the cobbler stick to his last"—which meant to him, "Let the merchant, the banker, the trader, the artisan and laborer in the fields stick to their jobs and not interfere with the affairs of state, which are such high mysteries as to be beyond the reach of common intellects." So the anti-suffragist has for his motto, "Let women stick to their jobs, and leave the affairs of state to my supreme wisdom—so celebrated through the ages ever since the apple episode in the Garden." He does not know that his ancestors won political power by agitation and violence, and were ridiculed with the very same "arguments" which he now addresses to the women . . .

There is no time now to tell the interesting and moving story of the long struggle by which the common man wrested from his political superiors the right to vote. I may say, however, that he employed argument, appeals to a sense of justice, the cry of "natural rights," petitions, parades, and sometimes mob violence. I may say also that nowhere were the disfranchised men required to submit to the tests now applied to women by the anti-suffragists. They were not required to show that they were the intellectual equals of the enfranchised. They were not required to prove that they would use wisely and for the benefit of the ruling classes the power they demanded. They were not required to show that voting would not interfere with their "natural" functions as fathers and supporters of homes. They were not required to prove that a majority of the disfranchised wanted the vote or would use it if they had it. Nowhere was the absurd idea adopted of allowing the disfranchised to vote on their own issue.

Every argument that has been brought against woman suffrage is already rusty with age, because it was used long ago against manhood suffrage by the privileged. Every argument which can be adduced in favor of allowing anybody except kings to share in the government can be employed in favor of women. The social and economic conditions which underlay the movement for manhood suffrage form the foundation for woman suffrage. The strength of these social and economic forces is irresistible. The women may lose their battle to-day, and to-morrow and the next day; but the sun of Austerlitz will yet rise over their field.

"WHO'S AFRAID? CONFESSION OF A SUFFRAGE ORATOR"

Max Eastman (1915)

It was never a question of making people believe in the benefits of women's freedom, it was a question of making them *like the idea.* And all the abstract arguments in the world furnished merely a sort of auction ground upon which the kindly beauties of the thing could be exhibited. Aristotle, in his hopeful way, defined man as a "reasonable animal," and the schools have been laboring under that delusion ever since. But man is a voluntary animal, and he knows what he likes and what he dislikes, and that is the greater part of his knowledge. Especially is this true of his opinion upon questions involving sex, because in these matters his native taste is so strong. He will have a multitude of theories and abstract reasons surrounding it, but these are merely put on for the sake of gentility, the way clothes are. Most cultivated people think there is something indecent about a naked preference. I believe, however, that propagandists would fare better, if they were boldly aware that they are always moulding wishes rather than opinions.

There is something almost ludicrous about the attitude of a professional propagandist to his kit of arguments—and in the suffrage movement especially, because the arguments are so many and so old, and so classed and codified, and many of them so false and foolish too. I remember that during the palmiest days of the abstract argument (before California came in and spoiled everything with a big concrete example) I was engaged in teaching, or endeavoring to teach, Logic to a division of Sophomores at Columbia. And there was brought to my attention at that time a book published for use in classes like mine, which contained a codification in logical categories of all the suffrage arguments, both pro and con, and *a priori* and *a posteriori,* and *per accidens* and *per definitionem,* that had ever been advanced since Socrates first advocated the strong-minded woman as a form of moral discipline for her husband. I never found in all my platform wanderings but one suffrage argument that was not in this book, and that I discovered on the lips of an historical native of Troy, New York. It was a woman, she said, who first invented the detachable linen collar, that well-known device for saving a man the trouble of changing his shirt, and though that particular woman is probably dead, her sex remains with its pristine enthusiasm for culture and progress.

But the day of the captious logician, like the day of the roaring orator, is past. What our times respond to, is the propagandist who knows how to respect the wishes of other people, and yet show them in a sympathetic way that there is more fun for them, as well as for humanity in general, in

Masses 7, *no. 1, issue no. 53 (October–November 1915).*

the new direction. *Give them an hour's exercise in liking something else*—that is worth all the proofs and refutations in the world.

Take that famous proposition that "woman's sphere is the home." A canvass was made at a woman's college a while ago to learn the reasons for opposing woman suffrage, and no new ones were found, but among them all this dear old saying had such an overwhelming majority that it amounted to a discovery. It is the eternal type. And how easy to answer, if you grab it crudely with your intellect, imagining it to be an opinion.

"Woman's sphere is the home!" you cry. "Do you know that according to the census of 1910 more than one woman in every five in this country is engaged in gainful employment?"

"Woman's sphere is the home! Do you know where your *soap* comes from?

"Woman's sphere is the home!—do you know that in fifty years all the work that women used to do within the four walls of her house has moved out into the—

"Woman's sphere is the home! Do you know that, as a simple matter of fact, the sphere of those women who most need the protection of the government and the laws, is *not* the home but the factory and the market!

"Why to say that woman's sphere is the home after the census says it isn't, is like saying the earth is flat after a hundred thousand people have sailed round it!"

Well—such an assault and battery of the intellect will probably silence the gentle idealist for a time, but it will not alter the direction of her will. She never intended to express a statistical opinion, and the next time you see her she will be telling somebody else—for she will not talk to you any more—that "woman's *proper* sphere is the home." In other words, and this is what she said the first time, if you only had the gift of understanding, "I like women whose sphere is the home. My husband likes them, too. And we should both be very unhappy if I had to go to work outside. It doesn't seem charming or beautiful to us."

Now there is a better way to win over a person with such a gift of strong volition and delicate feeling, than to jump down her throat with a satchel full of statistics. I think a propagandist who realized that here was an expression primarily of a human wish, and that these wishes, spontaneous, arbitrary, unreasoned, because reason itself is only their servant, are the divine and unanswerable thing in us all, would respond to her assertion more effectively, as well as more pleasantly.

The truth is that any reform which associates itself with the name of liberty, or democracy, is peculiarly adapted to this more persuasive kind of propaganda. For liberty does not demand that any given person's tastes or likings as to a way of life be reformed. It merely demands that these should not be erected into a dogma, and inflicted as morality or law upon everybody else. It demands that all persons should be made free in the pursuit of their own tastes or likings.

Thus the most ardent suffragist might begin by answering our domestic idealist—"Well, I suppose it is a charming and beautiful thing for you to stay in your home, since you are happy there. I myself have a couple of neighbors who have solved their problem of life that way too, and I never have an argument with them. Why? Because they recognize that all people's problems are not to be solved in the same way. They recognize the varieties of human nature. They recognize that each one of us has a unique problem of life to solve, and he or she must be made free to solve it in her own unique way. That is democracy. That is the liberty of man. That is what universal suffrage means, and would accomplish, so far as political changes can accomplish it.

"Let us agree that woman's proper sphere is the home, whenever it is. But there are many women who, on account of their natural disposition perhaps, or perhaps on account of their social or financial situation, can not function happily in that sphere; and they are only hindered in the wholesome and fruitful solution of their lives by the dogma which you and your society hold over them, and which is crystallized and entrenched as political inequality by the fundamental law."

Thus our agitation of the woman question would appear to arise, not out of our own personal taste in feminine types, but out of our very recognition of the fact that tastes differ. We would propagandize, not because we are cranks and have a fixed idea about what everybody else ought to become, and what must be done about it at once, but because we are trying to accept variety and the natural inclinations of all sorts of people as, by presumption at least, self-justified and divine. We want them all to be free.

Such is the peculiar advantage that the propaganda of liberty has over all the evangelical enthusiasms. It does not at the first gasp ask a man to mortify his nature. It merely asks him to cease announcing his own spontaneous inclinations as the type and exemplar of angelic virtue, and demanding that everybody else be like him. It tries to remove another old negative dogmatic incubus from the shoulders of life, aspiring toward variety and realization. That is what the suffrage propaganda is doing.

It would be folly to pretend, however, that the principle of equal liberty is the only motive behind the suffrage movement. I have said that it is the primary one. It is at least the broadest, the surest, the one upon which the conversion of a person whose taste opposes yours can be most graciously introduced.

But there is yet another way of changing a person's wish, and that is to show him that he himself has deeper wishes which conflict with it. And there is one deep wish in particular that almost all women, and most men possess, and that is a wish for the welfare and advancement of their children. And just as "Woman's sphere is the home" typifies the voluntary force opposing woman suffrage, so "Women owe it to their children to develop their own powers," typifies the force that favors it.

Universal citizenship has meant in human history universal education. That has been, next to a certain precious rudiment of liberty, its chief value. That will be its chief value to women for a long time to come. And by education I do not mean merely political education. I do not mean that it will awaken in women what we call a "civic consciousness," though it will, I suppose, and that is a good thing. I mean that by giving to women a higher place in our social esteem, it will promote their universal development.

We are not educated very much by anything we study in school or see written on the black-board. That does not determine what we grow up to be. The thing that determines what we grow up to be is the natural expectations of those around us. If society expects a girl to become a fully developed, active and intelligent individual, she will probably do it. If society expects her to remain a doll-baby all her life, she will make a noble effort to do that. In either case she will not altogether succeed, for there are hereditary limitations, but the responsibility for the main trend of the result is with the social conscience.

"Sugar and spice and everything nice,
That is what little girls are made of;
Snips and snails and puppy-dogs' tails,
That is what little boys are made of."

There is an example of what has been educating us. That kind of baby-talk has done more harm than all the dynamite that was ever let off in the history of the world. You might as well put poison in the milk.

All that is to be ended. And this is the chief thing we expect of women's citizenship. It will formulate in the public mind the higher ideal that shall develop the young girls of the future. They will no longer grow up, to be, outside the years of motherhood, mere drudges or parlor ornaments. They will no longer try to satisfy their ambitions by seeing who can parade the most extreme buffooneries of contemporary fashion on the public highway. They will grow up to be interested and living individuals, and satisfy their ambitions only with the highest prizes of adventure and achievement that life offers.

And the benefit of that will fall upon us all—but chiefly upon the children of these women when they are mothers. For if we are going anywhere that a sane idealism would have us go, we must first stop corrupting the young. Only a developed and fully constituted individual is fit to be the mother of a child. Only one who has herself made the most of the present, is fit to hold in her arms the hope of the future.

We hear a good deal about "child-welfare" in these days, and we hear the business of child-welfare advanced as one of the arguments for woman suffrage. To me it is almost the heart of the arguments, but it works in my mind a little differently from what it does in the minds of the people who write the child-welfare pamphlets. I do not want women to have, for the sake of their children, the control of the milk-supply and the food laws, half so much as I want them to have, for the sake of their children, all the knowledge-by-experience that they can possibly get. That is the vital connection between child-welfare and woman suffrage—that is the deeper ideal. No woman is fit to bring children into this world until she knows to the full the rough actual character of the world into which she is bringing them. And she will never know that until we lift from her—in her own growing years—the repressive prejudice that expresses itself and maintains itself in refusing to make her a citizen.

A man who trains horses up in western New York put this to me very strongly. "If you're going to breed race-horses," he said, "you don't pick out your stallions on a basis of speed and endurance, and your mares according to whether they have sleek hides and look pretty when they hang their heads over the pasture fence. And if you're going to raise intelligent citizens you'll have to give them intelligent citizens for mothers." I do not know whether he was aware that an actual tendency to *select* the more intelligent, rather than a mere training of the intelligence of all, is the main force in racial evolution. But that is what he said. And, either way, it is a piece of cold scientific fact. The babies of this world suffer a good deal more from silly mothers than they do from sour milk. And any change in political forms, however superficial from the standpoint of economic justice, that will increase the breadth of experience, the sagacity, the humor, the energetic and active life-interest of mothers, can only be regarded as a profound historic revolution.

In these broad effects upon the progress of liberty and life, not in any political result of equal suffrage, are to be found an object of desire which can rival and replace the ideal that opposes it. They are the material for the propaganda of the will. And while we noisy orators are filling the air with syllogisms of justice, and prophecies of the purification of politics, and the end of child labor, and what women will do to wars, and the police-department, and the sweat-shops, and the street-cleaning department, and the milk-wagons, and the dairy farms, and how they will reform the cows when they come into their rights, we ought to remember in our sober hearts that those large warm human values, which have nothing to do with logic or politics or reform, are what will gradually bend the wishes of men toward a new age.

"FIFTEEN REASONS WHY I AM IN FAVOR OF UNIVERSAL EQUAL SUFFRAGE"

Omar Elvin Garwood (CA. 1915)

1. Because for eighteen years I have seen the fairness and justice of the equal suffrage principle demonstrated in Colorado.

2. Because Colorado's experience shows that the vast majority of women exercise the privileges of the elective franchise wisely, conscientiously and intelligently.

3. Because I have yet to hear a single argument urged against woman-suffrage that cannot with equal force be urged against man-suffrage.

4. Because there is no logical reason why half of the American race should be denied a voice in making the laws and selecting the officers by which the whole race is governed.

5. Because since their enfranchisement, the women of Colorado have caused to be placed among the statutes the "sanest, most humane, most progressive and most scientific laws relating to the child to be found in any statute books in the world."

6. Because Colorado, with the help of its enfranchised women, has enacted model laws securing the property rights of married women, providing for the protection of widow's and orphan's estates and for the care of the delinquent and dependent classes.

7. Because since the enfranchisement of women in Colorado fifty towns, twelve counties and the principal residence portions of Denver, its largest city, have abolished the saloon evil.

8. Because I have never known an instance where the use of the ballot has caused a woman to lose her womanliness, or neglect her home or family.

9. Because there is no just basis for political inequality between men and women.

(SL, Harriet B. Laidlaw Papers.)

10. Because I have unbounded confidence in American womanhood.

11. Because by denying women the ballot, our political system places American women in the same class as other unfranchised members of society, viz: Minors, aliens, illiterates, imbeciles, idiots and convicts.

12. Because the denial to women of the right to vote violates the fundamental American doctrine that there shall be no taxation without representation.

13. Because since there is no sex distinction in the enforcement of the law, there should be none in the enactment of the law.

14. Because the correct solution of America's social and political problems—municipal, state and national—needs the active assistance, through the ballot, of American women.

15. Because tested by actual experience, equal suffrage means better laws, better candidates, better government and consequently a better society.

"NUTS TO CRACK"

Wilmer Atkinson (1916)

PUT CONSCIENCE into the ballot box on Tuesday next. Woman Suffrage is coming; get on the band wagon; help swing the old party to it. Lincoln was for it, Brumbaugh, Porter, Smith and Penrose are for it. How would you like to be taxed and not allowed to vote? Play fair; establish justice; your wife voted for you; now vote for her.

For you, Mr. Democrat: Take your cue from Woodrow Wilson, Wm. J. Bryan, Candidate Bromley; the democratic principle is for the people to rule—all people, not half of them. Women are people. *Vote "Yes" on November 2nd.*

For you, Any Other or No Party Man: Vote "Yes" on November 2nd.

For you, Mr. Lane and for you, Mr. McNichol: Don't hand out tips for your henchmen to work against the Woman Suffrage amendment. It is coming before long and you know it. Don't steer the party wrong on this issue; if you do, the women will not forget it after they get the vote. Stand for a square deal for the women. *Vote "Yes" on November 2nd.*

For you, the Vares: The women expect you to come out for Woman Suffrage. It is not like you to shiver on the brink. Say the magic word to your followers. *Vote "Yes" on November 2nd.*

For you, Mr. Man, who lives on Easy Street: Soften up a bit; think of the poor who fight the hard battle of life; the women who carry heavy burdens and plead for the protection the ballot will afford. *Vote "Yes" on November 2nd.*

Philadelphia: Men's League for Woman Suffrage, [1916]. *(SSL)*

For you, Veteran of the Civil War: The women of the 60's gave you and 1,500,000 other brave men to save the Union; they nursed you when sick and wounded. Help the mothers of today, who would not fail if called on for any patriotic duty, to obtain the same rights as you possess. *Vote "Yes" on November 2nd.*

For you, Mr. Colored Voter: Abraham Lincoln signed a proclamation emancipating your race. He was for Woman Suffrage. Wm. Lloyd Garrison, Frederick Douglass and Wendell Phillips were all for Woman Suffrage. By their help millions of your people were delivered from bondage and were given the vote. How can you turn down your benefactors; how can you deny the ballot to women? *Vote "Yes" on November 2nd.*

For you, Anti-Suffrage Clergymen: You know that the worst elements of society are arrayed against the ballot for women. Why help them to defeat the measure by your opposition or your silence? What would become of your church were it not for the women in it? *Vote "Yes" on November 2nd.*

For you, Mr. Working Man: Your hearts are right; life is hard for you; it is hard for your women; they plead for justice and equality. You may feel that they need no protection but what you can give them, but suppose you are suddenly called to your heavenly home, as many a healthy man is, then what? *Vote "Yes" on November 2nd.*

For you, Mrs. Militant Anti-Suffragist: Why are you against woman suffrage when you know the saloon men, dive-keepers and white slavers are all dead against it? Don't say you don't know it, for you do. You say woman's place is in the home. That is easy for you, but how about those who have no home of their own and who go out to earn their living? How many homes have you? Possibly two or three. Do you stay in any one of them long at a time? You say women should keep out of politics; then why don't you keep out of politics? You say that 90% of the women don't want to vote; how do you know? Did you make a count? What is the verdict of the General and State Federation of Women's Clubs? Come now, turn over a new leaf and use your indirect influence to persuade your men folks to *vote "Yes" on November 2nd.*

"WOMAN SUFFRAGE WOULD INCREASE CORRUPTION"

Lincoln Steffens (1917)

IT WOULD. But what of it?

We don't take the ballot from railroad presidents because railroads have to buy votes; nor from the colored voters of our cities and the good old American white stock of the rural districts of New England, Pennsylvania and Indiana because they sell their votes.

There is truth in the first implication in this: That women are morally as bad as men. Politically, I think they are worse. They must be. Morality is largely a matter of practice, and women had had no practice in political morality till the suffragists got into the game. And they are showing already that they are as prone to put the special interest of women above the common interest of all as a railroad, a church or a political party. And that's what political corruption is, in its final analysis. Let us grant then that woman suffrage would make our bad government worse for a while. What of it?

Good government is not what we are after. That's the second implication contained in this objection, and it is false and misleading. This is the assumption that makes the Goo-Goos wish for a limited, aristocratic franchise and look for a good man for mayor. And they are right, theoretically. If good government was what we are after, the thing to do is to get a good king.

From Anti-Suffrage Arguments Answered *(SL, Harnet B. Laidlaw Papers)*

But, practically, kings have failed, and aristocracies have failed, and now our plutocracy is failing. All these governments rule the people, not in the common interest, but in the special interest of the king, of the aristocracy, or with us, of business. We are being forced to turn to the people, all the people; not the best people, not even good people, but all the people, on the theory that if all the people are given the vote, all the interests of all the people will somehow be represented; that even if they all vote, even corruptly, in their special interests, the result will be an approximation to, possibly a conscious, intelligent perception of, the common interest of all the people as a people. And, as for morality, since representative government is no more an end than good government is an end; since government itself is but a means to an end; and since that end is the improvement, not of government, but of the brand of men and women, it follows that the participation of all men and women is good for them. No matter whether it is good for the government or bad, the voters' responsibility with power, the freedom of choice and the exercise of morality under temptations is good; good for men and, since women are so much worse than men politically, absolutely necessary for women. The worse they are, the more corrupt and corrupting, the more necessary it is that they vote. We must make the wives and mothers of men good, incorruptible and moral.

POSTSUFFRAGE STRUGGLES

"STATEMENT ON THE EQUAL RIGHTS AMENDMENT"

Henry A. Wallace (1944)

THE FIRST organized movement in the history of the world to free women from their age old shackles began in our own country almost one hundred years ago when a little group of undaunted women met at Seneca Falls, New York, and drafted a "DECLARATION OF PRINCIPLES," which has guided the movement in this country ever since.

No part of that program has been completely achieved except in the political field when the right of suffrage was granted to women. However, the Suffrage Amendment gave women only the right to vote and nothing more.

Having long advocated EQUALITY in DEMOCRACY it seems to me that it naturally follows that there should be no inequalities under the law because of sex. Every man and woman should have an equal right to earn a living, to control their earnings, and women should be freed from governmental restraints and handicaps, which now limit their wages and opportunities for advancement. The surest method to eradicate the many discriminations and injustices practiced against women is to pass the Equal Rights Amendment and thus complete the great movement for freedom begun at Seneca Falls in 1848.

However much the opponents of this Amendment may fear some possible temporary disadvantage to some women, may I suggest that in the end all such disadvantages, if they exist, weigh little beside the greater advantage of inner freedom which will come for all women when real equality is established.

From a letter to Mrs. E. G. Miller, 27 January 1944. (SL, Alma Lutz Papers)

"ON IMPROVING THE PARTY'S WORK AMONG WOMEN"

William Z. Foster (1948)

ONE OF THE GRAVEST weaknesses of the Communist movement in the various capitalist countries, including our own, is its relative failure to win the active support of decisive masses of women. It is a fact which we dare not ignore that the forces of reaction still have a strong hold on womankind, including proletarian women. This was again graphically demonstrated during the recent crucial elections in France and Italy, when an undue preponderance of women voted with the reactionary parties, especially those dominated by the Roman Catholic Church.

This shortcoming of the Communist parties becomes even more manifest today in view of the huge and increasing part that women are taking in all walks of life. This shortcoming must be quickly overcome inasmuch as the parties and organizations spearheading the drive to fascism and war hold the affiliation of very large masses of women. Obviously, therefore, a drastic improvement in their work among women is very much on the order of business for the Communist parties of the capitalist world, especially our Party here in the United States.

The basic cause of the more or less general weakness of the Communist parties' work among women in capitalist countries is due to an underestimation and general neglect of this vital work. Clearly, for Marxists, inadequacy in practical work implies inadequate grasp of theory. It is to this aspect of the question, the theoretical side, that this article especially addresses itself.

There has been a woeful theoretical neglect on the woman question, which, in turn, greatly hampers all practical educational and organizational work. This neglect is illustrated by the fact that we have had no detailed presentation of this most important matter since Engels wrote his fundamental work, *Origin of the Family, Private Property and the State,* 65 years ago and Bebel his *Woman and Socialism,* a generation later. This paucity of theoretical work is all the more deplorable because the role of woman is one of the most complex theoretical problems we have to deal with, and also because her position on a world scale has changed vastly since these famous books were written.

Only under Socialism can woman become truly free. Naturally, therefore, in the Soviet Union a revolutionary advance has been made in the whole status of women, economically, politically, socially, culturally. But the trouble is that, so far, little of the underlying scientific conclusions that have been drawn from all this advance of woman in the U.S.S.R. has reached the Communist

From Political Affairs: A Magazine Devoted to the Theory and Practice of Marxism-Leninism *(November 1948).*

Parties in the capitalist world. We have no contemporary work on the question of women, whether under Socialism or under capitalism, anywhere nearly satisfactory in scope. The Communist Parties are, therefore, literally starved theoretically on this vital matter. This dearth of theoretical material constitutes a challenge which should not go unanswered from Marxist-Leninist theoreticians. It is in order to make whatever contribution we can in this vital field that our Party has set up a theoretical subcommission on the woman question.

Theories of Male Superiority

One of the many aspects of the woman question where theoretical work is very necessary has to do with the "master idea," the widely current theories alleging the superiority of man over woman. These false notions, assiduously cultivated by all the forces of reaction, are widespread among the masses of the people. Obviously, our Party also is not free from the infection of these widely prevalent male superiority ideas. Such prejudices are extremely complex in character; they have roots dating back thousands of years, and they constitute serious obstacles to woman in her age-long fight for equality as a worker, a citizen, a homebuilder, and in her marital relations. In this article, it will be observed, I am only indicating the theoretical tasks involved in combating male superiority prejudices, rather than working out solutions.

It is a favorite trick, and a very effective one, for reactionary propagandists to base their anti-social arguments of all kinds upon pseudoscientific assumptions, particularly in the field of biology. To uninformed people this gives the so-called theories an air of finality. In the same way, reactionary propagandists argue that "Socialism is contrary to human nature"; that war is caused by "man's naturally combative character." They rationalize capitalist exploitation as an inevitable result of "man's acquisitive nature," and the like. Fascists especially go in for reactionary "biological" arguments on a big scale. Their theories of the "master-race" of the "elite" among the "Aryans," of the "inferiority" of Jews, Negroes, etc., are all clothed with false and preposterous biological conceptions. It is not surprising, therefore, that reactionaries throughout the ages have sought to justify the subjugation of woman with the aid of similar fake biological "theories." Such theories, alleging the biological inferiority of woman, have, of course, greatly facilitated the economic exploitation and political oppression of women under systems of society that have succeeded each other, from chattel slavery to capitalism.

For one thing, the male supremacists boldly claim that woman is, by her very make-up, intellectually inferior to man. Her brain is said to average somewhat less in weight than the man's and, therefore, the reactionaries argue that she cannot think as well as he does. They put woman's thinking capacity somewhere between the animal's and man's. That is, the animal is guided by its instincts, the woman thinks "intuitively," while the man reasons objectively. Such false arguments, contrary to science and experience, but widely current, have done and continue to do grave damage not only to woman's fight for equality, but to society as a whole.

There are, of course, physical differences between men and women. As Engels states, the first division of labor is that of men and women in procreation.

From these functional differences, bourgeois ideologists develop false conceptions. They seize upon the apparent greater muscular strength of man as the basis for the pseudoscientific theory that woman is generally physically inferior to man. They equate sameness with strength and difference with weakness. Thus they brush aside her greater ability to resist pain, her greater immunity to certain diseases, her greater longevity, etc. Such notions of woman's physical inferiority, cultivated by reactionaries for centuries, make for great handicaps to women, especially in industry.

The advocates of male superiority also claim that because of the far greater role played by the woman in child bearing and rearing, she is thereby constitutionally unfitted to enter into the hurly-burly competition of intellectual, economic, political, and social life. They claim that by her very nature her inevitable place is in the home. Not only is woman physically and mentally unfit for an active "career" and for participation in the social struggle, they argue, but it would also destroy her femininity and charm. All such contentions place high barriers in the way of women in many walks of life.

Then these reactionaries contend, by inference if not frankly, that since man plays the more positive and aggressive role sexually, he also should dominate the woman in her social life. They assert, in substance, that nature has made man the master and woman his slave. This reactionary notion, which is far more prevalent than most of us realize, hangs like a millstone about woman's neck in her fight for freedom; it flourishes and does immeasurable damage to women in innumerable respects. We must show that this whole conception is belied both by the findings of science and by the great struggle of woman for equality with the man.

Finally, to mention only one more aspect of the hydra-headed notion of male superiority, there is the reactionary contention that "nature has made man essentially polygamous and woman monogamous." This is the theory of the double standard of bourgeois morals, which seeks to justify the sexual exploitation of woman. We must show both from science and experience how such standards wrought incalculable harm (and continue to do so) to woman's happiness and to her position in society.

Equally insidious is the new twist being given to these reactionary male superiority notions by the bourgeois, pro-fascist, and Social-Democratic ideologists, who provide "scientific" garb for the myth of woman's inferiority by proclaiming that she is psychologically inferior. Thus, we witness a steady stream of such reactionary works as *Modern Woman—A Lost Sex,* by Dr. Marynia F. Fernham and Ferdinand Lundberg, which attempt to justify every anti-woman prejudice by psychological claptrap, in order to divert woman from progressive struggle and to reduce her to the fascist *Kinder-Küche-Kirche* level.

On the other hand, bourgeois feminism, which places the blame on men and not on the social system, for the oppression of women, can exert its influence in the absence of a sound theoretical position on the woman question. The bourgeois feminist would counterpose to the male superiority "theory" the equally unscientific notion of female superiority, which leads only into the blind alley of the "battle of the sexes."

The capitalists, in order to exploit the woman more effectively, make wide use of the male superiority theories in all their complexities and subtle ramifications. In this the capitalists are aided by reactionary church dogma. The general result is that harmful male supremacy notions have penetrated widely in all classes. Men especially readily absorb male superiority "theories"—little understanding that such noxious ideas injure them as well as they do women. Many women also accept the general notion that the man is the superior of the two sexes. Woman's painful struggle upward through the centuries, reaching heroic heights with the advent of the revolutionary struggle against feudalism and ever since, has been carried on in the face of the most savage interpretations and applications of male superiority theories.

V

THE STRUGGLE FOR SOCIAL EQUALITY, 1850–1960

WHAT IS FEMINISM?
COME AND FIND OUT

FIRST FEMINIST MASS MEETING
at the PEOPLE'S INSTITUTE, Cooper Union
Tuesday Evening, February 17th, 1914, at 8 o'clock, P. M.

Subject: "WHAT FEMINISM MEANS TO ME."

Ten-Minute Speeches by

ROSE YOUNG
JESSE LYNCH WILLIAMS
HENRIETTA RODMAN
GEORGE MIDDLETON
FRANCES PERKINS
WILL IRWIN
GEORGE CREEL
MRS. FRANK COTHREN
FLOYD DELL
CRYSTAL EASTMAN BENEDICT
EDWIN BJORKMAN
MAX EASTMAN

Chairman, MARIE JENNEY HOWE.

SECOND FEMINIST MASS MEETING
at the PEOPLES' INSTITUTE, Cooper Union
Friday, February 20th, 1914, at 8 o'clock, P. M.

Subject: "BREAKING INTO THE HUMAN RACE."

The Right to Work.—
RHETA CHILDE DORR

The Right of the Mother to Her Profession.—
BEATRICE FORBES-ROBERTSON-HALE.

The Right to Her Convictions.—
MARY SHAW.

The Right to Her Name.—
FOLA LA FOLLETTE.

The Right to Organize.—
ROSE SCHNEIDERMAN.

The Right to Ignore Fashion.—
NINA WILCOX PUTNAM.

The Right to Specialize in Home Industries.—
CHARLOTTE PERKINS GILMAN.

Chairman, MARIE JENNEY HOWE.

ADMISSION FREE. *NO COLLECTION.*

Handbill for feminist mass meeting, 1914. Library of Congress, George Middleton Papers.

"I SAY to Miss Anthony, you have to go deeper than the ballot. The question has got to go home," argued William Brown in a debate with Susan B. Anthony in Chicago in 1869. Women "must impregnate their husbands with the idea of giving women their rights socially and in the home circle. For while the ballot does a great deal[,] if you depend upon the ballot to bring you up, you will never come up" (*Chicago Times* [13 February 1869], cited in Buechler 1986, 72). Brown's argument expresses the logic by which feminists sought to transform social and personal life. From the earliest days of the women's movement, many feminists understood that the personal is political, that the feminist vision required the transformation of relations between women and men in the private sphere. "Woman suffrage," according to Unitarian minister Jesse Jones in 1874, "is not primarily a political but a social question; and means a profounder revolution in the whole structure of society, than many advocates seem ever to have dreamed of" (cited in Leach 1980, 15). Women have sought to enlarge their sphere of personal autonomy in their relations with men, with children, and with each other and to transform marriage, sexuality, housework, childbearing, and child rearing. They have fought against male violence against women, against a view of women's sexuality as passive, against marriage laws that give men control over women's bodies and women's property; they have fought for liberalized divorce laws, birth control,

An asterisk (*) indicates that a document is included in this volume.

abortion, "sex rights," and more involved (and equitable) parenting by husbands.

The documents in this section illustrate the range of issues that pro-feminist men addressed in their efforts to promote women's social equality. While anti-feminists relied on the standard plaint that women's place was in the home, pro-feminist men argued that the home needed to be transformed as well. The issues they raised included marriage, divorce, sexuality, and birth control. In several utopian communal experiments, in well-known and widely circulated medical treatises on women's physiology, in cross-cultural studies of male-female relations, and in marriage contracts, we find evidence that men supported social equality.

Later in the century, these modest, often idiosyncratic, and isolated efforts were legitimized by the development of American social science. While academic psychology had followed a largely anti-feminist course, from bowdlerized Freudians to followers of G. Stanley Hall's warnings to preserve American virility, many of the earliest anthropologists and sociologists weighed in on the side of gender equality. In the first few decades of the twentieth century, Bohemian radicals attempted to transform relations between women and men as part of their larger revolutionary program of socialist transformation. Inspired by social science writings on gender relations and socialist writings on political relations, these radicals sought to create relations without possessiveness or jealousy, in which women and men were equal.

Women's Social Equality

Some of the earliest texts about women's social equality argue that men have usurped social privilege and excluded women from the public arena. Theodore Dwight Weld's "Man's Disparagement of Woman in All Times and Climes"* (1855?) offers a cross-cultural chronicle of women's subordination and then examines English, French, and American literature to find their strains of misogyny. Consistent throughout is his belief that women's lower mental and physical capacity was *caused* by her oppression, not the other way around. "She has first been made the victim of a dementalizing process, then it has been assumed that this mental havoc is the natural outworking of her inferiority," Weld wrote. A second theme is the negative consequences for women of the simultaneous adoration of idealized womanhood and the subordination of real women in the real world. Free love advocate Ezra Heywood argued that woman's social status forces her into the manipulative posture that she is then accused of assuming by natural feminine wiles. "The victims of false deference on one hand and tyrannical subjection on the other, they win through diplomatic artifice, or by sacrifices inconsistent with personal sanctity and social well-being," he wrote in *Cupid's Yokes.**

One of the most intriguing indictments of the social origins of women's inferiority is Edward Bellamy's utopian novel *Equality* (1897), published nine years after his celebrated *Looking Backward.* Bellamy saw materialism, individualism, and sexism as the outcomes of capitalist greed; his Nationalist movement, which attracted reformers like the Women's Christian Temperance Union's Frances Willard, advocated the use of feminist principles to create social harmony and solidarity instead of class conflict (see Epstein 1981, 142). Women, he believed, would instill more virtue and selflessness into social life if they were equal. In *Looking Backward,* Bellamy examined the individual and social depredation that accompanied capitalism; in *Equality,* he took on gender relations directly, caustically dissecting "the utter hypocrisy underlying the entire relation of the sexes, the pretended chivalric deference to women on the one hand, coupled with their practical suppression on the other" (1897, 129). Bellamy advocated communal laundries and kitchens and women retaining their own names, to pass them on to their daughters, while men retained theirs, to be passed on to their sons.

Some black and Hispanic men also began to challenge existing gender relations. Alex Crummell's "The Black Woman of the South" (1883) presages efforts by Robert Terrell, Langston Hughes, and W. E. B. DuBois to honor black women for dignity during and after slavery and to restructure relations between women and men to accord as much dignity to black women as to black men. DuBois's essay "The Damnation of Women" (1920) is particularly powerful. Chicano writers saw the parallels between the two struggles. Praxedis Guerrero and Ricardo Flores Magon reject the artificial inferiority of women as the result of "enslavement" and blame the church for perpetuating women's second-class status (see Guerrero's "The Woman"*). Magon links women's struggle to class struggle. "Humiliated, degraded, bound by chains of tradition to an irrational inferiority, indoctrinated in the affairs of heaven by clerics, but totally ignorant of world problems, she is suddenly caught up in the whirlwind of industrial production which above all requires cheap labor to sustain the competition created by the 'princes of capital' who exploit her circumstances," he writes in "To Women."*

Transforming Marriage and Sexuality

Women's equality in the public sphere required transformation of relations between women and men in the private sphere. Since the mid-nineteenth century, women have struggled to base marriage on more egalitarian grounds, be protected from spouse abuse, and claim their own sexual agency. Men have often agreed with Henry Brown Blackwell's statement in a letter* to Lucy Stone that the "true degradation and disgrace rests not with the victim but with the oppressors."

Transforming marriage and sexuality was an important component of the communal experiments that sprang up in the Northeast and Midwest in the mid-nineteenth century. In some, women's equality depended on sexual abstinence, connecting "celibacy with the spiritual unity and social equality of the sexes." Sexual intercourse, they believed, symbolized a divisive, hierarchical society; celibacy was its opposite, "symbolic of unity, harmony, and equality" (Kitch 1989, 68, 74). The Shakers, for example, gave equal prominence to male and female deities and gave to "Shaker Sisters a corresponding place by the side of their Brethren at the speaker's desk" (Shaker Resolution, 25 October 1869, SRL, special collections, MS B41). The Koreshans believed in the spiritual bisexuality of God and promoted celibacy and the obliteration of all differences between women and men, including physical differences, until each person was an androgynous mix of male and female (see ibid.).

Some communal experiments saw sexual freedom, not celibacy, as the route to gender equality. Women at Modern Times, founded by Josiah Warren, enjoyed sexual freedom without censure and also maintained the right to set the price for their labor equal to, or even above, that set by men. "Every man and every woman has a perfect and inalienable right to do and perform, all and singular, just exactly as he or she may choose, now and hereafter," Warren told a visitor (cited in Muncy 1973, 204; see also 224). Women's equality was also promoted, to some degree, at Fruitlands, Brocton, Brook Farm, and Nashoba. Fourierist phalanxes followed their French utopian theorist's ideas that "the key to social harmony was the economic liberation of women" (see Brisbane 1840, 299). Albert Brisbane, the popularizer of Fourier's ideas in the United States, argued that women should be beyond the control of their husbands and have the privilege of changing companions when they chose to do so (Spurlock 1989, 146).

Women's equality was a central tenet at Oneida. Founder John Humphrey Noyes saw the parallels among the position of women, southern slaves, and children—all were placed "in a state of subordination and have not the advantage of personal independence" (cited in Thomas 1977, 124). In a short play, *Slavery and Marriage* (1850), Noyes expressly uses slavery as an extended metaphor for the position of women in American society. To Noyes, monogamous marriage and excessive childbearing "had made slaves of American women and they were as much entitled to emancipation in the ante-bellum years as the Negro slaves on Southern plantations" (Muncy 1973, 223). "At Oneida, women were to be freed from possessiveness, compulsory sex and childbirth, and the restraints of sex-determined occupational roles. No man had the right to demand the love of a woman, claim sexual privileges, or fertilize a woman without her consent" (Mandelker 1984, 121). Monogamy caused secret adultery, forced people who were not alike to stay together, demoted sexuality to a less important status, and allowed no room for divergent sexual appetites.

Noyes offered two solutions: complex marriage and male continence. Complex marriage made each member theoretically married to each member of the opposite sex. Women could give free reign to their sexual appetites; sexual encounters were always held in the women's private rooms, and each person (male or female) had the right to refuse the advances of any other member. Complex marriage freed women, Noyes argued, from household drudgery and sexual exploitation (see ibid., 18). Male continence was a birth-control system that enabled the male to refrain from ejaculation, even though he might experience the other physical sensations of orgasm, "by restricting the action of the organ to avoid the spasmodic crisis," as Noyes put it (see his "Male Continence"*). Intercourse could then last as long as the male could maintain his control, helping to increase women's pleasure and removing fear of pregnancy. Noyes's sexual and marital reforms opened up enormous possibilities for women's social equality. He offered a critique of the effects *on women* of monogamous marriage and enforced childbearing as forms of sexual slavery and placed the burden of providing sexual pleasure and preventing pregnancy entirely on the shoulders of men.

Robert Dale Owen also promoted sexual equality. Son of New Harmony founder Robert Owen, a pioneering social reformer who also had advocated equality in marriage, birth control, and women's rights, Dale Owen believed that marriage was a form of slavery; when a woman says "I do," he wrote, she places herself "as completely at the disposal and mercy of an individual, as the negro slave who is bought for gold in the slave market of Kingston or New Orleans" (*New Harmony Free Enquirer* [29 April 1829], cited in Muncy 1973, 198). Women were considered equal at New Harmony, with no distinction in rights and privileges made by sex. Owen's *Moral Physiology** (1830) was the first birth-control tract published in the United States. Owen believed that sexuality was the cause of debility, poor health, and the agony of childbirth for women, and he sought some method to alleviate women's pain. He opposed condoms because they allowed men to use women as sexual objects. "I do not write to facilitate, but on the contrary to prevent the degrading intercourse of which it is intended to obviate the penalty," he wrote (cited in Strauss 1982, 87). He advocated coitus interruptus, which placed responsibility for birth control in men's corner. Owen's own marriage to Mary Robinson proclaimed their equality.

Other mid-century marriages, such as Stephen Foster and Abby Kelly's and Samuel Blackwell and Antoinette Brown's, also attempted to repudiate male privilege and advocated equality within the marriage (see Hersh 1978). The century's most famous egalitarian marriage was Henry Brown Blackwell and Lucy Stone's. A dedicated pro-feminist, coeditor of the *Woman's Journal* from its founding in 1872 until his death in 1909, Blackwell offered powerful critiques of male privilege in marriage. In an editorial reply in The *Journal* in 1874, he raged against the "anachronism" of giving women away in marriage and urged wives not to promise to obey as part of their vows. "The word 'obey' means the subjection of the wife," he wrote. "A true marriage service will omit that word obey, in obedience to the command of Christ—'Call no man master" '. His own courtship letters to Stone stand as eloquent testimony to the struggle to make feminism an active principle in an intimate relationship (see Blackwell 1981). Blackwell's intention was, "as a husband, to *renounce* all the privileges which the law confers upon me, which are not strictly *mutual*" (letter to Lucy Stone, 3 January 1855, cited in ibid., 115). What he envisioned was a role of the husband as equal nurturer: "We will try to live so beautifully & so actively that every night we can compare notes together all by ourselves in one another's arms & say 'we have not lived today in vain'! We will plan together, lay out our own work, help each other to do it, & report progress every night" (letter to Lucy Stone, 13 February 1855, cited in ibid., 122). One letter* sums up Blackwell's position. "Equality with me is a passion," he wrote. "I *wish I* could take the position of the wife under the law and give you that of a husband. I would rather submit to the injustice a hundred times than subject you to it."

Their wedding, officiated over by the Reverend Thomas Wentworth Higginson, was marked by vows in which the couple disavowed male privilege. One suffragist, Josephine Henry, was inspired to write, "The domestic life of this couple who set up the standard of absolute equality of husband and wife was an exquisite idyl, fragrant with love and tenderness, a poem whose rhythm was not marred, a divine melody that rose above the discords and dissensions of domestic life upon the lowlands where man is the ruler and woman the subject" (*HWS*, 4:226).

Other couples also struggled to create egalitarian marriages. Wesley Clark Mitchell, a University of California economist, courted Lucy Sprague, a well-known suffragist, by arguing for an equality of passion and commitment to their work. He recognized that "the home in and of itself would not give adequate scope to your constructive energies" and that she was "a leader in the land of the present with an explorer's vision of the land of the future." He hoped she would not "think your companion, the one who loves you best of all the world—lacks virility" (cited in Antler 1987, 173, 175). Heywood Broun and Ruth Hale were active collaborators, even after their marriage failed. Hale was the founder of the Lucy Stone League, which consisted of women who retained their names after they were married. Broun campaigned for birth control and in such works as his "Holding a Baby" supported men doing housework and child care (see Broun 1941).

Campaigns against male violence also focused on transforming the subjection of women in marriage. Some were concerned with rape in marriage, the lack of protection that women had to refuse their husband's sexual advances. Stone and Blackwell campaigned to enact legislation to protect women from beating by their husbands; their failure strengthened their belief that women could never "be adequately protected," as Stone put it, "until women would help make the laws" (cited in Pleck 1987, 105). (Stone and Blackwell were the only ones to assert that suffrage would reduce wife beating.) By the late nineteenth century, most leaders of the campaigns against wife beating were men, whose opposition derived from an "objection to this form of coercing women, as signifying an unacceptable pattern of masculinity" (Gordon 1988, 254–55).

Finally, some men sought to support women's social equality at home personally, particularly in the division of household labor. To see men's household work as pro-feminist, we mean that it was done with some political awareness, as did William Sanger or Ramon Sanchez. In a letter* to his sister, Sanchez noted that he "consider[s] it the bounden duty of every husband to assist his wife in all things, and relieve her in every possible way, of as much care and labor as he can."

The Campaign for Birth Control

The transformation of marriage was often accompanied by advocacy of birth control as a means to provide women with control over their bodies. In the mid-nineteenth century, Robert Dale Owen's *Moral Physiology** was one of several tracts that advocated transformed sexual relations. Thomas Nichols's *Esoteric Anthropology* (1853) claimed that traditional marriage was but organized adultery. Marriage, Nichols wrote, "is the union of two persons in mutual love; and adultery is, perhaps, best defined as any gratification of mere lust, or the sensual nature, without the sanctification of true love, and apart from the lawful uses of marriage. According to these definitions, a true marriage may be what the laws call adultery, while the real adultery is an unloving marriage" (ibid., 96). T. R. Trall's *Sexual Physiology and Hygiene* promoted sexual pleasure as the end of sexual intercourse. "Whatever may be the object of sexual intercourse," he wrote, "whether intended as a love embrace merely, or as a generative act, it is very clear that it must be as pleasurable as possible to both parties" (Trall 1866, 291). Charles Knowlton's *The Fruits of Philosophy* ([1832] 1937) and Charles Woodruff's *Legalized Prostitution* (1862) also promoted birth control.

Edward Bliss Foote, a physician, wrote many of the century's most popular tracts on sex and birth control. *Dr. Foote's Replies to the Alphites* quotes the Reverend Jesse Jones about women's rights in sexual relations, that "the woman should bear rule in the sex relation instead of the man, that her body is her own, in her own charge," which Foote agreed would be a major change. "To teach that woman is to be set at the head of the family instead of the man is the most powerful and revolutionary form of the truth that can now be framed for utterance. It seizes men right where they now are, and heaves and whirls them right on to what is better" (Foote 1882, 50). Foote also advocated birth control, particularly the "womb veil" or diaphragm, because it "places contraception entirely under control of the wife, to whom it naturally belongs" (Foote 1864, 380). In *Medical Common Sense* (1864), he argued against a double standard that allowed for sexual activity only among young men.

Many advocates of "free love" also supported women's social equality. "When women are no longer owned," wrote Francis Barry in the *Revolution* in 1868, "when men are no longer slaveowners then . . . will men be manly, and just, and women be recognized and treated as equals" (cited in Spurlock 1989, 209). Moses Harmon's Kansas-based newspaper *Lucifer the Lightbearer* published articles supporting birth control and women's sexual expression and condemning marital rape (see ibid., 228). In 1883, the paper proposed to eliminate the word "male" from Kansas law, effectively granting suffrage to women. Harmon argued that women should retain their own names at marriage, lest they be "just as chattel slaves [who] were required to take the name of their master" (cited in Sears 1977, 83). His daughter Lillian's wedding to Edwin Walker was marked by passionate feminist speeches by both husband and wife. "Lillian is and will continue to be as free to repulse any and all advances of mine as she has been heretofore," said Walker. "In joining with me in this love and labor union, she has not alienated a single natural right. She remains sovereign of herself . . . and we . . . repudiate all powers legally conferred upon husbands and wives" (cited in ibid., 85).

Ezra Heywood, probably the era's leading free lover, also advocated birth control. He and his wife, Angela Tilton, published a newspaper, the *Word,* that championed birth control and criticized marriage from feminist principles. A woman's right to control her body was axiomatic; "of course it is a woman's right to protect herself, as best she can; if she chooses to use preventatives, I will defend her in that right," he wrote (cited in Blatt 1989, 149). Heywood called marriage the "penis trust" since it placed women under men's control (Spurlock 1989, 228). Harassed and arrested by anti-feminist morality crusader Anthony Comstock, Heywood's defenses invariably supported women's sexual freedom. "Since Comstockism makes male will, passion and power absolute to *impose* conception," he stated at one trial, "I shall stand with women to resent it" (cited in Blatt 1989, 146).

The campaign for birth control, and against Comstockism, continued into the twentieth century. Margaret Sanger was forced to flee to England because of police harassment; her supporters, such as Emma Goldman, Ben Reitman, and her husband William Sanger, all spent time in jail for distributing birth-control pamphlets. In the statement* given at his trial, Sanger linked his support for birth control to his manhood. Judge Ben Lindsey argued that birth control "ought to be available to all women who ask for it, married or unmarried, good health or bad" (Lindsey and Evans 1927, 242). The campaign for birth control was one of the first in which social science entered the fray with its new, scientific base. Several social scientists at the University of Chicago, like William Ogburn, W. I. Thomas, and Charles Henderson, supported various aspects of women's social equality, and many professors served as mentors for women who sought to become professional social workers, social reformers, or scholars and researchers (see Rosenberg 1982; see also Ogburn 1926). Edward Ross, of the University of Wisconsin, wrote favorably of women's right to divorce (Ross 1909). Henderson and Thomas were active suffragists (Thomas, n.d.; Henderson 1907). Thomas's treatise *Sex and Society* elaborated an anthropological history of women's degradation and linked it to "the development of private property and its control by man, together with the habit of treating her as a piece of property, whose value was enhanced if its purity was assured and demonstrable" (Thomas 1907, 297). (Of course, some opponents used social science methods to claim the inevitability of male dominance [see Schwendinger and Schwendinger 1974].)

Anthropologists also examined woman's lot in other cultures as a method of championing her cause in advanced society. In *Woman's Share in Primitive Culture* (1894), Otis Tufton Mason argued that women were responsible for the important work of daily life as well as most important inventions associated with agriculture, animal domestication, medicine, and pottery and tool making (see also Densmore 1907). Alexander Goldenweiser, an anthropologist at the New School for Social Research, argued that, in primitive society, women were freer and more creative: "Wherever she is permitted to apply her creativeness she makes good, and the excellence of her achievement is equal to that of man, certainly not conspicuously inferior to his" (Goldenweiser 1924, 132).

Lester Ward offered the most radical position. The former chief paleontologist for the U.S. Geological Survey and first president of the American Sociological Society, Ward used anthropology, the Darwinian theory of evolution, and sociology to argue that the female sex was both the original and the primary sex in evolutionary development. Men's dominance had its origin in women's selection of larger and stronger males as mates, but now men had usurped women's primacy by cunning. "Woman is the unchanging trunk of the great genealogic tree," he argued in the influential "Our Better Halves,"* "while man, with all his vaunted superiority, is but a branch, a grafted scion, as it were, whose acquired qualities die with the individual, while those of woman are handed on to futurity. Woman *is* the race, and the race can be raised up only as she is raised up." Against the illogical and unnatural "andrarchy" that silences one sex for the pleasure of the other Ward offered his "gynecocentric theory," which placed women at life's origins and saw patriarchy and monogamy as temporary evolutionary stages.

Ward argued that the state should regulate the family and marriage to ensure equality and that sex relations should be absolutely free (see May 1959, 309). He saw women's subordination as unnatural and politically insupportable. In *Pure Sociology,* he wrote that "throughout all human history woman has been powerfully discriminated against and held down by custom, law, literature and public opinion" (Ward 1903, 377). It was sexism that held women back, not biological or evolutionary inferiority. "The universal prevalence of the androcentric world view," he wrote in *Applied Sociology,* "acts as a wet blanket on all the genial fire of the female sex. Let this be once removed and woman's true relation to society will be generally perceived, and all this will be changed. We have no conception of the real amount of talent or of genius possessed by women" (Ward 1906, 233).

One woman who was particularly inspired by Ward's theories was Charlotte Perkins Gilman, "the most influential woman thinker in the pre–World War I generation" (Kraditor 1981, 97). Gilman thought Ward "quite the greatest man I have ever known" and his essay "Our Better Halves" "the greatest single contribution to the world's thought since Evolution," so she set out to make his gynecocentric theory accessible to all readers (Gilman [1935] 1990, 187). Her *Women and Economics* (1898), one of the most influential feminist books in U.S. history, and one that still reads as startlingly fresh and perceptive, was the result of that effort.

Ward was joined in his understanding of the social origins of women's subordinate status by Chicago economist Thorstein Veblen, perhaps America's foremost critic of the ideology of consumerism. Veblen's "Economic Theory of Woman's Dress"* examined fashion as an expression of the political relations between women and men. Eugene Hecker's *Short History of Woman's Rights* included a critique of woman's sphere as artificial. "The home is not necessarily every woman's sphere and neither is motherhood. Neither is it every woman's congenital duty to make herself attractive to men. The 'woman's pages' of newspapers, filled with gratuitous advice on these subjects, never tell men that their duty is fatherhood or that they should make themselves attractive or that their sphere is also the home" (Hecker 1914). Arthur Schlesinger took his fellow historians to task for ignoring women's contributions to history in *New Viewpoints in American History* (which includes his "The Role of Women in American History"*). Later in this century, sociologist Gunnar Myrdal (not included here because he was Swedish) drew a parallel between the position of women and the position of blacks in his brilliant and influential *An American Dilemma* (1944). Not since the abolitionists had any observer so carefully examined the similarities between sexism and racism.

Sex Radicals and Pro-Feminist Men in Greenwich Village

One group of men, the Greenwich Village radicals, stands out in their efforts to combine a militant critique of women's subordination with developing new types of living arrangements that would be based on equality. "The wish to live a free and real life, and to cherish and communicate its qualities in works of art, deserves the respect of every revolutionist," was how Max Eastman put it (cited in O'Neill 1978, 228). These prefigurative politics were short lived, enormously complex, and often contradictory, but they remind the contemporary reader of the necessity of fusing the personal and the political.

These writers and artists saw their support of feminism as part of a larger revolutionary struggle. In the pages of the *Masses,* in books and essays, and in salons and coffeehouses, the Greenwich Village radicals—among them Max Eastman and Ida Rauh, Hutchins Hapgood and Neth Boyce, John Reed and Louise Bryant, George Cram Cook and Susan Glaspell, Frederic Howe and Marie Jenny Howe, Floyd Dell, Randolph Bourne, and George Middleton—advocated socialism, feminism, and psychoanalysis. Walter Lippmann was a recent convert to feminism (see his "A Note on the Woman's Movement"*); a regular at Mabel Dodge's salon, there he met Elsie Clews Parsons, with whom he founded the *New Republic* (see Rosenberg 1982, 168). Some of the women were members of the famed Heterodox Club, founded by Marie Howe. The "lyrical left," as historian Henry May (1959) called them, fused economic, political, and social change and attempted to live the lives they envisioned for the future. "Bohemian feminists demanded that men and women be equal, not just as lovers, but also as friends, comrades, and intellectual peers. To thrive, free love required a context of shared responsibility, with men assuming equal roles in child care, housekeeping, and all the other daily chores that chained women to the home" (Jezer 1989, 64).

In their quest to fuse personal, literary, and political lives, many of the Greenwich Village radicals were inspired by Walt Whitman. Floyd Dell often quoted his poetry and saw him as a genuine believer in the absolute equality of women and men (expressed also, perhaps, in his supposed bisexuality). One fellow traveler of the Bohemian radicals, Mabel McCoy Irwin, wrote *Whitman: The Poet-Liberator of Woman* (1905).

Several saw women's emancipation as requiring economic change; see, for example, Upton Sinclair's "The Double Standard,"* published in the *Masses* in 1913. Hutchins Hapgood's influential *The Spirit of the Ghetto* ([1902] 1966) linked working-class struggle to women's struggles for birth control and sexual autonomy. Hapgood and Boyce, who collaborated on plays for the Provincetown Players, also tried to maintain free love within their marriage; Hapgood's claim that "the choice between a woman's work and marriage is a horrible choice and ought not to exist" (Hapgood 1915) prefigures contemporary feminists' critiques of the "second shift."

George Middleton's one-act plays were very influential. *Tradition* (1913) was first produced by the Woman Suffrage Party, and his full-length *Nowadays,* "the first attempt by an American author to treat radically the economic phase of the woman question," according to a review in the *Woman Voter,* "speaks for women in no uncertain terms" (cited in Middleton 1947, 427). In an interview in the *New Dramatic Mirror,* Middleton explained that the "whole movement is thrilling with drama waiting to be expressed, since it represents a great awakening in both men and women to a higher plane of mutual living"

(Krows 1914). Middleton was also an active campaigner for a broad feminist agenda; he marched with the Men's League in demonstrations and delivered "What Feminism Means To Me"* at the first feminist mass meeting in 1915.

Max Eastman, founder of the Men's League for Woman Suffrage, was an early pioneer of prefigurative political life in his marriage to Ida Rauh and his advocacy of birth control and sexual freedom. In "Revolutionary Birth Control," he tried to make the link between birth control and the working-class struggle: "Workingmen and women ought to be able to feed and rear the children they want—that is the end we are seeking. But the way to that end is a fight; a measure of working class independence is essential to that fight; and birth control is a means to such independence." Repression of birth control was based both on class power, since "the masters of the world, who use these untimely children in their workshops, are in great part responsible for the hoarding of this knowledge," and on patriarchy, since men were afraid "that women may become in reality free and self-dependent individuals" (Eastman 1915, 22, 6).

Floyd Dell may have been the most articulate advocate of women's liberation of all the Greenwich Village radicals. His novels, plays, books, and articles explored many aspects of the women's movement. His *Women as World Builders* celebrated a set of feminists, including Emma Goldman, Charlotte Perkins Gilman, Jane Addams, Ellen Key, and Beatrice Webb. In the section on Webb and Goldman, he gave a more personal side to women's liberation, arguing that "her development, her freedom, her independence, must come from and through herself" by "asserting herself as a personality and not as a sex commodity" and by "refusing the right to anyone over her body" (Dell 1913, 61). Dell consistently supported birth control. Suffrage should be enlisted to repeal the law, "which, by penalizing the spread of information in regard to the prevention of conception, attempts to enforce upon women the tyranny of accidental and unwelcome pregnancy." He continued the analogy to slavery. "There is certainly no kind of freedom where there is no command over one's own body. If a woman may not keep her body for her own uses as long as she wishes, and give it up to the service of the race when she chooses, she is certainly a slave" (Dell 1914, 351).

Dell's brief play *The Outline of Marriage,* written for the American Birth Control League, presented feminist thinking about birth control and marriage. The humorous dialogue between Myrtle and George, a typical couple, led to the conclusion that marriage must be based on love and companionship. He was bitingly critical of the double duty of women's work in the home and workplace:

> **Q:** You kept your job and were a wife at the same time. Didn't that involve a double burden?
> **A:** No. We ate at restaurants for the most part—at home only when we especially wanted to. And we both helped get those meals, as if we were on a picnic. We washed the dishes together—it's fun when you do it this way.
> **Q:** How about his buttons? Did you keep them sewed on for him?
> **A:** Not at all. He had managed about his buttons somehow before he married me. He didn't marry me to have his buttons sewed on.
> **Q:** What *did* he marry you for?
> **A:** For love—and companionship. [Dell 1916, 12]

To Dell, feminism meant that men and women could be friends since friendship "depends upon equality and choice" (Dell 1924, 183).

Dell linked women's liberation with men's. "Feminism is going to make it possible for the first time for men to be free," reads the first line of "Feminism for Men."* "Feminism is not only a revolt of women against conditions which hamper their activities," he wrote in "Socialism and Feminism"; "it is also a revolt of women *and men* against the type of woman created by those conditions" (Dell 1914, 349). Even though Dell (and several others) later repudiated his youthful personal and political radicalism, his efforts—rhetorical, political, and personal—to expand the scope of pro-feminist men's activity, to see the links between women's liberation and the development of a "liberated man," remain inspiring today.

SOCIAL EQUALITY FOR WOMEN

"MAN'S DISPARAGEMENT OF WOMAN IN ALL TIMES AND CLIMES"

Theodore D. Weld (1855?)

OUR PURPOSE in exploring this question is to determine what woman's actual condition and relations to man have been throughout history and to determine whether those relations were hers of necessity, or whether they were put upon her by man, according to "that good old rule" that "they may take who have the power, and they may keep who can."

In considering this subject, we shall deal with *facts* alone. Man's positive acts and declarations respecting woman furnish the only ground for judgment which is absolute. Of mens conventional bearing toward women there is no need to speak—it is full of cheap commonplaces, radiant with compliments to and genuflections "but in the deed, the unequivocal authentic deed, we find sound argument."

Man's physical structure marks him for strength. Among savages strength is gloried in and weakness scorned. The stronger man despises the weaker woman, and makes her his prey. She is his slave and beast of burden. The man takes the woman by the law of the strongest. Form is his title deed. . . .

To disparage woman has been a favorite pastime of our eminent English authors. To depreciate woman has been the fashion in English literature. . . . [L]et us end our illustrations with a single extract from one of our own most distinguished authors.

No one of them was for the first half of this century more widely known and admired at home and abroad than Washington Irving. Two lines from one of his papers in

Hyde Park, Mass., [1855?]. (WCL, Theodore Weld Collection)

the Sketch book reveal incidentally that estimate of the powers, sphere adaptation of women which marked his own times. Here it is.

"Woman who is the mere dependent and ornament of man in his happier hours will be his stay and solace when smitten with sudden calamity." This sentence emphasizes the then public estimate of the relations of women to man. . . .

Sixty years have passed since Irving wrote that sentence. His words accurately express the then current opinion of women. Since then signal changes have been wrought both in the appreciation and condition of women, tho she still bears burdens grievous to be borne, yet her legal, educational and professional disabilities have been greatly lessened. Far wider adaptations are conceded to her nature, her powers are more justly appreciated and her sphere of action and usefulness correspondingly enlarged.

The foregoing historic details establish and define man's estimate of women since the earliest records of the race. What do these facts in evidence prove? Answer first that while in savagism man's rational elements lie smothered under his animal nature, he seems hardly more than a human beast uses his power over woman. . . .

Second. When the savage develops into the barbarian he leaves behind some of his grossest elements, yet still holds woman as property: bought, sold and bartered like other property; a mere mercantile article and man her owner, she is rated like other serviceable things valuable only for the uses to which she is put.

Third. When barbarism first rises into civilization, tho its roughness is somewhat smothered, its ferocity tamed, and its appetite and passions held in check by laws, yet the wild pulse of its old self still throbs through its brain. . . .

The scores of quotations I have given prove that man has always determined woman's relations to himself, and exacted his conformity thereto. He has secured his own personal liberty to judge for himself, but has denied that liberty to woman. He makes all laws and subjects her to them. In short man's subjugation of woman in church and state reveal that barbarian estimate of woman bequeathed to modern civilization by the brutal ages which preceded it. . . .

In conclusion, What has been the result of man's estimate of woman?

1st her exclusion from all those rights, privileges employment and involvements that men enjoy.

2nd Man's universal estimate of woman has been woman's estimate of herself. She being the weaker and pressed upon by a public sentiment which he forms as the possessor of all power in church and state—can do no otherwise. The forced circumstances into which man has crowded her, the abnormal conditions and relations by which he has tethered her, have so jostled woman's *manifestations* that they only burlesque her real nature, exhibiting not its normal uses but its vast possibilities of abuse. Man's greater physical strength determined *at first* their relations. Through all time this fact has determined her condition.

Instead of having her nature free to work out its own symmetries, he has made his own will her propelling force. Man's maladministration of woman has made her what she is. The majority of women have had their natures so distorted by man's repressions, so tortured into parasite and fungous growth, so compelled into chaotic phases and ever shifting impulses that they but distort that nature, whose symmetries

God consecrated for the motherhood of the race. The woman that God made, man has blindly done what he could to unwoman. His influence upon woman in society is in many respects dementalizing and demoralizing. It tends to make women creatures of sensation, to feel rather than to think, to cultivate superficial graces rather than their rational natures. The social intercourse of men and women only mutually invigorates and elevates when sex is unthought of. Whereas the general tone which men give to society tends to make the *controlling* motive of women's lives to make themselves *agreeable to men*. . . .

"A WOMAN WAITS FOR ME"

Walt Whitman (1856)

A WOMAN WAITS for me, she contains all, nothing is lacking,
Yet all were lacking if sex were lacking, or if the moisture of the right man were lacking.

Sex contains all, bodies, souls,
Meanings, proofs, purities, delicacies, results, promulgations,
Songs, commands, health, pride the maternal mystery, the seminal milk,
All hopes, benefactions, bestowals, all the passions, loves, beauties, delights of the earth,
All the governments, judges, gods, follow'd persons of the earth,
These are contain'd in sex as parts of itself and justifications of itself.

Without shame the man I like knows and avows the deliciousness of his sex,
Without shame the woman I like knows and avows hers.

Now I will dimiss myself from impassive women,
I will go stay with her who waits for me, and with those women that are warm-blooded and sufficient for me,
I see that they understand me and do not deny me,
I see that they are worthy of me, I will be the robust husband of those women.

They are not one jot less than I am,
They are tann'd in the face by shining suns and blowing winds,
Their flesh has the old divine suppleness and strength,
They know how to swim, row, ride, wrestle, shoot, run, strike, retreat, advance, resist, defend themselves,

---

From Leaves of Grass and Selected Prose by Walt Whitman, *ed. John Kouwenhoven. New York: Modern Library, 1950.*

They are ultimate in their own right—they
are calm, clear, well-possess'd of
themselves.

I draw you close to me, you women,
I cannot let you go,, I would do you good,
I am for you, and you are for me, not only
for our own sake, but for others' sakes.
Envelop'd in you sleep greater heroes and
bards,
They refuse to awake at the touch of any
man but me.

It is I, you women, I make my way,
I am stern, acrid, large, undissuadable, but
I love you,
I do not hurt you any more than is
necessary for you,
I pour the stuff to start sons and daughters
fit for these States, I press with slow
rude muscle,
I brace myself effectually, I listen to no
entreaties,
I dare not withdraw till I deposit what has
so long accumulated within me.

Through you I drain the pent-up rivers of
myself,
In you I wrap a thousand onward years,
On you I graft the grafts of the best-loved
of me and America,
The drops I distil upon you shall grow
fierce and athletic girls, new artists,
musicians, and singers,
The babes I beget upon you are to beget
babes in their turn,
I shall demand perfect men and women
out of my love-spendings,
I shall expect them to interpenetrate with
others, as I and you interpenetrate now,
I shall count on the fruits of the gushing
showers of them, as I count on the fruits
of the gushing showers I give now,
I shall look for loving crops from the birth,
life, death, immortality, I plant so
lovingly now.

CUPID'S YOKES (excerpt)

Ezra Heywood (1879)

THE LEGAL SUBJECTION of women is thought to be justified by an assumed natural dependence on man. The old claim of tyranny, "The king can do no wrong," is reasserted by that many-headed monster, the majority, which widens the circle of despotism, but retains the fact. As people were to the king, so woman is now an appendage of man, who claims to be her "head," though nature seems not to have limited heads to the exclusive possession of either sex. That there is no natural feeling of dependence, on one hand, or of superiority on the other, is

Princeton, Mass.: Cooperative Publishing Co., 1879.

evident to the most casual observer of spontaneous dealings of the sexes. In practical sense and force a girl of fourteen is often ten years older than a boy of the same age; tells him how to act and protects him from the big boys at school. A widow lady who maintains herself and daughter and lays up money by keeping a half-dozen families in clean clothes, rejoices that she has no man on her hands to support. Her next door neighbor, who sold, one day, forty cents' worth of her husband's service for two pounds of beef, said that for another piece as large she would part with him entirely. At a court ball in Berlin, Bismarck, much pleased with the wife of a foreign diplomat present, with characteristic audacity, reached out to pluck a flower from the bouquet she carried; rapping his knuckles with her fan she said: "Pardon, Mr. Count, but that flower is not a German State; you must ask for it." Man instinctively defers to woman until poverty, marriage or ungentlemanly arrogance subjects her to his dictation. Popular reverence for her person forbids public laying on of hands to correct her, and private insolence dares not until she is under his legal thumb. She is a stronger body guard to man in a mob than a battalion of soldiers, and the sanctity of her person is the only barrier the savage atrocities of war never quite overleap. A body, ears, eyes, nose, taste, touch, sensitive to beauty of thought, color, sound; all requisites to admit men to the realm of sense, and a knowledge of material things, woman has; while, in intuition, the income of spiritual wealth, she is admitted to excel man. By what authority, then, is she required to look up to him for guidance, while he looks to Infinite Truth as the source of right and duty? The ruling class rarely yield a privilege until whipped out of it; so man now legislates with his fist rather than his conscience, robs his "better half" of all the ballot, simply because he is physically the strongest. To compel her to obey father before marriage, husband afterward, then her eldest son, may be consistent with Mormonism, which aspires to build an empire on Isaiah's prophecy that in the last days seven women shall cling to one man, and honors as "the wisest man" a patriarch who had seven hundred wives and three hundred concubines; it may be suited to a theology which makes man lord of creation and woman an afterthought, designates boys as the "sons of God" and girls as the "daughters of men," and paves hell, not in good intentions even, but with "infants' skulls not a span long;" it may be agreeable to her position in a Turkish harem, a Chinese palace, on a blazing funeral pile of a Hindoo husband, or in the hotter fires of a Boston brothel, but it is quite repulsive to the free ideas which transformed the dark realms of the American Indian into a constellation of powerful States.

The protesting indignation of some women who had the honor to be, at least, rebellious slaves, widespread and increasing unrest broke out in the first formal declaration of independence, issued in 1848, from Seneca Falls, N. Y., by Elizabeth Cady Stanton, Lucretia Mott, and others. It enumerated grievances equal in number and seriousness to those set down in the famous manifesto of '76, and is destined to work a more extended and beneficent revolution. Current objections to woman's enfranchisement can hardly be accounted for, except on the supposition that the sexes, even husbands and wives, are not yet personally acquainted with each other or truth. Justice unites persons widely remote; injustice separates infinitely those standing side by side. Men reputed to know something of the nature of liberty, so-called radicals who have ceased to represent the moral sense, or even the intelligence of the hour, talk flippantly of "universal suffrage" while shutting out one-half of human-kind. A wit believed in universal salvation, provided he could pick the men; so perhaps these recreant "radicals" will conquer their prejudice against impartial suffrage, when assured that new comers will vote their party ticket. The right of man to political freedom appears in the fact that he is a sentient being, capable of reason and choice, looking before and after. To rule adult citizens against their will is tyranny; women are adult citizens, hence those who deny them the ballot are tyrants. A dozen years ago or more, the writer, with other specimens of sophomoric assurance, one morning at breakfast, questioned the propriety of Lucy Stone's refusal to pay taxes, allowing her furniture to be sold in preference; the combined, college-learned, male wisdom thinking it a great ado about a small matter. A lady opposite, who first called his attention practically to peace and anti-slavery reform, flung over the table, "No taxation without representation. Did you ever hear of Sam. Adams and John Hampden?" It was the first and last argument he ever attempted to make against woman's suffrage. To justify himself, her oppressor must class her psychologically with brutes, deny her a soul, prove either that she has no functions equal with man, or that she is incapable of exercising them—neither of which can be done. Boys who toss their empty heads at this reform, use freely that epithet which reveals so much contempt for the human understanding—"strong-minded." Men are thought to personate reason, and women sentiment; but generally male objectors to this claim are noted for nothing more than their plentiful lack of logic and superabundance of mulish prejudice. Notwithstanding these disparaging exceptions, men yield to reason; and, at no distant day, physical strength will rally under the banner of moral beauty.

Whether suffrage is a right or privilege, natural or conventional, its denial to woman is equally indefensible. Minors become of age, slaves are emancipated, lunatics regain reason, idiots are endowed with intelligence, criminals are pardoned, traitors amnestied, disfranchised males of every class shed their disabilities and are restored to liberty; but the fact of sex—the crime of womanhood—dooms one to perpetual vassalage! Not the ability to drink, chew, smoke, lie, steal and swear, votes—though election day too often indicates these vices to be important conditions of membership in the male body politic—but intellect, conscience, character, are supposed to vote; and the boy proudly becoming "a man before his mother," is crowned a sovereign at twenty-one, because in thought and discretion he ceases to crawl as an animal, and stands an upright intelligence. Is she who endowed him with these royal qualities less capable of exercising them? If the admission fee to franchise is not age, but property, why are poor men received and rich women excluded? If the door swings open to integrity and courage, why are these turned away in women while their absence is welcomed in men? Simply because this booted, spurred and whiskered thing called government is a usurpation, and men choose to have it so. Since, then, custom not reason, fraud not justice, prejudice not good sense, object, this is a question not for argument, but for affirmation. Those who acknowledge the validity of existing government, by increasing its numerical power, not merely drop a stitch in their logic, but surrender the flag of impartial suffrage to its enemies. The negro certainly has quite as good a right to vote as his late masters. If ignorant, they made it a penal offence to teach him to read; if poor, they robbed him of his earnings by law. But who are negro men and Chinese that we should confer irresponsible power on them? To admit any man, be he black, red, yellow, or a minor—our curled, white darling just come of age—to the franchise, who is not pledged to share it with women, is treason to liberty, a desertion of the logical duty of the hour.

A cruel kindness, thought to be friendly regard, assumes to "protect" those who, by divine right of rational being, are entitled, at least, to be let alone. We are not among wild beasts; from whom, then, does woman need protection? From her protectors. While making marriage almost her only possible means of permanent subsistence, and working for a living unpopular, custom forbids her to "propose," to seek a husband; hence this vicarious theory of government owes her, what Socrates claimed for himself, a support at the public expense. If, in the old law phrase, "the husband and wife are one person, and he that one;" if, married or unmarried, her personality is buried in his, man should also embody her responsibility—be taxed for her food, clothing, leisure, pleasure, and punished for her sins. But, in practice, he does not recognize this obliging doctrine; for, while reserving the hottest corner of his future hell for her, in this life his responsibility ends with the gratification of his personal desires, and she his "abandoned"—thrown upon the tender mercies of public censure and charity. . . .

The imposing deference which, while it affects to regard woman as the pride and ornament of creation, degrades her to a toy, a cipher, fears natural order will not keep its footing, if she is allowed to go at large without keepers. But will the skeptic behind that objection please explain to us the nature of the tie which now joins, or may join him to the woman called wife? If it is force, who gave him authority to wield it! If it is fraud, the officers of justice should lay hands on him. If it is poverty, by what process did this once fascinating being, capable of infinite endeavor, become a menial in his service, dependent at his board? Is it not rather the memory of equality, of the hour when he, a glad suppliant, courted her, a free intelligence, able to accept or reject his proposals? Surrendering virgin liberty she entered his legal cage; the blooming maiden, "quickly scorned when not adored," is now the worn and faded wife, in the back-yard of his affections; and real respect for her has declined, just in proportion as she has lost the power of choice, and the control of her person. There may be men who, seeking a parlor ornament, or a subservient mistress, prefer languid helplessness to original strength in a wife; but the case of him who married the one he did, because she was the only girl in town he was not sure of before proposing, well indicates how much continent deference of the husband on the one hand, and free existence of the wife on the other, depend on her power to decline or even defy his advances. As one would rather be called a knave than a fool, so men respect woman's wickedness more than her weakness; the thorn and the bramble more than dependent vines wedded to masculine oaks. . . .

. . . In urging the political question, woman brings not mere avoirdupois weight, but living mind, to be admitted to citizenship. Her enfranchisement will prove the advent of reason and conscience to politics, obedience to "law whose throne is in the bosom of God, and whose voice is the harmony of the world." The prejudice against her fulfilling any function which makes her an independent, thoughtful, self-sustaining being is excited by narrow and despotic selfishness. We have created antagonism by establishing a privileged male class. . . .

It is thought that politics will unsex her, that she will "lose her tender little ways and bashful modesties, and the bloom be rubbed off every enjoyment." This is but the revival of an old cry of tyrants, now masquerading as republicans and democrats, that the people are incapable of self-government. As an exhausted receiver defines the sphere of a rabbit suffocated under it, so imprisoning conditions within which the ages have bound woman limit her natural right to life. While men's functions and opportunities are of their own choice, women's are forced on them by circumstances. Man's duties and avocations send the soul outward; woman must always stay at home with her heart. What right has one adult citizen to forcibly determine the *status* of another? The sphere of a slave is the circle described by his driver's lash; the sphere of woman free is the realm her heart fills, the range and height of her faculty. The ability of one marks the present sphere of that one, but leaves all space this side of God to enlarge upon. It is said that woman cannot engage in politics, or other business, because she must marry; but she is compelled to unpaid toil of many kinds, beside child-bearing, if married. Will it require more effort to go to the town hall twice than it does to attend church fifty-two times a year. Politics are merely a matter of business, the ways and means to certain ends. Principle is the what, policy is the how of affairs. The Queen of England is conceded to be, in the gentler traits, a model to her sex, though she rules an empire which encircles the globe; will our queen of hearts be less a woman when dropping a piece of paper into a box? Women in Congress at salaries of $5,000 a year, could hardly be more damaged or damaging than as waiter girls or mistresses of those august legislators. If politics are vicious, it is high time they were cured, for "sound policy always coincides with substantial justice." The plea that women will be rudely treated by men at the polls, so far as it has any weight, only proves that male ruffians should be disfranchised; but this "chivalry objection comes about two centuries too late, for the courtesy of men has increased as the freedom of woman has been accorded." If men are so bad they cannot be trusted to vote with women ought they to vote for women? Those accustomed to govern in schools, able to teach more than males can learn, will not consent to be lifelong vassals of boys they educate. The mother of nine children, successfully raised and started in life, why prefer a whiff of cigar smoke to her for President? Government is a bloody, barbarous thing, chiefly because it ignores ethics of which woman is the clearer and most steadfast exponent. . . .

A gentle bachelor fears conscriptions of war may invade his peace if women vote, and that our fair rulers may draft for husbands. Fatally married, the wife controls one-third his property, while he loses claim to any share in hers. He can deed nothing away without her signature, and has no use of her credit at the store, while she can buy heavily on his account, and law compels him to pay the uttermost. Withdrawing from his lordship's imperial nothingness she may levy perpetual alimony on him for a living, while he must delve to earn it, and count himself lucky to be rid of her at that. A gay creature, blushing behind her fan, outwits an elegant fop in lavender kids, who thinks all the girls dying to marry him, ensnares him in an engagement, provokes him to break it, and, in damages for breach of promise, carries off the bulk of his fortune. If this be his fate now, who can protect him when the "suppressed sex" are free, and he is obliged to risk his charms in an open market? Armed with jealousy and cunning, in the absence of better weapons of defence, ignorant, frivolous, exacting, woman now often drags man down; her subjected condition being fruitful in vices of artifice and power, of unnatural dependence, and imperious self-assertion, the aggressor, as usual, suffers most. Imbruted mind is the reflex result of the exercise of arbitrary power, and those who trample on the weak are the first to cringe to the strong. None but base natures assume to rule equals, or domineer over inferiors. We must count it, therefore, the first and chief of man's rights to undo, without asking, this injustice to woman; for in so far as he deprives her of vigor and scope does he maim himself. Alas! that any man can wish women perishing in luxurious inactivity, wedded to vice or imbecility, impaled on a needle, or starving in a garret, to be contented! Doubtless many superiors to Elizabeth Browning, Margaret Fuller, Charlotte Bronte, and George Sand are buried under our household, sewing shop, fashionable and factory life. England has one Stuart Mill, America one Emerson, but it were unlucky to have two; for why should nature be so given out as to repeat herself? In requiring woman to be the shadow, or echo of man, we mar creative intention, and rob society of the better service which intuitive sense waits to render. The value of self-supporting independence doubtless suggested the remark of a wit—"A wife is a fortune—when she is poor." As the adjective is said to be the greatest enemy of the noun, though agreeing with it in gender, number and person, so woman as an adjective, an appendage of man, is useless or worse to him, and a mockery to herself, having an inalienable right to be a noun, a person accountable to infinite intelligence. Since in correcting wrong we enact right, men's actual influence will not only not be lessened, but vastly increased, by abolishing the despotic and irresponsible power they now wield. If authority is natural and beneficent, the votes of a world united cannot overthrow it; if it is usurped, the quicker it falls the better.

Fascinating weakness, "sweet irresponsibility," becomes a nullity, or hostile, when allegiance is forced, and suggests truth in an old maxim, "As many slaves, so many enemies." Since we offer a premium to adverse influence, practical sense and persuasive eloquence are turned against us; "measures which statesmen have meditated a whole year may be overturned by women in a day," and often have they conquered a nation by simply making up faces. The victims of false deference on one hand and tyrannical subjection on the other, they win through diplomatic artifice, or by sacrifices inconsistent with personal sanctity and social well-being. Impulses, which rightly directed would outflow in tenderness and rectitude, invigorate, adorn and bless mankind, now take the sexes to houses of assignation, and the very materials with which perfect society will be constructed, when the builder arrives, are added fuel to flaming heats our ignorance kindles. The "social evil," which despairing philanthropy says "no law can restrain and no power suppress," is a vast business system of supply and demand, whose natural causes and retributive results point outcasts and outcasters to the ways of healthful sanity. Not to quote Solomon and Samson, the reputed wisest and strongest of men, both of whom were conquered by women, why in Europe and America to-day are men of genius, writers, statesmen and reformers, involved in family feuds, tenants of desolate homes, wanderers from what should be domestic quiet, or indulging in practices they dare not defend as right? These things cannot be dismissed with a sneer, or religiously attributed to the Prince of Evil; for the devil is only unexplained adversity, and may yet turn out to be Deity in disguise. The old theory of natural depravity and vicarious atonement will no longer serve to darken counsel with words; for the instincts and attractions God made are not essentially unclean. Conjugal law, which in all ages and nations has "confined woman to one man, has never confined man to one woman." Virtuous Congressmen, who urge war on Mormon polygamists, should first face domestic problems at home whose solution will require clearer heads and braver hearts than have yet appeared. In Utah husbands are responsible for their wives, required by law, at least, to provide them bread. In Boston and New York men are quite as much married, though in a clandestine and unscrupulous way. Spectacled bookworms may explore traditions of the past, grave divines declaim against laxity of morals, conceited stoics affect to be superior to fascination, but the fact remains that woman, incarnating love, has ruled and will rule man, for better for worse, just in proportion as she is assured or denied a right to herself. Not responsible to law, because unrecognized by it, she is now driven to secure recognition of her existence by depravity or rebellion. If frivolous or perverse, it is the result of false conditions; for nature has a seriously honest intent in creating a woman as in creating a man. If he makes badness a necessity and bribes to silence her moral sense, designed to call him to order, why may not the "weaker vessel" plot to upset the stronger? . . .

. . . [W]omen can afford to be indifferent to nothing which degrades women; the sad fact that "the contentment of slaves renders objection to liberty possible," makes it a more imperative duty to bestir ourselves to see justice done. Living in a world of petty details engenders narrow habits of mind, and the bounding aspirations of youth are killed out in the dull round of restricted life. "It might have been" is written over the tomb of many buried hopes. To think slavery liberty and dependence an honor; to be satisfied "with what we have rather than with what we want," that is the calamity. . . .

"OUR BETTER HALVES"

Lester F. Ward (1888)

THE PRACTICE of calling women better than men is purely chivalric—an empty compliment to the sex. The less enlightened regard them as inferior. The more enlightened consider them equal when all elements are taken into the account. The general opinion is that they are superior morally and inferior mentally and physically. But there are so many kinds of moral, mental, and physical qualities that each of these classes, when carefully analyzed, is found to contain some elements in which the one and some in which the other sex stands higher. It is therefore a difficult problem, increasing in intricacy with more thorough and candid investigation. Attempts have been made, often with much success, to point out the leading characteristics in which the sexes differ, especially in mental traits, and some have gone deeper and sought to explain these differences as arising from physical and social conditions.

Forum 6 (November 1888).

It is not my purpose to treat the subject from this standpoint, nor to attempt in any way to show wherein superiority consists. I propose simply to predicate of the female sex a particular kind of superiority and to offer some proofs on this single point. Whatever may be woman's present condition in civilized, barbaric, or savage society, and whatever may be the condition of the female sex in the different departments of animal life, I shall undertake to contend that in the economy of organic nature the female sex is the primary, and the male a secondary element. If this be a law, its application to the human race is readily made and its importance to social life cannot be ignored.

That such a view should be looked upon as unsound, and even absurd, by those who have only studied men is quite natural, but one would suppose that close students of nature, particularly such as have chosen the world of life as their special field of research, would pause at this question and seek to give it such a final solution as to prevent its return into the arena of discussion. I am sorry to say that they have not done so. In fact, so far as I have observed, they have treated it from the most superficial standpoint. Writers of this class have frequently drawn important practical conclusions from what I hope to show to be mere half-truths—conclusions bearing upon the future education, treatment, and position of woman in society. A quotation or two from authors of repute will make this point clear. Thus, in an article entitled "The Woman's Rights Question Considered from a Biological Point of View," in the "Quarterly Journal of Science" for October, 1878, the writer says:

"We propose, therefore, to examine this question in the light of the principles of natural selection, of differentiation and specialization, and to inquire whether the relations of the sexes in the human species and the distribution of their respective functions are or are not in general harmony with what is observed in that portion of the animal kingdom which lies nearest to man; to wit, in Mammalia. . . . Even a very superficial and popular survey of the class Mammalia will satisfy us that the structural differences between the males and the females of each species are by no means confined to the reproductive organs. The male ruminant, whale, bat, elephant, rodent, carnivore, or ape, is on the average a larger and heavier animal than his mate. The tiger, for instance, exceeds the tigress in size by a proportion of from ten to twenty per cent. In few, if any, species is the superior stature of the male more striking than in the one which approaches man most nearly in its physical development—the gorilla. But the mere difference in size is not all; the female is scarcely in any normal case a mere miniature copy of the male. Her proportions differ; the head and the thorax are relatively smaller, the pelvis broader, the bones slighter, the muscles less powerful. The male in many cases possesses offensive weapons which in the female are wanting. In illustration we need only to refer to the tusks of the elephant and the boar, and the horns of many spcies of deer. On the contrary, there is no instance of a female possessing any weapon which is not also found, to at least an equal degree, in the male. Further, the superior size of the head in the male is not merely due to the more massive osseous growth needful for the support of tusks, horns, etc., but to a proportionately larger development of brain."

And after much more in the same strain, this writer concludes:

> "We have, therefore, in fine, full ground for maintaining that the 'woman's rights movement' is an attempt to rear, by a process of 'unnatural selection,' a race of monstrosities—hostile alike to men, to normal women, to human society, and to the future development of our race."

Prof. W. K. Brooks, in a very able article in the "Popular Science Monthly" for June and July, 1879, succeeded, as I think, in proving that the well-known passivity of the female sex has the important significance that it represents the principle of heredity, or permanence of type, the male representing that of variability; thus completely reversing the *varium et mutabile semper femina.* But notwithstanding his lucid conceptions on this point, Prof. Brooks felt called upon in this article to write:

> "Our conclusions have a strong leaning to the conservative or old-fashioned view of the subject—to what many will call 'male' view of women. The positions which women already occupy in society and the duties which they perform are, in the main, what they should be if our view is correct; and any attempt to improve the condition of women by ignorning or obliterating the intellectual differences between them and men must result in disaster to the race, and the obstruction of that progress and improvement which the history of the past shows to be in store for both men and women in the future. So far as human life in this world is concerned, there can be no improvement which is not accomplished in accordance with the laws of nature; and, if it is a natural law that the parts which the sexes perform in the natural evolution of the race are complemental to each other, we cannot hope to accomplish anything by working in opposition to the natural method."

Utterances similiar to those above quoted have constantly found place for the last twenty years in our best scientific literature, and it may be fairly said to be the fashion among scientific men to treat the woman question from this point of view. A great array of evidence is brought to show that woman is physically inferior to man, that she is smaller in stature, and that her brain is not only absolutely smaller, but is smaller in proportion to her body; that she has less strength in proportion to her size, less power of endurance, and a greater number of ailments. This, it is said, is the natural result of her sex. Reproduction is so great a drain upon the female system that we should expect it to be attended with diminished strength and vitality. It is further argued that the smaller and weaker females of animals, as well as the young, are protected by the larger and stronger males, and the inference is freely drawn that the dependence of the females among animals is similar to that of women in society, which latter is therefore the natural condition.

I shall not deny the fact of woman's physical and mental inferiority, nor shall I deny that the differences are, in the main, due to causes analogous to those which have differentiated the sexes of the higher animals. I must, however, deny *in toto* that these causes are what they are assumed by these writers to be. It has always surprised me that those who start out avowedly from a Darwinian standpoint should so quickly abandon it and proceed to argue from pre-Darwinian premises. It was Darwin who taught us why the boar has tusks, the stag antlers, and the peacock gaudy tail-feathers. It is because the females chose mates that possessed these characters. The characters selected by the females have been, in the main, those that tended to insure success in rivalry for mates. The greater size and strength of the males, together with their powerful weapons, have not been acquired, as is implied in the argument above stated, for the purpose of protecting the dependent females; they have been acquired entirely for the purpose of combating rivals and winning mates. In very few such animals do the males ever attempt to protect the females, even where the latter have their young to take care of. When the hen with her brood of chickens is attacked, it is not the cock that ruffs his feathers and defends them with his spurs; it is the mother herself that defends them. The cock is always found with hens that have no chickens, and only uses his spurs in fighting with other cocks that have no notion of injuring the females. In the entire animal kingdom the cases where the male uses his great powers to protect the female or the young, or to bring them food, are so rare that where they are observed they are recorded as curious approximations to the social state of man. These "secondary sexual characters," as Darwin has named them, are generally adapted to aggressive warfare, not with the enemies of the species, but with the males of the same species for the possession of the females. All this has positively no analogy with the human condition, and those who cite these facts as a justification for retaining woman in a lower sphere of either mental or physical activity than that occupied by man, abandon the modern and correct interpretation of them and fall back upon the old interpretation which has been proved to be false.

That secondary sexual characters exist in man is, indeed, true. His beard is clearly one of the purely ornamental ones. His larger size and greater strength were doubtless acquired before his moral faculties had awakened, and are the result of his battles for his wives. The predominance of the male brain in the human species doubtless partakes of this nature, and is in a large degree attributable to this cause. The time came in the development of the race when brute force began to give way to sagacity, and the first use to which this growing power was put was that of circumventing rivals for female favor. Brain grew with effort, and like the other organs that are so strangely developed through this cause, it began to be more especially characteristic of the sex. The weaker sex admired success then as now, and the bright-witted became the successful ones, while the dull failed to transmit their dullness. There was a survival of the cunning.

The first use of mental power, as of physical power, was to defeat rivals and secure mates; it was not to protect female frailty or supply food to offspring. The females protected themselves and their progeny by maternal instinct. The females of all wild animals are more dangerous to encounter than the males, especially when they have young; and it has been observed that the male carnivores rarely attack man.

Nor do I deny that these agencies of selection are still at work, slowly, it is true, but perhaps as rapidly as at any previous period, producing physical modifications in man. But it is no longer simple female selection of male qualities, as in the lower animals; there is now going on an opposite class of influences by which a true male selection is bringing about modifications in woman, and this had progressed so far at the beginning of the historic period that the ornamental characters had been, as it were, transferred from the male to the female, and beauty, which in birds and many animals is the exclusive attribute of the males, had become the leading attribute of the women of the higher races. And while setting down this fact, let me call attention to its great significance as pointing to future possibilities in woman when men shall learn to select other qualities in their companions than mere beauty; for under the power of this comparatively modern male selection woman may become whatever man shall desire her to be, and the ideal woman, however high the standard, will become more and more the real woman.

The entire argument of those who would restrict woman's sphere because she is mentally and physically inferior to man would therefore fall to the ground, even if we were to admit that there was something in her sex that rendered that inferiority natural and essential. To be fully consistent, it would be necessary to insist that woman should defend both herself and her offspring from hostile influences of all kinds, and also assume the whole duty of supplying her children with food, while the sole function of man should be, as it is in most mammals and birds, to take care of himself and fight off rivals. This would be the "natural" state of society in the sense in which these philosophers employ that term. It is only distantly approached in a few of the very lowest tribes of savages.

But let us now inquire what grounds there are for accepting this mental and physical inferiority of women as something inherent in the nature of things. Is it really true that the larger part taken by the female in the work of reproduction necessarily impairs her strength, dwarfs her proportions, and renders her a physically inferior and dependent being? In most human races it may be admitted that women are less stalwart than men, although all the stories of Amazonian tribes are not mere fictions. It is also true, as has been insisted upon, that the males of most mammals and birds exceed the females in size and strength, and often differ from them greatly in appearance. But this is by no means always the case. The fable of the hedgehog that won the race with the hare by cunningly stationing Mrs. Hedgehog at the other end of the course, instructed to claim the stakes, is founded upon an exception which has many parallels. Among birds there are cases in which the rule is reversed. There are some entire families, as for example the hawks, in which the females exceed the males. If we go further down the scale, however, we find this attribute of male superiority to disappear almost entirely throughout the reptiles and amphibians, with a decided leaning toward female supremacy; and in the fishes, where male rivalry does not exist, the female, as every fisherman knows, is almost invariably the heavier game.

But it is not until we go below the vertebrate series and contemplate the invertebrate and vegetable worlds that we really begin to find the data for a philosophical study of the meaning of sex. It has been frequently remarked that the laws governing the higher forms of life can be rightly comprehended only by an acquaintance with the lower and more formative types of being. In no problem is this more true than in that of sex.

In studying this problem it is found that there is a great world of life that wholly antedates the appearance of sex—the world of asexual life—nor is the passage from the sexless to the distinctly male and female definite and abrupt. Between them occur parthenogenesis or virgin reproduction, hermaphroditism, in which the male being consists simply of an organ, and parasitic males, of which we shall presently speak, while the other devices of nature for perpetuating life are innumerable and infinitely varied. But so far as sex can be predicated of these beings, they must all be regarded as female. The asexual parent must be contemplated as, to all intents and purposes, maternal. The parthenogenetic aphis or shrimp is in all essential respects a mother. The hermaphrodite creature, whatever else it may be, is also necessarily a female. Following these states come the numberless cases in which the female form continues to constitute the type of life, the insignificant male appearing to be a mere afterthought.

The vegetable kingdom, except in its very lowest stages, affords comparatively few pointed illustrations of this truth. The strange behavior of the hemp plant, in which, as has long been known, the female plants crowd out the male plants by overshadowing them as soon as they have been fertilized by the latter, used to be frequently commented upon as a perverse anomaly in nature. Now it is correctly interpreted as an expression of the general law that the primary purpose of the male sex is to enable the female, or type form, to reproduce, after performing which function the male form is useless and a mere cumberer of the ground. But the hemp plant is by no means alone in possessing this peculiarity. I could enumerate several pretty well known species that have a somewhat similar habit. I will mention only one, the common cud-weed, or everlasting (*Antennaria plantaginifolia*), which, unlike the hemp, has colonies of males separate from the females, and these male plants are small and short-lived. Long after their flowering stalks have disappeared the female plants continue to grow, and they become large and thrifty herbs lasting until frost.

In the animal kingdom below the vertebrates female superiority is well-nigh universal. In the few cases where it does not occur it is generally found that the males combat each other, after the manner of the higher animals, for the possession of the females. The cases that I shall name are such as all are familiar with. The only new thing in their presentation is their application to the point at issue.

The superiority of the queen bee over the drone is only a well-known illustration of a condition which, with the usual variations and exceptions, is common to a great natural order of insects. The only mosquito that the unscientific world knows is the female mosquito. The male mosquito is a frail and harmless little creature that swarms with the females in the early season and passes away when his work is done. There are many insects of which the males possess no organs of nutrition in the imago state, their duties during their ephemeral existence being confined to what the Germans call the *Minnedienst.* Such is the life of many male moths and butterflies. But much greater inequalities are often found. I should, perhaps, apologize for citing the familiar case of spiders, in some species of which the miniature lover is often seized and devoured during his courtship by the gigantic object of his affections. Something similar, I learn, sometimes occurs with the mantis or "praying insect."

Merely mentioning the extreme case of Sphærularia, in which the female is several thousand times as large as the male, I may surely be permitted to introduce the barnacle, since it is one of the creatures upon which Prof. Brooks lays considerable stress in the article to which I have referred. Not being myself a zoologist, I am only too happy to quote him. He says:

> "Among the barnacles there are a few species the males and females of which differ remarkably. The female is an ordinary barnacle, with all the peculiarites of the group fully developed, while the male is a small parasite upon the body of the female, and is so different from the female of its own species, and from all ordinary barnacles, that no one would ever recognize in the adult male any affinity whatever to its closest allies."

The barnacle, or cirripede, is the creature which Mr. Darwin so long studied, and from which he learned so many lessons leading up to his grand generalizations. In a letter to Sir Charles Lyell, dated September 14, 1849, he recounts some of his discoveries while engaged in this study. Having learned that most cirripedes, but not all, were hermaphrodite, he remarks:

> "The other day I got a curious case of a unisexual instead of hermaphrodite cirripedge, in which the female had the common cirripedial character, and in two valves of her shell had two little pockets in each of which she kept a little husband. I do not know of any other case where a female invariably has two husbands. I have one still odder fact, common to several species, namely, that though they are hermaphrodite, they have small additional, or, as I call them, complemental males. One specimen, itself, hermaphrodite, had no less than seven of these complemental males attached to it."

Prof. Brooks brings forward facts of this class to demonstrate that the male is the variable sex, while the female is comparatively stable. However much we may doubt his further conclusion that variability rather than supplementary procreative power was the primary purpose of the separate male principle, we must, it would seem, concede that variability and adaptability are the distinguishing characteristics of the male sex everywhere, as the transmitting power and permanence of type are those of the female. But this is a very different thing from saying that the female sex is incapable of progress, or that man is destined to develop indefinitely, leaving woman constantly farther and farther in the rear. Does the class of philosophers to which reference has been made look forward to a time when woman shall become as insignificant an object compared to man as the male spider is compared to the female? This would be the logical outcome of their argument if based upon the relative variability of the male sex.

We have now seen that, whether we contemplate the higher animals, among which male superiority prevails, or the lower forms, among which female superiority prevails, the argument from biology that the existing relations between the sexes in the human race are precisely what nature intended them to be, that they ought not to be disturbed and cannot be improved, leads, when carried to its logical conclusion, to a palpable absurdity. But have we, then, profited nothing by the thoughtful contemplation of the subject from these two points of view? Those who rightly interpret the facts cannot avoid learning a most important lesson from each of these lines of inquiry. From the first the truth comes clearly forth that the relations of the sexes among the higher animals are widely abnormal, warped, and strained by a long line of curious influences, chiefly psychic, which are incident to the development of animal organisms under the competitive principle that prevails throughout nature. From the second comes now into full view the still more important truth with which we first set out, that the female sex is primary in point both of origin and of importance in the history and economy of organic life. And as life is the highest product of nature and human life the highest type of life, it follows that the grandest fact in nature is woman.

But we have learned even more than this, that which is certainly of more practical value. We have learned how to carry forward the progress of development so far advanced by the unconcious agencies of nature. Accepting evolution as we must, recognizing heredity as the distinctive attribute of the female sex, it becomes clear that it must be from the steady advance of woman rather than from the uncertain fluctuations of man that the sure and solid progress of the future is to come. The attempt to move the whole race forward by elevating only the sex that represents the principle of instability, has long enough been tried. The many cases of superior men the sons of superior mothers, coupled with the many more cases of degenerate sons of superior sires, have taught us over and over again that the way to civilize the race is to civilize woman. And now, thanks to science, we see why this is so. Woman is the unchanging trunk of the great genealogic tree; while man, with all his vaunted superiority, is but a branch, a grafted scion, as it were, whose acquired qualities die with the individual, while those of woman are handed on to futurity. Woman *is* the race, and the race can be raised up only as she is raised up. There is no fixed rule by which Nature has intended that one sex should excel the other, any more than there is any fixed point beyond which either cannot further develop. Nature has no intentions, and evolution has no limits. True science teaches that the elevation of woman is the only sure road to evolution of man.

"ANIMAL RIGHTS FOR WOMEN"

Judge Ben Lindsey (1890?)

TAKE THIS MATTER of providing for the care and support of mothers in order to assure the health and strength of the coming generation. Take, to be explicit, a case that I had in my court in Denver, before the war—the case of Mrs. N–.

Her husband had worked in the smelters. He had been employed there for sixteen years, from ten to twelve hours a day. Work in the smelters is a dangerous occupation, and under our Colorado law, he should not have been on duty more than eight hours a day; but, in order to evade the law, his employers had transferred the men in the smelters to the pay-roll of the railroad, where they might work twelve hours legally. At the end of a hard day, a tired workman stumbled against a pail of water and upset it on a slag pile. The slag exploded and killed Mr. N–. The railroad company paid Mrs. N– $250.00 for the life of her husband, and that was the end of the first chapter.

Mrs. N–, with six young children, settled down in a little house by the railroad tracks, to a life of poverty and ill-paid labor. The children were allowed to run wild, because she could not look after them, she had to leave home to earn for them. They were continuously hungry, because she could not earn enough to feed them. Near the house, the railroad's box cars were always standing as a temptation to mischief. Tommy, her eldest boy, broke into a box car, one day, stole two dollars' worth of lead that had come from the smelter—the smelter where

N.p., [ca. 1890]. (LOC, Judge Ben Lindsey Papers)

his father had been killed—sold it for sixty cents, and took the money to his mother. He was arrested and brought to Juvenile Court. End of chapter two.

The agents of our state Humane Society, so-called, here entered the case to report that they had investigated Mrs. N– and found that she was "bad." In an attempt to eke out her earnings, she had taken a boarder in her little shack. In the course of time and temptation, she had entered into relations with this boarder which the Humane Society described as immoral. Therefore, they proposed to take all her children away from her, and put them in an orphan asylum, and leave her to complete her ruin.

That is to say, society having killed her husband, by failing to enforce the laws for his protection—and having left her without the means to raise her six future citizens efficiently—and having forced her into the temptations of immorality in order to save them from starvation—and having debauched her boy Tommy in the same process of poverty—society now proposed to punish her and Tommy and all the other children for the acts and omissions of which society had been guilty.

Our Juvenile Court, of course, does not see the responsibilities of society fulfilled in this way, and we did what we could to save Mrs. N– and Tommy and her other little citizens from complete disaster. But as a result of this and many similar cases we lobbied the Colorado legislation for a Mother's Compensation Act that should allow us to pay such women as Mrs. N– as much as $50.00 a month to stay at home and rear their young families that these might be a profit to the state, instead of a loss. It was peace time. The war had not taught the world the value of mothers and children to the state. The legislature would not act.

In the meantime, a Progressive campaign in Colorado won the "initiative and referendum", by which the people themselves could initiate legislation. One of the first laws that we initiated was the Mother's Compensation Act. But the law contained no appropriation of money to carry it out. In Denver we had to ask the City Council for the money. We asked for an appropriation of $5000.

That seemed little enough, but it was too much for a committee of business men from the Denver Chamber of Commerce, who came to the hearings on the city budget and objected to giving $5000 to assist destitute mothers. They said it was "paternalism", "an encouragement to pauperism", "a fad", "the worst sort of socialism". They would have called it "Bolshevism", but that word had not yet been initiated itself. They argued against any appropriation for mothers.

While they were arguing, I glanced down the budget, and found an item reading: "For the dog catcher's department $8000." I called their attention to this item. The city was providing $8000 for the purpose of seeing that the streets were not over-run with homeless, ill-bred, and dangerous dogs. It was, in effect, an appropriation to provide for a good breed of well-cared for dogs, by catching and destroying all the poor mongrels for whom nobody would buy a tag. I pleaded for "dogs' rights for women." If they could appropriate $5000 for the better breeding of dogs, without being "paternalistic", couldn't they give $5000 to ensure a better breed of human beings? Would they do more for the offspring of a dog than for the children of a human mother? . . .

One of our greatest difficulties in the Juvenile Court had been to care for the young unmarried mothers who came before the court. They were not "bad" girls. The bad ones knew how to avoid motherhood. These were usually girls who had been betrayed by their own ignorance or innocence and the overpowering strength of natural instincts of which they had not been properly warned. They were about to give birth to children under conditions of ostracism and shame that were sure to blight the lives of their infants and themselves. That is to say, they were about to bring into the world future citizens who would surely be a liability to the state, instead of an asset. We had no way in which we could provide them with the care and attention they needed, and no way to protect them from the disgrace that was certain to destroy their social value to the state.

Equally, we were unable to provide in advance for the poverty-stricken young mother who abandoned her infant—because she foresaw no way of raising a child–and who was charged with a crime for deserting it. And equally, again, we had no way to help the poor mother who could not afford medical attention in child-birth, who could not even remain away from her work long enough to regain her strength after the birth of her child—with disastrous results to both parent and offspring.

One Sunday, after a week in which I had heard several such harrowing cases, my wife and I went motoring in the country. We passed the farm of a well-known stock breeder who hailed us and invited us in. He had a reputation all over the West for raising a very strong and enduring breed of horses; and in the West, where the horses have to climb hills and mountains, such a reputation must be well-deserved. I asked him how he had won it. He replied: "There's the reason in front of you," pointing to a pasture in which a score of mares with their colts were browsing and feeding and playing about in the sunlight. "We don't put the mothers at work for several months before and after foaling. We leave the colts with them as long as possible, to feed. It makes all the difference between our horses and inferior stock." And when I thought of all those pathetic young mothers whose tales I had been hearing in court, I cried out in despair to myself: "Why can't *they* have horses' rights."

So we began our slogan "Horses rights for women" in Colorado, and presented a bill in the legislature providing that any woman who was about to become a mother might make a private application to our court and receive a sufficient maintenance for her to bear her child in circumstances of health and comfort that somewhat approached the conditions enjoyed by my friend's horses on his stock farm. When it was discovered that this bill included the relief of unmarried mothers, all argument was useless. I was "encouraging immorality." I was seriously regarded as a questionable character. The bill never came any where near consideration by the legislature. It was damned in silence. . . .

"THE WOMAN"

Praxedis Guerrero (1910)

THE LUCK of women has varied. Among the Jews, women were impure and saleable slaves, absolute property of the father. In Egypt, they could exercise tyranny over the male; in India, they were an appendage which had to disappear with the owner; in China, victims of masculine sensuality and jealousy, they had and have a sad fate; in Greece, they were considered, with some exceptions, as objects; among the Hoyas, Bedouins, and other tribes, they have enjoyed relative liberty and very friendly rules. Let us look now at the equally diverse situation among modern nations.

The morality that ancient civilizations inherited from the earliest social groups, known as clans, has been modified with the evolution of customs, with the disappearance of some necessities and the birth of others; but in general, women remain outside the place they deserve and boys, who receive their first psychic impulses of life from women, will be responsible for perpetuating the discordance between the two parts that form humanity when they grow into men.

"Feminism" serves as a base for the opposition of the enemies of the emancipation of women. Certainly there is nothing attractive about a woman police officer, about a woman removed from the sweet mission of her sex to grasp the whip of oppression, about a woman fleeing from her gracious feminine individuality, in order to assume a hybrid "masculinization."

Inferiority of women! . . . [T]o be more truthful, we should say: Enslavement of women!

Innumerable generations have passed subjugating women to the rigors of such an education. Finally, when the results of this education are plain, when the prejudices accumulated in the feminine brain and the material burden that men impose on them, act as a ballast on their lives, impeding the unencumbered flight of their intellect in the free spaces of ideas, when everything that surrounds them is oppressive and untrue, one accepts the inferiority of women, in order not to admit nor confess the inequality of circumstances and the absence of opportunities which, in spite of everything, has not impeded the beginning of the emancipation of women, aided by the heroic efforts of women themselves. Revolutionary women, morally emancipated, respond victoriously to the charge of superficiality made against their sex; they make one ponder with respectful sympathy, on the amount of courage, energy, will, sacrifice and bitterness that their labor represents; it is the greatest merit of their rebellion, compared with that of men. . . .

Religion, of whatever denomination, is the worst enemy of women. On the pretext

---

Los Angeles, 1910. Reprinted in Juan Gomez-Quiñones. Sembradores, Ricardo Flores Magon y el Partido Liberal Mexicano: A Eulogy and Critique. *Los Angeles: University of California, Los Angeles, Chicano Studies Center, 1973. Translated by Maria Massolo.*

of consolation, it annihilates their conscience; in the name of a sterile love, it snatches away real love, the source of life and human happiness; with grotesque fantasies, sketched in a sickly poetry, separating her from the strong, real, immense poetry of free existence.

Religion is an auxiliary to the despots of the home and the nation; it mission is pacification; caress or lash, cage or lasso, everything it employs leads to one end: to tame, to enslave women in the first place, because women are mothers and teachers of boys, and boys will be men.

Women have another enemy no less terrible: established custom; these venerable customs of our elders, always broken by progress and always reestablished by conservatism. Women cannot live as free companions of men because custom opposes it, because violation of custom brings disdain, mockery, insults and curses. Custom has sanctified their slavery, their perpetual minority of age, and they must continue to be slaves and pupils according to custom, without remembering that other sacred customs of our ancestors were cannibalism, human sacrifices on the altars of Huitzilopochtli, the burning alive of children and widows, the piercing of noses and lips, the worship of lizards, calves, and elephants. Yesterday's sacred customs are crimes of stupidity today. Why, then, such respect and obeisance to customs which impede the emancipation of women?

Freedom surprises those who do not understand it and those who have made degradation and ignorant misery their medium; because of this, the emancipation of women encounters a hundred opponents for every man who defends it or works for it.

Free equality does not try to make men out of women; it gives the same opportunities to both halves of the human species so that both can develop without obstacles, supporting each other naturally, without taking away rights, without usurping the place each has in nature. We men and women must fight for this rational equality, which harmonizes individual happiness with collective happiness, because without it there will always be a seed of tyranny in the home, the sprout of slavery and social misery. If a custom is a yoke, let us break with that custom no matter how sacred it may seem; by offending custom, civilization advances. "What will people say?" is a restraint; but restraints have never liberated people, satisfied hunger, nor redeemed slaves.

A SHORT HISTORY OF WOMEN'S RIGHTS (excerpt)

Eugene Hecker (1910)

IN CONCLUDING this chapter, I wish to enlarge somewhat upon the philosophy of suffrage as exhibited in the preceding chapter. The "woman's sphere" argument is still being worked overtime by anti-suffrage societies, whose members rather inconsistently leave their "sphere," the home, to harangue in public and buttonhole legislators to vote against the franchise for women. "A woman's place," says the sage Hennessy, "is in th' home, darning her husband's childher. I mean—" "I know what ye mean," says Mr. Dooley. . . . A century ago, the home was the woman's sphere. To-day the man has deliberately dragged her out of it to work for him in factory and store because he can secure her labor more cheaply than that of men and is, besides, safer in abusing her when she has no direct voice in legislation. Are the manufacturers willing to send their 1,300,000 female employees back to their "sphere"? If they are not, but desire their labor, they ought in fairness to allow them the privileges of workmen—that is, of citizens, participating actively in the political, social, and economic development of the country. . . .

The home is not necessarily every woman's sphere and neither is motherhood. Neither is it every woman's congenital duty to make herself attractive to men. The "woman's pages" of newspapers, filled with gratuitous advice on these subjects, never tell men that their duty is fatherhood or that they should make themselves attractive or that their sphere is also the home. Until these one-sided points of view are adjusted to a more reasonable basis, we shall not reach an understanding. They are as unjust as the farmer who ploughs with a steam plow and lets his wife cart water from a distant well instead of providing convenient plumbing.

Women who are fitted for motherhood and have a talent for it can enter it with advantage. There is a talent for motherhood exactly as there is for other things. Other women have genius which can be of greatest service to the community in other ways. They should have opportunity to find their sphere. If this is "Feminism," it is also simple justice. One reason that we are at sea in some of the problems of the women's-rights movement, is that the history of women has been mainly written by men. The question of motherhood, the sexual life of women, and the position of women as it has been or is likely to be affected by their sexual characteristics, must be more exactly ascertained before definite conclusions can be reached. . . .

From A Short History of Women's Rights: From the Days of Augustus to the Present Time, with Special Reference to England and the United States. *New York: G. P. Putnam's Sons, 1910.*

"TO WOMEN"

Ricardo Flores Magon (1910)

COMPAÑERAS:

Revolution approaches! With angered eyes, and flaming hair, her trembling hands knock anxiously on the doors of our nation. Let us welcome her with serenity, for although she carries death in her breast, she is the announcement of life, the herald of hope. She will destroy and create at the same time; she will raze and build. Her fists are the invincible fists of a people in rebellion. she does not offer roses or caresses; she offers an axe and a torch.

Interrupting the millennial feast of the content, sedition raises her head, and the prophecy of Balthasar has with time become a clenched fist hanging over the heads of the so-called ruling class. Revolution approaches! Her mission will ignite the flames in which privilege and injustice will burn. Compañeras, do not fear the revolution. You constitute one-half of the human species and what affects humanity affects you as an integral part of it. If men are slaves, you are too. Bondage does not recognize sex; the infamy that degrades men equally degrades you. You cannot escape the shame of oppression. The same forces which conquer men strangle you.

We must stand in solidarity in the grand conquest for freedom and happiness. Are you mothers? Are you wives? Are you sisters? Are you daughters? Your duty is to help man; to be there to encourage him when he vacillates; stand by his side when he suffers; to lighten his sorrow; to laugh and to sing with him when victory smiles. You don't understand politics? This is not a question of politics; this is a matter of life or death. Man's bondage is yours and perhaps yours is more sorrowful, more sinister, and more infamous.

Are you a worker? Because you are a woman you are paid less than men, and made to work harder. You must suffer the impertinence of the foreman or proprietor; and if you are attractive, the bosses will make advances. Should you weaken, they would rob you of your virtue in the same cowardly manner as you are robbed of the product of your labor.

Under this regime of social injustice which corrupts humanity, the existence of women wavers in the wretchedness of a destiny which fades away either in the blackness of fatigue and hunger or in the obscurity of marriage and prostitution.

In order to fully appreciate women's part in universal suffering, it is necessary to study page by page this somber book called Life, which like so many thorns strips away the flesh of humanity.

So ancient is women's misfortune that its

"Editorial: To Women." Regeneracion *(24 September 1910). Translated by Prensa Sembradora, 8 March 1974. Reprinted in* Mexican Women in the United States: Struggles Past and Present, *ed. Magdalena Mora and Adelaida R. Del Castillo. Los Angeles: University of California, Los Angeles, Chicano Studies Research Center Publications, 1980.*

origins are lost in the obscurity of legend. In the infancy of mankind, the birth of a female child was considered a disgrace to the tribe. Women toiled the land, carried firewood from the forest and water from the stream, tended the livestock, constructed shelters, wove cloth, cooked food, and cared for the sick and the young. The filthiest work was done by women. Should an ox die of fatigue, the women took its place pulling the plow, and when war broke out between rivaling tribes, the women merely changed masters, and continued under the lash of the new owners, carrying out their tasks as beasts of burden.

Later, under the influence of Greek civilization, women were elevated one step in the esteem of men. No longer were they beasts of burden as in the primitive clan, nor did they lead secluded lives as in oriental societies. If they belonged to a free class, their role was one of procreators of citizens for the state; if they were slaves, they provided workers for the fields.

Christianity aggravated the situation of women with its contempt for the flesh. The founding fathers of the Church vented their outbursts of rage against feminine qualities. St. Augustine, St. Thomas, and other saints, before whose statues women now kneel, referred to women as daughters of the devil, vessels of impurity, and condemned them to the tortures of hell.

Women's position in this century varies according to their social stature; but in spite of the refinements of customs and the progress of philosophy, women continue subordinated to men by tradition and laws. Women are perpetually treated as minors when the law places the wife under the custody of the husband. She cannot vote or be elected, and to enter into civil contracts she must own a sizeable fortune.

Throughout history women have been considered inferior to men, not only by law but also by custom. From this erroneous and unjust concept derives the misfortune which she has suffered since humanity differentiated itself from lower animal forms by the use of fire and tools.

Humiliated, degraded, bound by chains of tradition to an irrational inferiority, indoctrinated in the affairs of heaven by clerics, but totally ignorant of world problems, she is suddenly caught in the whirlwind of industrial production which above all requires cheap labor to sustain the competition created by the voracious "princes of capital" who exploit her circumstances. She is not as prepared as men for the industrial struggle, nor is she organized with the women of her class to fight alongside her brother workers against the rapacity of capitalism.

For this reason, though women work more than men, they are paid less, and misery, mistreatment, and insult are today as yesterday the bitter harvest for a whole existence of sacrifice. So meager are women's salaries that frequently they must prostitute themselves to meet their families' basic needs, especially when in the marketplace of marriage they do not find a husband. When it is motivated by economic security instead of love, marriage is but another form of prostitution, sanctioned by the law and authorized by public officials. That is, a wife sells her body for food exactly as does a prostitute; this occurs in the majority of marriages. And what could be said of the vast army of women who do not succeed in finding a husband? The increasing cost of life's basic necessities; the displacement of human labor by the perfection of machinery; the ever-decreasing price of human labor—all contribute to the burden of supporting a family. The compulsory draft tears strong and healthy young men from the bosom of a society and lessens the number eligible for marriage. Migration of workers, caused by economic and political phenomena, also reduces the number of men capable of marriage. Alcoholism, gambling and other ills of society further reduce the number of available men. Consequently, the number of single women grows alarmingly. Since their situation is so precarious, they swell the ranks of prostitution, accelerating the degeneration of the human race by this debasement of body and spirit.

"THE ROLE OF WOMEN IN AMERICAN HISTORY"

Arthur Meier Schlesinger (1922)

AN EXAMINATION of the standard histories of the United States and of the history textbooks in use in our schools raises the pertinent question whether women have ever made any contributions to American national progress that are worthy of record. If the silence of the historians is taken to mean anything, it would appear that one-half of our population have been negligible factors in our country's history.

Before accepting the truth of this assumption, the facts of our history need to be raked over from a new point of view. It should not be forgotten that all of our great historians have been men and were likely therefore to be influenced by a *sex* interpretation of history all the more potent because unconscious. Furthermore, while it is indisputable that the commanding positions in politics, diplomacy, and the army have always been held by men, it is also true that our ideas of what is important in our past have greatly changed in recent years.

If, as the following sketch seeks to show, the women of the nation have played their full part in American development, the pall of silence which historians have allowed to rest over their services and achievements may possibly constitute the chief reason why the women have been so slow in gaining equal rights with the men in this the greatest democracy in the world. The men of the nation have, perhaps not unnaturally, felt disinclined to endow with equality a class of persons who, so far as they knew, had never proved their fitness for public service and leadership in the past history of the country. Any consideration of woman's part in American history must include the protracted struggle of the sex for larger rights

---

From New Viewpoints in American History. *New York: Macmillan, 1922.*

and opportunities, a story that in itself is one of the noblest chapters in the history of American democracy. . . .

Women are today standing upon the threshold of a new era in the history of their sex; and whatever affects the status of woman in America will affect the entire people of which they are so intimately a part. Women in the United States are now, in most respects, a part of human society literally and directly, not merely as represented by men to whom they "belong" in some relation. They are directly responsible for their choices and decisions and are placed in a position to increase immeasurably their contributions to American development. In speculating as to the use that women will make of the vote, it is not to be overlooked that the women are better prepared for their new responsibilities than any previous class admitted to the franchise. The beneficiaries of white manhood suffrage in Jackson's day were undisciplined and uneducated; and the black men, enfranchised a generation later, were on an infinitely lower plane of public morality and individual fitness. The value of the ballot to the women themselves as an educative force cannot be doubted; and any knowledge of the past services of women to American history is an assurance that the women will use their new power for the good of the nation and of humanity.

MARRIAGE AND DIVORCE REFORMS

"LOVE, MARRIAGE AND DIVORCE"

Stephen Pearl Andrews (1853)

WITH SOME MEN and some women, the instinct for Freedom is a domination too potent to be resisted. An association with angels under constraint would be to them a Hell. The language of their souls is "Give me Liberty, or give me death." Such natures have noble and generous propensities in other directions. Say to a man of this sort, abjure Freedom or abjure Love, and, along with it, the dear object whom you have already compromised in the world's estimation, and who can foresee the issue of that terrible conflict of the passions which must ensue? In the vast majority of such cases, notwithstanding all, Generosity and Love conquer, and the man knowingly sacrifices himself and all future thought of happiness, in the privation of Freedom, the consciousness of which no Affection, no amount of the World's Good Opinion, no consideration of any kind, can compensate him for, nor reconcile him to. It would be strange, on the other hand, if the balance of motive never fell upon the other side; and then comes the terrible desertion, the crushing weight of public scorn upon the unprotected head of the wretched woman, and the lasting destruction of the happiness of all concerned, in another of the stereotyped forms of evil.

I do not deny that, among those men, nor, indeed, that the great majority of those men who seduce and betray women, are bad men; that is, that they are undeveloped, hardened, and perverted beings, hardly capable of compassion or remorse. What I do affirm is, that there are, also, among them, men of the most refined, and delicate, and gentle natures, fitted to endure the most intense suffering themselves while they inflict it—none but their own hearts can tell how unwillingly—on those they most dearly prize in the world; and that Society is in fault to place such men in such a cruel conflict with themselves, in which some proportion of the whole number so tried is sure to fall. I also affirm that, of the former class—the undeveloped, hardened, and perverted—their undevelopment, hardening, and perversion are again chargeable upon our false Social Arrangements, and, more than all else, perhaps, upon that very exclusion from a genial and familiar association with the female sex, now deemed essential, in order to maintain the Marriage Institution in "its Purity." And, finally, I affirm, that, while such men

---

From Love, Marriage and Divorce and the Sovereignty of the Individual. *N.p.: Stringer & Townsend, 1853.*

exist, the best protection that Women *can* have against their machinations is more Development on her own part, such as can alone come from more Freedom, more Knowledge of the world, more Familiarity with Men, more ability to judge of character and to read the intentions of those by whom she is approached, more Womanhood, in fine; instead of a namby-pamby, lackadaisical, half-silly interestingness, cultured and procured by a nun-like seclusion from business, from Freedom of locomotion, from unrestrained intercommunication of thought and sentiment with the male sex, and, in a word, from almost the whole circle of the rational means of development.

He must be an unobservant man, indeed, who does not perceive the pregnant signs all around him that approximations toward the opinions now uttered by me are everywhere existent, and becoming every day nearer and more frequent. . . .

The restraints of Marriage are becoming daily less. Its oppressions are felt more and more. *There are to-day in our midst ten times as many fugitives from Matrimony as there are fugitives from Slavery; and it may well be doubted if the aggregate, or the average, of their sufferings has been less.* There is hardly a country village that has not from one to a dozen such persons. When these unfortunates, flying from the blessings of one of our *peculiar* and *divine* institutions, hitherto almost wholly unquestioned, happen to be Women—the weaker sex—they are contemptuously designated "Grass-Widows;" as "runaway" or "free nigger" is, in like manner, applied to the outlaws of another "domestic" arrangement—Freedom in either case becoming, by a horrible social inversion, a badge of reproach. These severed halves of the matrimonial unit are, nevertheless, achieving respectability by virtue of numbers, and in America, at least, have nearly ceased to suffer any loss of caste by the peculiarity of their social condition. Divorce is more and more freely applied for, and easily obtained. Bastard children are now hardly persecuted at all by that sanctimonious Phariseeism which, a few generations ago, hunted them to the death, for no fault of theirs. The Rights of Women are every day more and more loudly discussed. Marriage has virtually ceased to claim the sanction of Religion, fallen into the hands of the civil magistrate, and come to be regarded as merely a civil contract. While thus recognized as solely a legal Convention, the repugnance for merely *Conventional* marriages (*Marriages de Convenance*) is yet deepening in the public mind into horror, and taking the place of that heretofore felt against a genuine passion not sanctified by the *blessing of the Church.* I quote from one of the most Conservative writers of the age when I say, that "it is not the mere ring and the orange blossom which constitute the difference between virtue and vice."

Indeed, it may be stated as the growing Public Sentiment of Christendom already, that the Man and Woman who do not LOVE have no right, before God, to live together as MAN and WIFE, no matter how solemn the marriage service which may have been mumbled over them. This is the NEGATIVE statement of a grand TRUTH, already arrived at and becoming daily louder and more peremptory in its utterance. How long, think you, it will be before the Converse, or POSITIVE, side of the same TRUTH will be affirmed, namely, that the Man and Woman who do LOVE, can live together in PURITY without any mummery at all—that it is LOVE that *sanctifies*—not the Blessing of the Church?

Such is my doctrine. Such is the horrid heresy of which I am guilty. And such, say what you will, is the eternal, inexpugnable TRUTH of God and Nature. Batter at it till your bones ache, and you can never successfully assail it. Sooner or later you must come to it, and whether it shall be sooner or later is hardly left to your option. The progress of Opinion, the great growth of the world, in this age, is sweeping all men, with the strength of an ocean current, to the acceptance of these views of Love and Marriage, to the acceptance of Universal Freedom—Freedom to Feel and Act, as well as Freedom to Think—to the acceptance, in fine, of THE SOVEREIGNTY OF EVERY INDIVIDUAL, TO BE EXERCISED AT HIS OWN COST. If our remaining Institutions are found to be adverse to this Freedom, so that bad results follow from its acceptance, then our remaining Institutions are wrong, and the remedy is to be sought in still farther and more radical changes. . . .

"LETTERS TO LUCY STONE"

Henry Brown Blackwell (1853–1854)

13 June 1853

WHEN I BEGAN this note I intended to write six lines & then stop. But talking to you is like talking to myself & I find five thousand things that I should like to say, but will not. Only this much—You & I have talked frankly together & understand each other. Let me be *your friend* & write to you occasionally. If, as I believe, your views on certain subjects change, prove your consistency to Truth, by changing with them. If not stay—where you are. In any case, I shall esteem it a good fortune to have known & still to know you. If I know myself my object is not happiness in itself but to live a manly life and to aid everyone else to do so. Meantime try actual marriages not by your own standard, but by that of those who are parties to them. You will greatly modify your estimate of it. I believe it is as imperfect as the people themselves no more so. I believe some day you ought to & will marry somebody—perhaps not me, if not—a better person. Believe me, the mass of men are not *intentionally* unjust to women, nor the mass of women consciously oppressed. And just as soon and as fast as you can inspire women to step forward and take higher social positions, you will find Society after a period of probation, acquiesce as a matter of course. Positive action *proves itself* and always commands respect.

The difficulty our new theory meets with is, that people generally, wanting our ideal, criticize our position by their low standards of desire & possibility. I do hope & believe you are gradually awakening their minds & elevating their conceptions. But the great mass of people will only be convinced by *constructive* action on the part of women,

(LOC, Blackwell Family Papers)

practically achieving their claims. Let a woman prove that she can speak, write, preach, edit newspapers, practice medicine, law & surgery—carry on business & do every other human thing. And if possible let her prove too that she can do each & all of these & be a true woman in other relations also. If it be true that a woman *cannot be* a wife & mother consistently with the exercise of a profession, it justifies to a great extent the argument of our antagonists who say that very thing. For myself I protest against this doctrine. The more high our ideal of life, the more careful we should be against improper ties—the more dangerous is our experiment in marrying, but still the possibility & propriety of a connection with *an equal to ourselves* remains unaltered. I think if the pursuit of any human profession disqualified me for marriage or any other relation necessary to the highest development of the soul, I, as a man, should spurn the profession and prefer eternal exile from the paths of men, to falsehood to Nature & Destiny. But herein I think is the legitimate function of Reason, to so organize and construct our circumstances that we may reconcile the conflict of circumstances & duties and be true to our *whole nature* & live a symmetrical, rational life true to all our faculties. . . .

24 August 1853

I am glad you sympathize with my theory of *equality* in *marriage.* I knew you would do so of course but still it is satisfactory to hear you express it. But your lady friends were not far out, when they said "no man would ever submit to such a marriage." In practice a minority I think might do so, but *in theory* scarcely any. The *idea* of a loving & protective superiority is *ingrained* in men. They do not thereby suppose any conscious oppression—but regard it as a fixed fact that women do not & cannot desire absolute equality in the active affairs of life.

This summer, I have been travelling in a carriage with two business friends. Every day we discussed the anti-slavery & woman's rights. The former to a certain extent they could accept. But the whole womans movement they could not swallow *at all.* My idea of marriage especially struck them as ludicrous & unnatural. Yet both are honest, intelligent & affectionate & will make *excellent husbands.* For women, like men, in that stage of development, are incapable of appreciating the gospel of *individualism* & the glory of mental & material independence. I believe nineteen women out of twenty would be unhappy with a husband who, like myself, would repudiate supremacy. The proof of my opinion is that the great majority of people, in endeavoring to imagine a contrary state of things, conceive of the woman as the *leader* & the man as the *subservient.* Of course if there is to be a *head* to the family, while women are actually so inferior in developement of mind, no man can think with patience of playing the "hen-pecked husband." Hence the inveterate prejudice you have to contend with. Practically, the superior woman does oftentimes take the lead of the inferior husband & must always do so. But this to my mind is simply just as bad & no worse than, the opposite mismatch. But analyze the opposition to our view—it is based on an apparent *incapability* of understanding *absolute equality* between the sexes on the part of most people. Where there is no subjection on either side there can be, of course, no degradation or conflict of dignities. . . .

Now I have felt for years the most imperious necessity for marriage. At times I think I *must* quit dreaming & get a wife. But when it comes to the point, I find that I *cannot* forego my ideal. *Equality with me is a passion.* I dislike equally to assume, or to endure authority. But the great difficulty in realizing a true marriage after you find the right persons is that all the arrangements of Society are made for the average convenience—& fetter a woman with household cares & ties, while they impose on a man the whole burden of acquiring subsistence. I confess I see no hope of making the future of women *as a sex* what it should be, except by household association. So long as our present system of isolated families is maintained married women will be greatly precluded from public & professional pursuits. And indeed when I consider how degrading & unworthy all human pursuits not strictly scientific or literary are now, I do not feel any great anxiety to see many women undertake them. I feel so thorough a contempt for the whole sphere of business & am so desirous of getting out of it, that I am not able to get up any enthusiasm at the prospect of female merchants, or merchants clerks. I do indeed want to see the scope of women's employment enlarged, so that they may be better able to support themselves, when necessary, but it is only as a choice of evils.

You say in your letter that you never expect to give up lecturing & speaking but from death or old age. I certainly hope you never may, unless for some even wider sphere of action. As a writer if favorably situated, you might perhaps reach even more minds & in connexion with occasional public speaking be even more efficient. Such a position, with the ear of the public, is a grand one but somewhat difficult to attain. I hope to reach it some day through the medium of a widely circulated western newspaper. But surely you never did me the injustice to suppose that I could desire, under any circumstances, that you should withdraw yourself from public effort. . . . How much more should I desire that the glorious gift of eloquence which you certainly possess should not be withdrawn from the advocacy of great & unpopular Truths to be wasted upon a few, however dear. It would be like buying some beautiful spot of Nature hitherto the resort of hundreds & fencing it in with "no admittance" & "Spring guns" placarded in true "dog in the manger" fashion.

But for myself I dont see why, in order to do good, you should find it necessary to treat yourself a great deal worse than the Southerners treat their negroes, by depriving yourself of entrance into those personal relations which as you yourself acknowledge are a *want of our nature* & which I regard as a *duty* of our very organization. If this true idea of marriage cannot be realized, what is the use of having it? How can it be so eloquently preached as by *living it out* in practice. You speak of marriage to those in it. They may say to you with reason, as they have said to me—"you never have been married, or you would not so regard it. You know nothing about it." Your idea of the duty of sacrificing the lower to the higher I *fully approve.* But I think you estimate too low the sacred law of the affections, which Theodore Parker places with reason *above* the intellectual faculties—yes—& above even the *moral sense.* I, at first, thought Parker erred in setting the affections above the sense of right & wrong, but on reflection, I agree with him.

I think you are very right in saying that it is absolute madness to enter into marriage until *you know* thoroughly the whole nature of the other party. So I think, too. But if that nature possess the genuine affinity—are circumstances so satanic that marriage involves the withdrawal from public life? I do not see that. A woman unsuitably married like Mrs Stanton may find herself fettered—or in difficult circumstances like Mrs Weld formerly. But a woman who unites herself with a fellow worker with sufficient means & position to prevent the necessity of her drudging—free to be at home when she pleases & to leave it when she thinks it best—with a home of her own to rest & study & with friends to relieve her many responsibilities—is this a position necessarily less influential than your present one? I dont wonder at your resolving never to marry. Situated as women are I think you are wise in omitting the relation altogether from your prospectus of life. But if in the mysterious Providence of God you ever find the right person, you will have to enlarge & vary your theory to greet the unexpected Advent. I do not ask you to assume that I, or anyone else, am that person. I only wish I might prove to be so—that's all. . . .

3 January 1855

. . . I am sorry you should still feel as though *martyrdom* would demand *refraining* from marriage rather than *suffering* the law's injustice. . . . Why Lucy dear—You even now occupy a position similar in *kind* & differing only in *degree.* The law now says—You are not *fully* a citizen—You shall not *vote* shall not make laws, nor say who shall make them. You suffer this injustice for the same reason as you will the other. You *cannot help it.* "Ah, but I *can* avoid it in the one case and not in the other"—you will perhaps say. You *can* indeed avoid it *in both cases,* but in both it *costs too much.* You can avoid the political injustice you now suffer by retiring from civilization to some uninhabited, or barbarous country where individualism is the only law. You can avoid the additional injustice attached to marriage by *violating* the *divine law* which says *marry,* or by going to the same barbarous wilderness—& *in no other ways,* but these two.

Now then, if we could find a little band of men & women who, *to make a perfect State* would withdraw to some unclaimed wilderness & there found a nobler New England—I am ready to go. But I do not think any human laws have such claims upon my obedience as to *compel me* to go. I have a perfect right to stay & set the laws at defiance. We have a right to be a law unto ourselves. Would it not be a *slavish* doctrine to preach that we *ought* to sentence ourselves to celibacy because men have enacted injustice into a statute. But Lucy dear I want to make a *protest* distinct and *emphatic* against the laws. I wish, as a husband, to *renounce* all the privileges which the law confers upon me, which are not strictly *mutual* & I intend to do so. Help me to draw one up. When we marry, I will publicly state before our friends a brief enumeration of these usurpations & distinctly pledge myself to never avail myself of them *under any circumstances.* Surely *such a marriage* will not degrade you, dearest—Lucy, I *wish I* could take the position of the wife under the law & give you that of a husband. I would rather submit to the injustice a hundred times, than subject you to it. . . .

"PROTEST"

Henry Brown Blackwell and Lucy Stone (1855)

MARRIAGE OF LUCY STONE UNDER PROTEST.

It was my privilege to celebrate May day by officiating at a wedding in a farm-house among the hills of West Brookfield. The bridegroom was a man of tried worth, a leader in the Western Anti-Slavery Movement; and the bride was one whose fair name is known throughout the nation; one whose rare intellectual qualities are excelled by the private beauty of her heart and life.

I never perform the marriage ceremony without a renewed sense of the iniquity of our present system of laws in respect to marriage; a system by which "man and wife are one, and that one is the husband." It was with my hearty concurrence, therefore, that the following protest was read and signed, as a part of the nuptial ceremony; and I send it to you, that others may be induced to do likewise. REV. THOMAS WENTWORTH HIGGINSON.

WHILE ACKNOWLEDGING our mutual affection by publicly assuming the relationship of husband and wife, yet in justice to ourselves and a great principle, we deem it a duty to declare that this act on our part implies no sanction of, nor promise of voluntary obedience to such of the present laws of marriage, as refuse to recognize the wife as an independent, rational being, while they confer upon the husband an injurious and unnatural superiority, investing him with legal powers which no honorable man would exercise, and which no man should possess. We protest especially against the laws which give to the husband:

1. The custody of the wife's person.

2. The exclusive control and guardianship of their children.

3. The sole ownership of her personal, and use of her real estate, unless previously settled upon her, or placed in the hands of trustees, as in the case of minors, lunatics, and idiots.

4. The absolute right to the product of her industry.

5. Also against laws which give to the widower so much larger and more permanent an interest in the property of his deceased wife, than they give to the widow in that of the deceased husband.

6. Finally, against the whole system by which "the legal existence of the wife is suspended during marriage," so that in most

---

Reprinted in HWS, *vol. 1.*

States, she neither has a legal part in the choice of her residence, nor can she make a will, nor sue or be sued in her own name, nor inherit property.

We believe that personal independence and equal human rights can never be forfeited, except for crime; that marriage should be an equal and permanent partnership, and so recognized by law; that until it is so recognized, married partners should provide against the radical injustice of present laws, by every means in their power.

We believe that where domestic difficulties arise, no appeal should be made to legal tribunals under existing laws, but that all difficulties should be submitted to the equitable adjustment of arbitrators mutually chosen.

Thus reverencing law, we enter our protest against rules and customs which are unworthy of the name, since they violate justice, the essence of law.

(Signed), HENRY B. BLACKWELL,
LUCY STONE

"LETTER TO HIS SISTER"

Ramon Sanchez (1862)

I WAS NOT a little surprised last Tuesday morning by the receipt of your letter. I had abandoned all expectations of our getting a line from you, and I am truly glad to know that your correspondent in another direction, does not monopolize your entire time, and that for the future, there is a fair prospect of my receiving an occasional line from you.

Laura wrote you a long letter a few days since, so there is little left for me to say in addition to what she has told you all, in her numerous letters.

We have both been quite bussy [sic] for the past ten days in arranging and fixing up things generally, so that now we are pretty comfortably located. I can assure you it has been no small job, and this being our first attempt at house keeping of course there was much more to be done than I had any idea of. I was surprised to find that there could be so many little things to be done about a house necessary to comfort and neatness. . . .

Laura sent, in her last letter, a very correct plan of our house, which will give you a very good idea of how we are at present located. I have just had a high board fence put around the yard which makes the place quite secure and private.

Now I suppose you would like to have description of our mode of housekeeping and the part I take in the performance. Well here

(WCL, Crittenden Papers)

it is. We retire, generally, about two o'clock, sometimes earlier, if we are particularly tired and sleepy. We rise at six o clock in the morning if we wake up at that hour, (which does not always happen) I make a fire in the stove, put on the kettle of water, sweep out the kitchen, grind the coffee, open the doors and windows, and sweep out the hall and front porch. By the time I have finished doing all this, Laura makes her appearance in the kitchen, then I retire and finish my toilet. After that I set the breakfast table and fill the pitcher with fresh water; by that time breakfast is ready, and I assist in putting it on the table. After breakfast I help to clear off the table and do sundry other "chores", when it is time for me to go to the office. The dinner program is much the same as the above with the exception, that I assist Laura to wash the dishes and clean up the kitchen.

You will doubtless be very much amused at the idea of my doing so many things about the house that do not seem to be properly, any part of a man's duty. But I consider it the bounden duty of every husband to assist his wife in all things, and relieve her in every possible way, of as much care and labor as he can. I know that most married men pay very little attention to such things, and if they think of them at all, it is only to say that, "such trifles are beneath their manhood and no part of their duty." Now I would not give a copper cent for any man who would sit down in ease and idleness at home, or loaf around town, and let his wife toil and labor for his comfort and pleasure, and rarely, if ever, offer to assist her. Such a "fellow" is not worthy the name of "man."

Now let me give you this one little piece of advice. If you are ever married, and go to housekeeping, and should be so circumstanced as to be compelled to do your own house work, be sure to commence in time to break your "lord" into helping you in all things. He may at first neglect to do it from thoughtlessness, if so, a gentle reminder from you will soon bring him to his work. . . .

"PROSTITUTION WITHIN THE MARRIAGE BOND"

B. O. Flower (1880?)

FOR AGES men regarded women as slaves, whose duty it was to perform menial tasks, wait upon them, and be the instruments of their sensual gratification. Later, among the wealthier classes, woman became more or less a doll or petted child, who for sweetmeats, flattery, and fine presents was expected to give her body to her master. 'Still later, she was supposed to come into much higher and truer relations to man; but, unfortunately, this was more largely theoretical than actual. And at the present time, in order to consider one of the chief factors in the immorality of to-day, we must frankly face the problem of prostitution within the marriage relation. . . . A slothful conservatism seeks to impress woman with the idea that she is free, and that to be coddled or flattered in slavery is for her an ideal and ultimate condition. It even gravely informs her that she is the real ruler; and, sad to relate, this calumny is not infrequently parroted by women who instead of learning to think independently have been content for ages to take their ideas unquestioningly from their clergymen, their fathers, brothers, and husbands. It does not occur to these echoes that, if woman rules, she has sealed the age-of-consent statutes, or that she has championed injustice in the statutes which relate to marriage and which practically make her the dependent and, in a measure, the slave of her husband. Happily the echoes among women are rapidly giving place to independent thinkers, who appreciate the grave responsibilities woman owes to posterity, no less than to her sex; and in this recognition lies, to a great degree, the promise of the future.

No more unblushing falsehood has ever been made current by conventionalism than that woman is free in the marriage relation. Society clings most tenaciously to ancient ideals and customs, and is ever ready to cast discredit upon the outraged wife who braves the *dicta* of conservatism, even for the protection of posterity from disease and lust-cursed offspring. Law also places her at a disadvantage, in that the plea of sexual excess is not regarded as a crime by the courts, since the laws do not recognize the right of the wife to her body.

Our statutes, furthermore, do not protect the sacred rights of individuals by providing that divorce cases be heard in private; and this, in effect, would prevent a large majority of women from securing legal separation an account of sexual excesses, or what is virtually *compulsory prostitution*; not only because society has so long been accustomed to stone the woman that the unfortunate victim of lust would inevitably fall under the ban of conventionalism if she un-

Reprinted in Divorce: The First Debates, *ed. David J. Rothman and Sheila M. Rothman. New York: Garland, 1987.*

folded to the world the story of her enforced degradation, but because her innate moral sensibility would lead her in many cases to choose a life of physical and mental agony and an early grave in preference to having the details of her shame and humiliation made the subject of gossip at sewing circles, afternoon teas, and among men in their clubs, after being flaunted in the columns of the sensational press.

Again, a large number of women are rendered absolutely dependent upon their husband, because there is no equitable statutory provision for the wife's becoming possessor of a portion of her husband's property at the marriage altar. Hence if she leaves the man who has forfeited all claim to her love and respect by nameless abuses of that which must be regarded as holy if humanity is to rise and the children who come are to be clean and exalted natures; if she refuses to descend into the valley of death to bring forth children dowered with disease and inordinate passion, and thus destined to be a curse to themselves and to the society of to-morrow,—if she asserts the divinity within her, she must needs go forth penniless and under the ban of conventionalism *for being true to herself and for respecting the rights of the unborn and her obligations to posterity. . . .*

About all these most vital subjects a fatal silence has been maintained—at the fireside, in the pulpit, and in the educational training of the young. I am convinced that a very large proportion of the misery and prostitution now being undergone within the marriage relation is due to this widespread ignorance. Ignorance and thoughtlessness are filling prisons and insane asylums to-day and dowering the civilization of to-morrow with a generation whose moral sensibilities are necessarily blunted, and who, through heredity and prenatal and post-natal influences, are essentially creatures of lust rather than strong, clean-souled, clear-brained, heaven-aspiring men and women. . . .

In order that woman may cease to be in any sense the slave of her husband, provision should be made for her to become possessed at marriage of half the property the husband owns, with an additional amount to be hers whenever a child is born. If, on account of cruelty, abuse, or neglect, she finds life with her husband unbearable, she should have this property in her own right. The true interests of society and sound morality cannot be conserved by compelling a woman to live with a man who has forfeited her respect and love. When a woman is forced to bear children to a man she hates or no longer loves, she is by law obliged to prostitute her body, and the child is cursed before it is born. I yield to no man in my regard for the sacred relations of married life; the sanctity and purity of the home I believe to be essential to enduring civilization; but I am not blind to the fact that marriage, home, and posterity are alike dishonored when women are forced to submit to sexual abuses which are revolting to their souls and which wreck their physical health; and I can conceive of few crimes greater than the bringing into the world of children of lust or hate.

I believe that divorces should be freely granted to women when their husbands persist in indulging in sexual abuses, when they drink, or when they treat their wives with that cruel neglect which kills love. And I furthermore believe that divorce cases should be heard in private, that the press should be prohibited from parading the details of shame and humiliation which are filling the lives of so many suffering wives with untold misery. I believe that the jury in divorce cases should be composed of at least one-half women; and in the event of a divorce being granted, I believe that the mother who bore the children should have their custody unless there be special and obvious reasons for the court to decide otherwise. In a word, for the welfare of parenthood, for the rights of the unborn, and for the cause of sound morality, I would favor such wise and just legislation as would protect women from a life of prostitution under the sanction of law and respectability. . . .

It is idle and absurd to say she could leave him. The majority of women who are wrecked in health, and perhaps encumbered by one or more children, have no means of resource for a livelihood. The years they might have spent in learning a profession have been wasted in administering to a man who promised much, but who after marriage proved unworthy of love or respect. Now, to forbid such a woman to obtain a divorce, who through no fault or sin of her own is driven to that step, or to prohibit her from again marrying would be, in effect, to chain her for life to the debauched and debased creature she loathes, and in all probability to make her an unwilling instrument in cursing posterity with children born of rum and passion on the father's side and loathing on the part of the helpless but prostituted wife. Laws which would operate in such a way are not only cruelly unjust to the wife, but they are essentially criminal and immoral.

When justice is accorded to woman in the marital relation, and she shall be protected from enforced maternity and prostitution, then I believe the time will come when society will recognize the fact that true marriage is impossible where the two contracting parties are not drawn together by pure love; and the love which shall so unite husband and wife will not only hold them together, but will ever draw them upward toward the loftiest ideals, and the children of such a union will be the welcome offspring of love. I believe the time will come when civilization will recognize the injury inflicted on society by the grave infraction of the moral law by which children of lust or hate come as a fruit of enforced maternity. . . .

"SEX RIGHTS," SEXUALITY, AND BIRTH CONTROL

MORAL PHYSIOLOGY (excerpt)

Robert Dale Owen (1831)

It is evident, that, to married persons, the power of limiting their offspring to their circumstances is most desirable. It may often promote the harmony, peace, and comfort of families; sometimes it may save from bankruptcy and ruin, and sometimes it may rescue the mother from premature death. In *no* case can it, by possibility, be worse than superfluous. *In no case can it be mischievous.*

If the moral feelings were carefully cultivated—if we were taught to consult, in every thing, rather the welfare of those we love than our own, how strongly would these arguments be felt! No man ought even to *desire* that a woman should become the mother of his children, unless it was her express wish, and unless he knew it to be for her welfare, that she should. Her feelings, her interests, should be for him in this matter *an imperative law.* She it is who bears the burden, and therefore with her also should the decision rest. Surely it may well be a question whether it be desirable, or whether any man ought to ask, that the whole life of an intellectual, cultivated woman, should be spent in bearing a family of twelve or fifteen children—to the ruin, perhaps, of her constitution, if not to the overstocking of the world. No man ought to require or expect it.

Shall I be told, that this is the very romance of morality? Alas! that what ought to be a matter of every-day practice—a commonplace exercise of the duties and charities of life—a bounden duty—an instance of domestic courtesy too universal either to excite remark or merit commendation—alas! that a virtue so humble that its absence ought to be reproached as a crime, should, to our selfish perceptions, seem but a fastidious refinement, or a fanciful supererogation! . . .

But there are other cases, it will be said, where the knowledge of such a check would be mischievous. If young women, it will be argued, were absolved from the fear of consequences, they would rarely preserve their chastity. Unlegalized connections would be common and seldom detected. Seduction would be facilitated.—Let us dispassionately examine this argument.

I fully agree with that most amiable of

From Moral Physiology; or, A Brief and Plain Treatise on the Population Question. *New York: Wright & Owen, 1831.*

moral heretics, Shelley, that "Seduction, which term could have no meaning in a rational society, has now a most tremendous one." It matters not how artificial the penalty which society has chosen to affix to a breach of her capricious decrees. Society has the power in her own hands; and that moral Shylock, Public Opinion, enforces the penalty, even though it cost the life of the victim. The consequences, then, to the poor sufferer, whose offence is but an error of judgment or a weakness of the heart, are the same as if her imprudence were indeed a crime of the blackest dye. And his conduct who, for a momentary, selfish gratification, will deliberately entail a life of wretchedness on one whose chief fault, perhaps, was her misplaced confidence in a hypocrite, is not one whit excused by the folly and injustice of the sentence. . . . How then should he be regarded, who makes it a trade to win a woman's gentle affections, betray her generous confidence, and then, when the consequences become apparent, abandon her to dependence, and the scorn of a cold, a self-righteous, and a wicked world; a world which will forgive any thing but rebellion against its tyranny, and in whose eyes it seems the greatest of crimes to be unsuspecting and warm-hearted?

And, let me ask, what is it gives to the arts of seduction their sting, and stamps to the world its victim? Why is it, that the man goes free and enters society again, almost courted and applauded, while the woman is a mark for the finger of reproach, and a butt for the tongue of scandal? Is it not chiefly because she bears about her the mark of what is called her disgrace? She becomes a mother; and society has something tangible against which to direct its anathemas. Nine-tenths, at least, of the misery and ruin which are caused by seduction, even in the present state of public opinion, result from cases of pregnancy. Perhaps the unfeeling selfishness of him who fears to become a father, administers some noxious drug to procure abortion; perhaps—for even such scenes our courts of justice disclose—perhaps the frenzy of the wretched mother takes the life of her infant, or seeks in suicide the consummation of her wrongs and her woes! Or, if the little being lives, the dove in the falcon's claws is not more certain of death than we may be that society will visit, with its bitterest scoffs and reproaches, the bruised spirit of the mother and the unconscious innocence of the child. . . .

That chastity which is worth preserving is not the chastity that owes it birth to fear and ignorance. If to enlighten a woman regarding a simple physiological fact will make her a prostitute, she must be especially predisposed to profligacy. But it is a libel on the sex. Few, indeed, there are, who would continue so miserable and degrading a calling, could they escape from it. For one prostitute that is made by inclination, ten are made by necessity. Reform the laws—equalize the comforts of society, and you need withhold no knowledge from wives and daughters. It is want, not knowledge, that leads to prostitution.

For myself, I would withhold from no sister, or daughter, or wife of mine, any ascertained fact whatever. It should be to me a duty and a pleasure to communicate to them all I knew myself; and I should hold it an insult to their understandings and their hearts to imagine, that their virtue would diminish as their knowledge increased. Would we but trust human nature, instead of continually suspecting it, and guarding it by bolts and bars, and thinking to make it very chaste by keeping it very ignorant, what a different world we should have of it! The virtue of ignorance is a sickly plant, ever exposed to the caterpillar of corruption, liable to be scorched and blasted even by the free light of heaven; of precarious growth;

and even if at last artificially matured, of little or no real value.

I know that parents often think it is right and proper to withhold from their children—especially from their daughters—facts the most influential on their future lives, and the knowledge of which is essential to every man and woman's well-being. Such a course has ever appeared to me ill-judged and productive of very injurious effects. A girl is surely no whit better for believing, until her marriage night, that children are found among the cabbage-leaves in the garden. The imagination is excited, the curiosity kept continually on the stretch; and that which, if simply explained, would have been recollected only as any other physiological phenomenon, assumes all the rank and importance and engrossing interest of a mystery. Nay, I am well convinced, that mere curiosity has often led ignorant young people into situations, from which a little more confidence and openness on the part of their parents or guardians, would have effectually secured them. . . .

Among the modes of preventing conception which may have prevailed in various countries, that which has been adopted, and is now practised by the cultivated classes on the continent of Europe, by the French, the Italians, and, I believe, by the Germans and Spaniards, consists of complete withdrawal, on the part of the man, immediately previous to emission. *This is, in all cases, effectual.* It may be objected, that the practice requires a mental effort and a partial sacrifice. I reply, that, in France, where men consider this (as it ought ever to be considered, when the interests of the other sex require it,) a *point of honour, all* young men learn to make the necessary effort; and custom renders it easy, and a matter of course. As for the sacrifice, shall a trifling, (and it is but a very trifling) diminution of physical enjoyment be suffered to outweigh the most important considerations connected with the permanent welfare of those who are the nearest and dearest to us; Shall it be suffered to outweigh the risk of incuring heavy and sacred responsibilities, ere we are prepared to fulfil them? Shall it be suffered to outweigh a regard for the comfort, the well-being—in some cases, the *life* of those whom we profess to love? . . .

"MALE CONTINENCE"

John Humphrey Noyes (1877)

. . . THE FIRST QUESTION, or rather, perhaps I should say, the *previous* question in regard to Male Continence is, whether it is desirable or proper that men and women should establish intelligent voluntary control over the propagative function. Is it not better (it may be asked), to leave "nature" to take its course (subject to the general rules of legal chastity), and let children come as chance or the unknown powers may direct, without putting any restraint on sexual intercourse after it is once licensed by marriage, or on the freedom of all to take out such license? If you assent to this latter view, or have an inclination toward it, I would recommend to you the study of *Malthus on Population:* not that I think he has pointed out anything like the true *method* of voluntary control over propagation, but because he has demonstrated beyond debate the absolute *necessity* of such control in some way, unless we consent and expect that the human race, like the lower animals, shall be forever kept down to its necessary limits, by the ghastly agencies of war, pestilence and famine.

For my part, I have no doubt that it is perfectly proper that we should endeavor to rise above "nature" and the destiny of the brutes in this matter. There is no reason why we should not seek and hope for discovery in this direction, as freely as in the development of steam power or the art of printing; and we may rationally expect that He who has promised the "good time" when vice and misery shall be abolished, will at last give us sure light on this darkest of all problems—how to subject human propagation to the control of science.

But whether study and invention in this direction are proper or not, they are actually at work in all quarters, reputable and disreputable. Let us see how many different ways have already been proposed for limiting human increase.

In the first place, the practice of child-killing, either by exposure or violence, is almost as old as the world, and as extensive as barbarism. Even Plato recommended something of this kind, as a waste-gate for vicious increase, in his scheme of a model republic.

Then we have the practice of abortion reduced in modern times to a science, and almost to a distinct profession. A large part of this business is carried on by means of medicines advertized in obscure but intelligible terms as embryo-destroyers or preventives of conception. Every large city has its professional abortionist. Many ordinary physicians destroy embryos to order; and the skill to this terrible deed has even descended among the common people.

Then what a variety of artificial tricks there are for frustrating the natural effects of the propagative act. You allude to several of these contrivances, in terms of condemnation from which I should not dissent. The least objectionable of them (if there is any

---

Oneida, N.Y.: Office of the American Socialist, 1877.

difference), seems to be that recommended many years ago by Robert Dale Owen, in a book entitled Moral Physiology; viz. the simple device of withdrawing immediately before emission.

Besides all these disreputable methods, we have several more respectable schemes for attaining the great object of limiting propagation. Malthus proposes and urges that all men, and especially the poor, shall be taught their responsibilities in the light of science, and so be put under inducements *not to marry.* This prudential check on population—the discouragement of marriage—undoubtedly operates to a considerable extent in all civilized society, and to the greatest extent on the classes most enlightened. It seems to have been favored by Saint Paul; (see 1st Cor. 7); and probably would not be condemned generally by people who claim to be considerate. And yet its advocates have to confess that it increases the danger of licentiousness; and on the whole the teaching that is most popular, in spite of Malthus and Paul, is that marriage, with all its liabilities, is a moral and patriotic duty.

Finally, Shakerism, which actually prohibits marriage on religious grounds, is only the most stringent and imposing of human contrivances for avoiding the woes of undesired propagation.

All these experimenters in the art of controlling propagation may be reduced in principle to three classes, viz.:

1. Those that seek to prevent intercourse of the sexes, such as Malthus and the Shakers.

2. Those that seek to prevent the natural effects of the propagative act, viz., the French inventors and Owen.

3. Those that seek to destroy the living results of the propagative act, viz., the abortionists and child-killers.

Now it may seem to you that any new scheme of control over propagation must inevitably fall to one of these three classes; but I assure you that we have a method that does not fairly belong to any of them. I will try to show you our fourth way.

We begin by *analyzing* the act of sexual intercourse. It has a beginning, a middle, and an end. Its beginning and most elementary form is the simple *presence* of the male organ in the female. Then usually follows a series of reciprocal *motions.* Finally this exercise brings on a nervous action or ejaculatory *crisis* which expels the seed. Now we insist that this whole process, up to the very moment of emission, is *voluntary,* entirely under the control of the moral faculty, and *can be stopped at any point.* In other words, the *presence* and the *motions* can be continued or stopped at will, and it is only the final *crisis* of emission that is automatic or uncontrollable.

Suppose, then, that a man, in lawful intercourse with woman, choosing for good reasons not be beget a child or to disable himself, should stop at the primary stage and content himself with simple *presence* continued as long as agreeable? Would there be any harm? It cannot be injurious to refrain from voluntary excitement. Would there be no *good?* I appeal to the memory of every man who has had good sexual experience to say whether, on the whole, the sweetest and noblest period of intercourse with woman is not that *first* moment of simple presence and spiritual effusion, before the muscular exercise begins.

But we may go farther. Suppose the man chooses for good reasons, as before, to enjoy not only the simple *presence,* but also the *reciprocal motion,* and yet to stop short of the final *crisis.* Again I ask, Would there be any harm? Or would it do no good? I suppose physiologists might say, and I would acknowledge, that the excitement by motion *might* be carried so far that a voluntary suppression of the commencing crisis would be injurious. But what if a man, knowing his own power and limits, should not even *approach* the crisis, and yet be able to enjoy the presence and the motion *ad libitum?* If you say that this is impossible, I answer that I *know* it is possible—nay, that it is easy.

I will admit, however, that it may be impossible to some, while it is possible to others. Paul intimates that some cannot "contain." Men of certain temperaments and conditions are afflicted with involuntary emissions on very trivial excitement and in their sleep. But I insist that these are exceptional morbid cases that should be disciplined and improved; and that, in the normal condition, men are entirely competent to choose in sexual intercourse whether they will stop at any point in the voluntary stages of it, and so make it simply an act of communion, or go through to the involuntary stage, and make it an act of propagation.

The situation may be compared to a stream in the three conditions of a fall, a course of rapids above the fall, and still water above the rapids. The skillful boatman may choose whether he will remain in the still water, or venture more or less down the rapids, or run his boat over the fall. But there is a point on the verge of the fall where he has no control over his course; and just above that there is a point where he will have to struggle with the current in a way which will give his nerves a severe trial, even though he may escape the fall. If he is willing to learn, experience will teach him the wisdom of confining his excursions to the region of easy rowing, unless he has an object in view that is worth the cost of going over the falls.

You have now our whole theory of "Male Continence." It consists in analyzing sexual intercourse, recognizing in it two distinct acts, the social and the propagative, which can be separated practically, and affirming that it is best, not only with reference to remote prudential considerations, but for immediate pleasure, that a man should content himself with the social act, except when he intends to procreation.

Let us see now if this scheme belongs to any of the three classes I mentioned. 1. It does not seek to prevent the intercourse of the sexes, but rather gives them more freedom by removing danger of undesired consequences. 2. It does not seek to prevent the natural *effects* of the propagative act, but to prevent the propagative act itself, except when it is intended to be effectual. 3. Of course it does not seek to destroy the living *results* of the propagative act, but provides that impregnation and child-bearing shall be voluntary, and of course desired.

And now, to speak affirmatively, the exact thing that our theory does propose, is to take that same power of moral restraint and self-control, which Paul, Malthus, the Shakers, and all considerate men use in one way or another to limit propagation, and instead of applying it, as they do, to the prevention of the intercourse of the sexes, to introduce it at another stage of the proceedings, viz., *after* the sexes have come together in social effusion, and *before* they have reached the propagative crisis; thus allowing them all and more than all the ordinary freedom of love (since the crisis always interrupts the romance), and at the same time avoiding undesired procreation and all the other evils incident to male incontinence. This is our fourth way, and we think it the better way.

The wholesale and ever ready objection to this method is that it is *unnatural, and unauthorized by the example of other animals.* I may answer in a wholesale way, that cooking, wearing clothes, living in houses, and almost everything else done by civilized man, is unnatural in the same sense, and that a close adherence to the example of the brutes would require us to forego speech and go on "all fours!" But on the other hand, if it is natural in the best sense, as I believe it is, for rational beings to forsake the example of brutes and improve nature by invention and discovery in all directions, then truly the argument turns the other way, and we shall have to confess that until men and women find a way to elevate their sexual performances above those of the brutes, by introducing into them moral culture, they are living in *unnatural* degradation.

But I will come closer to this objection. The real meaning of it is, that Male Continence in sexual intercourse is a difficult and injurious interruption of a natural act. But every instance of self-denial is an interruption of some natural act. The man who virtuously contents himself with a look at a beautiful woman is conscious of such an interruption. The lover who stops at a kiss denies himself a natural progression. It is an easy, descending grade through all the approaches of sexual love, from the first touch of respectful friendship, to the final complete amalgamation. Must there be no interruption of this natural slide? Brutes, animal or human, tolerate none. Shall their ideas of self-denial prevail? Nay, it is the glory of man to control himself, and the Kingdom of Heaven summons him to self-control in ALL THINGS. If it is noble and beautiful for the betrothed lover to respect the law of marriage in the midst of the glories of courtship, it may be even more noble and beautiful for the wedded lover to respect the laws of health and propagation in the midst of the ecstacies of sexual union. The same moral culture that ennobles the antecedents and approaches of marriage will some time surely glorify the consummation. . . .

"SOCIO-SEXUAL INEQUALITIES"

Lester F. Ward (1883)

IT IS THIS general inequality which exists in the social position of the two sexes which especially interests us at present. It is too striking to be overlooked in an inquiry into the conditions of social progress, and, although a portion of it may be regarded as but the natural correlate to their physical inequality, the greater part must be accounted for in some other way. The inequalities which society has established between the sexes may be variously classified. The principal ones may be approximately ranged under the following heads: 1, inequality of dress; 2, inequality of duties: 3, inequality of education; and, 4, inequality of rights. Let us glance at each of these inequalities separately.

Inequality of Dress.—In all civilized countries the men dress differently from the

From Dynamic Sociology. *2 vols. New York: D. Appleton, 1883.*

women. There seems to be a tendency in society to separate the sexes by some distinguishing mark which enables people to determine the sex of one another at sight. Nature has done the same thing, it is true, through selection. The plumage of birds and the fur of animals are usually different in the males from what they are in the females. Mr. Darwin offers a very ingenious explanation of all this. So the physical appearance of the sexes in the human species differs in many important respects, only a few of which are explainable by their different habits. The absence of the beard in woman and the difference between the male and the female voice are among the best marked of these physical inequalities. Difference of stature, complexion, physical strength, and intellectual vigor may all be more or less satisfactorily accounted for by the difference in their respective social conditions and life, either as imposed by nature or by custom. And man has sought to imitate nature in this respect by clothing the sexes differently.

It is not probable, however, that the custom of dressing one sex differently from the other grew out of any attempt to copy from nature, and the process was certainly wholly unlike the selective processes of nature. If we will examine the matter closely, we shall discover that the dress of women resembles in its general design that of uncivilized races far more than does that of men. It is more as both sexes originally dressed, before the art had been improved upon and adapted to practical wants. Modifications and refinements in the dress of women took the direction of embellishment, while those of men tended toward utility. And thus, while the demands of active life have worked out for man a comparatively convenient and at the same time comely habit, the conditions which surrounded women, while they have made clothing a means of loading her with ornaments, have left her in the same or in many respects in a worse condition, as records her adaptation to active usefulness, than in the beginning. Nor has it been altogether because she has been inactive and useless to the industrial world that her mode of dress has not been improved, for she is generally compelled to perform her full share of the labor, especially of the lowest and most purely physical forms of it. It is due rather to her dependent and subordinate place in society which rendered her incapable of making innovations in behalf of her own sex.

The inactive state of the women of the middle and upper classes, however, is doubtless in great part produced by the inconvenient and unmanageable character of their dress; and the refinements which the rich, and some not so rich, have learned to load themselves down with, are the cause of an enormous amount of disease and suffering, and threaten to work a permanent physical deterioration of the race. The dress of men is not in all respects what it should be, but that of women is certainly the disgrace of civilization.

Inequality of Duties.—Next with regard to the inequality of duties. Independently of the duties of maternity, the sphere of woman's activity is wholly different from that of man's. If we grant that there is a certain natural connection between the bearing of offspring and the care of the household, which is probably true, there remains a chasm to be filled in order to equalize the duties of the two sexes. Among savages it is usually the women who perform all the real work of their societies. This they do in addition to their maternal and domestic duties. Among the lower classes of so-called civilized society, the case is almost the same. In Germany, women till the soil and tend the flocks, as of yore. Nearly all the menial service in Europe is performed by women. In our large cities thousands of women toil to support families, including often their indolent and inebriate husbands. Go into the great factories and see what proportion of the operatives are women. Consider the thousands of women who make their living, and a very scanty one, by their needle. Yet the most of these have their domestic duties to perform in addition to this labor. We see, then, how false is the assertion that men perform the labor of support, while women confine themselves to maternal and domestic duties. Women who profess to confine themselves to these duties usually seek in every way to escape them, and render themselves unfit to perform them by their devotion to fashion. This is because society has established two arbitrary sets of duties, and insists that woman can not perform the one and that man should not perform the other. This fact alone is a proof of the inferiority which society ascribes to woman, since it assigns her duties which it confesses are beneath the dignity of male labor. At the same time every attempt made by the more courageous of the female sex to encroach upon the domain of man, and seek to perform the duties which he has assigned to himself, is met by the chivalric remonstrance that men's duties are too severe for the delicate constitutions of the mothers of the race! Now, all this is excessively transparent and false, and indicates that it is not nature at all, but society, that has assigned to woman her duties.

If the delicacy of the female constitution is an objection to the admission of women to the harvest-field and the machine-shop, it is equally an objection to her admission to the laundry and the factory. If maternal and domestic duties are all that women can attend to in England, why can they attend to agricultural duties in Germany, pastoral duties in Switzerland, and mercantile duties in France? It will not be said that in these countries the men perform all the household duties.

But it is claimed that woman should by nature preside over the in-door interests and man over the out-door ones. This is probably the most fatal dogma to the health of woman and to the physical condition of the race which can be found in the whole social creed. It is in effect to assert that nature has designed woman to breathe carbonic acid and man oxygen; that sunlight is poisonous to woman, but exhilarating to all other animate beings; and that physical exercise, which is so necessary to the health of every other living thing, is fatal to the female portion of the human species. It is to make woman, in regard to her place and her duties, as she is made in regard to her dress, an entire exception to all the rules of hygiene. If this vicious dogma that woman's place is in the house is persisted in for a few more centuries, there can be no escape from a general physical and intellectual degeneracy of the whole human race.

Inequality of Education.—The third and not less important inequality between the sexes is that of education. Not content with shutting woman out of all opportunities for gaining knowledge by experience, society has seen fit to debar her also from the knowledge acquired by instruction. She has been pronounced incapable of coping with man in intellectual contests, and it has not, therefore, been thought worth while to provide her mind with any considerable amount of information. It seems to have been regarded as fitting to have woman's fund of knowledge correspond in quantity to the variety of her duties and be characterized by the same limitation. Her knowledge from instruction has, therefore, only kept pace with her knowledge from experience. Ignoring the important truth that all instruction is profitable to society, ignoring the fact that most of the knowledge imparted to men by educational processes is wholly within the capacity of women to acquire also, society has established schools and school systems for the education of the former, leaving the latter in their natural state of ignorance. Deprived, therefore, for ages of all facilities either of experience or instruction, woman presents herself to the wisdom of this age as a dwarfed and inferior being, destitute of both intellectual energy and intellectual aspiration. For it is in these two respects that her inferiority is chiefly manifest. It is these that produce originality and independence in intellectual labor, and it is originality and independence which distinguish masculine from feminine thought. . . . The fact that, wherever the youth of both sexes are permitted to vie with each other under equal circumstances, no marked average inferiority is observed in the females, is one of vital importance, and proves far more than the other fact that the males are more likely to distinguish themselves in after-life, since in women the spirit has been crushed and the opportunity denied.

Inequality of Rights.—Lastly, we find an inequality of rights. And here, as everywhere else, this inequality exists to the advantage of the males and to the disadvantage of the females. In all civilized countries the laws have been framed so as to discriminate severely against the personal and proprietary rights of women. Both in civil and political affairs they are usually without redress and without voice, and in the legislature they have always been without representation except by men, while in countries where representatives are chosen by suffrage, this simplest but most valuable of all rights has been persistently withheld. It is as a citizen that woman's position has reached its lowest and most dependent state, she being literally ignored in all matters relating to law or government.

We see therefore, generally, that, whether it be in matters of dress, of labor, of education, or of right, it is the female sex which has had to suffer from the discrimination. The clothing of the male sex is better, more convenient, more comfortable, more healthful. The duties of men are more agreeable, more dignified, more varied, and more interesting. Man's education is more general, more thorough, more profound. The rights of men are comparatively ample, liberal, and manifold. These are facts which, though they may bring the blush to the cheek of a truly chivalrous man, possess the highest interest for the thoughtful and philosophic student of society. . . . [T]he inferior position of woman, maintained through so many ages, has actually resulted in rendering her both physically and mentally inferior to man. . . .

If women were the recognized social equals of men, we should see a very different state of society from that which now exists. We should, in the first place, see men and women wearing nearly or quite the same kind of dress. The slight modifications necessary to adapt the dress of each sex to its peculiar physical constitution would not be sufficient to make the difference noticeable, and would not, as now, make the form of dress a badge of sex. For it can not be urged that the present dress of woman is rendered necessary by reason of its adaptation to her physical constitution. The least acquaintance with the comparative physiology of the sexes, on the contrary, is sufficient to show that it is precisely the reverse—that, if either sex can afford to wear heavy skirts hanging from the hips and wrenching the loins, it is the male; that, if either sex needs the lower extremities and parts of the body thoroughly protected from the exposure to currents of cold air, it is the female; that the practice of lacing the waist would be far less fatal to man than to woman, with her delicate uterine system so liable to displacement. And, even if nothing but the mere question of modesty were considered, it would be more proper for a woman than for a man to wear clothing to fit the body.

If the social equality of the sexes were recognized, we should see men and women performing substantially the same duties. In uncivilized races the drudgery and the honorable activities would be equally distributed between them. In civilized countries women would share all the varied occupations and professions with their husbands and brothers. There would be found very few avenues to wealth or happiness which women would be incapacitated to enter from purely physical reasons. There are, indeed, very few of them that women have not in some rare cases actually entered and successfully labored in. But, if their true equality were recognized, it would not be left for the few who dared to defy the rules of propriety to step forth into fields of usefulness to labor by the side of man. Not only would the duties, labors, and occupations of men be shared by women, but their pastimes, recreations, and pleasures as well. We should not see man amusing himself alone and in his own way, or in the society of men only, nor should we see women striving to become happy in the society of their own sex, and to derive pleasure from sources peculiarly their own, to which men are entire strangers. We should see a community of enjoyments, not differing materially, perhaps, from the present, but in which both sexes would join, adding to the animation which they otherwise afford the lively relish of sexual companionship. The present system, both of labor and of recreation, is calculated to bring out the worst side of sexuality. The separate duties and spheres in which the two sexes labor and move tend to render the desire for association a prurient one. The varied restraints of propriety and modesty have the effect of fanning human passions into a flame, and a consequence of this is that both sexes are liable to be whelmed in a vortex of crime, and their character and usefulness ruined. Equality in all respects would prove a certain antidote to all these social evils. It would do far more. It would transfer to the list of productive laborers the legion of women who now deem themselves wholly justified in occupying a position of dependency upon man, and consuming the fruits of his labor without adding the value of a loaf of bread to the wealth of the world. For this nonproducing condition of civilized women is an anomaly in the animal world, and even among human races. . . .

If the equality of the sexes were recognized, we should see both sexes educated alike. We should see women admitted along with men, not merely to the common schools, but to all the higher institutions of learning, to the professions and to the technical departments. We should see the principle applied that it is mind which needs instruction, not male mind. Men and women would then stand on an equal intellectual footing, and intellectual superiority, without regard to which sex it appeared in, would receive its just recognition. Then, if woman fell below, it would be just to infer a natural deficiency. Had the same opportunities and the same restraints existed for both sexes from the beginning, it would then be possible to judge of their relative merits.

If the equality of the sexes had been frankly recognized, both would have been accorded the same rights. Not only would both sexes have labored together in the great duty, along with others, of framing, interpreting, and executing the laws of society, but both would have enjoyed the same protection and advantages under those laws, and both would have been represented in all the branches of government by the same mode of representation, whatever that might be. Nor is it alone in political affairs that equal rights would have been extended. The social rights withheld from women are, if possible, worse than these. For under the head of rights may be ranged all the sexual inequalities named, and all that may be named. Education, industry, nay, even dress, are all of the nature of rights. To slight woman's education, to degrade and circumscribe her sphere of duty, to dress her with burdensome and unsanitary clothes—all these are deprivations of right of the most grievous nature. For every mind has a right to knowledge, every one has a right to choose his duties, and certainly all have the right so to clothe themselves as best to promote their comfort and successful activity.

But there are still higher rights, there is a still greater liberty which society withholds from one half its members. It is the right to themselves, the liberty of controlling their own persons, the possession of their own bodies. What a commentary upon professed civilization is the claim that the inactivity of the female sex is necessary to protect them from exposure to personal violence; that they can not pursue the free and honorable duties of men because thereby they would be exposed to insult! Or, if this be not feared, how shallow is the other plea that, if engaged in other duties than those to which society has restricted her, woman's modesty might be shocked by contact with the vulgar world! To so fine a point has this artificial sentiment been reduced! And this would be the place to show that it is this sentiment, more than any thing else, which has worked the degradation, the subjection, and the social enslavement of woman. To protect her from the rude advances of others, to preserve her in all purity for the use of her owner—these are the prime factors in the accomplishment of woman's present dependent condition. . . .

Although I have been careful to avoid all allusion to the question of who is responsible for this condition of things, I am aware that the human mind is prone to infer that where matters are bad some one must be to blame, and to assume that, where a state of things is so organized as to discriminate against one class and in favor of another, the class which derives the benefit must somehow be responsible; and I have feared that for these reasons some of my readers might class me in the list of those who see in the male sex only a confederacy of usurpers and tyrants, who do nothing but seek for further means of humiliating and subjugating the female sex for their own gratification and emolument. If any have been inclined to accuse me of this species of *misandry,* they need simply to be reminded that I have been only seeking to study the condition of society, not to criticise the conduct of its members. If there is any responsibility in a sociological phenomenon, it must rest upon society as a whole. If there is one social fact which has received the sanction and approval of all classes of society, it is the existing relations of the sexes. If there is an evil in the world for which nobody is to blame, it is the inequality of the sexes. If there is an illustration of the victims of an injurious system countenancing and upholding that system, it exists in the case of women and the system which holds them down. The mere handful of enlightened protesters, who have become aroused within the past few years to a vague sense of their true condition, is but the very embryo of the movement which would be required to accomplish the emancipation of woman. And it is not so much experience as philosophy which is agitating the question. The victims of the system are usually silent, or, if they speak, it is but the bitter language of discontent unsupported by the philosophic analysis of the subject which can alone give weight to their utterances. The greatest champions of social reform are, and will always be, those who possess the capacity to grasp great social truths and an insight into human nature and the causes of social phenomena deep enough to kindle a genuine sympathy, and a sound, rational philanthropy. . . .

A state of society, if it be bad for one class, is bad for all. Woman is scarcely a greater sufferer from her condition than man is, and there is, therefore, nothing either improper or inexplicable in man's espousing the cause of woman's emancipation. The freedom of woman will be the ennoblement of man. The equality of the sexes will be the regeneration of humanity. Civilization demands this revolution. It stands in the greatest need of the help which the female sex alone can vouchsafe. Woman is half of mankind. Civilization and progress have hitherto been carried forward by the male half alone. Labor and production are now also suffering from the same cause. It is high time that all the forces of society were brought into action, and it is especially necessary that those vast complementary forces which woman alone can wield be given free rein, and the whole machinery of society be set into full and harmonious operation. . . .

"THE ECONOMIC THEORY OF WOMAN'S DRESS"

Thorstein Veblen (1894)

UNDER the patriarchal organisation of society, where the social unit was the man (with his dependents), the dress of the women was an exponent of the wealth of the man whose chattels they were. In modern society, where the unit is the household, the woman's dress sets forth the wealth of the household to which she belongs. Still, even today, in spite of the nominal and somewhat celebrated demise of the patriarchal idea, there is that about the dress of women which suggests that the wearer is something in the nature of a chattel; indeed, the theory of woman's dress quite plainly involves the implication that the woman is a chattel. In this respect the dress of women differs from that of men. . . .

Woman, primarily, originally because she was herself a pecuniary possession, has become in a peculiar way the exponent of the pecuniary strength of her social group; and with the progress of specialisation of functions in the social organism this duty tends to devolve more and more entirely upon the

Popular Science Monthly *46 (November 1894).*

woman. The best, most advanced, most highly developed societies of our time have reached the point in their evolution where it has (ideally) become the great, peculiar, and almost the sole function of woman in the social system to put in evidence her economic unit's ability to pay. That is to say, woman's place (according to the ideal scheme of our social system) has come to be that of a means of conspicuously unproductive expenditure. . . . "Dress," therefore, from the economic point of view, comes pretty near being synonymous with "display of wasteful expenditure." . . .

It is not that the wearers or the buyers of these wasteful goods desire the waste. They desire to make manifest their ability to pay. What is sought is not the *de facto* waste, but the appearance of waste. Hence there is a constant effort on the part of the consumers of these goods to obtain them at as good a bargain as may be; and hence also a constant effort on the part of the producers of these goods to lower the cost of their production, and consequently to lower the price. But as fast as the price of the goods declines to such a figure that their consumption is no longer *prima facie* evidence of a considerable ability to pay, the particular goods in question fall out of favor, and consumption is diverted to something which more adequately manifests the wearer's ability to afford wasteful consumption. . . . [T]here is the evidence of expenditure afforded by a constant supersession of one wasteful garment or trinket by a new one. This principle inculcates the desirability, amounting to a necessity wherever circumstances allow, of wearing nothing that is out of date. . . .

This requirement of novelty is the underlying principle of the whole of the difficult and interesting domain of fashion. Fashion does not demand continual flux and change simply because that way of doing is foolish; flux and change and novelty are demanded by the central principle of all dress—conspicuous waste. . . .

But apart from the exhibition of pecuniary strength afforded by an aggressive wasteful expenditure, the same purpose may also be served by conspicuous abstention from useful effort. The woman is, by virtue of the specialisation of social functions, the exponent of the economic unit's pecuniary strength, and it consequently also devotes on her to exhibit the unit's capacity to endure this passive form of pecuniary damage. She can do this by putting in evidence the fact (often a fiction) that she leads a useless life. Dress is her chief means of doing so. The ideal of dress . . . is to demonstrate to all observers, and to compel observation of the fact, that the wearer is manifestly incapable of doing anything that is of any use. The modern civilised woman's dress attempts this demonstration of habitual idleness, and succeeds measurably.

Herein lies the secret of the persistence, in modern dress, of the skirt and of all the cumbrous and otherwise meaningless drapery which the skirt typifies. The skirt persists because it is cumbrous. It hampers the movements of the wearer and disables her, in great measure, for any useful occupation. So it serves as an advertisement (often disingenuous) that the wearer is backed by sufficient means to be able to afford the idleness, or impaired efficiency, which the skirt implies. The like is true of the high heel, and in less degree of several other features of modern dress.

Herein is also to be sought the ground of the persistence (probably not the origin) of the one great mutilation practiced by civilised occidental womankind—the constricted waist, as well as of the analogous practice of the abortive foot among their Chinese sisters. This modern mutilation of woman is perhaps not to be classed strictly under the category of dress; but it is scarcely possible to draw the line so as to exclude it from the theory, and it is so closely coincident with that category in point of principle that an outline of the theory would be incomplete without reference to it.

. . . The fact that voluntarily accepted physical incapacity argues the possession of wealth practically establishes the futility of any attempted reform of woman's dress in the direction of convenience, comfort, or health. It is of the essence of dress that it should (appear to) hamper, incommode, and injure the wearer, for in so doing it proclaims the wearer's pecuniary ability to endure idleness and physical incapacity.

. . . [T]his requirement, that women must appear to be idle in order to be respectable, is an unfortunate circumstance for women who are compelled to provide their own livelihood. They have to supply not only the means of living, but also the means of advertising the fiction that they live without any gainful occupation; and they have to do all this while encumbered with garments specially designed to hamper their movements and decrease their industrial efficiency. . . .

"STATEMENT AT HIS TRIAL"

William Sanger (1915)

. . . I AM CHARGED with having violated a statute of the Penal Law of this State which makes it a crime to furnish information regarding the prevention of conception. The District Attorney has brought into court a Comstock agent, to whom, it is charged, I gave a copy of my wife's pamphlet on "Family Limitation." I do not deny that I gave the pamphlet. I frankly admit it. Nor will Mr. Bamberger, the Comstock agent, deny that he came to me under a false name and obtained the pamphlet under false pretences.

I admit that I broke the law, and yet I claim that, in every real sense, it is the law, and not I, that is on trial here today.

Gives Story of Case

The immediate facts of the case and of my subsequent arrest are as follows: On December 18th a man came to my studio in my absence and left a card which gave the name of Mr. Heller, dealer in rubber goods and sundries. The following day, early in the morning, the man presented himself at my studio, and he proved to be this Mr. Heller who left his card the previous day. He asked if I were Sanger, to which I replied in the

"Trial Statement." Reprinted in Jailed For Birth Control: The Trial of William Sanger, September 10th, 1915, *ed. James Waldo Fawcett. New York, 1917. (SSL)*

affirmative. He stated that he knew of two books by Mrs. Sanger, "What Every Girl Should Know" and "What Every Mother Should Know," that he enjoyed reading them very much and that he was in sympathy with her work. He then asked me for a pamphlet called "Family Limitation," written by Mrs. Sanger. I told him that I did not have any, as far as I knew. He seemed insistent, and finally said that if he could only get a copy of this pamphlet he would have it printed in different languages to distribute amongst the poor people he worked with and did business with. I asked him whether he was the Mr. Heller that Mrs. Sanger knew and he replied that he was. I then told him that he would have to wait, and I would try and find a pamphlet for him. Thereupon I went and looked through the various books and pamphlets left in my care and found several copies, one of which I gave to him, and sent him, as I supposed, on his way rejoicing.

Arrest Followed Agent's Visit

The incident vanished from my mind entirely until a month later, when I was arrested by Anthony Comstock for violating the law against giving out "obscene, lewd, lascivious, filthy, indecent and disgusting" literature.

I was trapped into handing the pamphlet in question to an agent of Comstock. This self-appointed censor of our morality and his agent did not hesitate to use criminal methods to make a criminal out of me.

But I deny that I am a criminal. From my own inward feeling I did not wrong. Then why should I recognize the right of the State to brand me as a criminal?

I cannot claim the honor of connection with the writing, publication or circulation of this pamphlet. But it is true just the same that I had original convictions on this most vital subject years ago. I understand I have the right to summon six witnesses to testify as to my good character. I waive the privilege of getting character witnesses because I don't wish to stalk behind the reputation or standing of any one in this community. I stand here alone—on my own individuality as expressed in this statement.

I have lived here for thirty-five years. My life is an open book to anyone. I am the father of three children, and three lovely ones. Therefore, I feel I need no credentials from anyone.

Book Is Not Obscene

If this pamphlet on "Family Limitation" is considered obscene and indecent, then all the medical books on the subject are also obscene and indecent. There are books sold today at high prices by reputable publishers to anyone who has the price.

I was offered a suspended sentence by Comstock if I pleaded guilty. On the way to the Magistrate's Court on the day of my arrest, Comstock asked me three times the whereabouts of Mrs. Sanger. When I confronted him with the statement that he had no legal or moral right to ask me that question, there was no reply, but a cynical smile. The whole gist of his manner was that he had made a mistake in arresting me and wished to squirm out of it to save his face and his job by gracefully handing me a suspended sentence. He seemed peculiarly insistent, making the inquiry twice, the second time stating that he had prosecuted over thirty-nine hundred cases in his career and was invariably successful, and that, if he recommended to the court a suspended sentence, it would invariably comply. I told him that I would plead not guilty and not receive a suspended sentence from him under any consideration.

The fact is that Comstock does not dare to attack the more prominent, those able to withstand the expense of prolonged legal encounters, but he necessarily attacks me in the silence of my studio, because he thought that I would succumb at my arrest, plead guilty, and add another to his list of victims in his annual report.

Mrs. Sanger Is A Pioneer

I am proud to be identified with the work of that noble woman, Margaret Sanger. Even if she were not my wife I would consider it an honor to link my name with hers. I stand for everything in this pamphlet as written by this illustrious pioneer. I absolutely deny that there is anything obscene, indecent, lascivious or disgusting in this pamphlet.

Who is the man responsible for the obscenity law under which I am charged? The state of mind called Comstockery and Comstock in particular are responsible for this statute.

The facts are that this man who has received such an extraordinary power from the State is in reality a religious and pornographic fanatic. He is the victim of an incurable sexphobia. He believes he has a mission to extirpate what he calls obscenity by decoy letters, by bearing false witness. It makes no difference what the means is—that is a minor matter. The end to him justifies the means. The result has been suppression of investigation, experiment and expression.

Torquemada and Loyola attempted what Comstock has attempted, and failed, and time has linked their names with the Great Delusion—ending in fagots and the stake. The present inquisitor has not learned the lesson of history. Like the other inquisitors, he also has a mission; he also has energy and determination; but he is ignorant and without the intelligence to distinguish between pornography and scientific information. Sincerity is a great virtue, if it has brains and a fine sense of justice behind it. Without brains to guide it and the impulse of justice to temper it, it is bound to be a scourge to the race.

Scores Modern Witchcraft

The race has long ago emerged from the era of witchcraft, but yet today witchcraft exists in a different form, in the shape of obscenity laws. Obscenity statutes cannot be regarded in the same light as statutes dealing with concrete offences, such as criminal libel, arson, or the like, because they are based on a state of mind. Things obscene can only be detected when we think in terms of deformed mental process of reasoning. Obscenity, like witches, will cease to exist when men cease to believe in it.

The obscenity statute is therefore based on a belief rooted in the meanest, most cruel and ignorant censorship since the days of witchcraft. Shall any man or woman be liable to a fine or imprisonment based on a belief more or less religious and on the attitude of mind of those mentally deformed?

It can be shown that the framers of this obscenity statute knew nothing of the untold hardships endured by the workers in the past, because information in regard to birth control was withheld from them. They were indifferent to or sublimely ignorant of the fact that the statute, with others of the same character, were and are the message of death to the workers of this generation. It was a white-livered morality they had in mind and not the crying need of humanity.

Workers Need Birth Control

The result of the enforcement of the law is that it has caused untold hardships to that stratum of society least able to help itself. All because of this obscenity law and others, the relief asked for by the workers is denied them and the giving out of information on birth control is made a prison offence. But the workers keep on having children without any means for their support. The breeding, and not the rearing, of children goes on. These children come into the world not really wanted, because there is no place for them. They are shoved out in the streets, collect in gangs, are swatted like flies in places they call homes, largely because of these infamous obscenity laws. The homes of the very poor have been made brothels, instead of havens, for the rising generation, where these children might have a chance to grow up in beauty and love, basking in the sunshine of their parentage. It has been shown that among families earning 500 dollars a year one out of every four dies before he reaches one year of age. How about the unemployed? Their children become destitute and are thrown into orphan asylums and the like. If birth control information was not declared obscene, indecent, lascivious and disgusting, fewer and better children would be born and fewer children would die.

Birth Kills Mothers

Mainly on account of the law, thousands of women die yearly of miscarriage and abortion. We view with horror and righteous rage such disasters as the loss of life in the "Lusitania" tragedy, but yet pursue the even tenor of our way for the reason that it is not generally known that so many women yearly go to their untimely graves because the imparting of birth control information is declared obscene and indecent. The professional abortionist, midwives and other quacks would be driven from their practice if proper information in regard to birth control was disseminated. Eight thousand and odd women of the State lose their lives every year, but the quacks still remain to ply their vocation.

Comstockery, Prudery and its offspring, Ignorance, stalk behind every miscarriage and abortion. The State has given power to an irresponsible official of an irresponsible society; therefore the State is the real malefactor, the law is on trial, not I. Every fibre of my being revolts against the inhumane spectacle of insidious murder which this statute carries in its wake.

All because of the prudish censorship and these obscenity laws, we lag woefully behind the nations of Europe. For many years the English Government has allowed birth control information to be circulated. In France, it is not illegal. Birth control is a household term. The result has been the two-children family on the average. One sees little child labor in France and the children are well taken care of. In Spain, Italy and Germany it is not illegal and not declared obscene and indecent. In Belgium and Holland birth control information is not only not declared obscene and indecent, but is openly practised without legal restraint, Holland being in advance of all the nations by having free clinics in all its large cities, where women can get the benefit of the most advanced and enlightened information. For almost a half a century we have been under the ban of a prudish censorship. We are just beginning to emerge from this inquisition.

Ignorance Blights All

I sum up the indictment against the State on the following grounds: All on account of

Comstockery the legislature has been intimidated to pass obscenity laws, which have put the cowl of ignorance over the discussion and investigation of matters of birth control. I deny the right of the State to encroach on the rights of the individual by invading the most private and fundamental relations of men and women.

I deny the right of the State to compel the poor and disinherited to rear large families and to drive their offspring to child labor when they should be at school and at play. I deny the right of the State to exercise dominion over the souls and bodies of our women by compelling them to go into unwilling motherhood. I deny the right of the State to arm an ignorant, irresponsible and prudish censorship with the right of search and confiscation, to pass judgment on our art and literature, and I deny as well the right to hold over the entire medical profession, the legal ban of this obscenity statute. I deny the right of the State to heckle, hinder and deprive those best fitted by years of training and experience from aiding those who apply to them for vital information concerning their bodily well-being. The obscenity laws, State and Federal, as administered by Comstock and his inhuman and ignorant censorship, have driven the mother of my children into exile, separated from her children now for almost a year, and caused untold hardship to her and to me.

Why should I not despise these obscenity laws which have created so much ignorance, increased poverty and hardship, kept me personally away from creative work as an artist and decorator, deprived me of an income for my wife and children?

The court has the physical power to send me to prison, but it cannot take away from me my convictions and ideals. They are mine. I would rather be in prison with my ideals and convictions intact, than out it, stripped of my self-respect and manhood.

In the light of the facts, then, and of the circumstances of my arrest, I ask that I be acquitted here today.

EXPERIMENTING WITH EQUALITY: GREENWICH VILLAGE, 1900–1920

"THE DOUBLE STANDARD—A PARABLE OF THE AGES"

Upton Sinclair (1913)

ONCE upon a time a Man married a Woman.

Time passed and one day the Man said: "I love all women. I need a great deal of love."

And the Woman replied: "I love all men. I also need a great deal of love.

Said the Man: "If you talk like that, I will hit you over the head with a club."

And the Woman said: "Forgive me, Lord and Master."

Ten thousand years passed, and again the Man said: "I love all women. I need a great deal of love."

Masses 4, no. 11, issue no. 27 (August 1913).

And the Woman replied: "I love all men. I also need a great deal of love."

Said the Man: "If you talk like that, I will divorce you, and you will find it hard to earn your own living."

And the Woman said: "You are a Brute."

Another hundred years passed, and again the Man said: "I love all women. I need a great deal of love."

And the Woman replied: "I love all men. I also need a great deal of love. And, as you know, I can earn my own living."

Said the Man: "If you talk like that, I shall have to behave myself."

And the Woman said: "At last!"

"A NOTE ON THE WOMAN'S MOVEMENT"

Walter Lippmann (1914)

LIBERTY may be an uncomfortable blessing unless you know what to do with it. That is why so many freed slaves returned to their masters, why so many emancipated women are only too glad to give up the racket and settle down. For between announcing that you will live your own life, and the living of it lie the real difficulties of any awakening.

If all that women needed were "rights,"—the right to work, the right to vote, and freedom from the authority of father and husband, then feminism would be the easiest human question on the calendar. For while there will be a continuing opposition, no one supposes that these elementary freedoms can be withheld from women. In fact, they will be forced upon millions of women who never troubled to ask for any of these rights. And that isn't because Ibsen wrote the Doll's House, or because Bernard Shaw writes prefaces. The mere withdrawal of industries from the home has drawn millions of women out of the home, and left millions idle within it. There are many other forces, all of which have blasted the rock of ages where woman's life was centered. The self-conscious modern woman may insist that she has a life of her own to lead, which neither father, nor priest, nor husband, nor Mrs. Grundy is fit to prescribe for her. But when she begins to prescribe life for herself, her real problems begin.

Every step in the woman's movement is creative. There are no precedents whatever, not even bad ones. Now the invention of new ways of living is rare enough among men, but among women it has been almost unknown. Housekeeping and baby-rearing are the two most primitive arts in the whole world. They are almost the last occupations in which rule of thumb and old wives' tales have resisted the application of scientific method. They are so immemorially backward, that nine people out of ten hardly conceive the possibility of improving upon them. They are so backward that we have developed a maudlin sentimentality about them, have associated family life and the joy in childhood with all the stupidity and wasted labor of the inefficient home. The idea of making the home efficient will cause the average person to shudder, as if you were uttering some blasphemy against monogamy. "Let science into the home, where on earth will Cupid go to?" Almost in vain do women like Mrs. Gilman insist that the institution of the family is not dependent upon keeping woman a drudge amidst housekeeping arrangements inherited from the early Egyptians. Women have invented almost nothing to lighten their labor. They have made practically no attempt to specialize, to coöperate. They have been the great routineers.

From Drift and Mastery. *New York: M. Kennerly, 1914.*

So people have said that woman was made to be the natural conservative, the guardian of tradition. She would probably still be guarding the tradition of weaving her own clothes in the parlor if an invention hadn't thwarted her. She still guards the tradition of buying food retail, of going alone and unorganized to market. And she has been, of course, a faithful conservator of superstition, the most docile and credulous of believers. In all this, I am saying nothing that awakened women themselves aren't saying, nor am I trying to take a hand in that most stupid of all debates as to whether men are superior to women. Nor am I trying to make up my mind whether the higher education of women and their political enfranchisement will produce in the next generation several Darwins and a few Michelangelos. The question is not even whether women can be as good doctors and lawyers and business organizers as men.

It is much more immediate, and far less academic than that. . . . The day of the definitely marked "sphere" is passing under the action of forces greater than any that an irritated medical man can control. It is no longer possible to hedge the life of women in a set ritual, where their education, their work, their opinion, their love, and their motherhood, are fixed in the structure of custom. To insist that women need to be moulded by authority is a shirking of the issue. For the authority that has moulded them is passing. And if woman is fit only to live in a harem, it will have to be a different kind of harem from any that has existed.

The more you pile up the case against woman in the past the more significant does feminism become. For one fact is written across the whole horizon, the prime element in any discussion. That fact is the absolute necessity for a readjusting of woman's position. And so, every time you insist that women are backward you are adding to the revolutionary meaning of their awakening. But what these anti-feminists have in mind, of course, is that women are by nature incapable of any readjustment. However, the test of that pudding is in the eating. What women will do with the freedom that is being forced upon them is something, that no person can foresee by thinking of women in the past.

Women to-day are embarked upon a career for which their tradition is no guide. The first result, of course is a vast amount of trouble. The emancipated woman has to fight something worse than the crusted prejudices of her uncles; she has to fight the bewilderment in her own soul. She who always took what was given to her has to find for herself. She who passed without a break from the dominance of her father to the dominance of her husband is suddenly compelled to govern herself. Almost at one stroke she has lost the authority of a little world and has been thrust into a very big one, which nobody, man or woman, understands very well. I have tried to suggest what this change from a world of villages has meant for politicians, clergymen and social thinkers. Well, for women, the whole problem is aggravated by the fact that they come from a still smaller world and from a much more rigid authority.

It is no great wonder if there is chaos among the awakening women. Take a cry like that for a "single standard" of morality. It means two utterly contradictory things. For the Pankhursts it is assumed that men should adopt women's standards, but in the minds of thousands it means just the reverse. For some people feminism is a movement of women to make men chaste, for others the enforced chastity of women is a sign of their slavery. Feminism is attacked both for being too "moral" and too "immoral." And these contradictions represent a real conflict, not a theoretical debate.

There is in the movement an uprising of women who rebel against marriage which means to a husband the ultimate haven of a sexual career. There is also a rebellion of women who want for themselves the larger experience that most men have always taken. Christabel Pankhurst uses the new freedom of expression to drive home an Old Testament morality with Old Testament fervor. She finds her book suppressed by Mr. Anthony Comstock, who differs from her far less than he imagines. And she rouses the scorn of great numbers of people who feel that she is out, not to free women, but to enslave men. There is an immense vacillation between a more rigid Puritanism and the idolatry of freedom. Women are discovering what reformers of all kinds are learning, that there is a great gap between the overthrow of authority and the creation of a substitute. That gap is called liberalism: a period of drift and doubt. We are in it to-day. . . .

The effect of the woman's movement will accumulate with the generations. The results are bound to be so far-reaching that we can hardly guess them to-day. For we are tapping a reservoir of possibilities when women begin to use not only their generalized womanliness but their special abilities. For the child it means, as I have tried to suggest, a change in the very conditions where the property sense is aggravated and where the need for authority and individual assertiveness is built up. The greatest obstacles to a cooperative civilization are under fire from the feminists. Those obstacles to-day are more than anything else a childhood in which the anti-social impulses are fixed. The awakening of women points straight to the discipline of coöperation. And so it is laying the real foundations for the modern world.

For understand that the forms of coöperation are of precious little value without a people trained to use them. The old family with its dominating father, its submissive and amateurish mother produced inevitably men who had little sense of a common life, and women who were jealous of an enlarging civilization. It is this that feminism comes to correct, and that is why its promise reaches far beyond the present bewilderment.

"WHAT FEMINISM MEANS TO ME"

George Middleton (1914)

FEMINISM MEANS TROUBLE: trouble means agitation: agitation means movement: movement means life: life means adjustment and readjustment: so does feminism. It is an attack upon social opinion wherever it discriminates in its attitude toward man and woman on the basis of sex. It asks primarily that man and woman be considered as human beings. It recognizes that man and woman are made of the same soul stuff. It sees them respond to the same rhythm in music, the same beauty in verse and the same elemental emotions in life. . . .

With us our human attributes we have in common. Whatever difference in our human qualities there is, is individual. The variation is the same among men as it is among women. It is not however, a sex difference. Emotion and spirituality are bonds which men and women share in common. There are so-called masculine qualities in many women and much that is feminine in many men. The appelation, "maleness and femaleness" as applied to certain human characteristics, is purely arbitrary. We must recognize it has been environment not a biological necessity which in the past has differentiated the sexes in the certain channels. Basically men and women are human and from that standpoint, we face feminism. . . . Feminism does not therefore, believe in the effiminization of life but in its humanization. It is not a woman's movement exclusively: it pays equal dividends to men-as we shall see. It cannot achieve completion without the cooperation of men and women. It is not antagonism. It is mutuality. Feminism is not femaleness with fewer petticoats. It is not an assault on trousers. It does not seek to crinoline men. It asks a new change in the social garments of each. Feminism is therefore a state of mind and as a state of mind it faces many facts of life.

From one aspect feminism is an educational ideal. It asks that children be educated according to temperament and not according to sex. It asks a girl be educated for life and not for marriage alone. . . .

In another aspect feminism is an economic attitude. It is opposed to parasi[ti]sm in either male or female as a habit of thought. It asks equal opportunity to work. In England for example women can't practice law, neither can they in South Carolina. There have been these discriminations on the ground of sex all over the world. The brave struggle of women initiated by such leaders as Dr. Blackwell and Florence Nightingale, aided by the sympathetic help of men, are gradually breaking these restrictions down. With this equal opportunity to work and enter all professions, feminists demand equal pay for equal work. It asks that efficiency and not sex be the test of value. . . . Feminism asserts that there can never be any equality in the laws of marriage and divorce no matter how equal it phrases to-

---

Speech delivered at the Cooper Union, New York City, 17 February 1914. (LOC, George Middleton Papers)

ward each sex, if the letter of the law is made solely by man and its spirit interpreted solely by man. Feminism is of course in favor of a freer divorce, without inequal social penalties. . . .

Feminism seeks to change social opinion toward the sex relation; not to advocate license but to recognize liberty: not to encourage looseness but to dismiss the double standard of morality. It wishes to destroy that double standard between the sexes as between the classes. . . .

Woman suffrage is the political aspect of feminism. It is the kindergarten of feminism. Many people who believe in woman suffrage do not believe in all of the aspects of feminism. But all feminists are equal suffragists. Feminism believes that both men and women should have some say in the laws under which both are governed. It does not wish to resort to the subterfuges of indirect influence to obtain the things in legislation which are as much woman's right as man's. It recognizes no limitation in civic expression on the ground of sex. It sees too, the need of the vote for woman so that the part of the human race which she represents shall have representation and not charity. Feminism is democratic in its essence and there can be no democracy in the government which denies the suffrage to half its citizens simply because they wear skirts. It sees that one woman in every five is in modern industry, that they are supporting themselves even in whole or in part. It asks that these women, and all others, have the same right as men to express their need and relation to the community. It sees a great horde of women capable and efficient, who should help man with his civic burdens. It wishes, however, to compel no woman to vote if she does not wish to, but it demands that those who do wish to vote shall not be discriminated against because they are women. Feminists do not think all things will be accomplished through the ballot, they do see the great value of Woman's Suffrage as the fundamental first step in removing the political discriminations against her. With this removed they feel they will better be able to remove the other discriminations.

Feminism is thus a protest against further sex specialization. It wishes the sickening emphasis of sex differences to be taken out of discussion. It wants the energies which are now being wasted in getting certain rights to be expended in the fruitful and useful utilization of those rights.

Feminism therefore, is a mood as well as a movement. It is a high ideal of mutual understanding between the sexes working amid prejudice and tradition. Its aim is greater freedom. Its amunition is an appeal to common humanness. It is an awakening to the higher possibilities of life which lie in the changing social scheme. . . .

Its spirit is expansive. It asks that each sex separately may be able to give to the other more comradeship, more freedom, more self-realization, more honesty, more justice and I believe more beauty.

"LEARNING AND MARRIAGE"

Hutchins Hapgood (c. 1915)

THE CONDITIONS which tend to keep women professors in our universities unmarried was justly denounced with horror by President Thomas of Bryn Mawr College in an address the other day.

"They may have spent a lifetime in fitting themselves for a scholar's work, and then they may be asked to choose between it and marriage. No one can estimate the number of women who remain unmarried in revolt before such a horrible alternative. How many men scholars would there be if we compelled them to make such an inhuman choice?"

The social condition which tends to prevent or limit woman's independent work when she marries, not only in teaching but in every other occupation, is fortunately giving way to a more civilized and more productive state, the final forms of which are not clear to anybody. Some facts, however, are growingly felt by many people. It is beginning to be seen that women who work independently are, as a rule, more capable mothers and more interesting and attractive wives than those women who do not. Their natures are fed and enhanced by a vital relation to things outside the home, and thus greater spiritual and mental nutrition, and thus greater emotional enhancement, they bring to the home, to the children, to the husband.

Anything that increases life and vision and understanding in a woman helps her in every one of her life's relations. She becomes a better mother, a better lover, a better wife, a better citizen. We agree with Mrs. Thomas that the choice between a woman's work and marriage is a horrible choice and ought not to exist. It will be recognized some day as one of the barbarities of our time.

Chicago Evening Tribune *(n.d.). (SSL, Birth Control Pamphlets Collection)*

"FEMINISM FOR MEN"

Floyd Dell (1917)

The Emancipation of Man

FEMINISM is going to make it possible for the first time for men to be free.

At present the ordinary man has the choice between being a slave and a scoundrel. That's about the way it stands.

For the ordinary man is prone to fall in love and marry and have children. Also the ordinary man frequently has a mother. He wants to see them all taken care of, since they are unable to take care of themselves. Only if he has them to think about, he is not free.

A free man is a man who is ready to throw up his job whenever he feels like it. Whether he is a brick-layer who wants to go out on a sympathetic strike, or a poet who wants to quit writing drivel for the magazines, if he doesn't do what he wants to do, he is not free.

To disregard the claims of dependent women, to risk their comfort in the interest of self or of society at large, takes a good deal of heroism—and some scoundrelism, too.

Some of the finest natures to be found among men are the least free. It is the most sensitive who hesitate and are lost to the world and their own souls.

And this will be true so long as women as a sex are dependent on men for support. It is too much to ask of a man to be brave, when his bravery means taking the food out of the mouth of a woman who cannot get food except from him. The bravest things will not be done in the world until women do not have to look to men for support.

The change is already under way. Irresistible economic forces are taking more and more women every year out of the economic shelter of the home, into the great world, making them workers and earners along with men. And every conquest of theirs, from an education which will make them fit for the world of earning, to "equal pay for equal work," is a setting free of men. The last achievement will be a social insurance for motherhood, which will enable them to have children without taking away a man's freedom from him. Then a man will be able to tell his employer that "he and his job can go bark at one another," without being a hero and a scoundrel at the same time.

Capitalism will not like that. Capitalism does not want free men. It wants men with wives and children who are dependent on them for support. Mothers' pensions will be hard fought for before they are ever gained. And that is not the worst.

Men don't want the freedom that women are thrusting upon them. They don't want a chance to be brave. They want a chance to be generous. They want to give food and clothes and a little house with lace curtains to some woman.

Men want the sense of power more than they want the sense of freedom. They want

---

Masses 5, no. 20 (July 1917).

the feeling that comes to them as providers for women more than they want the feeling that comes to them as free men. They want some one dependent on them, more than they want a comrade. As long as they can be lords in a thirty-dollar flat, they are willing to be slaves in the great world outside.

They are afraid that woman will cease to ask them to do things, and say "Thank you!" They are afraid woman will lose the timidity and weakness which make them turn to men for help. They are afraid that woman will emancipate her legs with trousers. (And so she will; only they will not be so ugly as the garments at present worn by men, if Paul Poiret has anything to say about it!)

In short, they are afraid that they will cease to be sultans in little monogamic harems. But the world doesn't want sultans. It wants men who can call their souls their own. And that is what feminism is going to do for men—give them back their souls, so that they can risk them fearlessly in the adventure of life.

The fact is that this Occidental harem with its petty lordship over one woman, and its inefficient voluptuosities after the day's work, is not a fit place for a man. Woman has long since discovered that it is not a fit place for her.

The fit place for men and women is the world. That is their real home. The women are going there. The men are already there in one sense, but not in another. They own it, but do not inhabit it. They do not quite dare. The world is a home only for the free.

> "For there's blood on the field and blood
> on the foam,
> And blood on the body when man goes
> home.
> And a Voice valedictory, 'Who is for
> Victory?
> Who is for Liberty? Who goes Home!' "

Sweethearts and Wives

It is a time-honored masculine generalization that sweethearts are more fun that wives. This proposition really implies another, that wives and sweethearts are two distinct and different things. If we admit the validity of the latter proposition, the former stands unquestionably true.

This is, as somebody once pointedly remarked, a manmade world. Certainly the distinction in theory and practice between a wife and a sweetheart is a masculine creation. No woman, it may be affirmed, having once been a sweetheart, would ever cease to be one of her own free will and accord.

For observe what it means to be a sweetheart. In the first place, there is the setting, the milieu, the scene of action. This is definite by virtue of its remarkable diversity. One is a sweetheart in the park, in the theater, in the elevated train, on the front steps, on the fire escape, at soda fountains, at baseball games, in tea shops, in restaurants, in the parlor, in the kitchen, anywhere, everywhere—that is to say, in the world at large. When two people are being sweethearts, they inhabit the world.

And they inhabit it together—that is the next thing. It is one of the conditions of being a sweetheart that you are always "along" whenever possible—and it is generally found possible. It seems to be the proper thing for one sweetheart to be always where the other one is. There is never any reason, or any excuse, for a sweetheart staying at home. The fact that a man cannot take his sweetheart to work with him is universally held to justify him in neglecting his work. But when he plays, he can take her with him, and he does. He takes her to the theater, he takes her to the baseball park, he takes her out to Duck creek and teaches her how to fish.

That is the third thing about being a sweetheart. She is not shut out from his society by reason of differences in habits or tastes. The assumption is that their habits and tastes ought to be alike. If she doesn't understand baseball, he explains it to her. If he likes golf, he teaches her how to play. If he loves poetry, he sits up and reads her his favorite poets. He doesn't permit any trivial differences to come between them. If she has been brought up with the idea that it is wicked to drink, he will cultivate her taste in cocktails. He will give her lessons in Socialism, poetry and poker, all with infinite tact and patience. And he will do all of these things very humbly, with no pride in his own superiority. He will bring his most cherished ideas anxiously to her for her approval, and listen with the most genuine respect to her criticisms. They plan their future with the democratic equality of partners in the business of life.

Which is all very delightful. But in the course of time they are married, and very shortly after that the sweetheart becomes a wife. She is still the same person—she hasn't changed. But the conditions have changed. . . . There was once a man—I don't pretend to approve of him—who had a wife and also a sweetheart, and he liked the sweetheart so much better than the wife that he persuaded his wife to divorce him, and then married the sweetheart; whereupon he simply had to get another sweetheart, because it was just the same as it had been before. The poor fellow never could figure it out. He thought there must be some mysterious and baneful magic in the marriage ceremony that spoiled things. But that superstition need not detain us. Proceed we to an inquiry as to where the difference really is.

There is the matter of rendezvous. The whole spirit of meeting a sweetheart is that one is never quite certain whether she will really be there. Usually, as a matter of fact, she is late. One is anxious or angry, but one is never complacent about her coming. She may have misunderstood or misremembered the street corner. She may be waiting somewhere else. Or she may have changed her mind—a devastating thought. . . . But with a wife it is different. It is impossible for her to forget the place, for there is only one place. It is neither at the elevated station nor in the park nor on the library steps. It is a place quite out of the world. And she will always be there. Or, at least, if she isn't there, she ought to be. "A woman's place is in the home."

This saying applies only to wives. It does not apply to sweethearts. No man ever thought his sweetheart belonged at home. He regards her home with hostility and suspicion, and keeps her away from it as much as possible. It is only when she is a wife that he begins to think he has a right to expect her to be there. When he thinks of her, it is always in that setting. He thinks of her in that setting complacently. When he goes there to meet her he does not go anxiously, with a beating heart. The home is not a rendezvous. It is not one of the delightful corners of the world where two companions can meet for an adventure. It is a place out of the world where one keeps one's wife.

Home is a place quite different from the rest of the world. It is different by virtue of the things that are not done there. Out in the world, anything is likely to happen. Any restaurant may hatch a business deal. Any barber shop may be a polling place. But business and politics do not belong in the home. They are as out of place in that atmosphere as a "jag" or a display of fireworks. And from not being done in the home, they come not to be thought about there. Cooking, clothes, children—these are the topics of interest for the inmate of a home. These things are interesting. They are quite as important as baseball or politics. But they lack a certain imaginative appeal. They are not Homeric enough. A new dress is an achievement, but not the same kind of achievement as a home run. A new kind of salad is an interesting experiment, but one does not stand around offering to bet money on the results. In a word, the home is a little dull.

When you have got a woman in a box, and you pay rent on the box, her relationship to you insensibly changes character. It loses the fine excitement of democracy. It ceases to be companionship, for companionship is only possible in a democracy. It is no longer a sharing of life together—it is a breaking of life apart. Half a life—cooking, clothes and children; half a life—business, politics and baseball. It doesn't make much difference which is the poorer half. Any half, when it comes to life, is very near to none at all.

Of course, this artificial distinction does not strictly obtain in any particular marriage. There is an attempt to break it down. It is an honorable attempt. But our civilization is nevertheless built on that distinction. In order to break down that distinction utterly it will be necessary to break down all the codes and restrictions and prejudices that keep women out of the great world. It is in the great world that a man finds his sweetheart, and in that narrow little box outside of the world that he loses her. When she has left that box and gone back into the great world, a citizen and a worker, then with surprize and delight he will discover her again, and never let her go.

VI

CONTEMPORARY PRO-FEMINIST MEN

T-shirt design, 1981. Steve Rankin, San Francisco.

THE PUBLICATION of Betty Friedan's *The Feminine Mystique* (1963) heralded the revitalization of women's struggles for equality in the contemporary era. Following the enactment of suffrage of 1920, the feminist struggle continued in others arenas: the Equal Rights Amendment, recognition of women workers, birth control and abortion rights, child care, and equal admission to professional training were all important struggles from the end of the First World War to the beginning of the Kennedy administration (see Rupp and Taylor 1987). Friedan's indictment signaled a recharged feminism, allowing dissatisfaction with women's position to erupt with significant force. If women had achieved the vote, why were there so few women elected to public office? If women had equal right to the classroom, why were they so dramatically underrepresented in the professions? If the right to work was clearly established and women protected by the same laws that protected male workers, why were women's wages about three-fifths of men's, a level that had not changed since the year before the Civil War? If women had achieved at least part of the right to control their own bodies (birth control, but not abortion until 1973), why were they still so vulnerable to violence from men, to rape and battery?

Friedan offered a powerful critique of the suburban housewife's social position. Women controlled the home and child rearing, yet many felt empty, bored, unfulfilled, and angry; women were the ones living

An asterisk (*) indicates that a document is included in this volume.

lives of "quiet desperation." The modern women's movement was born from that anger and frustration. Over the last twenty-five years, it has grown in the United States and around the world because it stands for the equality of all persons, regardless of their sex. Today's feminist movement is concerned with the legacies of inequality and discrimination in the four arenas identified in this book: education, economic opportunity, political rights, and social equality. In each, women have faced enormous resistance from those men who are entrenched in their power and indifferent in their privilege. But there are also, today, men who stand with women in their struggle against inequality.

Education

Once women were granted entry into the academy, they discovered a curriculum flawed by centuries of male domination. In every subject area in the college curriculum, men were the subject matter, and the language used to describe that subject matter was masculine. Centuries of social invisibility had allowed the collegiate curriculum to make women invisible in the subject matter and in the ways in which that subject matter was discussed. Feminism offered a wide-ranging critique of academic sexism. Women have demanded their own curriculum, women's studies, devoted to recognizing the experience of women, which had not been integrated into the traditional curriculum. Women's studies made gender visible as one of the fundamental axes around which social life is organized.

Feminist researchers have worked to retrieve women's lives from obscurity, challenging how we think about social life and the means we use to express it. Feminism has challenged the appropriateness of the linguistic generic masculine and demanded that we use gender-specific language to refer to specific genders. Women's studies also challenges the institutional biases that construct the typical academic classroom as a masculine domain, to which women may be allowed entry, though always as "the other." This has meant challenging "objective" methodologies that eliminate emotion or experience and altering classroom politics, raising issues of sexual harassment and sexist language and humor.

Some men have actively supported these struggles. A few enrolled in women's studies courses to understand how women's experience of inequality constructs their lives and relationships with men and with other women (see William Alexander McDavid's "Feminism for Men 101"*). Some male professors have attempted to integrate women into their curriculum or to change their own use of language (Kampf and Ohmann 1983; Bezucha 1985; Schlib 1985; Baker 1981; and Folsom 1983). Others offer courses on men's experience as a way to apply the feminist insistence on the centrality of gender to men's lives. Such courses de-center the generic "man" and explore various masculinities (constructed by class, race, ethnicity, age) as specific constructions of gender, offering an implicit critique of men's power over women (see Harry Brod's "Scholarly Studies of Men"*; and also Kimmel and Messner 1989). Several academic books by men begin with feminist premises about the politics of male power and privilege. What seemed but a few voices in the 1970s has grown to a chorus of writers and scholars who use feminist insights to expand our understanding of men's lives with a political agenda of promoting gender equality.

Economic Equality

The contemporary women's movement has also been concerned with women's economic inequality. Pro-feminist men have supported women's right to enter professions previously closed to them (see Asimov 1971), to enjoy the protection of affirmative action and to enjoy union participation and leadership (see Milkman 1986). George Meany's 1977 speech to the Coalition of Labor Union Women (CLUW) suggests that union leadership was not uniformly opposed to feminist reform, from equality in the workplace to the ERA. "If supporting a living wage for all workers makes me a feminist, move over sisters; I've been called a lot worse," Meany declared. "ERA, full employment, minimum wage, labor law reform, pregnancy benefits, national health insurance—these are not women's issues. They are labor issues, trade union issues. They are fights all of us must win and win together" (cited in Balser 1987, 192).

Documents in this section indicate several ways in which men have supported these struggles, from women's wages (see Fred Small's "59 Cents"*) to academic discrimination (see Robert Reich's "Wake-Up Call"*). Since Antoinette Brown Blackwell, women have sought the right to minister to their faiths (see Jewett 1980). The Right Reverend Paul Moore, the Episcopal archbishop of New York, was the first to ordain a woman as a priest in the Episcopal church as well as the first to ordain an open lesbian, both in 1977 (see his "Statement at the Ordination of Rev. Mary Michael Simpson"*). Catholic theologian Leonard Swidler goes further. Christianity needs a thorough overhaul along feminist lines, he claims in "Jesus was a Feminist" (1971). (See also his "No Penis, No Priest."*) He urges women in the church, especially nuns, to "follow the example of Jesus, particularly, and to work most of all to bring to full maturity the most suppressed element of the world and of the Church: laywomen. If Jesus, a male, could identify with and champion the cause of the most oppressed of his society, women—for Jesus was indeed a feminist!—then surely nuns today can identify with and champion the cause of their sisters, laywomen" (Swidler 1976, 134).

Political Struggles

Central to the struggle for political equality has been the Equal Rights Amendment, which, though supported by a majority of American women and men, has failed to secure enough votes among state legislatures to become an amendment to the U.S. Constitution. Men have supported the ERA both individually and organizationally. Public statements by Howard Cosell ("Why I Support the ERA"*), Alan Alda ("Why Should Men Care?"*), and Jesse Jackson ("Ensuring the Dignity and Equality of Women"*) indicate support. Representative Don Edwards has introduced the ERA in the U.S. House of Representatives every year (see his speech* reintroducing the ERA), and there are numerous male cosponsors of the bill that attempt to have it enacted into law. (Edwards and Senator Alan Cranston also introduced the "Freedom of Choice Act," reaffirming the principles of *Roe v. Wade* and establishing women's right to choose as federal law.) Alda argued that he felt a special responsibility to speak out in support of the ERA because "men need to see other men expressing themselves and to know it's okay to get passionate about this," he told *Ms.* in 1975. "Feminism is not just women's business." Other male television celebrities appearing in *Ms.* supporting the ERA included Norman Lear, Henry Winkler, and Phil Donahue.

Men Allied Nationally for the Equal Rights Amendment (M.A.N. for the E.R.A.) was founded in 1978 by Barry Shapiro and had organizational branches in several states (see their "Eleven Ways Men Can Benefit from the ERA"*). Like the Men's League for Woman Suffrage seventy years earlier, its purpose was to organize men to march in demonstrations and take out advertisements in states then considering the amendment. Several other organizations, like the California Anti-Sexist Men's Political Caucus (CAMP Caucus) (see "Male Pride and Anti-Sexism"*) and the National Organization for Men Against Sexism (NOMAS) (see their statement* of principles), have made more diffuse efforts to raise issues of feminism for men, providing a model for the integration of support for changes among men and support for feminist reforms.

Social Equality

The struggle for social equality has been the most visible arena of struggle in the contemporary era since it has encompassed women's right to control her body and sexuality, to be protected from male violence and rape, to reform domestic life and share the work in the home, and to transform personal life and the relations between women and men. Several documents in this section provide powerful analyses of the ways in which various feminist struggles are interconnected. Blood, Tuttle, and Lakey's "Understanding and Fighting Sexism"* locates the source of male violence and women's oppression in socially derived definitions of masculinity. In "The Struggle to Smash Sexism is a Struggle to Develop Women,"* Kalamu ya Salaam links women's struggles to the struggle for African-American liberation. These are not sequential struggles, Salaam argues, but simultaneous and mutually reinforcing.

Many pro-feminist men have embraced a feminist analysis of male violence against women, particularly battery and rape. Senator Joseph Biden has introduced the Violence against Women Act in the U.S. Senate, where it is currently under debate. This bill would increase criminal penalties for rape and also make rape a gender-based hate crime and thus punishable under both federal civil rights statutes and state criminal codes. Other men work directly with violent men. Brotherpeace, a spinoff project of the Ending Men's Violence Task Group of NOMAS, sponsors an annual day for "breaking the silence to end men's violence." Dozens of organizations offer counseling to batterers in a collaborative arrangement with feminist shelters for battered women. Tim Beneke (1982) imagines the impact of rape of women's lives to illuminate the problem for men (see his *Men on Rape**).

Long before abortion was legalized, men supported women's right to choose. In the early 1960s, an Oklahoma doctor, William Jennings Bryan Henrie (whose namesake was another pro-feminist prairie populist), was openly performing illegal abortions for women who requested them (see his "A New Look at Abortion"*). Repeatedly arrested and jailed for his activities, his license revoked, Henrie believed that women's right to choose was more important than antiquated laws. "My relationship has always been with the woman who is burdened with an unwanted pregnancy, knows what she wants, knows what she needs, and is determined to have it [an abortion] regardless of any religious chastisement or legal punishment she might incur because of her action," Henrie wrote in 1967 (SL, MC 289, box 2, folder 35). Robert Bick, a California medical technologist, lost his job when it was revealed that he had been elected treasurer of the Society for Humane Abortion (SHA) in 1967 (ibid., box 1, folder 5). Richard Bowers, a Connecticut lawyer, was a member of the SHA and was also elected to the executive committee for the National Abortion Rights Action League (NARAL). "Compulsory Pregnancy Laws are *Social Insanity* in the 1970s" was Bower's suggestion for a masthead on SHA stationery in 1970. Bill Baird, a former medical student, "has devoted his life to changing our birth control laws" (*Boston Globe* [13 October 1968]: 35). After founding a free birth-control and abortion-referral service, Baird organized the Parents Aid Society, whose vans brought materials directly to women, especially in poorer neighborhoods, and established clinics to provide safe abortions.

A recent evocation of the simple eloquence of a doctor's responsibility to his patient's well-being is contained in John Irving's novel *The Cider House Rules* (1985). Irving "tries to show what the world was like before we could take a safe, legal abortion for granted," he commented in an interview. Bereft over a woman's death following a back-alley abortion, Dr. Wilbur Larch determines to use medically safe procedures to protect women's lives. "I'm not saying it's *right* you understand?" Larch says. "I'm saying it's her choice—it's a woman's choice. She's got a right to have a choice, you understand?" (Irving 1985, 110). Although Irving's earlier *The World According to Garp* suggested some ambivalence about feminism, *The Cider House Rules* is unequivocal. Irving has become an active campaigner for NARAL because he fears that the current agenda of the religious right augurs a "return to a kind of butchery [illegal abortions] that is really without social conscience and that really treats women not as second class citizens but *worse*" (cited in *New York Woman,* 1988, 57).

The anti-feminist vision lies behind much of the "pro-life" movement, whose judicial inroads and terrorist tactics have put women's right to choose again in jeopardy. So today pro-feminist men have joined with women to preserve the right to choose because it guarantees women equal rights and because, without it, equal relationships with men are virtually impossible. We close this volume with two statements by men in support of maintaining that right. "Why We March,"* the statement of the Men Who Care about Women's Lives, a San Francisco–based organization to support reproductive rights, parallels Justice Harry Blackmun's blunt, eloquent dissent* from the U.S. Supreme Court's decision on *Webster v. Missouri Reproductive Services.* Against the "callous" silence of the court's majority, Blackmun emerged as a guardian of women's "liberty to control their destinies." But, he concluded, "the signs are evident and very ominous, and a chill wind blows."

Today's Pro-Feminist Men

The resistance to women's equality expressed in that decision is becoming the minority opinion. Every Gallup poll since 1974 found a majority of American men have supported and continue to support the ERA and support a woman's right to choose (see Klein 1986). A majority of American men support women's equality in the workplace and the home and their political rights. About two-thirds of American men surveyed agreed with a statement that the "federal government should establish the principle of equal opportunity for women in hiring, training, and promotion in private employment," and nearly three-fourths agreed that there should be "professionally supervised child care facilities for children of working mothers" (Komorovsky 1976, 41). Despite this support, women's gains have been matched by persistent inequality at every level of American society. Today's feminist women stand for equality in every sphere, public and private. It is the side of justice and freedom, against which the conservative tides of reaction, privilege, and fear have always hoped to throw enough obstacles to block its success. Today's pro-feminist men stand with their feminist sisters, against the tide of men's resistance and for those social changes that will push this nation to honor its commitment to genuine democracy and equality.

STANDING UP FOR WOMEN

"WOMEN'S LIBERATION MEETS MILLER-MAILER-MANSON MAN"

Gore Vidal (1972)

THE RESPONSE to *Sexual Politics, Feminine Mystique,* et al. has been as interesting as anything that has happened in our time, with the possible exception of Richard Nixon's political career. The hatred these girls have inspired is to me convincing proof that their central argument is valid. Men do hate women (or as Germaine Greer puts it: "Women have very little idea of how much men hate them") and dream of torture, murder, flight.

It is no accident that in the United States the phrase "sex and violence" is used as one word to describe acts of equal wickedness, equal fun, equal danger to that law and order our masters would impose upon us. Yet equating sex with violence does change the nature of each (words govern us more than anatomy), and it is quite plain that those who fear what they call permissiveness do so because they know that if sex is truly freed of taboo it will lead to torture and murder because that is what *they* dream of or, as Norman Mailer puts if, "Murder offers us the promise of vast relief. It is never unsexual."

There has been from Henry Miller to Norman Mailer to Charles Manson a logical progression. The Miller-Mailer-Manson man (or M3 for short) has been conditioned to think of women as, at best, breeders of sons; at worst, objects to be poked, humiliated, killed. Needless to say, M3's reaction to Women's Liberation has been one of panic. He believes that if women are allowed parity with men they will treat men the way men have treated women and that, even M3 will agree, has not been very well or, as Cato the Censor observed, if woman be made man's equal she will swiftly become his master.

From Homage to Daniel Shays: Collected Essays, 1952–1972. *New York: Random House, 1972.*

M3 knows that women are dangerously different from men, and not as intelligent (though they have their competencies: needlework, child-care, detective stories). When a woman does show herself to be superior at, say, engineering, Freud finessed that anomaly by reminding us that since she is a bisexual, like everyone else, her engineering skill simply means that she's got a bit too much of the tomboy in her, as W. C. Fields once remarked to Grady Sutton on a similar occasion.

Women are not going to make it until M3 is reformed, and that is going to take a long time. Meanwhile the current phase of the battle is intense and illuminating. M3 is on the defensive, shouting names; he thinks that to scream "dyke" is enough to make the girls burst into tears, but so far they have played it cool. Some have even admitted to a bit of dyking now and then along with warm mature heterosexual relationships of the deeply meaningful fruitful kind that bring much-needed children into the world ("Good fucks make good babies"—N. Mailer). I love you Marion and I love you too Marvin. The women are responding with a series of books and position papers that range from shrill to literature. In the last category one must place Eva Figes who, of the lot, is the only one whose work can be set beside John Stuart Mill's celebrated review of the subject and not seem shoddy or self-serving. . . .

What does the American woman want? asks M3 plaintively. Doesn't she kill off her husbands with mantis-abandon, inherit the money, become a Mom to Attis-like sons, dominate primary education (most American men are "feminized" in what they would regard as the worst sense of that word by being brought up almost entirely by women and made to conform to American female values which are every bit as twisted as American male values)?

Yet the American woman who seems to have so much is still very much a victim of patriarchal attitudes—after all, she is made to believe that marriage is the most important thing in life, a sentiment peculiarly necessary to a capitalist society in which marriage is still the employer's best means of controlling the employee. The young man with a child and pregnant wife is going to do as he is told. The young man or woman on his own might not be so tractable. Now that organized religion is of little social significance, the great corporations through advertising (remember "Togetherness"?) and hiring policies favor the married, while looking with great suspicion on the bachelor who might be a Commie Weirdo Fag or a Pro-Crypto dyke. As long as marriage (and Betty Friedan's *Feminine Mystique*) are central to our capitalism (and to its depressing Soviet counterpart) neither man nor woman can be regarded as free to be human.

"In a society where men have an overriding interest in the acquisition of wealth, and where women themselves have become a form of property, the link between sexuality and money becomes inextricable." This is grim truth. Most men buy their wives, though neither party would admit to the nature of the transaction, preferring such euphemisms as Marvin is a good provider and Marion is built. Then Marion divorces Marvin and takes him to the cleaners, and he buys with whatever is left a younger model. It is money, not sex, that Puritans want. After all, the English word for "coming" used to be "spending": you spend your seed in the woman's bank and, if the moon is right, nine months later you will get an eight-pound dividend.

Needless to say, if you buy a woman you don't want anyone else using her. To assure your rights, you must uphold all the taboos against any form of sex outside marriage. . . .

Mailer's essential argument boils down to the following points. Masturbation is bad and so is contraception because the whole point to sex between man and woman is conception. Well, that's what the Bible says, too. He links homosexuality with evil. The man who gives in to his homosexual drives is consorting with the enemy. Worse, not only does he betray moral weakness by not fighting those drives but he is a coward for not daring to enter into competition with other Alpha males for toothsome females. This is dizzy but at least a new thought. One of the many compliments Mailer has tendered M3 over the years is never having succumbed to whatever homosexual urges M3 might have had. Now, to M2's shock, instead of getting at least a Congressional Medal of Honor for heroism, he sees slowly descending upon his brow an unmistakable dunce cap. All that hanging about boxers, to no good end!

Finally, Mailer's attitude toward woman is pretty much that of an VFW commander in heartland America. He can never understand that a woman is not simply a creature to be used for breeding (his "awe" at the thought of her procreative function is blarney), that she is a human as he is, and that he is dangerous to her since one of his most American dreams was of a man who murdered his wife and then buggered another woman against her will as celebration of the glorious deed. . . .

Those who have been treated cruelly will treat others cruelly. This seems to be a fact of our condition. M3 has every reason to be fearful of woman's revenge should she achieve equality. He is also faced with the nightmare (for him) of being used as a sexual object or, worse, being ignored (the menacing cloud in the middle distance is presently no larger than a vibrator). He is fighting back on every front.

Take pornography. Though female nudes have been usually acceptable in our Puritan culture, until recently the male nude was unacceptable to the Patriarchs. After all, the male—any male—is a stand-in for God, and God wears a suit at all times, or at least jockey shorts. Now, thanks to randy Lilith, the male can be shown entirely nude but, say the American censors, never with an erection. The holy of holies, the totem of our race, the symbol of the Patriarchs' victory over the Great Mother must be respected. Also, as psychologists point out, though women are not as prone to stimulus through looking at pictures as men (is this innate or the result of conditioning?), they are more excited by pictures of the male erect than of the male at ease. And excitement of course is bad for them, gives them ideas, makes them insatiable; even the ancient Greeks, though freer in sexual matters than we, took marriage seriously. As a result, only unmarried girls could watch naked young men play because young girls ought to be able to look over a field which married women had better not know about.

Today we are witnessing the breakup of patterns thousands of years old. M3's response is predictable: if man on top of woman has been the pattern for all our known history, it must be right. This of course was the same argument he made when the institution of slavery was challenged. After all, slavery was quite as old an institution as marriage. With the rejection of the idea of ownership of one person by another at the time of our Civil War, Women's Lib truly began. If you could not own a black man, you could not own a woman either. So the war began. Needless to say, the forces of reaction are very much in the saddle (in every sense), and women must fight for their equality in a system which wants to keep them in manageable family groups, buying consumer goods, raising future consumers, until the end of time—or the world's raw resources, which is rather closer at hand.

. . . It is very simple: we are breeding ourselves into extinction. We cannot feed the people now alive. In thirty-seven years the world's population will double unless we have the "good luck" to experience on the grandest scale famine, plague, war. To survive we must stop making babies at the current rate, and this can only be accomplished by breaking the ancient stereotypes of man the warrior, woman the breeder. M3's roar is that of our tribal past, quite unsuitable, as the old Stalinists used to say, to new necessities.

. . . Free the sexes first and the system will have to change. There will be no housewife to be conned into buying things she does not need. But all this is in the future. The present is the battleground, and the next voice you hear will be that of a patriarch, defending his attitudes—on a stack of Bibles.

"WOMAN IS THE NIGGER OF THE WORLD"

John Lennon (1972)

WOMAN is the nigger of the world.
Yes she is. Think about it.
Woman is the nigger of the world.
Think about it. Do something about it.

We make her paint her face and dance
If she won't be a slave we say that she don't love it.
If she's rude we say she's trying to be a man
We put her down by pretending that she's above us.

Woman is the nigger of the world, yes she is.

If you don't believe me, take a look at the one you're with.
Woman is the slave to the slave
If you believe me, you better scream about it.

We make her bear and raise our children
Then we leave her flat for being a fat old mother hen.
We tell her home is the only place she should be
Then we complain that she's too unworthy to be our friend.

Woman is the nigger of the world
If you believe me, take a look at the one you're with

From John Lennon: Live in New York City.

Woman is the slave to the slave
Yeah, you'd better scream about it.

We insult her every day on TV
And wonder why she has no guts or
confidence

When she's young we kill her will to be
free
We put her down for being dumb. . . .

"MARXISM AND FEMINISM"

Herbert Marcuse (1974)

I SHALL TAKE the liberty of beginning and ending with some rather personal remarks. For the beginning I just want to say that this is the only invitation to lecture which I have accepted during the entire academic year. The reason is a very simple one. I believe the Women's Liberation Movement today is, perhaps the most important and potentially the most radical political movement that we have, even if the consciousness of this fact has not yet penetrated the Movement as a whole. . . .

Now, two preliminary remarks on the situation of the Women's Liberation Movement as I see it. The Movement originates and operates within patriarchal civilization; it follows that it must be initially discussed in terms of the actual status of women in the male dominated civilization.

Secondly, the Movement operates within a class society—here is the first problem; women are not a class in the Marxian sense. The male-female relationship cuts across class lines but the immediate needs and potentialities of women are definitely class-conditioned to a high degree. Nevertheless there are good reasons why "woman" should be discussed as a general category versus "man." Namely the long historical process in which the social, mental and even physiological characteristics of women developed as different from and contrasting with those of men

Here, a word on the question whether the "feminine" or "female" characteristics are socially conditioned or in any sense "natural," biological. My answer is: over and above the obviously physiological differences between male and female, the feminine characteristics are socially conditioned. However, the long process of thousands of years of social conditioning means that they may become "second nature" which is not changed automatically by the establishment of new social institutions. There can be discrimination against women even under socialism.

Paper presented at Stanford University, 7 March 1974. Reprinted in Women's Studies *2, no. 3 (1974).*

In patriarchal civilization, women have been subjected to a specific kind of repression, and their mental and physical development has been channeled in a specific direction. On these grounds a separate Women's Liberation Movement is not only justified, but it is necessary. But the very goals of this Movement require changes of such enormity in the material as well as intellectual culture, that they can be attained only by a change in the entire social system. By virtue of its own dynamic, the Movement is linked with the political struggle for revolution, freedom for men *and* women. Because beneath and beyond the male-female dichotomy is the human being, common to male and female: the human being whose liberation, whose realization is still at stake.

The Movement operates on two levels; first, the struggle for full economic, social and cultural equality. Question: is such economic, social and cultural equality attainable within the capitalist framework? I will come back to this question, but I want to submit a preliminary hypothesis: there are no economic reasons why such equality should not be attainable within the capitalist framework, although a largely modified capitalism. But the potentialities, the goals of the Women's Liberation Movement go far beyond it, namely into regions which never can be attained within a capitalist framework, nor within the framework of any class society. Their realization would call for a second stage, where the Movement would transcend the framework within which it now operates. At this stage "beyond equality", liberation implies the construction of a society governed by a different Reality Principle, a society where the established dichotomy between masculine and feminine is overcome in the social and individual relationships between human beings.

Thus, in the Movement itself is contained the image, not only of new social institutions, but also of a change in consciousness, of a change in the instinctual needs of men and women, freed from the requirements of domination and exploration. And this is the Movement's most radical, subversive potential. It means, not only a commitment to socialism (full equality of women has always been a basic socialist demand), but commitment to a specific form of socialism which has been called "feminist socialism." I will return to this concept later.

What is at stake in this transcendence is the negation of the exploiting and repressive values of patriarchal civilization. What is at stake is the negation of the values enforced and reproduced in society by male domination. And such radical subversion of values can never be the mere by-product of new social institutions. It must have its roots in the men and women who build the new institutions.

What is the meaning of this subversion of values in the transition to socialism? And secondly, is this transition, in any sense, the liberation and ascent of *specifically feminine* characteristics on a social scale.

To start with the first question, here are the governing values in capitalist society: profitable productivity, assertiveness, efficiency, competitiveness; in other words, the Performance Principle, the rule of functional rationality discriminating against emotions, a dual morality, the "work ethic," which means for the vast majority of the population condemnation to alienated and inhuman labor, and the will to power, the display of strength, virility.

Now, according to Freud, this value hierarchy is expressive of a mental structure in which primary aggressive energy tends to reduce and to weaken the life instincts, that is, erotic energy. According to Freud, the destructive tendency in society will gain momentum as civilization necessitates intensified repression in order to maintain domination in the face of the ever more realistic possibilities of liberation, and intensified repression in turn leads to the activation of surplus aggressiveness, and its channelling into socially useful aggression. This total mobilization of aggressiveness is only too familiar to us today: militarization, brutalization of the forces of law and order, fusion of sexuality and violence, direct attack on the life instincts in their drive to save the environment, attack on the legislation against pollution and so on.

These tendencies are rooted in the infrastructure of advanced capitalism itself. The aggravating economic crisis, the limits of imperialism, the reproduction of the established society through waste and destruction, make themselves increasingly felt and necessitate more intensified and extended controls in order to keep the population in line, controls and manipulation which go down into the depth of the mental structure, into the realm of the instincts themselves. Now, to the degree to which the totalization of aggressiveness and repression today permeates the entire society, the image of socialism is modified at an essential point. Socialism, as a *qualitatively* different society, must embody the *antithesis,* the definite negation of the aggressive and repressive needs and values of capitalism as a form of male-dominated culture.

The objective conditions for such an antithesis and subversion values are maturing, and they make possible the ascent, at least as a transitory phase in the reconstruction of society, of characteristics which, in the long history of patriarchal civilization, have been attributed to the female rather than the male. Formulated as the antithesis of the dominating masculine qualities, such feminine qualities would be receptivity, sensitivity, non-violence, tenderness and so on. These characteristics appear indeed as opposite of domination and exploitation. On the primary psychological level, they would pertain to the domain of Eros, they would express the energy of the life instincts, against the death instinct and destructive energy. And the question here arises: Why do these life-protecting characteristics appear as specifically *feminine* characteristics? Why did the very same characteristics not also shape the dominant masculine qualities? This process has a history of thousands of years, during which the defence of the established society and of its hierarchy originally depended on physical strength, and thereby reduced the role of the female who was periodically disabled by bearing and then caring for children. Male domination, once established on these grounds, spread from the originally military sphere to other social and political institutions. The woman came to be regarded as inferior, as weaker, mainly as support for, or as adjunct to man, as sexual object, as tool of reproduction. And only as worker had she a form of equality, a repressive equality, with man. Her body and her mind were reified, became objects. And just as her intellectual development was blocked, so was her erotic development. Sexuality was objectified as a means to an end, procreation or prostitution.

A first countertrend became effective at the very beginning of the modern period, in the twelfth and thirteenth centuries, and, highly significantly, in direct context with the great and radical heretic movements with the Cathars and the Albigensians. In these centuries, the autonomy of love, the autonomy of the woman was proclaimed, contrasting and counteracting male aggressiveness and brutality. Romantic Love: I am perfectly well aware of the fact that these terms have become entirely pejorative terms, especially within the Movement. Still, I take them a little more seriously, and I take them in the historical context in which these developments should be taken. This was the first great subversion of the established hierarchy of values: the first great protest against the feudal hierarchy and the loyalties established in the feudal hierarchy, with its specifically pernicious repression of the woman.

To be sure, this protest, this antithesis was largely ideological, and confined to the nobility. However, it was not entirely ideological. The prevailing social norms were subverted in the famous Courts of Love, established by Elinor d'Aquitaine, where the judgment was practically always in favor of the lovers and against the husband, the right of love superseding the right of the feudal lord. And it was a woman who reportedly defended the last stronghold of the Albigensians against the murderous armies of the northern barons.

These progressive movements were cruelly suppressed. The weak beginning of feminism, anyway on a weak class basis, were destroyed. But nevertheless, the role of the woman gradually changed in the development of industrial society. Under the impact of technical progress, social reproduction depends increasingly less on physical strength and prowess, either in war or in the material process of production, or in commerce. The result was the enlarged exploitation of women as instruments of labor. The weakening of the social basis of male dominance did not do away with the perpetuation of male dominance by the new ruling class. The increasing participation of women in the industrial work process, which undermined the material grounds of the male hierarchy, also enlarged the human base of exploitation and the surplus exploitation of the woman as housewife, mother, servant, in addition to her work in the process of production.

However, advanced capitalism gradually created the material conditions for translating the ideology of feminine characteristics into reality, the objective conditions for turning the weakness that was attached to them into strength, turning the sexual object into a subject, and making feminism a political force in the struggle against capitalism, against the Performance Principle. It is with the view of these prospects that Angela Davis speaks of the revolutionary function of the female as antithesis to the Performance Principle, in a paper written in the Palo Alto Jail, "Women and Capitalism," December, 1971.

The emerging conditions for such a development are mainly:

—the alleviation of heavy physical labor,
—the reduction of labor time,
—the production of pleasant and cheap clothing,
—the liberalization of sexual morality,
—birth control,
—general education.

These factors indicate the social basis for the antithesis to the Performance Principle, the emancipation of female and feminine energy, physical and intellectual, in the established society. But at the same time, this emancipation is arrested, manipulated, and exploited by this society. For capitalism cannot possibly allow the ascent of the libidinal qualities which would endanger the repressive work ethic of the Performance Principle and the constant reproduction of this work ethic by human individuals themselves. Thus, at this stage, these liberating tendencies, in manipulated form, are made part of the reproduction of the established system. They became exchange values, selling the system, and sold by the system. The exchange society comes to completion with the commercialism of sex: the female body not only a commodity, but also a vital factor in the realization of surplus value. And the working woman continues, in ever larger numbers, to suffer the double exploitation as worker and housewife. In this form, the reification of the woman persists in a particularly effective manner. How can this reification be dissolved? How can the emancipation of the woman become a decisive force in the construction of socialism as a qualitatively different society?

Let's go back to the first stage in the development of this Movement, and assume the achievement of complete equality. As equals in the economy and politics of capitalism, women must share with men the competitive, aggressive characteristics required to keep a job and to get ahead in the job. Thus, the Performance Principle, and the alienation implied in it would be sustained and reproduced by a larger number of individuals. In order to achieve equality, which is the absolute prerequisite of liberation, the Movement must be aggressive. But equality is not yet freedom. Only as an equal economic and political subject can the woman claim a leading-role in the radical reconstruction of society. But beyond equality, liberation subverts the established hierarchy of needs—a subversion of values and norms which would make for the emergence of a society governed by a new Reality Principle. And this, in my view, is the radical potential of *feminist socialism.*

Feminist socialism: I spoke of a necessary modification of the notion of socialism, because I believe that in Marxian socialism there are remnants, elements of the continuation of the Performance Principle and its values. I see these elements, for example, in the emphasis on the ever more effective development of the productive forces, the ever more productive exploitation of nature, the separation of the "realm of freedom" from the work world.

The potentialities of socialism today transcend this image. Socialism, as a qualitatively different way of life would not only use the productive forces for the reduction of alienated labor and labor time, but also for making life an end in itself, for the development of the senses and the intellect for pacification of aggressiveness, the enjoyment of being, for the emancipation of the senses and of the intellect from the rationality of domination: creative receptivity versus repressive productivity.

In this context, the liberation of the woman would indeed appear "as the antithesis to the Performance Principle," would indeed appear as the revolutionary function of the female in the reconstruction of society. Far from fostering submissiveness and weakness, in this reconstruction, the feminine characteristics would activate aggressive energy against domination and exploitation. They would operate as needs and eventual goals in the socialist organization of production, in the social division of labor, in the setting of priorities once scarcity has been conquered. And thus, entering reconstruction of society as a whole, the feminine characteristics would cease to be specifically feminine, to the degree to which they would be universalized in socialist culture, material and intellectual. Primary aggressiveness would persist, as it would in any form of society, but it may well lose the specifically masculine quality of domination and exploitation. Technical progress, the chief vehicle of productive aggressiveness, would be freed from its capitalist features and channelled into the destruction of the ugly destructiveness of capitalism.

I think there are good reasons for calling this image of socialist society feminist socialism: the woman would have achieved full economic, political, and cultural equality in the all round development of her faculties, and over and above this equality, social as well as personal relationships would be permeated with the receptive sensitivity which, under male domination, was largely concentrated in the woman: the masculine-feminine antithesis would then have been transformed into a synthesis—the legendary idea of *androgynism.*

I will say a few words about this extreme of (if you wish) romantic or speculative thought, which I think is neither so extreme nor so speculative.

No other rational meaning can possibly be attributed to the idea of androgynism than the fusion, in the individual, of the mental and somatic characteristics, which in patriarchal civilization were unequally developed in men and women, a fusion in which feminine characteristics, in cancellation of male dominance, would prevail over their repression. But, no degree of androgynous fusion could ever abolish the natural differences between male and female as individuals. All joy, and all sorrow are rooted in this difference, in this relation to the other, of whom you want to become part, and who you want to become part of yourself, and who never can and never will become such a part of yourself. Feminist socialism would thus continue to be riddled with conflicts arising from this condition, the ineradicable conflicts of needs and values, but the androgynous character of society might gradually diminish the violence and humiliation in the resolution of these conflicts.

To conclude:

The Woman's Movement has gained political significance because of recent changes in the capitalist mode of production itself which provided the movement with a new material base. I recall the main features:

1) the increasing number of women employed in the production process,

2) the increasingly technical form of production, gradually diminishing the use of heavy physical labor power,

3) the spread of an *aesthetic* commodity form: systematic commercial appeal to sensuousness, luxuries; the diversion of purchasing power to pleasurable things and services.

4) the disintegration of the patriarchal family through "socialization" of the children from outside (mass media, peer groups, etc.)

5) the ever more wasteful and destructive productivity of the Performance Principle.

Feminism is a revolt against decaying capitalism, against the historical obsolescence of the capitalist mode of production. This is the precarious link between the Utopia and reality: the social ground for the movement as a potentially radical and revolutionary force is there, this is the hard core of the dream. But capitalism is still capable of keeping it a dream, of suppressing the transcending forces which strive for the subversion of the inhuman values of our civilization.

The struggle is still a political one, for abolition of these conditions, and in this struggle, the feminist movement plays an ever more vital part. Its mental and physiological forces assert themselves in the political education and action, and in the relationship between the individuals, at work and at leisure. I stressed that liberation cannot be expected as a by-product of new institutions, that it must emerge in the individuals themselves. The liberation of women begins at home, before it can enter society at large.

And here is my concluding personal statement. You may if you wish interpret it as a statement of surrender, or a statement of commitment. I believe that we men have to pay for the sins of a patriarchal civilization and its tyranny of power: women must become free to determine their own life, not as wife, not as mother, not as mistress, not as girl friend, but as an individual human being. This will be a struggle permeated with bitter conflicts, torment and suffering (mental and physical). Only the most familiar example today, which occurs again and again, where a man and a woman have jobs or can get jobs at places distant from each other, and the question naturally arises: who follows whom?

An even more serious example, the conflicting erotic relationships, which inevitably will arise in the process of liberation. These erotic conflicts cannot be resolved in a facile, playful way, nor by being tough, nor by establishing exchange relationships. That you should leave to the exchange society where it belongs. Feminist socialism will have to develop its own morality, which will be more, and other, than the mere cancellation of bourgeois morality.

Women's Liberation will be a painful process, but I believe it will be a necessary, a vital stage in the transition to a better society for men and women.

"SPEECH ON MEN SUPPORTING WOMEN"

Ed Asner (1987)

We've all heard how Abigail Adams urged her husband, John, to "remember the ladies" in the new Constitution. We also know he refused to take her seriously. Tonight, I'm happy to remind you of the gentlemen who have "remembered the ladies"—the men who stood up to be counted for the sake of their sisters, mothers, wives, daughters and just plain fairness. The really smart ones knew they were doing it for themselves as well.

There was John Quincy Adams, Abigail's son. In 1834, when a Southern Congressman claimed the Female Anti-Slavery societies had no right to petition Congress because their members couldn't vote, the former President—then serving in the House—asked, "Is it so clear they have no such right?" And for the next four days he spoke at length on the floor of the House about the bravery, the sacrifices, and the dedication of women in the American Revolution. He included his own mother, Abigail Adams, who had run a successful business and raised four children while her husband was away for 10 years during and after the war.

The women got their right to petition. Abigail would have been proud of her feminist son.

There was Frederick Douglass at the historic Seneca Falls Conference in 1848. The most illustrious Black spokesman of his time seconded Elizabeth Cady Stanton's

Manuscript courtesy of Ed Asner.

shocking proposal for women's suffrage when no one else would, and made such an impassioned speech in its support that the controversial resolution demanding the vote for women finally passed.

"All that distinguishes man as an intelligent and accountable being", said Douglass, "is equally true of woman. And if that Government only is just which governs by the free consent of the governed, there can be no reason in the world for denying to woman the exercise of the elective franchise, or a hand in making and administering the laws of the land. Our doctrine is that 'right is of no sex.' "

There's also John Stuart Mill, the English philosopher whose 1869 essay on "The Subjection of Women" became the bible of American and British suffragists. He presented the first bill for women's suffrage to England's House of Commons in 1867.

"We have had the morality of submission," wrote Mill, "and the morality of chivalry and generosity; the time is ripe for the morality of justice."

There's Al Smith, New York's tough-talking, newly-elected governor in 1919. I don't really know if Al was a feminist, but the "Happy Warrior" was a shrewd politician. He appointed the first woman ever to sit on the New York Industrial Commission.

"I've been thinking over my situation," the cigar-chomping Governor Smith told the press. "Women have got the vote. It's the first time. I thought I ought to bring women into the political picture in my administration."

Al made a good choice. His appointee was Frances Perkins who went on to become the first woman cabinet member. And she ended up serving four terms as Secretary of Labor in Franklin Roosevelt's cabinet.

Let's also remember Representative Daniel Anthony, Susan B. Anthony's nephew, and Senator Charles Curtis, who, in 1923, first introduced Alice Paul's Equal Rights Amendment in Congress.

There are also the feminist Congressmen like former Senator Birch Bayh and Representative Don Edwards—who helped get the ERA through Congress in 1972 and worked hard for the 1979 extension of the deadline for ratification.

There are many wonderful feminist men—lawyers, doctors, business leaders, clergymen, cartoonists, writers, producers, actors—too many to name tonight. But they believe in the feminist cause of equality, and they believe the feminization of power may be essential to our very survival.

As a feminist, I missed the presence of such women as Barbara Jordan and Elizabeth Holtzman on the Congressional panel investigating the Iran/Contra affair. Had they been on that panel, as they were during the Nixon impeachment hearings, I think the key questions would have been asked.

And as a feminist, I was offended to see an all male panel of senators sitting in judgment on the Bork nomination to the U.S. Supreme Court—an appointment that could have such devastating consequences for the women of this country.

The absence of women was flatly and simply—wrong!

So, I welcome this campaign for the feminization of power in this country and I'm proud to count myself as one of the feminist majority. . . .

"ENSURING THE DIGNITY AND EQUALITY OF WOMEN"

Rev. Jesse Jackson (1988)

Women are not a special interest group. They are the majority in our society and they have the right to a livable income, to freedom from discrimination in work and housing, to public policies which enable them to combine work and family life, and to respect.

IT IS A DISGRACE that the United States, the richest and most technologically advanced nation in the world, continues to deny full and equal citizenship to women. When we fail to pass the Equal Rights Amendment, when we impoverish women (and children) by job segregation and budget cuts, when we exploit women's sexuality, this nation is deprived of the potential gifts a majority of its citizens have to offer.

Despite the media images of women in high-paying positions, most women have fallen deeper into poverty and despair in the Reagan years. As women have filled three out of five new jobs they have joined the ranks of the working poor which have nearly doubled in the 1980s. Women today still earn only 67 cents of a man's dollar in wages and they are still largely segregated into low-paying "women's jobs" in the clerical, sales and service sectors. Minority women, facing the "double-jeopardy" of race and gender, are even worse off than white women—earning less, unemployed twice as often, and facing even greater job segregation.

No one should be forced to choose between work and family, between being able to afford to feed and clothe children and provide them proper supervision. Yet for all too many women this is their choice. We need a new set of rules—both at work and in law—that recognizes the importance of parenting and caregiving as well as work outside the home.

To ensure women's dignity and equality, I propose to:

Pass and Vigorously Enforce Anti-Discrimination Legislation

Women must be granted full protection under the law. We strongly support the passage and enforcement of the Equal (and Economic) Rights Amendment which would grant women the same constitutional rights as men. We must have an Attorney General who enforces the law of the land and a federal budget that gives greater funding to anti-discrimination agencies. We need . . . to guarantee that anti-discrimination laws will

Issue brief, 1988. Reprinted in Keep Hope Alive: Jesse Jackson's 1988 Presidential Campaign, *ed. Frank Clement and Frank Watkins. Boston: South End, 1989.*

be broadly interpreted, ensuring full access and participation on the part of women and minority groups.

Advance Economic Security

All workers must be guaranteed the right to a job at a living wage. We must significantly increase the minimum wage and link it to the average wage in the economy. We must reinvest in America, putting people to work to meet our needs in housing, health care, education, neighborhood revitalization and infrastructure repair. We need a new national commitment to strengthen workers' (especially service workers) rights to organize and represent their own interests. Women in unions earn a third more than women without unions.

We need a special effort to assure economic equality for women. We must break down the barriers in education, training and hiring which have created a sex-segregated workforce. "Women's work" must be eliminated. Vigorous affirmative action, with stated goals and timetables, must ensure equal access and participation for women in preparation for entrance into nontraditional fields and into higher paying and managerial positions. For the vast majority of women in traditional "women's jobs," we need a federal initiative establishing the principle of pay equity, so that jobs of comparable worth get similar pay. Part-time workers must be ensured minimum benefits, including pensions, on a pro-rated basis.

We must establish a uniform, national income benefit for needy families, most of whom are headed by women. We should explore a family allowance system which would supplement low earnings and ensure an adequate standard of living to families with children. Sixty-seven other countries have such a system. Finally, we must seek changes in the Social Security system and in private pension plans. Women should not be forced into poverty in old age because of discriminatory wages or because of lost wages due to motherhood.

Enable Women to Combine Work and Family

Women will never achieve equality in the marketplace until national and business policies on parental leave and child care change. Women—even women with small children—want work and not welfare. But to work they need decent pay, adequate health care and affordable childcare. Thus, we oppose current welfare and "workfare" proposals that would force poor women with very young children to go to work at low wages in return for their welfare checks. Such proposals are punitive and dangerous to families.

We need a comprehensive national childcare policy, with an increased federal childcare and credit, increased funding to states to develop and implement equal childcare programs, and the establishment of a national childcare office to promote long-range planning and implementation. We must also pass parental and medical leave legislation which would protect the jobs and incomes of workers who stay home to care for infants and for sick family members. The U.S. is the only industrialized country which does not guarantee women job-protected maternity leave. The lack of such a policy costs families and taxpayers nearly $400 million each year in lost earnings and public assistance.

Support Reproductive Choice

Decisions on the timing and size of one's family are a private responsibility. We must respect that right of privacy, while supporting family planning and making information available to reduce infant mortality and unintended adolescent pregnancy. The federal government must expand funding for family planning clinics and for research into safe and reliable methods of family planning. We oppose any attempts to repeal a woman's right to choose and must make sure that poor women have the same reproductive rights available to them as the rich—including Medicaid funding of abortion and the enforcement of informed consent laws to prevent involuntary sterilization.

Challenge Violence against Women

The president does much to set the tone of a nation. The Reagan administration's cutbacks in social services for poor women and their families, his attacks on reproductive rights, and his reversal of affirmative actions programs have all contributed to a climate allowing violence against women. We can create a different political climate, a climate in which women are treated with dignity and respect in every aspect of their lives. This includes adequately funding programs to stem violence against women and to protect those who have become the victims of such violence.

Women want equality, but equality cannot be achieved in a world in which the rules are stacked against them. Women want respect, but respect does not mean being put on a pedestal or into a gilded cage. Women want opportunity, not only in the home, but also in the workplace, the classroom and the athletic field. The time is now.

EDUCATIONAL EQUALITY

"MEN IN WOMEN'S STUDIES"

Louis Kampf and Dick Ohmann (1983)

MEN HAVE most of the power, prestige, and seniority in virtually every college and university. We deplore this fact; we should be trying to change it. Meanwhile, let us be practical about exploiting it. Those of us who are male, established, and committed to feminism and women's studies should not stand aside, feeling guilty and abstaining from participation because we think women should run this movement. They should and they will, but can they make use of our position and our support? Often the answer will be yes, and we should not hestiate to ask.

A fair number of men have gotten involved with women's studies in the last dozen years. Do women really need such favors? Often not, but men certainly do. For both Dick Ohmann and Louis Kampf, participation in the administration and teaching of women's studies has been a process

Radical Teacher *(Spring 1983).*

of self-education and consciousness-raising. Reading the appropriate journals and books is one thing; learning from day-to-day practice is quite another. We have been lucky in the specific institutional opportunities that have come our way. However, any man at an institution with a Women's Studies Program (or at least a few courses in the subject) can find a way of being involved. The particular situation may allow for no more than self-enlightenment. But even this, for the time being, ought to be rewarding enough. And sometimes more is possible.

The Institution

Assume this situation, which is the one Kampf and Ohmann are in: an overwhelming male hegemony in the institution; a nascent Women's Studies Program, poorly funded and relying on volunteers from various departments for most of the work; no departmental status or tenured chair; heavy reliance on students for energy and direction. A tenured man can contribute a lot to the public advancement of such a program without throwing his weight around in its internal processes.

Knowledge, for instance: how the Black Studies Program got established ten years earlier; what kind of argument has appealed to the provost, and to old so-and-so, chair of the educational policy committee; where to siphon off funds form other budgets to help with speakers, films, xeroxing; how to wrangle credit for students doing women's studies work; how the hiring process works, and how to intervene in it. If you attend women's studies meetings where practical needs come up, you'll probably find yourself able to pass on many small bits of information and counsel that will help avoid mistakes and smooth the bureaucratic path.

Second, and we need to be cautious here: clout. We think men in women's studies should never put themselves forward as spokespersons, ahead of or apart from the women in the program. But remember that many of our colleagues still simply don't hear what a woman says, until a man says it, too; nor will the old boys' network go away just because we choose to drop out of it. We can offer the supporting remarks in committee or in faculty meetings, endorsing the women's studies positions from a base of involvement and familiarity. We can raise hell within inner circles about obstacles to the tenuring of a feminist. We can go with the delegation to the dean, adding a few words now and then, repeating, insisting, seconding, translating into academese, showing our commitment.

Third: legitimation. More caution: we know that a movement can lose its power to subvert and alter, if it presents itself as too straight. All the same, we are not talking about revolution; we are talking about a program in a university. If we take part in the women's studies committee or collective, teach feminist ideas, advance them in meetings and colloquia, remind colleagues of the program's achievements, tell them about the new scholarship's challenge to old paradigms, we help combat the prejudice that "women's studies is not a discipline," and spread the conviction that it is a necessary part of the college's work.

These are ways men can advance women's studies by being directly active in its institutional life. Directly involved or not, we should obviously carry its discoveries and issues to our male colleagues, so that it does not seem "just" a women's concern. And our voices for feminism in classes convey the same message to male students. More concretely, we can intervene in our departmental hiring process to build the mass of young faculty members who will contribute to women's studies—and to combat the appointment of people who will be indifferent or opposed. We should contest the old male premises of the curriculum whenever it is up for revision. We can work for our departments to co-sponsor events with the Women's Studies Program, get courses cross-listed, order books and periodicals for the library. Unfortunately, at most places, women's studies cannot flourish without a parallel effort in departments.

The Department

Mainstreaming

Men can play an important role in keeping women's studies from, being ghettoized. We can call for women's studies courses within our departments, insisting that they are intellectually important to our own fields—rather than waiting until our departments grudgingly allow this or that course, taught by the department feminist, to be cross-listed. We should also find out from people in the Women's Studies Program what courses they most need, and see if we can reconcile those needs with departmental priorities.

Equally important, the curricular materials developed by feminists should be brought into the courses we ordinarily teach. Louis Kampf teaches one section of "Introduction to Fiction," a staff-taught course with the traditional, male-dominated syllabus. He introduced Doris Lessing, Colette, Edith Wharton, Tillie Olsen, Zora Neale Hurston, Toni Cade Bambara, and others into the course, and organized one large unit around the theme of relations between the sexes. There was some unpleasantness with the department's curriculum committee over this—a not uncommon occurrence, we suspect, but one which may be important in bringing the need for women's studies to the department's attention.

And, because departments are the planning units in universities, it is at the departmental level that mainstreaming will have to be raised, fought over, and resolved. The burden of restructuring courses cannot be entirely dumped on individual faculty members—male or female. Untenured people are rarely in a position to assert themselves. Even tenured people who want to do the right thing are often loath to risk isolating themselves from their colleagues. Kampf had the opportunity to propose to his department that American literature offerings be brought into line with feminist research. Only three of the thirty-two courses proposed for the catalogue by his department had women authors in their syllabi; only one course betrayed a feminist perspective in its catalogue description. Though several of the untenured women in the department were outraged, they could not afford to raise much of a fuss. Nothing much has happened as a result of the debate Kampf initiated, but there is a debate, and it will keep germinating. The untenured women now have at least a small space in which to assert themselves. Similarly, Ohmann was able to prevent a new, required course for majors from having an all-male (and all-white) reading list.

Beyond involving ourselves in skirmishes like these, we might also help organize faculty workshops, like those at Wheaton College, to explore the new research in women's studies and its implications for curricular change across the disciplines. An intellectual challenge of this sort may make more headway in some situations than the pressure of feminists demanding "their" share of the curriculum.

Teaching

Men have a responsibility to consult with people in women's studies about the content of the courses they teach. Have I absorbed work being done in women's studies? Have I overlooked sexist materials in the texts I use? How do I treat women students? Men should be particularly sensitive in how they teach feminist materials to women students. A woman student recently asked Kampf why he taught so many books by and about women. One's motives have to be honestly and seriously explained because women are, not surprisingly, suspicious.

In his teaching, a man can also initiate work at the intersection of his original discipline and women's studies, when no woman in his department has that specialty. For instance, Ohmann gave a group tutorial that explored (among other things) the study of women and language. He has also gradually made gender a central emphasis of his course in the structure and social functions of the mass culture industries, as in a unit on women's magazines, men's magazines, and pornography. And a male feminist colleague of his, who does bio-psychological research, will co-teach a course next year on sex and gender.

It is very important for men to team-teach some women's studies courses with women. It presents to the students a model for collaboration between men and women on a feminist project. Kampf is currently planning the introductory course to women's studies with a woman in another department. He has his doubts about doing this, but has no choice, since no other woman concerned with the subject has the time to organize and teach a new course. But for him the task is an opportunity rather than a burden. There is much for a man to learn in team-teaching any course with a committed feminist; all the more is to be learned in teaching the introductory course to women's studies. Obviously, the man, especially if he is tenured and his team-teacher is not, will have to be sensitive about dominating the class. He will have to be open to criticism from both his partner and the students. He'll have to learn when to be quiet and when to disappear. These are all lessons worth learning.

Research

An impressive body of research relating to the lives and history of women has been engendered by the development of women's studies. Women have done most of this research—which is as it should be. But we feel that it is important for men to be involved in the enterprise of discovery which has engaged so many women scholars. Male-dominated scholarship has done grievous injustice to women; it behooves men to work at correcting some of the injustices: male scholars must not ignore or misrepresent women in their research (be it concerned with peasants in twelfth-century China, the human brain, or the sociology of work) as they have in the past.

The dangers of men wanting to dominate research in women's studies are as real as they are with whites dominating scholarship about Blacks. Obviously, men's place in the enterprise of feminist scholarship should be a modest one. Our most important task may, in fact, be to bring the perspectives of feminist research to our studies of humanity as a whole.

Book Reviewing

How a book fares on the market usually depends on the nature of its reviews. Many works in women's studies have been reviewed by people who are ignorant, who hate women, or who have little sympathy for work that is openly committed to an ideological stance. We recall, for example, a particularly nasty review of Kate Millett's

Sexual Politics by Irving Howe. Men who are sympathetic and knowledgeable about women's studies should review books for both scholarly and popular journals. We do not mean that they should write puff pieces, merely that they be informative and fair.

We do not think of ourselves as pioneers among men in women's studies—some male colleagues, like Paul Lauter and Carl Degler, have been doing important work in the area for years. Nor do we imagine that our experience is typical. But we'd like to offer it as encouragement to others. There are small but significant ways we can help advance feminism and women's studies.

And not just out of altruism. Ohmann was reluctant to be co-coordinator of the Women's Studies Program at Wesleyan this year, agreeing only because the collective could not find a tenured woman to do the job. He planned to act as a front, signing papers and serving as go-between to the administration, while staying on the margins of the collective's work. He quickly discovered not only that his full participation was welcome but also that it was more exciting and rewarding than any other voluntary work he has recently done at his campus. The collective hums with energy and determination. Its consensual process is scrupulously democratic. The union of intellectual, political, and personal is tigher than he has ever experienced in an academic setting. And things get done: the collective got a part-time position authorized for a fine woman historian to teach about women and work in the United States; the program has tied into the hiring process in History and English (result: three new tenure-track people in Women's Studies); it has made progress toward rooting the program at Wesleyan by the time it undergoes review. Ohmann feels he has learned much and has made warm political friendships. For Kampf, too, the involvement with women's studies has been his most invigorating and intellectually significant academic experience since the teach-in movement inspired by the United States' aggression against Vietnam. Who, we are led to ask, is doing a favor for whom?

"FEMINISM FOR MEN 101"

Alex McDavid (1986)

Feminism for Men?

Frankly, it's about time.

It's about time that men studied feminism not just in the context of contemporary society, but in the context of all of human history. And it's about time that feminist men taught other men about feminism.

Men and women both need to know about feminism. Women need to know about it to give them many things including a history of themselves as women, a sense of shared experience with other women outside the isolation of the private sphere, the possibility of gender-created and defined language that acknowledges and explains their experiences from their own perspectives, a sense of self-worth that comes from being valued as full and complete members of society as a whole, and the ability to achieve personal and, therefore, political power in their own right for their own sake.

Men need to know about feminism for many reasons too. The first is to understand and acknowledge that patriarchy is the most basically practiced form of relationship between peoples and that it is also the most oppressive and destructive. Men need to know about feminism because it acknowledges that sexism pervades societies across cultures and history, and to make the connection that men have almost universally set the policies and values of those cultures and that history. Until that reality is understood and rejected by men as a gender, sexism and patriarchy ultimately cannot be eradicated. Unfortunately, sexism has popularly been considered a "woman's issue," but fundamentally it is not. No more than war, for instance, is a "man's issue." War involves women and sexism involves men. They are both human issues. The difference, of course, is that men, collectively, are usually responsible for war and they are also responsible for sexism. Women have not tended to have much of a voice in the perpetuation of either subject.

Sexism, in its many manifestations, is really a male problem. Women are the ones who experience its effects, but men and masculine-values are the instigators. Whether consciously or unconsciously, intentional or not, individually initiated, silently assumed as part of one's "birthright" or membership in the "brotherhood of man," or blatantly promoted or exercised, sexism is perpetuated by men and they are responsible for it. And, therefore, they must share in the responsibility for ending it.

. . . By suggesting that men have a responsibility to share in the ending of sexism, I am in no way suggesting that it is their battle, to be fought solely by them, using their own rules. The fight against sexism comes from those that are oppressed under the rule of patriarchy—that is, women—against a system that allows all men, regardless of personal culpability, the privilege of that

---

"Feminism for Men 101: An Introductory College Course." *M.A. thesis, California State University, Sacramento, 1986.*

system. Therefore, the theories, concepts, experiences and strategies developed by feminist women must be the foundation for and major portion of any attempt by feminist men in their work towards eradicating sexism and patriarchy.

. . . [S]ince women are responsible for feminism but men need to learn about feminist issues, should men get involved in feminism or would that involvement constitute infringement on women's right to their own struggle? This is particularly a concern since the struggle is with men's privileged status in the first place—a status which interferes with women's control of their own lives. If men need to recognize their role in the oppression of women and alter it, can they do so without a grounding in feminist education which offers the most thorough analysis of the problems of patriarchy for the lives of women? Can patriarchy be seriously questioned using patriarchal rules? Except for blatant cases of misogyny, it is assumed that most men will have little understanding of the effects of patriarchy unless they have a foundation in feminism. It can be concluded then, that there is no point in men unlearning sexism and rejecting patriarchal values outside the context of feminism. It can also be concluded however that women feminists are justifiably tired of explaining to men what feminism is all about. Therefore, if men, as the perpetuators of patriarchy, are to share in its eradication, some men must assume for themselves the responsibility of becoming educated in feminist theory and practice, and subsequently must share that information with other men.

Men who study feminism will have to do extensive work during their lives regarding their own socialization, status and behavior as men. It is, however, the belief of this author . . . to suggest that such men need to go beyond an enlightened perspective about themselves and women. These men must be taught particularly about women's experiences in a male-dominated world through the experiences and perspectives of women.

Cultures and history will only begin to consider women as full-fledged human beings, with as much value, rights, autonomy, freedom of movement, sense of self-worth and dignity as men have, when men truly respect women. But that can only happen if men listen to what is being, and has been, said by feminist women and accept responsibility for their participation in the causes, effects and continuation of sexism. . . .

"SCHOLARLY STUDIES OF MEN"

Harry Brod (1990)

IN SOMETHING of a turn of the tables, scholars in women's studies are having to decide what to do about a new field that is emerging in academe. The new kid asking to enter the club is "men's studies."

For some feminist scholars, the phenomenon seems either preposterous or dangerous, or more likely both. After all, the traditional curriculum that women's studies sought to reform was, in essence, men's studies. Other feminists, however, believe that the new field of men's studies is really a welcome extension of feminism's intellectual insights into hitherto male terrain. I believe that the field of men's studies is not only compatible with women's studies, but also an essential complement.

Men's studies begin by accepting as valid feminism's critique of traditional scholarship for its androcentric bias in generalizing from men to all human beings. The field adds the perspective that this bias not only excludes women and/or judges them to be deficient, but also ignores whatever may be specific to men *as men,* rather than as generic humans. The field also invokes feminist concepts that "gender" is not natural difference, but constructed power, to argue that the multiple forms of masculinities and femininities need to be re-examined.

The field of men's studies, for most of us anyway, thus is rooted in a feminist commitment to challenge existing concepts of gender. The debate within our still-nascent field over that commitment, however, has made some feminists skeptical about our entire enterprise. They see in the call for a new "gender studies" focused on both men and women the possibility that women's priorities and standpoints will again be subsumed and ignored under generic labels. Other feminists, though, find that the idea of a broadly conceived "gender studies," in which "gender" describes power and not just difference, does reflect the underlying conceptualization of their field. We should recognize, however, that the meaning of terms is still in flux. At my own institution, for example, our current solution is to develop a program in "Women's and Gender Studies."

Feminists' legitimate fear of once again having women's discourse subordinated to men's should not blind us to the very real and much-needed intellectual project that the field of men's studies is undertaking. To simplify a more extended argument, I believe the field is an essential complement to women's studies because neither gender ultimately can be studied in isolation. Gender is, itself, a relational concept: Masculinities and femininities are not isolated "roles," but contested relationships.

But it does not follow from my argument for men's studies as an intellectual enterprise that the field must be established in any particular form in academic institutions. Such decisions should be made by

---

"Scholarly Studies of Men: The New Field Is an Essential Complement to Women's Studies." Chronicle of Higher Education *(21 March 1990).*

women in women's studies. And any efforts to divert resources from women's studies to men's studies must be resisted; funds for the new men's studies must come from the old.

The new field has important implications for scholarship. For example, many explanations of the "gender gap" in political voting patterns have failed to see that it takes two to make a gap. Having noted the appearance of a "gap," social scientists have rushed to explain the changes in women that have produced it. Yet some of the evidence shows that the gap was produced more by a shift in men's than in women's political identification and voting patterns. By trying to understand the mutability and diversity of masculinities, men's studies avoid the pitfall of associating change only with women while assuming male constancy—a sexist bias.

By pointedly taking up the question of power relations among men in addition to those between the sexes, the new field also allows for a more differentiated conception of patriarchy. For the power of the real and symbolic father is not simply that of male over female, but also that of heterosexual over homosexual, one generation over another, and other constellations of authority. The field forces us to ask, Why does society privilege some men over others, even as it gives all men power over women? Why do so many of our founding myths contain fathers willing to kill their sons—the violence committed and permitted by Abraham against Isaac, Laius against Oedipus, the Christian God the Father against Jesus?

Further, the field of men's studies is not simply calling for sensitivity to diversity, though it surely does that, but also tries to apply an understanding of difference gained from radical feminism to men, arguing that sexuality is as socially constructed as identity. The field therefore is also forging special links to gay studies.

Two current phenomena show the need for men's studies to transcend a white, middle-class origin and orientation: the large number of suicides among Vietnam-era veterans and the huge number of college-age black men in prison rather than in college. When we speak of men's issues, there really is more to consider than the existential anxieties of middle-aged, middle-class executives and fathers, popular media treatments notwithstanding.

A final example from my own experience highlights the way feminism has helped me to ask new questions about men. I have noticed in recent years that many of the female political activists I know have devoted increasing attention to women's issues, for example moving from the peace movement to the women's peace movement or from environmentalism to the fusion of ecological and feminist concerns called ecofeminism.

At first, I simply contrasted this to the conventional wisdom that people become more conservative, *i.e.,* more "mature," with age. But I also recalled that the women's movement has been said to differ from others precisely because its members tend to become more radical as they age; it took only brief reflection to identify the conventional dictum as a male norm. Accordingly, I then asked myself what it was about women's lives that made them different. As I was coming up with various plausible answers I suddenly caught myself. I realized that I was committing the usual error of looking only to women to explain difference. In fact, as I started to see, if one believes as I do that there is validity in various radical social critiques, then the women's pattern should be the norm, as life experiences increasingly validate early perceptions of biased treatment of certain groups. Thus the question should not be, "What happens to women to radicalize them?" but rather "What happens to men to deradicalize them?" That question, more for men's studies than for women's studies, can open up fruitful areas of inquiry.

Indeed, I believe that any strategy for fundamental feminist transformation requires a more informed understanding of men. By exposing and demystifying the culture of male dominance from the inside out, the field of men's studies offers both women and subordinated men the empowerment such knowledge brings.

By elucidating the many and varied prices of male power—the drawbacks and limitations of traditional roles—the field helps motivate men to make common cause with feminist struggles, though not, it must be said, on the basis of any simple cost-benefit analysis, since the price men pay still purchases more than it pays for.

The field of men's studies, then, emerges not as some counterweight or corrective to women's studies, but as the extension and radicalization of women's studies. For it is the adoption of thoroughly women-centered perspectives, taking women as norm rather than "other," that helps us ask new questions about men.

ECONOMIC EQUALITY

"POLICY REGARDING CHALLENGE TO STATE PROTECTIVE LAWS"

Walter P. Reuther (1970)

MANY STATES have statutes which prohibit or limit . . . the employment of females in certain occupations, in jobs requiring the lifting or carrying of weights exceeding certain prescribed limits, during certain hours of the night or for more than a specified number of hours per day or per week. The Equal Employment Opportunity Commission (EEOC), the federal agency charged with enforcing Title VII, has now unequivocably ruled, with Court approval, that Title VII supersedes such state laws because they do not take into account the capacities, preferences, and abilities of individual females, and tend to discriminate against them rather than to protect them. This has been the position of the International Union since the enactment of the Title VII. . . .

Many employers have utilized the so-called "state protective laws" to deny women as a class, opportunities to work overtime, for recall, to bid on certain jobs,

U.S. Congress. Senate. Committee on the Judiciary. Equal Rights, 1970. *91st Cong., 2d sess., 5–7 May 1970.*

work in certain departments and on certain shifts, notwithstanding the fact that an individual woman might have had the seniority, skill and ability which should have been recognized in any of these situations. Employers have followed this course despite the absence of any contract language requiring women to be treated any differently from men. WHEREVER SUCH A PRACTICE STILL EXISTS, THE LOCAL UNION SHOULD CHALLENGE IT BOTH IN THE GRIEVANCE MACHINERY AND WITH THE EEOC.

There is a larger and fundamental point . . . regarding the Equal Rights Amendment which argues eloquently and imperatively for its enactment. The point is that . . . over 180 years since the ratification of the Constitution of the United States, American women are still second-class citizens. . . .

The Equal Rights Amendment is not a panacea, but it will bring us closer to the goal of equal justice under law. We in the UAW know no valid reason why this Amendment, which proposes equal treatment for men and women, should not be incorporated into the U.S. Constitution. . . .

"NO PENIS, NO PRIEST"

Leonard Swidler (1973)

THE READER may think at first that this title is mere sensationalism. It isn't! While at a discussion between Roman Catholic and Episcopal priests and theologians in the Philadelphia area last year, one young Episcopal priest insisted that women by nature were incapable of exercising the priesthood. When pressed for reasons he replied that the central priestly act was to celebrate the Eucharist, and that was a phallic act! Stunned incredulity was the response as he went on to explain in antiquated Aristotelean terms how it was the initiating male act of the priest that called Christ's presence down onto the altar; since women had no phallus, they obviously could not perform this phallic act essential to the priesthood. The Roman Catholic theologian present remarked: "I had intended to apply a *reductio ad absurdam* to your line of argumentation, but you have saved me the trouble."

Unfortunately it was made clear that such a mind-set still commands sufficient allegiance among the clergy . . . and laity of the Episcopal Church in the U.S. as to defeat once again a move to allow the ordination of women priests: this time it occurred at the 1973 triennial General Convention of the Protestant Episcopal Church of America at Louisville. Following the same political tactics as at the last Convention, the opposition clergy and laity in the House of Deputies called for a vote by order, allowing

---

Journal of Ecumenical Studies *10, no. 4 (Fall 1973).*

them to defeat the resolution favoring women priests, even though the individual vote was 488–400 in favor of ordaining women priests.

One of the favorite arguments used in the Episcopal Church against ordaining women is to claim that such a decision would make reconciliation with the Roman Catholic Church still more difficult. However, one becomes somewhat suspicious of such an argument when one hears a Roman Catholic churchman objecting to the ordination of women because it would make reconciliation with the Orthodox still more difficult! . . . Ecumenism is thus turned into a tool of reaction.

But this is surely not what ecumenism has meant up to now. It has been a mighty force for renewal in the churches. As one recent example, look at the Decree of Ecumenism of the Second Vatican Council: there renewal and reform of the Church were made essential prerequisites and concomitants of ecumenism. "In ecumenical work, Catholics must assuredly be concerned for their separated brethren . . . making the first approaches towards them. But their *primary duty* is to make an honest and careful appraisal of whatever needs to be renewed and achieved in the Catholic household itself . . . all are led to examine their own faithfulness to Christ's will for the Church and, where ever necessary, undertake with vigor the task of renewal and reform." (Section 4 of the Decree on Ecumenism) The peace and unity of the Church which is sought is that of the fullness of the stature of Christ, not the unity of the lowest common denominator, or the peace of the graveyard.

Furthermore, if Episcopalians were sincerely concerned about not allowing the issue of ordaining women priests to drive a greater wedge between them and the Roman Catholics, why have they not specifically dealt with the matter in their official bilateral consultations with Roman Catholics both on the national level in the U.S. and on the international level? The official consultation between Roman Catholics and Reformed/Presbyterian Christians in the U.S. took the issue up at length—and delivered a resounding resolution in favor of ordaining women . . .; here renewal and ecumenism were also seen as inextricably united.

If those who oppose the ordination of women on ecumenical grounds are not willing to stand accused of speciousness and fakery, they must submit the issue to a careful ecumenical analysis; the official bi-lateral Consultations are at least one very apt instrument for such an analysis. Hence, the Roman Catholic-Anglican Consultation (and the Lutheran-Catholic Consultation and other Consultations as well) would do their churches, and the cause of ecumenism, a great service if they would take up the issue of ordaining women priests, being certain they added competent women scholars to both sides of their now all male Consultations.

It is hoped that they, and their respective churches, would grow slightly more toward the fullness of Christ, who confirmed Mary in the "male" role of the intellectual and spiritual disciple when he said: "She has chosen the better part, and it shall not be taken away from her," and who, after his resurrection, chose to appear first to the *woman* Mary Magdalene and sent (*apostello*) her to give witness of this central Christian event to the (male) disciples, saying to her: "go and tell the brothers" (John 20:17). With Jesus it was the person, not the penis, that was primary.

"STATEMENT AT THE ORDINATION OF REV. MARY MICHAEL SIMPSON"

Bishop Paul Moore, Jr. (1979)

THIS," I said, "is a most historic moment. For the first time in the history of the Holy Catholic Church we gather to lay hands on a nun for the office of priest in the Church of God. We welcome you all, and especially the sisters from the Roman Catholic Church who are here to lend their prayers and support.

"Women were the first to embrace the religious life. The New Testament speaks of the widows and virgins who chose this special way of serving their Lord. Marcina, Sister of Gregory of Nyssa, started the first monastic community. Women joined the desert fathers of St. Anthony. Pachomius mentions communities of women in his account of the first monastic communities. The history of prayer, of sanctity, of martyrdom, is filled with the glories of women saints, women religious.

"Today, late in the course of time, we take a giant step, the opening up of the priesthood to this heritage of the past, this enormous potential for the future. There are those who say that a woman cannot be a priest. In a sense they are right, no human being can be a priest in and of him or herself. We believe that Christ alone is the great high priest and that all priesthood derives from Him. He made the one, true, pure, immortal sacrifice, He alone is worthy to stand as a mediator between God and man. Our priesthood only exists as an extension of His.

"The Church as a whole is His Body and as a whole exercises His priesthood here and now. This is the meaning of the phrase, the 'priesthood of all believers.' Women, as members of the Church, are *already* priests in this sense. Therefore, there can be no metaphysical or essential barrier to their priesthood. Ordained priesthood is an ordering of the priesthood of all believers, giving to certain persons the responsibility of being representatives of this priesthood. In ordering the instrumentality of his holy corporate priesthood there are different vocations. What we are doing and saying today is that response to these different vocations is not limited by sex any more than it is limited by nationality or race.

"I *feel* this to be true; I *know* this to be true. I have sensed this vocation deep in the hearts of Mary Michael and Carter, and of many other women. The Word became *flesh* and dwelt among us. Christ took on all humanity, not mere maleness. It has taken us so long to understand! 'In Christ is neither Jew nor Greek, male nor female.' In Christ's priesthood there is neither Jew nor Greek, black nor white, male nor female.

From Take a Bishop Like Me. *New York: Harper & Row, 1979.*

"God reveals His will over the years, reveals Himself, His nature gradually. The story of the Bible is the story of God revealing Himself to man when man has been able to comprehend the revelation. And the revelation is always from small to larger, from slavery to freedom. Our personal God is always too small. God as He is is too large for us. He continues to force us to understand the scope of His Being. Consider these times of revelation:

"First: Jahweh was thought to be the God only of Israel in the early days of that desert people. Through the exile in Babylon, He forced them to realize He was the God of the whole earth.

"Second: In the Old Testament of Jesus' day, He was thought of as a God of narrow law. Jesus forced us through His own death upon the Cross to realize Him to be a God of love far beyond the compassion of the law.

"Third: St. Paul, by his witnessing of the Holy Spirit coming to the Gentiles with whom he worked, was forced to understand that Christ was the Saviour of the Gentiles and not the Saviour only of the Jews.

"Fourth: The Reformation leaders returned the Bible to all men and gave them back their consciences.

"Last: Today, late in time, we have been forced by the work of God in the women's liberation movement to see that the ordained priesthood is open to all persons, not just men. What a marvelous Epiphany, what a marvelous breakthrough!

"I remember sitting in this very cathedral not many months ago as women ordinands knelt before me and feeling that my hands were tied behind my back. I struggled to loosen them. Today they are free to lay upon a woman's head.

"We open the priesthood to the flood of love God has given the world through the feminine, through the spiritual power of religious women.

"There is much still to do. This is but the first step in what will be a long, often painful, and dreary task of having the Church fully opened up to the ministry of women."

It is customary, at the end of an ordination sermon, to give a charge to the ordinand. For this the ordinand stands.

"Mary Michael, to this task you are called. To this task and indeed to the whole task of your priesthood you bring not only yourself but the strength of your whole community, the Order of St. Helena. You bring to this task the balance and discipline of the religious life, the internal certainty of prayer, and the perseverance brought by prayer. Our Church, our priesthood, sorely needs these gifts in the years ahead.

"Remember, however, first and foremost you are a priest in the Church of God. Like any other priest, pick up your Cross and follow Him." . . .

"59 CENTS"

Fred Small (1981)

HIGH SCHOOL DAYDREAMS come easy and free
When you're a working woman watcha gonna be?
A senator, a surgeon, aim for the heights
But the guidance office says lower your sights to

Chorus
Fifty-nine cents for every man's dollar
Fifty-nine cents it's a lowdown deal
Fifty-nine cents makes a grown woman holler
They give you a diploma it's your paycheck they steal.

She's off to college, the elite kind
To polish her manners, sharpen her mind
Honors in English, letter in lacrosse
Types her to type for her favorite boss at

Boston: Pine Barrens Music, 1981.

Chorus (They give you a degree . . .)

Junior executive on her way up
Special assistant to the man at the top
She's one in a million and all she found
Was her own secretary now to order around at

Chorus (They give you a title . . .)

But the word is being processed in the typing pool
A working woman ain't nobody's fool
She's telling the boss on Secretary's Day
You can keep your flowers, buddy, give me a raise more than

Chorus
Fifty-nine cents for every man's dollar
Fifty-nine cents—oh, the deal has changed
Fifty-nine cents makes a grown woman holler
You can keep your flowers, buddy, give us a raise.

"WAKE-UP CALL"

Robert Reich (1989)

LOST by four votes," she said simply. "I'll be home soon." I must have looked shaken as I put down the phone. Our precocious six-year-old, who had been eying me, summed up the situation: "They fired Mommy, didn't they?"

Sexism had always been something of an abstraction to me. It might show up in corporate bureaucracies or working-class communities where Rambo still reigned. But surely no such noxious bias would be found in our overwhelmingly liberal, intellectual university community.

Yet a string of white males had been voted into tenured professorships just before my wife's candidacy. Most had not written as much, nor inspired the same praise from specialists around the nation. None of their writings had been subjected to the detailed scrutiny—footnote by footnote—given her latest manuscript. Not one of the male candidates had aroused the degree of anger and bitterness that characterized her tenure review.

Why? I knew most of the men who had voted against her. Most were thoughtful, intelligent men who had traveled and read widely, and held positions of responsibility and trust. Gradually I came to understand that they were applying their standard of scholarship as impartially as they knew how. Yet their standard assumed that she had had the same formative intellectual experience as they, and had come to view the modes and purposes of scholarship as they do.

Through the years my wife had helped me to see the gender biases of these assumptions. Her experiences and understandings, and those of other women scholars, have been shaped by the irrefutable reality of gender. The values and perspectives she brings to bear on the world—and in particular the world of ideas—are different because she has experienced the world differently. In fact, it is the very uniqueness of her female perspective that animates her scholarship, that gives it its originality and intellectual bite.

Presumably the men who supported her had been able to imagine the life of the mind from a different perspective than their own. The majority of men on her faculty voted to grant her tenure. They had been able and willing to expand their standard—not to compromise or to reduce it, but to broaden it—to include a woman's way of knowing. I suspect that those who did not, did not care to try.

And why would they not have cared to try? Apart from the few diehards, they were kindly, tolerant men. But perhaps they did not feel that she had invited them to try. Early on, her closest friends on the faculty were a group of young professors who took delight in challenging the sacred cows of prevailing scholarship. Her early articles openly proclaimed a feminist perspective. She had not played at being a good daughter to the older and more traditional men on the

Ms. *18, no. 4 (October 1989).*

faculty, giggling at their jokes and massaging their egos. Nor had she pretended to be one of them, speaking loudly and talking tough. They had no category for her, and to that extent she had made them uncomfortable. So when it came time for them to see the world from her perspective, they chose not to.

Since the vote she has remained strong, and as certain of the worth of her scholarship as before. But the experience has shaken me. It has made me wary of my own limited perspective—the countless ways in which I fail to understand my female colleagues and students, and their ways of knowing the world.

I have begun to notice small things. A recruiter for a large company calls to ask about a student who is being considered for a job. "Does she plan to have a family?" he inquires, innocently enough. "Is she really, er, serious about a career?" It is not the first time such a question has been put to me about a female student, but it is the first time I hear it clearly, for what it is.

A male colleague is critical of a young woman assistant professor: "She's not assertive enough in the classroom," he confides. "She's too anxious to please—doesn't know her own mind." Then later, another colleague about the same young woman: "She's so whiny. I find her very abrasive." It is possible, of course, that she is both diffident and abrasive. But I can't help wondering if these characterizations more accurately reflect how my two colleagues feel about women in general—their mothers, wives, girlfriends—than about this particular young woman.

At a board meeting of a small foundation on which I serve, the lone woman director tries to express doubts about a pending decision. At first several loquacious men in the group won't give her a chance to speak. When finally she begins to voice her concern she is repeatedly interrupted. She perseveres, and eventually states her objection. But her concern goes unaddressed in the remainder of the meeting, as if she had never raised it. It seems to me that this isn't the first time she was ignored, but it is the first time I noticed.

In my class I present a complex management problem. An organization is rife with dissension. I ask: what steps should the manager take to improve the situation? The answers of my male students are filled with words like "strategy," "conflict," "interests," "claims," "trade-offs," and "rights." My female students use words like "resolution," "relationship," "cooperation," and "loyalty." Have their vocabularies and approach to problems always been somewhat different, or am I listening now as never before?

The vice president of a corporation that I advise tells me he can't implement one of my recommendations, although he agrees with it. "I have no authority," he explains. "It's not my turf." Later the same day, his assistant vice president tells me that the recommendation can be implemented easily. "It's not formally within our responsibility," she says off-handedly. "But we'll just make some suggestions here and there, at the right time, to the right folks, and it'll get done." Is the male vice president especially mindful of formal lines of authority and his female assistant especially casual, or do they exemplify differences in how men and women in general approach questions of leadership?

If being a "feminist" means noticing these sorts of things, then I became a feminist the day my wife was denied tenure. But what is my responsibility, as a male feminist, beyond merely noticing? At the least to remind corporate recruiters that they shouldn't be asking about whether prospective female employees want to have a family; to warn male colleagues about subtle possibilities of sexual bias in their evaluation of female colleagues; to help ensure that women are listened to within otherwise all-male meetings; to support my women students in the classroom; and to give explicit legitimacy to differences in the perceptions and leadership styles of men and women. In other words, just as I seek to educate myself, I must also help educate other men.

This is no small task. They day after the vote on my wife's tenure, I phoned one of her opponents—an old curmudgeon, as arrogant as he is smart. Without the slightest sense of the irony lying in the epithet I chose to hurl at him, I called him a son of a bitch.

POLITICAL EQUALITY

"WHY I SUPPORT THE ERA"

Howard Cosell (1975)

I SUPPORT the Equal Rights Amendment because, simply, it's right and necessary. It relates to the betterment of the society, it relates to the principles upon which the nation was supposed to be founded, principles which have not been lived up to. You do what is right and you stand for what is right. And the way you do that is with your mind, your heart, your vocalizations, and your general influence. It's very simple.

You see, I was born, bred, and grew up on the law. I practiced law for 10 years. I have deep convictions, morally, ethically, politically, and my position on the ERA is of a piece with those convictions.

Think about what the Constitution is supposed to mean, and in practice, *hasn't* turned out to mean. We have still not fulfilled the promise of the notion that all people are equal under the law, because certainly the blacks are not, and women are not. That's the only reason we need the ERA in the first place.

I think it's long since past time in this society that women were treated coequally with men and I don't think they are in many important areas of human existence, such as being able to get a bank loan or establish a charge account; getting equal wages and coequal treatment in physical education programs in college.

The way I can fight for equal rights is as a well-known American—perhaps the number one sports communicator in this country—making it clear by way of commentary on my shows that I believe in the new Title IX regulations (which the National Colle-

Ms. *4, no. 4 (October 1975).*

giate Athletic Association is strongly lobbying against) calling for much more equalization in the budget areas of physical education throughout the universities, colleges, and secondary schools of America. Generally, when I go on talk shows, I make my position clear, as I have with Dinah Shore, who wasn't given a membership in a country club because she was a woman.

But I think the battle is just about won for all women. We only need the ratification of four more states. And as to why the 16 states have not yet ratified, I think the principal opponents are women. Misguided, misled people like Phyllis Schlafly, who simply do not know what they are talking about, are not truly part of a contemporary society and are engaged in a self-destruct wish.

I think they do it out of ignorance. They do have the right to do what they want to, but they can't win. Their time is past. Their arguments are absurd, synthetic, like saying women will be drafted and fight in trenches. You don't even have to refute that kind of argument. It's *prima facie,* which is a term in law that more or less means "absurd."

"ALAN ALDA ON THE ERA: WHY SHOULD MEN CARE?"

Alan Alda (1976)

YES, men will benefit from the Equal Rights Amendment. But not at the expense of women—as some opponents would have us believe. The ERA would simply be a sex-blind leveler of laws which discriminate against or favor either women or men. All our lives will be improved both legally and personally. The legal benefits will be strong, clear protections under the Constitution, and the personal benefits will reach us as the "cultural fallout" from the amendment.

Most of the time, of course, the sex differential in our society discriminates against women, but in the case of wives who work outside the home, their husbands very often suffer right along with them.

In these hard times, a lot of men must depend, at least in part, on whatever inflated dollars their wives can bring into the family. According to the Department of Labor's *1975 Handbook on Women Workers,* 53 percent of all husband-wife families in 1973 had earning wives whose contribution averaged about 25 percent of the family income. It's likely that many men whose consciousness has been raised by the economy will be glad to see working wives afforded the same opportunities and rewards as working husbands.

Ms. *5, no. 1 (July 1976).*

"The entire family unit is injured when the wife fails to receive fair compensation because of her sex," says Kathleen Willert Peratis, a lawyer and director of the Women's Rights Project of the American Civil Liberties Union. "A husband may also suffer if his working wife is denied mortgage insurance, because if she should die, he would have neither her economic contribution toward the family's support nor any insurance to replace it. A bank's refusal to acknowledge a married woman's income for purposes of making a joint loan plainly hurts both spouses."

Many practices of this nature are already outlawed, but enforcement is something else again. "The ERA," Peratis says, "would put the moral force of our highest form of lawmaking—constitutional amendment—behind the equality principle so that statutes outlawing such discrimination are given added enforcement impetus."

It may surprise some men to realize that there are many laws that now deny them the same rights and privileges that women enjoy. Men whose wives work are excluded from retirement benefits that are received as a matter of course by women whose husbands work. Says Peratis, "Social Security laws deny certain retirement benefits to husbands and surviving husbands of working women unless they can show that their wives supported the family unit by earning at least 75 percent of the family's total income. Wives of working men receive the benefit automatically, whether or not their husbands supported them."

Former Congresswoman Martha Griffiths, cosponsor of the ERA and longtime proponent of Social Security reform, has pointed out the practical effect of this injustice. "If a husband doesn't work under covered employment—if he works for the government, for instance—and his wife *does* work under covered employment, the amount they can draw on retirement is reduced by one third. If the situation were reversed, if *she* were the one not covered, he'd be able to give her one half of his benefits." Several federal courts have found this scheme unconstitutional and have held that husbands are entitled to benefits on the same basis as wives. The government has appealed and the United States Supreme Court has agreed to hear the case. But, as Peratis remarks, "if there were an ERA, the eradication of the sex differential would be a certainty. Without it, we have high hopes but a big question mark."

The effect of the ERA on divorce and child-custody settlements has been the subject of great controversy. Because women have been denied equality in so many ways, some people fear that supporting rights that might also accrue to men in the domestic area may erode the few advantages that women now possess. In fact, the new fairness principle will give a winning edge neither to men nor to women, but to fairness itself. Each case will be determined according to the special factors in that case. And when parents dissolve their marriage, the fairness principle will look to the children's needs in rendering justice, not to the gender of the parents.

Peratis explains: "Matrimonial laws, including child custody, alimony, and child support, are more encrusted with sexual stereotypes and overbroad generalizations based on sex than any other area of the law. These outmoded laws hurt men, women and children—the human wreckage in family courts is a bitter reality for too many people."

Some custody disputes can be especially painful partly because of an old-fashioned bias against men as parents. It is still common for judges to presume that fathers, simply because they are men, are either not interested in nurturing their children, or automatically incapable of rearing children responsibly and lovingly. It is unfair to make this assumption of all men. Furthermore, a woman who does not feel herself to be the ideal custodian of her children is often viewed as an evil or unnatural person, which may coerce her to fight for total custody even if she feels the father is better suited.

Because of the prejudice against the male parent, a man who sues for custody of his children often must take part in discouraging, debasing, and costly battle.

Martha Griffiths tells of a custody case in one of the western states: a father felt he could provide a better home for his children than his former wife, who had enrolled the children in nine different schools in nine months. In order to counteract the normal bias favoring mothers in child-custody situations, the man found that he would have to present evidence in court that detailed the worst possible picture of the children's mother. He would have had to expose her as alcoholic and involved in prostitution. "Now of course," Griffiths says, "no one wants to bring all that out in court. He didn't, and he lost the children. And he should have had them. If the case were being decided on an equal basis, it would have been enough to point out that they had changed schools so often and that he had the ability to give them an uninterrupted education."

In some cases, men feel that for the welfare of the children they have no choice but to expose the mother's serious shortcomings. "I not only wanted them," said a Maryland father after a five-year battle for custody of his children, "but I felt they were endangered with their mother, and that made me fight hard."

"And you really have to fight," he said in an interview in the *Washingtonian*. "It's not pleasant. Evidence in this state has to be overwhelming for a man to prove his wife unfit. It took me three years to accumulate the evidence . . . we had detectives for adultery charges, we had alcohol and drug-abuse evidence. I had the backing of neighbors; the court-appointed social worker sided with me. The children wrote the judge letters; they told him they wanted to go with me."

He felt that although character assassination was not in his nature, he was forced to fight dirty because of the lesser status of the male parent. Nevertheless, he lost in court.

It wasn't until a year later, when she became involved with another man, that the mother decided to give her former husband legal custody of the children, now teenagers.

"The best interests of the children" is supposed to be the guiding principle in these cases, but when judges attempt to meet those interests by relying on sex-based bias and subjecting the entire family to unnecessary pain, then something is wrong.

This is far from saying that men should have an advantage in custody suits, or that they *would* have under the ERA. "The real beneficiaries," says Catherine East of the International Women's Year Commission, "will be the children."

The irony now is that forcing a husband to win custody by proving adultery on the part of the wife, plays into another kind of sexual bias: if she were to prove the same charge against him, it would carry far less weight against a man.

How great an effect will the ERA have in these sensitive matrimonial areas? Kathleen Peratis answers that "The ERA is not a cure-all, but it will go some distance to infusing sanity into these terribly painful proceedings. The principle is plain—people must be treated according to their *actual* capacities, abilities, and functions, not according to a sexual stereotype which has nothing to do with the real-live people before the court."

In a larger sense the problems for male parents go beyond custody. Any law which presumes that all men are indifferent fathers can make it difficult for men who are single parents to function at all.

Consider, for instance, the difficulty Basil Archey had when he was called to jury duty in San Antonio, Texas. Archey, who has legal custody of his two young sons, asked for the same consideration that is given to women in Texas. (Mothers of children under 10 are automatically exempt from jury duty.)

Since Archey has no one to help him care for his sons, who are both under 10, he was concerned about how he would manage. "It's one thing," he said, "to tell your boss you have to take the day off to take the kids to the doctor—but what do you do if you're in a sequestered jury?"

The judge—unimpressed with Archey's problem—charged him with being absent from jury duty without a reasonable excuse.

At one point during his legal battles, Archey was so frustrated that he considered dropping by the judge's house with his children to see if the judge would like to sit with them while Archey sat on the jury.

The fact is there are men who do care about their children. They diaper them, feed them, walk with them in their arms in the middle of the night, worry about their physical development and emotional growth. They side with them against unreasonable teachers and struggle through homework with them when it increases at a geometric rate. They put Band-Aids on their cuts and suffer with them the emotional bruises that will take no bandaging. They hug their children when they cry, and their own eyes can get wet at the sight of their kids growing into strength and grace and independence.

Certainly, there is the stereotype of the absent father who is absorbed in his work, cool and detached, and available only for the rewards but not the pain of parenting. But those men who do not conform to this unfortunate stereotype should certainly not be made to suffer for it, and those who *do* conform should not be reinforced in their behavior by laws and practices that accept this spiritual impoverishment as normal.

Ruth Bader Ginsburg, Professor of Law at Columbia University, feels that the greatest benefit a man will receive from the ERA will be a recognition of "his role in the family and his rights in relation to his children."

Ginsburg emphasizes that a man's relationship with his children can be warm and close rather than "just a question of laying out money for them."

However, men at every economic level are affected by laws that regard fathers simply as the ones who lay out the money.

Where men are too poor to fit that role different problems arise. Terrible indignities have been suffered by women whose personal lives are monitored by welfare investigators. In addition, Martha Griffiths has pointed out that welfare laws also discriminate against the father (and therefore against the whole family) by driving jobless men out of their homes: under current law in many states, mothers and children can collect welfare payments only if there is an absent father. This requirement institutionalizes broken families.

An additional, but optional program, Aid to Dependent Children–Unemployed Father (ADC-UF), is available in less than half the states. Here the family qualifies for welfare if the father is a temporarily unemployed breadwinner who is seeking work. But the family cannot qualify if the father is the homemaker/child-care parent and the mother is the unemployed potential breadwinner. The ERA would alter the "unemployed father" phrase to read unemployed *parent*—and doesn't that make sense when the welfare of dependent children is the key issue, not the sex of the breadwinner?

Whatever else the amendment does, of course, it will give all fathers, rich and poor, single and married, the satisfaction of seeing their daughters and sons enjoying the benefits of full citizenship and equal opportunities.

In addition to putting to rest certain myths about the parenting of children, there is the hope that the ERA will also revise some of the more rigid and unfair ideas about alimony.

For instance, men will not and *should* not escape the responsibility of continuing to support their families after divorce, ERA or not, if that was the economic basis of the marriage. Some husbands though, such as disabled men, have been dependent on their wives for support during the marriage. In many states, these dependent men are denied the right to alimony after a divorce. "The men affected are a minority," Catherine East says, "but still a significant number." More importantly, she says the automatic disqualification from alimony "indicates a basic attitude about men that puts an unfair pressure on them. It denies men the right to be dependent or in need of help. And they *are* in some cases—particularly if they're ill."

Law professor William B. Aycock of the University of North Carolina might have been considering such statutes as this when he referred to "those laws which perpetuate the notion that in some matters women are inherently inferior to men or that men should be discriminated against because they are inherently superior to women." Aycock sees the ERA as a source of encouragement to legislative bodies to accelerate the elimination of such laws.

Kathleen Peratis believes the amendment will force some legislatures to rethink the whole notion of support in a more rational and commonsense way: "Under the ERA, state laws would have to provide that support runs from the spouse who can afford it (the one who has been gainfully employed) to the spouse who needs it (the one who has stayed at home to care for house and family). Many states already mandate this kind of functional approach to support laws. The ERA would make it universal."

Other laws under which men suffer inequality are surprisingly varied. Young girls, for instance, are protected against sexual exploitation to a greater extent than are young boys. Protection against statutory rape often doesn't extend to males. "Legislators make a big joke of it," says Ginsburg. "They say, 'Do fourteen-year-old boys really need to be protected from twenty-five-year-old women?' People have thought for so long of men exploiting girls—but it can work the other way around as well. Lives can be damaged."

Frequently, laws governing the age of majority are also sex-biased. In some states, women may marry at an earlier age than men. Although a recent Supreme Court decision "has probably rendered such statutes unconstitutional," according to *IMPACT ERA: Limitations and Possibilities,* the Equal Rights Amendment Project of the California Commission on the Status of Women, "the Equal Rights Amendment will certainly have that effect."

Meanwhile, Oklahoma still says males cannot buy 3.2 beers until they are 21, although females can start at 18.

While it may seem frivolous to want the right at 18 to drink beer and get married, especially in that order, there is something basic going on here. Inequality under the law, even in small doses, is a reminder that we have not yet decided to provide for all people in this country the protection of equal laws.

These are some of the areas in which men as well as women will benefit legally after full ratification of the ERA. Important as they are, the strictly legal benefits may not influence us as strongly as what I've called the "cultural fallout" from the amendment—benefits of a personal nature that may be even more far-reaching. While it's true that the amendment is essentially a legal instrument and not one that will mandate a cultural revolution, there are surely going to be some very important changes in our lives after ratification. Some are very broad and may go unnoticed for a while, such as the fact that there will be an influx of new talent, energy, and insight in our work force. Sexual segregation in our society has been costly. How much closer might the moon have seemed if all of us were reaching for it together?

A more immediate benefit will be that men's working conditions will probably improve when there are more women on the job. Without ascribing to women any mystical and unattainable qualities of gentleness and wisdom, I think I have observed that where men work without women there is just a little less warmth, a little less laughter, and a little less relaxation. There seem to be culturally "feminine" qualities that have for too long been absent from our working environments. It is a small but significant point that men, with all their bravado, have seldom had the courage to stick a flower on their desk.

A longer-range benefit, but one that comes even closer to home, is the pleasure we will derive from the companionship of women who finally have the ability to make free choices in their lives and to develop themselves to their fullest potential. A number of men have noticed that those women who have spent years fulfilling the approved submissive role can make men pay for that dependence. (The clinging vine can be a Venus's-fly trap.) Women's independence will set those men free.

Some of the most personal benefits to men may be changes in the way we think, in the shifting of our expectations, the relinquishing of our stereotypes. The use of Title VII of the Civil Rights Act to prohibit sex discrimination in employment has already begun this process for us, but the ERA will carry it forward and will finally commit the country fully and publicly to equality under the law. As men increasingly fill jobs as secretaries, airline flight attendants, telephone operators, and receptionists we may find ourselves less likely to presume that people who fill these jobs are supposed to be servile, anonymous, and eager to fulfill our sexual fantasies. Similarly, as women fill traditionally male roles as police chiefs, gas station attendants, baseball players, and bankers, we may also begin to realize that wisdom, aggressiveness, and physical courage are not solely male attributes. The pressure to provide these qualities all by ourselves will be taken from men's shoulders. We can still be strong and brave, but we won't have to feel we're the only ones who are.

Finally, there's something at the very core of us that will benefit from the passage of the Equal Rights Amendment. It is our conscience.

How long can we live with a Constitution that is ambiguous about equality for every citizen, when the simple addition of a few words will put things right?

How long can we stand by and watch qualified people excluded from jobs or denied fair payment for their labor? How long can we do nothing while people are shut out from their fair share of economic and political power merely because they're women?

With your vote you have an opportunity to pass on to future generations the same kind of shelter for human dignity that the men who voted for the first 10 amendments passed on to us. Perhaps not every one of those men benefited personally from the Bill of Rights, but they all had one great overriding benefit—they had the knowledge that they did what was right.

"MEN'S POWER WITH WOMEN, OTHER MEN, AND SOCIETY: A MEN'S MOVEMENT ANALYSIS"

Joseph H. Pleck (1977)

MY AIM in this paper is to analyze men's power from the perspective afforded by the emerging antisexist men's movement. In the last several years, an antisexist men's movement has appeared in North America and in the Western European countries. While it is not so widely known as the women's movement, the men's movement has generated a variety of books, publications, and organizations,[1] and is now an established presence on the sex role scene. The present and future political relationship between the women's movement and the men's movement raises complex questions which I do not deal with here, though they are clearly important ones. Instead, here I present my own view of the contribution which the men's movement and the men's analysis make to a feminist understanding of men and power, and of power relations between the sexes. First, I will analyze men's power over women, particularly in relation to the power that men often perceive women have over them. Then I will analyze two other power relationships men are implicated in—men's power with other men, and men's power in society more generally—and suggest how these two other power relationships interact with men's power over women.

Men's Power over Women, and Women's Power over Men

It is becoming increasingly recognized that one of the most fundamental questions raised by the women's movement is not a question about women at all, but rather a question about men: Why do men oppress women? There are two general kinds of answers to this question. The first is that men

From Women and Men: The Consequences of Power, *ed. Dana Hiller and Robin Sheets. Cincinnati: University of Cincinnati, Center for Women's Studies, 1977.*

1. See, for example, Deborah David and Robert Brannon, eds., *The Forty-Nine Percent Majority: Readings on the Male Role* (Reading, Mass.: Addison-Wesley, 1975); Warren Farrell, *The Liberated Man* (New York: Bantam Books, 1975); Marc Feigen Fasteau, *The Male Machine* (New York: McGraw-Hill, 1974); Jack Nichols, *Men's Liberation: A New Definition of Masculinity* (Baltimore: Penguin, 1975); John Petras, eds., *Sex: Male/Gender: Masculine* (Port Washington, N.J.: Alfred, 1975); Joseph H. Pleck and Jack Sawyer, eds., *Men and Masculinity* (Englewood Cliffs, N.J.: Prentice-Hall, 1974). See also the *Man's Awareness Network (M.A.N.) Newsletter,* a regularly updated directory of men's movement activities, organizations, and publications, prepared by a rotating group of men's centers (c/o Knoxville Men's Resource Center, P.O. Box 8060, U. T. Station, Knoxville, Tenn. 37916); the Men's Studies Collection, Charles Hayden Humanities Library, Massachusetts Institute of Technology, Cambridge, Mass. 02139.

want power over women because it is in their rational self-interest to do so, to have the concrete benefits and privileges that power over women provides them. Having power, it is rational to want to keep it. The second kind of answer is that men want to have power over women because of deep-lying psychological needs in male personality. These two views are not mutually exclusive, and there is certainly ample evidence for both. The final analysis of men's oppression of women will have to give attention equally to its rational and irrational sources.

I will concentrate my attention here on the psychological sources of men's needs for power over women. Let us consider first the most common and commonsense psychological analysis of men's need to dominate women, which takes as its starting point the male child's early experience with women. The male child, the argument goes, perceives his mother and his predominantly female elementary school teachers as dominating and controlling. These relationships *do* in reality contain elements of domination and control, probably exacerbated by the restriction of women's opportunities to exercise power in most other areas. As a result, men feel a lifelong psychological need to free themselves from or prevent their domination by women. The argument is, in effect, that men oppress women as adults because they experienced women as oppressing them as children.

According to this analysis, the process operates in a vicious circle. In each generation, adult men restrict women from having power in almost all domains of social life except child rearing. As a result, male children feel powerless and dominated, grow up needing to restrict women's power, and thus the cycle repeats itself. It follows from this analysis that the way to break the vicious circle is to make it possible for women to exercise power outside of parenting and parentlike roles and to get men to do their half share of parenting.

There may be a kernel of truth in this "mother domination" theory of sexism for some men, and the social changes in the organization of child care that this theory suggests are certainly desirable. As a general explanation of men's needs to dominate women, however, this theory has been quite overworked. This theory holds women themselves rather than men ultimately responsible for the oppression of women—in William Ryan's phrase, "blaming the victim" of oppression for her own oppression.[2] The recent film *One Flew over the Cuckoo's Nest* presents an extreme example of how women's supposed domination of men is used to justify sexism. This film portrays the archetypal struggle between a female figure depicted as domineering and castrating and a rebellious male hero (played by Jack Nicholson) who refuses to be emasculated by her. This struggle escalates to a climactic scene in which Nicholson throws her on the floor and nearly strangles her to death—a scene that was accompanied by wild cheering from the audience when I saw the film. For this performance, Jack Nicholson won the Academy Award as the best actor of the year, an indication of how successful the film is in seducing its audience to accept this act of sexual violence as legitimate and even heroic. The hidden moral message of the film is that because women dominate men, the most extreme forms of sexual violence are not only permissible for men, but indeed are morally obligatory.

To account for men's needs for power over women, it is ultimately more useful to examine some other ways that men feel

2. William Ryan, *Blaming the Victim* (New York: Pantheon, 1970).

women have power over them than fear of maternal domination.[3] There are two forms of power that men perceive women as holding over them which derive more directly from traditional definitions of adult male and female roles, and have implications which are far more compatible with a feminist perspective.

The first power that men perceive women having over them is *expressive power*, the power to express emotions. It is well known that in traditional male-female relationships, women are supposed to express their needs for achievement only vicariously through the achievements of men. It is not so widely recognized, however, that this dependency of women on men's achievement has a converse. In traditional male-female relationships, men experience their emotions vicariously through women. Many men have learned to depend on women to help them express their emotions, indeed, to express their emotions for them. At an ultimate level, many men are unable to feel emotionally alive except through relationships with women. A particularly dramatic example occurs in an earlier Jack Nicholson film, *Carnal Knowledge.* Art Garfunkel, at one point early in his romance with Candy Bergen, tells Nicholson that she makes him aware of thoughts he "never even knew he had." Although Nicholson is sleeping with Bergen and Garfunkel is not, Nicholson feels tremendously deprived in comparison when he hears this. In a dramatic scene, Nicholson then goes to her and angrily demands: "You tell him his thoughts, now you tell me *my* thoughts!" When women withhold and refuse to exercise this expressive power for men's benefit, many men, like Nicholson, feel abject and try all the harder to get women to play their traditional expressive role.

A second form of power that men attribute to women is *masculinity-validating* power. In traditional masculinity, to experience oneself as masculine requires that women play their prescribed role of doing the things that make men feel masculine. Another scene from *Carnal Knowledge* provides a pointed illustration. In the closing scene of the movie, Nicholson has hired a call girl whom he has rehearsed and coached in a script telling him how strong and manly he is, in order to get him sexually aroused. Nicholson seems to be in control, but when she makes a mistake in her role, his desperate reprimands show just how dependent he is on her playing out the masculinity-validating script he has created. It is clear that what he is looking for in this encounter is not so much sexual gratification as it is validation of himself as a man—which only women can give him. As with women's expressive power, when women refuse to exercise their masculinity-validating power for

3. In addition to the mother domination theory, there are two other psychological theories relating aspects of the early mother-child relationship in men's sexism. The first can be called the "mother identification" theory, which holds that men develop a "feminine" psychological identification because of their early attachment to their mothers and that men fear this internal feminine part of themselves, seeking to control it by controlling thoe who actually are feminine, i.e., women. The second can be called the "mother socialization" theory, holding that since boys' fathers are relatively absent as sex-role models, the major route by which boys learn masculinity is through their mothers' rewarding masculine behavior, and especially through their mothers' punishing feminine behavior. Thus, males associate women with punishment and pressure to be masculine. Interestingly, these two theories are in direct contradiction, since the former holds that men fear women because women make men feminine, and the latter holds that men fear women because women make men masculine. These theories are discussed at greater length in Joseph H. Pleck's "Mens Traditional Attitudes toward Women: Conceptual Issues in Research" in *The Psychology of Women: New Directions in Research*, ed. Julia Sherman and Florence Denmark (New York: Psychological Dimensions, 1978).

men, many men feel lost and bereft and frantically attempt to force women back into their accustomed role.

As I suggested before, men's need for power over women derives both from men's pragmatic self-interest and from men's psychological needs. It would be a mistake to overemphasize men's psychological needs as the sources of their needs to control women, in comparison with simple rational self-interest. But if we are looking for the psychological sources of men's needs for power over women, their perception that women have expressive power and masculinity-validating power over them is critical to analyze. These are the two powers men perceive women as having, which they fear women will no longer exercise in their favor. These are the two resources women possess which men fear women will withhold, and whose threatened or actual loss leads men to such frantic attempts to reassert power over women.

Men's dependence on women's power to express men's emotions and to validate men's masculinity has placed heavy burdens on women. By and large, these are not powers over men that women have wanted to hold. These are powers that men have themselves handed over to women, by defining the male role as being emotionally cool and inexpressive, and as being ultimately validated by heterosexual success.

There is reason to think that over the course of recent history—as male-male friendship has declined, and as dating and marriage have occurred more universally and at younger ages—the demands on men to be emotionally inexpressive and to prove masculinity through relating to women have become stronger. As a result, men have given women increasingly more expressive power and more masculinity-validating power over them, and have become increasingly dependent on women for emotional and sex-role validation. In the context of this increased dependency on women's power, the emergence of the women's movement now, with women asserting their right not to play these roles for men, has hit men with a special force.

It is in this context that the men's movement and men's groups place so much emphasis on men learning to express and experience their emotions with each other, and learning how to validate themselves and each other as persons, instead of needing women to validate them emotionally and as men. When men realize that they can develop in themselves the power to experience themselves emotionally and to validate themselves as persons, they will not feel the dependency on women for these essential needs which has led in the past to so much male fear, resentment, and need to control women. Then men will be emotionally more free to negotiate the pragmatic realignment of power between the sexes that is underway in our society.

Men's Power with Other Men

After considering men's power over women in relation to the power men perceive women having over them, let us consider men's power over women in a second context: the context of men's power relationships with other men. In recent years, we have come to understand that relations between men and women are governed by a sexual politics that exists outside individual men's and women's needs and choices. It has taken us much longer to recognize that there is a systematic sexual politics of male-male relationships as well. Under patriarchy, men's relationships with other men cannot help but be shaped and patterned by patriarchal norms, though they are less obvious than the norms governing male-female relationships. A society could not have the kinds of power dynamics that exist between women and men in our society without certain kinds of systematic power dynamics operating among men as well.

One dramatic example illustrating this connection occurs in Marge Piercy's recent novel *Small Changes*. In a flashback scene, a male character goes along with several friends to gang rape a woman. When his turn comes, he is impotent; whereupon the other men grab him, pulling his pants down to rape *him*. This scene powerfully conveys one form of the relationship between male-female and male-male sexual politics. The point is that men do not just happily bond together to oppress women. In addition to hierarchy over women, men create hierarchies and rankings among themselves according to criteria of "masculinity." Men at each rank of masculinity compete with each other, with whatever resources they have, for the differential payoffs that patriarchy allows men.

Men in different societies choose different grounds on which to rank each other. Many societies use the simple facts of age and physical strength to stratify men. The most bizarre and extreme form of patriarchal stratification occurs in those societies which have literally created a class of eunuchs. Our society, reflecting its own particular preoccupations, stratifies men according to physical strength and athletic ability in the early years, but later in life focuses on success with women and ability to make money.

In our society, one of the most critical rankings among men deriving from patriarchal sexual politics is the division between gay and straight men. This division has powerful negative consequences for gay men and gives straight men privilege. But in addition, this division has a larger symbolic meaning. Our society uses the male heterosexual-homosexual dichotomy as a central symbol for *all* the rankings of masculinity, for the division on *any* grounds between males who are "real men" and have power and males who are not. Any kind of powerlessness or refusal to compete becomes imbued with the imagery of homosexuality. In the men's movement documentary film *Men's Lives*,[4] a high school male who studies modern dance says that others often think he is gay because he is a dancer. When asked why, he gives three reasons: because dancers are "free and loose," because they are "not big like football players," and because "you're not trying to kill anybody." The patriarchal connection: if you are not trying to kill other men, you must be gay.

Another dramatic example of men's use of homosexual derogations as weapons in their power struggle with each other comes from a document which provides one of the richest case studies of the politics of male-male relationships to yet appear: Woodward and Bernstein's *The Final Days*. Ehrlichman jokes that Kissinger is queer, Kissinger calls an unnamed colleague a psychopathic homosexual, and Haig jokes that Nixon and Rebozo are having a homosexual relationship. From the highest ranks of male power to the lowest, the gay-straight division is a central symbol of all the forms of ranking and power relationships which men put on each other.

The relationships between the patriarchal stratification and competition which men experience with each other and men's patriarchal domination of women are complex. Let us briefly consider several points of interconnection between them. First, women are used as *symbols of success* in men's competition with each other. It is sometimes thought that competition for women

4. Available from New Day Films, P.O. Box 615, Franklin Lakes, N.J. 07417.

is the ultimate source of men's competition with each other. For example, in *Totem and Taboo* Freud presented a mythical reconstruction of the origin of society based on sons' sexual competition with the father, leading to their murdering the father. In this view, if women did not exist, men would not have anything to compete for with each other. There is considerable reason, however, to see women not as the ultimate source of male-male competition, but rather as only symbols in a male contest where real roots lie much deeper.

The recent film *Paper Chase* provides an interesting example. This film combines the story of a small group of male law students in their first year of law school with a heterosexual love story between one of the students (played by Timothy Bottoms) and the professor's daughter. As the film develops, it becomes clear that the real business is the struggle within the group of male law students for survival, success, and the professor's blessing—a patriarchal struggle in which several of the less successful are driven out of school and one even attempts suicide. When Timothy Bottoms gets the professor's daughter at the end, she is simply another one of the rewards he has won by doing better than the other males in her father's class. Indeed, she appears to be a direct part of the patriarchal blessing her father has bestowed on Bottoms.

Second, women often play a *mediating* role in the patriarchal struggle among men. Women get men together with each other and provide the social lubrication necessary to smooth over men's inability to relate to each other noncompetitively. This function has been expressed in many myths, for example, the folk tales included in the Grimms' collection about groups of brothers whose younger sister reunites and reconciles them with their kingfather, who had previously banished and tried to kill them. A more modern myth, James Dickey's *Deliverance*, portrays what happens when men's relationships with each other are not mediated by women. According to Carolyn Heilbrun,[5] the central message of *Deliverance* is that when men get beyond the bounds of civilization, which really means beyond the bounds of the civilizing effects of women, men rape and murder each other.

A third function women play in male-male sexual politics is that relationships with women provide men a *refuge* for the dangers and stresses of relating to other males. Traditional relationships with women have provided men a safe place in which they can recuperate from the stresses they have absorbed in their daily struggle with other men, and in which they can express their needs without fearing that these needs will be used against them. If women begin to compete with men and have power in their own right, men are threatened by the loss of this refuge.

Finally, a fourth function of women in males' patriarchal competition with each other is to reduce the stress of competition by serving as an *underclass*. As Elizabeth Janeway has written in *Between Myth and Morning*,[6] under patriarchy women represent the lowest status, a status to which men can fall only under the most exceptional circumstances, if at all. Competition among men is serious, but its intensity is mitigated by the fact that there is a lowest possible level to which men cannot fall. One reason men fear women's liberation, writes Janeway, is that the liberation of women

5. Carolyn G. Heilbrun, "The Masculine Wilderness of the American Novel," *Saturday Review* 41 (January 29, 1972), pp. 41–44.

6. Elizabeth Janeway, *Between Myth and Morning* (Boston: Little, Brown, 1975); see also Elizabeth Janeway, "The Weak are the Second Sex," *Atlantic Monthly* (December 1973), pp. 91–104.

will take away this unique underclass status of women. Men will now risk falling lower than ever before, into a new underclass composed of the weak of both sexes. Thus, women's liberation means that the stakes of patriarchal failure for men are higher than they have been before, and that it is even more important for men not to lose.

Thus, men's patriarchal competition with each other makes use of women as symbols of success, as mediators, as refuges, and as an underlcass. In each of these roles, women are dominated by men in ways that derive directly from men's struggle with each other. Men need to deal with the sexual politics of their relationships with each other if they are to deal fully with the sexual politics of their relationships with women.

Ultimately, we have to understand that patriarchy has two halves which are intimately related to each other. Patriarchy is a *dual* system, a system in which men oppress women, and in which men oppress themselves and each other. At one level, challenging one part of patriarchy inherently leads to challenging the other. This is one way to interpret why the idea of women's liberation so soon led to the idea of men's liberation, which in my view ultimately means freeing men from the patriarchal sexual dynamics they now experience with each other. But because the patriarchal sexual dynamics of male-male relationships are less obvious than those of male-female relationships, men face a real danger: while the patriarchal oppression of women may be lessened as a result of the women's movement, the patriarchal oppression of men may be untouched. The real danger for men posed by the attack that the women's movement is making on patriarchy is not that this attack will go too far, but that it will not go far enough. Ultimately, men cannot go any further in relating to women as equals than they have been able to go in relating to other men as equals—an equality which has been so deeply disturbing, which has generated so many psychological as well as literal casualities, and which has left so many unresolved issues of competition and frustrated love.

Men's Power in Society

Let us now consider men's power over women in a third and final context, the context of men's power in the larger society. At one level, men's social identity is defined by the power they have over women and the power they can compete for against other men. But at another level, most men have very little power over their own lives. How can we understand this paradox?

The major demand to which men must accede in contemporary society is that they play their required role in the economy. But this role is not intrinsically satisfying. The social researcher Daniel Yankelovich[7] has suggested that about 80 percent of U.S. male workers experience their jobs as intrinsically meaningless and onerous. They experience their jobs and themselves as worthwhile only through priding themselves on the hard work and personal sacrifice they are making to be breadwinners for their families. Accepting these hardships reaffirms their role as family providers and therefore as true men.

Linking the breadwinner role to masculinity in this way has several consequences for men. Men can get psychological payoffs from their jobs which these jobs never provide in themselves. By training men to accept payment for their work in feelings of masculinity rather than in feelings of satis-

7. Daniel Yankelovich, "The Meaning of Work," in *The Worker and the Job*, ed. Jerome Rosow (Englewood Cliffs, N.J.: Prentice-Hall, 1974).

faction, men will not demand that their jobs be made more meaningful, and as a result jobs can be designed for the more important goal of generating profits. Further, the connection between work and masculinity makes men accept unemployment as their personal failing as males, rather than analyze and change the profit-based economy whose inevitable dislocations make them unemployed or unemployable.

Most critical for our analysis here, men's role in the economy and the ways men are motivated to play it have at least two negative effects on women. First, the husband's job makes many direct and indirect demands on wives. In fact, it is often hard to distinguish whether the wife is dominated more by the husband or by the husband's job. Sociologist Ralph Turner writes: "Because the husband must adjust to the demands of his occupation and the family in turn must accommodate to his demands on behalf of his occupational obligations, the husband appears to dominate his wife and children. But as an agent of economic institutions, he perceives himself as controlled rather than as controlling."[8]

Second, linking the breadwinner role to masculinity in order to motivate men to work means that women must not be allowed to hold paid work. For the large majority of men who accept dehumanizing jobs only because having a job validates their role as family breadwinner, their wives' taking paid work takes away from them the major and often only way they have of experiencing themselves as having worth. Yankelovich suggests that the frustration and discontent of this group of men, whose wives are increasingly joining the paid labor force, is emerging as a major social problem. What these men do to sabotage women's paid work is deplorable, but I believe that it is quite within the bounds of a feminist analysis of contemporary society to see these men as victims as well as victimizers.

One long-range perspective on the historical evolution of the family is that from an earlier stage in which both wife and husband were directly economically productive in the household economic unit, the husband's economic role has evolved so that now it is under the control of forces entirely outside the family. In order to increase productivity, the goal in the design of this new male work role is to increase men's commitment and loyalty to work and to reduce those ties to the family that might compete with it. Men's jobs are increasingly structured as if men had no direct roles or responsibilities in the family—indeed, as if they did not have families at all. But paradoxically, at the same time that men's responsibilities in the family are reduced to facilitate more efficient performance of their work role, the increasing dehumanization of work means that the satisfaction which jobs give men is, to an increasing degree, *only* the satisfaction of fulfilling the family breadwinner role. That is, on the one hand, men's ties to the family have to be broken down to facilitate industrial work discipline; but on the other hand, men's sense of responsibility to the family has to be increased, but shaped into a purely economic form, to provide the motivation for men to work at all. Essential to this process is the transformation of the wife's economic role to providing supportive services, both physical and psychological, to keep him on the job, and to take over the family responsibilities which his expanded work role will no longer allow him to fulfill himself. The wife is then bound to her husband by her economic dependency on him, and the husband in turn is bound to his job by his family's economic dependence on him.

8. Ralph Turner, *Family Interaction* (New York: Wiley, 1968), p. 282.

A final example from the film *Men's Lives* illustrates some of these points. In one of the most powerful scenes in the film, a worker in a rubber plant resignedly describes how his bosses are concerned, in his words, with "pacifying" him to get the maximum output from him, not with satisfying his needs. He then takes back this analysis, saying that he is only a worker and therefore cannot really understand what is happening to him. Next, he is asked whether he wants his wife to take a paid job to reduce the pressure he feels in trying to support his family. In marked contrast to his earlier passive resignation, he proudly asserts that he will never allow her to work, and that in particular he wil never scrub the floors after he comes home from his own job. (He correctly perceives that if his wife did take a paid job, he would be under pressure to do some housework.) In this scene, the man expresses and then denies an awareness of his exploitation as a worker. Central to his coping with and repressing his incipient awareness of his exploitation is his false consciousness of his superiority and privilege over women. Not scrubbing floors is a real privilege, and deciding whether or not his wife will have paid work is a real power, but the consciousness of power over his own life that such privilege and power given this man is false. The relative privilege that men get from sexism and, more importantly, the false consciousness of privilege men get form sexism plays a critical role in reconciling men to their subordination in the larger political economy. This analysis does not imply that men's sexism will go away if they gain control over their own lives, or that men do not have to deal with their sexism until they gain this control. I disagree with both. Rather, my point is that we cannot fully understand men's sexism or men's subordination in the larger society unless we understand how deeply they are related.

To summarize, a feminist understanding of men's power over women, why men have needed it, and what is involved in changing it, is enriched by examining men's power in a broader context. To understand men's power over women, we have to understand the ways in which men feel women have power over them, men's power relationships with other men, and the powerlessness of most men in the larger society. Rectifying men's power relationship with women will inevitably both stimulate and benefit from the rectification of these other power relationships.

"ELEVEN WAYS MEN CAN BENEFIT FROM THE ERA"

Men Allied Nationally for the Equal Rights Amendment (1978)

1. Freedom from Being a Success Object

As men, we do not want to spend our lives supporting not only ourselves, but women, children (at $100,000 per child), a mortgage, and an image of ourselves.

Until women share that support we, as men, do not have the freedom to take risks on our job, or the freedom to fail taking those risks, for fear that if we do fail our family will end up in the poor house.

We cannot depend on women to share that support equally until women are paid equally. Nor can we expect women to share that support equally until women have equal access to trade union membership, to seniority positions within the unions, to in-house training for advancement once hired, to graduate education, law schools, medical schools and jobs at every level. And women cannot gain access to these jobs if the "buddy boy" system of hiring is not checked by affirmative action programs to balance the distorted hiring practices resulting from that system.

So, as the ERA helps check the distortion of hiring practices, men become freer to experiment with our lives—to escape the straight jacket of spending our lives getting the approval of the person above us at work so we can get to the next highest step on the ladder so we can get the next highest salary to support the next highest mortgage—a path that discourages men from asking ourselves "is this what I really want to be doing with my life?"

M.A.N. for the E.R.A. leaflet (Collection of Barry Shapiro.)

2. Child Nurturance

As the E.R.A. allows women the option to really share in the responsibilities of earning the income, it allows men more time to nurture our children.

3. Child Custody and Child Support

The E.R.A. will prevent states from depriving men of child custody merely because we are men. It will prevent us from being forced to declare our wives unfit mothers in order to gain equal access to custody.

Once custody is equalized, child support becomes equalized rather than being demanded of us because we are men. And we obtain as much right to the emotional support many mothers now find children provide rather than returning to the lonely house after the loss of a loved one through divorce. To be used financially while barely being allowed contact with the people we are financing reinforces our role of unfeeling provider.

4. Alimony—Legality

The E.R.A. will make it illegal for states to automatically assign alimony payments to men based only on our sex. (Although only 14% of divorced women are awarded alimony).

5. Alimony—Necessity

Courts will have less *reason* to assign alimony payments to men when women have had access to the training and income that makes alimony less necessary.

6. Divorce Training

When legal inequities push men into working outside the home and women into working inside the home this division of labor leads to a division of interests. The opposite interests push the sexes apart, (e.g., the "opposite sex"), encouraging divorces. Training men and women to be opposite each other is, in essence, divorce training.

Psychologically, divorces are one of the most traumatic experiences in men's lives. Personality differences always lead to some divorces. We do not need laws to exacerbate these differences.

7. Prostitutes and Security Objects

Women who hang onto relationships with men because society gives us the easier road to providing financial security make us into security objects and make themselves into prostitutes. When women must keep their misgivings about these relationships to themselves for fear of losing the financial security, men often find ourselves "shocked" when what we thought was a good relationship "suddenly" blows up.

8. Protective Labor Laws

The E.R.A. will allow extension to men of the protection of numerous labor laws in health, safety and overtime pay that now applies only to women. And those protective labor laws that are facades for keeping women out of selected jobs can be eliminated.

9. Inheritance

Many common law states require a husband to have a living child born of the marriage prior to receiving inheritance of his wife's realty. This is not required of the women. Women are hurt by other inheritance provisions. The ERA will force an equalization of these provisions.

10. Sexual Molestation of Boys

A number of states protect female children from adult male sexual molestation but do not protect male children from adult molestation by either sex. While carressing of children sexually may or may not need to be interpreted as molestation, the law should not eliminate boys from protection in clear cases of abuse while protecting females in such cases.

11. Corporate Benefits

The ERA will prevent major corporations from providing automatic salary continuations, insurance and pension benefits for widows only, while not providing similar benefits to widowers. Seventy percent of women work out of economic necessity. A woman working outside of the home who dies leaves the husband with little ability to nurture his children at the time of their mother's death if the effect of the death is to increase the pressure on him to provide.

"MALE PRIDE AND ANTI-SEXISM"

Tim Wernette, Alan Acacia, and Craig Scherfenberg (1980)

What Is the CAMP Caucus

The California Anti-Sexist Men's Political Caucus (C.A.M.P.) is a statewide alliance of men committed to pro-feminist, anti-sexist political work and to understanding how sexism, heterosexism, racism and classism affect the way we see ourselves and live in the world.

C.A.M.P. was established in November, 1979 at the Second Annual California Men's Gathering by men who needed and wanted support in our efforts to make broad changes in society and in our personal lives.

Our goal is to transform the traditional cultural and politcal aspects of our male role so that we might create a new and growing community of men who care for and respect our planet, our sisters and brothers, and ourselves.

N.p.: California Anti-Sexist Men's Political Caucus, 1980.

Principles of Unity

We, as members of the C.A.M.P. Caucus, agree that we live in a patriarchal society in which men have and use socially approved oppressive power over women, and in which some men oppress other men according to class, race and sexual orientation.

Our experience of loving and working together with other men and women leads us to respect effective anti-sexist action as an expression of self-respect, love, anger and justice.

Male Pride and Anti-Sexism

Personal Growth and Social Action

Knowing our feelings is a key source of political understanding. So often it seems that our problems are unique, highly personal, private only to ourselves. But, as soon as we begin to share our doubts, worries and problems with other men, we come to see that we are not alone, and that our difficulties are shared by others as well.

It is not too long before we begin to understand that many of the stresses and barriers that hinder us as men have a common root in the ways we have been brought up to *be* men. We see that personal problems have their origins in social problems, which require political solutions. In other words, we cannot overcome the blocks to our own growth without also confronting the social climate that builds them.

Individual development and social action go hand in hand. Our personal and political lives are interwoven. Because we are alive and changing, with our lives touching other people, the question we ask ourselves is not: "Do I want to be political?", but rather "What are my politics and how can I express my values in ways that are life-affirming for me and my society?"

Obstacles that Prevent Us from Being Ourselves and Living in Harmony and Justice with Others

The roles we are taught to live as men are designed to support social and economic structures that keep other people down. These structures are supported by us when we live out myths we are trained to have about ourselves and other people. In order for us to grow as human beings, we need to identify and confront attitudes which force us to ignore people's needs.

Here is a discussion of some of the more destructive lies about the world that lead to the oppression of many people, as well as isolating and making shallow the lives of men. The following definitions refer to attitudes that support *hierarchies,* or social structures of authority, in which those at the top have power and privilege (special benefits and options) over those on lower steps.

Sexism is the unequal treatment of people based on sex or gender. Sex itself is biological and/or surgical; gender is our learned masculine and feminine roles. Sexism involves the exaggeration of gender differences and the objectification of others, usually to the disadvantage of women. It begins when baby girls and boys are treated differently, given different toys and taught to do/not do very different things.

Women in particular—our sisters, mothers, daughters, wives, lovers, friends, coworkers—endure many kinds of oppression because of sexism, ranging from job and salary barriers to the terror of sexual assault. The contempt for women, the limits placed on what sorts of work they can do, the belittling of the opinions they hold or the values they esteem, arise from *misogyny,* a hatred or distrust of women. Misogyny, being a crucial part of patriarchal ideology, poisons our society.

Sexism hurts men as well, by directing us to abandon our feelings of caring, equality and sensitivity. Along with capitalism, sexism offers instead a glittering promise of privilege, influence and control over others. In reality, however, many of us are left without a sense of real power in our lives. Masculine roles tell us to struggle and compete for success, not to be tender or vulnerable. Domination over others is extended to include domination even over our own feelings.

Sexist behavior isolates us from ourselves and others in the world. Divided from and competing with each other, we seldom have either a basis for trust or the energy to build a community for social change.

Homophobia is the fear of homosexuality, or being labelled homosexual, and/or of same-sex closeness and affection. Homophobia prevents us, as men (regardless of our sexual orientation), from giving and getting support or affection with each other. Homophobia combines with misogyny to prevent men from forming equal alliances with women and each other, calling those who do "sissies", "unmanly", or "losers".

Heterosexism is not the same as heterosexuality. Heterosexism is the assumption that everyone is sexually attracted (or ought to be) only to persons of the other sex. Heterosexism forces lesbian women, gay men and bisexual people to keep rich and vital aspects of their lives in hiding, or else face discrimination and violence.

There are other attitudes that are not the same as sexism, yet which function in many of the same ways that sexism does, and are very much connected with it. For example, prejudice towards people of different racial or ethnic groups and towards people of other socio-economic groups also hurts and isolates people from each other. Each of these offer material comforts to some of us, but poverty and a theory of inferiority to others of us. Both of them are promoted by special myths. One is that in this country race or class background are not real obstacles to the person who wants to achieve "the good life." Another is that people of color or of the working class are poor because they are incompetent or unwilling to work as hard as other people. These lies overlook the special benefits and privileges of many people. They work to keep people "in their place" in the hierarchy.

There are other kinds of discrimination, among them the prejudices towards people of different ages—children and older people especially (ageism), towards those who are physically or mentally different from many of us, and towards various sexual minorities. All of these hierarchial attitudes poison our worlds, and alienate us from who we really are.

The Difference between Men's Liberation and Male Anti-Sexist Activities

In the face of challenges to our life-styles, it is tempting to try to solve our problems on an individual basis. We learn to cry, to touch other men, to feel our emotions. Without these abilities, we are damaged.

Choosing to work out a personal solution is an option taken by some men within the men's movement. Some of us can *afford* to keep our solutions on this personal level, because we are not oppressed. This choice is often called "men's liberation".

Men's liberation is in touch with many truths. For example, it is undeniably true that the "John Wayne Syndrome" prevents us from leading lives of emotional richness, or from becoming close with other men. Sex-role stereotyping of men hurts us, just as it hurts women too. We need to overcome the roles that are dictated to us if we are to become fully human beings.

Yet in addition to the damage that each of us suffers because of our roles, there are also injuries that happen to certain people only because of their sex, race or class position. For instance, the woman who overcomes her conditioning and seeks to work in the traditionally male job of fire-fighting still has to face the possible contempt of her employers and co-workers, as well as the actual threat of rape or sexual assault. These dangers face her above and beyond any "role" she might take. Some of us who are racial or sexual minority men, or who realize our economic exploitation, also recognize that similar dangers confront us as well.

We in the C.A.M.P. Caucus believe that it is not enough to work only for men's liberation. We think that oppression of others, on any basis, is an *insult* to our own feelings of justice and caring for others. In addition, we oppose discrimination against any less-favored group because we value belonging to a diverse *community* of people. We want to overcome the segregation imposed on us as men, even if that segregation offers us benefits.

Patriarchal capitalism in which we live commands all men to sell out our capacity to care for and learn from others. Let us encourage each other to resist that pressure. We have too much self-respect to keep silent while others get worked over.

Because we love and have pride in ourselves, we feel a need to become involved in anti-sexist work that includes and yet goes beyond, men's liberation. Perhaps it is talking with our friends, telling each other the truths about male socialization, working for gay or reproductive rights, or working against domestic violence. Whatever it may be, there are no strictly personal solutions. The call to nurture ourselves includes a call to action when those we love are under attack.

Growing Beyond Guilt: Justice, Community and Self-Respect

Our awareness of injustice and discrimination can frequently involve feelings of guilt and self-blame. We may collaborate with, yet feel ashamed of a system in which we're not truly comfortable. We may also feel trapped and powerless to transform our society.

We do not believe that guilt is an answer. The responsibility of men as a class for the oppression of women is a reality. But feeling hopeless about it is not effective. Feeling self-blame doesn't change anything. We need to replace it with pride in ourselves and the actions we undertake. We work past self-blame when we (1) work on ourselves—raise our consciousness, and (2) work to change those conditions in society which make us feel guilty. We diminsh guilt when we take the responsibility for personal and political behavior that makes us feel good about ourselves.

We have many positive motivations for our growth and work:

—*love* for ourselves and others,
—*anger* at the way little boys are rewarded for becoming insensitive; and *anger* at the ways we, our loved ones, and others have been hurt by the patriarchy,
—*self-respect* in our commitment to equality and our sensitivity to justice and injustice,
—*desire for community* which thrives when we break through the isolating prejudices based on sex, sexual orientation, race, class background, age, physical status, etc.

We will solve the problems that face us as changing men not through guilt, avoidance, or denial, but rather through our joining together in a community to work towards better lives for all people. We believe that we can experience our fullest sense of growth by recognizing that our path is both personal and political.

We will work together on a *personal* level (1) because of a sense of pride in our emotions and actions, and (2) in order to end our isolation from women and from each other. We will work together on a social level (1) because all oppression is clearly unjust and hurtful, and (2) in order to achieve common goals with women and others.

Individual and Collective Actions Men Can Take

Individual Actions

—tell men that you don't think rape jokes are funny
—set time aside to talk with the women in

your life about working towards equal relationships

—when approaching a woman in a deserted area, keep your hands visible, walk so that women have a clear path, and be aware that to every woman, any man is a potential rapist

—wear a pink triangle, the symbol that Nazis forced Gay people to wear in German concentration camps, to demonstrate solidarity with Gays and Lesbians

—confront men who are hassling women on the street

—practice giving and getting attention from other men

—wear buttons that reveal your opposition to oppression

—spend more time with children because they have much to teach and because their natural sense of emotional freedom needs support

—learn to listen better to women, children and other men

—point out sexist comments and behavior with your friends and co-workers

—be willing to be self-critical, or recount your own past sexist behavior

—try wearing a skirt sometime

—write male anti-sexist grafitti on bathroom walls, billboards, anywhere

—come out if you are gay or bisexual, or come out as an open supporter of gays and lesbians and bisexual people

—be ready to hear critical feedback from minority groups you are not a member of. At the same time, it is not the responsibility just of minority groups (the physically different, for example) to raise our consciousness (say, concerning accessibility to public places). It is *everybody's* responsibility (including the physically unchallenged) to confront oppression or discrimination.

—donate money to anti-sexist or other efforts—funds for resistance do not come out of thin air

—subscribe to the CAMP Caucus Newsletter, or to *M.*, the national anti-sexist men's publication

—don't use the word "fuck" as a curse

—spend a period of time as a househusband

—read feminist historical and political literature

—listen hard to hear the everyday terror of sexual assault and other sexist violence experienced by women

—tell people you have good heterosexual friends who are feminist and anti-homophobic and a pleasure to be with

—buy anti-sexist men's music (Geof Morgan, Charlie Murphy, etc.) and poetry, and support cultural work by attending readings and concerts.

—buy yourself some flowers and let the florist know they are for you

Collective Actions

—share with other men common experiences about growing up male

—form a support group with other men

—form a consciousness-raising group with other men

—start a local men's center

—find out how to start a counseling program for men who batter

—offer a workshop or plan a men's sharing day

—participate in a protest demonstration or parade

—sign petitions, write letters, or join lobbying efforts

—join the CAMP Caucus—it really needs men who actually are ready to work in its task forces and committees

—organize childcare for Take Back the Night marches and other feminist events

—leaflet movies depicting and supporting violence against women

—write articles on your ideas and experiences for the CAMP newsletter, or for *M.*

—support abortion clinics and women's reproductive rights groups
—work with parents to end sexism in school curriculum and career planning
—discuss with other men the threat that pornography has toward the submission of women, and the damage that it does to our own sexuality
—carry anti-sexist male values to organizations of which you are a member
—organize a study group to read feminist literature
—keep your spirits up! The patriarchy is slowly crumbling, and despite the long struggle the energy of anti-sexist men is growing.

"STATEMENT ON THE FORMATION OF THE NATIONAL ORGANIZATION FOR CHANGING MEN"

Robert Brannon (1983)

THIS AFTERNOON marks the first public appearance of a new national organization. It is one composed primarily of American men, and devoted to a wide range of issues and actions which especially affect the lives of men in this society.

We wish to make clear also that together with our concern for the lives and welfare of men, we are committed to changing other injustices which have since ancient times been associated with a human being's sex. We are committed to full equality and justice for women, and with equal conviction, to full equality and acceptance of those who have been stigmatized because of their sexual preference. We believe, in fact, that all of these issues are far more closely connected than most human beings have recognized in the past.

There have been other, previous groups of men who were concerned about one or another of the many special problems and issues of men. There are today organizations of women who demand equal treatment, and organizations of gay men and Lesbian women who are asking for the simple justice of being treated fairly and equally. Although less well-known, there have also been

"Press Conference Statement of March 12, 1983." Brother *1, no. 2 (1983).*

groups of men in the past who fought valiantly for the rights of women, and there have been heterosexual men who worked for an end to prejudice against gays. But the record will show that there has never been an organized national movement of men with the breadth of concern, and the determination to bring about social change, as the one that we are launching today.

Here, in brief form, is our agenda for change. This organization and the broader men's movement out of which it evolved over the past few years, are working for basic social changes in at least three major and equally important arenas, all connected in different and yet related ways with the fact of a person's sex:

First, we are saying and feel with great conviction that the average man's life could be a great deal more happy and satisfying, if he could learn to escape from what we have come to recognize as this culture's "Male Sex Role." American men are taught from childhood to be unemotional, aggressive, un-nurturing, mainly directed toward work and career achievment, unconcerned with the quality of personal relationships, exploitative of women, wary of other men, reflexively competitive, isolated from children, and profoundly afraid of admitting to any interest, hobby, attitude, or other quality that might somehow suggest, to someone, that they might be that most terrible of all things . . . a homosexual.

Our society's conception of masculinity also includes some good qualities, it is true. But the total package is both limiting and often destructive, to us and to others. As men who care about the quality of our own lives, we are working to *unlearn* our lifelong indoctrination in the male sex role, and to discover new ways of living and relating to others which will make us freer, happier, and . . . healthier, in every sense of that word.

A second, and today especially urgent goal of the men's movement, is to join immediately in the unfinished fight for full equality for women. We are dismayed that in this huge and rich nation, with its proud rhetoric and claims of Liberty And Justice For All, our own mothers, sisters, wives, daughters, and many women friends still suffer the innumerable minor and major abuses and indignities of sexism. The terrible recent statistics—e.g. of rape (a woman is raped every three minutes somewhere in this country, night and day); domestic violence and battering; burgeoning pornography (now a billion-dollar industry in the U.S., and growing rapidly); and widespread incest and child abuse—*sicken* us, as we feel they must sicken any thinking human being who cares about others. We are determined, therefore, to become a *strong, vocal, visible,* and *effective* force, in the difficult fight for justice and equality for women. We take special pride in the work of men within our movement who have already been active in working for reproductive choice; for the ERA; against domestic violence and battering; and against rape and pornography. We promise that there will be much more of this work to come.

The third very deep concern of our movement—and in no way less important than the other two—is the insanity which has long gripped our society concerning the little-understood issue of sexual preference. We are profoundly disturbed by the immense power of "homophobia" in the minds of so many American men. ("Homophobia" is a term meaning the intense and irrational fear of and hostility toward the idea of homosexuality.) Over the past ten years we have come to believe that this illogical but widespread fear is probably the single most powerful source of opposition among men to changing traditional masculine behaviors. The reasons for this self-defeating rigidity are clear. American men are taught to consider almost any behavior which differs from traditional masculinity as somehow related to homosexuality. Thus they live within the invisible cage of their secret fear, afraid to try any path which might lead to a charge of being gay.

The other side of homophobia is the cruel and primitive oppression which this society directs toward the minority of its citizens who are homosexual. Outside of a few major urban areas, these millions of stigmatized Americans are perhaps the most bizarrely and universally oppressed minority in this country today. Small wonder that the average man will go to any length to avoid being called gay, even making himself a swaggering caricature of masculinity, when he sees the incredible, mindless hostility directed toward those men who are gay.

We believe that the only way out of this psychological swamp of ignorance, fear, and hostility is to confront it directly. Thus, this organization considers it one of its major objectives to free heterosexual men from the needless burden of homophobia. We encourage free communication and cooperation among gay and straight men, as a way of reducing fears and misconceptions. We are totally opposed to all forms of discrimination based on sexual preference.

To some casual observers, it might perhaps seem that this new organization is spreading its concerns and energies over many issues which are not, by usual standards, closely related to each other. The truth, however, is the opposite. The oppression of women, male homophobia, the oppression of gays, and the numerous burdens, fears, and wounds of the average American man are all part of the same basic pathology of what social scientists have called a "patriarchal" way of life. Each injustice associated with sex contributes to all of the others. Even if we wished to, there would be no logic at all in attacking just one of these problems, and leaving the others untouched.

The very special beauty—and great potential strength—of this men's movement is that we encompass and embody *all* of these concerns.

Most people in the United States have never heard gay men speak up for women's rights.

Most people have not heard heterosexual men speak out forcefully for the civil rights of gay men and Lesbians.

Most people have not heard women speak knowledgeably and sympathetically about men's sex role burdens.

In our movement, all of these things take place at every conference and meeting. There is something very special, powerful, and wonderful to be part of, in the breadth and vision of an organization of American men devoted to helping themselves and to helping others, by unraveling the ancient Gordian knot of sex roles and sex oppression which has for so long bound and afflicted all of us. We seek nothing less than a world in which *everyone* is free to be whomever they are, to achieve whatever they can.

We ask our fellow American men to join us in this effort.

"SPEECH REINTRODUCING THE ERA"

Rep. Don Edwards (1989)

THE ROAD to equal rights for women has been a long one. Gathered in Seneca Falls, New York, in 1848, women used the Declaration of Independence as a model to argue for the first time for full rights as American citizens.

Seventy two years later, in 1920, women finally gained the first right of citizenship—the right to vote—after overcoming enormous opposition. Opponents claimed that women's suffrage would not help women, but would destroy them, the family and the nation. Today we know how silly those arguments were.

Yet we hear the same tired arguments against the Equal Rights Amendment. Instead of recognizing that American women are entitled as part of their birthright to full rights of citizenship, we hear contradictory arguments that ERA is either not needed (because the states will do it), or that it would destroy women, the family and our country.

Typescript courtesy of Rep. Don Edwards.

Only one woman at the Seneca Falls meeting lived to see women get the vote. The Equal Rights Amendment was first introduced in Congress in 1923, on the 75th anniversary of Seneca Falls. Another 75 years have passed since then. Women have waited long enough: the ERA needs to be incorporated into our Constitution now.

ERA is more than a symbol of full citizenship. Yes, there are laws protecting women from discrimination in employment, education, credit and so forth. But enforcement of those laws is subject to the whim of every Administration. We have seen in recent years that the commitment to eradicate discrimination is not always there. When the signal goes out that if it's OK for the federal government to back off of its commitment, it's OK for others, too.

The ERA would stand as a permanent, unassailable commitment by creating a constitutional standard of equality against which the actions of Congress, federal and state and local governments and ultimately the private sector would have to be measured.

SOCIAL EQUALITY

"A NEW LOOK AT ABORTION"

William Jennings Bryan Henrie, D.O. (1966)

. . . It is always an honor for an ex-convict to be asked to speak to any group on any subject. It is especially so in this case.

I have been told not to say that I am an ex-convict but I ask, why should I be ashamed of being an ex-convict if I am not ashamed of the things I did that caused me to become a convict? I am ashamed of a law that must be broken to save the honor and respect of many women. I am ashamed of a law that must be violated to help other women live better lives, and I am certainly ashamed of a law that must be disobeyed in order to make a better world in which to live and to help people live better in that world.

I am not ashamed that I took the time to listen to those pleading women for now I can stand proud and erect, as I do, to give thanks that I had the heart to understand their problems; and I am glad that I had the courage to abandon the ethics of my training to practice the convictions of my conscience and perform the services those patients demanded, so willingly paid for, and in so many, many, many cases were so gratefully satisfied.

I have been asked how I was able to practice so long and so openly without prosecution. I think the question was answered best by one County Attorney who said: "Sure. I'm ready to send Dr. Henrie to the penitentiary anytime because the law says it is illegal to perform an abortion; but, the law also says it is illegal to seek and have an abortion performed. Bring me five women who will testify that they sought such an abortion and whom I can send to the penitentiary with him, then I will act; but I do not propose to send my Doctor to the penitentiary and let all the guilty women run free to repeat their illegal acts with impunity."

This prompted the statement I have written: The weakness of the abortion laws were bred with its own conception, born as its Siamese twin and cannot be separated except with the death of both. Neither the patient nor the abortionist can testify to an abortion without incriminating herself or himself and to be granted immunity from the law makes the grantor wantonly hypocritical. This may be an honored and respected procedure within the law but hardly complies with more integrity than that the

---

Statement to the San Francisco Conference on Abortion and Human Rights, 9 January 1966. (SL)

end justifies the means; in which case we ask then, when does an end not justify the means? And does not the end results obtained justify the means of abortion? The women who demand abortions believe it does and none have ever denied it.

In many cases where the choice of the woman involved could solve many personal problems, all too often a third party entirely alien to the case, unrelated, unaffected and certainly not involved, demands their plan be followed. Then we see this woman stripped of every vestige of personal privacy, draped in the ominous veil of morbid curiosity, lying helpless on the consultation table of the lawyers, in the amphitheatre of publicity, under the searchlight of an inquisition, and suffering the agony of despair without even the aspirin of hope while the lawyers piously thumb their law books as they ponder their dilemma, but denying to doctors any value to their many hours of study, the voice of their experience, any right to their judgement or use of their ability to treat the patients and correct the problem. . . .

"UNCERTAIN, COY, AND HARD TO PLEASE"

Isaac Asimov (1969)

WHAT WITH ONE THING and another, I have been doing a good deal of reading of Shakespeare lately, and I've noticed a great many things, including the following: Shakespeare's romantic heroines are usually much superior to his heroes in intelligence, character and moral strength.

Juliet takes strenuous and dangerous action where Romeo merely throws himself on the ground and weeps ("Romeo and Juliet"); Portia plays a difficult and active role where Bassanio can only stand on the sidelines and wring his hands ("Merchant of Venice"); Benedick is a quick-witted fellow, but he isn't a match for Beatrice ("Much Ado About Nothing"). Nor is Berowne a match for Rosaline ("Love's Labor's Lost") or Orlando a match for Rosalind ("As You Like It"). In some cases, it isn't even close. Julia is infinitely superior in every way to Proteus ("Two Gentlemen of Verona") and Helena to Bertram ("All's Well That Ends Well").

The only play in which Shakespeare seems to fall prey to male chauvinism is "The Taming of the Shrew," and a good case can be made out for something more subtle than merely a strong man beating down a strong woman—but I won't bother you about that here.

Fantasy and Science Fiction *36, no. 2 (February 1969).*

Yet, despite all this, I never hear of anyone objecting to Shakespeare on the ground that he presents women inaccurately. I have never heard anyone say, "Shakespeare is all right but he doesn't understand women." On the contrary, I hear nothing but praise for his heroines.

Shakespeare—who, by common consent, has caught the human race at its truest and most naked under the probing and impersonal light of his genius—tells us women are, if anything, the superior of men in all that counts. How is it, then, that so many of us nevertheless remain certain that women are inferior to men. I say "us" without qualification because women, by and large, accept their own inferiority.

You may wonder why this matter concerns me or this magazine. Well, it concerns me (to put it most simply) because everything concerns me. It concerns this magazine because science fiction involves future societies, and these, I hope, will be more rational in their treatment of 51 percent of the human race than our present society is.

It is my belief that future societies *will* be more rational in this respect, and I want to explain my reasons for this belief. I would like to speculate about Woman in the future, in the light of what has happened to Woman in the past and what is happening to Woman in the present.

To begin with, let's admit there are certain ineradicable physiological differences between men and women. (First one to yell "Vive la différence!" leaves the room.)

But are there any differences that are primarily non-physiological? Are there intellectual, temperamental, emotional differences that you are *sure* of and that will serve to differentiate women from men in a broad, general way? I mean differences that will hold for all cultures, as the physiological differences do, and differences that are not the result of early training.

For instance, I am not impressed by the "Women are more refined" bit, since we all know that mothers begin very early in the game to slap little hands and say, "No, no, no, nice little girls don't do that."

I, myself, take the rigid position that we can never be sure about cultural influences and that the only safe distinctions we can make between the sexes are the physiological ones. Of these, I recognize two:

1—Most men are physically larger and physically stronger than most women.

2—Women get pregnant, bear babies, and suckle them. Men don't.

What can we deduce from these two differences *alone*? It seems to me that this is enough to put women at a clear disadvantage with respect to men in a primitive hunting society, which is all there was prior to, say, 10,000 B.C.

Women, after all, would be not quite as capable at the rougher aspects of hunting and would be further handicapped by a certain ungainliness during pregnancy as well as distractions while taking care of infants. In a catch-as-catch-can jostle for food, she would come up at the rear every time.

It would be convenient for a woman to have some man see to it that she was thrown a haunch after the hunting was over and then see to it, further,that some other man didn't take it away from her. A primitive hunter would scarcely do this out of humanitarian philosophy; he would have to be bribed into it. I suppose you're all ahead of me in guessing that the obvious bribe is sex.

I visualize a Stone Age treaty of mutual assistance between Man and Woman—sex-for-food—and as a result of this kind of togetherness, children are reared and the generations continue.

I don't see that any of the nobler passions can possibly have had anything to do with this. I doubt that anything we would recognize as "love" was present in the Stone Age, for romantic love seems to have been a rather late invention and to be anything but widespread even today. (I once read that the Hollywood-notion of romantic love was invented by the medieval Arabs and was spread to our own western society by the Provençal troubadours.)

As for the concern of a father for his children, forget it. There seem definite indications that men did not really understand the connection between sexual intercourse and children until nearly historic times. Mother-love may have its basis in physiology (the pleasure of suckling, for instance), but I strongly suspect that father-love, however real it may be, is cultural in origin.

Although the arrangement of sex-for-food seems a pretty reasonable *quid-pro-quo,* it isn't. It is a terribly unfair arrangement, because one side can break the agreement with impunity and the other cannot. If a woman punishes by withholding sex and a man by withholding food, which side will win out? "Lysistrata" to the contrary, a week without sex is a lot easier than a week without food. Furthermore, a man who tires of this mutual strike can take what he wants by force; a woman can't.

It seems to me, then, that for definite physiological reasons, the original association of men and women was a strictly unequal one, with man in the role of master and woman in the role of slave.

This is not to say that a clever woman, even in Stone Age times, might not have managed to wheedle and cajole a man into letting her have her own way. And we all know that this is certainly true nowadays, but wheedling and cajolery are slave-weapons. If you, Proud Reader, are a man and don't see this, I would suggest you try to wheedle and cajole your boss into giving you a raise, or wheedle and cajole a friend into letting you have your way, and see what happens to your self-respect.

In any master-slave relationship, the master does only that portion of the work that he likes to do or that the slave cannot do; all else is reserved for the slave. It is indeed frozen into the slaves' duties not only by custom but by stern social law that defines slaves' work as unfit for free men to do.

Suppose we divide work into "big-muscle" and "little-muscle." Man would do the "big-muscle" work because he would have to, and the women would then do the "little-muscle" work. Let's face it; this is usually (not always) a good deal for men because there is far more "little-muscle" work to do. ("Men work from sun to sun; women's work is never done" the old saying goes.)

Sometimes, in fact, there is no "big-muscle" work to do at all. In that case the Indian brave sits around and watches the squaw work—a situation that is true for many non-Indian braves, who sit and watch their non-Indian squaws work. Their excuse is, of course, that as proud and gorgeous males they can scarcely be expected to do "women's work."

The social apparatus of man-master and woman-slave was carried right into the most admired cultures of antiquity and was never questioned there. To the Athenians of the Golden Age, women were inferior creatures, only dubiously superior to domestic animals, and with nothing in the way of human rights. To the cultivated Athenian, it seemed virtually self-evident that male homosexuality was the highest form of love, since that was the only way in which a human being (male, that is) could love an equal. Of course, if he wanted children, he had to turn to a woman, but so what; if he wanted transportation, he turned to his horse.

As for that other great culture of the past, the Hebrew, it is quite obvious that the Bible accepts male-superiority as a matter of course. It is not even a subject for discussion at any point.

In fact, by introducing the story of Adam and Eve, it has done more for woman's misery than any other book in history. The tale has enabled dozens of generations of men to blame everything on women. It has made it possible for a great many Holy Men of the past to speak of women in terms that a miserable sinner like myself would hesitate to use in referring to mad dogs.

In the ten commandments themselves, women are casually lumped with other forms of property, animate and inanimate. It says, in Exodus 20:17 "Thou shalt not covet they neighbour's house, thou shalt not covet they neighbour's wife, nor his man-servant, nor his maid-servant, nor his ox, nor his ass, nor any thing that is thy neighbors."

Nor is the New Testament any better. There are a number of quotations I can choose from, but I will give you this one from Ephesians 5:22–24: "Wives, submit yourselves unto your own husbands, as unto the Lord. For the husband is the head of the wife, even as Christ is the head of the church: and he is the saviour of the body. Therefore as the church is subject unto Christ, so let the wives be to their own husbands in every thing."

This seems to me to aspire to a change in the social arrangement of man/woman for master/slave to God/creature.

I don't deny that there are many passages in both the Old and New Testaments that praise and dignify womankind. (For example, there is the Book of Ruth.) The trouble is, though, that in the social history of our species, those passages of the Bible that taught feminine wickedness and inferiority were by far the more influential. To the self-interest that led men to tighten the chains about women was added the most formidable of religious injunctions.

The situation has not utterly changed in its essence, even now. Women have attained a certain equality before the law—but only in our own century, even here in the United States. Think how shameful it is that no woman, however intelligent and educated, could vote in a national election until 1920—despite the fact that the vote was freely granted to every drunkard and moron, provided only that he happened to be male.

Yet even so—though women can vote, and hold property, and even own their own bodies—all the social apparatus of inferiority remains.

Any man can tell you that a woman is intuitive rather than logical; emotional rather than reasonable; finicky rather than creative; refined rather than vigorous. They don't understand politics, can't add a column of figures, drive cars poorly, shriek with terror at mice and so on and so on and so on.

Because women are all these things, how can they be allowed an equal share with men in the important tasks of running industry, government, society?

Such an attitude is self-fulfilling, too.

We begin by teaching a young man that he is superior to young women, and this is comforting for him. He is automatically in the top half of the human race, whatever his shortcomings may be. Anything that tends to disturb this notion threatens not only his personal self-respect but his very virility.

This means that if a woman happens to be more intelligent than a particular man in whom she is (for some arcane reason) interested, she must never, for her very life, reveal the fact. No sexual attraction can then overcome the mortal injury he receives in the very seat and core of his masculine pride, and she loses him.

On the other hand, there is something infinitely relieving to a man in the sight of a woman who is manifestly inferior to himself. It is for that reason that a silly woman seems "cute." The more pronouncedly male-chauvinistic a society, the more highly valued is silliness in a woman.

Through long centuries, women have had to somehow interest men if they were to achieve any economic security and social status at all, and those who were not stupid and silly by nature had to carefully cultivate such stupidity and silliness until it came naturally and they forgot they ever were intelligent.

It is my feeling that all the emotional and temperamental distinctions between men and women are of cultural origin, and that they serve the important function of maintaining the man/woman master/slave arrangement.

It seems to me that any clear look at social history shows this and shows, moreover, that the feminine "temperament" jumps through hoops whenever that is necessary to suit man's convenience.

What was ever more feminine than Victorian womanhood, with its delicacy and modesty, its blushes and catchings of breath, its incredible refinement and its constant need for the smelling-salts to overcome a deplorable tendency to faint? Was there ever a sillier toy than the stereotype of the Victorian woman; ever a greater insult to the dignity of Homo sapiens?

But you can see why the Victorian woman (or a rough approximation of her) had to exist in the late 19th Century. It was a time when among the upper classes, there was no "little-muscle" work for her to do since servants did it. The alternative was to let her use her spare time in joining men in their work, or to have her do nothing. Firmly, men had her do nothing (except for such make-work nothings as embroidery and hack-piano-playing). Women were even encouraged to wear clothes that hampered their physical movements to the point where they could scarcely walk or breathe.

What was left to them, then, but a kind of ferocious boredom that brought out the worst aspects of the human temperament and made them so unfit an object, even for sex, that they were carefully taught that sex was dirty and evil so that their husbands could go elsewhere for their pleasures.

But in this very same era, no one ever thought of applying the same toy-dog characteristics to the women of the lower classes. There was plenty of "little-muscle" work for them to do, and since they had no time for fainting and refinement, the feminine temperament made the necessary adjustment, and they did without either fainting or refinement.

The pioneer women of the American West not only cleaned house, cooked, and bore baby after baby, but they grabbed up rifles to fight off Indians when necessary. I strongly suspect they were also hitched to the plow on such occasions as the horse needed a rest, or the tractor was being polished.—And this was in Victorian times.

We see it all about us even now. It's an article of faith that women just aren't any good at even the simplest arithmetic. You know how those cute little dears can't balance a checkbook. When I was a kid, all bank-tellers were male for that very reason. But then it got hard to hire male bank-tellers. Now 90 percent of them are female, and apparently they can add up figures and balance checkbooks after all.

At one time all nurses were males because everyone knew that women were simply too delicate and refined for such work. When the economic necessities made it important to hire females as nurses, it turned out they weren't all that delicate and refined after all. (Now nursing is "woman's work" that a proud man wouldn't do.)

Doctors and engineers are almost always men—until some sort of social or economic crunch comes—and then the female temperament makes the necessary change, and, as in the Soviet Union, women become doctors and engineers in great numbers.

What it amounts to is best expressed in a well-known verse by Sir Walter Scott:

O woman! in our hours of ease,
Uncertain, coy, and hard to please,
. . .
When pain and anguish wring the brow,
A ministering angel thou!

Most women seem to think this is a very touching and wonderful tribute to them, but I think that it is a rather bald exhibition of the fact that when man is relaxing he wants a toy and when he is in trouble he wants a slave, and woman is on instant call for either role.

What if pain and anguish wring *her* brow? Who's *her* ministering angel? Why, another woman who is hired for the occasion.

But let's not slip to the other extreme either. During the fight for women's votes, the male chauvinists said that this would wreck the nation since women had no feeling for politics and would merely be manipulated by the men-folks (or by their priests, or by any political quack with a scalp-ful of curls and a mouth-ful of teeth).

Feminists, on the other hand, said that when women brought their gentleness and refinement and honesty to the polling booth, all graft, corruption and war would be brought to an end.

You know what happened when women got the vote? *Nothing.* It turned out that women were no more stupid than men—and no wiser, either.

What of the future? Will women gain true equality?

Not if basic conditions continue as they have ever since Homo sapiens became a species. Men won't voluntarily give up their advantage. Masters never do. Sometimes they are forced to do so by violent revolution of one sort or another. Sometimes they are forced to do so by their wise foresight of a coming violent revolution.

An *individual* may give up an advantage out of a mere sense of decency, but such are always in the minority, and a group as a whole never does.

Indeed, in the present case, the strongest proponents of the status quo are the women themselves (at least most of them). They have played the role so long they would feel chills about the wrists and ankles if the chains were struck off. And they have grown so used to the petty rewards (the tipped hat, the offered elbow, the smirk and leer, and, most of all, the permission to be silly) that they won't exchange them for freedom. Who is hardest on the independent-minded woman who defies the slave-conventions? Other women, of course, playing the fink on behalf of men.

Yet things will change even so, because the basic conditions that underlie woman's historic position are changing.

What was the first essential difference between men and women?

1) Most men are physically larger and physically stronger than most women.

So? What of that today? Rape is a crime, and so is physical mayhem even when only directed against women. That doesn't stop such practices altogether, but it does keep them from being the universal masculine game they once were.

And does it matter that men are larger and stronger, in the economic sense? Is a woman too small and weak to earn a living? Does she have to crawl into the protecting neck-clutch of a male, however stupid or distasteful he may be, for the equivalent of the haunch of the kill?

Nonsense! "Big-muscle" jobs are steadily disappearing, and only "little-muscle" jobs are left. We don't dig ditches any more, we push buttons and let machines dig ditches.

The world is being computerized, and there is nothing a man can do in the way of pushing paper, sorting cards, and twiddling contacts, that a woman can't do just as well.

In fact, littleness may be at a premium. Smaller and slenderer fingers may be just what is wanted.

More and more, women will learn they need only offer sex-for-sex and love-for-love and nevermore sex-for-food. I can think of nothing that will dignify sex more than this change, or more quickly do away with the degrading master/slave existence of "the double standard."

But how about the second difference:

2) Women get pregnant, bear babies, and suckle them. Men don't.

I frequently hear that women have a "nest-building" instinct, that they really *want* to take care of a man and immolate themselves for his sake.—Maybe so, under conditions as they used to be. But how about now?

With the population explosion becoming more and more of a cliffhanger for all mankind, we will, before the end of the century, have evolved a new attitude toward babies or our culture will die.

It will become perfectly all right for a woman not to have babies. The stifling social pressure to become a "wife and mother" will lift, and that will mean even more than the lifting of the economic pressure. Thanks to the pill, the burden of babies can be lifted without the abandonment of sex.

This doesn't mean women *won't* have babies; it means merely they won't *have* to have babies.

In fact, I feel that female slavery and the population explosion go hand in hand. Keep a woman in subjection and the only way a man will feel safe is to keep her "barefoot and pregnant." If she has nothing to do except undignified and repetitive labor, a woman will want baby after baby as the only escape to something else.

On the other hand, make women truly free and the population explosion will stop of its own accord. Few women would want to sacrifice their freedom for the sake of numerous babies. And don't say "No" too quickly; feminine freedom has never been truly tried, but it must be significant that the birth rate is highest where the social position of women is lowest.

In the 21st Century, then, I predict that women will be completely free for the first time in the history of the species.

Nor am I afraid of the counter-prediction that all things go in cycles and that the clearly visible trend toward feminine emancipation will give way to a swing back to a kind of neo-Victorianism.

Effects can be cyclic, yes—but only if causes are cyclic, and the basic causes here are non-cyclic, barring world-wide thermonuclear war.

In order for the pendulum to swing back toward feminine slavery, there would have to be an increase in "big-muscle jobs" that only men could do. Women must begin once more to fear starvation without a man to work for them. Well, do you think the present trend toward computerization and social security will reverse itself short of global catastrophe? Honestly?

In order for the pendulum to swing back, there would have to be a continuation of the desire for large families and lots of children. There's no other way to keep women contented with their slavery on a large scale (or too busy to think about it, which amounts to the same thing). Given our present population explosion and the situation as it will be by 2000, do you honestly expect women to be put to work breeding baby after baby?

So the trend toward woman's freedom is irreversible.

There's the beginning of it right now, and

it is well established. Do you think that the present era of sexual-permissiveness (almost everywhere in the world) is just a temporary breakdown in our moral fiber and that a little government action will restore the stern virtues of our ancestors?

Don't you believe it. Sex has been divorced from babies, and it will continue to be so, since sex can't possibly be suppressed and babies can't possibly be encouraged. Vote for whom you please, but the "sexual revolution" will continue.

Or take even something so apparently trivial as the new fad of hairiness in man. (I've just grown a pair of absolutely magnificent sideburns myself.) Sure, it will change in details, but what it really stands for is the breakdown of trivial distinctions between the sexes.

It is indeed this which disturbs the conventional. Over and over, I hear them complain that some particular long-haired boy looks just like a girl. And then they go on to say, "You can't tell them apart any more!"

This always makes me wonder why it is so important to tell a boy from a girl at a glance, unless one has some personal object in view where the sex makes a difference. You can't tell at a glance whether a particular person is Catholic, Protestant, or Jew; whether he/she is a piano-player or a poker-player, an engineer or an artist, intelligent or stupid.

After all, if it were *really* important to tell the sexes apart at the distance of several blocks with one quick glance, why not make use of Nature's distinction? That is *not* long hair since both sexes in all cultures grow hair of approximately equal length. On the other hand, men always have more facial hair than women; the difference is sometimes extreme. (My wife, poor thing, couldn't grow sideburns even if she tried.)

Well, then, should all men grow beards? Yet the very conventionals who object to long hair on a man, also object to beards. *Any* change unsettles them, so when change becomes necessary, conventionals must be ignored.

But *why* this fetish of short hair for men and long hair for women, or, for that matter, pants for men and skirts for women, shirts for men and blouses for women? Why a set of artificial distinctions to exaggerate the natural ones; why the sense of disturbance when the distinctions are blurred?

Can it be that the loud and gaudy distinction of dress and hair between the two sexes is another sign of the master-slave relationship? No master wants to be mistaken for a slave at any distance, or have a slave mistaken for a master, either. In slave societies, slaves are always carefully distinguished (by a pigtail when the Manchus ruled China, by a yellow Star of David when the Nazis ruled Germany, and so on). We ourselves tend to forget this, since our most conspicuous non-female slaves had a distinctive skin-color and required very little else to mark them.

In the society of sexual equality that is coming, then, there will be a blurring of artificial distinctions between the sexes, a blurring that is already on the way. But so what? A particular boy will know who his particular girl is and vice versa, and if someone else is not part of the relationship what does he/she care which is which?

I say we can't beat the trend, and we should therefore join it. I say it may even be the most wonderful thing that has ever happened to mankind.

I think the Greeks *were* right in a way, and that it *is* much better to love an equal. And if that be so, why not hasten the time when we heterosexuals can have love at its best?

"A GAY MANIFESTO"

Carl Wittman (1972)

On Women

1. *Lesbianism:* It's been a male-dominated society for too long, and that has warped both men and women. So gay women are going to see things differently from gay men; they are going to feel put down as women, too. Their liberation is tied up with both gay liberation and women's liberation.

This paper speaks from the gay male viewpoint. And although some of the ideas in it may be equally relevant to gay women, it would be arrogant to presume this to be a manifesto for lesbians.

We look forward to the emergence of a lesbian liberation voice. The existence of a lesbian caucus within the New York Gay Liberation Front has been very helpful in challenging male chauvinism among gay guys, and anti-gay feelings among women's liberation.

2. *Male chauvinism*: All men are infected with male chauvinism—we were brought up that way. It means we assume that women play subordinate roles and are less human than ourselves. (At an early gay liberation meeting one guy said, "Why don't we invite women's liberation—they can bring sandwiches and coffee.") It is no wonder that so few gay women have become active in our groups.

Male chauvinism, however, is not central to us. We can junk it much more easily than straight men can. For we understand oppression. We have largely opted out of a system which oppresses women daily—our egos are not built on putting women down and having them build us up. Also, living in a mostly male world we have become used to playing different roles, doing our own shitwork. And finally, we have a common enemy: the big male chauvinists are also the big anti-gays.

But we need to purge male chauvinism, both in behavior and in thought among us. Chick equals nigger equals queer. Think it over.

3. *Women's liberation*: They are assuming their equality and dignity and in doing so are challenging the same things we are: the roles, the exploitation of minorities by capitalism, the arrogant smugness of straight white male middle-class Amerika. They are our sisters in struggle.

Problems and differences will become clearer when we begin to work together. One major problem is our own male chauvinism. Another is uptightness and hostility to homosexuality that many women have—that is the straight in them. A third problem is differing views on sex: sex for them has meant oppression, while for us it has been a symbol of our freedom. We must come to know and understand each other's style, jargon and humor.

From Out of the Closets: Voices of Gay Liberation, *ed. Karla Jay and Allen Young. New York: Douglas, 1972.*

"THE STRUGGLE TO SMASH SEXISM IS A STRUGGLE TO DEVELOP WOMEN"

Kalamu ya Salaam (1980)

THE STRUGGLE to eradicate sexism, develop women and establish progressive relationships between African-american women and men is, in our opinion, a key and critical aspect of our national liberation movement, a movement against capitalism, racism and sexism, and for African-american political self-determination and economic self-reliance.

This presentation will attempt to point out why eradicating sexism, developing women and building progressive relationships is important to the future of our people as a whole, and also will suggest beginning steps toward accomplishing that purpose.

Defining Feminism as an Integral Aspect of Our Struggle

The battle against sexism is not a war of the sexes. It is not a battle of women against men. It is a battle against an exploitative social system, a political battle—political in the sense that it is about us as a people, and, in this case, specifically our women, gaining the power to self-determine, self-defend and self-respect ourselves as human beings.

From Our Women Keep Our Skies from Falling. *New Orleans: Privately printed, 1980.*

Our national liberation work must have a feminist aspect as the dialectical complement of our anti-sexist position. From a political philosophical point of view, it is important for us to grasp that ultimately, the only effective "anti" position is a "pro" position. It is not enough to be against sexism, we must also be for feminism.

Feminism, at root and in its most positive sense, is simply political and economic power for women. Feminism is an integral part of our national liberation struggle precisely because there is no such thing as partial freedom or freedom in the abstract. Either all of us must have access to political and economic power, or else we as a people are not free.

In our view feminism does not necessarily result in, nor does it require espousing as its main goal, the turning of women into "men," or the development of an androgynous or uni-sex society. Some slick opponents of feminism make this claim in order to create erroneous and easily refuted "straw women." Concretely, women are not men, nor is it necessary for them to become men-like in order to self-determine, self-defend, and self-respect their own lives as women and to decisively and collectively contribute to the upliftment of our people.

Additionally, we assert that the contributions of women are unique contributions.

The uniqueness of these contributions is precisely that they are reflective of and deeply rooted in the specific reality of what it means to be a woman in general, and also, what it specifically means to be an African-american woman in modern America.

Unlike those who, in a zeal to achieve social equality for women, put forward the concept that there is no essential difference between women and men, we believe that there are obvious and essential differences which concretely lead to a basis for women making distinctive inputs into the structuring and maintenance of society. However, it is imperative to simultaneously assert that these real differences in no way should be twisted or construed to be a basis for denying power to women, or for justifying that women are inferior, weaker, or less capable of thinking than men because of these differences.

Difference is not a measure of worth. Both the earth and the sun, which are undeniably different in essence and function, are necessary for life as we know and live it. In a similar fashion, in order to develop the liberated life we need and desire, and for the establishment of which we struggle against sometimes seemingly insurmountable odds, we need unfettered and mutually respecting women and men maximally contributing to society, each in their own unique and profoundly human ways.

In order to bring into being such women and men it will be necessary not only to refute sexism, but also we will need to establish a meaningful feminism. The struggle to gain and maintain a meaningful feminism will produce women and men who are whole human beings.

Although there is some resistance on the part of many men and a significant element of our women, the facts are that there is a real basis, in both history and our present conditions, for the construction of feminism within the context of our culture and struggles. Our history and current conditions, both as Africans and African-americans, include women such as Nzinga and Harriet Tubman, or the militants of PAC, ANC, ZANU, ZAPU, SWAPO and other African liberation movement and the female cadre of various African-american liberation organizations. These women in the past voluntarily and valiently went to war with our enemies, and in the present continue to confront our enemies. They have in the past and continue today to actively participate in and help lead wars of national liberation and resistance.

Also, presently there are literally millions of women who, due to force of exploitative and oppressive circumstance, have to fend for and feed self and dependents as single heads of households without spouses or with only minimal outside support in the thousands of ghettoes which litter the American urban-scape and thousands of miles of Bantustans which pollute the South African countryside. Such women are the key to our struggle precisely because they are the most exploited and therefore are the most in conflict with the status quo. They comprise the single greatest pool of potential revolutionaries.

Another importance of such history and current conditions is that they offer concrete examples and bases on which can be built a genuine, indigenous and self-serving feminism which interacts as a vital part of our overall liberation struggle. If we would only but make a realistic assessment of our history and conditions, we would find that we have the basis for the development of a political and progressive feminism rather than a biological and reactionary feminism. As our history and current conditions make clear, feminism is not foreign to us. The only question is will we develop feminism as a specific aspect of our liberation struggle.

We must specify feminism as a component of our struggle rather than maintain, as we too often did in the past, that once we are free from white domination our women will be free. Just as we rightly argue that racism will not simply disappear with the destruction of capitalism, or that capitalism doesn't disappear simply because Blacks are put in control, in similar fashion, we should understand that sexism will not simply disappear with the eradication of white male domination.

Sexism is a philosophy and practice that has its own internal dynamics and existence. To root it out will require special attention or else we will find it with us long after the last shot is fired. Particular problems demand particular attention.

Unity in Struggle

We must demonstrate in practice, through the establishment of specific and effective programs, that we are for the defense and development of African-american women, and also for the combating of sexist ideas and behavior in our men (*and* our women). Some argue that such a course of action actually divides our people. But, for the following three reasons, we believe that the course of action we outline here unites rather than divides us both as a people and also as individual women and men.

First, the internal struggle to defend and develop women and to raise men past being macho machines is generally a non-antagonistic contradiction among our people. It is generally non-antagonistic because we will be or should be able to resolve the majority of our internal differences without having to resort to killing each other. It is a contradiction because there are distinct and identifiable wrongs which must be eradicated and divergences which must be united.

However, because the internal struggle to defend and develop our women is generally non-antagonistic and among our people, it is therefore, a contradiction which can be solved through political action in the form of democratic discussion, ideological struggle, criticism and self-criticism, and the enactment of progressive programs.

In its external aspect, defending and developing women and raising men clearly falls into the context of an antagonistic contradiction between our people and our enemies and the struggle should be waged as such, i.e., using every resource at our command including warfare.

Second, we believe that the defense and development of women will raise our women, our organizations, and, ultimately, all of our people to a significantly higher level of social development. We will gain more revolutionaries, leaders and workers in the vein of Sojourner Truth, Harriet Tubman and Mary McLeod Bethune.

Additionally, as many of our social scientists are quick to point out, there is a shortage of African-american men and a surplus of African-american women. Given that our women are a numerical majority and also face a triple oppression and exploitation, then certainly particular attention should be paid to encouraging their full participation in our people's national liberation struggle.

Third, as Dr. Karenga correctly points out, if we ignore the problems and potentials of African-american women, we will create confusions and antagonisms where none need exist. Failing to get attention through peaceful means, women will rightfully disrupt a sexist status quo. Should disruption fail, women will correctly define us as collaborators and traitors who are little better than our people's historic enemy.

The truth is that our failure to fight sexism, our failure to help defend and develop our women, and our failure to raise the consciousness and behavior of our men will be the ultimate wedge which will keep us from getting together. The status quo argues for a false unity based on the relegation of women to a lower status. But, since when does unity mean one being on top of the other?

Only those consciously or unconsciously in favor of present social constructs and sexist hierarchies would argue that struggling to smash sexism and develop women is unnecessary and/or disruptive. But those of us who want to make change, who want to see women active at a higher level of social life, who want to see true liberation, we should understand that smashing sexism and developing women will bring women and men closer together as comrades, complements and lovers who work in principled and practical unity to build and defend a better and more beautiful world for ourselves, our people, and ultimately all peoples on the planet.

In order to effectively and efficiently accomplish our important task, it is crucial that we begin by grasping three key elements: (1.) put politics in the lead, (2.) develop organization, (3.) be scientific.

Put Politics, and Not Biology, in the Lead!

First, put politics, and not biology, in the lead. Among many other considerations, this view unequivocably asserts the position that men can and should participate in this struggle. Those of us who consider ourselves progressive men should be in the forefront of not only support work but also in the forefront of actual front line struggle against sexism and for the empowerment of women. Additionally, we should, in practical terms, work on the day to day improvement of our relationships with women.

Many men do not struggle in this way because we are, as a result of our American socialization, thoroughly indoctrinated with sexism. Those of us in this category see no need, nor have any desire, to struggle against sexism in ourselves, as well as in other men, and to struggle for the development of women. Others of us don't struggle because of our ideological errors and deficiencies, i.e. a shaky and/or incorrect analysis and understanding of what we are fighting against, what we are fighting for, and who will benefit from our struggles.

Also, many men react negatively and incorrectly to those women who attempt to exclude men from the feminist struggle based on a reduction of the feminist struggle to a biological factor, i.e. biological determinism or putting biology, rather and politics, in the lead.

It is wrong to believe that biology or physiological differences determine social relationships. Social relationships are determined by the ideas and actions of both women and men acting either as individuals or, as in the overwhelming majority of cases, as self-defined groups.

Because women, or anyone else in a given struggle, make the error of biological determinism or other errors, that does not mean that either the struggle itself or those individuals who make mistakes while struggling are of no or little value and can be dismissed.

Also, in order for men to make significant contributions to the struggle to defend and develop women, it is not necessary for men to be in every organization formed to achieve that goal.

There is nothing inherently wrong with "women only" caucuses and organizations established to fight sexism and develop women. In fact, tactically speaking, such a move will often be necessary in order to advance.

But, on the other hand, there is something

wrong with the outlook and behavior of men who do not struggle against sexist wrongs and for women's rights unless they have a say so in everything that women say and do. This is nothing but a continuance of male domination.

We not only affirm the right of women to meet and organize among themselves, we also denounce the position which would lead us to believe that such actions are inherently incorrect. At the same time, however, we believe that it is both possible and important for women and men to live, struggle, work and create together as politically and economically equal parts of a larger society.

This is why our organization has both female and male cadre on an equal standing, and why we sponsor programs which speak directly to the defense and development of women, and why we include men in such programs. But, on the other hand, recognizing the importance and sensitiveness of initial mobilization—gathering together people of common interest to confront a particular problem or make productive a particular potential—our organization continues to offer opportunities for women to get together, in the absence of men, in order to address questions of their choice. However, it is important to recognize that "female only" mobilization is only a secondary tactic, rather than a primary tactic, of our overall strategy for smashing sexism and developing women.

Furthermore anti-sexism and feminism are, in our view, but one part of our greater national liberation struggle; an indispensable part, a part of high priority, but, nonetheless and in the final analysis, still a part and not a whole in and of itself.

We do not believe that the defense and development of women, nor men, can be realized separate from our overall national liberation. We believe that while there will be no true liberation without women's liberation, it is also true that women's liberation (or men's liberation) can not be achieved and maintained separate from our over all liberation struggle. It is a serious error to believe and act otherwise.

However, it is also a serious error to spend valuable time attacking women who make mistakes in the process of waging struggle (which is qualitatively different from women or men who consciously side with, and thusly, become agents of our enemy).

Initially, we will all make mistakes, for that is part of the necessary process of acquiring theoretical and practical knowledge and skills. Once we recognize the inevitability of mistakes, then we should also recognize the importance of compassion, understanding and assistance.

Men who are genuine in this struggle will make every effort to help rather than hurt, to rectify rather than simply refute, to defend rather than denounce women who are struggling to defend and develop themselves, *particularly when women make mistakes.* To persist in putting down women in the name of correcting or criticizing their mistakes, rather than supporting and encouraging women who struggle, is a serious error.

These and other errors are, to a great extent, due to our lack of or deficiency in an ideology based on dialectical praxis, i.e., a development of theory and practice grounded in: (1.) *perception* of concrete reality through observation investigation, (2.) *reflection* or deductive "thinking about" what we have perceived, (3.) *conception* of logical conclusions which flow out of our reflections and perceptions, (4.) *formulation* of specific hypotheses or ideas as guides for action, (5.) *application* in practice of the hypothesis, (6.) and *evaluation* of the results of our practice.

Instead of choosing this methodology, most of us think as we have been taught to think, i.e. metaphysically, fatalistically, and/or individually. As I have previously pointed out,

> If we weren't so metaphysical (attributing material and social development to unknown and/or incomprehensible nonmaterial, nonhuman forces) and fatalistic (believing that our future is predetermined and/or beyond the influence of our struggle to transform ourselves and the world) we would look beyond the image to the controllers of the image and the mechanisms of image making; we would look for the hidden hand of humans acting in their own interest rather than the invisible hand of "our God(s)" allegedly manipulating reality. Furthermore, what we "think" or "believe" about reality does not determine reality or necessarily aid us in confronting and changing it. We can create better and more beautiful lives only by critically and concretely investigating and transforming material and social reality.

Furthermore, because we have been taught to take an "individualistic" approach, many of us do not understand and/or accept that every so-called "personal" issue is also inevitably and overwhelmingly a political issue. "Personal" problems are, at root, nothing more than particular examples of general social problems. These social problems are necessarily defined within a larger and specific social/political context. In fact, our individual personalities are nothing more than the result of our socialization and the response of each of us to this socialization.

We are not saying that personal problems do not exist. But rather, we are saying that the existence of each and every personal problem has its origins and maintenance in our overall social conditions. Personal problems can be solved by either altering individual responses to social conditions and/or by altering social conditions which effect the individual. The former choice maintains the status quo, the latter choice changes the status quo. Obviously then, for those of us who are systematically exploited and oppressed within this social context, the most appropriate and effective choice, although certainly not the easiest choice to make or carry through to completion, is to challenge and change society.

In order to successfully challenge and change society, we as a people will have to obtain power, which we define as the capability (will and ability) to self-determine, self-defend and self-respect our lives. The struggle to control society and our lives, which is also the essence of our national liberation struggle, is then what we must be about if we are to solve our so-called "personal problems."

Additionally, women and men who participate in this struggle, will find that active participation offers both an opportunity to work on these problems in meaningful manners, and also provides, in many cases, the opportunity to resolve or at least ameliorate the personal problems of those who are struggling for national liberation.

Although we do have an ultimate destination, an ideal social goal, the reality is that social upliftment is not deferred pending realization of "utopia," but rather, social upliftment is a dialectical and necessary outgrowth of the struggle to reach our goal, particularly when our goal is a better society, a qualitatively higher development of human life.

By putting politics, rather than biology, in the lead we can break through the estrangement and alienation of women from men and vice versa; we can recognize that biological differences do not necessarily lead to political and economic differences; and we can understand that the political and economic differences that do exist between women and men in America are engineered by the architects of a profit-oriented, white supremacists, male chauvinist society which has intentionally built into the society, mechanisms of political economic, racial and sexual division in order to ensure the maintenance of white, male, ruling class domination.

By putting politics in the lead we not only make ourselves conscious of the sources of division and the reasons for division, but more importantly, we also decisively contribute to our own transformation which gives us the revolutionary capacity to both theoretically and practically confront our real enemies by uniting and fighting for a national liberation program of (1.) political and economic sovereignty, (2.) international solidarity of peoples of African descent, and (3.) the institution of a controlled and collective, creative and productive social system.

Second, in addition to putting politics in the lead, we must organize ourselves. The struggle against sexism and for power is not a struggle that any of us can take on single-handedly, although each of us will certainly have to make individual contributions. We must always remember that power comes from people organized and actively working to transform themselves and their material and social conditions. Those of us who recognize this usually concurrently recognize that, since power comes from the creative and productive work of people, only a people organized can defeat exploitation and oppression, only people organized can become self-determining and self-reliant.

Every organization, regardless of its collective character, individual constituents, or its purpose and programs, in the final analysis, is politically either progressive, regressive or status quo oriented. In order to be progressive, organizations will have to pay great attention to the social relationships active within the organization and between the organization and other organizations, individuals, institutions and issues.

Again, this is ultimately a political question. Even an all female caucus or organization must make a decision about how it will relate to or not relate to progressive peoples and issues, almost all of whom will include men. An all woman organization is no guarantee of progressiveness, just as an all Black, an all male or "all whatever" organization can not guarantee progressiveness. Progressiveness is determined by the philosophy and programs of an organization and the specific contributions of those who make up the organization.

So then we are saying that the struggle to smash sexism and gain power requires not only a different ideology, a different way of thinking and acting, but also requires that we either form distinct organizations to address these issues or else set up specific programs within existing organizations to take up the work of defending and developing women.

To the degree that we do not address the question of sexism within the organizations that we form, to that same degree our organizations will contain fatal flaws which will ultimately undermine and doom the organization to failure.

This task will not happen by accident. Our organizations must plan to pay attention to and solve the problems of women. We must consciously work at developing the potential of women. The issue can not be put on a back burner. It must be a priority issue of organizational work if it is to be adequately addressed. This organizational priority must run the gamut of activities from childcare to political education; from organizational support in confronting, in both individual and collective instances, the reluctance of both men and women to face up to and transform socially induced weaknesses, to the structuring of specific sessions and programs which address the issues and concerns of women within and without the organization.

In Order to Overcome, Be Scientific!

Third, in addition to ideology and organization, we must be scientific in our methods of struggle. The dialectical method of investigation is the cornerstone of science. But, in relation to using the scientific method, the most important and underlying assumption is that we as human beings can transform ourselves and our environment.

This belief in self is revolutionary optimism; revolutionary, because we believe in our own ability to make decisive change and optimism because we are confident that Pamoja Tutashinda (Together We Will Win)! Additionally, in order to be truly optimistic, we must be honest in our evaluation of ourselves, each other and our capabilities. So then, those who employ scientific methods are invariably optimistic in outlook and honest in the evaluations.

Optimism. For too long we as a people, and particularly those of us who are women, have not believed in our own collective and individual capacity to make change.

Women have suffered the stringent controls of a sexist society which, ideologically, politically, economically and in countless other concrete ways, binds the feet of women.

This process of footbinding has been so horribly thorough that often women will bind the feet of both themselves as well as the feet of other women in an effort to conform to a detrimental and self-destructive image which they have been taught to believe is what women are supposed to be. Thus, society not only creates a dependency complex in both the minds and the lives of women, but also, society sometimes successfully uses women as agents to perpetuate this dependencycomplex.

We African-americans should not be surprised by the "victim-turned-oppressor" syndrome. We should be very familiar with this phenomenon. For just as America changed the African and created the self-destructive "negro," so too, America has helped change women into "the American girl." The only two distinctions being that (1.) whereas our indoctrination into "negroness" began with the slave trade, the sexist indoctrination of women preceded that time period, and (2.) whereas we had our names changed to negroes, the sexist modification of women's consciousness was accomplished without a name change, thusly making it even more difficult to recognize.

But whether or not we recognize or understand this terrible reality, women will not be able to walk on their own two legs until the theoretical and practical footbindings of women are unraveled and discarded. Until women's feet are free, regardless of how much they may want to walk unassisted, they will in reality remain physically, emotionally, and otherwise dependent on others for support.

The fact that some women have tried removing the bindings on their own, the fact that some have been partially successful at slipping out of the bindings but still have not as a whole been able to walk as whole human beings, all of this and more, has served to discourage women and men from struggling for the development of women.

Regrettably after falling once or twice, some of us have concluded that women will never walk upright, just as many of us believe that our people as a whole will never be liberated and self-reliant. Some of us are convinced that regardless of what we do we can not win. Unfortunately, at this time, more than a few of us believe that we can not significantly change our conditions.

This lack of belief in ourselves when coupled with our reluctance to honestly and fearlessly, materially and socially, criticize each other and our collective situations has been a more effective fetter on our progress than any chain or physical force used by our enemy.

In order to be optimistic it will be necessary to adopt a revolutionary ideology, i.e. guiding principles and values which are change-oriented (in a self-defined progressive and positive sense) rather than status quo oriented. We need an ideology which is collective rather than individual in orientation and which affirms that conscious people can adequately defend themselves from physically more powerful people and can overcome past and current material deficiencies. This is important. If we lack a belief in our own ability to make change, we will certainly not be willing to go against the tide of the status quo, or in cases when we do go against the tide, we will allow small setbacks or the rigors and tests of protracted struggle to overwhelm and defeat us.

But in order for us to adopt such an outlook it will be necessary to strip ourselves of old indoctrinations, and it will be necessary, although certainly painful at times, to learn new ways of looking at and living in the world. This in turn will require a degree of honesty about ourselves that we previously have not yet achieved and a simultaneous degree of hard and conscious Kazi (work) that we previously have avoided.

Honesty. The best honesty, in a collective setting, is serious criticism/self-criticism. Criticism, or a critique, is simply an accurate assessment of reality, a weighing. We should decide what is good, what is bad, what is real, what is abstract, why and when we do what we do and don't do.

Critiques should in no way imply condemnation. Most of us, as a result of our socialization within this society, take a dim view of criticism and self-criticism. We have been taught to think that not only are critiques unnecessary, unhealthy, and ultimately destructive, but also, we have been taught that critiques are personal attacks.

However, the important and indispensable purpose of principled political critiques is to reveal the reality of our everyday individual and collective lives, to expose the material and social forces at work, and to help us determine what course of action is best in order to achieve our own goals.

In developing the capacity to critique each other and our external reality, we will necessarily have to critique and confront both our external opposition and our internal weaknesses. Such critiques, particularly in the case of self-criticisms and criticisms of internal weaknesses shall come only as a result of conscious efforts and can be successful only within a context where it is clear that it is done out of concern for both the individual and the collective.

To tell the truth to each other is sometimes very difficult, but it can be done if we make one of our organizational priorities truth telling and the establishment of an atmosphere that promotes standing up for the truth with positive reenforcements.

Political critiques necessarily demand ideological study, demand the acquiring of skills not only of thinking but also acquiring a practical understanding of history and contemporary conditions, how the world and people within it have worked and how they work today.

There is no simple road to smashing sexism and to developing women and men into whole human beings. But we reiterate our firm conviction, based on history and our present practice, we can win this struggle. If Sojourner Truth and Frederick Douglas could recognize, critique, fight against, and overcome the negative effects of their own sexist socializations in a slave society then we today can certainly also do at least the same and based on building on their historical accomplishments, we should be able to do more.

Critiques are welcomed among those of us who are genuinely optimistic based on a belief in our own human capacity to transform self and society, a belief which is validated by both history and practice. We do not fear our weaknesses nor the "might" of those problems we must face precisely because we know that we can change for the better. We know that we can transform ourselves and our society.

Individually, whether male or, especially, if female, we must dare greatness, go against the tide and oppose the multitude who have been trained by society to protect and promote the status quo. This is especially important for females as this is the only way to develop.

In any and all human societies only those who materially and socially produce goods and services actually develop. The way to develop muscles is to exercise them. The way to improve ourselves as social beings is to struggle to change and control society in general, as well as struggle to change and control specific social relationships within society. Social development is no abstract concept; it is real and practical.

Our organizations, if nothing else, must be structures which facilitate social change both internally—among the members who make up the organization, and externally—in the society at large within which the organization exists.

The struggle to smash sexism must be viewed in a positive manner. It is not just a matter of convincing men not to be sexist, it is more importantly a matter of convincing women not to accept sexism, to fight against it and to defend and develop themselves as women in the process of fighting sexism.

Above all else the smashing of sexism is a struggle to develop women. Why? Because developed women can not be contained by primitive or punitive sexist social systems. Developed women will transform themselves and the society within which they live, will determine their own lives. Developed women will fight back, will defend themselves. Developed women will put an end to degradation, will respect themselves.

Women must be armed with the theory necessary to refute the specious and sexist arguments of male chauvinism, especially when it is put forward by someone who is liberal or left, and particularly when the proponent of sexism is female. For finally, no soldier is a soldier unless they are able to fight, to shoot, to confront the enemy.

But again, there is much more to this than memorizing political formula. Grasping ideology necessarily includes not only study but also struggle. But ideology, or politics, alone, although necessary, is not sufficient. Women must also develop their creative and productive capacities in order to make socially relevant and ultimately indispensable contributions to our overall struggle and future societies.

For too long we have overlooked the concrete task of supporting women acquiring knowledge and skills which will be useful both to them as women and to our people's collective national liberation struggle.

We must go all out to create more women who, in addition to being theoretically advanced, are also proficient in the arts, sciences and skilled areas of productive labor. Women must also be encouraged to enter the so-called "non-traditional jobs" not to be tokens or firsts but rather because these job areas are, in most cases, the productive backbones of this and any society.

Within our organizations we should emphasize the development of women, pay attention to issues such as child care and birth control, communicative skills such as public speaking and writing, and self-defense. We must insure women the opportunity to travel and to meet people of various backgrounds and areas of expertise.

Women must insist on these opportunities which are the basic stepping stones of development. Women must not be discouraged by failure upon first attempting to work in new areas, nor be discouraged by the misunderstandings and ill-feelings that will inevitably surround them, nor stop short of success because of the temporary alienation that may exist between the emergent new woman and old friends, family and acquaintances.

Regardless of what happens or how long it takes to happen, all of us must recognize and reaffirm that it is primarily the ways in which society is organized and the ways in which women and men have been socialized that accounts for the position and dispositions of women in today's society. It is important to realize that women were not born with their feet bound but rather their feet were bound by a society which wishes to hobble them. There is no fatal flaw in the nature of women, just as there is no fatal flaw in the nature of our people as a whole.

Ideology and organization without optimism and criticism will not work simply because we will not be able to maintain a commitment to and faith in social relationships and organizations which we do not understand and over which we have little control.

When "things fall apart" we must be able to discover the cause and we must have confidence that we can reverse a negative trend. Lacking this confidence, we will desert, will quit, will revert back to the ways in which we were reared. Without a knowledge of what is wrong and why, we will never be able to overcome the odds against us, we will never truly recognize reality. Instead we will fool ourselves and, under the influence of a pervasive, enemy-led, mass media, we will nickname the truth and pathetically try to find ways to coexist with rather than challenge and change an exploitative and oppressive status quo.

Optimism and criticism are a necessary connective which holds together our theoretical (ideology) and concrete (organizational) work in the face of inevitable material and social stresses and strains.

A Collective and Scientific Struggle of Conscious Comrades!

Ideology, organization, and a scientific methodology based on optimism and criticism are necessary prerequisites to any successful struggle to smash sexism (or capitalism and racism) because these are the basic building blocks of a social system. Furthermore, in our case, the social system which exploits and oppresses us will not be totally defeated until and unless it is replaced by a different social system.

Sexism will not be totally defeated until this society is replaced by a non-sexist society. But the process of replacement requires an effort which is conscious (ideology), collective (organization), and scientific (criticism/optimism).

In order to smash sexism we must smash the weaknesses which provide fertile ground for sexism in ourselves, within our organizations, and within the society in which we live, struggle and die. In a similar fashion, we must work to develop women and also to raise the consciousness and behavior of men in order to establish positive social relationships between women and men. While at any given time any one of the three areas (individual, organization, society) may take priority, generally the case is that work must occur in all three in order for any of the three to be thorough.

Those who would depreciate the need to work in these areas; those who would have us believe that it is possible to make change without changing ourselves; those who deny, in either theory or practice, the need for organizational work; and those who suggest that we can forget about the larger society within which we exist and suggest that we isolate ourselves into some ideal utopian enclaves, these are people who are either ignorant of the lessons of history or agents of the status quo.

Beware of guides who claim that the road is smooth sailing. We who are active and aware know that the struggle to smash sexism is a difficult road, especially for women whose feet have been bound for centuries and especially also for men who have been blinded by sexism and who are too often reluctant to give up their position of "lord and master" over women.

But, all of these problems considered, there is no cause for despair, for as we struggle to achieve ideological clarity, and individual as well as organizational higher levels of socially significant practice, it becomes clearer and clearer that we can make change, that we can create a better and more beautiful human being and world.

Based on the lessons of history, our practice of today, and our vision of the future, there is no doubt but that we will win. We who are active and aware know that the struggle to smash sexism, the struggle to develop women, individually, organizationally and within society at large is a struggle which grows stronger every day and is a struggle which will both strengthen and institutionalize new interrelationships between women and men.

Those whose feet once were bound are now walking and running the way of the new world. Those whose minds once were bound up in sexist and other equally erroneous ways of thinking, are now taking a different view of themselves, each other and the world. As the bindings are removed, as we stretch and struggle forward, success does not any longer seem so far away nor so unaccessible.

Politicized, organized and scientific about our struggle, most certainly we can all run on together to live, love, struggle and die in a world made better and more beautiful by our work and the ways we interrelate with each other!

"UNDERSTANDING AND FIGHTING SEXISM: A CALL TO MEN"

Peter Blood, Alan Tuttle, and George Lakey (1981)

Understanding the Enemy: How Sexism Works in the U.S.A.

What Is Sexism?

Sexism is much more than a problem with the language we use, our personal attitudes, or individual hurtful acts toward women. Sexism in our country is a complex mesh of practices, institutions, and ideas which have the overall effect of giving more power to men than to women. By "power" we mean the ability to influence important decisions—political decisions of government on every level, economic decisions (jobs, access to money, choice of priorities), and a wide variety of other life areas down to the most personal concerns, such as whether two people are going to make love on a given night or not. The word "patriarchy" is sometimes used to refer to the actual power structure built around men's domination of women. Two key areas where women are denied power are the area of jobs and the area of violence directed toward women.

Women have much less earning power in our labor market than men do. Reasons for this include the fact that much of women's labor is unwaged (housecleaning, childrearing, little services to please bosses or lovers); the low status and pay of most of the traditionally women's jobs that are waged (secretary, sales clerk, childcare, nursing home attendant); the non-union status of most women workers; and the discriminatory practices such as the recent Supreme Court decision allowing companies to exclude pregnancy from their medical insurance and sick leave benefits.

Women face a constant threat of physical violence and sexual aggression in our society. As men we are rarely aware of how pervasive this is or the powerful effect it has on women's outlook on themselves and the world. Actual rape or sadistic violence is the tip of the iceberg. Physical abuse of wives and lovers is common and rarely publicized. A majority of women have probably experienced some form of sexual abuse as children. The memory of these experiences often gets suppressed because they feel so humiliated and scared, and because adults deny repeatedly that such a thing could happen. Society is filled with messages pressuring women to provide men with sexual pleasure.

All of the above combine with differences in physical strength, voice, acculturated ways of dealing with anger, and the very concrete power men hold in other areas of life to keep many women intimidated, passive, and unable to even acknowledge their own fear openly. The rapist is the shock trooper for an overall system of unequal power.

Patriarchy is not just a power structure

From Off Their Backks and On Our Own Two Feet. *Philadelphia: Men against Patriarchy, Movement for a New Society, 1981.*

"out there"; it is mainly enforced by our own acceptance of its character ideals for our lives. The character ideal which is held up for men to reach toward is "masculinity." A masculine man is supposed to be tough, good at abstract reasoning, hard-working, unfeeling except for anger and sexual desire, and habitually taking the initiative. Masculinity exists only in contrast to femininity, the model for women. Feminine characteriscs include cooperativeness, emotionality, patience, passivity, nurturance, and sexual appeal.

We all know that human characterisics are *not* distributed neatly between the sexes that way. A nursery school will often include girls who do abstract reasoning and get into fights and boys who cry easily. We also know that the culture does not leave them alone—the tomboy usually learns to become a lady, and the gentle boy develops armor to protect him from the jibes of his mates. They also learn that masculinity is valued in our culture more than femininity, especially when it comes to gaining power. In fact, the characteristics which are assigned to men by the patriarchy are the power-linked characterisics. In other words, by accepting masculinity as an ideal for ourselves, men buy into a system which keeps women down. . . .

Taking Responsibility without Guilt

We need to take responsibility as men for the continuation of the oppression of women—and commit ourselves to ending it. Guilt is a poor motivator for change, primarily because it gets people doing things to feel better, without really thinking through whether these are the most effective steps for us to be taking. As none of us asked to be born into a sexist culture, we will be more effective fighters for change if we can blend a clear understanding of sexism and commitment to end it with pride in ourselves. And pride in all the tremendously creative, industrious, and caring things men *have* done over the centuries.

There are many ways we can take on this responsibility. We can organize and support fights against institutional sexism. This could include work around forced sterilization of poor and Third World women, companies' restrictive maternity/paternity leave policies, organizing officeworkers, pushing affirmative action programs in hiring and promotion, demanding the expansion of high-quality publicly-financed daycare, etc. . . .

Supporting Women as They Stand Up

We need to be supporting the women's movement and individual women we know as they assume more power over their lives. The most important way we can support women is by doing the kinds of things described above, by developiong and sharing our feminist and socialist analysis in groups we are part of, and by building effective strategy. Another important way is to identify and interrupt sexism when it appears in ourselves or other men we know, rather than relying upon women to do this. We can also interrupt put-downs and jokes about "women's lib" or assertive strong women. We can listen to women think out loud about issues they are wrestling with, projects they are planning, and just listen to their anger and frustration. We can join in and otherwise support women-initiated actions against sexism. We can offer practical support like childcare, helping with a mailing, or cooking for a meeting.

MEN ON RAPE (excerpt)

Tim Beneke (1982)

A WOMAN, having been harassed by men, protested: "Why are they *so angry*?"

It will take much thought as yet unthought, by men in states of perception as yet unattained, to answer her. And any answer must serve primarily to assure women's safety. At this point in history men have only begun to acknowledge their anger at women, to reflect on its origins, to confront its manifestations. This book is, in part, an exploration of that anger, an attempt to give it air and light. In a culture where women are brutalized, where few men acknowledge that brutalization and fewer still evince indignation over it, just getting men to talk (more or less) honestly about rape has value. If a major attempt is to be made to confront the problem of rape, many things must happen. I will mention a few.

First, rape (and violence against women generally) must be perceived, pure and simple, as a *man's problem* and one that results directly from the way men regard women in American culture. Since 1971, when women first made of rape a contemporary political issue, women have agitated, educated, lobbied, learned self defense, formed rape crisis centers, rewritten archaic rape laws, provided better treatment for rape survivors, and given each other strength, confidence, comfort, and love. But what of the response of men? It is men who rape and men who collectively have the power to end rape. The enormous resources of American men—intellectual, economic, political—must be marshaled to that end. This will only begin to happen when men cease blaming women for rape. The many insidious and cruel maneuvers by which this is done—treating rape as natural, relating a woman's appearance to a weapon, regarding women as commodities, projecting sexual desire onto women, treating rape survivors as dupes, distrusting women's credibility, and generally imputing motives alien to women's intentions—must be clearly confronted.

Second, rape must be comprehended both in terms of the crime itself and the effect of its threat on women's lives. The ways in which the threat of rape alters the meaning and feel of the night and nature, inhibits the freedom of the eye, hurts women economically, undercuts women's independence, destroys solitude, and restricts expressiveness must be acknowledged as part of the crime.

Third, rape must be seen as part of a continuum of acts of violence against women which together constitute a major mental health issue for all women in American culture. Starting at the less severe end of the continuum such acts might include: harassment—rude stares and noises accompanying women as they walk down the street, grabbing or touching women's bodies without permission, unwanted attentions and intrusions, and suggested rewards for sexual favors in work situations; obscene phone calls; exhibitionism; Peeping Toms; spouse

---

From the Introduction to Men on Rape. *New York: St. Martin's, 1982.*

battering; dating rape, marital rape, and rape by strangers; incest; and femicide, the murder of women because they're women.

Fourth, marital rape must be given its full acknowledgment as a crime; laws must be passed in the forty states where it is currently legal.

And finally, a conversation must begin between men and women. Perhaps for a long time, the most urgent part of that conversation will consist of men listening to women describe their sufferings. In the past, most men have not listened. It is painful but necessary to acknowledge the sense in which men benefit from violence against women. Men compete with women in myriad ways, both professional and personal; the threats to women give men definite advantages. It is sometimes said that men tolerate violence against women *because* they benefit from it. This is doubtless true of some men. But few men seem to *consciously* tolerate it because they perceive benefits. And it is only from a competitive or antagonistic view of women that men can ultimately claim benefits. For men who care about women or (finally) themselves, violence against women benefits no one. It mystifies and poisons relations between men and women and vitiates the potential for trust, love, and surrender. I am convinced there are many men who, if they were to listen to women, would awaken to the reality of violence against women and take action. And "action" can range from contributing to a rape crisis center to joining an anti-rape group to talking to one's son.

How much longer will men accept as normal lives of constraint and abuse for women? I don't know. American men have an opportunity to reverse a part of history as old as history itself. History can happen fast. We must see that it happens soon.

"AN OPEN LETTER TO CAROLINA"

Abelardo Delgado (1982)

LAST TUESDAY I received your letter. I thought it was rather long. I went home and thought about it . . . I meant to answer it right away but the many unasked questions you raised in it merited some more thinking . . . much more thinking. This Thursday afternoon I try to put together those thoughts, both yours and mine, in a way that they make some sense to both of us. Let me start that orderly answer by stating right out that answering you does me much more good than it will probably do you. I gathered from your letter that you merely wished to be listened to and that answering you didn't really matter.—the subject I want to talk (write) to you about concerns women and men.—U said at the bottom of the first page. You thought I might laugh at you. I didn't. We can begin three ways, Carolina, in even approaching the subject. God, the sexist, in Genesis does two things which symbolically have served to attach the label of inferiority on women. He created Adam first. He created "her" out of one of his ribs. (not even two ribs . . . one rib) He goes on to make her the instigator in the downfall of all humankind by falling prey to the guile of the serpent and tempting the innocent Adam. The second approach would be an animalistic one which would have men and women emerge through evolution simultaneously but yet burdening the women to reproduce the species and to carry what is commonly referred to as the curse: menstruation. The third historical distinction is the value given to the first females as far as anthropologists can determine. It isn't very romantic to picture a female dragged by the hair by a caveman with a big garrotote in case she would complain of the treatment. He, the hunter. She the keeper of the cave.

It is obvious that the relationship between men and women has never been on an equal basis. Since we are Chicanos we have our own origin to look back to. The Indian side of us did not assign better roles for females. Our whole raza is the product of the "raped one." We Chicanos paradoxically know not whether to bless our creation or damn it. Octavio Paz in *El Laberinto de la Soledad* has much to say as to how we as Chicanos see our women. I recommend you go through it. For now let it suffice to say that as far as our wives and mothers we make saints of them but remain always in search of a lover with macho characteristics. It is not easy, Carolina, to change the attitudes which literally have turned to stone by now; it's a hell of a challenge. What I say publicly on the subject is that we as males are not about to initiate the change because quite bluntly the double standard suits us best. I believe, though, that any one of us with an ounce of intelligence sees that the double standard is an abusive one and that we cannot honestly continue to pursue our inde-

From A Decade of Hispanic Literature: An Anniversary Anthology, *Nicholas Kanellos. Houston: Arte Publico/University of Houston, 1982.*

pendence and total liberation while we do not abandon the role of abusers. Customs are the manifestations of our double standards and sexist behavior. If you notice what I am saying, then you will know that within me some growth has taken place to even admit to all this accumulated guilt. . . .

. . . [W]e Chicanos have to find our power within ourselves or else it loses the meaning. Women too must realize that they have value and power of themselves and not try to obtain it "from men." You tend to personalize your question and I like that since that facilitates my putting my answer on a more intimate and personal level. I came upon an article in the latest issue of *Psychology Today* which deals with the question of "power" in men-women relationships, most particularly of lovers or husband and wife relationships. It approaches the question from a perspective I had not given much thought to. In our relationships, whether they be friend to friend, brother to sister, father to daughter, son to mother, husband to wife, lover to lover or co-workers or members of a movement, the question of who has the advantage or the power to either determine what must be done and how it is to be done or exactly how the roles of each are to be carried out is not the kind of question that is resolved with an either-or answer. That is to say that in our relationships there are areas in which women have the power and areas in which men have the power. It is for balance that we strive. It is for respect that we search. The problems arise precisely because in interpreting those various areas of power we tend to dehumanize one another and to foolishly place more value on one role than on the other. It would be foolish for me to say that the way things are presently between the sexes there is a balance of power. Much more of a difference exists in our Chicano culture. There is no other way to describe what goes on than to label it by the proper name: abuse. For whatever reason I believe myself to be gifted in terms of seeing things (life) with such clarity. This in no way means that because I see things clearly I myself do not wind up being a willing abuser myself. It only means that in my own personal case I cannot plead ignorance. It also means that if we talk in terms of sin, then mine is a greater one because I know the difference.

It is so simple, Carolina, to begin to make the changes we should have initiated long ago. All it takes is a simple refusal on the part of women to be abused by us men. I believe we always have the potential to say no to abuse. Granted most of us are victims of convenience and fear and therefore wind up compromising the hell out of our convictions and thus making life very miserable. I was thinking of how we betray our sexist attitudes in our very vocabulary. Take the questions of sex and see if the terminology is not a misleading one favoring us males. We say I fucked her. Yo me la coché. She is assigned a passive role of a recipient in an act which all of us know is, or should be, a sharing one. No one sexes the other. Both males and females share in an act of love and yet we males proudly announce, if not to others then to ourselves, that we "laid her." Perhaps our relationships will begin improving with merely being honest.

Dear Carolina, you say:—. . . a woman envies a man in the acceptance he automatically receives from other men, but she falls prey to the ugly mentalities that exist and they can be considered avenues of recourse when she finds herself unable to grow . . .—

No one can truly say that he is unable to grow unless he is dead and, being dead, he or she cannot say it. Again I take you to measure yourself, a female, trying to compete and gain acceptance in the world of men. The error is that there is no such thing as the world of men but a world of humans and other things. The heart of your comment indicates clearly that while men build relationships among themselves women do not penetrate those and thus the root of the envy is that a man does not accept a woman as he does other men. I find a lot of truth in this and going first to the Chicano way I find it even more pronounced that the question of trust and love (in a Platonic sense) is much more stronger between a man and a man than between a man and a woman. Thus even the question of husband-wife versus husband-male friend is not as binding. I myself have been puzzled about these relationships and have asked students in my classes to speak about this. I have raised this question with other male friends and female friends to get their reactions and feelings. I conclude that the degree of intimacy reached even in sex is often surpassed by that of compañerismo. I am not so sure that it is a phenomenon peculiar only to men. Many men also envy the close relationships that exist between females.

Why this is so has been explained to me by those I question. A man and another man find much more in common to relate to each other on a physical and emotional plane. Certainly a woman and another woman can relate as well. Just to complicate matters I have posed the question if it is possible to carry out a Platonic relationship between a man and a woman without at one point becoming sexually involved. It is so easy to either transcend or mistake the relationship. I personally sense that there is a barrier of fear between our two sexes that prevents our relating intellectually or spiritually and that because such a barrier does not exist between members of the same sex that they get along better and also stronger ties develop. Maybe a man and a woman do not feel competitive or fearful with their sex peers whereas they might with members of the opposite sex.

The question remains one of power use and abuse and consequentially that of role assignment. I just returned from a conference in Chicago where the customary women's workshop was part of the program. Only another carnal and I attended as men. The women in the workshop raised the question as to why many more men had not attended their workshop. This can be taken to mean that men considered it non-important or non-relevant. This led them to conclude, and me as well, that to discuss relationships you need both parties to enter into the dialogue. I presume that is exactly what I am doing when I write you these open letters in response to your letter (which without your permission I have made public . . . one more sign of male prerogative and abuse). . . .

Carolina, que tal,

Here we are again trying to deal with the ancient dilemma of how we relate to one another as humans . . . as members of the two sexes. I picked up on a line you phrased which has a lot to offer as food for thought. You said, and I quote—We cannot rely on our feelings to explain for us what we mean.—As a female you and all females are categorized as people who deal mostly on feelings, thus what a woman says we place in a different slot in our male computer minds. We rationalize that you are saying whatever it is you are saying because that is the way that you feel. I guess when you say to me that such a way of speaking is not to be trusted I kind of understand your comment to mean that.

One of the obvious manifestations of our sexism is that we find it very odd that women can speak to us with their intelligence instead of with their "feelings." When you are among men, in this case Chicano men, tradition is on your shoulders but it is also on our shoulders and so we respond traditionally. What it means, Carolina, that women, Chicano women in particular, have learned to manipulate tradition and achieve their ends whether it is with their emotions or with their intelligence. I would argue that in order to manipulate tradition it requires a lot of intelligence so that the option is simply to continue to let us men think you are creatures of feelings without much mind and then go on to use your minds to get your way by displaying the right kind of feelings at the right time and place.

To break away from that you must earn the respect of those around you whether it be from those most intimately associated with you to those who merely remotely deal with you. You must show them all that your mind is on par or above theirs. You must be careful that you do this with some grace, dignity and humility so that you do not merely win a battle and lose the war. Men might accept your challenges a few times and let it go but if our ego happens to be wounded, then watch out, Carolina, because what follows is cold rejection and a new assigned role of a feme-macho. If you notice what I am saying then you know why women do not see it profitable to approach their liberation on an individual basis as much as we Chicanos do not accept that liberation is the business of one or a few individuals but of all Chicanos. This is to say that to fight tradition it requires a collective effort and the foreign taste of success. If you noticed what you said about our feelings being poor conveyors of meaning then you must also agree that intellectualizing things is just as bad, if not worse. We are made in a way that mind and feelings balance out. In this case we men suffer too because while we have agreed that it is ok for you women to be creatures who can display your feelings at the drop of an eyelid we must be machos and hold on to ours and keep them in our darkest mind chambers till we crack unable to suppress them anymore.

It is for this reason, this craving to be ourselves in our entirety, without a mask that we seek a lover, husband, a friend. Someone who will not find it repulsive to accept us with our bundles of weaknesses. We are able to define intelligence only in this context, a collective, social struggle, rejection and acceptance. We must not select to sacrifice that which makes us humans . . . displaying our feelings publicly, and in our minds, but that task is neither male or female but human in nature.

"FOLLOWING A WIFE'S MOVE"

Gordon Mott (1985)

MY WIFE'S announcement was not dramatic. She walked into the house after work and said, "They want me for the Paris job." The offer was not unexpected nor unattractive. The bank my wife works for was giving her a promotion and transferring her to its Paris office. I reacted with excitement. I imagined all the wonderful aspects of a life in Paris: springtime, restaurants, the Louvre and weekend jaunts to quaint country inns.

The announcement did not violate the set of rules established by our two-career couplehood. Seven years ago, I ambushed her outside a New York City squash court with the declaration that I'd been transferred to Mexico. She made the move and began work in her company's Mexico City office. Ever since, I have been reminded that living in the third world had been my idea and that the next move, in our two-career couple jargon, was "hers."

But within days of letting "Sure, sure, sounds great" slip out I succumbed to second guessing, reluctance and terror. This wasn't for play. We were moving. My rationalizations about the career flexibility of freelance journalists crumbled. I was forced to face the reality that I would be throwing away a network of contacts in Central America that I had built up over the years; I was also abandoning work as a stringer for *The New York Times* after months of struggling to get my freelance writing off the ground. I envisioned weeks of inactivity, huddled with my dog, Nica, in our Paris apartment, waiting for my wife to return from her job.

Then it struck me where my fears came from. The man in the family—me—was putting his career at the mercy of his wife's. In the starkest psychological terms, I was following her and abdicating my traditional male role.

I can't deny that special factors, some sounding exotic and glamerous, distinguish a move between Mexico City and Paris from, let's say, a move between New York and Boston. However, the same emotions, career concerns and the reactions of colleagues are probably common to most professional men confronted with making career choices dictated by their wife's job.

My psychological reactions are the toughest to understand and verbalize. My generation—men and women in their thirties and forties—had the rules switched. I grew up believing that I would be the breadwinner and those little girls across the schoolhouse aisle would be housewives and mothers, not professional competition or providers. Although I have embraced the notion of career women for the last ten years, the move opened mental cubbyholes in which the idea of a working woman just didn't seem right. Even though I cringe at the admission, I've had strong emotional responses that I'm less of a man for not putting my foot down and

New York Times *(14 April 1985). Reprinted in* About Men, *ed. Edward Klein and Don Erickson. New York: Poseidon, 1987.*

saying, "Stop this career stuff, woman, and get into the kitchen." That reaction is probably unavoidable because of my background and expectations. But the anxiety also undermined my resolve and led to arguments with my wife about whether we would leave at the same time, about where we'd live in Paris.

Professional colleagues and acquaintances betrayed their own prejudices and unease. Innocent queries such as, "Well, isn't that nice, but what are you going to do?" rang with not-so-subtle implications. The questioners' tone suggested that I was giving up the rest of my professional life and denying my own personal desires for my wife's career. The offhand, joking remarks about "How does it feel to be a kept man?" or "What will you do in your spare time?" revealed inflexible attitudes about the best way to pursue a career and an unwillingness to accept women as equal partners. On the other hand, not many men have the opportunity to explore alternative career options or take a break from the career-ladder syndrome. My wife's move is giving me that chance. Even though I know I will now be forced to devote long and difficult hours to establishing a new network of people and publications, the freelancer's lifeblood, there also will be time for improving my French, visiting and writing about the eight countries in which my wife will be traveling for business, immersing myself in European politics and finishing a novel.

I'm also glad that I've opted for what is perceived as the uncommon choice. I've heard complaints from many single women that they can't trust any man's willingness to promote their careers. At least I know I'm not in that category. My worries about losing my self-worth or masculinity are offset by feeling courageous.

Another benefit has been the strengthening of my marriage. I think my declaration that being with my wife is more important than anything else is an absolute expression of love. I think she understands my commitment more clearly because of my willingness to take a chance with my own career. In addition, our ability to work out the problems caused by the stress of moving has deepened the bond between us.

A subtle shift has occurred, too, in our perceptions of each other. I've always been the one to initiate change. This time, it was her turn, and I'm the one enjoying the results of our belief that it's good to be adventuresome in our lives, jobs and relationships. That has enhanced my trust and respect for my wife.

Finally, I've experienced something broader. Like the characters in the movie *The Big Chill,* I've been dismayed as many ideals espoused by me and my friends in the early 1970s slipped quietly out of vogue. One thing that didn't change was my relentless support for women's rights. But until now my advocacy existed in the abstract. It was never tested, even as I enjoyed the benefits of a two-salary family and a dynamic, involved partner.

The issue of women's rights is real for me now, although it's still not easy for me. I know my fears are not going to disappear magically, nor is this move the last time we'll have to juggle our careers. But I'm actively challenging my assumptions about traditional male roles and forcing myself to live the beliefs about women that I've held for the last ten years. That seems right.

"WHY WE MARCH"

Men Who Care about Women's Lives (1989)

TODAY we are witnessing the bloom of a new force in feminism—the power and conviction of thousands of men across the nation proclaiming their interest in shaping and sharing their futures with women as free and equal partners.

Men are marching for women's lives because we are challenging from within the status quo which has ingrained in us a tradition of oppressing both women and minorities. So stigmatized is the feminine side of our culture that many men are unable to utter the words, "I am a feminist."

But it is feminists—women and men working together—who have already begun dismantling the structures and traditions of oppression which victimize both sexes. Without fighting for the freedom of all we cannot expect to preserve freedom for anyone.

Feminist Men's Alliance. "Men Who Care About Women's Lives: Keep Abortion Safe and Legal—A Statement of Purpose, a Call to Action." San Francisco, 1989.

Gay and bisexual men share a common oppression with women, and have a history of support from the feminist community. The threat to women's privacy rights is already a dark reality to gay and bisexual men. By marching, gay and bisexual men fly in the face of deeply rooted homophobia and shatter the shallow logic which labels inequality a "woman's issue."

Abortion could be illegal in most states in the 1990s. Here in California, the Assembly has consistently voted to eliminate the Medi-Cal funding for abortions, and low-income women are threatened by a two-thirds budget slash for the Office of Family Planning. Forty percent of these women receive no other health care, an indication that California's state government cannot be trusted to protect women's health.

Women's freedom of choice is severely threatened; one of the most significant and personal decisions in a woman's life is on the verge of becoming legislated by the state. We are Men Who Care About Women's Lives and we will not stand for it.

PRO-FEMINIST MEN INTO THE 1990s

"STATEMENT OF POSITION ON SEXUAL ABUSE"

Pi Kappa Phi Fraternity (1985)

WHEREAS we, the members of Pi Kappa Phi Fraternity, believe that the attitudes and behavior exhibited by members of the collegiate population have direct bearing on the quality of their present and future lives, and

Whereas there is an increased consciousness of sexual exploitation and violence and incidences thereof not just on the nation's college campuses but in society, and

Whereas the Greek community has stated its responsibility in leadership, scholarship, community service, human dignity and respect, and

Whereas Pi Kappa Phi is committed to excellence in the Greek community, and this requires us to identify and solve serious problems that prevent the growth and development of our brothers, and

Whereas Pi Kappa Phi strives to foster an atmosphere of healthy and proper attitudes and behavior towards sex and the sex roles, and wishes that the incidences of sexual abuse (mental and physical abuse—coercion, manipulation, harassment) between the men and women of the collegiate community be halted,

Therefore

Be it resolved that Pi Kappa Phi Fraternity will not tolerate or condone any form of sexually-abusive behavior (either physically, mentally or emotionally) on the part of any of its members, and

Be it further resolved that the Pi Kappa Phi Fraternity encourages educational programming involving social and communication skills, interpersonal relationships, social problem awareness, etiquette and sex-role expectations; and will develop a reward system to recognize chapters and individuals that lead in fostering a healthy attitude towards the opposite sex.

Pi Kappa Phi, Charlotte, N.C., 13 August 1985.

"THE PROFEMINIST MEN'S MOVEMENT: NEW CONNECTIONS, NEW DIRECTIONS"

John Stoltenberg (1988)

. . . I WANT to bring into this room tonight a sense of what the profeminist men's movement has achieved in these last few years. And there are two important areas I want to talk about: our work to end homophobia and our work to end violence against women.

From the beginning, men have come to the profeminist men's movement from across the whole spectrum of "sexual orientation." I'm not crazy about those words, but you know what I mean: we have a fine history of honoring one another's loving. And this sets us quite apart from just about any bunch of men you could name.

So over the years gatherings like this one have become a safe space for us to let go of a lot of dumb stuff. There are thousands of stories of acceptance among us, thousands of stories of compassion and gentle regard. We who were all terrorized in one way or another to have a sexual orientation in one way or another—together we learned to let go of some dread. . . . [F]rom this particular assembly of grappling lives grew a brand-new political agenda: a commitment to eradicate homophobia completely—a commitment made *jointly* by both those whom homophobia targets to be the hated and those whom homophobia enlists to be the haters. We stood together. We said homophobia must end.

We were perhaps already familiar with the pain of those of us who have felt ashamed and despised for being queer. But we had not clearly realized homophobia's wounding impact on men who are not. What we learned—and the insight we have brought to the campaign to end social homophobia—is that homophobia gets internalized and intrudes at the most intimate moments of your life, whomever you're making love with, in the form of forces in your head demanding you be the man there, demanding you be a man's man every instant of your life, and threatening to wither away your sense of selfhood if you don't. Homophobia does that. Interpersonally, the forces of homophobia kill off reciprocity and empathy, without which intimacy can't possibly happen. Like a weapon gone berserk, homophobia doubles back, diminishing the lives even of those whose much-prized sexual orientation it is supposed to protect and defend.

This connection came from us. It drew on the life experience and political conviction of those who identify with the profeminist men's movement. It happened here. We did it. And we're taking this insight and vision to the world.

Address presented at the thirteenth National Conference on Men and Masculinity, Seattle University, 8 July 1988. Reprinted in Changing Men 20 *(Winter/Spring 1989).*

Another achievement grew out of this movement and our connectedness: it grew up among those of us doing work counseling men who batter, among those of us organizing programs to stop rape, among those of us joining the fight to get the pornography industry off women's backs. What happened here was an insight about traditional masculinity and the forms of sexual violence we saw it needing to act out in order to *be.* We drew on our personal connections to the feminist antibattery movement, the feminist antirape movement, the feminist antipornography movement, the nonviolence movement, but we also drew on our awareness of our own lives as men. We looked inside at the patterns of sexualized angers we'd picked up, the habits of depersonalizing sexual objectification, the little routines of sexual bullying we'd learned so well; when we talked among ourselves, as we did often, we sometimes disclosed our own anguished efforts not to stumble into the very behaviors we were trying to persuade other men to stop.

Violence against women is part of a continuum, we realized—a continuum that contains an awful lot of day-in-day-out stuff: put-downs and dismissals, manipulations and numbers, the whole gamut of things you'd only do to someone who didn't matter as much as you, someone you outrank.

So when we talk now to other men about their antiwoman pornography consumption, their acceptance of rape myths, their violent and brutal tempers, we speak from a particular and hardwon perspective: We know the continuum extends to us. But through our feminist activism we are building up a sense of who we are and who we can be that no longer depends on sexual domination. We always knew that was necessary. We've come to learn it's possible.

In both these contexts—our work to end homophobia and our work to end violence against women—an active profeminist theory and practice has evolved, through the work itself and the think-tanking around it, through sharing and self-honesty, through the courage to take our insights and visions out into the world. Sure, the world doesn't yet know very well who we are—but we know ourselves a lot better than we did. And sure, the work is not anywhere near over and done with—it's really only just begun—but we know we're in it for the long haul. As I was thinking about how our purpose and connectedness has already brought forth these original and responsible achievements, I got to wondering: what *else* might we be able to do—what *other* issues are we in a unique historical position to address?

So what I want to do next is to sketch out two specific areas where I believe that we could make a distinct and unique contribution to radical social change. They are areas in which we could take our self-honesty, our think-tanking, and our activism next—some areas in which, I believe, we could do some original and profoundly important connection making.

I want to talk first about the relationship between racial hate and woman hate. There are many historical parallels between the way that racism has worked and the way sexism has worked. The laws and institutions that enforce second-class status on account of sex and race are interlocking and interconnected. For example: the culture-wide belief that women want to be raped—the belief that that's what women are for. This belief not only justifies but necessitates sexual violence. Pornography keeps the belief alive and virulent. The legal system keeps rape victims from much chance of justice. Over a third of all women are raped in their lifetime. And institutionalized male supremacy rolls on its merry way.

Now turn and look—simultaneously, if you will—at the system of white supremacy in this country, and look in particular at the mythology that portrays Black men as rapists. Historically, this mythology has functioned to justify and necessitate countless vicious killings and beatings of Black men by whites, and the mythology pervades the criminal justice system to this day.

What do these two mythologies have in common?: She (female) wants to be raped. He (Black male) wants to rape. In the interlocked systems of white and male supremacy, where do these parallel phenomena intersect—and why?

I believe the profeminist men's movement has some essential answers to divulge. And I believe that the more we tell the truth, the more our movement will be of use. Here's what I mean:

Many of us have looked searchingly into the training we got to be men, our socialization into masculinity. It was an imposed process of personal-identity formation that required of us an enormous amount of *dis*-identification. We weren't supposed to be a sissy. We weren't supposed to be anything like a girl. And this fear of *contamination* by anything female, this dread of *being confused* with someone female, became a touchstone of our masculinity. If we didn't always stay on guard against the hazard of feminization, we might not appear manly enough, and we might not experience ourselves as masculine enough. That's why so many men use violence against women—to act out through domination just how different from women men need to be to be men.

Our personal sense of masculinity might not come from overt complicity in the system of male supremacy. But we can recognize in ourselves, if we are honest, the dynamic of disidentification that keeps the system going. It's a long way from "Nyah, I don' wanna be a sissy!" to "Take that, you bitch!" We don't all have to go the distance, but we all have to crave the difference—the difference of us from women that the system is set up to keep real.

The whites who beat and lynched Black men acted out of an analogous and parallel dynamic. They were terrified that their racial identity would be contaminated and defiled. It's as if they needed that murderous rage in order to be white, in order to still their fears that their racial identity would dissolve.

Dread of contamination. Differentiation through dominance. In the interlocked systems of white and male supremacy, the identity you're supposed to have as white and/or as male is the identity that can only come through disidentification. And in these systems, the myth that women want to be raped and the myth of the Black male rapist justify whatever it takes to experience real manhood, whatever it takes to feel racially pure.

Tonight I challenge the profeminist men's movement to make this personal connection and bring it to light politically. I challenge us to dig deep, to look truthfully inside ourselves and at the machinations of our society, and to generate a new consciousness about the nexus of racism and sexism that has never before been politically explored—a new awareness of how racial hate and woman hate have a common source in the drive to defend an identity that cannot withstand equality.

The other area I want to talk about tonight is the relationship between capitalism and the sex industry (by which I mean pornography and prostitution, in particular). If the first area I described was mainly a race and sex connection, this one is mainly a class and sex connection.

Economically, society is organized to make sure that men are never confused with women. Men earn more than women. Women are segregated into "women's jobs." The only jobs in which women outnumber men and earn more than men are modeling and prostitution. This is no accident. This is an economic advantage handed to men, an economic reinforcement of the sex-class hierarchy.

The liberal left in this country has challenged capitalism only up to a point, and that point is where the sex industry begins. In general, the U.S. liberal left has celebrated and defended the sex industry's commoditization of sex and its trafficking in the subordination of women. Recently, for instance, a political line has emerged that virtually applauds prostitution as a viable career path for women. If you think about the exploitation—sexual and economic—that defines the domestic sex industry, and if you think about it from the point of view of an authentically revolutionary economic analysis, such liberal-left positions are absolutely outrageous. In Europe there are countries where the Left has articulated a very sharp critique of the pornography/prostitution business. In the U.S., however, the liberal left shills for it, turning pimps and pornographers into political heroes, and feminist antipornography activists into dirty jokes.

Now, I believe that we as a movement of profeminist men could be a brave and prophetic voice here, especially those of us with connections already to movements for economic justice, especially those of us who care deeply about the intensely alienating effect of ownership of other people's labor and lives. Most of the money that goes into the sex industry does not get to the women. And even if it did, what kind of society would consign a whole class of people to do work that is sexually degrading and dangerous in order to earn a decent wage? We in the profeminist men's movement are in a unique historical position. As men we are supposed to reap the psychic and sexual rewards of the sex industry. As men of conscience we can see through that sham. I challenge us as men who care about both sexual and economic justice to rage against the sex industry and shut it down.

We in the profeminist men's movement have a lot of work cut out for us. We share a diverse range of commitments and carings about people; many of us have grown up and matured within the context of various visions of justice and peace; many of us have been working hard to make those visions a reality. What I want to stress most tonight is that we can learn something important from what we have achieved—something of our capacity to connect and to act. And with that capacity, there's more ahead of us that we can do—more that we *especially* can do.

"DISSENT ON *WEBSTER V. REPRODUCTIVE SERVICES*" (excerpt)

Justice Harry Blackmun (1989)

TODAY Roe v. Wade, and the fundamental constitutional right of women to decide whether to terminate a pregnancy, survive but are not secure. Although the Court extricates itself from this case without making a single, even incremental change in the law of abortion, the plurality and Justice Scalia would overrule Roe (the first silently, the other explicitly) and would return to the states virtually unfettered authority to control the quintessentially intimate, personal and life-directing decision whether to carry a fetus to term.

Although today, no less than yesterday, the Constitution and the decisions of this Court prohibit a state from enacting laws that inhibit women from the meaningful exercise of that right, a plurality of this Court implicitly invites every state legislature to enact more and more restrictive abortion regulations in order to provoke more and more test cases, in the hope that sometime down the line the Court will return the law of procreative freedom to the severe limitations that generally prevailed in this country before January 22, 1973. Never in my memory has a plurality announced a judgment of this Court that so foments disregard for the law and for our standing decisions.

Nor in my memory has plurality gone about its business in such a deceptive fashion. At every level of its review, from its effort to read the real meaning out of the Missouri statute to its intended evisceration of precedents and its deafening silence about the constitutional protections that it would jettison, the plurality obscures the portent of its analysis. With feigned restraint, the plurality announces that its analysis leaves Roe "undisturbed," albeit "modif[ied] and narrow[ed]." But this disclaimer is totally meaningless.

Winks, Nods and Knowing Glances

The plurality opinion is filled with winks and nods and knowing glances to those who would do away with Roe explicitly, but turns a stone face to anyone in search of what the plurality conceives as the scope of a woman's right under the due process clause to terminate a pregnancy free from the coercive and brooding influence of the State. The simple truth is that Roe would not survive the plurality's analysis, and that the plurality provides no substitute for Roe's protective umbrella.

I fear for the future. I fear for the liberty and equality of the millions of women who have lived and come of age in the 16 years

United States Reports *492 (1989): 537.*

since Roe was decided. I fear for the integrity of, and public esteem for, this Court.

I dissent. . . .

It is impossible to read the plurality opinion, and especially its final paragraph, without recognizing its implicit invitation to every state to enact more and more restrictive abortion laws, and to assert their interest in potential life as of the moment of conception. All these laws will satisfy the plurality's non-scrutiny until sometime, a new regime of old dissenters and new appointees, will declare what the plurality intends: that Roe is no longer good law. . . .

Thus, "not with a bang, but a whimper," the plurality discards a landmark case of the last generation and casts into darkness the hopes and visions of every woman in this country who had come to believe that the Constitution guaranteed her the right to exercise some control over her unique ability to bear children.

The plurality does so either oblivious or insensitive to the fact that millions of women and their families have ordered their lives around the right to reproductive choice, and that this right has become vital to the full participation of women in the economic and political walks of American life.

Back-Alley Abortions Feared

The plurality would clear the way once again for government to force upon women the physical labor and specific and direct medical and psychological harms that may accompany carrying a fetus to term. The plurality would clear the way again for the State to conscript a woman's body and to force upon her a "distressful life and future."

The result, as we know from experience, would be that every year hundreds of thousands of women, in desperation, would defy the law and place their health and safety in the unclean and unsympathetic hands of back-alley abortionists, or they would attempt to perform abortions upon themselves, with disastrous results. Every year many women, especially poor and minority women, would die or suffer debilitating physical trauma, all in the name of enforced morality or religious dictates or lack of compassion, as it may be.

Of the aspirations and settled understandings of American women, of the inevitable and brutal consequences of what it is doing, the tough-approach plurality utters not a word. This silence is callous. It is also profoundly destructive of this Court as an institution.

To overturn a constitutional decision is a rare and grave undertaking. To overturn a constitutional decision that secured a fundamental personal liberty to millions of persons would be unprecedented in our 200 years of constitutional history. . . .

For today, at least, the law of abortion stands undisturbed. For today, the women of this Nation still retain the liberty to control their destinies. But the signs are evident and very ominous, and a chill wind blows.

I dissent.

"STATEMENT BEFORE THE SENATE JUDICIARY COMMITTEE ON THE 'VIOLENCE AGAINST WOMEN ACT OF 1990'"

Sen. Joseph R. Biden, Jr. (1990)

THE PURPOSE of today's hearing is completely non adversarial. We fully understand—as much as anyone can who has not undergone it themselves—the trauma that some of the people who will testify here have undergone. We fully understand the difficulty of recounting, regardless of how many times it has been done before, recounting a horrible tragedy that some of the women who will testify today have undergone. It is not an easy thing. Any of you who have had a tragedy occur in your life or your family—a severe loss that you have suffered—will understand this.

Imagine sitting before these lights, with all of us sitting up here like we're a bunch of judges looking down on a witness table, with a number of people scribbling notes, including us. Imagine what it would be like to have to recount one of the most frightening or sorrowful days in your life. No matter how many times you have done it, it's a very difficult thing to do. And I want the witnesses to know that, although we cannot totally appreciate that, we have some sense of how difficult it is.

We are truly grateful that you were willing to come and testify for us. You have come in order to help us, hopefully, draft a meaningful piece of legislation—one that I already introduced, but we're here to hear your suggestions as to whether it should be changed. It may not be correct the way I introduced it—some of it may be wrong, none of it may be wrong. But that's the purpose of today's hearing.

If we look at what is happening in society, there are several things that come across very clearly—at least to me. And one of them is that no matter how much we say we've changed as a society, there's something wrong, something terribly wrong, when over the last 15 years, violence against young men has dropped by 12 percent while violence against young women in America has increased 50 percent. Something is wrong.

I'm not going to attempt to be an armchair psychiatrist or psychologist today and try to psychoanalyze society and why this is happening. The only thing I can say is that I know it has happened. It's not getting better. It's getting worse.

I personally think there are several things that have to be done in order to be able to, at a minimum, change that god-awful trend that exists in society. There's violent sex-

---

20 June 1990. Courtesy of Sen. Joseph R. Biden, Jr.

ism. We're not talking in this hearing today merely about the sexism that exists in society that's so sophisticated that it does not give a woman a job, but gives a man a job. That's a serious flaw in our national psyche. What we're talking about is violence: Violence that is directed against women for the sole reason that they are women—not because they happen to be there and not because they happen to be the bank teller between the criminal and the vault. It's because they are women.

You know, just since I've introduced this bill it has created a bit of a furor—furor may be the wrong word—a good deal of discussion already, and I only introduced it yesterday. I hear commentators on television and the press saying, "Well, will this stop violence against women by making it a civil rights violation?" The answer is no. That is not my intention.

My intention in making this a civil rights violation is to change the nation's attitude. I know of no circumstance under which the nation has concluded that there is a serious problem where that problem has not been reflected in legislative form. I know of none.

Reducing the drunk driving level from .1 to .08 blood alcohol does not stop drunk driving. But it does say society is tired of it. We're going to make it tougher. So what happens is it generates discussion at cocktail parties. It generates discussion in carpools. People start to say, "My god, this isn't what we thought it was." Alright for ole' Harry to go out and have four beers because he's just a jolly good guy and get in his car. No more.

So I don't expect that making this a civil rights violation will solve this problem. People will not say, "I was thinking of committing a crime of violence and raping that woman, but now that it' a civil rights violation I won't do it because I may be sued in federal court." But it does say—not unlike what President Kennedy said about the need to deal with the civil rights of black Americans—that there is a need for the national psyche to acknowledge that there is something horribly wrong. There's something horribly wrong. The law should reflect that attitude.

There is a second practical reason for the civil rights remedy. I want women to be able to get into the best court system in the world, with the most educated judges in the world, and with a set of rules and regulations and a degree of sensitivity that is uniform. So when she does conclude after the criminal matter is settled, that she wishes to pursue the civil matter, she has the best, most honest, most even, most uniform chance of succeeding.

So part of what I have in mind here is to heighten public awareness and change as a priority in America, this notion of violence against women. I still think we have some arcane notions—notions that are changing, I hope. And that is that it's alright for a man in anger to grab his wife's arm and put it behind her back while they're arguing. It's never alright—never, ever, under any circumstances.

One of the things we have to change is the attitude about rape. I don't know how to do it, unless we begin to discuss it. Do you know how many times I read statistics and studies and juror after juror says "well maybe the woman invited it."

Consider this: If I walk from here, out across the mall to the Capitol, waving two thousand dollar bills in front of everyone for all to see, and someone comes and grabs them out of my hand and runs. The young woman or man who grabbed the two thousand dollar bills that I was waving and flaunting in front of the public cannot say in court, "by the way, he invited it—Biden was walking down the street waving two thousand dollar bills." They cannot use that as a defense.

So even if a woman—no matter how suggestive—no matter how she was dressed, no matter what she was doing—walked in the most promiscuous and inviting manner from here to the Capitol across the way, no one under any circumstance has any right, for any reason, to violate her physically. And it should be no defense to say she invited it. Yet I'll bet you there are some in society hearing me today saying "Biden, you're crazy." Why should it be no defense for a robbery and a defense for rape?

The third point I would like to make is that if we don't prioritize this crime against women, it's going to get worse, and we can't afford for it to get much worse. It seems to me (again from my experience here over the years) that unless we start to say enough is enough, not much begins to happen. Something may happen if we start to point out those charts, as I pointed out the change in the rates of assaults since 1974 against young male victims versus young female victims, and the number of murders since 1974, older males down 5.6 percent, older females up 29.9 percent.

What reason can there be for that? We as a society have to change.

I would very briefly like to suggest that one of the reasons for this particular hearing is to look not only at the growing problem, but the proposed solution that I put forward. Again, I'm not suggesting that the solution that I put forward is the totality of the solution. Parts of it may be wrong. That's why I've asked some of the experts to come today, as well as some of the victims.

Let me very briefly explain how we will proceed. First, with the help of two very courageous survivors of violent crime, we'll take a look at the staggering human impact of crime on those who survive the crimes. And, second, with the help of three distinguished legal experts, we'll look at what role the federal government can play in this fight. I have a number of questions for the witnesses, many of which focus on the legislation that I introduced yesterday—the Violence Against Women Act of 1990.

I will not take the time here to explain in detail each aspect of the comprehensive legislation. The bill contains many significant legislative proposals—too many to summarize at this time. But I would like to make some general points about the legislation and what I am trying to achieve.

The bill has three broad, but simple goals to make streets safer. The first goal is to try to make streets a little bit safer for women; the second is to make their homes a little bit safer; and the third is to protect their civil rights.

To meet the first goal, there are some very practical suggestions that we know from experience work. Title I of the bill provides significant new resources for state and local law enforcement agencies. It grants $200 million dollars for 40 areas in the country found by the Justice Department to be the most dangerous for women. In addition, it grants $100 million for the remainder of the states.

These grants will significantly boost the number of police officers on the streets and prosecutors in the court, and police and prosecutors targeting violent crime against women. Title I also helps prevent street crime against women by providing very basic things like lights and cameras in public transit areas, and punishing sex crimes more severely by doubling the penalties for rape and aggravated rape tried in federal courts.

To meet the second goal—making homes safer for women—the legislation confronts a growing crisis of millions of women each year who are the victims of violent crime in their own homes—what we often call domestic violence. "Domestic" violence often connotes something more benign than street crime. But it's far from tame. One million women every year require medical attention for injuries inflicted by abusing spouses.

My proposal provides new laws, encourages new policies, and adds new funds to help in the fight against domestic violence. For example, the bill protects women who flee from their abusers by making protective court orders issued in any state legal in every state. This way, when a woman crosses a state line, she does not lose the benefit of a judge-issued order aimed at keeping her abusive spouse or lover away from her, which is the case now.

In addition, the bill uses federal grant programs to encourage states to treat domestic violence as a crime, and not as a quarrel, by encouraging states to arrest abusive spouses. The data are clear: in many states, that does not occur. The arresting officer comes in, the woman is clearly the victim of violence and has been beaten, but there is no arrest made. In almost all of those states, the officer has the power to be the complaining witness filing the complaint, and we want that to happen. So a condition to getting this money will be: pass some laws in your own state making it a priority to arrest these people. This part of the bill also includes increased funding for shelters that house battered women and funds for training prosecutors and court personnel in handling spouse abuse cases.

Finally, and perhaps most importantly, the third goal of this bill is to protect and declare that sex crimes violate a woman's federally protected civil rights. For too long we have ignored the right of women to be free from the fear of attack based on their gender. For too long we have kept silent about the obvious. 97 percent of sex crimes in this country are sex crimes against women. We know this, indeed we assume it, but we ignore the implications.

A rape or a sex assault should be deemed a civil rights crime just as hate beatings aimed at blacks or asians are widely recognized as violations of their civil rights. Creating a civil rights remedy can never blunt the pain that a survivor of a sex crime feels, but it does say that we as a nation—as a whole nation—will not tolerate crimes perpetrated against women because they are women.

In conclusion, I want to thank all of our witnesses for appearing here today. I look forward to all the help they can give me and other Senators here in understanding this growing and troubling problem. I stand ready for advice and seek advice on how we can deal with this problem.

"STATEMENT OF PRINCIPLES"

National Organization for Men against Sexism (1990)

THE National Organization For Men Against Sexism is an activist organization of men and women supporting positive changes for men. NOMAS advocates a perspective that is pro-feminist, gay-affirmative, and committed to justice on a broad range of social issues including race, class, age, religion, and physical abilities. We affirm that working to make this nation's ideals of equality substantive is the finest expression of what it means to be men.

We believe that the new opportunities becoming available to women and men will be beneficial to both. Men can live as happier and more fulfilled human beings by challenging the old-fashioned rules of masculinity that embody the assumption of male superiority.

Traditional masculinity includes many positive characteristics in which we take pride and find strength, but it also contains qualities that have limited and harmed us. *We are deeply supportive of men who are struggling with the issues of traditional masculinity. As an organization for changing men, we care about men and are especially concerned with men's problems, as well as the difficult issues in most men's lives.*

As an organization for changing men, we strongly support the continuing struggle of women for full equality. We applaud and support the insights and positive social changes that feminism has stimulated for both women and men. We oppose such injustices to women as economic and legal discrimination, rape, domestic violence, sexual harassment, and many others. Women and men can and do work together as allies to change the injustices that have so often made them see one another as enemies.

One of the strongest and deepest anxieties of most American men is their fear of homosexuality. This homophobia contributes directly to the many injustices experienced by gay, lesbian, and bisexual persons, and is a debilitating restriction for heterosexual men. We call for an end to all forms of discrimination based on sexual-affectional orientation, and for the creation of a gay-affirmative society.

We also acknowledge that many people are oppressed today because of their race, class, age, religion, and physical condition. We believe that such injustices are vitally connected to sexism, with its fundamental premise of unequal distribution of power.

Our goal is to change not just ourselves and other men, but also the institutions that create inequality. We welcome any person who agrees in substance with these principles to membership in the National Organization For Men Against Sexism.

September 1990.

ABBREVIATIONS

LIBRARIES AND ARCHIVES

BHL Bentley Historical Library, Michigan Historical Collection, Ann Arbor
BL Beinecke Rare Book and Manuscript Library, Yale University
CHSL California Historical Society Library, San Francisco
CU Columbia University
EI Essex Institute, Salem, Mass.
HL Houghton Library, Harvard University
HUA Harvard University Archives
JHL John Hay Library, Brown University
LCP Library Company of Philadelphia
LOC Library of Congress
MCP Medical College of Pennsylvania
MEL Milton S. Eisenhower Library, The Johns Hopkins University
NHS Nevada Historical Society, Reno
NL Newberry Library, Chicago
NYPL New York Public Library
OL Olin Library, Wesleyan University
OSU Ohio State University Library
PHS Pennsylvania Historical Society, Philadelphia
SFPL San Francisco Public Library
SHSI State Historical Society of Iowa, Woman's Suffrage Collection, Iowa City
SL Arthur and Elizabeth Schlesinger Library on the History of Women in America, Radcliffe College
SRL Spencer Research Library, University of Kansas
SSL Sophia Smith Library, Smith College
UCB University of California, Berkeley
UCD University of California, Davis
UCI University of California, Irvine
UCL University of Chicago Library
URL University of Rochester Library
VCA Vassar College Archives
WCL William Clements Library, University of Michigan
WRC Woodson Research Center, Rice University
WRH Western Reserve Historical Society

OTHER

GERR Gerritsen Collection of Women's History: 1543–1945.
HWS *The History of Woman Suffrage*
WJ *The Woman's Journal*
WSL *Woman Suffrage Leaflets*

SELECT BIBLIOGRAPHY

GENERAL WOMEN'S HISTORY

Primary Sources

Documentary Collections

Baxandall, Rosalyn, Linda Gordon, and Susan Reverby, eds. *America's Working Women.* New York: Random House, 1976.

Buhle, Mari Jo, and Paul Buhle, eds. *The Concise History of Woman Suffrage.* Urbana: University of Illinois Press, 1978.

Cohart, Mary, ed. *Unsung Champions of Women.* Albuquerque: University of New Mexico Press, 1974.

Cott, Nancy, ed. *Root of Bitterness: Documents of the Social History of American Women.* New York: Dutton, 1972.

Cott, Nancy, and Elizabeth H. Pleck, eds. *A Heritage of Her Own: Toward a New Social History of American Women.* New York: Simon & Schuster, 1979.

Frey, Sylvia, and Marian Morton. *New World, New Roles: A Documentary History of Women in Pre-Industrial America.* New York: Greenwood, 1986.

Lerner, Gerda. *Black Women in White America: A Documentary History.* New York: Pantheon, 1972.

Loewenberg, Bert James, and Ruth Bogin, eds. *Black Women in Nineteenth-Century American Life.* University Park: Pennsylvania State University Press, 1976.

Marcus, Jacob R., ed. *The American Jewish Women: A Documentary History, 1654–1980.* New York: KTAV, 1981.

Martin, Wendy. *American Sisterhood: Feminist Writings, Colonial to Present.* New York: Harper & Row, 1972.

Rossi, Alice S., ed. *The Feminist Papers.* New York: Columbia University Press, 1973.

Schneir, Miriam, ed. *Feminists: The Essential Historical Writings.* New York: Random House, 1972.

Sochen, June, ed. *The New Feminism in Twentieth Century America.* New York: Heath, 1971.

Stanton, Elizabeth Cady, Susan B. Anthony, and Matilda Joslyn Gage, eds. *History of Woman Suffrage.* 6 vols. Reprint. New York: Arno, 1969.

Microfilm Collections

The Cornell University Collection of Women's Rights Pamphlets: 1814–1914. Wooster, Ohio: Bell & Howell, 1974.

Gerritsen Collection of Women's History, 1543–1945. Glen Rock, N.J.: Microfilming Corporation of America, 1983.

History of Woman Microfilm Collection. New Haven, Conn.: Research Publications, 1976.

Microfilm Edition of the Gerrit Smith Papers: 1775–1924. Glen Rock, N.J.: Microfilming Corporation of America, 1974.

Woman Suffrage Leaflets. New Haven, Conn.: Research Publications, 1977.

The Woman's Journal (Boston, Chicago), vols. 1–48, 1870–1917. New Haven, Conn.: Research Publications, 1975.

Periodicals

The Crisis. New York: National Association for the Advancement of Colored People, 1910–.

M.: Gentle Men for Gender Justice. The name of this publication was changed in 1985 to *Changing Men: Issues in Gender, Sex and Politics.* Madison, Wisc.: Feminist Men's Publications, 1979–.

The Masses. New York, 1911–17.

Social Progress Studies in The Gospel of the Kingdom. New York: American Institute of Social Service, 1908–21.

Woman Suffrage Leaflets. Boston: American Woman Suffrage Association, 1888–94.

The Woman's Journal. Boston: National American Woman Suffrage Association, 1870–1917.

PART I: BEFORE SENECA FALLS, 1775–1848

Primary Sources

Branagan, Thomas. *The Excellency of the Female Character Vindicated; Being an Investigation Relative to the Cause and Effects of the Encroachments of Men upon the Rights of Women, and the Too Frequent Degradation and Consequent Misfortunes of the Fair Sex.* 1807. Reprint. New York: Arno, 1972.

Carey, Mathew. *Miscellaneous Essays.* Research and Source Work Series no. 135. New York: Burt Franklin, 1830.

———. "On the Rate of Wages Paid to Women." Letter to the editor of the *New York Daily Sentinel* (1830). Reprinted in *Miscellaneous Essays.* Philadelphia, April, 1831.

———. "Female Wages and Female Oppression." No. 1 (22 June 1835), no. 2 (3 July 1835), and no. 3 (4 July 1835). (PHS)

———. "A Letter Addressed to the Particular Attention of the Ladies of the United States." 23 July 1835. (PHS)

———. *Mathew Carey Autobiography.* 1837. Reprint. Brooklyn: E. L. Schwaab, 1942.

Forten, James, Sr. "The Minutes and Proceedings of the First Annual Meeting of the American Moral Reform Society, Philadelphia, 1837." Reprinted in *Afro-American History Series,* ed. Maxwell Whiteman. Wilmington, Del. Scholarly Resources, 1971.

Fuller, Margaret. *Women in the Nineteenth Century.* New York: Greeley & McElrath, 1845.

Garrison, William Lloyd. "Boston Female Anti-Slavery Society: Letter of October 13, 1840 to Mrs. Maria Chapman for the Annual Meeting." *Liberator* 10, no. 42 (16 October 1840): 167.

Gray, James. "Female Education." *Portfolio* 4. Philadelphia: Bradford & Inskeep, July 1810.

Harris, Walter, A.M. *Discourse Delivered to the Members of the Female Cent. Society.* Concord, N.H.: G. Hough, 1814.

Johnston, William. "An Address on Female Education, Delivered at Columbus, December 31, 1844." N.p.: C. Scott, 1845.

Jones, Samuel. *A Treatise on the Right of Suffrage*. Boston: Otis, Broaders, 1842.

Paine, Thomas. "Letter To Kitty Nicholson Few" 6 January 1789. Reprinted in *The Complete Writings of Thomas Paine*, ed. Philip S. Foner. 2 vols. New York: Citadel, 1945.

Remond, Charles L. "Letter to Rev. C. B. Ray of June 30, 1840." *Liberator* 10, no. 43, whole no. 511 (16 October 1840): 165.

Ruggle, David. "Woman's Rights." *Ladies Mirror of Liberty* (July 1838).

Tuckerman, Joseph. "An Essay on the Wages Paid to Females in the Form of a Letter from a Gentleman in Boston to his Friend in Philadelphia." 25 March 1830. Reprinted in *Low Wages and Great Sin: Two Antebellum American Views on Prostitution and the Working Girl*, ed. David J. Rothman and Sheila M. Rothman. New York: Garland, 1987.

Weld, Theodore Dwight. "Letter on Preaching to Sarah and Angelina Grimké." 22 July 1837. (WCL)

———. "Letter on Suffrage to Sarah and Angelina Grimké. 15 August 1837. (WCL)

———. "Letter on Marriage to Angelina Grimké." 7 May 1838. (WCL)

Secondary Sources

Ayer, A. J. *Thomas Paine*. New York: Atheneum, 1989.

Barker-Benfield, Ben. "Anne Hutchinson and the Puritan Attitude towards Women." *Feminist Studies* 1 (Fall 1972).

Berg, Barbara J. *The Remembered Gate: The Origins of American Feminism, the Woman and the City, 1800–1860*. New York: Oxford University Press, 1978.

Bradsher, Earl L. *Mathew Carey: Editor, Author and Publisher: A Study in American Literary Development*. New York: Columbia University Press, 1912.

Clarke, David Lee. "Brockden Brown and the Rights of Women." *University of Texas Bulletin*, no. 2212 (22 March 1922).

Cott, Nancy. *The Bonds of Womanhood: "Woman's Sphere" in New England, 1780–1835*. New Haven, Conn.: Yale University Press, 1977.

De Pauw, Linda Grant. *Remember the Ladies: Women in America, 1750–1815*. New York: Viking, 1976.

de Tocqueville, Alexis. *Democracy in America*. 1836. 2 vols. Reprint. New York: Schocken, 1961.

"Domestic Relations in a Utopian Community." *Phalanx* 1, no. 21 (8 February 1844).

Epstein, Barbara. *The Politics of Domesticity: Evangelism and Temperance in Nineteenth Century America*. Middletown, Conn.: Wesleyan University Press, 1981.

Fleischmann, Fritz. *A Right View of the Subject: Feminism in the Works of Charles Brockden Brown and John Neal*. Erlangen: Palm & Enke, 1983.

George, Carol V. R. *Remember the Ladies: New Perspectives on Women in American History*. Syracuse, N.Y.: Syracuse University Press, 1975.

Hammond, Charles A. *Gerrit Smith: The Story of a Noble Man's Life*. Geneva: W. F. Humphrey, 1900.

James, Janet Wilson. *Changing Ideas about Women in the United Statees, 1776–1825*. New York: Garland, 1981.

Kerber, Linda. *Women in the Republic: Intellect and Ideology in Revolutionary America*. Chapel Hill: University of North Carolina Press, 1980.

Melder, K. E. "The Beginning of the Women's Rights Movement in the United States, 1800–1840." Ph.D. diss., Yale University, 1963.

Melder, Reita. *Beginnings of Sisterhood: The American Woman's Rights Movement, 1800–1850*. New York: Schocken, 1977.

Ryan, Mary. *Womanhood in America from Co-*

lonial Times to the Present. New York: New Viewpoints, 1975.

———. *Cradle of the Middle Class: The Family in Oneida County, New York, 1790–1865*. New York: Cambridge University Press, 1981.

Sanders, Thomas E., and Walter W. Peek, eds. "The Law of the Great Peace of the People of the Longhouse." In *Literature of the American Indian*. New York: Glencoe, 1973.

Wagner, Sally Roesch. "The World Anti-Slavery Convention of 1840: Three Anti-Sexist Men Take a Stand." *M.*, no. 12 (Spring-Summer 1984): 35–41.

———. "Samuel Joseph May." *Changing Men*, no. 14 (Spring 1985): 28–29.

———. "The Iroquois Confederacy: A Native American Model for Non-Sexist Men." *Changing Men*, no. 19 (Spring-Summer 1988): 32–34.

PART II: THE STRUGGLE FOR EQUAL EDUCATION, 1850–1960

Primary Sources

Women's Right to Higher Education

Bowditch, Henry, M.D. "On the Education of Women, the Hostile Position of Harvard University and of the Massachusetts Medical Society. What Remedies Therefore Can Be Suggested?" *Boston Medical and Surgical Journal* (September 1881): 289–92.

Breckinridge, William C. P. "Letters of October 8, 1884 and December 17, 1884." Reprinted in "With More Love Than I Can Write: A Nineteenth Century Father to His Daughter," by Helen Lefkowitz Horowitz. *Wellesley Alumnae Magazine* (Spring 1985): 16–20.

Buchanan, Joseph. "The Sphere of Woman." In *Proceedings of the Woman's Rights Convention, Akron, Ohio, May 28–29, 1851*. Cincinnati, 1851.

Butterfield, L. H., Wendell D., Garrett, and Marjorie E. Sprague, eds. *Adams Family Correspondence*. 2 vols. Cambridge, Mass.: Harvard University Press, 1963.

Clarke, Edward H. *Sex in Education; Or a Fair Chance for the Girls*. Boston: Osgood, 1873.

Comfort, George F., and Anna Manning Comfort, M.D. *Woman's Education and Woman's Health*. Syracuse, N.Y.: Thomas Durston, 1874.

Eliot, Charles W. "The Higher Education of Woman." *Harper's Bazaar* (1908): 161–67.

Gilman, Arthur. "Women Who Go to College." *Century* (September 1888): 714–18.

Harris, Samuel. *A Report Presented to a Convention of the Friends of Education, Assembled March 31, 1853 at the Chapel of the Young Ladies Institute, Pittsfield, Mass.* New Haven, Conn.: T. J. Stafford, 1853.

Higginson, Thomas Wentworth. "Higher Education of Woman." Paper read at the Social Science Convention. Reprinted in *Woman Suffrage Tracts*, no. 9 (14 May 1873), and in *The Liberal Education of Women: The Demand and the Method. Current Thoughts in America and England*, ed. James Orton. New York and Chicago: A. S. Barnes, 1873.

———. "Review of *Sex in Education*." *WJ* 4, no. 45 (8 November 1873): 353–54, and no. 46 (15 November 1873): 361. Reprinted in *Sex and Education: A Reply to Dr. E. H. Clarke's "Sex in Education,"* ed. Julia Ward Howe. 1874. Reprint. New York: Arno, 1972.

———. "Editorial: Sex and Education." *WJ* (1874). Reprinted in *HWS*, vol. 3.

Higginson, Thomas Wentworth, with Lucy Stone, comps. *Woman's Rights Almanac for 1858*. Worcester: Z. Baker, 1858.

Jordan, David Starr. "The Question of Coeducation." *Muncey's Magazine* 34 (March 1906).

———. *The Woman and the University*. San Francisco: Whitaker & Ray-Wiggin, 1912. (SFPL)

Male Teachers' Association of New York City. "Are There Too Many Women Teachers?" *Educational Review* 28 (1904).

Stevens, W. LeConte. *The Admission of Women to Universities*. New York: S. W. Green, 1883.

———. "University Education for Women." *North American Review* 136 (January 1883).

Tefft, Benjamin Franklin. "An Inaugural Address as President of Genesee College." Cincinnati: R. P. Thompson, 1851.

Thompson, W. O. "The Educated Woman and the New World: Commencement Address Delivered at Western College for Women, Ohio." 13 June 1917. (OSU)

Todd, John. *Women's Rights*. Boston: Lee & Shepard, 1867.

Establishing Colleges for Women

"Addresses of President Rhoads, Daniel C. Gilman, President of the Johns Hopkins University and President Thomas Chase of Haverford College at the Inauguration of Bryn Mawr College, Bryn Mawr, 1885." Philadelphia: Sherman, 1886.

"Editorial: Colleges for Both." *Golden Ages* (November 1871). Reprinted in *The Liberal Education of Women: The Demand and the Method. Current Thoughts in America and England*, ed. James Orton. New York and Chicago: A. S. Barnes, 1873.

Emerson, Joseph. *Female Education: A Discourse Delivered at the Dedication of the Seminary Hall in Saugus, January 15, 1822*. Boston: S. T. Armstrong and Crocker & Brewster, 1822.

Higginson, Thomas Wentworth. "The Wellesley College for Women." *WJ* (28 November 1874).

Jewitt, Milo P. "The Origins of Vassar College." 1879. (VL, Vassar Archives).

MacCracken, Henry Noble. "Progress, The Founder's Motto." Commencement address, Vassar College, 10 June 1919. (VCA)

———. "Educated Women in American Life." *Columbia* 450 (September 1923).

———. "Letter to a Gratified Husband." *Women's Home Companion* (March 1925). (VCA)

Nielson, William Allan. "The Inaugural Address of the President of Smith College." *School and Society* 8 (20 July 1918).

Orton, John. "Vassar College." *Old and New Age* (August 1871). Reprinted in *The Liberal Education of Women: The Demand and the Method. Current Thoughts in America and England*, ed. James Orton. New York and Chicago: A. S. Barnes, 1873.

———, ed. *The Liberal Education of Women: The Demand and the Method. Current Thoughts in America and England*. New York and Chicago: A. S. Barnes, 1873.

Raymond, John. "The Demands of the Age for a Liberal Education for Women and How it Should be Met." In *The Liberal Education of Women: The Demand and the Method. Current Thoughts in America and England*. ed. John Orton. New York and Chicago: A. S. Barnes, 1873.

———. *Vassar College: A College for Women*. New York: S. W. Green, 1873.

Rice, William North. "Report to the Board of Trustees of Wesleyan University." 20 March 1900. Reprinted in *Papers on the Relation of Wesleyan University to the Higher Education of Women*. Middletown, Conn.: Wesleyan University. (OL)

Royce, Josiah. "Letter on Teaching at the Harvard 'Annex.'" 1886. (SL)

Tappan, Henry. *A Discourse on Education Delivered at the Anniversary of the Young Ladies Institute, Pittsfield, Mass., October 2, 1846*. New York: Roe, Lockwood & Son, 1846.

Thomas, M. Carey. "Present Tendencies in Women's College and University Education." *Publications of the Association of Collegiate Alumnae*, ser. 3, no. 17 (February 1908).

Vassar, Mathew. "Farewell Speech to Trustees of Vassar." Vassar College, June 1868. (VCA)

White, Andrew D. "Report Submitted to the Trustees of Cornell University in Behalf of a Majority of the Committee on Mr. Sage's Proposal to Endow a College for Women, Albany, February 13, 1872." Ithaca, N.Y.: Cornell University Press, 1872.

The Argument for Coeducation

Allen, W. F. "The Sexes in College." *Nation* 10, no. 244 (1870). Reprinted in *The Liberal Education of Women: The Demand and the Method. Current Thoughts in America and England*, ed. James Orton. New York and Chicago: A. S. Barnes, 1873.

Angell, James. "Coeducation at Michigan University." *Pennsylvania School Journal* 29 (1881).

Blanchard, President. "The Experience at Knox College." *Independent* (January 1870). Reprinted in *The Liberal Education of Women: The Demand and the Method. Current Thoughts in America and England*, ed. James Orton. New York and Chicago: A. S. Barnes, 1873.

Buckley, J. W. "The Education of Boys and Girls Together." *New York Teacher* 5 (1855).

Clarke, James Freeman. "Co-Education In Harvard: From a Report to the Committee of the Board of Overseers, 1872." Reprinted in *The Liberal Education of Women: The Demand and the Method. Current Thoughts in America and England*, ed. James Orton. New York and Chicago: A. S. Barnes, 1873.

Cutler, Carrol. "Shall Women Now Be Excluded from Adelbert College of Western Reserve University: An Argument Presented to the Board of Trustees." 7 November 1884. Cleveland: A. W. Fairbanks, 1884.

Dewey, John. "Education and the Health of Women." *Science* 6 (March 1885).

———. "Health and Sex in Higher Education." *Popular Science Monthly* 28 (1886): 606–14.

———. "Letter to President William Rainey Harper." 25 July 1902. (UCL)

Dix, Morgan, William C. Schermerhorn, Talbot W. Chambers, Cornelius R. Agnew, and John J. Townsend. "A Report to the Trustees of Columbia College of the Select Committee: Subject of Admission of Women to College." 23 April 1884. (CU)

Draper, Ander. "Coeducation in the United States." *Educational Review* 25 (February 1903).

Duffey, Elizabeth. *No Sex in Education; Or An Equal Chance for Both Girls and Boys*. Philadelphia: J. M. Stoddart, 1874.

Fairchild, James Harris. "The Joint Education of the Sexes: A Report Presented to a Meeting of the Ohio State Teachers Association." Oberlin, Ohio, 1852.

———. *Oberlin: The Colony and the College, 1833–1883*. Oberlin: E. J. Goodrich, 1883.

Hall, G. Stanley. *Adolescence: Its Psychology and Its Relation to Physiology, Anthropology, Sociology, Sex, Crime, Religion, and Education*. 2 vols. New York: Appleton, 1904.

Howe, Julia Ward, ed. *Sex and Education: A Reply to Dr. E. H. Clarke's "Sex in Education."* Boston: Roberts Bros., 1874. Reprint. New York: Arno, 1972.

Hutchins, President [Robert Maynard]. "The University and Co-Education: Extracts from an Address Recently Delivered by President Hutchins at Grand Rapids, Michigan, before the Ladies Literary Society." *Michigan Alumnus* (January 1911): 179–86. (BHL)

Magill, Edward H. *An Address Upon the Co-Education of the Sexes*. Philadelphia: Swarthmore College, 1873.

Mann, Horace. *A Few Thoughts on the Powers and Duties of Women: Two Lectures*. Syracuse, N.Y.: Hall, Mills, 1853.

Stevens, W. Le Conte. "The Admission of Women to Universities." New York: S. W. Green, 1883.

Whittier, John Greenleaf. "Letter to Richard Atwater on the Opening of Brown University to Women, August 10, 1881." In *The Letters of John Greenleaf Whittier*, Vol. 3, *1861–1892*, ed. John B. Pickard. Cambridge, Mass.: Harvard University Press, 1975.

"The Woman Peril." *Educational Review* 47 (February 1914).

Secondary Sources

Becker, Carl. *Cornell University: Founders and Founding*. Ithaca, N.Y.: Cornell University Press, 1943.

Buck, Paul. "Harvard Attitudes toward Radcliffe in the Early Years." *Massachusetts Historical Society* 74 (May 1962).

Comfort, George F., and Anna Manning Comfort, M.D. *Woman's Education and Woman's Health*. Syracuse, N.Y.: Thomas Durston, 1874.

Conable, Charlotte, W. *Women at Cornell: The Myth of Equal Education*. Ithaca, N.Y.: Cornell University Press, 1977.

Conway, Jill. "Perspectives on the History of Women's Education in the United States." *History of Education Quarterly* 14, no. 1 (Spring 1974).

Curtis, Wardon A. "The Movement against Coeducation at the University of Wisconsin." *Independent* 65 (6 August 1908).

Edelstein, Tilden. *Strange Enthusiasms: A Life of Thomas Wentworth Higginson*. New York: Atheneum, 1970.

Fletcher, Robert. *A History of Oberlin College from Its Foundation through the Civil War*. Oberlin, Ohio: Oberlin College Press, 1943.

Gordon, Lynn. *Gender and Higher Education in the Progressive Era*. New Haven, Conn.: Yale University Press, 1990.

Graham, Patricia. "Expansion and Exclusion: A History of Women in American Higher Education." *Signs* 3 (Summer 1978).

Green, Elizabeth Alden. *Mary Lyon and Mount Holyoke: Opening the Gates*. Hanover, N.H.: University Press of New England, 1979.

Haines, Patricia Foster. "Women, Men and Coeducation: Historical Perspectives from Cornell University, 1868–1900." Paper presented at the Berkshire Conference on the History of Women, 1976. (SL)

Horowitz, Helen Lefkowitz. *Alma Mater: Design and Experience in the Women's Colleges from Their Nineteenth Century Beginnings to the 1930s*. New York: Knopf, 1984.

———. ". . .'The Most Beautiful Female Seminary the World Had Ever Seen.'" *Wellesley Alumnae Magazine* (Spring 1985).

Kaledin, Eugenia. *The Education of Mrs. Henry Adams*. Philadelphia: Temple University Press, 1981.

Keller, Arnold Jack. "An Historical Analysis of the Arguments for and against Coeducational Schools in the United States." Ph.D. diss., Teachers College, Columbia University, 1971.

Knight, Louise. 'The 'Quails': The History of Wesleyan University's First Period of Coeducation, 1872–1912." B.A. honors thesis, Wesleyan University, 1972.

Komorovsky, Mirra. *Women in the Modern World: Their Education and Dilemmas*. New York: Little, Brown, 1953.

Lord, John. *The Life of Emma Willard*. New York: Appleton, 1873.

Maxwell, John. "Should the Education of Boys and Girls Differ? A Half-Century of Debate, 1870–1920." Ph.D. diss., University of Wisconsin, 1966.

Miller, Alice Duer, and Susan Myers. *Barnard College: The First Fifty Years*. New York: Columbia University Press, 1939.

Newcomer, Mabel. *A Century of Higher Education for Women*. New York: Harper & Bros., 1959.

Rosenberg, Rosalind. *Beyond Separate Spheres: Intellectual Roots of Modern Feminism*. New Haven, Conn.: Yale University Press, 1982.

———. "The Limits of Access: The History of Coeducation in America." In *Women and Higher Education in American History*, ed. John Faragher and Florence Howe. New York: Norton, 1988.

Solomon, Barbara. *In the Company of Educated Women*. New Haven, Conn.: Yale University Press, 1985.

Stoddard, George. *On the Education of Women*. Kappa Delta Phi Lecture Series. New York: Macmillan, 1950.

Synott, Marcia Graham. *The Half-Opened Door: Discrimination and Admissions at Harvard, Yale and Princeton, 1900–1970*. Westport, Conn.: Greenwood, 1979.

Tyack, David and Elizabeth Hansot. *Learning Together: A History of Coeducation in American Public Schools*. New Haven, Conn.: Yale University Press, 1990.

White, E. E. "Separate Education of Boys and Girls." *Common School Journal*, 13, no. 6 (15 March 1851).

———. "Coeducation of the Sexes." *National Teacher* 2 (1872).

White, Lynn. *Educating Our Daughters: A Challenge to the Colleges*. New York: Harper & Bros., 1950.

Woody, Thomas. *A History of Women's Education in the United States*. 2 vols. New York: Science, 1929.

PART III: WOMEN'S STRUGGLES FOR ECONOMIC EQUALITY, 1850–1960

Primary Sources

Women's Economic Independence

Blackwell, Henry Brown. "Wages for Women." *WJ* (18 July 1874).

Bowditch, William I. *Taxation of Women in Massachusetts*. Cambridge, Mass.: John Wilson & Son, 1875.

———. "The Forgotten Woman in Massachusetts." *WSL* 2, no. 15 (1 March 1889): 1–4. (EI)

Butts, Bryan J. "Material Independence of Woman." In *Miscellaneous Speeches*. Hopedale, Mass., 1871.

Dall, Caroline. *Women's Right to Labor*. Boston: Walker, Wise, 1860.

Ecob, James H. "Work Versus The Worker." *Social Progress Studies in The Gospel of the Kingdom* 4, no. 5 (May 1912): 68.

Fuller, Margaret. *Woman in the Nineteenth Century*. New York: Greeley & McElrath, 1845.

Phillips, Wendell. "Woman's Rights and Woman's Duties: Address delivered in New York City, 10 May 1866." In *Speeches, Lectures and Letters*. Boston: Lee & Shepard, 1891.

Strong, Josiah D. "Women in Industry." *Social Progress Studies in The Gospel of the Kingdom* 1, no. 2 (November 1908): 10–16.

Women in the Trades

Alaska Fishermen's Cooperative Association. *Resolutions and Instructions Authorizing Bargaining Agency: Instructions and Credentials of Delegates or Business Agents; By-Laws of Fishermen's Collective Marketing Agency*. Juneau: Alaska Fishermen's Cooperative Association, 1943.

Andrews, John, and W. D. P. Bliss. *A History of Women in Trade Unions*, vol. 10 of *Report on Conditions of Woman and Child Earners in the United States*. S.Doc. 645, 61st Cong., 2d sess. Washington, D.C.: U.S.A. Government Printing Office, 1911. Reprint. Arno, 1974.

Ames, Azel, Jr., M.D. *Sex in Industry: A Plea for the Working Girl*. Boston: James Osgood, 1875.

Binder, Rudolph M. "Minimum Wage for Women." *The Gospel of the Kingdom* 10, no. 8 (May 1918): 70–74.

Cheesewright, Charles. "The Factory Girl." *Labor Enquirer* (16 July 1887).

Edelshtadt, David. "To The Women Workers." Reprinted in *American Labor Songs of the Nineteenth Century*, ed. Philip S. Foner. Urbana: University of Illinois Press, 1975.

Gompers, Samuel. "Should the Wife Help Support the Family?" *American Federationist* 13, no. 12 (January 1906): 36. (UCB)

———. "The Woman Movement." *American Federationist* (August 1913).

———. "Woman's Work Rights and Progress." *American Federationist* 20, no. 8 (August 1913): 624–27.

———. "Coming Into Her Own." *American Federationist* 22, no. 7 (July 1915): 517–19.

———. "Women's Work." In *Seventy Years of Life and Labor: An Autobiography*, vol. 1. New York, Dutton, 1925.

Owen, Robert Dale. "Rights of Women in the Old Immoral World." Parts 1–5. *Robert Owen's Journal* 2, no. 29 (13 May 1851); 2, no. 30 (26 May 1851); 2, no. 32 (7 June 1851); 2, no. 33 (14 June 1851); and 2, no. 34 (21 June 1851).

———. "Testimonial to Robert Dale Owen from the Women of Indiana." *Robert Owen's Journal* 2, no. 33 (14 June 1851).

Phelan, Raymond V. "Living Wages and the Ballot." New York: National American Woman Suffrage Association, 1913.

Pritchett, Henry Smith. "A Woman's Opportunity in Business and the Industries: An Address given at the Second Annual Commencement of Simmons College, Boston." 12 June 1907. Boston: The College, 1907. (*GERR*)

"Solidarity?" *New Republic* 19, no. 241 (14 June 1919): 208–9.

Wright, Carroll. *The Working Girls of Boston.* 1889. Reprint. New York: Arno, 1969.

Women in the Professions

Brown, William Symington, M.D. "The Capability of Women to Practice the Healing Art." In *Lecture at Ladies Medical Academy*. Boston: Ripley, 1859.

Byford, William Heath, M.D. "Doctorate Address Delivered at the Commencement of the Women's Medical College by President Byford." 22 April 1884. *Chicago Medical Journal and Examiner* 48, no. 6 (June 1884).

Cabot, Richard C., M.D. "Women in Medicine." Paper presented at the Woman's Medical College, Philadelphia. Reprinted in *Journal of the American Medical Association* 65, no. 11 (11 September 1915): 947–48. (MCP)

Cohen, Henry. "Ordination of Women as Rabbis." 1922. Reprinted in *American Reform Responsa: Collected Responsa of the Central Conference of the American Rabbis, 1889–1983*, ed. Walter Jacob. New York: The Conference, 1983.

Cornell, William M., M.D. "Woman The True Physician." *Godey's Magazine and Lady's Book* 46 (January 1855).

Dewey, Melvil. "Women in Libraries." 1887. Typescript. (CU)

Foote, C. C. "Woman's Rights and Duties: On Women as Preachers." *Oberlin Quarterly Review.* Oberlin, Ohio: James M. Fitch, 1849.

Fussell, Edwin, M.D. "Valedictory Address to the Graduating Class of the Female Medical College of Pennsylvania at the Tenth Annual Commencement." Philadelphia: J. R. Chandler, 1861.

Gardner, A. K., M.D. "Women Doctors." *Frank Leslie's Illustrated Newspaper* (16 April 1870).

Gregory, Samuel, M.D. "Letter to the Ladies in Favor of Female Physicians." American Medical Education Society, 1850. Reprinted in *Sex, Marriage and Society: The Male Mid-Wife and the Female Doctor*, ed. Charles Rosenberg and Carroll Smith-Rosenberg. New York: Arno, 1974.

———. "Female Physicians." *Living Age* 73 (April–June 1862): 243–49.

Knopf, S. Adolphus, M.D. "The Woman Physician and Professor Cabot." *Woman's Medical Journal* 25, no. 7 (July 1915): 159–60.

Longshore, J. S., M.D. "An Introductory Lecture at the Opening of the Female Medical College of Pennsylvania." Philadelphia: James Young, 1850.

Mead, George H. "On Training Women Physicians." 1917. Typescript. (UCL)

Osler, William. "On The Opening of the Johns Hopkins Medical School to Women." [1891.] (SL)

Truman, James. "An Account of the Admission to Women into Dental Surgery." 1875. Reprinted in *HWS*, vol. 3.

Wise, Isaac Mayer. "Woman in the Synagogue." 1876. Reprinted in *The American Jewish Woman: A Documentary History, 1654–1980*, ed. Jacob R. Marcus. New York: KTAV, 1981.

Secondary Sources

Abbot, Edith. *Women in Industry: A Study in American Economic History*. New York: Appleton, 1910.

Abrams, Ruth J. *"Send Us a Lady Physician."* Toronto: Penguin, 1985.

Balser, Diane. *Sisterhood and Solidarity: Feminism and Labor in Modern Times*. Boston: South End, 1987.

Basch, Norma. *In the Eyes of the Law: Women, Marriage, and Property in 19th Century New York*. Ithaca, N.Y.: Cornell University Press, 1982.

Billington, Ray. *American History after 1865*. Totowa, N.J.: Rowman & Littlefield, 1967.

Buhle, Mari Jo. *Women and American Socialism: 1870–1920*. Urbana: University of Illinois Press, 1981.

Calhoun, Arthur. *A Social History of the American Family from Colonial Times to the Present*. 3 vols. Cleveland: Arthur Clark, 1917–19.

Cott, Nancy. *The Bonds of Womanhood: "Woman's Sphere" in New England, 1780–1835*. New Haven, Conn.: Yale University Press, 1977.

Davies, Margery. *Women's Place Is at the Typewriter: Office Work and Office Workers, 1870–1930*. Philadelphia: Temple University Press, 1982.

Dublin, Thomas. *Women at Work: The Transformation of Work and Community in Lowell, Massachusetts, 1826–1860*. New York: Columbia University Press, 1979.

Dye, Nancy Schrom. *As Equals and Sisters: Feminism, the Labor Movement, and the Women's Trade Union League of New York*. Columbia: University of Missouri Press, 1980.

Epstein, Cynthia Fuchs. *Woman's Place: Options and Limits in Professional Careers*. Berkeley and Los Angeles: University of California Press, 1970.

———. *Women in Law*. New York: Basic, 1981.

Foner, Philip S., ed. *American Labor Songs of the Nineteenth Century*. Urbana: University of Illinois Press, 1975.

———. *Women and the American Labor Movement: From Colonial Times to the Eve of World War I*. New York: Free Press, 1979.

———. *Women and the American Labor Movement: World War I to the Present*. 2 vols. New York: Free Press, 1980.

Frankfort, Roberta. *Collegiate Women: Domesticity and Career in Turn of the Century America*. New York: New York University Press, 1977.

Glazer, Penina Migdal, and Miriam Slater. *Unequal Colleagues: The Entrance of Women into the Professions, 1890–1940*. New Brunswick, N.J.: Rutgers University Press, 1987.

Greenberg, Blu. *On Women and Judaism*. Philadelphia: Jewish Publication Society of America, 1981.

Hammond, Charles A. *Gerrit Smith: The Story of a Noble Man's Life*. Geneva, N.Y.: W. F. Humphrey, 1900.

Henry, Alice. *Women and the Labor Movement*. 1923. Reprint. New York: Arno, 1971.

Kessler-Harris, Alice. *Out to Work: A History of Wage Earning Women in the United States*. New York: Oxford University Press, 1982.

Lehrer, Susan. *The Origins of Protective Labor Legislation for Women, 1905–1925*. Albany: State University of New York Press, 1987.

Milkman, Ruth, ed. *Women, Work and Protest: A Century of U.S. Women's Labor History*. Boston: Routledge & Kegan Paul, 1985.

———. *Gender at Work: The Dynamics of Job Segregation by Sex during World War II*. Urbana: University of Illinois Press, 1987.

Morello, Karen Burger. *The Invisible Bar*. New York: Random House, 1986.

Oppenheimer, Valeria Kincaid. *The Female Labor Force in the United States: Demographic and Economic Factors Governing Its Growth and Changing Composition*. Westport, Conn.: Greenwood, 1976.

Raybeck, Joseph G. *A History of American Labor*. New York: Free Press, 1966.

Scharf, Lois. *To Work and to Wed: Female Employment, Feminism and the Great Depression*. Westport, Conn.: Greenwood, 1980.

Tax, Meredith. *The Rising of the Women*. New York: Monthly Review Press, 1980.

Tentler, Leslie Woodcock. *Wage-Earning Women: Industrial Work and Family Life in the United States, 1900–1930*. New York: Oxford University Press, 1979.

Waskow, Arthur. *God Wrestling*. New York: Schocken, 1978.

———. *Seasons of Our Joy*. Toronto: Bantam, 1982.

Weiner, Lynn. *From Working Girl to Working Mother: The Female Labor Force in the United States, 1820–1880*. Chapel Hill: University of North Carolina Press, 1985.

Weisberg, D. Kelley. *Women and the Law: The Social Historical Perspective*. New York: Schenkman, 1982.

Wertheimer, Barbara. *We Were There: The Story of Working Women in America*. New York: Pantheon, 1977.

Zipser, Arthur. *Working Class Giant*. New York: International, 1981.

PART IV: THE MOVEMENT FOR POLITICAL EQUALITY, 1850–1960

Primary Sources

From Abolition to Suffrage

Beecher, Henry Ward. "Women's Influence in Politics." Boston: R. F. Wallcut, 1860. (*GERR*)

———. "Address to Congress." 10 May 1866. Reprinted in *HWS*, vol. 2.

———. "Woman's Duty to Vote: A Speech at the 11th National Woman's Rights Convention Held in New York on May 10, 1866." New York: The Revolution, 1868. (*GERR*, SSL)

———. "Liberty for Soul." *The Agitator: Devoted to the Interests of Woman* (Chicago) (5 June 1869): 3.

———. "Statement to Suffrage Convention." 1870. Reprinted in *HWS*, vol. 2.

Bellows, Henry. "The Woman's Rights Convention at Worcester." *New York Christian Inquirer* (1851). Reprinted in *HWS*, vol. 1.

Blackwell, Henry Brown. "What the South Can Do." 15 January 1867. Reprinted in *HWS*, vol. 2: 929–31.

———. "Comments at the Convention." 1873. Reprinted in *HWS*, vol. 2.

———. "Woman Suffrage Problems Considered." *Forum* 3 [1887?]: 131–41.

———. "Objections to Woman Suffrage Answered." *WSL* 1, no. 3 (1 September 1888): 1–2.

———. "How to Win Woman Suffrage." *WSL* 5, no. 6 (November 1892): 1–2.

———. "Eminent Opinions on Woman Suffrage." *WSL* 6, no. 1 (January 1893): 1–2.

———. "Objections of Woman Suffrage Answered." *WSL* 5, no. 2 (March 1896).

———. "Woman Suffrage and the Home: Statement to the National American Convention." 1898. Reprinted in *HWS*, vol. 4.

———. "Woman Suffrage and Municipal Reform." N.d. (SFPL)

Brough, William. "Let Us All Speak Our Minds." Reprinted in *All Our Lives: A Women's Songbook*, ed. Joyce Cheney, Marcia Deihl, and Deborah Silverstein. Baltimore: Diana, 1976.

Buchanan, Joseph. "The Sphere of Woman." In *Proceedings of the Women's Rights Convention* [Akron, Ohio, 28–29 May 1851]. Cincinnati, 1851.

Bushnell, Horace. *Woman Suffrage: The Reform Against Nature*. New York: Scribner's, 1870.

Cattell, J. D., and H. Canfield. *Report of the Select Committee of the Ohio Senate on Giving the Rights of Suffrage to Females*. Columbus, Ohio, 1858. (*GERR*)

Caverno, Charles. "Social Science and Woman Suffrage." *Transactions of the Wisconsin Academy of Science, Arts, and Letters* 1 (1872): 72–89.

Channing, William Ellery. "Letter to the President and Members of the Woman's Rights Convention." 3 October 1852. Reprinted in *HWS*, vol. 1.

———. *The Complete Works of William Ellery Channing: 1780–1842*. London: Christian Life, 1884.

Chapman, Ray. *The Rights of Woman*. New York: D. M. Bennett Liberal, 1878. (SSL)

Clarke, James Freeman. "Statement to Suffrage Convention." 1870. Reprinted in *HWS*, vol. 2.

———. *Autobiography*. Boston: Houghton Mifflin, 1891.

Fairchild, James H. *Woman's Right to the Ballot*. Oberlin, Ohio: George H. Fairchild, 1870. (*GERR*)

Greeley, Horace. "Letter to Woman's Rights Convention." 22 November 1856. Reprinted in *HWS*, vol. 1.

———. "Women in Politics." *Tribune* (26 July 1867). Reprinted in *HWS*, vol. 2.

Grover, Alonzo, J. "The Bible Argument Against Women Stated and Answered from a Bible Standpoint." Earlville, Ill.: Cook County Woman's Suffrage Association, 1870. (LCP)

Higginson, Thomas Wentworth. "Speech before the Committee of the Constitutional Convention on the Qualifications of Voters." 3 June 1853. Reprinted in *HWS*, vol. 1.

———. "Address to 7th National Convention." November 1856. Reprinted in *HWS*, vol. 1.

———, ed. *Consistent Democracy: The Elective Franchise for Women: Twenty-Five Testimonies of Prominent Men*. Worcester, Mass., 1858. (SSL)

———. "Statement at Convention, Cleveland." November 1870. Reprinted in *HWS*, vol. 1.

———. "Statement at Suffrage Meeting." May 1870. Reprinted in *HWS*, vol. 2.

———. "Unsolved Problems in Woman Suffrage." 1886. Reprinted in *Forum* 2 (January 1887): 439–49.

———. "The Nonsense Of It: Short Answers to Common Objections Concerning Woman Suffrage." *WSL* 2, no. 23 (1 July 1889): 1–2.

———. "Straight Lines or Oblique Lines?" *WSL* 6, no. 6 (November 1893): 1–2.

———. "Should Women Vote: Important Affirmative Authority." Rochester, N.Y.: Equal Rights Association, 1 March 1896.

———. "Wendell Phillips." In *The Writings of Thomas Wentworth Higginson*, vol. 2. Cambridge, Mass.: Riverside, 1900.

———. *The Writings of Thomas Wentworth Higginson*. 7 vols. Cambridge, Mass.: Riverside, 1900.

Hoar, George F. "Woman Suffrage: Essential to the True Republic." An Address at the annual meeting of the New England Woman

Suffrage Association, 27 May 1873. Reprinted in *Woman Suffrage Tracts*, no. 8. Boston: Woman's Journal Office, 1873.

Hooker, John. *The Bible and Woman Suffrage*. Tracts of Connecticut Woman Suffrage Association, no. 3. Hartford, Conn.: Case, Lockwood & Brainard, 1874. (*GERR*)

Johnson, Samuel. "Letter to the Woman's Rights Convention." 4 October 1856. Reprinted in *HWS*, vol. 1.

Longfellow, Samuel. "Speech at New York Convention." [1856.] Reprinted in *HWS*, vol. 1.

Love, Alfred H. "Statement to Suffrage Convention." 1870. Reprinted in *HWS*, vol. 2.

Mahan, Asa. "Remarks Made at the Sessions of the Convention on the Subject of Seneca Falls Declaration." [1853.] Reprinted in *HWS*, vol. 1.

Owen, Robert. "Speech in Indiana Constitutional Convention." 1850. Reprinted in *HWS*, vol. 1.

———. "Remarks at Indiana Constitutional Debate." 1853. Reprinted in *HWS*, vol. 1.

Parker, Theodore. *Additional Speeches, Address and Occasional Sermons*. 3 vols. Boston: Little, Brown, 1855.

———. *Theodore Parker: An Anthology*. Edited by Henry Steele Commager. Boston: Beacon, 1960.

———. *The Collected Works of Theodore Parker: 1863–1871*. Edited by Frances P. Cobbe. New York: Garland, 1973.

Phillips, Wendell. "Introductory Remarks to Reading the Resolutions Prepared for Consideration of the Convention." 15 October 1851. Reprinted in *HWS*, vol. 1.

———. "Women's Rights Speech of Wendell Phillips, Esq., to the Worcester Convention." 15, 16 October 1851. (SL)

———. "The Education of the People." Address delivered in the Representatives' Chamber, Boston, 10 March 1859. Reprinted in *Speeches and Lectures and Letters*. Boston: J. Redpath, 1863.

———. "Suffrage for Women: Address delivered at the Tenth Woman's Rights Convention, Cooper Institute, New York, 10 and 11 May 1861." In *Speeches, Lectures and Letters*. Boston: Lee & Shepard, 1891.

———. "The Fifteenth Amendment." *Woman's Advocate* 2, no. 1 (July 1869): 34–39.

———. "Shall Women Have the Right to Vote?" 1851. Reprint. Philadelphia: Equal Franchise Society of Pennsylvania, 1910.

———. *Wendell Phillips on Civil Rights and Freedom*. Edited by Louis Filler. New York: Hill & Wang, 1965.

Reed, Charles. "Report from Vermont." 1870. Reprinted in *HWS*, vol. 3.

Sargent, Aaron A. "Statements on Woman Suffrage during the Debate on the Formation of the Territory of Pembina (later North Dakota)." *Congressional Record*. 43d Cong., 1st sess., 1874. Vol 2, pt. 5

———. "Statement in the U.S. Senate." 1876. Reprinted in *HWS*, vol. 3.

Sayers, Joseph. *Women's Rights*. Cincinnati, 1856.

Smith, Gerrit. "Letter to Susan B. Anthony." 7 May 1853. Reprinted in *HWS*, vol. 1.

———. "Speech at the Convention." [1853.] Reprinted in *HWS*, vol. 1.

———. "Letter to Elizabeth C. Stanton." 1 December 1855. Reprinted in *HWS*, vol. 1.

———. "Woman Suffrage above Human Law." 15 August 1873. Reprinted in *HWS*, vol. 2.

"Thomas Wentworth Higginson: Early Advocate of Equal Suffrage." [Editorial/obituary.] *La Follete's Weekly Magazine* 3, no. 21 (27 May 1991): 11.

Whittier, John Greenleaf. "The Women's Convention." *National Era* (6 November 1851).

———. "Letter # 1140." 1869. In *The Letters of John Greenleaf Whittier*, ed. John B. Pickard, vol. 3. Cambridge, Mass.: Harvard University Press, 1975.

———. "Woman Suffrage." Letter to the Newport Convention, 12 August 1869. In *The Prose Works of John Greenleaf Whittier*, vol. 3. Boston: Houghton, Mifflin, 1892.

———. "Suffrage for Women." Read at the Woman's Convention at Washington, 8 March 1888. In *The Prose Works of John Greenleaf Whittier*, vol. 3. Boston: Houghton, Mifflin, 1892.

The Woman's Rights Convention. Akron, Ohio, 1851.

Wright, Henry C. "Letter to the Woman's Rights Convention." Flushing, Long Island, 14 October 1851. Reprinted in *HWS*, 1:310.

Working for Suffrage

Adams, F. G. "The Women's Vote in Kansas." *WSL* 1, no. 9 (1 December 1888): 1–4.

Addams, Jane. "Why Women Should Vote." 1909. Reprinted in *A Centennial Reader*, ed. Emily Cooper Johnson. New York: Macmillan, 1960.

Alcott, A. Bronson. "Letter to Suffrage Convention." 1874. Reprinted in *HWS*, vol. 3.

Bashford, J. W. "The Bible for Woman Suffrage." *WSL* 2, no. 29 (1 October 1889): 1–2.

Beecher, Henry Ward. "Henry Ward Beecher on Suffrage." Speech presented at Cooper Institute, 2 February 1860. Reprinted in *WSL* 3, no. 2 (15 January 1890): 1–2.

———. "Woman Suffrage Man's Rights." Speech presented at Cooper Institute, 2 February 1860. Reprinted in *WSL* 3, no. 1 (1 January 1890): 1–2.

Blair, Henry W. "Woman Suffrage in Utah." *Congressional Record*. 49th Cong., 1st sess., 1886. Vol. 17, pt. 1.

———. "Woman Suffrage Resolution." *Congressional Record*. 49th Cong., 1st sess., 1886. Vol. 17, pt. 8

Bourne, Randolph. "The Later Feminism." *Dial* 63, no. 747 (16 August 1917): 103–4.

———. *The Radical Will: Selected Writings, 1911–1918*. Edited by Olaf Hansen. New York: Urizen, 1977.

Bowditch, William I. "Address at the Annual Meeting of the Massachusetts Woman Suffrage Association." 1853. (EI)

———. "Woman Suffrage—A Right, Not A Privilege." Cambridge, Mass.: Wilson, 1879. (*GERR*)

———. "The Right to Govern Ourselves." Woman's Suffrage Association Tract, 1894. (EI)

Bowditch, William I., and Sarah R. Bowditch. "To the Women of Brookline—A Letter to the Women of the State on their Right to Vote." 17 June 1879.

"Brandeis for Suffrage." *New York Times* (11 June 1911).

Brewer, David J. "Summing Up the Case for Woman Suffrage." New York: National American Woman Suffrage Association, n.d.

Bruns, Henry Dixon. "Liberty, Male and Female: Statement at the National American Convention." 1903. Reprinted in *HWS*, vol. 5.

Bryan, William Jennings. "An Enemy of Woman Suffrage." *Commoner* 15, no. 9 (September 1915): 4.

———. "Three Great Reforms." *Commoner* 15, no. 12 (December 1915): 5.

———. "Equal Suffrage." *Commoner* 16, no. 3 (March 1916): 10–11.

———. *William Jennings Bryan: Selections*. Edited by Ray Ginger. Indianpolis: Bobbs-Merrill, 1967.

Bush, W. S. "Suffrage in Washington Territory." *Chicago Law Times* 3, no. 1 (January 1889): 47–57.

Carey, Joseph M. "Suffrage Statement at the National American Convention." 1891. Reprinted in *HWS*, vol. 4.

Catt, Carrie Chapman, and Nettie Rogers Schuler. *Woman Suffrage and Politics*. 1923. Reprint. Seattle: University of Washington Press, 1969.

Chadwick, John W. "The Enfranchisement of Women. An Address at the Annual Meeting of the Pennsylvania Woman's Suffrage Society." Philadelphia: Published by the Society, 27 October 1886. (SSL)

Chambers, Raymond, "Why Women Should Vote." Paper presented at the Evanston Political Equality League. Reprinted in *Evanston Press* (19 September 1908). (SL)

Clark, Frederick Converse. "Woman vs. the State." Paper presented at the Century Club of San Francisco, 18 January 1893. Reprinted in *Ann Arbor Register* (1893). (*GERR*)

Clute, Oscar. "Suffrage Statement." Reprinted in *HWS*, vol. 2.

Cobbe, Frances Power. "A Duty of Woman." *WSL* 1, no. 3 (15 October 1888): 1–2.

Cody, William F. [Buffalo Bill]. "Statement in Favor of Women Suffrage." *New York Sun* (3 April 1898).

Curtis, George William. "An Address Vindicating the Right of Woman to the Elective Franchise." N.p.: C. T. Munson, 1858.

———. "Equal Rights for Woman Speech in the Constitutional Convention of New York at Albany, July 19, 1867." Reprinted in *Equal Rights for Women*. Boston: C. K. Whipple, 1869.

———. "Fair Play for Women: An Address before the American Woman-Suffrage Association at Steinway Hall, New York." 12 May 1870. Reprinted in *Orations and Addresses of George William Curtis*, ed. Charles Eliot Norton, vol. 1. New York: Harper & Bros. 1894.

———. "Equal Rights for Women." *WSL* 2, no. 12 (15 January 1889): 1–4.

Davis, Charles. *Why Not Now?* Boston: Badger, 1909.

Davison, John. "Fair Play for Women." Paper presented at the Women Suffrage Convention, Cedar Point, Ohio, 27 June 1911. (WRH)

De Leon, Daniel. "Woman's Suffrage: An Address Delivered by Daniel De Leon Under the Auspices of the Socialist Women of Greater New York." 8 May 1909. (UCD)

Dell, Floyd. "Woman Suffrage." *Masses* 4, no. 1 (July 1912): 3.

———. "Confessions of a Feminist Man." *Masses* 5, no. 6, issue no. 34 (March 1914): 8.

———. "Feminism for Men." *Masses* 5, no. 10, issue no. 38 (July 1914): 19–20.

———. "Adventures in Anti-Land." *Masses* 7, no. 1, issue no. 53 (October–November 1915): 5–7.

———. "Men and Women." *Liberator* (n.d.).

"Denver's Business Men Repudiate Slanderers of Woman's Suffrage." *Denver News* (17 May 1916). (LOC)

Douglass, Frederick. *My Bondage and My Freedom*. 1885. Reprint. New York: Arno, 1968.

———. "Address before Woman Suffrage Association." *WJ* (14 April 1888). Reprinted in *Frederick Douglass on Women's Rights*, ed. Philip S. Foner, Contribution in Afro-American and African Studies, no. 25. Westport, Conn.: Greenwood, 1976.

———. "Address on Men Supporting Women." 1894. Reprinted in *HWS*, vol. 4.

———. *The Life and Writings of Frederick Douglass, 1817–1860*. Edited by Philip S. Foner. 2 vols. New York: International, 1950.

DuBois, W. E. B. "Women." *Horizon* 5, no. 2 (December 1909): 2.

———. "Black Women." *Horizon* 5, no. 4 (February 1910): 4.

———. "The Woman." *Crisis* 2, no. 1 (May 1911): 19–21.

———. "Ohio." *Crisis* 4, no. 4 (August 1912): 181–82.

———. "Suffering Suffragettes." *Crisis* 4, no. 2 (June 1912): 74–77.

———. "Votes for Women." *Crisis* 4, no. 5 (September 1912): 234.

———. "Woman's Suffrage." *Crisis* 4, no. 5 (September 1912): 233.

———. "Votes for Women." *Crisis* 8, no. 4 (August 1914): 179–80.

———. "Votes for Women: A Symposium by Leading Thinkers of Colored America." *Crisis* 10, no. 4 (August 1915): 177.

———. "Woman Suffrage." *Crisis* 9, no. 6 (April 1915): 285.

———. "Woman Suffrage." *Crisis* 11, no. 1 (November 1915): 29–30.

———. "The Ballot." *Crisis* 17, no. 2 (December 1918): 62.

———. *Darkwater: Voices from Behind the Veil.* New York: Schocken, 1920.

———. "Sex Equality." *Crisis* 19, no. 3 (January 1920): 106.

———. "Triumph." *Crisis* 20, no. 6 (October 1920): 261.

———. "Woman Suffrage." *Crisis* 19, no. 5 (March 1920): 234.

Eaton, William J. "A Plea for Woman's Suffrage." N.d. (SL)

Ellis, A. Caswell, "Why Men Need Equal Suffrage for Women." In *War Messages to the American People,* no. 3. New York: National Woman Suffrage Publishing Co., [1918].

Emerson, Ralph Waldo. "A Reasonable Reform." *WJ* (26 March 1881). Reprinted in *The Early Lectures of Ralph Waldo Emerson,* ed. Stephen E. Wicker and Robert E. Spiller. Cambridge, Mass.: Harvard University Press, 1959–72.

Foulke, William Dudley. "Hon. Wm. Dudley Foulke on Equal Rights: Speech at the American Woman Suffrage Association in Washington, D.C., 18 February 1890." *WSL* 3, no. 7 (15 May 1890): 1–3.

Fowler, Nathaniel Clark, Jr. *Principle of Suffrage.* New York: Sully & Kleintech, 1916. (*GERR*)

"Freedom for Men!" *Masses* 5, no. 2 (November 1913): 18.

Garrison, William Lloyd. *The Letters of William Lloyd Garrison.* Edited by Walter M. Merrill, 6 vols. Cambridge, Mass.: Harvard University Press, 1971–81.

Gibbon, Gen. John. "Why Women Should Have the Ballot." *North American Review* 163, no. 476 (July 1896): 91–97.

Gregg, David. "Dr. Gregg on Equal Rights." *WSL* 5, no. 3 (May 1892): 1–4.

Hale, General Irving. "General Hale on Colorado Women's Votes." Political Equality Pamphlet Series, vol. 3, no. 8. Warren, Ohio: National American Woman Suffrage Association, 1909.

Harrah, C. C. "The Equal-Rights Banner." In "Song Leaflet For Woman Suffrage, W.C.T.U., and Other Reform Meetings." *WSL* 2, no. 32 (15 November 1889).

Heaton, George N. "Ballots for the Beautiful; or Words for Woman Suffrage." Privately printed, 1896. (SL, Woman Suffrage Collection)

Henderson, Charles. "Statement to Suffrage Convention." 1907. Reprinted in *HWS,* vol. 5.

Hertwig, John George. "Woman Suffrage: Equal Rights to All in All Matters of Public Concern." Washington, D.C.: Eckler, 1883. (URL)

Heywood, Ezra H. "Statement to Suffrage Convention." 1870. Reprinted in *HWS,* vol. 2.

Hillyer, C. J. "Woman Suffrage: Speech Delivered in the Nevada State Assembly." 16 February 1869. Carson City, Nev.: Henry Mighels, 1869. (BL)

———. *The Winning of Nevada for Woman Suffrage.* Carson City: Nevada Printing Co., 1916. (*GERR*)

Hoar, Sen. George F. "Women's Right and the Public Welfare: Remarks to the Massachusetts Legislature." *Woman's Suffrage Tracts,* no. 6 (14 April 1869). Boston: C. K. Whipple. (*GERR*)

———. "Report to the Senate." 1 February 1879. Reprinted in *HWS,* vol. 3.

———. "Woman's Co-operation Essential to Pure Politics." *WSL* 1, no. 7 (1 November 1888): 1–4.

———. "Women and the State." *WSL* 4, no. 12 (December 1891): 1–4.

———. "The Right and Expediency of Woman Suffrage." *Century Magazine* 48 (August 1894): 605–13.

Howard, Clifford. "Why Man Needs Woman's Ballot." *Los Angeles Graphic* ("Woman Pamphlets"), no. 2 (1912).

Howard, Frank. "We'll Show You When We Come To Vote." N.d. (JHL)

Howe, Frederic C. "Frederick C. Howe on Suffrage." *Political Equality Leaflet.* National American Woman Suffrage Association, 1906. Reprinted in *HWS,* vol. 5.

———. "What The Ballot Will Do For Women

And For Men." *Colliers'* (1911). Reprint. New York: National American Woman Suffrage Association, 1912.

"How it Feels to be the Husand of a Suffragette." By "Him." New York: Doran, 1915. (SL)

Hoyt, John. "Thirteen Years' Experience of Woman Suffrage in Wyoming." *WSL* 3, no. 11 (1 November 1890).

Hughes, Charles E. "Women's Interest in the Big Questions of the Day." *Woman's Home Companion* 43, no. 11 (November 1916). (LOC)

Illinois Equal Suffrage Association. *The Suffrage Dime Speaker*. Rockford, Ill.: Glen & Kneeland, 1893.

Journal and Debates of the Constitutional Convention of the State of Wyoming at Cheyenne, 2–3 September 1889. Cheyenne: Daily Sun Book and Job Printing, 1893.

Kent, William. "Concerning Woman Suffrage From a Man's Viewpoint: Speech of August 31, 1913 in Washington, D.C." *Congressional Record*. 63d Cong., 1st sess., 1913. Vol. 5, pt. 7.

Laidlaw, Harriet Burton. *Twenty-Five Answers to the Antis*. New York: National American Woman Suffrage Association, 1912. (SSL, Ethel Dreier Papers)

Leigh, Robert Devore. "More than the Vote: the Woman and Her City." New York: Woman's Press, 1920. (*GERR*)

———. "A Spur to the Reluctant Voter." New York: Woman's Press, 1920. (*GERR*)

Lindsey, Judge Ben B. "Judge Lindsey on Suffrage." Political Equality Pamphlet Series, vol. 1, no. 5. Warren, Ohio: National American Woman Suffrage Association, July 1904.

———. "Judge Lindsey on Woman Suffrage in the West." *New York Times* (7 February 1909): 5.

———. "If I Were a Woman." New York: National American Woman Suffrage Association, 1912.

———. "The Voice of Colorado." *Harper's Weekly* 60, no. 3046 (8 May 1915): 450. (SSL)

———. "Woman Suffrage in Colorado." N.d. (LOC)

Livermore, Daniel P. *Arguments Against Woman Suffrage, by Rev. H. M. Dexter, Carefully Examined and Completely Answered*. Boston: Lee & Shepherd, 1885. (*GERR*)

———. *Female Warriors*. In *The Ballot and the Bullet*, comp. Carrie Chapman Catt. National American Woman Suffrage Association. Philadelphia: A. J. Ferris, 1897.

London, Meyer. "Woman Suffrage." *Congressional Record*. 65th Cong., 1st sess., 1917. Vol. 53, pt. 7.

Long, John D. "No Distinction of Sex in the Right to Vote: An Address Delivered October 20, 1885 at Melrose, Massachusetts." *WSL* 1, no. 11 (1 January 1889).

McCullough, Frank H. "Woman and The Home." Chicago: Chicago Political Equality League, 1912. (SL)

McGraw, Lou. "Annual Report of the Legislative and Congressional Chairman of the Illinois Equal Suffrage Association." Chicago, 7–9 October 1920. (SL)

MacKaye, Percy. "Hymn For Equal Suffrage." In *The Present Hour: A Book of Poems*. New York: Macmillan, 1914.

Massachusetts State Branch American Federation of Labor. "Organized Labor Endorses Equal Suffrage." 1914.

Minor, Francis. "Woman's Legal Right to the Ballot, An Argument in Support of." *Forum* 2 (December 1886): 351–62. (SSL)

———. "Woman's Political Status." *Forum* 9 (April 1890): 150–58.

Morrow, Edwin. "Message to the Legislature in Support of Ratification." [1919.] Reprinted in *HWS*, vol. 6.

Morton, Senator. P. "Suffrage Statement." Reprinted in *HWS*, 2: 549–52.

Munger, George G. *Shall Women Vote? An Argument in Favor of Woman Suffrage*. New York: L. K. Strouse, 1882. (*GERR*)

Murray, John F. "Equal Suffrage Resolution Proposal to the National Education Association." N.d. (NHS)

———. "Give Women the Ballot." N.d. (NHS)

National American Woman Suffrage Association. "Woman Suffrage Endorsed by The American Federation of Labor." *Political Equality Leaflet*. [1908.]

———. "Prominent Speakers in Favor of Woman Suffrage." N.d.

Osborne, Edmund Burke. "A Monologue on Equal Suffrage." *Newark Evening News* (19 October 1913).

———. "The Proof of the Woman Suffrage Pudding is the Eating of It." *Newark Evening News* (17 July 1913).

Palmer, Thomas W. "Resolution for Suffrage." 6 February 1885. Reprinted in *HWS*, vol. 4.

———. "The Woman Voter Hits the Color Line." *Nation* 111 (6 October 1920). Reprinted in *The Black Man and the American Dream*, ed. June Sochen. Chicago: Quadrangle, 1971.

Phelan, Raymond V. "Democracy Demands Woman Suffrage." Warren, Ohio: National American Woman Suffrage Association, 1909.

Pillsbury, Parker. "Statement at Suffrage Convention." 1870. Reprinted in *HWS*, vol. 3.

Pittman, Key. "Mr. Hughes on Suffrage." *Congressional Record*. 64th Cong., 1st sess., 1916. Vol. 8, pt. 12.

Rainsford, William S. "Why Women Should Vote." New York: Ronald's, n.d.

Randolph, A. Phillip. "The Pickets of the White House." *Messenger* 2, no. 1 (January 1918), 8.

———. "Woman Suffrage and the *Messenger*." *Messenger* 2, no. 1 (January 1918): 9.

"Reform Rabbis on Women's Suffrage." In *The American Jewish Woman: A Documentary History, 1654–1980*, ed. Jacob R. Marcus. New York: KTAV, 1981.

The Remonstrance (1890). (SL)

Richardson, Willis. "The Deacon's Awakening: A Play in One Act." *Crisis* 21, no. 1 (1 November 1920): 10–15.

Roe, Clifford G. "What Women Might Do with the Ballot." New York: National American Woman Suffrage Association, n.d. (URL)

Ryckman, J. H. "Thirty-four Reasons Why I Believe in Votes for Women." *California Social Democrat* (30 September 1911).

Shafroth, John F. "Should Woman Have Equal Suffrage?" Statement before the Committee on Woman Suffrage of the United State's Senate on Senate Joint Resolution 81. Washington, D.C.: U.S. Government Printing Office, 1910. (SSL)

———. "Remarks on the Equal Suffrage Amendment." *Congressional Record*. 64th Cong., 1st sess., 1916. Vo. 53, pt. 7.

Shurter, Edwin DuBois, ed. *Woman Suffrage: Bibliography and Selected Arguments. Bulletin of the University of Texas*, no. 233. Austin: University of Texas, 1 June 1912.

Steunenberg, Frank. "Statement." 1900. Reprinted in *HWS*, vol. 4.

Stevens, Isaac N. *An American Suffragette*. New York: William Rickey, 1911.

Strong, Josiah, ed. "Woman Suffrage." *Social Progress Studies in The Gospel of the Kingdom* 4, no. 6 (June 1912): 86–87.

Strong, Josiah, and W. D. P. Bliss, eds. "Suffrage for Women." *Social Progress Studies in The Gospel of the Kingdom* 6, no. 2 (February 1914): 26–27.

Sylvis, William H. "Female Suffrage." In *The Life, Speeches, Labors and Essays of William H. Sylvis*, ed. James C. Sylvis. Philadelphia: Claxton, Remsen & Haffelfinger, 1872.

Taft, William Howard. "Votes for Women." *Saturday Evening Post* 188, no. 11 (11 September 1915).

Thomas, Thaddeus P. "Why Equal Suffrage Has Been a Success: Address to the Equal Suffrage League of Baltimore." Hartford: Connecticut Woman Suffrage Association, [1910].

Tilton, Theodore. "A Law Against Women." *New*

York Independent (1866). Reprinted in *HWS*, vol. 3.

———. "Speech at 11th National Woman's Rights Convention, New York, 10 May 1866." Reprinted in *HWS*, 2:154–67.

———. "Letter to Henry Ward Beecher." 11 May 1870. Reprinted in *HWS*, vol. 3.

———. "The Constitution: A Title Deed to Woman's Franchise." *Golden Age Tracts*, no. 2. New York: Golden Age, 1871. (SSL)

———. "The Rights of Women: A Letter to Horace Greeley." *Golden Age Tracts*, no. 1. New York: Golden Age, 1871.

Train, George Francis. *Championship of Woman: Thirty Speeches During Two Weeks Delivered in All Parts of Kansas*. Leavenworth, Kans.: Prescott & Hume, 1867.

———. "Statement at Suffrage Convention." 1870. Reprinted in *HWS*, vol. 2.

Twenty Opinions on Woman Suffrage by Prominent Californians. November 1896. (SFPL)

U.S. Congress. "Woman Suffrage Speeches in the House of Representatives for Tuesday, January 12, 915." *Congressional Record*. 63d Cong., 2d sess., 1915. Vol. 55, pt. 2.

U.S. Congress. Senate. Committee on Woman Suffrage. *Proposing an Amendment to the Constitution of the United States to Secure the Right of Woman Suffrage, with Minority Report*. 47th Cong., 1st sess., 1882. S. Rept. 686.

Waite, Charles B. "Suffrage a Right of Citizenship." *Chicago Law Times* 1, no. 3 (July 1887): 3.

Waite, Davis H., and Lorenzo Crounse. "Woman Suffrage in Practice." *North American Review* 158. no. 451 (1894): 737–41.

Walker, Timothy. "The Legal Condition of Women." *Western Law Journal* 1, no. 4 (January 1849): 145–59.

Weisman, Henry. "On Woman Suffrage." N.p.: German-American Committee of the Woman Suffrage Party, [1915].

Wendte, W. C. "Statement at Suffrage Convention." 1870. Reprinted in *HWS*, vol. 2.

Wentworth, Franklin H. "The Woman's Portion: An Address Delivered in Carnegie Hall, New York City, Sunday, February 27, 1918, Under the Auspices of the Women of the Socialist Party." New York: Socialist Co-operative Publishing Associaton, 1910. (*GERR*)

White, John D. "Political Rights of Women." *Congressional Record*. 48th Cong., 1st sess., 1884. Vol. 15, pt. 6.

Wilder, Amos. "Claims of Woman Suffrage: An Address Delivered to the Joint Legislative Committees on State Affairs." Madison, Wisc., 13 March 1895.

Willcox, Hamilton. "Debaters Guide for Friends of Woman Suffrage—Showing How to Win Debate and Carry Audience from 35 Years Experience in the Cause." New York: Published by the author, 1890. (*GERR*)

———. "Freedom's Conquest: the Great Spread of Woman Suffrage." 1890. (*GERR*)

Willcox, James K. H. "Suffrage a Right, Not a Privilege." Speech before the Universal Franchise Association, Washington, D.C., 19 July 1867. Washington, D.C.: Universal Franchise Association, 1867.

———. "Call for the First Woman Suffrage Convention in Washington; Twenty-One Years Since." Washington, D.C.: Universal Franchise Association, 1868.

———. "Wyoming: The True Cause and Splendid Fruits of Woman Suffrage There." New York, 1890. (UCB)

Williams, Jesse Lynch. *A Common-Sense View of Woman Suffrage*. Warren, Ohio: National American Woman Suffrage Association, [1910].

———. "A Woman's Last Word." *Harper's Weekly* 40, no. 4036 (8 May 1915): 451.

Wilson, J. Stitt. "After Suffrage—What?" *California Social Democrat* (13 June 1914).

———. "To the Women Voters of Berkeley." *City for the People* 1, no. 3 (21 April 1915): 3. (UCB)

Wilson, Woodrow. "Remarks at the National American Convention." 1916. Reprinted in *HWS*, vol. 5.

Winston, Edward M., ed. "Clergymen for Woman Suffrage." *WSL* 2, no. 21 (1 June 1889): 1–2.

"Would Extending the Ballot to Women Tend to Better City Government? Well-Known Men Express Varying Views and Give their Reasons for Their Opinions." *New York Times* (9 January 1910): sec. 5, pp. 1–2.

Yale University Debating Team. *A Discussion of Woman Suffrage By the Yale University Debating Teams in the 1914 Triangular Debates with Harvard and Princeton*. Yale University Debating Association Handbook, no. 1. New Haven, Conn.: Yale Co-Operative Corp., 1915.

Organizing Men for Feminism: The Men's League for Woman Suffrage

"Anti-Suffrage Arguments Answered." [1915.] (SL)

Atkinson, Wilmer, President, Pennsylvania's Men's League for Woman Suffrage. "A Statement, A Comparison, And An Appeal," Philadelphia, June 1914. (SL)

———. "Defining the Attitude of the Pennsylvania Men's League Toward Other Woman Suffrage Organizations and Toward the Cause." Philadelphia, April 1916. (SL)

Boyce, Neith, and Hutchins Hapgood. "Enemies." In *The Provincetown Plays*, ed. George Cram Cook and Frank Shay. Cincinnati: Stewart Kidd, 1921. (BL)

California Men's League for Woman Suffrage. "Constitution." [1912.] (CHSL)

College Equal Suffrage League of Northern California. "Men Supporting Suffrage." In *Winning Equal Suffrage in California*. San Francisco: National College Equal Suffrage League, [1913].

Creel, George. "Chivalry versus Justice: Why the Women of the Nation Demand the Right to Vote." *Pictorial Review*. Reprint. New York: National Woman Suffrage Publishing Co., 1915.

———. "What Have Women Done with the Vote?" New York: National Woman Suffrage Publishing Co., 1915.

Creel, George, and Ben B. Lindsey. "Measuring Up Equal Suffrage." *Delineator* (February 1911). (LOC)

Dewey, John. *The Middle Works of John Dewey, 1899–1924*, vols. 6, 7. Edited by Jo Ann Boydston. Carbondale and Edwardsville: Southern Illinois University Press, 1978–79.

"Dynamite, Cries Steffens. Tells Suffragists Women Should Not Hesitate to Destroy." *New York Times* (13 January 1914): sec. 2, p. 5.

Eastman, Max. "Woman's Suffrage and Sentiment." New York: Equal Franchise Society, 1909.

———. "Democracy and Women: Speech to the National American Convention." 1910. Reprinted in *HWS*, vol. 4.

———. "Is Woman Suffrage Important?" New York: Men's League for Woman Suffrage, 1912.

———. "Values of the Vote." Address before the Men's League for Woman Suffrage of New York, 21 March 1912. New York: Men's League for Woman Suffrage, 1912.

———. "Values of the Vote." New York: Men's League for Woman Suffrage, 1914.

———. "What Do You Know About This?" *Masses* 5, no. 6, issue no. 34 (March 1914): 7.

"Expects 10,000 Men in Suffrage March: James Lees Laidlaw Has 5,000 Enrolled Already for Next Saturday's Parade." *New York Times* (20 October 1915).

"George Foster Peabody Asks Five Definite Questions and Suggests the Answers." *New York Times* (14 February 1915).

"In the 'Men's Brigade': Pennsylvanians to March." *New York Times* (5 May 1912): 22.

"Iowa Men Form League to Help Women Win." 29 January 1916. (SHSI)

Laidlaw, James L. "Flyer for Men Marchers in Woman Suffrage Parade." 1 May 1915.

———. "Letter to George Foster Peabody on Inviting President Woodrow Wilson to be Honorable Chairman of the Men's League for Woman Suffrage." 21 November 1916. (LOC)

Massachusetts Men's League for Woman Suffrage. "Massachusetts Men's League for Woman Suffrage." Boston, 24 February 1910. (SL)

———. "Statement of Purpose." 22 February 1912. (SL)

"Men for Suffrage Parade." *New York Times* (3 May 1911): sec. 2, p. 5.

"Men in Suffrage Parade." *New York Times* (24 April 1913): sec. 8, p. 7.

"Men Plan Suffrage Parade." *New York Times* (28 June 1912): sec. 9, p. 4.

Ohio Men's League for Equal Suffrage. "Petition for a Constitutional Amendment." 23 September 1914. (OSU)

Olmsted, A. S. "Letter to the President and Fellows of Harvard College." 1913. (HL)

"Parade of Women as Well as Men." *New York Times* (19 July 1912).

Pennsylvania Men's League for Woman Suffrage. "Pennsylvania Men's League: A Call to Action—The Great Parade—Mass Meeting Victory at the Polls!" N.d. (SL)

Pinchot, Amos. "Team Work." *Harper's Weekly* 40, no. 3046 (8 May 1915): 450.

"Real Beauty Show in League Pageant: Handsomest of Their Sex Chosen for Suffrage Allegorical Scene." *New York Times* (18 April 1914): sec. 11, p. 5.

Strong, John F. A. "Letter to Thomas Hotchkiss of New York." 16 October 1915. (WRC)

"Watch For Blue Button. Men Suffragists Wearing One Will Give Up Seats to Women." *New York Times* (21 July 1913): sec. 2, p. 7.

Postsuffrage Struggles

Adams, James Truslow. "James Truslow Adams Endorses the Equal Rights Amendment." National Woman's Party, [1930]. (SL)

Arlen, Harold, and E. Y. Harburg. "The Eagle and Me." In *Bloomer Girl*. New York: Chappell, 1944.

Burt, Struthers. "Men Speak for the Equal Rights Amendment." National Woman's Party, [1943]. (SSL)

Cousins, Norman. "The Women Are Coming." *Saturday Review of Literature* 31, no. 29 (17 July 1948): 18.

Hepbron, James M. "Women on Juries." *Baltimore Evening Sun* [29 May 1930].

Schlesinger, Arthur Meier. "Arthur Meier Schlesinger Endorses the Equal Rights Amendment." National Woman's Party, [1930]. (SL)

Swing, Raymond Gram. "Raymond Gram Swing Endorses the Equal Rights Amendment." National Woman's Party, [1930]. (SL)

Walsh, Richard J. "Men Speak for the Equal Rights Amendment." National Woman's Party, [1930]. (SL)

"Why Not Equality for Women?" *New York World Telegram* (14 December 1943).

Secondary Sources

Ashby, LeRoy. *William Jennings Bryan: Champion of Democracy*. Boston: Twayne, 1987.

Bartlett, Irving H. *Wendell Phillips: Brahmin Radical*. Boston: Beacon, 1961.

———. *Wendell and Ann Phillips: The Community of Reform, 1840–1880*. New York: Norton, 1979.

Becker, Susan. "An Intellectual History of the National Woman's Party, 1920–1941." Ph.D. diss., Case Western Reserve University, 1975.

———. *The Origins of the Equal Rights Amendment: American Feminism between the Wars*. Westport, Conn.: Greenwood, 1981.

Buechler, Steven M. *The Transformation of the Woman Suffrage Movement: The Case of Illinois, 1850–1920*. New Brunswick, N.J.: Rutgers University Press, 1986.

———. "Elizabeth Boynton Harbert and the

Woman Suffrage Movement." *Signs* 13, no. 1 (1987): 78–97.

———. "Conceptualizing Radicalism and Transformation in Social Movements: The Case of the Woman Suffrage Movement." Mankato State University, 1989. Typescript.

———. *Women's Movements in the United States*. New Brunswick, N.J.: Rutgers University Press, 1991.

Cott, Nancy. *The Grounding of Modern Feminism*. New Haven, Conn.: Yale University Press, 1987.

Davis, Paulina, ed. *A History of the National Woman's Rights Movement for Twenty Years, With the Proceedings of the Decade Meeting held at Apollo Hall, October 20, 1870, From 1850 to 1870*. New York: Journeymen Printer's Co-operative Association, 1871.

DuBois, Ellen. *Feminism and Suffrage: The Emergence of an Independent Woman's Movement in America, 1848–1869*. Ithaca, N.Y.: Cornell University Press, 1978.

DuBois, W. E. B. *The Autobiography of W. E. B. DuBois*. New York: International Publishers Co., 1968.

Edelstein, Tilden G. *Strange Enthusiasm: A Life of Thomas Wentworth Higginson*. New York: Atheneum, 1970.

Flexner, Eleanor. *Century of Struggle: The Woman's Rights Movement in the United States*. New York: Atheneum, 1970.

Forster, Margaret. *Significant Sisters: The Grassroots of Active Feminism, 1839–1939*. New York: Knopf, 1984.

Frauenglass, W. "Attitudes towards Suffrage in Popular Humor Magazines, 1911–1920." Ph.D. diss., New York University, 1967.

Hersh, Blanche. *The Slavery of Sex: Feminist-Abolitionists in America*. Urbana: University of Illinois Press, 1978.

Hewitt, Nancy. *Women's Activism and Social Change: Rochester, New York, 1822–1872*. Ithaca, N.Y.: Cornell University Press, 1984.

Higginson, Mary Thatcher. *Thomas Wentworth Higginson: The Story of His Life*. Boston: Houghton Mifflin, 1914.

Johnson, Donald Bruce, and Kirk H. Porter, eds. *National Party Platforms, 1840–1956*, vol. 1. Urbana: University of Illinois Press, 1956.

———. *National Party Platforms, 1960–1976*, vol. 2. Urbana: University of Illinois Press, 1978.

Klein, Ethel. *Gender Politics*. Cambridge, Mass.: Harvard University Press, 1984.

Kraditor, Aileen. *The Ideas of the Woman Suffrage Movement, 1890–1920*. New York: Norton, 1981.

Kugler, Israel. *From Ladies to Women: The Organized Struggle for Woman's Rights in the Reconstruction Era*. New York: Greenwood, 1989.

Lerner, Gerda. *The Grimké Sisters from South Carolina: Pioneers for Women's Rights and Abolition*. New York: Schocken, 1971.

Levine, Lawrence. *Defender of the Faith: William Jennings Bryan; the Last Decade, 1915–1925*. New York: Oxford University Press, 1965.

Livermore, Mary A. "Does the Ideal Husband Exist?" *North American Review*, 1895. Reprinted in *HWS*, vol. 5.

Lutz, Alma. *Crusade for Freedom: Women of the Anti-Slavery Movement*. Boston: Beacon, 1968.

McPherson, James. "Abolitionists, Woman Suffrage, and the Negro, 1865–1869." *Mid-America: An Historical Review* 47, no. 1 (January 1965): 40–47.

Marable, Manning. *W. E. B. DuBois, Black Radical Democrat*. Boston: Twayne, 1986.

Meyer, Howard N. *Colonel of the Black Regiment*. New York: Norton, 1967.

Myerson, Joel. *Theodore Parker: A Descriptive Bibliography*. New York: Garland, 1981.

Noun, Louise R. *Strong Minded Women: The Emergence of the Woman Suffrage Movement in Iowa*. Ames: Iowa State University Press, 1986.

O'Neil, William. *Everyone Was Brave: The Rise*

and Fall of Feminism in America. Chicago: Quadrangle, 1969.

———. *The Last Romantic: A Life of Max Eastman*. New York: Oxford University Press, 1978.

Porter, Kirk H. *A History of Suffrage in the United States*. Chicago: University of Chicago Press, 1918.

Rampersad, Arnold. *The Art and Imagination of W. E. B. DuBois*. Cambridge, Mass.: Harvard University Press, 1976.

Ripley, C. Peter, ed. *The Black Abolitionist Papers*. 2 vols. Chapel Hill: University of North Carolina Press, 1985–87.

Robinson, Harriet Jane Hanson. *Massachusetts in the Women's Suffrage Movement*. Boston: Roberts Bros., 1881.

Rupp, Leila J., and Verta Taylor. *Survival in the Doldrums: The American Women's Rights Movement, 1945 to the 1960s*. New York: Oxford University Press, 1987.

Salvatore, Nick. *Eugene V. Debs: Citizen and Socialist*. Urbana: University of Illinois Press, 1982.

Scharf, Louis, and Joan M. Jensen. *Decades of Discontent: The Women's Movement, 1920–1940*. Westport, Conn.: Greenwood, 1983.

Severn, Bill. *Free but Not Equal: How Women Won the Right to Vote*. New York: Julian Messner, 1967.

Silber, Irwin. *Songs America Voted By*. Harrisburg, Pa.: Stackpole, 1971.

Sillen, Samuel. *Women against Slavery*. New York: Masses and Mainstream, 1955.

Simmons, William J. *Men of Mark: Eminent, Progressive and Rising: The American Negro: His History and Literature*. 1887. Reprint. New York: Arno, 1968.

Strauss, Sylvia. *"Traitors to the Masculine Cause": The Men's Campaigns for Women's Rights*. Westport, Conn.: Greenwood, 1982.

Terrell, Mary Church. *A Colored Woman in a White World*. Washington, D.C.: Ransdell, 1940.

Tuttleton, James. *Thomas Wentworth Higginson*. Boston: Twayne, 1978.

Wagner, Sally Roesch. "Parker Pillsbury: A Forgotten Anti-Sexist Man." *M.*, no. 11 (Winter 1983–84): 22–23.

———. "William Lloyd Garrison." *M.*, no. 13 (Fall 1984): 20–21.

———. "Suffrage in the 1870's and Anti-Pornography in the 1980's." Pts. 1, 2. *Changing Men*, no. 15 (Fall 1985): 26–27; and no. 16 (Summer 1986).

———. *A Time of Protest: Suffragists Challenge the Republic, 1870–1887*. Carmichael, Calif.: Sky Carrier, 1988.

———. "How the East Was Won: The 1915 Report on Woman's Suffrage of the New York Men's League." *Changing Men*, no. 20 (Winter-Spring 1989): 40–41.

———. "Woman's Suffrage in South Dakota." *Changing Men*, no. 21 (Winter-Spring 1990): 39–40.

Ward, William E. "Charles Lenox Remond: Black Abolitionist, 1838–1873." Ph.D. diss., Clark University, 1977.

Ware, Susan. *Beyond Suffrage: Women in the New Deal*. Cambridge, Mass.: Harvard University Press, 1981.

———. *Holding Their Own: American Women in 1930*. Boston: Twayne, 1982.

PART V: THE STRUGGLE FOR SOCIAL EQUALITY, 1850–1960

Primary Sources

Social Equality for Women

Bellamy, Edward. *Equality*. New York: D. Appleton, 1897.

Binder, Rudolph M. "Preliminaries to the Woman Problem." *Social Progress Studies in The Gospel of the Kingdom* 10, no. 7 (April 1918): 109–12.

Brisbane, Albert. *The Social Destiny of Man; or, Association and Reorganization of Industry*. Philadelphia: C. F. Stollmeyer, 1840.

Bullock, Alexander H. "The Centennial Situation of Woman: Address at the Commencement Anniversary of Mount Holyoke Seminary." Worcester, Mass.: Charles Hamilton, 1876. (SSL)

Cronau, Rudolph. *Woman Triumphant: The Story of Her Struggles for Freedom, Education and Political Rights*. New York: Published by the author, 1919.

Crummell, Alex. "The Black Woman of the South: Her Neglects and Her Needs—Address before the Freedman's Aid Society, Methodist Episcopal Church, Ocean Grove, New Jersey, August 15th, 1883." Reprinted in *Africa and America: Addresses and Discourses*. Springfield, Mass.: Willey, 1891.

Dell, Floyd. "Feminism and Literature." *Chicago Evening Post* (15 September 1911).

———. "The Quality of Woman." *Chicago Evening Post* (15 December 1911).

———. *Women as World Builders: Studies in Modern Feminism*. Chicago: Forbes, 1913.

———. "Socialism and Feminism: A Reply to Belfort Bax." *New Review* 2 [1914]: 349–53.

———. "A Discontented Woman." *Masses* 7, no. 1, issue no. 53 (October–November 1915): 11.

———. "The Nature of Woman." *Masses* 8, no. 3, issue no. 55 (January 1916): 16.

———. *Moon-calf*. New York: Knopf, 1920.

———. "Feminism and Socialism." *New Masses* (1921): 352.

———. *Homecoming: An Autobiography*. New York: Farrar & Rinehart, 1933.

Dewey, John. *The Later Works of John Dewey, 1925–1953*, vol. 6. Edited by Jo Ann Boydston. Carbondale: Southern Illinois University Press, 1985.

DuBois, W. E. B. "The Damnation of Women." In *Darkwater: Voices from Within the Veil*. New York: Schocken, 1920.

Foulke, William Dudley. "Men's View of Women's Clubs: A Symposium of Men Who Are Recognized Leaders in the Philanthropic and Reform Movements of America." *Federation Bulletin* 2, no. 9 (June 1905): 291–96. (LOC)

Hapgood, Hutchins. "Women in Society." [1915.] (SSL)

———. *Women and Men*. New York: Harper & Bros., 1888. (*GERR*)

Higginson, Thomas Wentworth. "Women and Her Wishes." New York: Fowlers & Wells, 1853.

Heywood, Ezra H. "Uncivil Liberty: An Essay to Sow the Injustice and Impolicy of Ruling Woman Without Her Consent." Princeton, N.J.: Cooperative Publishing Co., 1872. (NYPL)

Hoyt, John W. "On the Revolutionary Movement Among Women." *Transactions of the Wisconsin Academy of Sciences, Arts and Letters* 3 (1875–76): 161–76.

Hughes, Langston. "The Negro Mother." In *The Negro Mother and Other Dramatic Recitations*. New York: Golden Stair, 1931.

Hutchins, Harry. "The Individual Responsibility of College Women." 1912. (BHL)

Krows, Arthur Edwin. "The Feminist Movement as a Dramatic Theme." *New York Dramatic Mirror* 71, no. 1848 (20 May 1914): 1.

Montagu, Ashley. "The Intellectual and Bodily Superiority of Women." In *The Natural Superiority of Women*. New York: Macmillan, 1952.

Phillips, Wendell. "Women." In *Wendell Phillips on Civil Rights and Freedom*, ed. Louis Filler. New York: Hill & Wang, 1965.

Pickens, William. *The New Negro, His Political, Civil and Mental Status*. New York: Neale, 1916.

Randle, Frederick Alanson. *Woman Among the Illustrious: A Lecture*. 3d ed. New York: J. B. Alden, 1890.

Rose, Kenneth. "Excerpts from an Address Outlining Plans for the First Nationwide Planned Parenthood Campaign." February 1947. (SL, Planned Parenthood Papers)

Shakers. "Resolutions Passed at the Convention at Worcester, Mass. on October 25, 1869 Concerning Behavior During the Convention." Worcester, Mass., 1869. (SRL)

Sinclair, Andrew. *The Emancipation of American Women*. New York: Harper & Row, 1966.

Smith, Paul Jordan. *The Soul of Woman: An Interpretation of the Philosophy of Feminism*. San Francisco: Paul Elder, 1916. (*GERR*)

Smith, Thomas Robert, ed. *The Woman Question*. New York: Boni & Liveright, 1923.

Terrell, Robert. "The New Era Women." [1920.] (LOC)

Marriage and Divorce Reforms

Blackwell, Henry Brown. *Loving Warriors: Selected Letters of Lucy Stone and Henry B. Blackwell, 1853–1893*. Edited by Leslie Wheeler. New York: Dial, 1981.

Blackwell, Henry Brown. "Obey." *WJ* (May 1874)

Dell, Floyd. *The Outline of Marriage*. New York: American Birth Control League. [1916]. (NL)

———. "Can Men and Women be Friends?" In *Our Changing Morality*, ed. Freda Kirchway. New York: Albert & Charles Boni, 1924.

———. *Love in the Machine Age*. New York: Farrar & Rinehart, 1930.

Ecob, James H. "Woman in the Home." *Social Progress Studies in The Gospel of the Kingdom* 4, no. 49 (April 1912): 49–50.

Foote, Edward Bliss, Jr., M.D. *Divorce*. New York: Murray Hill, 1884.

Greeley, Horace. "Marriage and Divorce: A Discussion between Horace Greeley and Robert Dale Owen in the *New York Tribune*, March and April 1860." In *Recollections of A Busy Life* . . . . New York: J. B. Ford, 1868.

Hapgood, Hutchins. "Learning and Marriage." 1915. (SSL)

Lindsey, Ben B. "Wisdom For Parents." In *Sex in Civilization*, eds. V. F. Calverton and S. D. Schmalhausen. Garden City, N.Y.: Garden City Publishing, 1929.

———. "A Word About Divorce and Birth Control." N.d. (LOC)

Lindsey, Ben B., and Wainright Evans. *The Companionate Marriage*. New York: Boni & Liveright, 1927.

Noyes, John Humphrey. "Slavery and Marriage: A Conversation Between Judge North, Major South and Mr. Free Church." 1850. (WRC)

Parker, Theodore. "Marriage and Divorce." In *Divorce: A Review of the Subject from a Scientific Standpoint*, ed. Edward B. Foote. New York: Murray Hill, 1887.

Woodruff, Charles. *Legalized Prostitution; or, Marriage as It Is, and Marriage as It Should Be, Philosophically Considered*. Boston: Bela Marsh, 1862.

"Sex Rights," Sexuality, and Birth Control

Baber, Ray Erwin. "Birth Control: A Balance Sheet." *Forum* 32 (November 1932): 294–99.

Cooper, James F., M.D. "Some Reasons For the Popularity of the Birth Control Movement."

New York: American Birth Control League, [1920]. (SSL)

Densmore, Emmet. *Sex Equality: A Solution of the Woman Problem*. New York: Funk & Wagnalls, 1907.

Eastman, Max. "Revolutionary Birth Control." *Masses* 6, no. 10, issue no. 50 (July 1915): 21–22.

Eliot, Dr. Charles. "The Double Standard on Chastity." *The Gospel of the Kingdom* 1, no. 2 (November 1908): 10–16.

Foote, Edward Bliss, Jr., M.D. *Medical Common Sense*. New York: Murray Hill, 1864.

———. *Dr. Foote's Letters*. New York: Health Monthly, 1881.

———. *Dr. Foote's Replies to the Alphites Giving Some Cogent Reasons for Believing that Sexual Continence is Not Conducive to Health*. New York: Murray Hill, 1882.

———. *The Radical Remedy in Social Science; Or, Borning Better Babies through Regulating Reproduction by Controlling Conception*. New York: Murray Hill, 1889.

Goldenweiser, Alexander. "Man and Woman as Creators." In *Our Changing Morality*, ed. Freda Kirchway. New York: Albert & Charles Boni, 1924.

Henderson, Charles. "Statement of Suffrage Convention." 1907. Reprinted in *HWS*, 5:198–99.

Himes, Norman. "Next Steps in the Movement." *Birth Control Review* 13, no. 11 (November 1929): 317–19.

———. "The Truth About Birth Control." New York: John Day Pamphlets, 1931.

Hodak, John. "Birth Control." In *The Council*. Salt Lake City, August 1919.

Knowlton, Charles. *Fruits of Philosophy; or, the Private Companion of Adult People*. 1832. Reprint. Mount Vernon, N.Y.: Peter Pauper, 1937.

Lewis, Denslow, M.D. "The Gynecologic Consideration of the Sexual Act." Paper presented at the fiftieth annual meeting of the American Medical Association, Columbus, Ohio, 1899. Chicago: Henry O. Shepard, 1900. Reprinted in *Journal of the American Medical Association* 250, no. 2 (8 July 1983): 222–29.

Mason, Otis Tufton. *Woman's Share in Primitive Culture*. New York and London: D. Appleton, 1894.

Nichols, Thomas. *Esoteric Anthropology*. [1853.] Reprint. New York: Arno, 1972.

Ogburn, William F. "Birth Control and Early Marriage." *Birth Control Review* 10, no. 12 (December 1926): 363–64.

Ross, Edward Alsworth. "The Significance of Increasing Divorce." *Century* (1909).

Sanger, William. "Prostitution." In *A History of Prostitution*. New York: Medical Publishing Co., 1898.

Thomas, W. I. "The Adventitious Character of Woman." *American Journal of Sociology* 12 (July 1906).

———. *Sex and Society*. Chicago: University of Chicago Press, 1907.

———. "The Psychology of Woman's Dress." *American Magazine* 65 (November 1908).

———. "The Mind of Woman." *American Magazine* 67 (December 1908).

———. "Votes for Women." *American Magazine* 68 (July 1909).

———. "Woman and the Occupations." *American Magazine* 68 (September 1909).

———. Statement on suffrage published in "Prominent Speakers in Favor of Woman Suffrage." New York: National American Woman Suffrage Association, n.d.

Trall, R. T. *Sexual Physiology and Hygiene*. New York: Fowler & Wells, 1866.

Veblen, Thorstein. "The Barbarian Status of Women." *American Journal of Sociology* 4 (January 1899). Reprinted in *Essays in Our Changing Order*, ed. Leon Ardzrooni. New York: Viking, 1954.

———. *The Theory of the Leisure Class*. New York: Macmillan, 1899.

Ward, Lester Frank. *Pure Sociology*. New York: Macmillan, 1903.

———. *Applied Sociology*. Boston: Ginn, 1906.

Experimenting with Equality: Greenwich Village, 1900–1920

Broun, Heywood. *Seeing Things at Night*. New York: Harcourt, Brace, 1921.

———. "After Six Years." *New York Telegram* (17 April 1929).

———. *Collected Edition of Heywood Broun*, ed. Heywood Hale Broun. New York: Harcourt, Brace, 1941.

Eastman, Max. "Is the Truth Obscene?" *Masses* 6, no. 6, issue no. 46 (March 1915): 5–6.

———. *Enjoyment of Living*. New York: Harper & Bros., 1948.

Hapgood, Hutchins. *The Spirit of the Ghetto: Studies of the Jewish Quarter of New York*. 1902. Reprint. New York: Schocken, 1966.

Krows, Arthur Edwin. "The Feminist Movement as a Dramatic Theme." *New York Dramatic Mirror* (20 May 1914).

Middleton, George. *Tradition*. New York: Henry Holt, 1913.

———. *Back of the Ballot: A Woman Suffrage Farce in One Act*. New York: Samuel French, 1915.

———. *Criminals, A One-Act Play About Marriage*. New York: B. W. Huebsch, 1915.

———. *Possession With: The Groove, The Unborn, Circles, A Good Woman, The Black Tie; One-Act Plays of Contemporary Life*. New York: H. Holt, 1915.

———. *These Things Are Mine: The Autobiography of a Journeyman Playwright*. New York: Macmillan, 1947.

Middleton, George, and Guy Bolton. *Polly with a Past*. New York: Samuel French, 1923.

Williams, Jesse Lynch. *"And So They Were Married": A Comedy of the New Woman*. New York: Scribner, 1914.

Secondary Sources

Abrahams, Edward. *The Lyrical Left: Randolph Bourne, Alfred Stieglitz and the Origins of Cultural Radicalism in America*. Charlottesville: University Press of Virginia, 1986.

Antler, Joyce ed. *Lucy Sprague Mitchell: The Making of a Modern Woman*. New Haven, Conn.: Yale University Press, 1987.

Banner, Lois. *Women in Modern America: A Brief History*. New York: Harcourt Brace Jovanovich, 1974.

Barker-Benfield, B. A. *The Horrors of the Half Known Life*. New York: Harper & Row, 1976.

Beard, Mary. *America through Women's Eyes*. New York: Macmillan, 1933.

Blair, Karen. *The Clubwoman as Feminist: True Womanhood Redefined, 1868–1914*. New York: Holmes & Meier, 1980.

Blatt, Martin Henry. *Free Love and Anarchism: The Biography of Ezra Heywood*. Champaign: University of Illinois Press, 1989.

Bordin, Ruth. *Women and Temperance: The Quest for Power and Liberty, 1873–1900*. Philadelphia: Temple University Press, 1981.

Buechler, Steven M. *The Transformation of the Woman Suffrage Movement: The Case of Illinois, 1850–1920*. New Brunswick, N.J.: Rutgers University Press, 1986.

Chafe, William Henry. *The American Woman: Her Changing Social, Economic and Political Role, 1920–1970*. New York: Oxford University Press, 1972.

———. *Women and Equality: Changing Patterns in American Culture*. New York: Oxford University Press, 1977.

Chafetz, Janet Saltzman, and Gary Dworkin. "In the Face of Threat: Organized Antifeminism in Comparative Perspective." *Gender and Society* 1 (1987): 31.

Clark, Leadie. *Walt Whitman's Concept of the American Common Man*. New York: Philosophical Library, 1955.

Clinton, Catherine. *The Plantation Mistresses:*

Women's World in the Old South. New York: Pantheon, 1982.

———. *The Other Civil War: American Women in the 19th Century*. New York: Hill & Wang, 1984.

Cohart, Mary, ed. *Unsung Champions of Women*. Albuquerque: Univeristy of New Mexico Press, 1974.

Cook, Blanche Wiesen, ed. *Toward the Great Change: Crystal and Max Eastman on Feminism, Antimilitarism and Revolution*. New York: Garland, 1976.

Cott, Nancy. *The Grounding of Modern Feminism*. New Haven, Conn.: Yale University Press, 1987.

Dash, Joan. *A Life of One's Own: Three Gifted Women and the Men They Married*. New York: Paragon, 1988.

Degler, Carl. "What Ought to Be and What Was: Women's Sexuality in the Nineteenth Century." *American Historical Review* 79, no. 5 (December 1974): 1467–90.

———. *At Odds: Women and the Family from the Revolution to the Present*. New York: Oxford University Press, 1980.

Dubbert, Joe. *A Man's Place: Masculinity in Transition*. Englewood Cliffs, N.J.: Prentice-Hall, 1980.

Evans, Richard. *The Feminists: Women's Emancipation Movements in Europe, America and Australia, 1840–1920*. New York: Barnes & Noble, 1977.

Feldman, David M. *Marital Relations, Birth Control and Abortion in Jewish Law*. New York: Schocken, 1974.

Fishbein, Leslie. *Rebels in Bohemia: The Radicals of The Masses, 1911–917*. Chapel Hill: University of North Carolina Press, 1982.

Forster, Margaret. *Significant Sisters: The Grassroots of Modern Feminism*. New York: Knopf, 1985.

Foster, Lawrence. *Religion and Sexuality: Three American Communal Experiments of the Nineteenth Century*. New York: Oxford University Press, 1981.

Giddings, Paula. *"When and Where I Enter . . .": The Impact of Black Women on Race and Sex in America*. New York: Morrow, 1984.

Gilman, Charlotte Perkins. *The Living of Charlotte Perkins Gilman*. 1935. Reprint. Madison: University of Wisconsin Press, 1990.

Gordon, Linda. *Women's Body, Women's Rights: A Social History of Birth Control in America*. New York: Grossman, 1976.

———. *Heroes of Their Own Lives: The Politics and History of Family Violence*. New York: Viking, 1988.

Hansen, Karen. "'Helped Put in a Quilt': Men's Work and Male Intimacy in Nineteenth-Century New England." *Gender and Society* 3, no. 3 (1989): 334–54.

Hantover, Jeffrey. "The Boy Scouts and the Validation of Masculinity." In *The American Man*, ed. Joseph Pleck and Elizabeth Pleck. Englewood Cliffs, N.J.: Prentice-Hall, 1980.

Harding, Susan. "Family Reform Movements: Recent Feminism and Its Opposition." Michigan Occasional Paper. Ann Arbor: University of Michigan, Women's Studies Program, 1979.

Harrison, C. E. "Prelude to Feminism, 1942–1968." Ph.D. diss., Columbia University, 1982.

Harrison, J. F. C. *Quest for the New Moral World: Robert Owen and the Owenites in Britain and America*. New York: Scribner's, 1969.

Hart, John E. *Floyd Dell*. New York: Twayne, 1971.

Hartman, Mary. "Sexual Crack-Up: The Role of Gender in Western History." Rutgers University, 1984. Typescript.

Hersh, Blanche. *The Slavery of Sex: Feminist-Abolitionists in America*. Urbana: University of Illinois Press, 1978.

Holloway, Emory. "Whitman as a Journalist." *Saturday Review of Literature* 8 (September 1928).

Huff, Ronald P. "Social Christian Clergymen and Feminism during the Progressive Era, 1890–

1920." Ph.D. diss., Union Theological Seminary, 1978.

Hull, Gloria, and Patricia Bell Scott, eds. *All of the Women Are White, All the Blacks Are Men, but Some of Us Are Brave*. Old Westbury, N.Y.: Feminist, 1982.

Hynes, Terry. *Magazine Portrayal of Women, 1911–1920*. Lexington, Mass.: Association for Education in Journalism, 1981.

Irwin, Mabel MacCoy. *Whitman: The Poet-Liberator of Woman*. New York: Privately printed, 1905.

Jezer, Marty. "The Problems and the Promise of the Bohemian Left." *Z Magazine* (November 1989): 58–62.

Keller, Betty. *Black Wolf: The Life of Ernest Thompson Seton*. Vancouver: Douglas & McIntyre, 1984.

Kern, Louis J. *An Ordered Love: Sex Roles and Sexuality in Victorian Utopias—the Shakers, the Mormons, and the Oneida Community*. Chapel Hill: University of North Carolina Press, 1981.

Kimmel, Michael S. "Men's Responses to Feminism at the Turn of the Century." *Gender and Society* 1, no. 3 (1987).

Kirchway, Freda, ed. *Our Changing Morality: A Symposium*. New York: Albert & Charles Boni, 1924.

Kitch, Sally L. *Chaste Liberation: Celibacy and Female Cultural Status*. Champaign: University of Illinois Press, 1989.

Kraditor, Aileen. *The Ideas of the Woman Suffrage Movement, 1890–1920*. New York: Norton, 1981.

Larsen, Charles. *The Good Fight: The Life and Times of Ben Lindsey*. Chicago: Quadrangle, 1972.

Leach, William. *True Love and Perfect Union: The Feminist Reform of Sex and Society*. New York: Basic, 1980.

Lear, Martha. "The Second Feminist Wave." *New York Times Magazine* (10 March 1968).

Lemons, J. Stanley. *The Woman Citizen: Social Feminism in the 1920s*. Urbana: University of Illinois Press, 1973.

Lerner, Gerda. "Women's Rights and American Feminism." In *The Majority Finds Its Past*. New York: Oxford University Press, 1979.

Macleod, David. *Building Character in the American Boy: The Boy Scouts, YMCA, and Their Forerunners, 1870–1920*. Madison: University of Wisconsin Press, 1983.

Mandelker, Ira L. *Religion, Society and Utopia in Nineteenth Century America*. Amherst: University of Massachusetts Press, 1984.

Maraccio, Michael D. *The Hapgoods: Three Earnest Brothers*. Charlottesville: University Press of Virginia, 1977.

Marriner, Gerald. "A Victorian in the Modern World: The 'Liberated' Male's Adjustment to the New Woman and the New Morality." *South Atlantic Quarterly* 76 (1977): 190–203.

May, Henry. *The End of American Innocence*. New York: Knopf, 1959.

Muncy, Robert Lee. *Sex and Marriage in Utopian Communities in Nineteenth Century America*. Bloomington: Indiana University Press, 1973.

Nierman, Judith. *Floyd Dell: An Annotated Bibliography of Secondary Sources, 1910–1981*. Metuchen, N.J.: Scarecrow, 1984.

O'Neill, William. *The Last Romantic: A Life of Max Eastman*. New York: Oxford University Press, 1978.

Owen, Robert. *The Life of Robert Owen*. New York: Knopf, 1920.

Pleck, Elizabeth. *Domestic Tyranny: The Making of Social Policy against Family Violence from Colonial Times to the Present*. New York: Oxford University Press, 1987.

Reed, James. *From Private Vice to Public Virtue: The Birth Control Movement and American Society since 1830*. New York: Basic, 1978.

Rosen, Ruth. *The Lost Sisterhood: Prostitution in America, 1900–1918*. Baltimore: Johns Hopkins University Press, 1982.

Rosenberg, Rosalind. *Beyond Separate Spheres:*

Intellectual Roots of Modern Feminism. New Haven, Conn.: Yale University Press, 1982.

Rosenthal, Michael. *The Character Factory: Baden-Powell's Boy Scouts and the Imperatives of Empire*. New York: Pantheon, 1986.

Rothman, Sheila. *Women's Proper Place: A History of Changing Ideals and Practices, 1870 to the Present*. New York: Basic, 1978.

Schramm, Sarah Slavin. *Plow Women Rather than Reapers: An Intellectual History of Feminism in the United States*. Metuchen, N.J.: Scarecrow, 1979.

Schwarz, Judith. *Radical Feminists of Heterodoxy*. Norwich, Vt.: New Victoria, 1986.

Schwendinger, Herman, and Julia Schwendinger. *The Sociologists of the Chair: A Radical Analysis of the Formative Years of North American Sociology, 1883–1922*. New York: Basic, 1974.

Sears, Hal D. *The Sex Radicals*. Lawrence: University Press of Kansas, 1977.

Smith-Rosenberg, Carrol, and Charles Rosenberg. "The Female Animal: Medical and Biological Views of Woman and Her Role in Nineteenth Century America." *Journal of American History* 2 (1973): 332–56.

Sochen, J. "Feminism in Greenwich Village, 1910–1920." Ph.D. diss., Northwestern University, 1967.

Spurlock, John C. *Free Love: Marriage and Middle Class Radicalism in America, 1825–1860*. New York: New York University Press, 1989.

Sterling, Dorothy. *We Are Your Sisters: Black Women in the Nineteenth Century*. New York: Norton, 1984.

Strauss, Sylvia. *"Traitors to the Masculine Cause": The Men's Campaigns for Women's Rights*. Westport, Conn.: Greenwood, 1982.

Stricker, Frank. "Socialism, Feminism, and the New Morality: The Separate Freedoms of Max Eastman, William English Walling, and Floyd Dell, 1910–1930." Ph.D. diss., Princeton University, 1974.

Taylor, Barbara. *Eve and the New Jerusalem: Socialism and Feminism in the Nineteenth Century*. New York: Pantheon, 1983.

Thomas, Robert David. *The Man Who Would Be Perfect: John Humphrey Noyes and the Utopian Impulse*. Philadelphia: University of Pennsylvania Press, 1977.

Trachtenberg, Alan. *The Incorporation of America: Culture and Society in the Gilded Age*. New York: Hill & Wang, 1982.

Trimberger, Ellen Kay. "Feminism, Men and Modern Love: Greenwich Village, 1900–1925." In *The Powers of Desire: The Politics of Sexuality*, ed. Ann Snitow, Christine Stansell, and Sharon Thompson. New York: Monthly Review Press, 1984.

Wagner, Sally Roesch. "Moses Harman: Champion of Reproductive Rights." *Changing Men*, no. 18 (Summer-Fall 1987): 29–30.

Wagner, Sally Roesch, with Thomas Mosmiller. "Martin R. Delaney." *Changing Men*, no. 17 (Winter 1986): 24–26.

Ware, Caroline F. *Greenwich Village, 1920–1930*. New York: Harper & Row, 1935.

PART VI: CONTEMPORARY PRO-FEMINIST MEN

Primary Sources

Educational Equality

Baker, Robert. "'Pricks' and 'Chicks': A Plea for Persons.'" In *Sexist Language: A Modern Philosophical Analysis*, ed. Mary Vetterling-Braggin. Totowa, N.J.: Littlefield, Adams, 1981.

Brod, Harry, ed. *The Making of Masculinities: The New Men's Studies*. Boston: Allen & Unwin, 1987.

Folsom, Jack. "Teaching about Sexism and Language in a Traditional Setting: Surmounting the Obstacles." *Women's Studies Quarterly* 11, no. 1 (Spring 1983): 12–14.

Kampf, Louis, and Dick Ohmann. "Men in Women's Studies." *Women's Studies Quarterly* 11, no. 1 (Spring 1983): 9–11.

Kimmel, Michael S. "Teaching about Men: Retrieving Women's Studies' Long Lost Brother." *Journal of the National Association for Women Deans, Administrators and Counselors* 49, no. 3 (Summer 1986): 13–21.

———. "Toward a Sociology of Men: A Teaching and Research Agenda." *Journal of the National Association for Women Deans, Administrators, and Counselors* 49, no. 4 (Summer 1986): 42–43.

Pratt, Ray. "Reflections on Teaching about Women in Two Courses in Political Thought." *Women's Studies Quarterly* 11, no. 1 (Spring 1983): 15–19.

Economic Equality

Asimov, Isaac. "No Space for Women?" *Ladies Home Journal* 88, no. 3 (March 1971): 115, 201–4.

Chafe, William. "Woman, Society and Change." In *The Rise of Modern Woman*, ed. Peter N. Stearns. St. Louis: Forum, 1978.

Cooper, George. *Fair Employment Litigation Text and Materials for Student Practitioner*. St. Paul, Minn.: West, 1975.

Copus, David, and Linda E. Rozenzweig, eds. *OFCCP and Federal Contract Compliance*. New York: Practicing Law Institute, 1981.

Crocker, Lawrence. "Preferential Treatment." In *Feminism and Philosophy*, ed. Mary Vetterling-Braggin, Frederick A. Elliston, and Jane English. Totowa, N.J.: Rowman & Littlefield, 1977.

Fuchs, Victor R. *Women's Quest for Economic Equality*. Cambridge, Mass.: Harvard University Press, 1988.

Fullinwider, Robert K. "On Preferential Hiring." In *Feminism and Philosophy*, ed. Mary Vetterling-Braggin, Frederick A. Elliston, and Jane English. Totowa, N.J.: Rowman & Littlefield, 1977.

Goldman, Alan H. "Limits to the Justification of Reverse Discrimination." *Social Theory and Practice*, no. 3 (Spring 1975). Reprinted in *Feminism and Philosophy*, ed. Mary Vetterling-Braggin, Frederick A. Elliston, and Jane English. Totowa, N.J.: Rowman & Littlefield, 1977.

Grim, Patrick. "Sexism and Semantics." In *Feminism and Philosophy*, ed. Mary Vetterling-Braggin, Frederick A. Elliston, and Jane English. Totowa, N.J.: Rowman & Littlefield, 1977.

Jewett, Paul K. *The Ordination of Women: An Essay on the Office of Christian Ministry*. Grand Rapids, Mich.: Eerdmans, 1980.

Lannon, Al. "ILWU Local 6: Antisexism at Work." Paper presented to the Labor Panel at the Men and Women in Struggle for Community Conference in Oakland, Calif., April 1977. Reprinted in *The Women Say, the Men Say*, ed. Evelyn Shapiro and Barry Shapiro. New York: Dell, 1979.

McBrien, Richard. "Women's Ordination: Effective Symbol of the Church's Struggle." In *Women and the Catholic Priesthood: An Expanded Vision: Proceedings of the Detroit Ordination Conference*, ed. Anne Marie Gardiner. New York: Paulist, 1976.

Mathias, Charles McC., Jr. "Remarks before the Annual Conference of Federally Employed Women." 13 July 1974. (MEL)

Men and Class. Special issue of *Brother: A Forum for Men against Sexism*, no. 14–15 (Summer 1976).

Men's Studies Bibliography. Cambridge: Massachusetts Institute of Technology, Human Studies Collection, Humanities Library, 1977.

Novack, George. "Revolutionary Dynamics of Women's Liberation." New York: Pathfinder Pamphlet, 1969. (UCI)

Sordill, Willie. "Please Tip the Waitress (Waiter)." *M.*, no. 3 (Summer–Fall 1980): 34.

Swidler, Leonard. "Jesus Was a Feminist." *Catholic World* (January 1971): 171–83.

———. "Sisterhood: Model of Future Priesthood." In *Women and the Catholic Priesthood: An Expanded Vision: Proceedings of the Detroit Ordination Conference*, ed. Anne Marie Gardiner. New York: Paulist, 1976.

———. "Seven Reasons for Ordaining Women." *U.S. Catholic* (May 1977): 34–35.

Von Hoffman, Nicholas. "My Mother, the Dentist." *Ms.* 4, no. 51 (20/27 December 1971): 60–62.

Political Equality

Bell, Tony, and Sam Diener. "Pro-Feminism: Men's Nonviolent Approach to Feminism." New York: War Resisters League, [1988].

Brod, Harry. "Fraternity, Equality and Liberty." *Changing Men* 16 (Summer 1986).

Brother: A Forum for Men against Sexism (Berkeley). 1971–75.

Brother: The News Quarterly of the National Organization for Men against Sexism. 1983–.

Dansky, Steven, John Knoebel, and Kenneth Pitchford. "The Effeminist Manifesto." *Double-F: A Magazine of Effeminism*, no. 2 (Winter–Spring 1973).

Ellsberg, Daniel. "Daniel Ellsberg Talks about Women and War." *Ms.* (Spring 1972): 36–39.

Fasteau, Marc Feigen. "The Roots of Misogyny." In *The Male Machine*. New York: McGraw-Hill, 1974.

A Forum for Changing Men. Portland, Oreg.: Men's Resource Center, 1973–76.

Gius. Joe. "ERA Speech." In *The Women Say, the Men Say*, ed. Evelyn Shapiro and Barry Shapiro. New York: Dell, 1979.

Harrison, Harvey L. "State ERAs: Learning from Iowa." *M.*, no. 8 (Spring 1982): 21.

Hesburgh, Theodore M. "Civil Rights and the Women's Movement." In *The Higher Education of Women: Essays in Honor of Rosemary Park*, ed. Helen S. Astin and Werner Z. Hirsch. New York: Praeger, 1978.

Kanowitz, Leo. *Women and the Law*. Albuquerque: University of New Mexico Press, 1969.

———. *Sex Roles in Law and Society*. Albuquerque: University of New Mexico Press, 1973.

———. "The Male Stake in Women's Liberation." In *Equal Rights: The Male Stake*. Albuquerque: University of New Mexico Press, 1981.

Kennedy, Edward M. "Statements on the Equal Rights Amendment." 1 July 1982, 3 January 1985.

———. "Statement on the Equal Rights Amendment and the Military." 1 November 1983.

———. "Statement on Reintroduction of the Equal Rights Amendment." 6 January 1987, 25 January 1989.

Mathias, Charles McC., Jr. "The National Organization of Women." *Congressional Record*. 93d Cong., 1st sess., 1973. Vol. 119, pt. 17.

———. "Remarks before the Annual Conference of Federally Employed Women." 13 July 1974. (MEL)

———. "Remarks before the Women's Political

Caucus, Prince Georges County, Adelphi, Maryland." 23 August 1974. (MEL)

———. "Women's Rights." 31 May 1974. (MEL)

Marcuse, Herbert. "Capitalism and Women's Liberation." In *Counterrevolution and Revolt*. Boston: Beacon, 1972.

Men Allied Nationally for the Equal Rights Amendment (M.A.N. for the E.R.A.) Newsletter. 1978–80.

Morning Due (Seattle). 1974–77.

Mosmiller, Tom, Mike Bradley, and Michael Biernbaum. "Are We the First? A Call for a Feminist Men's History." *M.*, no. 4 (Fall/Winter 1980).

Rosenfield, Allan, M.D. "Washington March." 9 April 1989.

Sawyer, Jack. "On Male Liberation." *Liberation* 15, nos. 6, 7, 8 (August, September, October 1970): 32.

———. "On the Politics of Male Liberation." *WIN* 8, no. 13 (1 September 1971: 20–21.

Shapiro, Barry. "Father's Day for the Equal Rights Amendment Resolution." San Francisco National Organization for Women, 5 October 1979.

———. "Organizing Men in the Struggle for a Sex-Fair Society." *M.*, no. 5 (Spring 1981).

Snodgrass, Jon. "The Women's Liberation Movement and the Men." Paper presented at the meeting of the Pacific Sociological Association, Victoria, British Columbia, 17–19 April 1975.

———. ed. *For Men against Sexism*. Albion, Calif.: Times Change, 1977.

Steiner, Claude. "Reflections on Men's Liberation." *Issues in Radical Therapy* 1, no. 1 (15 January 1973).

Stoltenberg, John. *Refusing to Be a Man: Essays on Sex and Justice*. Portland, Oreg.: Breitenbush, 1989.

Stone, Jay. "Rethinking Masculinity and Sexual Politics." *Days of Decision: Journal of the Youth Section of the Democratic Socialists of America*, no. 20 (Winter 1988).

Social Equality

Alda, Alda. "What Every Woman Should Know about Men." *Ms.* 4, no. 4 (October 1975): 15–16.

Beneke, Tim. "Male Rage: Four Men Talk about Rape." *Mother Jones* 7, no. 9 (July 1982): 13–23.

Bond, Julian. "Self-Defense against Rape: The Joanne Little Case." *Black Scholar* 6, no. 6 (March 1975): 29–31.

Borowitz, Eugene B. *Liberal Judaism*. New York: Union of American Hebrew Congregations, 1984.

Brod, Henry. "Pornography and the Alienation of Male Sexuality." *Social Theory and Practice* 14, no. 3 (Fall 1988): 265–84.

———. "Toward a Male Jewish Feminism." In *A Mensch among Men: Explorations in Jewish Masculinity*. Freedom, Calif.: Crossing, 1988.

Buhler, Franchot. "Protest." *Glamour* (November 1970).

Castleman, Michael. "If Your Friend Gets Raped." *M.*, no. 4 (Fall–Winter 1980): 9–10.

Center for Men's Health Education. "Men and Abortion: Facts for Men." Oakland, Calif., 1984.

Cohen, Steven M., Susan Dessel, and Michael Pelavin. "The Changing Role of Women in Jewish Communal Affairs: A Look into the U.S.A." In *The Jewish Woman: New Perspectives*, ed. Elizabeth Koltun. New York: Schocken, 1976.

Cuomo, Mario M. "New York Governor Speaks Out about Religion" [excerpts from the speech "Religious Belief and Public Morality: A Catholic Governor's Perspective." *St. Petersburg Times* (15 September 1984).

East Bay Men's Center. "Statement on Rape." In *For Men against Sexism: A Book of Readings*, ed. Jon Snodgrass. Albion, Calif.: Times Change, 1977.

Farrell, Warren. "The Resocialization of Men's Attitudes towards Women's Role in Society." Paper presented at the meeting of the

American Political Science Association, New York, 9 September 1970.

Flynn, Patrick. "It's a Ford." *New York Times* (13 February 1989).

Goldin, Rick. "Them Playboy Days Is Over." *Changing Men*, no. 15 (Fall 1985): 29.

Goldolf, Edward. *Man against Woman: What Every Woman Should Know about Violent Men*. Blue Ridge Summit, Pa.: Tab, 1989.

Hearn, Thomas K., Jr. "Jesus Was a Sissy after All." *Christian Century* 87 (7 October 1970): 1191–94.

Hellerstein, David. "Multiplying Roles: The Next Stage." *Ms.* 16, no. 4 (October 1987): 48–50.

Irving, John. *The World According to Garp*. New York: E. P. Dutton, 1978.

———. *The Cider House Rules*. New York: William Morrow, 1985.

Kendall, Mark William. "Glad to Be a Feminist Man." *M.*, no. 8 (Spring 1982).

Kenin, Elliot. "The Housewife Syndrome." *People's Daily World* (15 May 1971): 9.

Kimmel, Michael, ed. *Men Confront Pornography*. New York: Crown, 1990.

Kokopeli, Bruce, and George Lakey. "More Power than We Want: Masculine Sexuality and Violence." *WIN* 22, no. 27 (29 July 1976): 4–8.

Lieberknecht, Greg, and Kay Lieberknecht. "What Is a Feminist Man?" *M.*, no. 8 (Spring 1982): 14.

McCormick, Andrew J. "Men Helping Men Stop Woman Abuse." *State and Mind* 7, no. 3 (Summer 1980): 46–50.

Maguire, Daniel C. "A Catholic Theologian at an Abortion Clinic." *Ms.* 13, no. 6 (December 1984): 129–32.

Marable, Manning. *Sexism and the Struggle for Black Liberation: Two Essays*. Black Praxis Series, Occasional Paper no. 5. Dayton, Ohio: Black Research Associates, n.d.

Marx, George. "Men Working to End Rape!?" *Nurturing News: The Quarterly for Nurturing Men* 8, no. 3 (19896).

Men. Special Issue of *WIN* 10, no. 13 (11 April 1974).

Miller, S. M. "The Making of a Confused Middle-Class Husband." *Social Policy* (July/August 1971): 33–39.

National Technical Assistance Center on Family Violence. "Guidelines for Funding Batterers Programs." *Monthly Memo* 3, no. 1 (Winter 1981): 1.

O'Rourke, James. "Byron Demystified." [Letter to the editor.] *New York Times* (11 March 1989).

Pogrebin, Bertrand B. "How Does It Feel to Be the Husband Of . . . ?" *Ms.* 1, no. 3 (September 1972): 26–27.

Rogow, Z. "Her Choice." *M.*, no. 3 (Summer–Fall 1980): 12.

Salaam, Kalamu ya. "Revolutionary Struggle/Revolutionary Love." *Black Scholar* 8–9 (May–June 1979): 20–24.

———. *Our Women Keep Our Skies from Falling*. New Orleans: Published by the author, 1980.

———. *Somewhere in the World (Long Live Assata)*. New Orleans: Published by the author, 1988.

Santa Cruz Men against Rape. "Men: We Are Men against Rape." Santa Cruz, Calif.: 1986.

Seattle Men against Rape. "Men Taking Action to Help Stop Rape: A Statement." Seattle, 1980.

Sordill, Willie. "The Woman She Hold Up." *M.*, no. 14 (Spring 1985): 19.

Steiner, Claude. "Feminism for Men." Parts 1–3. *Changing Men*, no. 54 (May–June 1979), no. 55 (1979), and no. 56 (December 1979).

Stevens, Mark, and Randy Gebhardt. *Rape Education for Men Curriculum Guide*. Columbus: Ohio State University Rape Education and Prevention Program, 1985.

Straton, Jack. "Stopping Rape: It's Up to Men." Speech presented during Anti-Rape Week at Indiana University. 19 September 1988.

Tapia, Michael. "On Machismo." In *The Women Say, the Men Say*, ed. Evelyn Shapiro and Barry Shapiro. New York, Dell, 1979.

Tynan, Ed. "Strategies of the Left and Gay Liberation." *Gay Community News* 2, no. 12 (14 September 1974): 5.

Vasquez, Carlos. "Women in the Chicano Movement." In *From Mexican Women in the United States: Struggles Past and Present*, ed. Magdalena Mora and Adelaida R. Del Castillo. Los Angeles: University of California, Los Angeles, Chicano Studies Research Center Publications, 1980.

Warshaw, Robin. *I Never Called It Rape: The Ms. Report of Recognizing, Fighting and Surviving Date and Acquaintance Rape*. New York: Harper & Row, 1988.

Wetzsteon, Ross. "The Feminist Man?" In *The Women Say, the Men Say*, ed. Evelyn Shapiro and Barry Shapiro. New York: Dell, 1979.

Widmer, Kingsley. "Reflections of a Male Housewife: On Being a Feminist Fellow-Traveller." *Village Voice* (10 June 1971).

Secondary Sources

Abzug, Bella. "Martin, What Should I Do Now?" *Ms.* 19, no. 1 (July/August 1990): 94–96.

Adam, Barry. *The Rise of a Gay and Lesbian Movement*. Boston: Twayne, 1987.

Antler, Joyce. "The Educated Woman and Professionalization: The Struggle for a New Feminine Identity." Ph.D. diss., State University of New York at Stony Brook, 1977.

Aptheker, Bettina. *Woman's Legacy: Essays on Race, Sex and Class in American History*. Amherst: University of Massachusetts Press, 1982.

Balser, Diane. *Sisterhood and Solidarity: Feminism and Labor in Modern Times*. Boston: South End, 1987.

Berman, David K. "Male Support for Woman Suffrage: An Analysis of Voting Patterns in the Mountain West." *Social Science History* 11 (1978): 281–94.

Bezucha, Robert. "Feminist Pedagogy as a Subversive Activity." *Gendered Subjects: The Dynamics of Feminist Teaching*, ed. Margo Culley and Catherine Portuges. Boston: Routledge & Kegan Paul, 1985.

Brannon, Robert, and Deborah David, eds. *The Forty-Nine Percent Majority*. Reading, Mass.: Addison-Wesley, 1976.

"Britt Leads San Francisco March for Abortion Rights." *San Francisco Chronicle* (19 June 1989).

Brittan, Arthur. *Masculinity and Power*. New York: Blackwell, 1989.

Bronski, Michael. *Culture Clash: The Making of Gay Sensibility*. Boston: South End, 1984.

Carden, Maren Lockwood. *The New Feminist Movement*. New York: Russell Sage, 1974.

Carroll, Berenice A. *Liberating Women's History: Theoretical and Critical Essays*. Urbana: University of Illinois Press, 1976.

Connell, R. W. *Gender and Power*. Stanford, Calif.: Stanford University Press, 1988.

Davidson, Nicholas. *The Failure of Feminism*. Buffalo, N.Y.: Prometheus, 1988.

de Beauvoir, Simone. *The Second Sex*. New York: Vintage, 1973.

DeLeon, David. *Everything Is Changing: Contemporary U.S. Movements in Historical Perspective*. New York: Praeger, 1988.

Degler, Carl N. "Is There a History of Women? An Inaugural Lecture Delivered before the University of Oxford, March 14, 1974." Oxford: Clarendon, 1975.

D'Emilio, John. *Sexual Politics, Sexual Communities: The Making of a Homosexual Minority in the United States, 1940–1970*. Chicago: University of Chicago Press, 1983.

Douglas, Ann. *The Feminization of American Culture*. New York: Knopf, 1977.

Doyle, James. *The Male Experience*. 2d ed. Dubuque, Iowa: William C. Brown, 1989.

Evans, Sara. *Personal Politics: Roots of Women's Liberation in the Civil Rights Movement and the New left*. New York: Knopf, 1979.

Farrell, Warren. *The Liberated Man*. New York: Random House, 1975.

———. *Why Men Are the Way They Are*. New York: McGraw-Hill, 1986.

Farson, Richard. "The Rage of Women." *Look* 33, no. 25 (16 December 1969): 21–23.

Fass, Paula. *Outside In: Minorities and the Transformation of American Education*. New York: Oxford University Press, 1989.

Fasteau, Marc Feigen. *The Male Machine*. New York: Delta, 1975.

Ferree, Myra Marx, and Beth B. Hess. *Controversy and Coalition: The New Feminist Movement*. Boston: Twayne, 1985.

Filene, Peter. *His/Her Self: Sex Roles in Modern America*. 2d ed. Baltimore: Johns Hopkins University Press, 1986.

Fox, Matthew. *Original Blessing: A Primer in Creation Spirituality Presented in Four Paths, Twenty-Six Themes, and Two Questions*. Santa Fe: Bear, 1983.

Franklin, Clyde. *The Changing Definition of Masculinity*. New York: Plenum, 1984.

———. *Men and Society*. Chicago: Nelson-Hall, 1989.

Freeman, Jo. *The Politics of Women's Liberation*. New York: McKay, 1975.

Friedan, Betty. *The Feminine Mystique*. New York: Dell, 1963.

———. *It Changed My Life: Writings on the Women's Movement*. New York: Random House, 1976.

Gatlin, Rochelle. *American Women since 1945*. Jackson: University Press of Mississippi, 1987.

Gerzon, Mark. *A Choice of Heroes*. Boston: Houghton Mifflin, 1983.

Hall, Margaret C. *Women Unliberated: Difficulties and Limitations in Changing Self*. Washington, D.C.: Hemisphere, 1979.

Hardin, Garrett. "Abortion and Human Dignity." Public lecture at University of California, Berkeley, 29 April 1964. (SSL)

Hartmann, Susan M. *The Homefront and Beyond: American Women in the 1940s*. Boston: Twayne, 1982.

Hearn, Jeff. *The Gender of Oppression*. London: Harvester/Wheatsheaf, 1988.

Hole, Judith, and Ellen Levine. *The Rebirth of Feminism*. New York: Quadrangle, 1971.

hooks, bell. *Ain't I a Woman: Black Women and Feminism*. Boston: South End, 1981.

Juda, Daniel. "An Interview with William Baird." *Boston Globe* (13 October 1968).

Kaledin, Eugenia. *Mothers and More: American Women in the 1950s*. Boston: Twayne, 1984.

Katz, Jonathan. *Gay American History*. New York: Crowell, 1976.

———. *Gay/Lesbian Almanac*. New York: Harper & Row, 1983.

Kaufman, Michael, ed. *Beyond Patriarchy*. Toronto: Oxford University Press, 1987.

———. *Cracking the Armor*. New York: Ballantine, in press.

Kelly-Gadol, Joan. "The Social Relation of the Sexes: Methodological Implications of Women's History." *Signs* 1, no. 4 (1976): 809–23.

Kimmel, Michael S., ed. *Changing Men: New Directions in Research on Men and Masculinity*. Newbury Park, Calif.: Sage, 1987.

Kimmel, Michael S., and Michael Messner, eds. *Men's Lives*. New York: Macmillan, 1989.

Komorovsky, Mirra. *Dilemmas of Masculinity*. New York: Norton, 1976.

Kriegel, Leonard. *On Men and Manhood*. New York: Hawthorn, 1979.

Leahy, John. "Ex-D.O. Henrie: 'A Matter of Principle.'" *OP/The Osteopathic Physician* (July 1970).

Lewis, Robert, ed. *Men in Difficult Times*. Englewood Cliffs, N.J.: Prentice-Hall, 1981.

Mansbridge, Jane. *Why We Lost the ERA*. Chicago: University of Chicago Press, 1986.

Mattfield, Jacquelyn A., and Carol G. Van Aken. *Women and the Scientific Professions*. Cambridge: MIT Press, 1965.

Merriam, Eve. *After Nora Slammed the Door: American Women in the 1960s—the Unfinished Revolution*. Cleveland: World, 1964.

Messner, Michael. "The Life of a Man's Seasons: Male Identity and the Lifecourse of the Jock." In *Changing Men: New Directions in Research on Men and Masculinity*, ed. Michael Kimmel. Newbury Park, Calif.: Sage Publications, 1987.

———. "The Meaning of Success: The Athletic Experience and the Development of Male Identity." In *The Making of Masculinities: The New Men's Studies*, ed. Harry Brod. Boston: Allen & Unwin, 1987.

———. *Power at Play: Sports and the Problem of Masculinity*. Boston: Beacon. In press.

Morain, Thomas J. "Emergence of the Women's Movement, 1960–1970." Ph.D. diss., University of Iowa, 1974.

Nash, Jennie. "John Irving's Grand Passion." *New York Woman* (May 1988).

Nichols, Jack. *Men's Liberation: A New Definition of Masculinity*. New York: Penguin, 1975.

Pleck, Joseph H. "Men's Responses to the Changing Consciousness of Women." In *Women and Men: Roles, Attitudes and Power Relationships*, ed. Eleanor L. Zuckerman. New York: Radcliffe Club of New York, 1975.

———. *The Myth of Masculinity*. Cambridge: MIT Press, 1981.

Pleck, Joseph H., and Elizabeth Pleck, eds. *The American Man*. Englewood Cliffs, N.J.: Prentince-Hall, 1980.

Pleck, Joseph H., and Jack Sawyer, eds. *Men and Masculinity*. Englewood Cliffs, N.J.: Prentice-Hall, 1974.

Robb, Christina. "The Lonely Warrior." *Boston Globe* (9 June 1985).

Roszak, Betty, and Theodore Roszak, eds. *Masculine/Feminine*. New York: Harper & Row, 1969.

Rotundo, E. Anthony. "Manhood in America: The Northern Middle Class, 1770–1920." Ph.D. dissertation, Brandeis University, 1982.

———. "Body and Soul: Changing Ideals of American Middle-Class Manhood: 1770–1920." *Journal of Social History* 16, no. 4 (1983): 23–28.

———. "Learning about Manhood: Gender Ideals and the Middle Class Family in Nineteenth Century America." In *Manliness and Morality: Middle Class Masculinity in Britain and America, 1800–1940*, ed. J. A. Mangan and James Walvin. New York: St. Martin's, 1987.

Rupp, Leila J., and Verta Taylor. *Survival in the Doldrums: The American Women's Rights Movement, 1945 to the 1960s*. New York: Oxford University Press, 1987.

Sanford, Nevitt. "Is Coeducation Wasted on Women?" *Ladies Home Journal* 74 (May 1957).

Schlib, John. "Pedagogy of the Oppressors?" In *Gendered Subjects: The Dynamics of Feminist Teaching*, ed. Margo Culley and Catherine Portuges. Boston: Routledge & Kegan Paul, 1985.

Seidler, Victor. *Rediscovering Masculinity: Reason, Language, Sexuality*. New York: Routledge & Kegan Paul, 1989.

Shapiro, Evelyn, and Barry Shapiro, eds. *The Women Say, the Men Say*. New York: Dell, 1979.

Silverman, Jerry. *The Liberated Woman's Songbook*. New York: Macmillan, 1971.

Slater, Philip. *Footholds*. New York: Dutton, 1977.

Stearns, Peter. *Be a Man!* New York: Holmes & Meier, 1979.

Telander, Rick. "Not a Shining Knight." *Sports Illustrated* (9 May 1988): 122.

Todd, Richard. "My Son, the Feminist." *Atlantic Monthly* 234, no. 5 (November 1974): 104–10.

Vetterling-Braggin, Mary, ed. *Sexist Language.* Totowa, N.J.: Rowman & Littlefield, 1981.

———, ed. *Femininity, Masculinity and Androgyny.* Totowa, N.J.: Rowman & Littlefield, 1982.

Vetterling-Braggin, Mary, Frederick A. Elliston, and Jane English, eds. *Feminism and Philosophy.* Totowa, N.J.: Rowman & Littlefield, 1977.

Wandersee, Winifred. *On the Move: American Women in the 1970s.* Boston: Twayne, 1988.

CREDITS

Alda "Alan Alda on the ERA: Why Should Men Care?" by Alan Alda. Originally published in *Ms.* 5, no. 1. Copyright © 1976 by Alan Alda. Reprinted by permission of the author.

Asimov Excerpt from "Uncertain, Coy, and Hard to Please," by Isaac Asimov. Originally published in *Fantasy and Science Fiction* 36, no. 2 (February 1969). Copyright © 1968 by Mercury Press. Reprinted by permission of the author.

Asner Excerpt from "Speech on Men Supporting Women," by Ed Asner. Copyright © 1987 by Edward Asner. Reprinted by permission of the author.

Beneke Excerpt from *Men on Rape,* by Tim Beneke. Copyright © 1982 by St. Martin's Press, Inc., New York. Reprinted by permission of St. Martin's Press.

Brannon Excerpt from "Press Conference Statement of March 12, 1983," by Robert Brannon. Originally published in *Brother* 1, no. 2. Copyright © 1983 by Robert Brannon. Reprinted by permission of the author.

Brod Excerpt from "Scholarly Studies of Men: The New Field Is an Essential Complement to Women's Studies," by Harry Brod. Originally published in the *Chronicle of Higher Education* (21 March 1990). Copyright © 1990 by Harry Brod. Reprinted by permission of the *Chronicle of Higher Education* and the author.

Cosell "Why I Support the ERA," by Howard Cosell. Originally published in *Ms.* 4, no. 4. Copyright © 1975 by Howard Cosell. Reprinted by permission of the author.

Delgado "An Open Letter to Carolina . . . or Relations between Men and Women Part I," by Abelardo Delgado, from *A Decade of Hispanic Literature,* ed. Nicolas Kannelos. Copyright © 1982 by Arte Publico Press. Reprinted by permission of Arte Publico Press.

Estabrook "The Taxation Tyranny," by General E. Estabrook. Originally published in *Songs America Voted By,* by Irwin Silber. Copyright © 1971 by Irwin Silber. Reprinted by permission of Stackpole Books and the author.

Guthrie "Union Maid." Words and Music by Woody Guthrie. Copyright © 1963 by Ludlow Music, Inc., New York. Reprinted by permission of Ludlow Music, Inc.

Jackson Excerpt from "Ensuring the Dignity and Equality of Women," by Jesse Jackson, from *Keep Hope Alive: Jesse Jackson's 1988*

Presidential Campaign, ed. Frank Clemente and Frank Watkins. Copyright © 1989 by Keep Hope Alive PAC. Reprinted by permission of Lois Hayes, South End Press.

Kampf and Ohmann "Men in Women's Studies," by Louis Kampf and Dick Ohmann. Originally published in *Radical Teacher*. (Spring 1983). Copyright © 1983 by *Radical Teacher*. Reprinted by permission of Louis Kampf.

Lennon Excerpt from "Woman is the Nigger of the World," by John Lennon. Copyright © 1972 by Ono Music. All rights administered by Sony Music Publishing, 8 Music Sq. West, Nashville, TN 37203. Reprinted by permission of the publisher.

McDavid Excerpt from "Feminism for Men 101—Educating Men in 'Women's Studies,'" by W. Alexander McDavid, Jr. Copyright © 1986 by W. Alexander McDavid, Jr. Reprinted by permission of the author.

Marcuse Excerpt from "Marxism and Feminism," by Herbert Marcuse. Originally published in *Women's Studies* 2, no. 3. Copyright © 1974 by Harwood Academic Publishers. Reprinted by permission of Harwood Academic Publishers.

Mead Excerpt from "George Herbert Mead's Ideas on Women and Careers: A Letter to His Daughter-in-Law, 1920: Archives," by Steven Diner. Originally published in *Signs* 4, no. 2. Copyright © 1978 by Steven Diner. Reprinted by permission of the University of Chicago Press and the author.

Moore Excerpt from *Take a Bishop Like Me*, by Paul Moore, Jr. Copyright © 1979 by Paul Moore, Jr. Reprinted by permission of Harper and Row, Publishers, Inc.

Mott Excerpt from "Following a Wife's Move," by Gordon Mott. Copyright © 1987 by the *New York Times* Syndication Sales Corp. Reprinted by permission of Poseidon Press, a division of Simon & Schuster, Inc.

New York Times "The Heroic Men." Copyright © 1912 by the *New York Times*. Reprinted by permission of the *New York Times*.

Pickens Excerpt from "The Kind of Democracy the Negro Race Expects," by William Pickens, from *The Voice of Black America*, ed. Philip S. Foner. Copyright © 1972 by Philip S. Foner. Reprinted by permission of Simon & Schuster, Inc.

Pleck "Men's Power with Women, Other Men, and Society: A Men's Movement Analysis," by Joseph Pleck. Copyright © 1977 by the Center for Women's Studies, University of Cincinnati. Reprinted by permission of the Center for Women's Studies, University of Cincinnati.

Reich "Wake-Up Call," by Robert Reich. Originally published in *Ms.* 18, no. 4. Copyright © 1989 by *Ms.* Reprinted by permission of *Ms.*

Salaam Excerpt from "The Struggle to Smash Sexism is a Struggle to Develop Women," by Kalamu ya Salaam, from *Our Women Keep Our Skies from Falling*. Copyright © 1980 by Kalamu ya Salaam. Reprinted by permission of the author.

Schlesinger Excerpt from "The Role of Women in American History," by Arthur M. Schlesinger. Copyright © 1922 by the Macmillan Publishing Co. Reprinted by permission of Arthur Schlesinger, Jr.

Small "Fifty-Nine Cents," by Fred Small. Copyright © 1981 by Pine Barrens Music (BMI). Reprinted by permission of the author.

Stoltenberg Excerpt from "The Profeminist Men's Movement: New Connections, New Directions," by John Stoltenberg. Originally published in *Changing Men* 20 (Winter/Spring 1989). Copyright © 1988 by John Stoltenberg. Reprinted by permission of the author.

Swidler Excerpt from "No Penis, No Priest," by Leonard Swidler. Copyright © 1973 by the *Journal of Ecumenical Studies*. Reprinted by permission of Nancy E. Krody, managing editor of the *Journal of Ecumenical Studies*.

Vidal Excerpt from "Women's Liberation Meets Miller-Mailer-Manson Man," from *Homage to Daniel Shays: Collected Essays, 1952–1972*, by Gore Vidal. Copyright © 1968, 1970, 1972 by

Gore Vidal. Reprinted by permission of Random House, Inc.

Wittman Excerpt from "A Gay Manifesto," by Carl Wittman. Originally published in *Out of the Closets: Voices of Gay Liberation*, ed. Karla Jay and Allen Young. Copyright © 1972 by Karla Jay and Allen Young. Reprinted by permission of Karla Jay.

Essential Forensic Biology